LABOR ECONOMICS
AND INSTITUTIONS

THE MACMILLAN COMPANY
NEW YORK · CHICAGO
DALLAS · ATLANTA · SAN FRANCISCO
LONDON · MANILA

IN CANADA
BRETT-MACMILLAN LTD.
GALT, ONTARIO

LABOR

ECONOMICS

AND

INSTITUTIONS

Arthur D. Butler

ASSOCIATE PROFESSOR OF ECONOMICS

THE UNIVERSITY OF BUFFALO

THE MACMILLAN COMPANY   NEW YORK

© Arthur D. Butler 1961

Second Printing 1963

Library of Congress catalog card number: 61-5946

The Macmillan Company, New York
Brett-Macmillan Ltd., Galt, Ontario

Printed in the United States of America

PREFACE

In our modern affluent society, the plight of the worker no longer arouses the concern it did during the Great Depression of the 1930's when labor courses first became popular. At that time many students were interested in learning about the "wickedness of management and the excesses of capitalism" and studied to become leaders in the rising labor unions and government institutions. Experience since then has taught us that labor problems cannot be eliminated by mere institutional innovations because they are rooted too deeply in basic economic, social, and psychological conflicts of interest. The study of labor problems, therefore, must not be devoted solely to shifting institutional arrangements.

This book is concerned primarily, though not entirely, with an economic analysis of workers in their relations with one another and with other groups. The economic relationships cannot be examined usefully apart from non-economic forces: a worker's attitude toward his job is affected by his discussions with fellow employees, his attitude toward his union is affected by the views of his neighbors and the newspapers he reads. Hence, the social, psychological, and political factors influencing the economic variables should receive some of our attention.

Logically, the starting point for an exposition of labor's **economic** problems should be wages and employment theory. Once this theoretical framework is established, individual and institutional responses to shifting economic, social, and political forces can more easily be fitted into place. However, the abstractions and generalizations necessary for a purely theoretical analysis may seem unreal and irrelevant to beginning students. The first half of the book is therefore concerned with the institutional setting.

Part 1 describes the demographic and sociological characteristics of the labor force and the history and the nature of the growth of unions. Part 2 is devoted to the conflict between worker and management organizations and discusses their tactics and objectives in dealing with each other, concluding with an analysis of collective bargaining legislation. These two parts, though largely institutional, are written to complement the theoretical sections which follow. Furthermore, where it is appropriate, additional institutional material is integrated with the chapters on wages and employment. Part 3 is concerned with wage theory and its applications to wage differentials and the impact of unions and the government on the labor market. Part 4 examines the employment problems of workers, and the efforts to alleviate the hardships of unemployment, particularly in the years since World War II, with special attention given to the relation between collective bargaining and inflation. Part 5 is a brief chapter in which the author takes the liberty of airing his prejudices and views on fundamental labor problems in a dynamic economy.

In a one-semester course with its interruptions, this book will be a reference for the student, giving coherence to the material he has studied. Nevertheless, it must be more than a crutch; it should also stimulate the serious student to reconsider old thought patterns and to read further in those areas which particularly interest him. For this purpose, a series of discussion questions and suggested readings concludes each chapter. The instructor, for his part, is enabled by this text to emphasize his favorite topics, or those of current interest, without fear that other important subjects will be neglected. He is also free, for the same reason, to introduce more recent research and to present opposing views.

"No man is an island unto himself," particularly when producing a textbook. The inspiration of former instructors, the challenges and criticisms of colleagues, the patience of friends—all these are indispensable. The two teachers who most greatly influenced my thinking, and for whom my appreciation has steadily grown, were Edwin Witte and Selig Perlman; both passed away while the book was in process. Myron Joseph of Carnegie Institute of Technology, Gardner Ackley of the University of Michigan, Mark Kahn of Wayne State University, Theresa Wolfson of Brooklyn College, Roscoe Hinkle of Ohio State University, and Hildegarde Shinners of The Univeristy of Buffalo read part or all of the manuscript, and George Strauss of The University of Buffalo read two drafts and answered innumerable questions. They are only to be thanked, not blamed. Mrs. Carol Boteler and Miss Mary Zagarino were accurate and critical typists. Mrs. Mary Coulter and Mrs. Ruth Berger contributed generously in the final stages of manuscript preparation. The usual thanks are due to my wife for doing all the unusual things necessary for keeping the project from becoming unhitched.

ARTHUR D. BUTLER

The University of Buffalo

CONTENTS

LABOR ECONOMICS
AND INSTITUTIONS

PART

1

UNIONS AND
THE LABOR FORCE

Economic problems arise from the scarcity of resources for satisfying human desires. One of the resources, labor, is not only a scarce factor of production, but is simultaneously the major source of consumption demand. What do we mean by labor? What are the conflicts between its roles as producer and consumer, and how are they resolved? What is the relationship of the labor force to the total population? How has the labor force been changing in size and composition, and how is this related to population growth? What are the effects of rising educational standards and improved methods of production technology?

Why is it that some workers join unions and others do not? What are the characteristics of our society which cause worker organizations to be so different in the United States and Canada than they are in other countries? What has been the pattern of union growth and what is the outlook for its future? What changes have occurred in the organizational structure of American unions? How have they adjusted to differing political and economic challenges? Have they accumulated enough economic power to dominate our society, or are they submerged in the rush of changing events? Finally, is there some central motivation which is common to the great variety in American unionism, and, if so, what is it?

1 { LABOR IN THE
AMERICAN ECONOMY

In a modern industrialized economy, a worker acts in many different roles simultaneously. He is a *producer*—a member of the labor force
—one of the scarce factors of production necessary to provide material
goods and services for satisfying human wants. He is a *consumer*—a
source of demand for the goods produced. But above all else, he is an
individual with his own special needs, desires, and motivations deriving
from his home, community, and working environment. As a producer he
sells his services to an employer, attempting to make as favorable a sale
as possible. As a consumer he has insatiable needs and desires which he
satisfies as best he can within the limits of his income. As an individual
he wants to be able to respect himself, earn the respect of his associates,
work in pleasant working conditions, and enjoy a reasonable amount of
leisure time.

The worker serving in his role as a producer forms the central theme of
this book. His activities as consumer and individual cannot be ignored,
however, for the way he functions as a producer is influenced by how
well he fulfills his desires and aspirations in these other capacities. His
approach to his job will certainly be different if he believes he is forced
to suffer an unfairly low standard of living and occupy an inferior social
status. And of course, his attitudes toward what constitutes a fair standard of living will be continually revised upward as the economy grows.

As a producer the worker must make a bargain with an employer. The
bargaining may be done either on an individual basis or in cooperation

with a group of fellow workers. Cooperation may be informal and perhaps temporary, or it may be formal, through an established organization —a union. In the latter case, workers join together to protect and promote their interests as producers. Their objective is to change the relationship between themselves and the employer, to force a change in their relative bargaining power. In short, collective bargaining replaces individual bargaining. Hence, any analysis of the activities of workers as producers must take into account unions and collective bargaining.

To set the stage for an analysis of the conditions surrounding this bargaining—whether between an individual worker and his employer, or a group of workers and their employer—something must be known about the way in which workers participate in the labor market. Who goes into the labor market—what segments of the population? Are there patterns of change in the way different groups participate in the labor market? How are the workers distributed among the different occupations and industries, and what patterns of change are discernible here?

THE LABOR FORCE

A definition of the labor force must draw an arbitrary line between who is and who is not to be included. The most widely used definition, developed by the Bureau of the Census, includes all persons aged fourteen and older who are gainfully employed or actively seeking gainful employment. This includes the self-employed, and part-time as well as full-time employees. The age fourteen was chosen because state legislation requires children to attend school at least up to that age. Those who are not looking for work because they think they have no chance of finding it are excluded. This definition, then, includes only those persons currently active in the labor market. The total potential labor supply is of course much larger.[1]

Obviously, not all of our population of 180 million people can be gainfully employed. Some people are either too young or too old, or are physically handicapped. Some prefer to be full-time students, and others are out of the labor market tending to children and household chores.

---

[1] This concept of the labor force was developed by the Bureau of the Census, of the Department of Commerce, in order to meet the need for reliable data on the amount of employment and unemployment. The present method of collecting these data, called the current population survey, was devised in 1940 and has been modified a number of times since then. For a discussion of the development of the labor force concept, see A. J. Jaffe and Charles D. Stewart, *Manpower Resources and Utilization* (New York: John Wiley & Sons, Inc., 1951), pp. 1–118, and U. S. Congress, *Employment and Unemployment Statistics*, Hearings before the Subcommittee on Economic Statistics of the Joint Committee on the Economic Report, 84th Cong., 1st Sess., November 7 and 8, 1955 (Washington: Government Printing Office, 1955).

Approximately seventy-five million people, about 41 per cent of the population, are in the labor force. This figure includes about three million who are in the armed services.

Statistics on the labor force have many valuable uses. They give us a measure of the total productive capacity of the economy since, together with the techniques of production which prevail at any given moment, the number of workers sets the upper limit to the amount of output. The statistics also give us a picture of how well the economy is operating: during a period of prosperity, they indicate those areas of activity which are expanding and those which are contracting. They provide information useful for guiding resources from the declining to the expanding industries and occupations. During a depression, labor force statistics measure the degree of unemployment and indicate which areas of the economy feel the most severe effects of the depression. Thus, government planners are in a better position to determine what action would be most appropriate for combating the depression. During a period of defense mobilization, such statistics are essential for making rational decisions on the number of people available for military service and for defense production, and for considering what additional sources of labor might be tapped for these purposes.

Factors Which Control Labor Force Participation

The labor force is not an unchanging number of people or even a fixed percentage of the population. What determines the size of the labor force?

The participation of individuals in the labor force—their willingness to seek gainful employment—is determined by a complex of socio-economic factors. For example, in our society the husband is expected to be the primary breadwinner for his family; however, in other societies this duty may fall upon the wife, or the entire family. Furthermore, we seem to be motivated by an urge to live beyond a bare minimum of subsistence, driving ourselves to ever higher standards of living. Many cultures place a greater value on other activities, such as religious and ritual ceremonies or just plain leisure.

The participation of different social groups in the labor force is further affected by the economic development of the country. A highly industrialized economy is very different from a primitive, agricultural economy, where all persons are compelled to work just to eke out a meager subsistence. In such preindustrialized economies, the communities cannot afford to give up the work of the young or the aged. Even the religious and political leaders must work in the field.

Such factors as marital status and accepted educational standards, as well as age and sex, are also important determinants of participation in the labor force. That is, an individual's attitude toward accepting a job is substantially influenced by the customs and traditions of the social group to which he belongs. For instance, members of different age and sex groups living in rural areas seek gainful employment in proportions very different from the corresponding groups living in urban areas. Rural males tend to enter the labor force at an earlier age than urban males, and rural females are less likely to seek employment than urban females.

The effects of the socio-economic factors on labor force participation vary from one time period to another. As a consequence, the labor force has a continually changing age and sex composition. This is so even though the bulk of its members remain permanently in the labor market.

Seasonal Changes in Labor Force Participation

The seasons of the year substantially influence the size of the labor force. Seasonal fluctuations—the annual recurrence at about the same time each year of periods of expansion and contraction—are present in almost all types of economic data. For the labor force, the high point occurs early in the summer and the low point at midwinter. There are approximately four million more persons in the labor force at the peak than at the low point.

Besides this significant change in size, there are seasonal changes in the sex and age composition caused by the fact that the workers whose participation varies seasonally are generally women and young people. Almost all male seasonal workers are fourteen to twenty-four years old, largely students working at summer jobs. Almost half of the female seasonal workers are more than twenty-five years old. They are mainly housewives supplementing family income. Many of them remain employed on into November. The primary sources of employment for these seasonal workers are the agricultural, food-processing, and construction industries.

The seasonal change in size of four millions understates the amount of movement into and out of the labor force in a typical year. Some temporary workers are entering the labor market while others are leaving; housewives, for instance, accept employment in the fall after their children return to school at the same time that students are leaving their summer jobs. Therefore, the total number of workers who engage in labor force activity during the year is about 20 per cent more than its average size.[2]

These impermanent attachments to the labor market have many important consequences. They adjust the labor supply to seasonal changes in consumer demand and to the special needs of industries affected by weather conditions. At the same time, they complicate the organization problems of unions in those industries where seasonal employment fluctuates widely.

Short-run Changes in Labor Force Participation

The labor force is affected significantly by the short-run fluctuations in employment opportunities associated with the business cycle. For our purposes at this point, let us define the business cycle as expansions and contractions in employment and income recurring with imperfect regularity every three to five years. Although there is no doubt that short-run changes in income and employment change attitudes toward accepting gainful employment, it is not clear just what effect the summation of these changes has on the over-all size and composition of the labor force. Nevertheless, it is interesting and useful to consider the following questions: What changes occur in the labor force when wages are falling and family breadwinners are becoming unemployed? Do these conditions induce more people to enter the labor market, hoping to restore their family income to its previous level? What happens to the labor force when real income rises? Do more people seek employment because of more attractive wages and working conditions? Do some age and sex groups change their rate of participation in the labor force as employment opportunities change? Or is the supply of labor generally unresponsive to such conditions?

One group of labor market theorists claims that persons who would not otherwise seek employment enter the labor market whenever there is a decline in income and employment. They argue that the size of the labor force is inversely related to the level of income; that is, a change in income produces a change in the opposite direction in the labor force. Others claim that there are additional workers who are available for employment during extremely prosperous times as well as depressions.

[2] For a more detailed discussion of the patterns of labor force participation, see Clarence D. Long, *The Labor Force Under Changing Income and Employment* (Princeton: Princeton University Press, 1958); Gertrude Bancroft, *The American Labor Force* (New York: John Wiley & Sons, 1958); and Sophia Cooper and Stuart Garfinkle, *Population and Labor Force Projections for the United States, 1960 to 1975,* U. S. Department of Labor, Bulletin No. 1242 (Washington: Government Printing Office, 1959).

During periods of prosperity, they argue, the attractiveness of jobs induces older people to delay retirement or to return to the labor force,
housewives to enter the labor market, and students to forgo, or at least
postpone, their education. During periods of severe depression, additional workers enter the labor market hoping to supplement family
income or to replace the income of the unemployed breadwinner. According to the additional-worker hypothesis, then: 1) during depression,
the forced reduction in living standards *pushes* additional workers into
the labor market even though jobs are hard to find, and 2) during boom
times the attractiveness of good wages *pulls* more workers into the labor
force causing it to be larger than normal.

Other labor market economists doubt that additional workers appear
under extreme economic conditions. They believe that although some
workers may be forced to enter the labor market during a depression,
others drop out for lack of employment opportunities or are discouraged
by the harsh discipline and severe competition for jobs; the number
going out offsets the number coming in. The part played by women
in the labor force illustrates the point. Women living in urban areas
are more inclined to enter the labor market during depression years,
but this is offset by the decline in farm-to-city migration, and the fact
that those living in rural areas are less likely to seek gainful employment.[3]

Our knowledge of the labor market is not sufficiently detailed to accept
or reject the additional-worker hypothesis. By and large, the main
part of the labor force, males between the ages of twenty-five and fifty-
five years, continue in the labor market regardless of the extremes in
economic conditions. During a depression, some young people, being
unable to afford continued education, enter the labor force earlier. The
effect of this is partially reduced by other young people remaining in
school because of inability to find jobs. The response of women and
older persons to the depression is similarly conflicting. Some women
enter the labor market to supplement family income; others become
discouraged because of the prevailing working conditions and the
lack of employment opportunities, and therefore retire from the labor
force. Many older workers who lose their jobs become discouraged over

---

[3] W. S. Woytinsky, "Seasonal and Cylical Variations in the Labor Force," in W. S.
Woytinsky and Associates, *Employment and Wages in the United States* (New York:
The Twentieth Century Fund, 1953), pp. 321–23; Clarence D. Long, "The Labor
Force and Economic Change," *Insights into Labor Issues*, ed. by Richard A. Lester
and Joseph Shister (New York: The Macmillan Co., 1948), pp. 329–55; and John
D. Durand, *The Labor Force in the United States, 1890–1960* (New York: Social
Science Research Council, 1948), pp. 84–121.

their inability to find other jobs and therefore leave the labor market. Many employed older workers, however, delay retirement in order to supplement family income. It is not clear, then, whether these changes constitute net additions to the total size.

The experience during and after World War II was in accordance with the prosperity phase of the additional-worker hypothesis: the labor force expanded at a time when there was a great increase in the demand for labor. Compulsory military service brought many young men into the labor force—which includes the armed services—who would otherwise have been pursuing their education. Abundant job opportunities and rising wages, as well as patriotism, induced many women and older persons to accept employment. Teen-agers accepted part-time jobs in much greater numbers. In the postwar period, while jobs were plentiful, some of these additional workers remained in the labor force. This experience may have represented no more than a retardation in the return to the former attitudes toward participation in the labor force. It does not clearly indicate what to expect in a future period of high demand for labor.

The type of fluctuations associated with the business cycle appears to have only a modest effect on the size of the labor force, either during depression with unemployment or during prosperity with rising wages. The habits and traditions which determine whether individuals will enter the labor market do not change rapidly enough to adjust to cyclical fluctuations. Only a cataclysm such as war can overwhelm these habit patterns and bring an increase in the willingness to take part in the productive process.

Long-run Changes in Labor Force Participation

When a longer period than that encompassed by the business cycle is considered, it is possible to observe the evolution of the customs and traditions influencing participation in the labor force. These long-run trends are only temporarily affected by seasonal and cyclical fluctuations; their full effects are usually discernible only after a period of two or three decades.

Young people in the labor force. The greatest source of increase in the labor force is, of course, the growth of the population. Since 1890, the average age at which people start work has risen from fifteen to eighteen, largely the result of higher educational standards. A one-year increase in the average entry tends to reduce the labor force by approximately 4 per cent, about three million young workers. In the near future, educational standards will probably continue their slow upward trend, and therefore be a continually depressing factor on the proportion of the population in the labor force.

The decline in the birth rate, which continued until World War II, was a second factor causing young people to be a decreasing proportion of the labor force. In 1955 the fourteen to twenty-four year age group contributed 12.7 million workers to the labor force, 18 per cent of the total. This compares to 21 per cent in 1950 and 31 per cent in 1900. The twenty-five to forty-four age group will remain unchanged between 1955 and 1965 while the rest of the labor force is increasing by more than ten million.[4]

The average age of the labor force has been rising, then, because of the rise in the average age of entry and because the proportion of the population reaching that age has been declining. This trend began to reverse itself in 1960, because of the higher birth rate since 1940, as shown in Figure 1-A. The increasing tendency of teen-agers to work part-time also serves to counteract this trend.

FIGURE 1-A

**Changes in the Number of Workers in Each Age Group
1950 to 1960 and 1960 to 1970**

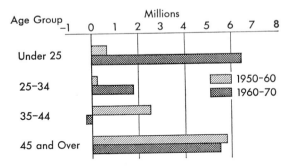

Source: U. S. Department of Labor, *Manpower, Challenge of the 1960s* (Washington: Government Printing Office, 1960), p. 6.

Old people in the labor force. The proportion of the old people in the labor force—those over sixty-five—has been declining for many decades. In 1920, 57 per cent of the men over sixty-five were in the labor force; in 1960, only 36 per cent were. Although the labor market conditions associated with World War II caused a temporary leveling off, the downward trend has reappeared. It is true that many older workers

[4] Cooper and Garfinkle, *op. cit.*, pp. 22–30.

have their jobs protected by seniority, but those who lose their jobs experience great difficulty in becoming re-employed, a difficulty which, incidentally, applies to ages considerably below sixty-five. Opportunities for self-employment in agriculture and other industries have been declining in past decades. The substitution of machinery and semi-skilled workers for skilled labor has deprived many older workers of a chance to capitalize on a lifetime of experience, while their age makes it difficult for them to readjust to the changing conditions. The direction of public opinion in favor of earlier retirement has been strengthened and institutionalized by the government's old age insurance program and by private pension programs. Futhermore, employers often feel that it is socially more acceptable—and more profitable—to discharge older rather than younger workers who are likely to have more dependents. Thus older workers tend to leave the labor force at earlier ages than in past decades.

A number of factors have been in operation recently which may reverse this trend. These are discussed below along with the special problems of an aging labor force.

Women in the labor force. Since young people are entering the labor market in smaller proportions and old people are leaving sooner, what prevents the labor force from being a declining percentage of the population? The major counterbalancing factor has been the increase in the willingness of women to seek gainful employment. In fact, for the ten-year period from 1955 to 1965, women will account for more than half of the increase in the labor force, and by the end of the period will be one-third of the total.

Many of the changing customs which induce a greater participation by females in gainful employment have an economic basis. Increasing mechanization has opened up many semi-skilled jobs which do not require heavy physical energy. This and continuing lower wages for women cause employers to hire them for a variety of jobs. Occupations traditionally filled by women—teaching, clerking, and other white-collar jobs—have grown more rapidly than other occupations. The decreasing rate of entrance of young people perhaps contributed to an easier job market, and the trend toward shorter hours has made it possible for women to secure remunerative employment and still have time left to devote to their families.

Changing social attitudes have also broadened the employment horizons for women. It is no longer considered wicked or a sign of an inferior social position for a woman to accept a paying job. Smaller families, day nursery care for children, household gadgets which simplify the wife's daily chores, and many other factors have decreased the amount of time she must spend at home. The variety of assignments which women capably filled during World War II weakened the remaining barriers and traditions standing in the way of their increasing participation in the labor force.

Marriage and children traditionally have been the major social obstacles preventing women from accepting jobs. Yet their increased labor market activity has occurred despite a rise in the proportion of them marrying and having children. In 1940, 60 per cent of all women were married; in 1950, 66 per cent were. Married women now constitute a much larger segment of the female portion of the labor force than in the past: in 1940, 36 per cent, but by 1950, more than 50 per cent.

Our customs have changed to the point where a "two-phase" working life for women is now socially approved. After completing their education, young women enter the labor force, particularly those living in urban areas. Most of them quit after marriage and the birth of children, but return when their children reach school age: the ages thirty-five to forty-four are the most typical for married women in the labor force. Although some are employed only part-time, most have full-time jobs.[5]

Rural-urban migration. The growth of large metropolitan areas has had a significant impact on the size and composition of the labor force. Rural farm residents accounted for 30 per cent of the population in 1920; the proportion had dropped to less than 15 per cent by 1950. During World War II, the migration away from farms continued at an accelerated rate and will probably do so for decades to come.

In rural areas young and old people are more likely to be in the labor force than in urban areas, partly because of the nature of the work available and partly because of the social customs prevailing in rural areas. However, the proportion of women in the labor force, according to the census computations, is much lower in rural areas. Thus, the population movement from rural to urban areas brings fewer young and old into the labor market, but more women between the ages of twenty-five and fifty. The net effect is to increase the labor force.

In the long run, then, the growth of the labor force depends on the growth of the population; but the two may grow at different rates. This is well illustrated by the changing roles of young people, old people, and women. The one tradition important to the labor force, which

[5] Gertrude Bancroft, "Trends in the Labor Force," *Manpower in the United States,* ed. by William Haber, Frederick H. Harbison, Lawrence R. Klein, and Gladys L. Palmer (New York: Harper & Brothers, 1954), pp. 132–42.

has remained largely unchanged, is that the husband and father should be the primary breadwinner for his family. The solid core of our labor force continues to consist of males between the ages of twenty-five and sixty-five, with other groups changing in their participation.

Whether these changes will be exactly offsetting in the future—whether the labor force will continue to be a constant proportion of the population—cannot be predicted with certainty. The concern over juvenile delinquency may keep more women at home and may lead to organized attempts to find employment for young people. Legislation to combat discrimination against hiring old people may cause a rise in the average retirement age. It may be that when evolving social customs cause some age-sex groups to enter the labor market at a reduced rate, a vacuum is created which attracts more people from other age-sex groups. Or it may be only accidental that the changing rates of participation of different groups have offset each other in the past. The former hypothesis would lead us to expect the labor force to be a stable fraction of the population; the latter would make the outlook uncertain.

The Aging Population and the Labor Force

For both the labor force and the population as a whole, the proportion in the upper age groups has been increasing over the past decades. Between 1900 and 1950, the percentage of the population sixty-five years old and older doubled, and this percentage continues to grow. During the same period, the fastest growing segment of the labor force was the forty-five and older group, which rose from less than 23 per cent to more than 35 per cent of the total. At the same time, as we saw, there has been a long-run decline in the percentage of people over sixty-five who are employed.

The increasing average age of the population and of the labor force gives rise to a number of special economic and social problems. There is first the need for maintaining the income of older people. Second, there is a loss of production to society caused by their exit from the labor market. And third, there is the problem of maintaining their self-respect; many of them do not want to live out their last years in wasteful idleness.

The first problem results from changing labor market conditions which have eliminated employment as the typical source of income for older persons, and from changing social customs which discourage them from living in the same household with their children. Reliance is now placed on group rather than family support for their financial needs, entailing expensive public insurance and private pension programs.

Nevertheless, the standard of living of old people averages much less than that of the rest of the population. This may have dangerous political implications because of the increasing numbers of older people.

The loss of production as a consequence of retiring older workers—our second problem—places a greater burden on those within the productive ages. In 1950, there were 718 persons between twenty and sixty-four for every 100 over that age; for 1970, the estimate is 575 persons of working age for every 100 of retirement age. Some day we may decide we cannot afford the luxury of retiring workers at the age of sixty-five.

The advancements made in medical science continue to increase the average length of life. After a worker reaches sixty-five, life expectancy is approximately fifteen years. Many people, of course, live longer than that. Those who retire at sixty-five, still with many years to live, are forced to reorient their lives completely, and to make this adjustment at a very late age. Unless interesting social and economic incentives are provided, they may easily lose their self-respect.

This feeling of being left out of the mainstream of economic activity also attacks workers who have not yet reached sixty-five. Middle-aged persons, as noted earlier, who are discharged often have great difficulty in finding new employment. Recent experience has shown that the older the worker, the longer the unemployment. The occupations which have been expanding most rapidly—e.g., professional and technical, clerical, and sales—are very difficult to enter at an advanced age. Low educational accomplishments prevent many from being eligible for the training necessary for the new jobs in the expanding occupations. Thus many are forced into early retirement with ten or twenty years of potential working life remaining.[6]

PATTERNS OF OCCUPATIONAL AND INDUSTRIAL DISTRIBUTION OF THE LABOR FORCE

In a complex economy with a high degree of division of labor, workers fill a wide variety of jobs. These jobs are classified both by occupation and by industry. Occupational classification depends on the nature of the job regardless of the final product, e.g., foreman, drill press operator, common laborer. Industrial classification depends on the goods or services produced, e.g., automobiles, food products, television repair services. Each industry includes a number of occupations, and the typical occupation is found in many different industries.

[6] John J. Corson and John W. McConnell, *Economic Needs of Older People* (New York: The Twentieth Century Fund, 1956).

Changes in the nature of the economy are mirrored in the changing occupational and industrial distribution of the labor force. The movement from a rural agricultural economy to an urban manufacturing economy is an example. To understand the labor market, it is necessary to be cognizant of the occupational and industrial distribution of the labor force and the pattern of the changes therein. Changes in either of these categories will have profound effects on the kind of work people do, on the wages they are paid, and on the nature of unionization.

Trends in Occupational Distribution

The changing occupational picture of the American economy is depicted in Table 1-A. (The figures for May, 1959, are affected by seasonal fluctuations and therefore are not fully comparable with the annual data.) The shifting patterns are clear in the table but deserve some additional emphasis. The occupation of manager, official, and proprietor and the occupation of laborer each accounted for 25 per cent of the labor force in 1910, whereas the two together barely exceeded 25 per cent in 1959. The main declines occurred among farm managers and farm laborers. Big increases—more than 150 per cent—were scored by clerical workers, while the number of professional and technical workers more than doubled. Operatives (semi-skilled workers) increased by 50 per cent, but began to decline after 1950. Skilled workers have not lost ground with the increasing mechanization of industry. The modern skilled workers are mechanics, maintenance men, and foremen rather than artisans.

These occupational trends reflect the changing manpower requirements of a developing economy. In fact, the stage of economic development can be measured by the proportion of the labor force engaged in occupations requiring a high degree of training. The increasing amount of capital investment per worker places more emphasis on occupations involving brain-power and machine manipulation.

Will innovations change the trends observable in Table 1-A? This is most unlikely. To illustrate, consider the implications of the spread of automation—one of the most widely heralded of recent innovations. Automation is the chaining together of several separate production processes into one integrated process, automatically transferring the work materials from one operation to the next. It often involves complicated electronic equipment and feed-back, self-regulating control mechanisms. A familiar example is the thermostat that automatically regulates the temperature of a house more accurately and consistently

TABLE 1-A

Major Occupational Groups of Employed Workers*

Major occupational group	Number (000's omitted)				Percentage			
	1910	1940	1950	May, 1959	1910	1940	1950	May, 1959
Total employed [a]	35,469	44,888	56,239	66,016	100.0	100.0	100.0	100.0
Professional, technical, and kindred workers	1,642	3,566	4,910	7,154	4.6	7.9	8.7	10.8
Managers, officials, proprietors	8,695	8,764	9,327	10,165	24.5	19.5	16.6	15.4
Farmers and farm managers	6,129	5,144	4,309	3,217	17.3	11.4	7.7	4.9
Managers, officials, and proprietors except farm	2,566	3,620	5,018	6,948	7.2	8.1	8.9	10.5
Clerical and kindred workers	1,952	4,371	6,895	9,063	5.5	9.7	12.3	13.7
Sales workers	1,759	3,072	3,927	4,265	5.0	6.8	7.0	6.5
Craftsmen, foremen, and kindred workers	4,139	5,152	7,783	8,653	11.7	11.5	13.8	13.1
Operatives and kindred workers	5,019	8,470	11,872	11,868	14.1	18.9	21.1	18.0
Service workers	3,391	5,271	5,694	8,086	9.6	11.8	10.1	12.3
Laborers	8,872	6,222	5,831	6,761	25.0	13.9	10.4	10.3
Farm laborers and foremen	4,745	3,099	2,400	2,938	13.4	6.9	4.3	4.5
Laborers, except farm and mine	4,127	3,123	3,431	3,823	11.6	7.0	6.1	5.8

* Gladys L. Palmer and Ann R. Miller, "The Occupational and Industrial Distribution of Employment, 1910–1950," *Manpower in the United States*, ed. by Haber *et al*, p. 87. Table 1-A and Table 1-B are reproduced by permission of Harper & Brothers, New York.

[a] Excludes Armed Forces and persons under 14 years of age. Percentages computed on unrounded data.

Sources: Data for 1910 have been converted to 1950 classifications from original published figures for that year. Data for 1940 and 1950 from published tabulations of the U. S. Bureau of the Census. Persons not reporting occupation have been included with "Operatives and kindred workers" for purposes of greater comparability with 1910. Figures for May, 1959, from Department of Commerce, Bureau of the Census, *Current Population Reports*, Series P–57.

than could be done manually. Although simple automatic control devices have been used for centuries, it is only in the last decade that complicated devices have spread widely beyond such processing industries as oil, chemicals, and pulp and paper-making.

Extending the applications of automation requires a great deal of research and development and thus accelerates the demand for scientific and technical personnel, and for maintenance employees trained to repair more complicated equipment. Automation also substantially modifies the nature of the work done by production employees. For example, before automation, workers in a factory making automobile engine blocks were required to drill, inspect, and transport the heavy castings from one drilling machine to the next. Using one-tenth the number of workers, an automated factory turns out the same number of engine blocks of a better quality with the workers now devoting their efforts to watching an instrument board and occasionally throwing switches. Thus, automation will augment rather than change the present trends in occupational distribution.

To college students, one of the most interesting developments is the increase in professional and technical employment, the fastest growing occupational category in the coming years. New scientific discoveries have created a demand for scientists, engineers, and technicians to do applied research and developmental work necessary to convert these discoveries into practical production techniques. Hence, more technical skills are needed in production, marketing, and other positions. The various functions of management are also becoming increasingly specialized and technical.[7]

Trends in Industrial Distribution

The trends in the industrial distribution of the labor force are shown in Table 1-B. Over the past few decades, manufacturing has replaced agriculture as the dominant industry, with wholesale and retail trade moving into second place. Although manufacturing scored the greatest absolute increase, in terms of number of workers, between 1910 and 1950, many industries had relatively much larger increases, e.g., professional and related services, public administration, and finance. When the statistics from the 1960 census are finally tabulated, they will show a relative decline for the manufacturing industry. Using data presented on a somewhat different basis from that in Table 1-B, in 1950, manu-

[7] Helen Wood, "Trends in the Specialization of Occupational Requirements," *op. cit.,* ed. by Haber *et al,* pp. 103–16.

TABLE 1-B

Major Industry Groups of Employed Workers*

	Number (000's omitted)			Percentage		
Major industry group	1910	1940	1950	1910	1940	1950
Total employed [a]	35,469	44,888	56,239	100.0	100.0	100.0
Agriculture, forestry, and fisheries	10,987	8,498	7,007	31.0	18.9	12.4
Mining	989	930	944	2.8	2.1	1.7
Construction	2,178	2,112	3,493	6.1	4.7	6.2
Manufacturing	7,279	10,777	14,822	20.5	24.0	26.3
Transportation, communication, and other public utilities	3,076	3,166	4,439	8.7	7.1	7.9
Wholesale and retail trade	4,170	7,698	10,733	11.8	17.1	19.1
Finance, insurance, and real estate	584	1,502	1,951	1.6	3.3	3.5
Business repair services	278	908	1,434	0.8	2.0	2.6
Personal services	3,491	4,071	3,558	9.8	9.1	6.3
Entertainment and recreation services	175	427	563	0.5	1.0	1.0
Professional and related services	1,676	3,365	4,764	4.7	7.5	8.5
Public administration	586	1,434	2,531	1.7	3.2	4.5

* Palmer and Miller, *loc. cit.*, p. 90.

[a] Excludes Armed Forces and persons under 14 years of age. Percentages computed on unrounded data.

Sources: The original published figures from the 1910 Census of Population have been converted to 1950 classifications. Data for 1940 and 1950 are from published tabulations of the Bureau of the Census. Persons not reporting industry have been distributed in nonagricultural employment as persons reporting industry.

facturing accounted for a third of all workers in nonagricultural establishments, but only 30 per cent in 1959. The downward trend began with the recession of 1954, and has been especially marked among production employees. In fact, white-collar employees in manufacturing have been increasing rapidly relative to blue-collar workers.

A close relationship obviously exists between the trends in industrial and occupational distribution. Just as the rise of manufacturing brought the need for more foremen, skilled workers, and operatives, so the rise of wholesale and retail trade increased the demand for clerical and sales workers.

The rising standard of living in the United States is mirrored in the relative decline of the industries producing goods compared to those producing services. As the output per worker of food, clothing, coal, refrigerators, etc. increases, we can afford to devote a larger portion of our labor force to education, recreation, and medical services. Since 1940, slightly over half of our workers have been employed in industries producing services rather than physical goods. The expanding application of automation techniques will probably accelerate this trend.

The changing industrial distribution of the labor force has a substantial impact on the nature of labor problems. How can workers who are replaced by technological improvements be guided into new jobs? How can financial rewards be adjusted to take into account the new technical, skilled, and semi-skilled jobs that appear in the new industries? What new labor legislation will be needed to meet these problems? What policies will unions follow on these questions? Some of the industries expanding most rapidly are the ones where unions have made only a negligible penetration. What organizing techniques will unions devise to break into these expanding areas of employment? Will they be forced to modify some of their basic policies? Or will these growing industries remain unorganized?

Before we can discuss these questions, we must know more about the labor force, the union movement, and collective bargaining.

SUMMARY

Customs and traditions play a major role in determining what portion of the population seeks gainful employment. Over long periods of time, modifications occur in the customs and traditions, thus inducing changes in the size and composition of the labor force. The central core of the labor force consists of males between the ages of twenty-five and sixty-five. However, there are other groups—young people, old people, and women of all working ages—who regularly augment the working population. It is for these groups that changes in customs and traditions are crucial.

During a typical year, the labor force exhibits a seasonal pattern, reaching its peak during May and June, and its low mark, some three to four million fewer workers, in January and February. Changes in the labor force also occur during the course of a cyclical fluctuation in income and employment. These cyclical changes, which tend to counterbalance each other, are prevalent among young people, old people, women of all working ages, and rural-to-urban migrants. Although the evidence is not clear, it appears that at the very peak of a booming prosperity, the excess demand for labor attracts some additional workers into the labor force, increasing its size beyond what it would otherwise be.

Over the long run, women have been participating in the labor market at a greater rate. Young people, because of higher educational standards, have been entering the labor force at increasingly older ages. The trend toward an earlier retirement age for older people—which may reverse itself—has reduced the number of older people in the labor force. The fact that the number of older persons is increasing, both absolutely and relatively to both population and labor force, leads to economic and social problems that we are only beginning to understand.

Changes in the occupational and industrial distribution of the labor force have reflected the dynamic nature of our economy. The most obvious industrial change over the last fifty years has been the shift away from agriculture and the extractive industries. The manufacturing, trade, and service industries have registered large increases while transportation and construction have remained relatively constant. During the first half of the century there was a marked rise in the professional and technical, clerical, and operative occupations. The decline in common laborers and in managers has been just as striking.

DISCUSSION QUESTIONS

1. What interests does the typical worker have that might be in conflict with his interests as a producer?

2. The definition of the labor force emphasizes attachment to the labor market. What does this mean? This definition arbitrarily excludes some groups who might enter the labor force under different labor market conditions. Describe some of these groups and explain how they are excluded by the definition.

3. Explain a number of different ways in which labor force statistics are useful in interpreting our economy.

4. As automation is widely adopted throughout American industry, what effect do you expect it to have on the size and composition of the labor force? Explain.

5. What seasonal changes take place in the size of the labor force? What groups of workers account for these changes?

6. Discuss the factors which would tend to lead to an increase in the size of the labor force during a decline in employment. What are the counteracting factors?

7. List the customs and traditions which determine who will enter the labor force and discuss their changing importance over the last few decades.

8. What special problems appear with an aging labor force? Do you think that the increasing average age of the population will have any effects on the proportion of the population in the labor force? Explain.

9. Which are our most rapidly expanding industries and occupations? What effect do you expect automation will have on these trends? Explain.

10. The changing industrial distribution of the labor force reflects our rising standard of living. Explain how this is so.

BIBLIOGRAPHY

Bancroft, Gertrude. *The American Labor Force.* New York: John Wiley & Sons, 1958.

Cooper, Sophia, and Garfinkle, Stuart. *Population and Labor Force Projections for the United States, 1960 to 1975.* U. S. Department of Labor, Bulletin No. 1242. Washington: Government Printing Office, 1959.

Corson, John J., and McConnell, John W. *Economic Needs of Older People.* New York: The Twentieth Century Fund, 1956.

Durand, John D. *The Labor Force in the United States, 1890–1960.* New York: Social Science Research Council, 1948.

Haber, William; Harbison, Frederick H.; Klein, Lawrence R.; and Palmer, Gladys L., eds. *Manpower in the United States.* New York: Harper & Brothers, 1954.

Jaffe, A. J., and Stewart, Charles D. *Manpower Resources and Utilization.* New York: John Wiley & Sons, Inc., 1951.

Long, Clarence D. *The Labor Force under Changing Income and Employment.* Princeton: Princeton University Press, 1958.

Woytinsky, W. S., and Associates. *Employment and Wages in the United States.* New York: The Twentieth Century Fund, 1953.

2

STRATIFICATION

IN THE LABOR FORCE

In every economy, there are many organized groups—employers, workers, farmers—competing for the fruits of production, each seeking to protect its special interest and to increase its share of the total output. Sometimes conditions favor one group vis-à-vis its rivals: employer groups held the advantage in the nineteenth century when political attitudes and economic forces encouraged rapid exploitation of our natural wealth. Each organization, in adopting its rules of conduct and techniques of battling its opponents, is circumscribed by the environment. For example, our laws and social customs rule out revolutionary violence as a technique for worker organizations. And so we must examine the socio-economic environment which surrounds the birth and development of unions.

One of the most important of the environmental factors is the degree of class consciousness prevailing in society. When class lines are clear-cut and easily recognized, workers consider themselves a group set apart from the rest of society. They are separate from the owners, managers, and persons in professional occupations, and expect that neither they nor their sons will ever rise to these higher status occupations. The working class will be underprivileged as compared to the other classes in receiving such rewards as income, education, political power, and social esteem. Such conditions would certainly affect the willingness of workers to join unions and the kinds of union policies they would support.

SOCIAL STRATIFICATION

Systems of social stratification are found in every known society. They consist of ranking individuals on a superiority-inferiority scale according to the valuation placed on them by other members of society. In America, the commonly accepted basis for evaluation includes: the amount of a person's income, how he earns it, his influence in community affairs (Does he dominate the Community Chest Board of Directors?), how much power and authority he wields over other persons (Does he have control over hiring and firing large numbers of workers?), the amount of deference accorded to him by others (Is he seated at a place of honor at social functions?), and many other factors. In some societies, a person's ranking depends on the class into which he is born. This attitude was prevalent in Europe during the Middle Ages and is reflected in India's caste system today.

What is the nature of social stratification in America? Rank is not inherited, but is our society divided into discrete and easily recognized classes? Some scholars believe they have found evidence that class lines do exist. Some have even argued that these class lines are hardening and that members of different classes are becoming more aware of their status positions, making it more difficult for manual workers, and the sons of manual workers, to move into non-manual occupations. In its extreme form, the argument states that a working class is emerging with its own unique political and social outlook, and that all workers tend to have the same motivations and goals.

Other scholars claim that while there is a diversity in the status positions of individuals and families which is closely related to the way in which they earn their living, our social stratification is a continuous gradation from the bottom to the top. In other words, while there are variations in the social and economic rewards received by different individuals, there is no clearly recognized line separating a workers' class from the rest of society.

Evidence of Class Lines

To begin our study of social stratification and its impact on unions, we will examine some of the evidence indicating the existence of clearly defined class lines. The three pieces of evidence we are going to consider, prepared by E. W. Bakke, Richard Centers, and W. Lloyd Warner, must be interpreted in the light of their methodology and dates. The class attitudes and reactions of Americans today are certainly different from what they were during the depression and unemployment of the 1930's and different from World War II and the immediate postwar period. In another decade or so, they may change again.

Class Lines During the Depression

Bakke studied unemployed workers and their families in New Haven, Connecticut, between 1932 and 1939, and found that they had not developed a mature working-class philosophy. But he did record the following factors which tended to encourage the development of a moderate form of class consciousness: 1) There was a tradition of industrial work running through the families; 62 per cent of those who provided information were the children of industrial workers. 2) The unemployed workers suffered from a common set of dissatisfactions and frustrations; and though their economic and social goals were not basically different from those of other members of society, the unemployed were more modest in their expectations for achieving the goals. 3) They were aware of outgroupers, e.g., executives and professional people, who looked, lived, and dressed in a manner different from them. 4) They had a tendency to divide people into those who do the planning as opposed to those who work with their hands. 5) They were aware that an upper-status person had greater scope in his personal affairs. The "boss" could decide, for instance, to move to a new neighborhood, and would be in an economic position to do it, whereas the worker might just as well not consider the matter. 6) There was a widespread belief that the working people had only a very limited chance for "getting ahead." 7) Their common problems led to common leisure time activities, e.g., cheap movies and inexpensive recreation in public parks.

At the same time, Bakke found some important barriers which tended to prevent the development of class consciousness: 1) The workers' closest ties were with their jobs rather than with workers as a class: they were job-conscious and not class-conscious. 2) There was no constant opponent, no identifiable group rising to wealth and power on the backs of the workers. 3) The workers did not generalize on their daily experience, considering their hardships as individual problems, and hence did not fit the pieces together into a working class philosophy. 4) The variety of nationalities prevented them from fully understanding and trusting each other.

Bakke's final conclusion was that these barriers were weakening and that a solidified working class was already well started in its development.

In the future, economic and political institutions would reflect this class character.[1]

Postwar Class Lines

Richard Centers interviewed a nation-wide sample of 1,100 white males in 1948. He wanted to learn whether people identified themselves with a particular social class, whether this identification was determined by their occupations, and whether it influenced their social and political attitudes.

Each person interviewed was asked to name the class to which he belonged, choosing among upper, middle, working, and lower classes. Centers found that slightly more than half of the people identified themselves with the working class, and about 40 per cent with the middle class. No allowance was made for those who thought they did not belong in any one of the classes.

After he had identified his class, the person was presented with a list of occupations. He was asked to mark the ones he considered to be in his own class. There was agreement on some occupations, considerable disagreement on others. About half of those who identified themselves with the middle class assigned doctors, lawyers, salesmen, office workers, and farmers to some other class. Those who claimed to be in the working class were about equally divided as to whether office workers, waiters and bartenders, and servants belonged in their class. Centers' study, then, shows some relationship, but an inconclusive one, between class identification and occupation.

Centers found some interesting differences in social and political attitudes. The "working class" was more likely to favor government ownership of large enterprises and public utilities, government guarantees of full employment, and a larger voice in government for the working people. The "middle class" was more likely to believe that success depended on ability rather than luck and that their children had a good opportunity to rise to higher status positions. Those in the lower occupations—generally accepted as working class occupations—showed a greater tendency to approve of unions, but people in every class believed workers improved their economic position through union membership.[2]

[1] E. Wight Bakke, *Citizens Without Work* (New Haven: Yale University Press, 1940), pp. 86–105.
[2] Richard Centers, *The Psychology of Social Classes* (Princeton: Princeton University Press, 1949), pp. 55–85.

From Upper Upper to Lower Lower

W. Lloyd Warner, one of the most widely recognized writers on social stratification, has studied social classes for a period covering more than twenty years. He divides society into six classes: upper upper, lower upper, upper middle, lower middle, upper lower, and lower lower. According to his measurements, some communities have all six classes, others may have only five classes, and others, particularly smaller communities, may have only two or three.[3]

What determines the class to which a person belongs? Warner believes he can determine this by examining the social affiliations and membership connections of the individual—country clubs, churches, ladies' auxiliaries, etc. Certain social groups are typically associated with a given class. Thus, membership in those groups indicates the class to which the person belongs. Warner also suggests a more direct method —giving approximately the same results—involving an evaluation based on four factors: occupation, size and construction of home, nature of the immediate area in which the home is located, and whether income is earned or received as dividends, rents, or otherwise. An individual is then assigned a score which determines his class.

If Warner had found, in computing a large number of these scores, that they tended to cluster around six separate points, corresponding to the six classes, he would have convincing evidence of a society with definite class lines. He does not claim such a clustering of his scores, yet he maintains that class lines do exist.

Warner and his associates made some interesting discoveries concerning the relationship between education and social status. Public schools were found to make the path to college easier and more stimulating for the upper status children. Furthermore, since income helps to determine social status, children from higher status families were more likely to complete high school and go on to college. In short, the expense of acquiring an education tends to perpetuate the existing degree of social stratification. At the same time, Warner and his associates found a number of exceptions, students whose social position improved as they took advantage of the opportunities provided by free public education.[4]

[3] W. Lloyd Warner, Marchia Meeker, and Kenneth Eells, *Social Class in America* (Chicago: Social Science Research Associates, Inc., 1949). The subtitle of this book is "Manual of Procedure for the Measurement of Social Status."

[4] W. Lloyd Warner, Robert J. Havighurst, and Martin B. Loeb, *Who Shall Be Educated?* (New York: Harper & Brothers, 1944), especially pp. 62–95.

Evidence That Class Lines Do Not Exist

Some sociologists believe that there are no clear lines separating social classes in the United States. A survey conducted in Columbus, Ohio, designed to test Warner's hypothesis and using the approach he suggested, failed to reveal any clustering of social status positions into six classes, or into two or four or any other number of classes. Just as we have an age continuum, yet call people young, middle-aged, or old, so we have a social continuum and yet speak of lower, middle, and upper classes.[5]

There are many factors operating in the American society which prevent the appearance of class lines. Among the most important of these is the tenacity with which we hold the belief that all people are equal and should have equal political and economic opportunity. So we grant all citizens the right to vote and to hold public office, we equalize the burdens of military service and jury duty, and provide free public education and a host of public services. Furthermore, the symbols of class position are not consistently possessed by individuals: one person may have a middle class home, an upper class income, a middle class occupation, a lower class education, and almost no organizational affiliations. Such crisscrossing of symbols is not at all uncommon and acts as a strong barrier to the development of a consciousness of class lines.[6]

Other barriers include the rapid growth of the American economy and our restless geographical mobility. The growing economy has brought a continual stream of new industries and occupations which have provided new opportunities for members of every status group. Hence, any class lines which begin to appear are blurred by the shifting patterns of income. Of course, as Bakke found, a prolonged depression, which stifles economic opportunities, would alter this picture.

Geographical mobility breaks down old traditions and class lines at the same time. Such mobility, of course, does not create economic equality between persons of greatly different wealth. But when an individual moves from the East to the West or from a small town to a metropolitan area, he loses old status symbols, particularly those based on family background.

To deny that there are well-defined class lines is not the same as

[5] John F. Cuber and William F. Kenkel, *Social Stratification in the United States* (New York: Appleton-Century-Crofts, 1954), pp. 137–50.
[6] Robin M. Williams, *American Society* (New York: Alfred A. Knopf, 1954), pp. 115–25.

claiming that everybody is in one big middle class. Within the American stratification system, there is a wide range of inequality in social and economic rewards. There is no difficulty in distinguishing between those at the top of the range and those at the bottom, between a corporation executive and an irregularly employed common laborer. But it is difficult to find a permanent and well-recognized demarcation between an upper middle class and a lower middle class, or between a lower middle class and an upper lower class. And whatever demarcation does exist is in a constant state of flux.

Conclusion on Social Stratification

Every dynamic economy has some degree of stratification. Higher rewards, socially and economically, are probably necessary to induce persons to accept the more arduous, more responsible, or more risky tasks. For example, positions of union leadership must carry certain prestige and power rewards if they are to attract capable personnel. In order to induce an adequate flow of trained personnel, it is perhaps necessary to offer higher rewards to the educated who sacrificed income by postponing their entrance into the labor market. Whether or not the range between the highest and lowest rewards is too great is a question of value standards and is not discussed here.

In the United States, stratification takes the form of a range of social classes, but without rigid class lines, with the exception of racial and ethnic groups who are the victims of discrimination. Although there is some evidence that people identify themselves as members of a class, they are not at all class-conscious in a Marxian sense. There are common attitudes and opinions held by people in similar occupations. But at the same time people from almost all income groups own cars, watch the same television programs, read the same newspapers and magazines.

The American class system is an open class system. That is, the opportunity to rise from one status position to a higher one prevents the development of hardened class lines. Since social class is closely related to occupation, the extent of this upward social mobility depends on the amount of upward occupational mobility.

OCCUPATIONAL MOBILITY

Occupational mobility is the movement of workers from one occupation to another. It is upward occupational mobility when workers shift from one occupation to another with higher prestige. Some occupations carry high prestige value: physician, corporation executive, and scientist;

others are at the bottom of the scale: domestic worker and common laborer. In general, white-collar jobs possess higher prestige than blue-collar jobs. The degree of rigidity of social stratification depends on the individual's opportunity to move up the occupational ladder, and on his opportunity to achieve a higher status occupation than that of his father.

Occupational Mobility: the Amount

The typical American worker changes his occupation at least once during his working life. For example, only about one-fifth of the young men who begin their working careers as clerical and sales workers remain in that occupation to the end of their careers. About three-tenths of them become managers, officials, proprietors, or professional persons, about one-tenth craftsmen or foremen, and two-fifths go to other manual occupations. Workers who begin their careers in other occupations also show a high degree of mobility.[7] Such labor market conditions serve as a major barrier to the development of a rigidly stratified society.

The question of father-son (intergenerational) occupational mobility was analyzed in a comprehensive study conducted by Natalie Rogoff in 1949–1950.[8] She investigated the occupations of more than 10,000 men and their fathers in 1940, and found that the over-all mobility rate had remained unchanged: the tendency for the son to follow the same occupation as his father was neither stronger nor weaker in 1940 as compared to 1910. In each period the occupational differences between sons and fathers was about four-fifths of what would be expected if the son's occupation was entirely independent of his father's. To make this clear, consider two possibilities: 1) the son's occupation depends 100 per cent on the father's occupation, and 2) the son's occupation is completely independent of the father's occupation. The first possibility would cause all sons to follow in their fathers' footsteps. The second possibility would cause sons to be in the same trade as their fathers only as a matter of chance.

Although the over-all father-son mobility was four-fifths of what would have resulted from completely random factors, different occupations

---

[7] A. J. Jaffe and R. O. Carleton, *Occupational Mobility in the United States, 1930–1960* (New York: King's Crown Press, 1954), pp. 54–57.

[8] Natalie Rogoff, *Recent Trends in Occupational Mobility* (Glencoe: The Free Press, 1953). The sample was taken from Marion County, Indiana, which includes the city of Indianapolis.

showed very different rates of mobility. In 1910, sons of professional, semiprofessional, proprietor, and clerical fathers were more mobile than sons of industrial workers. By 1940, however, the sons of blue-collar workers were about as mobile as sons of white-collar fathers. The white-collar sons concentrated most of their movement into relatively few occupations, whereas the blue-collar sons moved into a wider range of occupations. In other words, blue-collar sons showed a greater tendency to shift into white-collar positions than white-collar sons into blue-collar positions.

The son is more likely to choose his father's occupation than any other single occupation out of the wide range of possibilities. The tendency varies in different occupations, with the pattern of variation being about the same in 1940 as in 1910. The sons of fathers whose occupations were either at the top or at the very bottom of the occupational ladder showed a greater tendency to follow in their fathers' footsteps than did the sons whose fathers were in the middle of the occupational ladder. That is, father-son mobility was greatest in the lower middle and the upper lower classes, embracing a crucial range of occupations where, if there were no mobility, there would be a greater tendency for a working class consciousness to appear.

Vertical Mobility

Upward mobility is the most important element in the relation of occupational mobility to the development of a working class conscious-ness, even more important than the over-all mobility trends described above. On the basis of data from 1930 to 1950, it is estimated that for every 100 men who move down the occupational scale, there are 300 who move up over their lifetime. Of the men who enter at the bottom of the occupational ladder—laborers, operatives, and service workers— about 60 per cent move to higher status occupations. Even within these lower occupations there is considerable upward movement from laborer to operative.[9]

Even though there is a considerable amount of vertical mobility, there are many workers who are left behind and become entrenched in their jobs at an early age. This appears to be particularly true of workers in large factories, as revealed in a postwar study of automobile workers in a middle-sized midwestern city. Many of the workers ac-cepted their jobs, with starting rates of pay that were comparatively

[9] Jaffe and Carleton, *op. cit.*, pp. 55–56.

high, with the anticipation of saving enough to go into business for themselves. However, after marriage and adjusting their standard of living to their pay scale, these workers generally found it impossible to leave the factory to fulfill their early aspirations. With the accumulation of seniority, they had become trapped in a job which provided them with almost no opportunity for vertical mobility. Since the wage range was narrow and the pace of the job was set by the machine, they could not significantly raise their income by demonstrating unusual ability on the job. Their economic advancement, then, depended on how successful the union was in winning wage increases.[10]

What is the picture for intergenerational occupational mobility? To what extent is it possible for sons of unskilled and semi-skilled industrial workers to become physicians, technicians, or executives? If the opportunity is severely restricted, or if the opportunity is decreasing from year to year, a basis is provided for a class-conscious society.

It appears that this is not the case. Rogoff found that upward mobility was about the same in 1940 as 1910, while downward mobility had decreased.[11] Other evidence indicates that the sons of fathers in nonmanual occupations are more likely to enter the higher status occupations than are the sons of fathers in manual occupations. Nevertheless, the latter also show a substantial amount of upward mobility.[12]

This evidence permitted an analysis of the relationship between the father's occupation, the son's education, and the son's occupation. A positive relationship between the father's occupation and the amount of education of the son was found; that is, the higher the status of the father's occupation, the greater the amount of education of the son. There was also a positive correlation between the amount of education and the job at which the son entered the labor market. Even where education between the sons was equal, the sons of the manual workers were more likely to enter the labor market in a manual job then were the sons of the nonmanual workers. Whenever college education was attained, it seemed to be an equalizer between the sons of manual and nonmanual fathers. The jobs of college graduates appeared to have little correlation with the fathers' occupations. Since a larger and

[10] Ely Chinoy, *Automobile Workers and the American Dream* (New York: Doubleday & Co., 1955).

[11] Rogoff, *op. cit.*, p. 61.

[12] Reinhard Bendix, Seymour M. Lipset, and F. Theodore Malm, "Social Origins and Occupational Career Patterns," *Industrial and Labor Relations Review*, Vol. VII (January, 1954), pp. 246–61. This study was conducted in the Oakland, California, labor market in 1949 and 1950.

larger portion of young people are attending college, this equalization of opportunities may be further extended.

As the American economy has grown over the past decades, the non-manual occupations have expanded more than the manual occupations. (See Chapter 1.) Thus, the average occupation today has a higher prestige status than it did in the past. This change in our occupational structure has contributed significantly to intergenerational upward mobility.[13]

Mobility and the Business Elite

Movement into the occupation of corporation executive constitutes one of the most interesting areas of study in vertical mobility. Where do these executives come from? Is theirs a closed occupation to be filled only by sons of executives? Or may persons of humbler origins rise to these positions?

In 1952, Warner and Abegglen collected biographical information from 8,000 corporation executives, from board chairmen to secretaries and treasurers, covering all industries and geographical regions of the United States. A disproportionately large percentage of these corporation executives were the sons of business executives or the sons of owners of large businesses. Other occupations in which fathers contributed more than their proportion of corporation executive sons were small business owners, professional men, and foremen.[14]

This study was just one generation later than a similar one,[15] thus permitting interesting comparisons between the results. The proportion of corporation executives coming from lowly origins had increased in 1952 as compared to 1928. The proportion who were sons of professional men and business owners and executives had declined. With the passage of a generation, there has been an increase in the amount of vertical mobility into the business elite. The data studied by Warner and Abegglen permitted comparison of the fathers of the business elite. Again, a large amount of vertical occupational mobility was found. It would appear, then, that vertical occupational mobility is a pervasive

[13] Nelson N. Foote and Paul K. Hatt, "Social Mobility and Economic Advancement," *American Economic Review*, Vol. XLIII (May, 1953), pp. 370–75.

[14] W. Lloyd Warner and James C. Abegglen, *Occupational Mobility in American Business and Industry, 1928–1952* (Minneapolis: University of Minnesota Press, 1955).

[15] F. W. Taussig and C. S. Joslyn, *American Business Leaders* (New York: The Macmillan Company, 1932).

characteristic of the American economy which shows no tendency to diminish.

CONSEQUENCES FOR UNIONIZATION

The evidence presented in this chapter supports the argument that the American society is not rigidly stratified, but is characterized more accurately as a continuous gradation from lower class laborers to upper class executives. Furthermore, there is a considerable amount of over-all occupational mobility with substantial vertical mobility. The amount of this vertical mobility is at least as great today as it was three or four decades ago, and therefore prevents the development of rigid stratification. What does all of this mean for unionization of the labor force? How does it affect the growth of union membership, union goals and tactics?

Union Growth

A well-developed working class consciousness would materially aid the growth of unionism. In some European countries, with more rigidly stratified societies than ours, the proportion of the labor force that is unionized is much greater than here. The reason is obvious. A man who sees his lifetime destiny dependent on the progress of manual workers as a group is likely to be willing to make sacrifices to promote the organization of that group, whereas a man who expects to move into nonmanual occupations would not be so inclined.

What does this mean from the point of view of union growth? Workers in this country see unions as organizations to protect their immediate economic interest rather than long-run class interests. If unions were class organizations in a class society, workers would join without a second thought; but as economic organizations, workers will join only if they see positive short-run economic gains.

The Oakland labor market study showed that vertically mobile workers were less likely to become union members than were their fellow-workers. This held true regardless of whether it was upward or downward mobility. In fact, those who were downwardly mobile were least likely to join unions. Although this was only one study in a single labor market, and may therefore not be typical, there are two reasonable explanations for this type of behavior by downwardly mobile workers. Workers may have resisted unions because membership would have entailed admission of their lower status on the occupational ladder. Or they may have absorbed anti-union attitudes from their earlier middle class environment.[16]

Since workers in many occupations do not automatically become members, unions must resort to expensive organizing campaigns. Furthermore, once organized, the workers will not necessarily give their first loyalty to the union. They may be more devoted to their church, lodge, veterans' organization, or employer. In fact, their tenure as union members may be temporary, despite the union's efforts to hold their loyalty.

One of the major problems of American unions, therefore, is holding the membership together. Obviously, efforts expended in this direction dilute the union efforts to increase membership. Union growth in this country is restricted—and will continue to be—by the lack of class consciousness. The rapid growth of unions in the 1930's was partially the consequence of some degree of class feeling appearing at that time; vertical mobility was negligible during the depression. The evidence found by Bakke supports this position.

Union Goals

To be successful over the long run, workers' organizations must be in tune with workers' experience. A union movement which emphasizes class-conscious goals, e.g., government ownership of the means of production or abolition of the wage system, is out of harmony with our socio-economic environment. It would arouse large-scale opposition throughout society, and probably also lose the allegiance of large groups of workers. Unless our society becomes more rigidly stratified, the development of class-conscious unionism is well-nigh impossible.

The absence of class consciousness also makes it more difficult for unions to win general public support for even more moderate goals. Outside of the unions themselves, there is no large group which will consistently follow the "union line." Under these circumstances, the rise of a labor party, particularly a class-conscious party, is not likely on our political horizon. Such a party would probably receive little or no support outside of unions, and it is doubtful whether union members themselves are sufficiently unified in their political objectives to promote their own party. Manual workers who have aspirations to become nonmanual workers, particularly those who have had some experience

[16] Seymour M. Lipset and Joan Gordon, "Mobility and Trade Union Membership," *Class, Status and Power,* ed. by Reinhard Bendix and Seymour M. Lipset (Glencoe: The Free Press, 1953), p. 492.

in white-collar occupations, tend to assume the attitudes and values of the "middle class." Although in the same economic boat as other manual workers, they become very unreliable political allies.

Another barrier to union adoption of class-conscious political goals stems from a peculiar characteristic of our social mobility. The mobility has left behind racial and ethnic minority groups who generally fill the lower status occupations. These racial and ethnic groups have demonstrated an effective political cohesion, particularly in large cities. Thus, we have minority-group-conscious rather than class-conscious political action.[17] The attachment of individuals to these racial and ethnic groups acts as a divisive factor in union affairs as well as in politics.

Class consciousness would lead all workers to believe that they are in conflict with a common enemy, the exploiting class. Unions and other workers' organizations would present a united front in this battle. The lack of class consciousness leads to disunity and internecine struggles within unions. American unions have devoted an excessive amount of time and funds to fighting each other. These fights between unions represent a conflict over narrow economic interests. They are the antithesis of a battle for broad class goals.

Even within a two-party political system, unions are unable to agree on a common set of goals. Union leaders—the professionals who articulate their members' goals—are divided over which political party to support; and they take widely varying stands on important political issues, e.g., tariffs and government ownership of public utilities.

Union Tactics

In attempting to achieve their goals, what tactics do unions adopt and how are the tactics affected by our system of social stratification? The most powerful weapon of American unions is the strike, but there are many environmental limitations on its use. Workers enthusiastically support strikes only for immediate economic benefits. They have no inclination to go without wages in order to win long-run political and social goals. Tactics of this type would cause workers to desert the unions.

The failure of other tactics demonstrates the impact of our open society. Union-sponsored educational ventures—daily newspapers, radio stations, political meetings—are comparatively scarce and sparsely attended. Union-sponsored social programs have never achieved the stat-

[17] Reinhard Bendix, "Social Stratification and Political Power," *The American Political Science Review*, Vol. XLVI (June, 1952), p. 364.

ure of the church supper or bingo party, or of the neighborhood poker club. In short, unions have been signally unsuccessful in spreading their tentacles into our daily lives.

Another characteristic of union tactics results from high mobility: union members themselves give less than full allegiance to their organizations. It was found that active union members—those who participate the most in union affairs—were less mobile, both occupationally and geographically, than the inactive. Also, the active members were the ones whose degree of skill was neither higher nor lower than their fathers'.[18] In other words, mobility not only inhibits the growth of unions, it also causes the members to be less interested in union activity, less willing to make sacrifices for the union. This means that unions can count on membership support for only a limited variety of tactics.

SUMMARY

In attempting to understand the behavior of American unions, it is necessary to take into account our degree of social stratification. Although we have a range of occupational and status positions, we do not have a rigidly stratified society. During the depression of the 1930's, there were tendencies for a class consciousness to develop. Since that time, the development of class consciousness appears to have made very little progress. Nevertheless, in the American stratification system, an individual's political and social attitudes are related to his identification with the "middle class" or the "working class." In the past these class distinctions were perpetuated by our educational system. However, with college education becoming more widely available, the reverse may now be true.

Instead of a rigidly stratified society, we have a range of socio-economic status positions. The difference between the top and the bottom, however, is sufficiently great to lead one to expect those at the lower end of the range to act differently from those at the upper end. Although such differences appear, they have not hardened into a class ideology.

One factor which helps to maintain our open society is the high degree of occupational mobility. Much of the mobility is up the occupational ladder, both for single working lifetimes and for father-son comparisons. This vertical mobility is at least as substantial now as in the past.

This lack of rigid stratification associated with the high degree of occupational mobility has a number of important consequences for

[18] Lipset and Gordon, *loc. cit.,* pp. 493, 498–99.

unions. It inhibits their growth, since mobile persons are less likely to become union members. Unions must concentrate much of their effort on merely retaining the allegiance of present members. Union goals and tactics cannot be of a broad class-conscious variety since they would receive very little support from union members, not to mention other segments of society.

DISCUSSION QUESTIONS

1. Define social stratification.
2. Why is it necessary to take into account the nature of social stratification in order to understand the union movement?
3. Differentiate between a society with a continuous gradation of social status positions and one with a rigid class stratification.
4. Citing evidence which you see about you in your daily life, write an essay either in support of or against the proposition that we have a rigidly stratified society.
5. Write an essay on the changes you believe would occur in our system of social stratification if we suffered a prolonged and severe depression.
6. What is the relationship between occupational mobility and social stratification?
7. What is vertical mobility and how is it likely to affect the growth of unions?
8. How do you explain the presence of a large amount of vertical occupational mobility in this country?
9. Vertical mobility will probably decrease in the next twenty years. Explain to what extent you agree or disagree with this statement.
10. How would union goals and tactics be affected if there were a sharp decrease in the amount of vertical mobility?
11. In the long run, more education for the population as a whole will lead to less union membership and less active union members. Explain to what extent you agree or disagree.

BIBLIOGRAPHY

Chinoy, Ely. *Automobile Workers and the American Dream*. New York: Doubleday & Co., 1955.

Cuber, John F., and Kenkel, William F. *Social Stratification in the United States*. New York: Appleton-Century-Crofts, 1954.

Jaffe, A. J., and Carleton, R. O. *Occupational Mobility in the United States, 1930–1960*. New York: King's Crown Press, 1954.

Mayer, Kurt B. *Class and Society*. Garden City: Doubleday & Co., 1955.

Rogoff, Natalie. *Recent Trends in Occupational Mobility*. Glencoe: The Free Press, 1953.

Warner, W. Lloyd; Meeker, Marchia; and Eells, Kenneth. *Social Class in America*. Chicago: Social Science Research Associates, Inc., 1949.

Williams, Robin M. *American Society*. New York: Alfred A. Knopf, 1954.

3 { GROWTH OF UNIONS

Unions today, their goals and tactics, are what they are as a result of their experience over the past 170 years. Born and reared in a hostile environment, American unions have had to battle tenaciously for their very existence. Since they could not rely on class consciousness to hold together, other methods had to be found by pragmatic, trial-and-error adjustments to each new crisis. In the course of making these adjustments, traditions were established which exercise a controlling influence over unions today.

Our survey of union growth can be more conveniently managed if it is divided into four periods: 1) the early gropings for a permanent adaptation to the American environment, 2) the growth of the American Federation of Labor (AFL) from the 1880's to the 1930's, 3) the rise of the Congress of Industrial Organizations (CIO) from the 1930's to the end of World War II, and 4) the current period of consolidation with stagnation in membership growth. Our attention is directed in this chapter to the first three periods.

EARLY TRIBULATIONS

The American labor movement vacillated for over ninety years before finally achieving a philosophy and approach which were adjusted to the American environment. Many different philosophies were examined and found wanting.

Unions first had to develop a range of goals possessing a permanent appeal to the American workers. Then the unions experimented with different techniques designed to secure these goals, including political and direct economic action. This experimental process reached a major turning point with the founding of the AFL in 1886.

Effects of Business Cycles

The outstanding characteristic of the first period of union growth was the impact of economic fluctuations on union membership and goals. During prosperous times, as employment and prices moved upward, workers frequently found that their wages lagged behind the rising cost of living. Under this pressure membership increased and unions concentrated on economic goals. Besides wage increases, they bargained for reductions in the length of the work day, in some places as long as fourteen and sixteen hours, and for the closed shop—the employer could hire only union members—in order to gain control of the job territory and ration it according to union rules.[1]

In depressions, unions declined sharply in membership and effectiveness. They were no longer able to win improvements in wages and working conditions. Workers then turned their attention to a variety of utopian plans to reshape the entire socio-economic structure. These utopian plans were completely out of harmony with short-run economic goals.

The first organizations of wage earners in this country, not counting the benevolent societies, some of which existed among skilled artisans before the Declaration of Independence, appeared in the last quarter of the eighteenth century. There were strikes—or "turnouts" as they were called—against wage decreases, involving shoemakers, printers, carpenters, and seamen. These groups, which never included all the workers involved, fell apart soon after the strikes. In 1792, the Philadelphia cordwainers (shoemakers) established the first organization of workers which had a continuous existence of more than a few years. They conducted a nine-week strike in 1799, during which the journeymen picketed their masters' shops.

The formation of the Mechanics' Union of Trade Associations in 1827 marks the real beginning of the labor movement. Striking for the ten-hour day, the Philadelphia carpenters sought the aid of other associations of building tradesmen in the city. Although the strike itself was unsuccessful, the idea of bringing together unions of workers from dif-

[1] These are typical of the goals of *business unions,* unions which accept the capitalistic wage system, rather than attempting to overthrow it, and which work for improvements in that system. Business unions are more fully discussed in Chapter 7.

ferent occupations caught on. All Philadelphia unions were invited to join the Mechanics' Union. Similar organizations—called city centrals in modern terminology—appeared in New York, Boston, and a number of other cities. Some of these Mechanics' Unions became active in support of workingmen's parties, particularly the one in New York City.

During the period of rising prices in the early 1830's, unions placed their main trust in economic techniques to improve working conditions. Many strikes were successful; a number of the craft unions won the ten-hour day. At this time, the National Trades' Union was established, a loose organization of the general unions (the city centrals) from many cities. It brought together labor leaders from all over the country for an exchange of opinions and experiences. The financial panic of 1837, and the consequent decline in union strength, doomed the National Trades' Union. The unions, however, were successful in their support of free public education, the abolition of imprisonment for debt, and mechanics' lien laws—laws which give workers first claim to the assets of bankrupt employers.

Whenever the unions were successful in holding their organization together for any length of time and in securing real economic gains, they were confronted with newly formed employers' associations. During the beginning stages of union organization, these were no more than associations of master craftsmen. The master craftsmen worked along with their journeymen employees sharing many of their interests. As transportation improved and wholesaling and manufacturing replaced the "bespoke" system—production directly for the consumer, almost always done in a small shop—the separation between employer and worker became greater, and the employers' associations began to resemble those of the present time more closely.

These early employers' associations succeeded in arousing public antipathy toward unions. Furthermore, the courts frequently found unions, when they promoted strikes, to be guilty of criminal conspiracy, and imposed fines on the union leaders. The combined opposition of courts, employers, and much of the general public, as well as the successive economic crises, shortened the life of these early unions and induced the workers to aim for the stars, to give their support to utopian programs.

Utopias

Utopias were "dreamed-up" by radical intellectuals who sought the support of unions to put their programs into effect. Utopians believed there was an abundance of economic opportunity, but that it was not available on a fair basis to all of the citizens. Institutional barriers blocked the way to the good life. If the capitalistic wage system could be eliminated, all workers would enjoy a higher standard of living. Religious and other idealistic groups, often motivated by the spread of factories and their surrounding tenement houses, established rural communities based on cooperative production and equal sharing of the output. The philosophy of the utopians undermined the unions which had grown during the prosperous periods: as long as the workers believed their salvation lay in substituting another system for the wage system, they were not inclined to develop strong economic organizations to win wage increases and improvements in working conditions.

A major theme of most utopian plans was opposition to monopoly. Among the primary targets of antimonopoly sentiment were the banks and financial institutions of the East, railroads and other distributive businesses, and land speculators. Farmers, shopkeepers, and owners of small factories believed they were oppressed by the monopolists and therefore joined with workers in support of some of the utopias.

Perhaps the most extreme of the utopian programs was that proposed by Thomas Skidmore. He gave it the name: *The Rights of Man to Property; Being a Proposition to Make it Equal among the Adults of the Present Generation; and to Provide for its Equal Transmission to Every Individual of Each Succeeding Generation, on Arriving at the Age of Maturity.* The plan called for periodically dividing the land of the country among all adult males, a non-Marxian type of communism, and was supported by the unions in New York City in 1829. The New York Workingmen's Party was successful in getting a substantial portion of the popular vote that year.

The advantages gained by the New York Workingmen's Party were almost immediately dissipated by factionalism between the radical intellectuals, among whom were Robert Dale Owen, advocating universal compulsory education in free boarding schools, and Frances Wright, advocating women's rights and easy divorce laws. The workers revolted against the radical leadership of Skidmore and the others. Furthermore, the middle class strongly opposed the utopias, showing their overwhelming desire to preserve private property rights. The unions, by temporarily supporting the utopias, gained a very radical reputation, incurring the wrath of the middle class, and were not able to live down the effects, particularly in New York City, until a generation had passed.

Supporting utopian schemes proved very costly to unions. A large measure of public support was transformed into widespread antipathy.

Energy that could have been used to extend union membership and to press for higher wages was frittered away in a vain attempt to win "pie in the sky." It was a matter of the unions, once achieving organization, being uncertain about quite what to do next. They fell apart quibbling over what direction to take. The bitter experience taught some segments of the union movement, particularly the skilled workers, strong negative lessons: what they should *not* adopt as goals and techniques. However, the lessons were not fully learned until the 1880's.

The Knights of Labor

Utopian programs attracted the attention of American workers until well after the Civil War. The last one to win widespread support was sponsored by the Noble and Holy Order of the Knights of Labor. Since the Knights engaged in normal union activity, besides pursuing long-run utopian goals, they did not constitute a pure utopia in the same sense as the earlier Skidmore program. Their so-called first principles, or utopian goals, included: seeking one big union of all trades, educating workers on the evils of capitalism, and promoting producers' cooperatives.[2]

The Knights generally tried to avoid strikes, which in their opinion were time and energy wasted on inconsequential short-run goals. They preferred the long-run objective of making every worker an entrepreneur.

The Knights had two unusual organizational features, both of which contributed to their eventual downfall. First, any "producer" was eligible for membership. Producers included anyone who worked with his hands and thereby contributed to the total output of goods, but excluded doctors, lawyers, bankers, and other "economic parasites." Workers were to be in the same organization with farmers, shopkeepers, and small employers; highly skilled journeymen were to join forces with unskilled workers.

The second peculiar aspect of the organization was its strong centralization. All members joined local assemblies which were directly under the control of the district assemblies. At the top of the centralized structure was the General Assembly, with complete and final power. Terence V. Powderly, Grand Master Workman, a spell-binding orator, completely dominated the General Assembly during the Knights' most active years.

[2] A producers' cooperative is an enterprise in which all employees are owners; all the workers are capitalists and share in the profits in proportion to the amount of work they perform. Producers' cooperatives had been a popular part of a number of the earlier utopian programs.

In actual practice the structure of the Knights was less centralized than it appeared on paper. While idealistically pursuing the goal of one big union, the Knights included trade assemblies—workers organized according to their craft or industry—which often showed greater interest in their own immediate economic concerns than in the long-run goals of the Noble and Holy Order. The centralization was more visible in the mixed assemblies—groups which included farmers, small employers, and workers who joined as individuals rather than as employees in a particular firm or as craftsmen in a particular trade. Naturally, the mixed assemblies showed less interest in strikes and more in producers' cooperatives and other reform movements. After the Knights passed the peak of their power, the mixed assemblies became the dominant group.

In spite of the Knights' objections to strikes, the members' opposition to employers became so strong in some cases that Powderly had to condone a number of strikes. Those in 1883 and 1884 were lost by the Knights. However, in 1885 two were won against the railroad system controlled by Jay Gould, including the Wabash, the Missouri, Kansas and Texas, and the Missouri Pacific. The end of the second strike marked the first time a leading capitalistic organization recognized a labor union as a force equal to itself.

The late 1880's was a period of spontaneous class conflict, to which the severe depression of the previous decade served as the prelude. The strikes on the railroads in the late 1870's were marked by violence and rioting, and order was restored by federal troops. An economic crisis struck again in the 1880's. Protest rallies of unemployed workers were held in many large cities, frequently terminating in pitched battles with the police. There were many strikes, with the eight-hour day being a major union goal.

During this period an anti-big-business attitude appeared in many segments of the public. The merger of smaller firms into giant combines with plants located all across the country contributed to this attitude. Ostentatious displays of wealth also evoked sympathy for workers and for the unemployed. As a result of the successful strikes on the Gould railroads, the desire to shorten the work day, and the anti-big-business attitudes, the Knights reached their peak membership of 700,000.

The Haymarket bomb explosion in 1886 caused a substantial loss in public sympathy for unions. In stopping a battle between strikers and strike-breakers near the McCormick Reaper Works in Chicago, the police killed four workers and wounded many others. The Black International [3] conducted a protest meeting the next day on Haymarket Square. Permission had been granted for holding the meeting and a number of public officials gave speeches. It proceeded peacefully until the police marched on the gathering. Then someone threw a bomb which killed and wounded a number of policemen. The police then fired into the crowd, killing several people. This episode brought on a period of police terror in Chicago, hysterical tirades in the press, and general panic on the part of the local citizens. Once more, the American labor movement—although innocent in the bomb-throwing—learned how easily the government and the public were aroused to a fever pitch by what they considered to be revolutionary activity threatening the rights of private property. Today it is difficult for us to imagine strikers in violent combat against strike-breakers and police, bringing death to many and a nation-wide desire for revenge. Yet this happened all too often in American union history.

The Decline of the Knights

While the Knights were achieving dominance in the American labor movement, other unions were also active, but aiming for different goals and employing different tactics. The trade unions, primarily consisting of highly skilled workers, preferred separate organizations, one for each trade or craft, rather than lumping all workers into one big union, and they supported strikes to win wage increases. When the Knights' membership stood at 700,000, the trade unions had approximately 250,000.

In the early 1880's the trade unions launched a campaign—involving a large number of strikes—to win the eight-hour day. The campaign was successful for as many as 200,000 workers, but by 1887 employers' associations, using lockouts, blacklists, strike-breakers, and plant guards, and aided by the reaction to the Haymarket bombing, were able once more to reduce the power of the unions and to win back this concession from most of them. Although the Knights took little active part in the drive, they received much of the credit from workers and condemnation from employers and the press. Most people did not differentiate between the two union groups, considering the skilled workers as a branch of the Knights.

The Knights and the trade unions soon became locked in a death struggle in the competition for the allegiance of American workers. The trade unions wanted the Knights to abandon all jurisdiction over

[3] The Black International was a group of anarchists, persons who favor eliminating all governments and vesting authority directly in workers as individuals. It consisted mainly of immigrants who thought in European rather than American terms.

skilled workers. The Knights refused, since such action would cause many of the assemblies to become impotent. The conflict reached its zenith in New York City in the battle between the cigar makers and District 49 of the Knights. The latter, realizing that they needed the skilled workers if they were to be successful, set out to bring the cigar makers into the Knights. The cigar makers' trade union sought to remain independent, believing it could maintain a stronger bargaining position vis-à-vis the employers if it excluded the unskilled segments of the industry. When District 49 engaged in strike-breaking activities during a strike against a wage reduction, the dispute reached a point beyond reconciliation. The trade unions consolidated their ranks, formed the AFL, and carried the fight beyond New York to all parts of the country.

The trade unions appealed directly to the self-interest of the skilled workers. Their leaders were more capable of conducting a strike than were the leaders in the Knights. Furthermore, they entered strikes with vigor, whereas the Knights of Labor considered a strike an undesirable and temporary means to a short-run end. The final triumph of business unionism over the utopias was a survival of the fittest: The victorious group recognized that the great majority of workers would be employees all of their lives, while the defeated group wanted to convert all workers into self-employed capitalists. The trade unions represented a much better adjustment to the American environment than did the Knights.

RISE OF THE AMERICAN FEDERATION OF LABOR

The cigar makers and two of their leaders, Samuel Gompers and Adolph Strasser, provided the dynamic force in forming the American Federation of Labor. The fight with the Knights convinced Gompers and Strasser that an altogether new kind of organization was needed. As a result of their interpretation of the American scene and their study of the British experience, they advocated the following general principles: Each trade union should 1) manage its own affairs with authority concentrated in the hands of the national officers, 2) maintain a large strike fund by charging sufficiently high dues, and 3) finance a broad benefit system, including payments to the aged and widows, as a technique for securing membership loyalty. This organizational structure was deemed to be most effective for improving wages and working conditions. Union energy was not to be wasted in vain chase of such utopian goals as overthrowing the capitalistic system.

The National Labor Unions

To find the chief building blocks of the AFL, we have to back up a couple of decades. Labor unions with a nation-wide membership first appeared in the 1850's among the printers, carpenters, tailors, machinists, painters, and other crafts. New economic conditions created problems which could be adequately handled only with national organizations and stimulated many strikes as unions attempted to adjust to the changes. With the continuing growth of railroads, goods produced in different parts of the country came into competition with each other in a national market. Thus, if the stove-molders in Detroit worked for lower wages than those in St. Louis, the wages of the latter would soon be forced down. In order to maintain the union wage rate, the workers in all stove manufacturing centers would have to be organized and uniform conditions imposed on all employers. From this economic motivation the National Molders' Union appeared, which later became the Iron Molders' International Union. Under the leadership of William H. Sylvis, it grew into one of the most powerful unions in the country at the end of the Civil War.

The wider use of machinery and the increased division of labor threatened the economic position of a number of the crafts. Further complicating this problem was the large number of immigrant workers willing to work at extremely low wages. Many of the immigrants were imported by employers' associations or large corporations seeking cheap labor, and in some cases they were used as strike-breakers. To distinguish themselves from the unskilled and semi-skilled workers and to protect the standards of their trade, the craft unions sought nation-wide organization. National unions on an industrial basis—rather than a craft basis —were also attempted, notably in coal mining, to prevent the threatened deterioration of wage rates resulting from the employment of immigrant workers.

Another factor promoting national unions was the traveling journeyman. The movement of journeymen from city to city was proportionately greater during the last half of the nineteenth century than it was before or has been since. These workers, searching for the high-wage cities, could be controlled only if they were union members; otherwise they would undermine union conditions, and even serve as strike-breakers. Furthermore, such control would have to be through uniform rules, administered in a like manner by all locals of the union. To achieve equal application of the rules, a national union with authority over its local units was necessary. The presence of traveling journeymen was instrumental in bringing about national organization in both the building trades and the printing trade.

It would seem that the next logical step would be the creation of a federation of these national unions, but that did not follow easily. In 1866, the National Labor Union was established; it held an annual meeting each year until 1872. The president was William H. Sylvis, up to his death in 1869. In his later years, however, Sylvis was more interested in long-run political goals than in the immediate economic interest of the craft unions. In 1872 the National Labor Union became a political party, but when its presidential candidate withdrew, the organization collapsed.

The Federation of the Organized Trades and Labor Unions of the United States and Canada (the forerunner of the AFL) was founded in 1881. Its main functions were 1) to assist in organizing new members, 2) to adjudicate jurisdictional disputes between affiliated unions, and 3) to press for favorable legislation. This organization was clearly at variance with the Knights of Labor from a structural point of view. It gave full recognition and independence to each craft, as opposed to the Knights' centrally dominated organization.

The conflict with the Knights forced the national trade unions together, and they formed the American Federation of Labor in 1886, absorbing the Federation of the Organized Trades and Labor Unions.

Craft Autonomy

One of the keystones of the structure of the AFL was—and still is— craft autonomy. Each craft remained autonomous in disciplining its members and in collective bargaining with employers. The AFL protected the crafts by guaranteeing jurisdictional rights to the affiliated unions. It would not charter a new union with authority to organize workers covered by an existing union. In fact, it would come to the aid of any union threatened by dual unionism.

Craft autonomy had been suggested by the lessons of labor history. It was felt that each craft union, fighting for its own immediate concerns within its own limited economic sphere, would be better able to maintain a stable membership over a long period of time. The skilled workers were able to weld together powerful economic units because they held strategic technological positions and could not easily be replaced in case of a strike.

The fight with the Knights of Labor had convinced the AFL that a strongly centralized organization was not necessarily a good fighting organization in this economy. If there had been a real feeling of class solidarity on the part of all workers, skilled and unskilled, then perhaps the Knights would have had a better chance of success. The AFL, however, felt that such class solidarity did not exist and therefore appealed to the self-interest of the workers within the existing capitalistic system.

The AFL was a decentralized federation; that is, it allowed each of its affiliated national organizations to develop more or less as it pleased (a structural characteristic which still prevails). Hence, each union, taking advantage of its autonomy, made its own adjustment to the economic and political conditions in its trade. Some struck frequently, others rarely; some emphasized wage increases, others control of working conditions; some stressed democratic procedures, others showed interest only in economic improvements. The AFL, by not imposing its will on the constituent national unions, became sufficiently all-inclusive to permit these wide differences.

Growth of the AFL

The new stability of the American labor movement was proved in the financial panic of 1893 to 1899. Up to that time depressions had always depleted the unions, but the AFL maintained 275,000 members throughout. During the years from 1898 to 1904 the AFL expanded from 275,000 to 1,676,000. From 1910 until 1914 it again made a spurt, reaching 2,000,000. There were an additional 700,000 workers who were members of unions not affiliated with the AFL. These independent unions, operating on the same business-union philosophy as the AFL, were the bricklayers, who joined the AFL in 1917, and the railroad brotherhoods.

During this period of growth, unionism spread into new industrial and geographical areas; nevertheless, with the exception of the miners and the clothing workers, the membership consisted almost entirely of skilled or higher-level semi-skilled workers. An outstanding example of the rise of unionism in the early days of the AFL occurred in 1892. John Mitchell led the United Mine Workers in a strike for union recognition, a nine-hour day, and better working conditions. They won a contract covering 100,000 workers, the entire anthracite coal industry.

The employers did not stand idly by during this period. In the depression of 1907–1908, they ended many trade agreements and established employers' associations. One outstanding example was the Employers' Association of Dayton, Ohio. It had a labor bureau which supplied strikebreakers, offered rewards to workers who did not go out on strike, and funds to employers who were struck. The National Association of Manufacturers, organized in 1895, came under the influence of the Dayton Association in 1903. The NAM became—and continues to be—an effective lobbyist in Congress and state legislatures.

The outbreak of war in Europe, August, 1914, found the country in a depression with a considerable amount of unemployment. During 1915 and 1916 the AFL stayed relatively stable in membership. The entrance of the United States into the war proved to be a great opportunity for union growth. Union leaders, as well as management personnel, were appointed to the War Labor Board, established by President Wilson to oversee union-management relations and to reduce work stoppages in defense industries. The War Labor Board recognized the workers' right to organize, prevented employer discrimination against union members, supported the eight-hour day, and recognized the right to strike limited only by self-restraint. Here, for the first time, an important federal government agency took a strong stand in favor of collective bargaining. In this environment of comparative government friendliness and high employment, the AFL grew rapidly. From 1916 to 1919, it rose from 2,070,000 to 3,260,000 members. The main increases occurred among meat cutters and butchers, machinists, and railroad workers. Immediately following the war, employers again organized to combat union growth. Nevertheless, the AFL had more than 4,000,000 members in 1920.

During the 1920's the AFL slid from its high point immediately after World War I to a membership in the neighborhood of 3,000,000. Most of this decline occurred during the short, sharp depression of 1921–1922. The rest of the decade was a period of stagnation in union growth, to which many factors contributed. The shifting industrial distribution of the labor force, particularly the rapid rise of such manufacturing industries as automobile, rubber, glass, and chemicals, increased employment in areas not organized by the craft unions. Workers looked upon the improvements in real wages as resulting more from prosperity in the capitalistic system than from union efforts, hence leading to the belief that unions were unnecessary.

Union expansion in the 1920's was further frustrated by employer opposition. This often took the form of public espousal of the open shop. Supposedly the open shop was a firm which employed both union and nonunion workers, but as a matter of fact, it usually excluded union members. Many companies relied on blacklists, lists of union organizers and sympathizers circulated among employers, to maintain the open shop. In some cases company spies mingled with the workers, and even joined unions, and then reported their findings to their employers. If unions grew strong enough to strike, in spite of blacklists and spies, armed guards were hired to escort strike-breakers across picket lines.

A more subtle form of employer opposition was the promotion of welfare capitalism as an alternative to unions. This program included company-sponsored employee representation plans, a form of company unionism in which the employer dominated the employees' organization and decided which issues were proper subjects for bargaining. In some companies, welfare capitalism included employer-financed pension plans, and in other companies the employees were permitted to purchase shares of the corporation's stock at special prices.

The AFL found it difficult to adjust its organizing drives to this type of environment. Many segments of the public considered unions radical organizations upsetting the peaceful serenity of the capitalistic system. The AFL made abortive efforts to organize workers in the steel industry, the auto industry, and in the South, but always became entangled on craft independence. The craft approach to the mass production industries clearly demonstrated its inadequacy during the twenties.

Challenges from the Left

The AFL, an essentially conservative labor organization, has frequently been challenged from the left. The first such challenge to gain considerable headway reached its peak at the AFL convention in 1893. The socialists were able to convince the convention that it ought to adopt a political program containing such provisions as: municipal ownership of utilities, nationalization of telephones, telegraphs, railroads, and mines, and the collective ownership by the people of all means of production and distribution. Although the majority of the affiliated unions endorsed the program, the conservative leaders strongly opposed it. In the 1894 convention the program was voted down. The price which Gompers had to pay for his fight with the socialists was the loss, for one year, of the presidency of the AFL. Otherwise, he was the president from its founding until his death in 1924.

After the turn of the century, the socialists divided into two groups. One was headed by Daniel De Leon, who, after being defeated by Gompers at the convention in 1894, formed the Socialist Trade and Labor Alliance, an unsuccessful attempt at dual unionism. Daniel De Leon, who bitterly denounced Gompers and the AFL, was one of the foremost Marxists in this country, but after leaving the AFL he never had a large following. The other faction split off from De Leon's Social-ist Labor Party and joined the Debs-Berger movement in the Socialist Party. These more moderate socialists remained within the AFL. They did not aim for control, but merely attempted to propagandize among the union leaders, hoping to win AFL support for socialistic programs.

One of the most radical organizations to challenge the AFL's leader-ship of American labor was the Industrial Workers of the World. This organization had its inception in the Western Federation of Miners, which staged several bitter strikes in the 1890's. It was separated from the AFL by geography, policy, and program. In 1905 the Western Federation of Miners merged with the De Leon group and others to form the IWW.

"Big Bill" Haywood, from the Western Federation of Miners, domi-nated the IWW from the beginning. He believed the emancipation of labor could be achieved only with violence and direct action. This caused the more moderate union members to leave the Wobblies as the IWW was called. Later, the De Leon group split off to pursue politi-cal activity. Although rent by factionalism, the Wobblies organized migratory workers, lumbermen, and miners in the West. In 1912 the IWW won a major strike in the textile industry in Lawrence, Massa-chusetts, but was unable to establish a permanent organization. The IWW then went into a rapid decline; it had, however, dramatized the deplorable wages and working conditions of unskilled workers. The Wobblies, in spite of their continual criticism of the AFL leadership, were no real threat in the sense of winning members away from the AFL. Furthermore, the total size of the IWW was never more than a small fraction of the AFL.

The challenges from the left demonstrated two chinks in the armor of the AFL. First, it was too conservative to suit some of the idealistic labor leaders. The most radical accused the AFL of conniving with the "exploit-ing class," the employers. Left-wing splinter movements were a constant threat. On the other hand, conservatism was one of the AFL's chief sources of strength in making a long-run adjustment to its environment. The second weakness was more serious: its inability—or even lack of interest—in organizing the semi-skilled and unskilled workers.

ORGANIZATION OF THE
CONGRESS OF INDUSTRIAL ORGANIZATIONS

The AFL's concentration on skilled crafts was a major factor in split-ting the house of labor. In the early 1930's, many of the largest and most rapidly growing industries were almost completely without unionization, e.g., steel, automobiles, electrical equipment, farm machinery, rubber, oil, and chemical. There were two methods of handling this problem which gained a considerable amount of support among the critics of the AFL. One approach was the "one big union," advocated by the IWW and the Knights of Labor. The second proposal was to organize by industry without regard to craft, each industry having its own separate union. Within the AFL there was some precedent for this method, both the miners' union and the clothing workers' union being organized along industrial lines.

When the conflict within the AFL over the question of craft vs. industrial unions appeared to be stalemated, those who favored the latter took independent action. The inability of the AFL to assimilate this industrial type organization led to a separate federation, the Congress of Industrial Organizations. The CIO rapidly developed into a powerful and permanent force in the labor movement. It was favored by a changed legal environment, a changed public attitude, and a group of vigorous leaders. The sudden rise of a potent rival sparked the AFL into its own new period of rapid growth.

Changed Public Attitude

Many drastic changes in the American economy and society came with the depression which started with the crash of 1929 and from which we never really recovered until the beginning of World War II. During much of this period more than 10,000,000 people were unemployed; one out of every four workers was without a job. The rising real income of the twenties was reversed and almost all workers were living in substantially poorer circumstances. Many families who had known better times suffered from genuine hunger, with plans for their children's future demolished by the bleak and idle factories. People were in desperate need of more housing, clothes, refrigerators, automobiles, etc. The machines and workers were present to produce them. Anybody could see that! Yet the wheels of production were halted by some force incomprehensible to the ordinary citizen.

As a consequence, the attitude of the public changed considerably: no longer was the capitalistic system looked upon as the infallible provider of a high standard of living. The new attitude favored some experimenting or tampering with the system, and it was more tolerant of union organization and activity.

In the election of 1932, the Democrats came into power for the first time since World War I. President Roosevelt and the New Deal brought a major change in the role played by the government in our economy. As a part of this picture, much legislation favorable to unions and workers was passed, e.g., the National Labor Relations Act, commonly referred to as the Wagner Act, the Social Security Act, and the Fair Labor Standards Act.[4] In fact, these new trends were visible even before the election of Roosevelt, as demonstrated by the passage of the Norris-LaGuardia Act in 1932. Furthermore, throughout the 1930's, the government spent comparatively large sums of money for public works programs and relief, which directly benefited low income receivers and unemployed workers.

AFL Versus CIO

The conflict within the AFL concerning industrial type organization was more than merely a disagreement over structure. The AFL leadership, with a few exceptions, believed they represented a special group of workers: highly skilled craft workers, the elite of labor. This attitude prevailed even though the AFL had long included some industrial unions. Internal power politics acted as a second factor inhibiting the development of industrial type organization. The influence of a union leader within the AFL depended on the proportion of the total membership he represented; for example, Bill Hutcheson exercised a great deal of control over AFL policies because he was president of the largest affiliated union, the carpenters. To allow new unions to come into the AFL, such as an auto workers' or steel workers' union, with a potential membership of millions, would mean a substantial reduction in authority for those leaders who dominated the AFL. And finally, it was feared that an industrial union could not properly represent the craft workers within the industry. Although the highly skilled craftsmen—e.g., those who maintained the machines or built and repaired the blast furnaces—constituted far less than half of the total employment in mass production industries, they were numbered by the hundreds of thousands. The carpenters, machinists, bricklayers, and other craft unions were concerned lest these workers be swallowed up by an omnipotent industrial union. Therefore, the minority of AFL leaders who promoted industrial unions were continually frustrated.

The dispute reached its climax at the AFL Convention in 1935. The majority of the committee reporting on problems of industrial organization favored the approach used unsuccessfully in the previous decade: to allow some of the craft unions to join forces in an effort to organize.

---

[4] These laws will be discussed in detail in later chapters.

This was a rejection of the proposal to establish new and independent organizing campaigns on an industrial basis. A minority of the committee, however, expressed vigorous opposition. When the majority report was adopted by the Convention delegates, the minority held a rump session and decided to go ahead on their own. They created the Committee for Industrial Organization which was the forerunner of the Congress of Industrial Organizations. Leaders in this precedent-breaking movement included John L. Lewis of the United Mine Workers, David Dubinsky of the International Ladies' Garment Workers, and Sidney Hillman of the Amalgamated Clothing Workers.

The Committee sponsored successful organizing campaigns in a number of industries and grew rapidly in membership. The AFL leaders who had opposed industrial organization immediately became alarmed. They went to William Green, then president of the AFL, and put pressure on him to force the Committee to cease its operations. Green and the AFL executive committee expelled everyone associated with the CIO who refused to "admit his errors and mend his ways." At the AFL Convention in 1938 this action of the executive committee was ratified.

Instead of repenting their sins and returning to the AFL, the Committee established itself as a permanent organization and adopted the name: Congress of Industrial Organizations. Since this smacked of dual unionism, a number of the original adherents of the CIO resigned and went back to the AFL, notably David Dubinsky and the International Ladies' Garment Workers.

Growth of Industrial Unions

The new unions spread rapidly, partly because of a bold and dedicated leadership. In the forefront was John L. Lewis, who rose from the minepits to become a ferocious orator, filling his speeches with choice passages from Shakespeare, learned by studying at night under the guidance of his wife, a former schoolteacher.

In industry after industry the CIO found workers who were anxious to join. In many industries, the employers' personnel programs had included employee representation plans. The workers had found that these company unions did not prevent wage reductions during the early 1930's. And furthermore, they felt that the organizations were not really independent of the employers, who ignored them whenever they pleased.

The industrialization of the 1920's had created working conditions in many factories which allowed the worker little or no control over his destiny—little opportunity to rise to a higher status job. Where previously skilled workers had produced a few automobiles a year, masses of workers with very little training were turning out thousands each day. The engineering miracle was founded on the interchangeability of the parts: a crankshaft could be taken from one Ford and put on any other. And the workers were equally interchangeable.

Once caught in the whirl of factory production, a worker's chances of rising to a management position or to a white-collar job were slim. The speed and quality of his output were determined by the machines, largely independent of his own efforts. In short, he felt that he was an inconspicuous element in a giant enterprise—and he was often treated as such. The new unions held out the promise of some control over his job; they gave him a vehicle through which he could express his complaints and assert his personality.

The CIO concentrated a large portion of its early organizing zeal in the steel industry, bypassing the old and inept AFL union, the Amalgamated Association of Iron, Steel, and Tin Workers. By 1936 many of the workers had become disillusioned with the company-sponsored employee representation plans. The Steel Workers' Organizing Committee, operating on funds borrowed from the United Mine Workers, found that the officials of these company unions, elected by the employees, were fertile organizing material, and the SWOC eventually included a number of them in its leadership. When the SWOC's influence in the employee representation plans in its plants became overwhelming, United States Steel (Big Steel) recognized the union and signed a contract in March, 1937. This was accomplished without a strike—quite amazing in the light of the company's long tradition of vigorous anti-unionism.

SWOC organizers often were required to ply their trade in "company towns" where the steel mill owned the houses, the newspaper, the stores, and other places of business, and in almost like manner, the city's officials and police force. Election results altered this picture in many parts of the country. For example, when a former secretary-treasurer of the United Mine Workers became Lieutenant-Governor of Pennsylvania, he could speak to union rallies, receiving protection from the same state police who prevented such rallies in earlier years.

The contract with Big Steel—along with the re-election of President Roosevelt and the victory of the auto workers at General Motors—appeared to open the floodgates, and many other companies followed suit. This was not a reaction to low wages; the new union members were among the highest paid in the country. Rather, it was a reaction against the insecurity of employment, representing a desire to gain control over the job.

The sharp recession of 1937 stunted the drive of the CIO. When orders for steel dropped, the companies had little to lose by holding out against a strike. And unemployed workers could be recruited to serve as strike-breakers when needed. Therefore, Little Steel (Bethlehem, Republic, Youngstown, and Inland, the major producers other than United States Steel) offered determined resistance. SWOC was involved in more or less unsuccessful strikes with each of these companies—strikes which involved much violence and bloodshed. A number of strikers were killed by police whose armaments were furnished by the corporations.

The rapid rise of the United Auto Workers also included violent encounters. In organizing General Motors, the workers engaged in a widespread sit-down strike, focused on Flint, Michigan. Although there was considerable pressure on the Governor to call out the militia to drive the workers out of the factory, no such action was taken. General Motors finally capitulated in February, 1937. Chrysler followed soon after, but the Ford Motor Car Company held out against the union for another four years. However, widely publicized pictures of Ford service men physically assaulting union organizers aroused an adverse public reaction and ended the corporation's overt efforts to prevent workers from joining. Recognition of the union soon followed.

The CIO, as a new and fast-growing organization, hired many young organizers, often college graduates who believed they were enlisting in a crusade to bring about a radical change in the economic system. Many entered the union movement with a religious zeal, willing to work long hours at great personal sacrifice and often quite successfully when measured in terms of recruitment of members. They believed they were replacing an old and decadent union organization with a vibrant driving force and expected the CIO to develop in a political direction, eventually leading to a labor party. Among these young organizers were a number of adherents to the Communist Party, some of whom rose to important positions in several of the CIO unions.[5]

In spite of these pressures to become a political movement, the CIO concentrated most of its efforts on winning wage increases and improved working conditions rather than striving for utopian goals. However, it did show a greater interest in political activities than did the AFL.

[5] The Communist Party members caused the CIO many headaches. These are discussed in the next chapter.

Unions During World War II

In the 1940's employment conditions were completely reversed from the previous decade. During most of World War II and the next few years, jobs were looking for men rather than men looking for jobs. Unemployment fell as low as 200,000, an irreducible minimum of people moving between jobs. Since much of the additional employment occurred in industries already well along the road to unionization—machinery, automobiles, heavy construction, ship–building, and aircraft —membership rose rapidly, from 9,000,000 in 1940 to 14,750,000 at the end of the war.

Immediately after our entrance into World War II, the AFL and CIO gave the President a no-strike pledge and implemented this pledge by taking active part in a variety of government programs. Unions were represented on many of the important government agencies, e.g., the War Labor Board and the War Production Board. Since these boards operated at regional and local levels, as well as in Washington, many union officials actively participated in the defense program and as equals with the management representatives. John Lewis and his United Mine Workers—at this time an independent union no longer affiliated with the CIO—were the major exception to union cooperation. The UMW conducted long strikes and took no part in the defense bureaucracy. The War Labor Board, in attempting to maintain industrial peace and full production, gave considerable emphasis to collective bargaining as a means of handling industrial disputes. This helped unions to increase their membership.

Unions not only gained in membership during the war period, but also made a number of innovations in collective bargaining. When the government imposed wage ceilings in order to stem inflationary pressures, this temporarily eliminated one of the traditional subjects of negotiation. Unions then switched their war-enhanced bargaining power into other channels. Clauses were written into contracts which protected the unions' long-run position in many industries where they were new and uncertain in their hold on employees. Innovations were also made in benefit programs for those unemployed because of sickness or retirement.

By the end of World War II, unions had become solidly entrenched in many basic industries. They had achieved a degree of public respect and legal recognition never before accorded to them—somewhat tarnished by the record of the United Mine Workers. It seemed that the union movement was in an excellent position to make still greater advancements. Instead, it became the victim of the shifts in postwar economics and politics and of its own internal bickering.

Peace had barely been achieved when we encountered, in 1946, the worst strike year in our history, losing 116,000,000 man-days of production as a result of 4,985 work stoppages, nearly 1.5 per cent of total working time. Upsetting conditions were only to be expected in the mad scramble to convert factories from defense to consumer goods. The anxiety was all the greater because of the large savings accumulated while incomes were rising and goods were unavailable. Unions had a backlog of unsettled grievances and had been prevented from getting satisfaction through striking. Inefficiencies which had developed in many firms under the aegis of cost-plus contracts were being fought by employers who wanted greater output per man-hour. Furthermore, many workers and employers were just beginning to learn what collective bargaining really meant. These employers wanted to go back to the "good old days" and their employees wanted to experiment with new-found powers. Under such circumstances, a major strike wave was inevitable, and so was a strong public reaction to it.

SUMMARY

Throughout their history, American unions have reflected their environment. The first organizations which resembled unions were short-lived, engaging in turnouts and then dissolving. The first enduring association was founded in Philadelphia in 1792, and the first grouping together of unions from several trades appeared in the same city thirty-five years later. These early associations were quite different from modern unions, although they made the familiar demands for wage increases and the closed shop. They were local in character with little or no affiliation which reached beyond the city limits, and easily committed themselves to political activity and utopian schemes designed to replace the capitalistic wage system.

Prior to 1886, unions bounced back and forth between business union activity and the utopian plans. During prosperous periods they engaged in economic activity and during depressions they engaged in star-gazing. During the prosperous 1850's, unions began to develop national organizations. With the social upheaval of the 1880's new heights in membership were achieved. At this point, workers had to choose between the Knights of Labor, a final utopian fling, and the AFL. The skilled craftsmen—with few exceptions, the only workers capable of holding an organization together—chose the latter.

The organization of the AFL and its success in withstanding the depression of the 1890's, as well as later depressions, represented a triumph for business unionism. The AFL emphasized craft autonomy, a basic structural characteristic which can be traced to the conflict with the Knights. The AFL withstood several challenges from the left. The socialists and the IWW attacked its essentially conservative program and its tender regard for the craft workers as opposed to the unskilled workers.

The refusal of the AFL to modify its structure to include industrial unions brought about the formation of a new federation, the Congress of Industrial Organizations, which grew rapidly in the favorable legal and social climate of the late thirties. During World War II, the AFL and the CIO continued their rapid growth and reached the end of the war period as substantial and permanent institutions in the American environment.

DISCUSSION QUESTIONS

1. Explain why American unions grew at an uneven rate.

2. What are producers' cooperatives? Why did they win the allegiance of so many workers?

3. To what extent were the utopias incompatible with trade unionism? Explain.

4. Explain, in economic terms, why national unions became prominent in the 1850's and 1860's.

5. In what respects was the structure of the Knights of Labor poorly adjusted to the American labor scene?

6. Unions substantially increased their membership during the Civil War, World War I, and World War II. How do you explain this?

7. Contrast the position of unions during World War I and World War II.

8. What is craft autonomy? Why did it become so important in the American labor movement?

9. What factors caused the AFL to be reluctant to engage wholeheartedly in organizing mass production industries?

10. What characteristics of the American environment facilitated the rapid growth of the CIO in its early years?

11. What was the relationship between the Steel Workers' Organizing Committee and the employee representation plans sponsored by the steel corporations?

BIBLIOGRAPHY

Beard, Mary. *A Short History of the American Labor Movement.* New York: Harcourt, Brace and Company, 1921.

Brooks, Robert R. R. *As Steel Goes, . . .* New Haven: Yale University Press, 1940.

Commons, John R., and Associates. *History of Labour in the United States, 1896–1932.* New York: The Macmillan Company, 1918, 1935. Volumes I, II, and IV.

Dulles, Foster Rhea. *Labor in America—A History.* New York: Thomas Y. Crowell Co., 1949.

Foner, Philip S. *History of the Labor Movement in the United States.* New York: International Publishers, 1947, 1955. Volumes I and II.

Harris, Herbert. *Labor's Civil War.* New York: Alfred A. Knopf, 1940.

Perlman, Selig. *A History of Trade Unionism in the United States.* New York: The Macmillan Company, 1922.

Taft, Philip. *The A. F. of L. in the Time of Gompers.* New York: Harper & Brothers, 1957.

Ulman, Lloyd. *The Rise of the National Trade Union.* Cambridge: Harvard University Press, 1955.

Ware, Norman J. *The Labor Movement in the United States, 1860–1895.* New York: D. Appleton and Company, 1929.

Woolman, Leo. *Ebb and Flow in Trade Unionism.* New York: National Bureau of Economic Research, 1936.

CONSOLIDATION OR STAGNATION

4

Perhaps the title of this chapter should be followed by a question mark, since there is much disagreement over which term properly defines this fourth period of union history. There has been consolidation in the sense that the AFL and CIO have merged into a single federation and that unions are more solidly entrenched in many industries. Stagnation, however, more aptly describes the rate of increase in membership and the lack of new techniques to meet the challenge of the second half of the twentieth century. In many respects the period following World War II paralleled the decade after World War I, with unions on the defensive and barely holding their own.

In this chapter we will devote most of our attention to the consolidation aspects, and particularly to the merger, the most significant incident in the labor movement since 1950. After twenty years of animosity, with occasional periods of lukewarm cooperation, the two dominant groups in American labor joined forces to become a single federation. All during this period efforts had been made to mend the breach, both by labor leaders and the friends of labor, including President Roosevelt. Before reviewing the events leading up to the merger, we must consider the gains and losses from the split in labor's ranks.

CONSEQUENCES OF THE CONFLICT

From the union point of view, perhaps the most obvious gain from the split was the organization of the mass production industries. The CIO was successful on this score probably sooner, and more completely, than the AFL would have been if it, as then constituted, had led the organizing drive. The union movement, as a whole, grew rapidly after 1935—more than doubling its membership by 1940—partially as a result of the competition between the two organizations. The rise of the CIO infused new life into the AFL.

Establishing the new federation resulted in another gain. An opportunity was presented for new young leaders to rise to important positions in the labor movement, e.g., Walter Reuther of the automobile workers, David McDonald of the steel workers, and James Carey of the electrical workers. These people probably would not have been able to rise as rapidly in the already institutionalized hierarchy of the AFL.

The most important loss to the unions was the lack of a single voice to represent labor politically, economically, and socially. Efforts to work together politically fell apart in 1937. In its convention that year, the AFL decided to oppose any candidate for public office who encouraged or supported John L. Lewis and the Committee for Industrial Organization. The CIO henceforth became politically more active, with little or no aid from the AFL. In fact, in their testimony before Congress, the two rivals took opposite positions on the National Labor Relations Act. The AFL, in 1939, urged Congress to abolish the legislation, while the CIO vigorously supported it. During World War II, jealousies arose over the proper representation each should have on the defense and mobilization boards. Such conflicts diluted their effectiveness in advocating labor's cause.

In the immediate postwar period, there was a wave of strikes as unions attempted to maintain the wartime levels of take-home pay. Coming at a time when veterans were returning to civilian life in large numbers and just when consumers were anxious to convert their savings into automobiles, refrigerators, etc., these strikes aroused great public antipathy, leading to popular support for a more conservative Congress and eventually to the Taft-Hartley Act. The division within the ranks of labor was a severe handicap in counteracting this trend.

The split also led to expensive internecine warfare. Unions from the two rival organizations were in competition with each other for many groups of workers, spending large sums of money battling one another, rather than seeking out workers who otherwise would not be organized. The wrangling aroused the distrust of many unorganized workers and inhibited organization in the South, as well as among a number of industrial and occupational groups.

FORERUNNERS OF THE MERGER

The merger did not represent a sudden change of heart by either the AFL or the CIO. Rather, there were a number of forerunners presaging the marriage ceremony. Although significant barriers remained, certain developments on the national scene contributed strong pressures toward merger. The almost simultaneous change in the top leadership of both organizations in 1952 provided the necessary catalyst, and the No-Raiding Pact signed in 1954 set the final stage.

National Developments Promoting Unity

Two important developments on the national scene produced reactions in the two federations which stimulated greater cooperation. These were 1) the Taft-Hartley Act and 2) the Korean War.

The Taft-Hartley Act [1] contained many provisions designed to restrict union activity and was unanimously condemned as anti-labor legislation by leaders in both the AFL and CIO. This Act aroused them to a greater awareness of the importance of a unified approach to Congress. In the following years they attempted joint, but unsuccessful, efforts to bring about changes in this law. Nevertheless, both organizations were convinced more vigorous political action was necessary.

The national defense emergency during the Korean War induced the federations to create the United Labor Policy Committee, whose chief function was to establish labor's policy for the developing problems in the regulation of manpower, wages, and prices. It provided labor with a single voice in advising the many government agencies set up at that time, particularly the Wage Stabilization Board. For a brief period the United Labor Policy Committee exhibited an unprecedented degree of unity. The AFL, however, abandoned the Committee nine months after it was formed because of a jealous belief that the CIO was receiving at least as much recognition from the government even though the AFL was much the larger of the two.

Some people thought that these two events might well be the prelude to real labor unity, but the two federations still were unable to reach agreement. At the local level, greater success was achieved in a few areas. For example, in New York City, the local representatives of the two federations operated on a united basis for political action.

[1] The Taft-Hartley Act is discussed in detail in Chapter 13.

Continuing Barriers to Unity

One of the perennial causes of division was the dispute over how to proceed toward merger: by organic unity or by functional cooperation. In general the AFL favored organic unity, that is, complete amalgamation as a first and final step in bringing the two sides together. The CIO interpreted this to mean dissolving its organization and bringing its unions "contritely back home to mother." The CIO favored functional cooperation, that is, cooperating on specific projects as a first step toward unity. Among the specific projects proposed were political action and elimination of jurisdictional disputes.

The AFL frequently accused the CIO of having affiliated unions which were dominated by Communist Party members and sympathizers. When a number of its unions appeared to be following the Communist Party line in their support of Henry Wallace during the 1948 presidential elections, the CIO leadership decided to force the issue. After an investigation, it expelled eleven of its national affiliates, with nearly a million members, including the United Electrical Workers, the International Longshoremen's and Warehousemen's Union, and the International Fur and Leather Workers' Union. The CIO immediately set in motion a vigorous organizing campaign to win back the rank and file membership from the unions it had thrown out. The campaign was long and expensive, but largely successful, notably among the electrical workers. Two of the expelled unions, however, were able to maintain their membership while operating independently: the Longshoremen's and Warehousemen's Union with its membership along the Pacific Coast and in Hawaii, and the Mine, Mill and Smelter Workers' Union, located mainly in the Rocky Mountain area. This direct attack on the left-wing union leaders removed a major barrier to unity, but it left the CIO with membership about half that of the AFL.

Another barrier was the CIO's temporary affiliation with the World Federation of Trade Unions. This organization, founded during World War II, included the labor federations of many nations. The AFL objected to the World Federation on the grounds that it included the Russian unions, which were instruments of the Soviet government and did not really represent the workers. In 1949 the CIO withdrew from the World Federation because the unions from behind the Iron Curtain blocked the organization's endorsement of the Marshall Plan to rehabilitate Europe. The AFL and CIO then cooperated with labor federations from democratic nations in establishing the International Confederation of Free Trade Unions.

A further barrier to unity grew out of a CIO complaint accusing the AFL of willingness to harbor corrupt union leaders. In 1953 the AFL expelled the International Longshoremen's Association, one of its most corrupt affiliates.[2] This union has its membership among the longshoremen in seaports from New England to New Orleans, with headquarters in New York City. Many of its leaders were either criminals or had close ties with criminals of all types. In fact, many of the members supplemented their regular income with petty thievery from the boats they were unloading. When the union was unable, or unwilling, to eliminate either its most outstanding rackets or most undesirable leaders in spite of numerous warnings and a final trial period, the AFL expelled it and chartered a rival union, the International Brotherhood of Longshoremen, which made some progress in the Great Lakes area but not elsewhere.

Finally, the CIO was much more active politically and too far to the left to suit many of the AFL leaders. The latter preferred to stay out of most national elections, relying on lobbying for their special interests.

New Leadership in the AFL and CIO

William Green, president of the AFL, and Philip Murray, president of the CIO, died within two weeks of each other in November, 1952. Green had held his position for twenty-eight years, and Murray for twelve years. Both had been personally involved when the split between the two federations occurred and both had been involved in the futile attempts to bring the two sides together. Confronting each other only brought back memories of earlier bitterness. The coincidence of their deaths gave both federations an opportunity to install younger leaders.

George Meany was elected president of the AFL without opposition. He had risen to the position of secretary-treasurer of the AFL in 1940 by way of the plumbers' union and the New York State Federation of Labor. Walter Reuther became president of the CIO after a convention battle which pitted the two largest unions—the auto workers and the steel workers—against each other. He had risen through the ranks of the United Automobile Workers, of which he is still president. Meany was fifty-eight years old and Reuther forty-five at the time they assumed their new positions.

---

[2] Later in this chapter, actions against other unions with corrupt leadership will be described.

During his presidency of the New York State Federation of Labor, Meany was successful in promoting much state legislation favorable to labor. While secretary-treasurer of the AFL he earned a reputation as a peacemaker through his efforts to settle jurisdictional disputes between the craft unions. Reuther came from a family with a long socialist and union tradition. In his early working career he was discharged a number of times for union activity. He won control of the UAW after defeating powerful pro-communist forces within the union.

The No-Raiding Pact

One of the major barriers to unity was the overlapping jurisdictions of unions affiliated with each federation. To cite a typical case, the CIO brewery workers' union and the AFL teamsters' union both claimed jurisdiction over the truck drivers who distributed beer. Furthermore, national unions in both the CIO and the AFL felt free to raid the membership in affiliates of the rival federation. For example, if the United Electrical Workers, CIO, had organized the employees of a firm, the International Brotherhood of Electrical Workers, AFL, might enter the situation, attempt to stir up factional disputes and dissatisfaction with the CIO union's leadership, and then seek to win the workers to its banner. In short, unions were expending much energy in reorganizing the already organized.

Jurisdictional disputes had become one of the major causes of loss of public respect. Furthermore, workers caught between raiding unions became confused and disillusioned with unionism. These disputes brought large financial losses for the competing unions as well as employers. Meany reported that the AFL and CIO had spent nearly $11,500,000 fighting each other within the space of just three years, and the results were: the AFL gained 44,000 members from the CIO and lost 40,000 members to it, a net change of 4,000 at a cost of nearly $3,000 each.[3]

Less than one year after taking office, Meany and Reuther reached agreement on a No-Raiding Pact, designed to prevent unions affiliated with one federation from raiding those affiliated with the other. This was the first real step toward organic unity. It had been preceded by no-raiding agreements between individual unions, notably the International Association of Machinists, AFL, and the United Automobile Workers, CIO.

After some delay caused by a number of reluctant unions, the No-Raid-

[3] A. H. Raskin, "Labor Unity Pacts Sealed by Unions," *New York Times*, May 15, 1954, p. 11.

ing Pact was officially signed in June, 1954, by ninety-four unions, sixty-five AFL affiliates, and twenty-nine CIO affiliates, covering approximately 10,000,000 workers. Forty-five AFL unions stayed out of the pact, two-thirds of whom had no jurisdictional counterparts in the CIO. However, the teamsters' union, the largest in the AFL, also refused to agree to give up raiding. Four CIO unions did not sign, including the steel workers', the second largest within the CIO. This illustrates some of the limitations on the power of a federation president. The refusal to join the pact by these two big unions was an expression of internal politics, a power play on the part of the leaders of the nonsigning unions against the leaders of the federations.

Under the No-Raiding Pact, which was continued in effect after the merger, a raided union could carry its grievance to the secretary-treasurers of the two federations. If these officials could not achieve a settlement, the dispute was taken to an impartial umpire who conducted a hearing and then rendered a final and binding decision, enforceable in the courts.[4] The union designated as the violator by the impartial umpire was required to give up its claim to the disputed workers. The principles of the No-Raiding Pact have been ingrained in the Constitution of the AFL-CIO.

THE MERGER

Immediately after assuming office, Meany and Reuther took steps toward merging the two federations. Besides promoting the No-Raiding Pact, they appointed committees to inquire into the problems of unity and to write a constitution for a combined organization. Such committees had been appointed in the past, but had made little real progress.

The major stumbling block centered around the problem of integrating the national unions into a single organization while at the same time preserving their individual character. The CIO unions had no intention of giving up the principles which had originally motivated their independent action. Their individuality could be lost, they feared, in amalgamation with an organization twice their size. At the same time the AFL unions did not intend to permit the large CIO unions to absorb some of their smaller affiliates. They did not want the skilled workers, who were members of their craft unions, but employed in large industrial plants, to be claimed by their new brothers.

A solution was found by guaranteeing the integrity of all existing

---

[4] David Cole was selected as the first impartial umpire. He was formerly chairman of the Federal Mediation and Conciliation Service and is a prominent arbitrator of labor disputes.

unions and at the same time creating an industrial union department within the merged federation—an acceptance of structural pluralism: organization by trade and organization by industry. The new department includes the CIO unions and those AFL workers who are organized along industrial lines.[5]

The unity proceedings were not entirely free of dissension. At the final pre-merger convention of each federation, some opposition was expressed. Among some of the leaders of the AFL there was a feeling that they would lose power to the top executives of the merged federation. Others expressed concern over the nature and direction of political activity under the influence of the politically more active CIO. The primary CIO dissident was Michael Quill of the Transport Workers' Union. He argued that the merger should be delayed until the AFL cleaned out corruption in some of its unions and until it eliminated all racial segregation. In spite of these objections, the overwhelming majority of the leaders and the rank and file of both federations favored unity without further delay.

On December 5, 1955, the new Federation, called the American Federation of Labor and Congress of Industrial Organizations since neither party wanted to give up its old name, was brought into existence with the constitution signed by all the affiliates of its two predecessors. Thus, twenty years of division within the ranks of labor came to an end. The new AFL-CIO claimed. sixteen million members as compared with the five million in the AFL just prior to the split.

Whenever two institutions with proud histories are merged, whether it be churches, corporations, or unions, there is always the knotty problem of apportioning the scarce leadership positions. There can only be one president, one director of research, etc. Considering the amount of acrimony which could have developed, differences were settled quite amicably. Since the AFL was by far the larger, it was awarded the positions of president and secretary-treasurer, filled respectively by Meany and William Schnitzler. The top positions in the industrial union department went to former CIO officials, Reuther as president and James Carey as secretary-treasurer. Of the twenty-seven AFL-CIO vice presidents, seventeen were formerly with the AFL and ten came from the CIO. The position of Director of Organization went to a former CIO leader, John W. Livingston, a vice president of the United Automobile Workers.[6]

[5] Its functions and position in the AFL-CIO are described in Chapter 6.
[6] The organization and structure of the AFL-CIO are fully discussed in Chapter 6.

In a sense the merger will not be complete until the unions with overlapping jurisdictions either combine into a single union or make concessions to each other. Some unions have begun the process. The most outstanding was consummated in 1957, between the International Brotherhood of Paper Makers (formerly AFL) and the United Paperworkers of America (formerly CIO). The two barbers' unions, the two insurance workers' unions, and the two marine engineers' unions have merged; and the metal engravers joined the International Association of Machinists. The Amalgamated Meat Cutters and Butcher Workmen of North America (formerly AFL) and the United Packinghouse Workers (formerly CIO) agreed to merge in early 1956. Many delays have occurred, but their plans have not been abandoned. The typographers and lithographers began similar efforts in 1959. In time, others will perhaps follow, but it will be many decades—at best—before all the jurisdictional conflicts are settled.

CONSEQUENCES OF THE MERGER

What has been accomplished by the merger? Has it merely amounted to a change in the formal organizational structure of unions which has not and will not have any effects on their operations? Or does it portend great changes in the functioning of unions in our economy? Since we have had only a few years to observe the new Federation, answers to these questions must be partially speculative. Potentially, almost all aspects of unionization will be influenced, although in some matters the effects will not be discernible until many years have passed.

Political Activity

Before the merger, union efforts in the political arena were poorly coordinated. The CIO would be button-holing Congressmen with certain legislative goals in mind, while the AFL was completely unconcerned or going off in a different direction. This disparity occasionally reached the extreme of endorsing opposing candidates for the same office. Duplications and contradictions have largely been eliminated in political research, publicity, lobbying, and spending for election campaigns. Political spending has increased and is more judiciously distributed in areas where the money can be effective. At least, AFL-CIO money is no longer going to each of two opposing candidates.

The merger has not ended all political differences between unions. In the first place, the Federation leadership, which includes both staunch Republicans and staunch Democrats, does not always agree on which candidates to support and what form the support should take: merely endorse, supply funds, provide campaign workers. Secondly, some of the affiliated unions, believing they have unique political needs, insist on acting independently, supporting their own slate of candidates and doing their own research and publicity. It is unlikely that individual unions will ever stop advocating special interest legislation in the areas of tariffs, subsidies, government expenditures, and legally imposed working rules.

The Federation intends to follow the traditional principle of avoiding entangling alliances with either political party. Nor does it have any plans for setting up an independent labor party. Support will be given to politicians of either party who vote the "right way" on collective bargaining, social security, minimum wage, and civil rights legislation and on government spending and taxing to affect levels of employment and income distribution.

Organizing Activity

Now that competition between rival unions is no longer the chief motivating force behind organizing campaigns, efforts can be concentrated on the more fertile areas of unorganized workers. Approximately half of the expenditures of the old AFL and CIO had been devoted to programs for increasing membership, a total of more than $6,500,000 for the two federations. This money may now be more wisely spent on integrated drives. Winning new members continues to be primarily a responsibility of the internationals, but the Federation can help with planning and funds. A unified, well-financed approach to organizing the unorganized should—in the long run—be more successful than efforts made in the past, e.g., among chemical workers and Southern textile workers.

Organizing activity in the first years after the merger produced rather dismal results for the unions. "Operation Dixie," after much publicity, failed to produce any real increases in membership. One important reason was the attitude, widely held in the South, toward the consequences of union growth for racial integration. After the Supreme Court decision (May, 1954) ordering the admission of white and Negro students to the same schools on an equal basis, the AFL-CIO found itself in a very awkward position. Along with many, but not all, of its affiliated unions, it had taken a public stand in favor of ending legal barriers to equal treatment for all races, religions, and nationalities. Many public officials in the South, ranging from state governors to county clerks, held the directly opposing view. White Citizens' Councils were established in many cities to protect the Southern way of life by bringing effective economic and political sanctions against individuals or groups who promoted integration. This created an environment much too hostile for union growth. In fact, it brought considerable internal confusion, with some union leaders playing prominent roles in the White Citizens' Councils while others were fighting determinedly against them. This serves as another example of the age-old problem of American unions: how to adjust their goals to the community's institutional structure.

The agreement between the International Association of Machinists and the United Automobile Workers covering the aircraft industry, where they have overlapping jurisdiction, is an example of the type of joint approach that could follow from the inspiration of the merger. Each union agreed not to begin an organizational campaign where the other had already organized more than 50 per cent of an employer's workers. Whenever both unions approached the same group of employees at the same time, the campaign was to be conducted in a gentlemanly fashion with no disparaging remarks made about the rival.

It would be expecting too much to predict that there will be no more competition in organizing drives. Some unions complain of having been grievously raided in the past and want to recover their losses. Others are led by empire builders who see almost no limits to their jurisdiction, e.g., the carpenters' union. However, the ambitious leaders, including those outside the AFL-CIO, can be more effectively curbed under unification than by two separate federations.

Suppression of Communism and Corruption

There were great expectations that the merger would give the Federation increased flexibility in dealing with affiliates dominated by corrupt or communist leadership. Prior to the merger, if one of the federations expelled a wayward union, it ran the risk of having that union find a new home in the rival federation. Hence, to police its affiliates vigorously might cost a federation part of its membership and bring no improvement in the ethical standards of unions. The threat of expulsion now carries greater weight since the convicted union has potential allies only in the unions outside the AFL-CIO and must contend with a much more powerful organization which may charter and support a rival union covering the same jurisdiction.

Two outstanding cases demonstrate the increased power of the Federation for dealing with corruption in its midst and the limitations on that power. The first test case, involving the International Longshoremen's Association, reached a peak at the time of the merger preparations. The teamsters' union began negotiations to absorb the ILA even though the latter had been expelled from the AFL for corrupt leadership. Meany prevented the two unions from joining together and stopped a proposed loan of $400,000 from the teamsters to the ILA. The best the teamsters could arrange was a mutual assistance agreement between three of its regional divisions and the ILA. Although this was a compromise, the Federation did exhibit a far greater willingness to take strong action against corruption than had been demonstrated in the past. The ILA, however, continued in full operation independent of the AFL-CIO even though a rival union was chartered. After a substantial amount of housecleaning, it rejoined the Federation in 1959.

Whether the strong stand taken by the Federation had much to do with the improvement in the ILA is doubtful. More likely, the Waterfront Commission of New York Harbor, created by special bistate legislation in New York and New Jersey, served as the chief purifying ingredient. The Waterfront Commission is a special police agency, established to eliminate crime from the docks of our biggest seaport. It operates employment offices where all longshoremen must register, thus replacing the shape-up, a hiring system which made the workers absolutely dependent on the pier bosses for their jobs each day. This reduced the power of the pier bosses, leaders in the ILA, some of whom sold labor peace to the shipping companies for under-the-table fees and extorted money from the rank and file members through bogus memorial funds, special fees, and enforced gambling.

The Teamsters and Jimmy Hoffa

An even more important test of the firmness of the AFL-CIO's attitude on corruption rose in 1957. An investigation of the teamsters' union by the Senate Select Committee on Improper Practices in the Labor and Management Field [7] revealed misappropriations of large sums of money by Dave Beck, president of the union, Frank Brewster, head of its Western Conference, and Jimmy Hoffa, head of its Central, Eastern, and Southern Conferences. The findings of the Senate Committee put the AFL-CIO in an embarrassing position, since Beck was a vice-president

[7] The Committee, commonly called the McClellan Committee after its chairman, Senator John McClellan of Arkansas, investigated officials of many unions, exposing a wide variety of racketeering. The hearings received much publicity and helped rouse sentiment which led to the Labor-Management Reporting and Disclosure Act of 1959, often called the Landrum-Griffin Act, since it was sponsored by these two members of the House of Representatives.

of the Federation as well as president of its largest affiliate. The time-honored policy of hands-off, an almost untenable position in the light of the publicity given to the case, could have been followed. Instead, Beck was relieved of his vice-presidency and pressures were exerted on the teamsters' union, causing Beck to withdraw his name from its presidential election.

The Federation's Ethical Practices Committee conducted its own investigation of the charges against the teamster officials and reported numerous instances of corruption to the Executive Council, including: 1) indicted and convicted criminals holding office, 2) misappropriation of union funds, 3) teamster officials owning part or all of companies selling services to employers with whom they bargained, 4) charters issued to paper locals (with few or no members) that were used by corrupt "union leaders" to shake down small employers and to pad the vote in regional and national elections of the teamsters' union, and 5) clauses in the constitution that permitted undemocratic practices. The Executive Council ordered the offending international to correct these abuses at its forthcoming convention, remove the corrupt officials, and report back on its progress within a month. At the end of September, 1957, the teamsters defied the Federation by promoting some of the accused officials; Hoffa was elected president and John O'Rourke and Owen (Bert) Brennan were elected vice-presidents. The report of the Ethical Practices Committee was read to the convention and then immediately expunged from the minutes, and no effort was made to eliminate the abuses cited.

The Executive Council had no choice: the teamsters were suspended. The conditions imposed for lifting the suspension were removal of Hoffa and cooperation with a specially appointed Federation committee to correct all abuses. During its biennial convention at the end of 1957, the AFL-CIO took the final step and expelled the teamsters. A great deal of sacrifice and risk was involved in this drastic measure: sacrifice because the Federation gave up nearly 1,500,000 members, the source of 10 per cent of its revenue, and risk because of the powerful economic position of the teamsters resulting from the importance of trucking to almost all employers. In fact, it was the fear of the economic power of the teamsters that prevented the AFL-CIO from chartering a rival international to raid the membership of the expelled union.

In the meantime, the teamster leaders were being attacked from another side. Thirteen rank and file members secured an injunction staying the seating of Hoffa as president on the grounds that the convention was rigged. After a long trial examining whether the convention was in violation of the union constitution, Judge F. Dickenson Letts, of the Federal District Court, issued a consent decree based on a compromise: Hoffa became provisional president, elections were to be conducted at a future convention in not less than one year or more than five years, and a board of monitors was to keep the teamsters under surveillance. Three monitors were selected, one by Hoffa, one by the rank and file members, and the third, to act as chairman, by agreement of the other two. They became officers of the court with duties and responsibilities of: 1) counseling the teamsters' executive board, 2) drafting a model code of local union by-laws, and 3) consulting and recommending on accounting and financial procedures. The court ordered the officers to end their financial interest in companies doing business with employers who bargained with the teamsters.

The monitors could have resigned themselves to filing perfunctory semi-annual reports; instead, they vigorously pressed their mandate with Hoffa as the chief target. They sought his removal on the grounds that he violated the court decree and his oath of office by accepting re-election to the presidency of the Detroit local, with 17,000 members, even though the teamsters' constitution requires a full-time president, and by transferring $400,000 of the Detroit local's money to a no-interest deposit in a Florida bank as collateral for a loan to a real estate company he partly owned. Hoffa acquiesced to the demands of the monitors on some points, but fought shrewdly on matters affecting his control of the union. Very competent legal talent was hired to contest the monitors, appealing many cases through the federal courts to the Supreme Court. Although the monitors won on all basic legal issues, Hoffa won long delays, making it more difficult to dislodge him before the next convention.

An ordinary person would have fallen before such an onslaught, but Hoffa is no ordinary person. While being grilled by the McClellan Committee, fighting the AFL-CIO, and side-stepping the monitors, he came out successfully in two separate court cases, one charging him with illegal wire-tapping and the other with attempting to bribe an investigator employed by a congressional committee. He also attended to the normal business of his union, leading it to increases in membership and better collective bargaining agreements while the rest of the AFL-CIO was losing members. To the embarrassment of Meany and the Executive Council, Hoffa worked out cooperative agreements with at least ten affiliated internationals for collective bargaining and organization drives.

Two of these unions had presidents who served on the Ethical Practices Committee, Albert Hayes, the Committee's chairman, of the International Association of Machinists, and Joseph Curran of the National Maritime Union. The Executive Council demanded that all internationals sever their ties with expelled unions, but did permit local arrangements to continue. After all, almost every union comes into contact with the truckers.

It may seem strange that the membership, employers, and public indignation are unable to force a person such as Hoffa out of positions of responsibility. In some teamster locals, individuals may fear for their personal safety, and therefore keep quiet. Nevertheless, the members, as a group, have the advantage of numbers and if they made a concerted effort, the leadership could no doubt be changed. But, with the exception of a minority, they are willing to tolerate tainted leadership in return for regular wage increases. Employers are willing to bargain with this type of official, preferring stability to the upsetting labor-management relations associated with a democratic battle for union office. Public indignation is expressed in moralistic after-dinner speeches and pious editorials, but retires with smug satisfaction after a law has been passed, with no realization of how little difference the law can make when the regulated parties are determined to circumvent it.

The teamsters' story—still unfinished while this book was being written —was described in so much detail for a number of reasons: 1) it illustrates how the AFL-CIO through its Ethical Practices Committee attempts to reduce corruption in unions; 2) the weakness of the Federation in dealing with a powerful international is portrayed; 3) the case sets a precedent for court interference in internal union affairs, after many years of judicial reluctance to regulate voluntary organizations; 4) the publicity given to Hoffa and other teamster officials provided an important impetus toward passing the Labor-Management Reporting and Disclosure Act; 5) finally, the story shows how difficult it is to change the traditions of an institution whose leaders resist and whose members "don't care," even when outside forces seem overwhelming. After all, the truck driver may argue that his union is no more corrupt than the radio-television industry, as other congressional investigations revealed, with its rigged quiz shows and "payola" (bribes to disk jockeys for plugging particular records).

Although the Ethical Practices Committee has not accomplished as much as it would like, some genuine progress has been made. The United Textile Workers (formerly AFL) were forced to clean house and the newly chartered bakery workers' union has won most of the membership from the union which was expelled in 1957 for its corrupt leadership. The Allied Industrial Workers, under the threat of expulsion, eliminated some of the most infamous racketeers from their leadership, the Distillery Workers were placed on probation, and the Laundry Workers were expelled. By investigating and exposing, the Ethical Practices Committee limits many of the more flagrant abuses of crooked union leaders.

Effect on Collective Bargaining

The direct impact of the merger on collective bargaining has been small, and will undoubtedly continue to be. Since the demise of the Knights of Labor and the Industrial Workers of the World, collective bargaining in this country has been a function performed solely by the national unions and their affiliated local bodies. Neither the AFL nor the CIO interfered in bargaining—a reflection of one of the most important lessons learned by the AFL in its struggle with the Knights.

In a few instances two or more national unions have joined forces to bargain with an employer or group of employers. More of this will probably occur in the future, but for economic reasons rather than as a consequence of the merger. That is, national unions coordinate their demands and strike threats whenever it appears economically advantageous for them to do so. The Industrial Union Department encourages such cooperation where two or more unions are involved in the same industry or related industries. But the Federation itself will probably neither encourage nor enter into such bargaining. Nevertheless, those who frequently criticize unions charge that the merger has created a giant labor monopoly. They claim that it may lead to nation-wide demands and strikes involving several unions and industries at one time.[8] Such a development does not seem likely in the near future, and certainly not as a result of the merger.

The merger may eventually have a number of important indirect effects on collective bargaining. Anything which increases the strength of unions generally is bound to affect union-employer relationships. Therefore, if the AFL-CIO is able to extend unionization into new areas of the economy, the bargaining power of all unions will tend to be greater because this reduces the threat of nonunion plants undermining the union wage scales and working conditions. Furthermore, with less of their energies expended on jurisdictional wrangling, unions will be in a

---

[8] National Association of Manufacturers, *Industry's View on Organized Labor and the Antitrust Laws,* March, 1956, p. 3.

position to devote more of their efforts to winning concessions from employers.

CONCLUSIONS ON MERGER

Whether the merger will contribute to the effectiveness of unions depends to a large extent on the sincerity of the cooperation between the leaders. Conceivably, a new spark could be ignited leading to a far larger and more powerful labor organization. In any case, there appears to be little doubt that the political voice of labor will become more potent. The organizing and bargaining activities have been given at least a modest boost. And the ability of unions to deal with corruption and communism in their midst has been improved.

Contrariwise, it has been predicted by some that the marriage will end in annulment. Many of the old disputes between various union leaders continue to smolder behind the scenes. There is still disagreement about who should have jurisdiction over plant maintenance, painting, small-scale remodeling—the industrial union which has organized the plant or the local unions which have organized the carpenters, painters, and other craftsmen. John L. Lewis predicted that the merger would "part like the rope of sand it is" because of these long-standing rivalries.[9] But at least the marriage did not have the earmarks of being a shotgun affair, and it has weathered the first years, the most trying times of any new partnership.

The merger, however, is not complete. Many of the affiliates have overlapping jurisdictions. Also, there are a number of important independent unions outside the AFL-CIO, notably the teamsters, the United Mine Workers, and some of the railroad brotherhoods.

SUMMARY

Interpreted in even the most favorable terms, the record of unions since World War II is spotty, even though some progress was made toward consolidating the ranks of labor. After twenty years of conflict mingled with abortive efforts at cooperation, the AFL and CIO finally merged. During these two decades, the American union movement more than tripled in size, expanding particularly in manufacturing industries. To some extent, the competitive aspect of the split stimulated this growth. On the other hand, the breach in the labor movement prevented the unions from acting in concert on a number of crucial political, social, and economic questions.

[9] *New York Times*, September 5, 1955, p. 22.

The need for unity became more impressive with the passage of the Taft-Hartley Act in 1947 and again during the Korean War. However, the efforts to work together at that time were only temporary. The AFL insisted on organic unity while the CIO preferred functional cooperation. Each accused the other of harboring undesirable elements, either as communist or corrupt leaders.

The appearance of new presidents in both federations at the end of 1952 marked the real turning point in the direction of unity. The merger did not bring complete serenity to the relations between all unions and their leaders. Nevertheless, it fostered a degree of cooperation far beyond anything which had occurred over the previous twenty years. Combining the political arms of the two federations has led to more effective political activity. With organizing efforts coordinated, the possibility of expanding union membership is increased; however, other factors have prevented any realization of this possibility.

Even though the merger permits greater flexibility in dealing with unions dominated by communist or corrupt leaders, the AFL-CIO is not capable of doing a thorough housecleaning job on a large national union. In fact, inability to deal effectively with the teamsters' union reveals a substantial blemish on its record of consolidation. Lack of development of new techniques for rooting out corruption and failure to launch a successful membership campaign suggest that a degree of stagnation is present in the American union movement.

DISCUSSION QUESTIONS

1. In what respects can the 1950's be called a period of union consolidation, in what respects a period of stagnation? Explain.

2. "The split between the AFL and the CIO aided rather than hindered the growth and development of unions." Critically evaluate this statement.

3. Trace the significant events between 1950 and 1955 leading to the merger of the AFL and CIO.

4. What were the bases of the argument between the AFL and CIO over "organic unity" as opposed to "functional cooperation"? Explain how the merger was a compromise between these two positions.

5. Do you think unity would have been achieved without a change in the leadership in the AFL and CIO? Explain.

6. What was the No-Raiding Pact of 1954? Why was it an important document?

7. Describe the pressures that were applied and explain why they were

far from completely successful in changing the policies of the teamsters' leadership.

8. "In dealing with corruption, the AFL-CIO and its Ethical Practices Committee are no more effective than the pre-merger federations." Write an essay critically appraising this statement.

9. What do you think have been the most important consequences of the merger? Why?

10. What effects has the merger had on union organizing and political activities? Explain.

BIBLIOGRAPHY

Bloch, Joseph W. "Founding Convention of the AFL-CIO," *Monthly Labor Review*, Vol. LXXIX (February, 1956), pp. 141–49.

Goldberg, Arthur J. *AFL-CIO Labor United*. New York: McGraw-Hill Book Company, 1956.

Harris, Herbert. *Labor's Civil War*. New York: Alfred A. Knopf, 1940.

Industrial and Labor Relations Review, Vol. IX (April, 1956). (The entire issue is devoted to the merger, the events leading up to it and its possible consequences.)

Seidman, Joel. *American Labor from Defense to Reconversion*. Chicago: The University of Chicago Press, 1953.

Taft, Philip. *The A. F. of L. from the Death of Gompers to the Merger*. New York: Harper & Brothers, 1959.

———. *Corruption and Racketeering in the Labor Movement*. Ithaca: New York State School of Industrial and Labor Relations, Bulletin No. 38, 1958.

5

PROSPECTS FOR THE FUTURE

Are unions, as the result of their 150 years of growth, approaching the point of dominating our economic life? Are they imbued with a vitality driving them to higher levels of membership and greater influence over all community affairs? Or has the labor movement lost its spark, become stagnant and unable to rise to new challenges? Are unions becoming satisfied with a humdrum continuation of time-worn patterns of behavior? Does the existence of many unorganized areas dilute their power into relative ineffectiveness?

POSITION OF UNIONS IN THE ECONOMY

The position of unions today is certainly far different from that of a century ago, or even twenty-five years ago. They are no longer looked upon as a temporary phenomenon which will be eliminated with the first fierce wind of economic adversity. The Taft-Hartley Act and the Landrum-Griffin Act, even though condemned by labor leaders, recognize unions as legitimate organizations, protecting them in some activities and regulating them in others. Business firms, of course, object to some things which unions do, but it is no longer a common practice for corporations to spend large sums of money in expectation of driving the unions out of their plants. Unions today are an accepted part of the American economic scene.

Students of the union movement do not agree on just how powerful unions are. Some believe that unions possess tremendous monopoly

81

power and are destroying the capitalistic system.[1] Their constant upward pressure on wages, it is argued, is upsetting the market structure and price system. Another extreme position claims that: "Inside this country today, the labor leaders are the strategic actors: they lead the only organizations capable of stopping the main drift towards war and slump." [2] This argument has also been made in slightly different terms: "The trade unions are the most powerful economic organizations . . . the community has ever seen. Their policies will be a major influence in determining how much the community produces, how rapidly it adds to its capital, and how the product of industry is divided." [3] A more moderate view holds that unions

. . . do not . . . have monopolistic control of wages or other conditions of employment, to say nothing about production, prices, or profits. They do not control government and, acting alone, have little prospect of gaining such control in the foreseeable future . . . In dealings with employers and in substantially everything else, the unions of this country never act as a unit. Nearly everywhere, the organized workers, including their families, are only a minority in the population, and their leaders are socially unacceptable in the so-called "best circles." Our society is "laboristic" only in the sense that unionism has made great gains and is beginning to challenge the dominance of our great corporations. But the unions have neither monopoly control over industry nor the main say in public affairs in the contemporary United States.[4]

In view of this disagreement among impartial observers who have carefully studied workers and their organizations, what conclusions can we draw? Four factors must be considered. Each is subject to qualification and amplification which will be made here and in later chapters. 1) In certain industries unions are quite powerful, e.g., in automobiles, steel, and construction in large cities. But even here they cannot dictate wages, amount of employment, and working conditions. 2) In other industries, unions are weak, e.g., agriculture, services, retail trade. In these industries, they have no direct effect on wages and working conditions. 3) With respect to certain variables in our national economy, unions are very influential, but not omnipotent, e.g., concerning the general level of wages and the taxing and spending policies of the federal government. The latter is affected indirectly: failure to manipulate the

[1] See especially Charles E. Lindblom, *Unions and Capitalism* (New Haven: Yale University Press, 1949).

[2] C. Wright Mills, *The New Men of Power* (New York: Harcourt, Brace and Company, 1948), p. 3.

[3] Sumner H. Slichter, *The Challenge of Industrial Relations* (Ithaca: Cornell University Press, 1947), p. 4.

[4] Edwin E. Witte, "Role of the Unions in Contemporary Society," *Industrial and Labor Relations Review*, Vol. IV (October, 1950), p. 4.

government's fiscal affairs so as to deal effectively with a recession and unemployment will bring workers to the polls in large numbers to defeat the party in power. 4) With respect to many other economic variables, unions are weak, although not entirely powerless, as in the questions of money supply and other monetary policies, the goods and services involved in international trade, and the rate of technological improvement in production methods. In a few industries, notably construction, they have been able to delay the use of some technological improvements. However, in no industry or occupation are they capable of preventing changes in consumers' tastes, which could decrease or eliminate the employment of their members.

If the first and third of these factors are considered the most important, then the conclusion would be that unions are extremely powerful in the American economy. However, the second and fourth factors cannot be ignored, and they materially reduce the economic and political power of the labor movement. Unions, then, are powerful economic organizations, but they operate within an environment over which they have only limited control.

UNORGANIZED AREAS

One of the restrictions on union power is the presence of large groups of unorganized workers. A number of large geographical areas in the United States are almost untouched by unionism, and the same is true of many occupations and industries. It is in these unorganized areas that significant increases in union growth will occur—if they are to occur at all.

Percentage of the Labor Force Organized

The magnitude of this problem—from the union point of view—is portrayed by the fact that out of approximately seventy million workers in the civilian labor force only seventeen million are organized. The latter figure is subject to some error since the statistics on actual membership are difficult to secure, because some unions underestimate their union membership in order to reduce the per capita tax they must pay to the AFL-CIO, and other unions overestimate their actual membership in order to increase their voting power in the Federation. Using these figures, which are probably as accurate as any, we find that approximately 25 per cent of the civilian labor force is organized.

Expressing union membership as a percentage of the civilian labor force is misleading because the latter includes farmers and other self-employed persons and corporation officials and managers. If the unorganizable groups are eliminated, we have approximately fifty million potentially organizable workers; and two-thirds of them have *not* joined unions.

Geographical Areas

The most completely organized areas of the country are the Northeast, the eastern sections of the Midwest, and the Pacific states. Areas in which the unions have met the greatest opposition are the South and the Rocky Mountain areas. Viewed differently, large cities are more highly unionized than small cities and rural areas. Workers in medium-sized cities are more likely to be organized in the Northeast than in the South. These observations are exceedingly broad and there are many exceptions.

What explains this geographical pattern of union organization? First, the area north of the Ohio River and east of the Mississippi River, historically, has been more heavily industrialized; and more recently, the Pacific Coast has become a major industrial area. These areas are characterized by large cities and large firms with indirect relationships between employers and employees. As a result of this impersonality, workers are more willing to pledge allegiance to a union. In the small shops, more typical of small towns, the relationship between the workers and the owner or top management is more direct and personal. The worker is more likely to feel that he has a stake in the success of the firm and that his productive contribution is of some consequence. Furthermore, in a small firm, an employee's union affiliation is more quickly spotted by the employer and becomes an open invitation to retaliation.

Secondly, in large cities, the customs and traditions of factory life are more clearly etched in the workers' minds. The widespread unemployment during a depression weighs heavily on each worker and his neighbor, and becomes the major topic of discussion in every local "gin mill." Alternately, the great demand for labor during prosperous periods, with pay increases and overtime work, spreads a bond of fellowship among the workers. In short, the waves of economic activity are shared in common by the majority of city workers. In large cities most workers have no hope—or soon lose what hope they ever had—of becoming independent entrepreneurs with their own farms, stores, or small shops. With their economic destiny tied to the impersonal factory, and with little opportunity to attain the ranks of management, the city workers are more likely to turn to the union to improve their status.

The third factor explaining the geographical distribution of unionism is that once an important segment of workers is organized, it becomes easier to organize other industries and occupations in the same geographical area. Why is this? A union, when it first appears, is a new institution, threatening the old institutional arrangements and upsetting the existing balance of power. Individuals, groups, and organizations currently holding power will generally resist such a change. Once a major union or a group of unions has achieved some status within the community, resistance declines, or at least becomes less effective. The importance of local institutions is well illustrated by what has happened to union-organizing drives in the South, where there is comparatively little unionization. Union organizers have been given the coolest of welcomes by the local citizenry, have been denied the use of public facilities and private meeting halls, and in some instances have been unceremoniously escorted out of town by police officers. This hostile reception is partly the consequence of the threat of unionism to the existing patterns of racial segregation. In some cities a union organizer is required to purchase a license costing up to $1,000 and to pay a fee for each worker organized or for each day he practices his profession. Although such legislation has been declared unconstitutional, its continual appearance in different forms indicates the strength of community feeling. In one South Carolina town a manufacturer asked for an expression of local opinion on doubling the size of his plant, on condition that it be unionized. The merchants and other local businessmen were unanimously opposed, even though the increased payrolls would have brought them greater profits. In the face of such official and unofficial opposition, it is not surprising that unions have made little headway in the South.

What is likely to happen to the geographical distribution of union membership in the future? There will probably not be any great shift in the next several years for reasons discussed in a following section on the growth potential of unions. Whatever geographical redistribution does occur, however, will be caused more by the relocation of industry than by union-organizing drives. Southern states and cities have offered substantial inducements to encourage business firms to settle within their borders, e.g., temporary exemptions from taxes and plant facilities at low rents. Furthermore, wages in many occupational classifications are lower in the South than elsewhere. Hence, more than a proportional share of the industrial expansion of the last decade has occurred in the South. The government's desire to decentralize industries vital to national defense will also cause firms to build new plants in areas less heavily unionized. Whenever these new plants are subdivisions of completely organized firms, union recognition may be somewhat easier to secure. The advancing wave of industrialization will tend slowly—perhaps very slowly—to break down the barriers to organization in these communities.

Occupational and Industrial Groups

By referring to Chapter 1, the reader may refresh his memory on the occupational and industrial distribution of the labor force and the changing trends therein. White-collar workers constitute one group of occupations which has been an expanding portion of the labor force and has been a "tough nut" for the unions to crack. Included are: professional, technical, and kindred workers, managers and officials, clerical and kindred workers, sales workers, and a portion of the service workers. White-collar workers account for nearly 50 per cent of the labor force, occupy many different work situations, and encompass a wide variety of skills.

Some of the white-collar workers are in daily contact with management and therefore tend to identify with management, thus creating a significant barrier to union organization. They fear that unionization will not only mean the loss of this status-giving identification, but also that they may become wallflowers within a production workers' union not at all familiar with their special problems.

The organizing tactics designed for blue-collar workers do not have the same appeal to white-collar workers. Furthermore, techniques which will be successful for one group of white-collar workers are likely to be highly inadequate in approaching another group. For example, it is generally easier to organize office workers in a plant where the production employees have a successful union, whereas clerks in a department store or tellers in a bank require an altogether different approach.

Service and clerical workers are often difficult to organize because they work in small firms with a closer employer-employee relationship, as in a gasoline station. In other cases the employees are largely, or entirely, females who have little expectation of remaining in the labor market for any length of time, and therefore are less willing to make the sacrifices which go along with establishing a permanent and successful union. Furthermore, since their jobs frequently require only a short training period, they can be easily replaced by another group of female workers.

The professional and technical occupations are rapidly increasing in importance in our economy. Traditionally, they have been nonunion, having instead professional organizations of their own. However, in sev-

eral instances these professional organizations are acquiring characteristics more closely approximating those of a union. For example, the
National Educational Association has found it necessary to become
concerned over the salaries of elementary and high school teachers,
partly because of the spread of unionization among teachers in some
cities. The nurses' associations have likewise shown a greater interest
in the economic condition of their members. In many situations, particularly among the engineers, the professional and technical worker is
taking on the characteristics of the production worker. That is, he is
separated from his employer by two or three levels of supervisory
employees and works on specific assignments under direct supervision.
Frequently he is not required to carry any project through to its conclusion, but only to contribute a small and routine effort to the total
project. Potentially, professional and technical employees are a fertile
field for union organization. This would be particularly true if the unions
could integrate the existing professional associations into their organizations.[5]

The problems faced by unions in organizing the white-collar occupations become more pressing because of the continuing rise of the service
industries. Of course, not all employees in the service industries are white-
collar workers, but a large portion of them are. With increasing levels
of income, greater urbanization of the population, and higher educational
standards, the service industries have been employing a larger and larger
share of the labor force.[6] Hotels and restaurants, cleaning and laundry
establishments, retail and wholesale trades, and entertainment are partly
organized, but mainly in large cities. Other major branches are almost
entirely unorganized, e.g., domestic service, medical and health care,
insurance and real estate, and banking and finance. The service industries,
with the exception of wholesale trade, are characterized by small firms,
predominantly proprietorships and partnerships. The business owners
constitute a significant portion of the labor force and generally work
directly with the employees.

One of the service industries which has become increasingly important
over the past decades is the government. As an employer, it occupies a
position different from that of a private firm. Many public agencies
refuse to recognize, or are prohibited by law from recognizing and

[5] Herbert R. Northrup, "Collective Bargaining by Professional Societies," *Insights
into Labor Issues*, ed. by Richard A. Lester and Joseph Shister (New York: The
Macmillan Company, 1948), pp. 142–62.
[6] George J. Stigler, *Trends in Employment in the Service Industries* (Princeton:
Princeton University Press, 1956).

bargaining with, unions. Ever since the famous strike of Boston policemen (1919) it has been assumed in many quarters—in the words of Calvin
Coolidge, then Governor of Massachusetts—that "there is no right to strike
against the public safety . . ." Since many of the unionized government
workers voluntarily renounce the right to strike and the majority of
others resort to strikes only under extreme circumstances, they are cut
off from the ordinary stream of the labor movement. That is, the unions
tend to look upon public employees and their unions as outside of their
normal range of interest, a group which wins economic improvements
through political action rather than strikes.[7] However, in recent years,
some governmental units have shown a greater willingness to deal with
unions.

The agricultural industry continues to employ approximately 2,000,000
workers, in spite of its declining importance in the labor force. It has
been particularly resistant to unionization, largely because of the small
size of the employing unit and the close personal relationship between
employer and employee. Furthermore, many agricultural jobs are of
short duration, filled by unskilled casual labor with only temporary
attachments to the farm labor market. The trend toward the development
of "factory farms"—farms with a permanent work force—has created
conditions conducive to organization, but the unions of agricultural workers have made little progress. The city unions have not seen fit to give
their "country cousins" any real aid and support.

If unions are ever going to be successful in organizing agricultural
workers, the service industries, and the white-collar occupations, they
will have to change their approach, and recognize that the methods
which have been successful for dealing with factory workers' problems
may not be successful for other workers. For example, a strike is the
most effective bargaining weapon for production employees, but in the
case of white-collar, government, or professional and technical employees,
it may be out of the question for legal reasons or because it "lacks
dignity." Hence, the unions will have to devise a new technique, perhaps
with a longer-range goal than that associated with a strike. Unions
will also have to be willing to give a real voice in their organization
to these new groups if they are to be attracted. Whether the AFL-CIO
possesses the flexibility and imagination necessary for this task is yet
unknown. It will require breaking old traditions and rearranging union
power relationships.

[7] Sterling D. Spero, *Government as Employer* (New York: Remsen Press, 1948).
The role of the government as an employer is discussed in detail in Chapter 18.

Foremen

The rise and decline of unionization among foremen makes an interesting case study of the problems which unions face in extending their organization. In many respects they fall into a special category, primarily because of their quasi-management position.

Prior to World War II, foremen were almost entirely unorganized, with major exceptions in printing and building trades where they belonged to the same union as other employees. A number of factors contributed to the rapid growth of foremen's unions, and especially to the aggressiveness of the Foremen's Association of America, during and immediately after World War II. The changed attitude of the National Labor Relations Board (as expressed in the Maryland Dry Dock [1943] and the Packard Motor Car Company [1945] cases) brought them under the protection of the Wagner Act. This meant that the employers could not discharge them solely for engaging in union activity and that foremen and their unions could go before the National Labor Relations Board for representation elections. If they won these elections, the employers were compelled to bargain with the union.

During World War II, with the rapid expansion in employment, particularly in heavy manufacturing industries, new foremen had to be recruited rapidly. In many cases they were brought up from the ranks of the production workers and hence had a union background. Many believed that their new position was temporary and were anxious to maintain their union contracts.

Management was unwilling to put authority in the hands of their new foremen, partly because of the unionization of the production workers. If one supervisor made a grievance settlement particularly favorable to the union, the settlement would be claimed as a precedent to be applied to all other divisions of the plant. Since this could raise the company's labor costs substantially, foremen were granted very little jurisdiction in settling many types of grievances. Their power to discipline the workers under them had been taken away.

The crowning insult to the foreman's prestige was the decline, and in many cases disappearance, of his pay differential over that of the production workers. Being on a fixed salary, he frequently found that the employees whom he was directing earned more, including their overtime, than he did.

As organization among foremen increased, employers began to offer more resistance. They pressed successfully for a change in the supervisors' status under the National Labor Relations Act. The passage of the Taft-Hartley Act in 1947 brought with it an exclusion of all supervisors from the protection of the Act. Many firms, furthermore, made efforts to increase the authority of the foremen and engaged in a public relations program to convince them that they were really a part of management, e.g., they were often consulted on management policy, given special reserved areas in the parking lot, provided with impressive desks, etc. Pay increases were granted. At the end of World War II there was a decline in the amount of overtime worked by the production employees and thus the traditional pay differential reappeared. The finishing blow to foreman unionization was administered by the Ford strike, when the Foremen's Association lost in its effort to retain collective bargaining status with the corporation.

Management's techniques have effectively closed off the foremen as potential union members. Will the pendulum swing back again? Not necessarily! Although the Taft-Hartley Act does not make foremen's unions illegal, it does permit discharging a supervisor for joining a union, thus giving the employer a lethal weapon for combating unionization in the management family. Furthermore, employers learned their lesson during and after World War II, and will likely exert greater efforts in the future to woo the foremen in terms of salary, authority, and status within the firm. This experience demonstrates a weakness in the American labor movement: an inability to outmaneuver management and environmental forces to win the allegiance of many special groups of workers.

GROWTH POTENTIAL OF UNIONS

What are the prospects for union growth? What are the factors which will shape whatever growth occurs? Will unions be able to extend their membership into the geographical, occupational, and industrial areas that are now largely unorganized? Certain obvious factors can be cited immediately. The continued growth of the labor force, at the rate of about 2 or 3 per cent per year, will probably lead to an increase in union membership. The relative growth of industries and occupations which are already highly organized will affect the growth of unions. But will unions significantly increase in proportion to the size of the labor force?

In suggesting a framework for analyzing these possibilities, Joseph Shister identified three determinants of union growth: work environment, sociolegal framework, and nature of union leadership.[8] One dimension

[8] Joseph Shister, "The Logic of Union Growth," *The Journal of Political Economy,* Vol. LXI (October, 1953), pp. 413–33.

of the work environment is occupational mobility. Our earlier discussion of this subject showed that the high rate of mobility has retarded the growth of unions. Of course, if our economy changes so as to erect insurmountable barriers between occupations, organization would be encouraged.

A second dimension of the work environment is fluctuations in employment. In the past, cycles in business activity have affected the pace of union growth. Generally, prosperity favors the expansion of membership and depression discourages it. The important exception to this occurs during later stages of long depressions marked by considerable unemployment, as in the 1880's and the 1930's. In each of these instances, organization increased substantially, to a large extent because workers wished to register their objections to the harsh working conditions, low wages, and uncertainty of their jobs. Unions were vehicles of social protest. If such severe cyclical movements never occur again—and many economists make this prediction—union growth will be denied this impetus. Certainly, the prosperity of the last fifteen years interspersed with relatively mild recessions has *not* stimulated a rapid rate of growth.

Another important aspect of the work environment is the structure of the industry which is potentially to be organized. The resistance to unionization is less, if job conditions make it difficult to replace workers, e.g., a rapidly expanding industry, or employees who require a considerable amount of training. The nature of the product being sold and the patterns of competition among firms will also be important. If the employer is likely to suffer a permanent loss of business as a result of a strike, the union's organizing opportunities are greater. If the industry is characterized by large-sized firms, the distance between top management and the rank and file worker is great, and the worker is more likely to feel that a union is necessary to protect his interests. Nevertheless, many firms characterized by these factors are still unorganized. In some cases they represent islands of resistance in industries otherwise completely unionized; perhaps the most outstanding example is Weirton Steel, geographically in the middle of the United Steel Workers and the United Mine Workers.

The sociolegal framework—Shister's second determinant—is the complex of social attitudes and legislation, court decisions, etc., which exist at the time. It has been fickle toward unions, sometimes favorable and at other times hostile. Thus, a major shift occurred in the sociolegal framework in the 1930's, and had a profound effect on union growth. One of its aspects—higher educational standards—appears to be an inhibitor of union growth. This is not to say that educated people do not join unions, but rather that much of the higher education today is designed to train people for professional, technical, and supervisory jobs—occupations which are largely unorganized. The work environment and the sociolegal framework are closely related; and in the long run the latter is determined by the factors which control the former.

The role of the leader in fostering the union's growth—Shister's third determinant—is played within the limits set by the work environment and the sociolegal framework. If an imaginative union leader is successful in capitalizing on the social unrest associated with a depression, for example, he is able to increase rapidly the membership of his union. If he is shrewd in appraising the vulnerable spots in the structure of the industry, he will be able to extend his organization. An outstanding example is John L. Lewis, who led the rapid rise of the mineworkers' union in the first years of the New Deal, and then held his organization together in spite of many technological changes in mining and the use of coal.

What, then, are the prospects for union growth in the coming years? The barriers to union penetration into the presently unorganized industries and occupations are all but overwhelming, and these are the ones which are growing most rapidly. Unless substantial changes occur in the work environment, such as a severe depression, or in the sociolegal framework, unions are not likely to achieve much success in these unorganized areas. Well-directed organizing campaigns financed by the AFL-CIO might gain members in such geographical areas as the South, but the obstacles are almost insurmountable. Over-all there appears to be no convincing reason to expect that the percentage of the labor force which becomes organized will do more than increase modestly, if at all, within the foreseeable future.[9]

Special Benefits to Members

Concluding that the growth potential of unions is very limited does not imply that they are in great danger of losing a large portion of their present membership. In fact, their special benefits programs serve as one of the incentives—though not the most important—for members to continue their loyalty.

[9] For varying opinions on this conclusion, see: Irving Bernstein, "The Growth of American Unions," *American Economic Review*, Vol. XLIV (June, 1954), pp. 301–18; Irving Bernstein, "Union Growth and Structural Cycles"; and the following discussion by Daniel Bell, Lloyd Ulman, and Russell Allen, *Proceedings of the Seventh Annual Meeting of the Industrial Relations Research Association*, December, 1954, pp. 202–46.

"Special benefits programs" is a name given to a variety of off-the-job benefits provided to members free or below market prices. No two unions offer the same package of special services, each program being tailor-made to the needs of the constituency. Some are financed solely through the union, others receive contributions from employers.

One of the most typical benefits is medical care. The United Mine Workers have built hospitals in coal fields previously lacking in adequate medical facilities. In all, unions have established more than sixty health centers throughout the country, with a special emphasis on preventive medicine.

Homes for retired members are operated by the typographers, carpenters, ladies' garment workers, printing pressmen, and others. Low rent housing cooperatives, financed by unions, are expanding rapidly, particularly in New York City, with members having priority in occupancy. Nearly 5,000 credit unions are serving the banking needs of union members, making low-interest loans and paying interest on deposits.

Union experts counsel workers on their rights under the social security laws, and in some cases give free legal advice on any personal problem. Many unions perform social counseling, helping members to contact appropriate community chest and welfare agencies. Organized labor is contributing over a half-million dollars annually for college scholarships. Buying clubs and other consumer services are being promoted.

Recreation—one of the fastest growing claims on the time of all American citizens—has not been neglected. A few unions operate resort facilities making possible low-cost vacations for members and their families. Unions have sponsored dancing classes, theatre parties, week-end trips, and similar social functions.[10]

The special benefits constitute a technique for retaining loyalty of members in a period when unions have to fight hard just to maintain their present size. As long as incomes are rising and jobs secure, members may become lackadaisical, but these programs act as a constant reminder of the presence of their union.

NATURE OF UNION LEADERSHIP

Since the leaders play a key role in the growth potential of unions and since they are "strategic actors" in our society, it is appropriate to inquire into their characteristics. In personal attributes they are similar to leaders of other American institutions. They must have a boundless

[10] For a more complete discussion of special benefits to members, see Morris Maken, "Union Card 'Dividends,'" *Industrial Bulletin*, N. Y. Department of Labor, October, 1959, pp. 3–9.

energy, be willing to sacrifice their family life, be constantly engaged in planning future events, and possess a strong urge for power. Like politicians, they must know how to win friends and influence people, and avoid unnecessarily making enemies.[11] These attributes of a union leader have been summarized in a striking but slightly exaggerated fashion:

> The labor union is an army; the labor leader is a generalissimo. The union is a democratic town meeting; the leader is a parliamentary debater. The union is a political machine; the leader is a political boss. . . . The labor union is a regulator of the workingman's industrial animosity; the labor leader is a salaried technician of animosity, gearing men at work into an institution and then easing that institution through the slumps and wars and booms of American society.[12]

Backgrounds of Union Leaders

Where do labor leaders come from? What sort of background propels people in this type of activity? The background of labor leaders differs from that of the rest of the male population of this country only to a small extent. Well over half of them were the sons of wage workers, less than 10 per cent the sons of white-collar workers, and approximately one-third the sons of entrepreneurs, farmers, small shopkeepers, etc. The leaders who were sons of wage workers had as fathers primarily foremen and skilled workers.

Approximately three-fourths of the union leaders held jobs as wage workers prior to assuming their union position. Approximately half of them had been foremen or skilled workers.[13] American labor leaders, then, are a product of their own work environment. They are not middle class "intellectuals" who have usurped power among the workers in order to lead them to some brave new society.

Tenure in Office

Although there are many exceptions, union leaders at the top level generally have a long tenure in office. This is particularly true of the presidents of national unions, who, prior to World War II, had served

[11] Eli Ginzberg, *The Labor Leader* (New York: The Macmillan Company, 1948), p. 28. This study of American labor leaders was conducted prior to World War II. Ginzberg's sample included the executive boards of ten international unions, two of them quite large and two quite small. The sample was representative but had two important biases. The unions were all well established, having an extensive history behind them. None were from the CIO, since they were too young to have an established leadership at the time of Ginzberg's study.

[12] Mills, *op. cit.*, pp. 3–4.

[13] *Ibid.*, pp. 88–93.

on their executive boards for an average of twenty-six years, twenty years of this time as president. In other words, the presidents arrived at their top position early in their careers and then held the position for a long time. In the lower levels of officialdom, particularly in the local units, the turnover is much greater.[14]

Since unions are comparatively new institutions, the average length of tenure of top office-holders has been increasing. But this trend has probably reached its peak, because the presidents who rose to power during the thirties, or earlier, have passed from the scene or are reaching retirement age. Phil Murray of the steel workers, Bill Hutcheson of the carpenters, John L. Lewis of the mine workers, and Dan Tobin of the teamsters were long-tenure leaders who have been replaced since 1950. A new generation of executives will have to be found for others, such as George Harrison of the railway clerks and David Dubinsky of the ladies' garment workers.

Professionalization of Leadership

The complex nature of the modern corporation has created the need for a managerial group possessing a wide range of specialized talents. The unions which deal with these corporations must develop an adept leadership to match the managerial group or else be at a disadvantage in bargaining. Thus, unions have found it necessary to employ their officials on a full-time basis. For the national union, this means a staff of professional experts, including statisticians and accountants as well as organizers and bargainers. Many of the locals, particularly among the skilled trades, employ a full-time official—generally a business agent. Running the affairs of a union has become a professionalized occupation, even though there is no educational curriculum leading to a degree in union leadership. (A member of unions, however, conduct special institutes, sometimes on college campuses.)

There is tremendous variation in the income paid to different union presidents. A few of them receive salaries of $50,000 or more. The majority of them, however, receive more modest incomes in the neighborhood of $15,000 or less, often much less. One constant difficulty of the full-time official is to avoid creating a gulf between himself and the rank and file workers whom he leads, because it interferes with his effectiveness in his job. Both his salary and his status in the community may contribute to widening the gulf. The large number of votes cast for the defeated candidate in the contested election, in 1957, of David McDonald

[14] Ginzberg, *op. cit.*, pp. 63–66.

as president of the United Steel Workers appeared to be partially the result of rank and file reaction to his $50,000 salary and his fraternization with corporation executives.

Union leaders, particularly those in the upper echelons, strive not only for the loyalty of their membership but also for the respect of the community. Achieving a position as a recognized social and political leader satisfies the union official's ego and at the same time allows him to spread more effectively the influence of unionism among political groups and social agencies, such as community planning boards, public housing agencies, and the like. However, going to the country club to attend luncheon meetings with bankers, newspaper editors, and society matrons may increase the distance between the official and the members. They may feel he no longer understands or cares about their job problems.

Leadership and Union Growth

We began our discussion of leadership by pointing out the important role it plays in union growth. In past times, dynamic personalities have risen from the ranks and inspired workers to join successful fighting organizations. But has the American labor movement become too "flabby" —Walter Reuther's term to describe the condition[15]—to respond to present-day challenges? When protected by long tenure, receiving comfortable salaries, and enjoying professional status, do union officials become devoid of ideas capable of igniting the loyalty of new groups of workers?

Answering these questions is at least partially speculative, but lessons from the past are helpful. The restrictions on union growth in the 1950's have many parallels to the 1920's. The economy is prosperous and growing, with almost all segments participating in the rising standard of living. Workers—particularly unorganized workers—see no reason to attribute their higher real incomes to union activity. Management has shown vigor and imagination in resisting union penetration into new territories, e.g., those of foremen and engineers. The tenor of public opinion and the legislation adopted from 1947 on more closely resemble the situation of the 1920's than the 1930's.

To triumph over these obstacles requires a most imaginative type of leadership. And this has been lacking! There has been some progress in terms of consolidating the gains made up to the end of World War II. The merger is a creditable achievement, but more than patching old differences is needed if membership and economic influence are to be

[15] In a speech to the Industrial Union Department convention in 1959, Reuther used this term to describe the union movement. *New York Times,* November 10, 1959.

significantly increased. The record of lagging growth since 1947 is evidence of the need for a change in policies.

The cause of the stagnation which seems to be spreading through the modern American labor movement is perhaps the heritage of the limited range of goals sought and the ingrained pragmatism of unions, stunting the imagination of the leadership and failing to fire the enthusiasm of the members. In earlier days, unionism distinguished itself as something different from the rest of the community, even while striving for only short-run economic improvements; it held out the promise of major changes in wages, working conditions, freedom on the job—a chance for the worker to hold his head high. This was a shining vision worthy of great sacrifice. But unions and the community have changed. The differences between union and nonunion workers are not so great as they once seemed. Nonunion workers tend to improve themselves, economically and otherwise, at about the same rate as union workers. There are exceptions, of course, but this cuts both ways; some groups of nonunion workers are among the leaders in making economic improvements.

These provocative statements are not made as condemnation of the present union leadership. It may be a wise choice to play safe, to continue to operate within the framework of a limited economic philosophy called business unionism (discussed in Chapter 7). To rush into new and uncharted areas would perhaps bring heavy losses in members, or be lacking in membership support. American workers seem to care little about the strength of unions so long as their standard of living is rising and their on-the-job problems are reasonably well cared for. They prefer unions that stick to a limited range of economic goals and tactics, and might well withdraw their loyalty from organizations that set out in radically different directions. The leaders then are shackled by the members and must confine their imagination to immediate economic benefits and resign themselves to plodding efforts to maintain a growth rate that keeps membership, at best, a constant percentage of the labor force.

POLITICAL POWER OF UNIONS

In evaluating the power status of unions in our present economy, some consideration must be given to their political influence. Unions have always been involved in political activity. Historically, this has taken two opposing directions: establishing an independent labor party, or working through one or both of the existing parties. In Chapter 3 some of the independent party activities of the nineteenth century were discussed and therefore need not be recounted here. The final major effort of this type was made in 1924. At that time the AFL, the railroad brotherhoods, and the Socialist Party combined with midwestern agricultural groups to support Robert M. LaFollette, Sr., for President of the United States. Although it was an amalgamation of political parties from diverse backgrounds, it was able to win five million votes in the popular election. In spite of this rather impressive showing, unions decided that independent political activity was not a promising avenue for improving their status, and therefore the AFL and the brotherhoods ended their support for third parties even though farmer-labor parties continued to be active in a number of midwestern states. The chief gains made by unions through the independent party approach came when the dominant parties adopted many of the platform planks of the labor parties, such as anti-injunction laws, minimum wage legislation, and so on.

After the founding of the AFL, unions concentrated most of their political efforts within the two-party system, relying on Gompers' guide: "Reward your friends and punish your enemies." There are two aspects to this approach: endorsing and supporting candidates friendly to unions and lobbying for legislation favorable to unions. In some cases, unions have sought narrow job goals, e.g., ship builders and maritime workers favoring the expansion of the American merchant marine, and railroad workers seeking laws compelling the use of full crews. In other cases, unions have sought to make substantial over-all changes in legislation, affecting all workers, as in liberalization of the unemployment compensation and fair labor standards laws. Prior to the 1930's, AFL political activity was mainly of the former type; in fact, during the 1920's, its leaders opposed unemployment compensation.

The depression and the influence of the CIO brought changes in the AFL's political goals and tactics. In 1936 the AFL and CIO combined their political activities to form Labor's Nonpartisan League, which worked actively for the election of Roosevelt in 1936. It became dominated to a large extent by the CIO, and consequently the AFL dropped out. As a result of disappointments with the 1942 election, the CIO established its Political Action Committee in 1943. This committee was active at national, state, and local levels in almost all important elections until the merger in 1955. In some instances it materially contributed to the vote of the labor-supported candidate. In other instances the PAC appeared to be quite ineffective. The AFL established a corresponding political organization called Labor's League for Political Education.[16] It is impossible to predict correctly whether in close elections endorsement by unions will be a real benefit to the candidate or a kiss-of-death. When unemployment is high, union support seems to be persuasive. In other conditions, endorsement probably leads to an increase in the number of union members who will cast their votes for that candidate, but it may also cause persons unsympathetic to unions to vote for the opposing candidate.

The political power of unions is most evident, on a continuing basis, in large cities which are dominated by one or two industries whose employees are fully organized, e.g., Pittsburgh, Seattle, Akron, Toledo, and Detroit. In these areas no politician can afford to be "anti-labor" and most public agencies—elective or appointive—will contain a high proportion of union representation.

The Taft-Hartley Act restricted union political activity by forbidding the allocation of regular funds collected through dues, fees, and assessments for the support of any candidate for public office. In response to the law, political agencies were established as separate affiliates financed by voluntary donations collected through the union structure. Unions are permitted, however, to endorse candidates through their regularly sponsored newspapers and radio programs.

Potentially, unions possess tremendous political power in any national election, or in state elections in the Northeast. The voting power of seventeen million members and their families constitutes the nation's largest single pressure group. However, this ignores the all-important point that members follow their own whims rather than mechanically accepting the political dictates of their leaders. Except during depressions, they are as apathetic toward "getting out the vote" as they are toward attending union meetings. The fact that television, newspapers, and other sources of public information are usually pro-management increases the difficulties of unions in selling their program.

Another dimension of union political power can be measured in terms of general influence in the community, separate from elective office. Local affairs in most American cities have traditionally been dominated by a small group of people, usually including the chief executives of the largest corporations, bankers, editors of newspapers, the most prosperous lawyers and physicians, and a few who have inherited prestige or wealth

[16] Henry David, "One Hundred Years of Labor in Politics," *The House of Labor,* ed. by J. B. S. Hardman and Maurice F. Neufeld (New York: Prentice-Hall, Inc., 1951), pp. 104–10, and Edwin E. Witte, "The New Federation and Political Action," *Industrial and Labor Relations Review,* Vol. IX (April, 1956), pp. 406–18.

or both. Not that each city is the same, but the direction of events is usually controlled by some such group. Since the end of World War II, union leaders have begun to infiltrate these select circles. They have been appointed to planning agencies, hospital and education boards, full-employment committees, community chests, Y.M.C.A. boards, etc. And they are often consulted when not officially represented. As yet their degree of influence is not proportional to the membership of the organizations they lead, but it is increasing.

Union Political Goals

Because of their emphasis on economic gains for the membership, unions do not formulate any consistent long-range political program, or at least not one which is uniquely their own. This is not to say that American unions do not have political goals, but they are specific and short-run. Union leaders do think they have a program: soon after World War II, about half of the AFL leaders thought that unions had a political program and nearly four-fifths of the CIO leaders thought so. However, they were probably talking about short-run demands or vaguely generalized principles.[17]

There are a number of reasons why unions do not have a clearly formulated political program. The foremost is the acceptance of the free enterprise system. As long as unions do not advocate a basic change in the structure of our economy, their "program" cannot be more than a collection of proposals for tampering with the existing system, e.g., modifying the tax structure, liberalizing social security benefits, and so forth.

Membership apathy also restricts the development of a political program. The leadership is generally more concerned than the rank and file about public affairs and their implications for unions. In fact, a large fraction of the members "don't care" or actually prefer that their union stay out of politics. And among those who are more favorably disposed toward active participation, there is much disagreement over tactics: how much time at local meetings should be used to discuss issues and candidates, how should political funds be collected.

Another reason why unions have not formulated a long-run political program is that they operate in a generally hostile environment: they are constantly forced to be on the defensive against specific offenses of the "opposition," hence, the adoption of short-run goals. For example, when employer organizations conduct a campaign in support of legislation

[17] Mills, *op. cit.*, pp. 159–60.

to restrict unions, the political energies of unions are directed toward the short-run goal of counteracting this campaign, leaving them no time for developing a long-run political program.

Furthermore, union leaders must be administrators of the day-to-day organizational problems of the union, which consumes a tremendous amount of their time. An ambitious young man may enter the union leadership hierarchy with a broadly conceived program, but he finds that his status as a leader depends on how well he satisfies the immediate goals of his constituents, again putting pressure on him to concentrate on a short-run program. Walter Reuther is an example of a union leader who entered the labor movement as a socialist, at one time advocating an independent labor party. After assuming the responsibilities of the presidency of the UAW, and later the CIO, his goals became more immediate and short-run.

Union short-run political goals fall into four categories. First, unions are always directly concerned with collective bargaining legislation, favoring laws which tend to extend collective bargaining while placing a minimum number of restrictions on their freedom of action. Unions will cooperate in drafting regulations of their internal affairs if the regulations strengthen the hand of the AFL-CIO in dealing with racketeering, corruption, and undemocratic practices. Second, unions favor governmental policies aimed at increasing employment, for the labor force as a whole and for special groups of organized workers. But this does *not* include striving for the goal of maximum long-run growth for the economy, since growth implies greater output per worker, the equivalent of fewer workers to produce a given amount. Unions, of course, favor rapid economic growth in the sense of rising standards of living, but when it comes to specific cases of replacing workers with new efficient machinery, their enthusiasm diminishes. The third area of short-run goals is maintenance of stable demand and prices for final goods, and thus stable wages and employment, in industries where their influence is effective. Included here are the promotion of building codes and licensing laws and lobbying before public service commissions for higher prices for public utilities whose workers are organized. Finally, unions seek liberalization of benefits under workmen's compensation, unemployment insurance, old age, survivors, and disability insurance laws, and higher minimum wages.

There are some reasons to expect that unions in the future may become more active politically even though making no major changes in their goals. The stakes in increased influence over public decisions are becoming greater for many reasons, among them increased government participation in collective bargaining and in providing economic security. Furthermore, the environment is somewhat less hostile to union political action, at least when compared with thirty years ago. One of the important motivations of the AFL-CIO merger was the hope of becoming more effective in the public arena. On the other hand, so long as the economic desires of American workers are satisfied through short-run economic tactics, there may be little direct pressure on union leaders to extend significantly their political activity.

SUMMARY

Although unions have succeeded in organizing only a third of the organizable labor force, they constitute a powerful institution, because 1) they have almost completely organized several of the basic industries, and 2) they are the only recognized voice of labor, both for the organized and the unorganized workers. No major change can occur in the American economic system without being at least partially influenced by unions. Nevertheless, their power is much less than it otherwise would be because there are large groups of unorganized workers. They have made only modest penetration into a number of important geographical areas. Many occupations and industries, including some of those which are growing most rapidly, are almost untouched by unionization.

In the meantime unions will probably continue to grow. But whether this growth will be faster than the growth of the labor force is uncertain. Since recent economic expansion has been greater in the unorganized industries and occupations, the outlook is not favorable. One of the important factors shaping this growth is the nature of union leadership. Workers do not automatically join unions in this country, therefore expansion of membership depends to a large extent on dynamic leadership. The officials have risen from the membership and tend to reflect the attitudes and desires of their constituents. In recent years, union leadership has assumed some of the characteristics of a professional occupation. Professionalization, along with incomes well above those of the best-paid rank and file members, has caused a gap to develop between the top leaders and the membership.

The political outlook of unions and their leaders is rather narrowly confined. The acceptance of the American economic system as it is and the emphasis on immediate short-term goals prevent the development of a political program radically different from that of many other interest groups.

DISCUSSION QUESTIONS

1. Union leaders are the "strategic actors" in our economy. What does this statement mean? To what extent do you agree?

2. How do you explain the fact that unions have organized only 25 per cent of the labor force and yet are able to exert such a great influence over our economy?

3. How do you explain the greater degree of union organization in the North as compared with the South?

4. Using your knowledge of which industries and occupational groups are heavily organized, explain why workers join unions.

5. Using the case study of foremen, explain why workers join unions.

6. "American unions will probably not make any significant increases in membership in the next five years." To what extent do you agree with this statement?

7. The growth of unions is largely determined by economic and social conditions and has little to do with the quality of union leadership. Discuss, indicating to what extent you think this is a correct statement.

8. What characteristics are generally common to American union leaders?

9. Union leadership is becoming a professionalized occupation. What does this mean? What are some of the probable consequences?

10. "Current labor leaders show a woeful lack of imagination in adjusting union traditions to present economic and social conditions." Write an essay in support of or in opposition to this proposition.

11. Under what economic and political conditions would you expect American unions to develop a consistent and unique long-range political program, if at all?

12. "With seventeen million members, unions are our most powerful political pressure group." Comment.

BIBLIOGRAPHY

Barbash, Jack. *The Practice of Unionism.* New York: Harper & Brothers, 1956.
——— (editor). *Unions and Union Leadership.* New York: Harper & Brothers, 1959.
Ginzberg, Eli. *The Labor Leader.* New York: The Macmillan Company, 1948.
Madison, Charles A. *American Labor Leaders.* New York: Harper & Brothers, 1950.
Mills, C. Wright. *The New Men of Power.* New York: Harcourt, Brace and Company, 1948.
Shister, Joseph. "The Logic of Union Growth," *The Journal of Political Economy,* Vol. LXI (October, 1953), pp. 413–33.

Slichter, Sumner. *The Challenge of Industrial Relations.* Ithaca: Cornell University Press, 1947.

Stigler, George J. *Trends in Employment in the Service Industries.* Princeton: Princeton University Press, 1956.

"Union Growth." Part VII, *Proceedings of the Seventh Annual Meeting of Industrial Relations Research Association,* December, 1954, pp. 201–46.

Witte, Edwin E. "Role of the Unions in Contemporary Society," *Industrial and Labor Relations Review,* Vol. IV (October, 1950), pp. 3–14.

6

THE STRUCTURE AND
GOVERNMENT OF UNIONS

In joining a union, a worker, at one and the same time, may become a member of a local and an international, and indirectly a member of a city central, a state organization, a national federation, and one or more departments. Why all these different appendages to the union organization? How are they run? What are their functions? How do they relate to each other? How do they make and administer union policies?

The structure of the American labor movement is the result of a pragmatic adjustment to the American environment. While adapting its goals and tactics to the challenges it has encountered, it has also devised a governmental system which is especially designed for living in a hostile community. Like all vital institutions, it is continually changing, continually experimenting with new power arrangements, although there is always resistance from those who lose power or status. The vicissitudes of the economic, political, and social framework within which the unions operate compel them to make occasional readjustments in their formal structure and frequent readjustments in the functions and powers of the various segments of the structure. The split between the AFL and CIO in 1935 and the merger in 1955 are outstanding examples.

THE FEDERATION

The structure of the AFL-CIO represents an amalgamation of the structural forms of the two predecessor federations, which were basically quite similar. The schematic arrangement of the constituent elements of

105

the AFL-CIO is shown in Figure 6-A. The arrows indicate the sources of authority; e.g., the members of the locals elect the officers of the internationals, and the officers of the internationals control the officers and policies of the departments. The most crucial power relationships are those between the local, the international, and the Federation—the heavy line up the middle of the figure. These statements, like the chart itself, are oversimplifications and are enlarged upon in the following sections of this chapter.

FIGURE 6-A

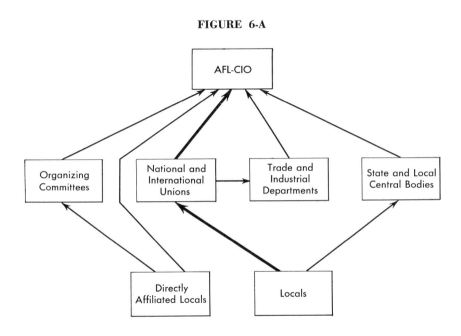

The placing of the Federation at the top of the structure (Figure 6-A) does not imply that it dominates or rules the other segments; rather, the AFL-CIO depends on the affiliated unions for its existence. It is a federation in the full sense of the word, with limited powers delegated to it by the autonomous internationals. The internationals are self-governing bodies, financed independently of the Federation, and free to disaffiliate—to leave the Federation—at their own discretion. If an international does disaffiliate, it loses the aid and services of the Federation, but many of them are sufficiently powerful to operate effectively as independent organizations. In short, the powers of the AFL-CIO are no greater than those the internationals are willing to grant it.

Functions of the Federation

One of the primary functions of the AFL-CIO is to promote the organization of the unorganized workers. This is accomplished through the Department of Organization (a Staff Department, to be distinguished from the Trade and Industrial Departments discussed in a later section of this chapter), created at the merger convention of the AFL-CIO. The Department of Organization operates at two different levels. First, it works in cooperation with the international unions—who have primary responsibility for bringing new members into the fold—providing them with funds and organizers. It may coordinate the efforts of two or more internationals in a joint campaign, e.g., in the South. The second level of organizing activity of the AFL-CIO is conducted through directly affiliated locals, which are attached directly to the AFL-CIO rather than to any international. When enough directly affiliated locals fall into a particular jurisdiction, but clearly outside of the jurisdiction of any existing international, they are organized into a fledgling international known as an organizing committee. As soon as they are able to stand on their own feet, an international charter is issued to them. The AFL-CIO may also acquire new members by persuading a non-affiliated international to join the Federation.

The second important function of the AFL-CIO is the settlement of jurisdictional boundaries between the internationals. Prior to the merger, both the AFL and the CIO performed this function, issuing charters to their affiliated internationals which described each international's jurisdiction. Partly as a consequence of changing technology, these jurisdictional areas inevitably overlapped. After 1900 the AFL was continually plagued by jurisdictional disputes between its internationals; therefore, adjudicating such disputes has been a historic function of the AFL. The jurisdictional battles between the CIO and AFL were discussed in Chapter 4 in relation to the No-Raiding Pact; the constitution now provides machinery which replaces the pact. In spite of this machinery, peace-making efforts in jurisdictional disputes continue to be a major function of the AFL-CIO.

Two other major functions of the AFL-CIO are the coordination of labor's political activities and the policing of all parts of the union structure to eliminate communism and corruption. Allied with these two functions, particularly with the former, is that of being public spokesman for unions, and, in fact, for all workers. It is up to the Federation to create, as far as possible, a climate of public opinion favorable to union growth.

Beyond these functions the AFL-CIO offers a multitude of services to the internationals and organized labor in general. An indication of the nature of these services is seen from a listing of some of the committees established by the constitution: civil rights, community services, housing, safety and occupational health, social security, and research. However, there is one major function which the AFL-CIO does not perform. It does not engage directly in bargaining; that is the domain of the locals and internationals.

State and Local Central Bodies

The state organizations engage in political and educational activities at a state level similar to those of the AFL-CIO at the national level. In a sense they are the state-wide representatives of the AFL-CIO; however, they are not directly dominated by the Federation. Their personnel indicates the type of work they do: among their employees are thirty-nine education directors, twenty-four research directors, and sixty-three legislative representatives.[1] Not all eligible unions belong to the state organizations. They are not required to belong in order to be affiliated with the national Federation. Some refuse to join the state organizations for personal and political reasons; for example, they may disapprove of the extent of support given to certain legislative proposals, or industrial unions may refuse to take part in activities controlled by craft union officers and vice versa.

Similarly to the state organizations, the city and county organizations engage in political and educational activities on a local basis. Again unions are not required to belong to the city centrals and again the same reasons appear for some unions deciding not to join.

In almost all cases these state and local organizations are not very powerful. Within any given community, union influence is generally wielded by the locals of two or three internationals, e.g., automobile workers and teamsters in Detroit, steel workers in Pittsburgh. In many local areas, the unions in the building trades act as an independent power bloc.

Even though the state and local bodies do not exercise a great deal of influence, in some circumstances a union or its leadership may suffer loss of face if it is excluded. Thus, when expelled by the AFL-CIO

[1] *Directory of National and International Labor Unions in the United States,* 1957, Bureau of Labor Statistics Bulletin No. 1222, p. 1.

in 1957, the teamsters were forced to cut their ties with all state and local bodies because an unaffiliated union cannot belong. Since Detroit is the base of operations of both James Hoffa and Walter Reuther, bitter rivals for many years, the latter could express his opinions and make his political pronouncements through the Detroit union council, while the former was denied the use of this sounding board.

Trade and Industrial Departments

The AFL had five departments, all of which were retained in the new Federation. Four of these grew out of the problem of overlapping jurisdictions. For example, as the technology of construction changed, the question of just which union should have control of particular jobs became a matter of dispute. When metal doors replaced wooden doors, the carpenters claimed to have continuing jurisdiction over putting up doors, but the metal workers also claimed the jurisdiction. In its efforts to settle jurisdictional disputes, the AFL established a building and construction department, a metal trades department, a railway employees department, and a maritime trades department. As well as attempting to settle jurisdictional disputes between the members, the departments encourage joint bargaining among their members.

The AFL also had a union label department. The function of this department was to promote wider use of the union label and encourage purchases of goods so marked.

As a consequence of the merger, a sixth department was created to give special representation to the former CIO unions. This department, the Industrial Union Department, also includes a portion of the members of former AFL unions, such as the carpenters' and machinists' unions, part of whose membership is organized on an industrial basis. More than 2,500,000 members joined with the 4,500,000 from the CIO, giving the Industrial Union Department nearly half of the membership of the Federation.

The chief functions of the youngest Department are maintaining the solidarity of the industrial unions and promoting organization of new members on an industrial basis. It provides a forum where the former CIO leaders are dominant and can pass resolutions and take political positions free from restraints imposed by craft unions. Furthermore, the Department constitutes an already established structure in case the industrial unions should some day feel they must leave the AFL-CIO. This possibility, of course, enhances their bargaining power within the Federation.

The Industrial Union Department was born with a silver spoon in its mouth, inheriting approximately one million dollars from the old CIO treasury. Its regular income, two cents per capita per month, is forwarded to it by the member internationals, the former AFL unions paying only for that fraction of their members who are included in the Department. The other departments also collect monthly dues of one or two cents per capita. Hence, the departments are financed independently of the Federation, but completely dependent on the internationals.

Government of the Federation

The supreme governing body of the AFL-CIO is the biennial convention. Each national or international union and each organizing committee is entitled to send delegates in accordance with the size of its membership.[2] Directly affiliated locals, departments, and state and local central bodies are entitled to one delegate each. Thus, the internationals, particularly the large ones, exercise the dominant authority in the decision-making of the AFL-CIO convention.

Between conventions the government of the AFL-CIO rests with the Executive Council which is to meet at least three times a year. It consists of the president, secretary-treasurer, and twenty-seven vice presidents, all of whom are elected at the biennial convention. The Executive Council is an extremely powerful body, with authority to put into effect the decisions of the conventions and to enforce the provisions of the AFL-CIO constitution. One source of its power stems from its size. Compared with the large amorphous group of delegates at the biennial conventions, it is better able to grapple with problems, work out compromises, and reach decisions.

The Executive Council may investigate any affiliate accused of infiltration by communism, fascism, or corruption, and, on a two-thirds vote, suspend such an affiliate from the Federation. Such action may be appealed to the convention. The membership of the Executive Council is made up largely of top officers from the large internationals, another avenue through which the large internationals dominate the Federation.

The Executive Council creates its own "inside ruling group" by electing an Executive Committee consisting of six of its members and the president

[2] National and international unions are entitled to send delegates on the following scale: one for less than 4,000 members, two for over 4,000 members, three for over 8,000 members, four for over 12,000 members, five for over 25,000 members, six for over 50,000 members, seven for over 75,000 members, eight for over 125,000 members, nine for over 175,000 members, and one additional delegate for each additional 75,000 members.

and secretary-treasurer of the Federation. This Executive Committee, which meets at least every two months, assists the Federation's officers in carrying out their duties. As well as performing the usual duties of a president and secretary-treasurer, they must act as the country's chief spokesmen for labor and must take the initial steps in almost all of the Federation's activities, e.g., settling a jurisdictional dispute, appointing convention committees, and hammering out the AFL-CIO's policy in legislative matters.

Since the AFL-CIO conventions are biennial, some mechanism had to be created to reflect the views of the total membership during the two-year interval. Hence, the General Board was established consisting of the Executive Council and the president of each affiliated international. It is to meet at least once a year and to decide all policy matters referred to it by the executive officers or the Executive Council. Questions coming before the General Board are decided by roll-call vote with the president of each international having votes equal to the membership of his union.

The ruling bodies of the AFL-CIO are the biennial convention, the Executive Council, the Executive Committee, and the General Board. However, it is the internationals and their presidents who are the major sources of power. True, the executive officers of the Federation have extensive authority, certainly far beyond that exercised by the executive officers of the old AFL. Nevertheless, in effectuating any major decision, the president and secretary-treasurer need the support of the majority of the presidents of the large internationals.

THE INTERNATIONALS

There are about 200 national and international unions, generally referred to as internationals. Many of them have members in Canada, hence the title: international. These vary in size from a few hundred to well over a million members. Three are in the million member class, the automobile workers', teamsters', and steel workers' unions. These three plus the machinists' and the carpenters' unions accounted for one-third of the AFL-CIO membership before the teamsters were expelled. The AFL-CIO originally included 138 internationals; 108 were formerly affiliated with the AFL and 30 with the CIO. The remaining internationals were independents, that is, not affiliated with the AFL-CIO. Among the independents were the railroad brotherhoods, with more than 400,000 members, and the United Mine Workers with approximately 300,000 members. The independent internationals had about 1.8 million members,[3] and, including the teamsters, the total now comes to about 3.2 millions, just under one-fifth of all union members.

Functions of Internationals

The main functions of the internationals are to organize and charter new locals and to provide them with services. These services, which amount to control of the locals in many instances, include aid in bargaining and handling grievances, providing strike benefits, help in organizing new members, and advice on all matters ranging from an educational program or political activity to aiding members in relation to unemployment compensation, workmen's compensation, etc.

This general description of the functions of the internationals obscures many variations in the relationship between the parent body and its locals. In some cases the locals are the dominant power. This tends to be the case in industries where the competition between the employers is largely within a local market, as in construction. But where competition is on a nation-wide basis, the internationals usually dominate the locals. In the steel industry, for example, the international does the bargaining and signs the basic contract.

In order to carry out their functions, many internationals have organized district councils, primarily administrative units, supervising the relationship between the international and several locals in a given geographical area. Practically all unions have employees known as international representatives, who are on-the-spot personal representatives of the top officers of the international. An international representative is generally an experienced union man serving in his capacity on a full-time paid basis. He may have been a successful organizer in the early stages of his union's growth, or he may have distinguished himself as the president of a local. In almost all cases he must be loyal to the top officers of the union, or he will be replaced. Even if he is elected by the membership, support of the international officers is usually necessary if he is to retain his position. The international representative exerts a powerful influence in the area under his supervision, particularly over all aspects of collective bargaining.

Some internationals conduct a substantial amount of research into the economics of their industries, employing a staff of professional

---

[3] *Directory, op. cit.*, pp. 3–4, 7. Four of the traditionally independent railway unions have joined the AFL-CIO: the Brotherhood of Locomotive Firemen and Enginemen (1956), the American Train Dispatchers' Association (1957), the American Railway Supervisors' Association (1957), and the Brotherhood of Railroad Trainmen (1957).

economists, statisticians, and other trained specialists. This includes studying market trends, profits, technological changes, and anything else which might have a bearing on the jobs of the members and the bargaining position of the union. The internationals also engage in political activity, apart from the Federation. This often takes the form of promoting their special self-interest, e.g., seeking a tariff to protect their particular industry, or special laws which might affect the number of jobs available in the industry. Most internationals publish a regular newspaper or periodical.

Government of Internationals

Each international has its own history, its own structure, and its own internal power relationships. Although it is impossible to generalize for all internationals, Figure 6-B is illustrative of the relationship between the internationals and the membership.

FIGURE 6-B

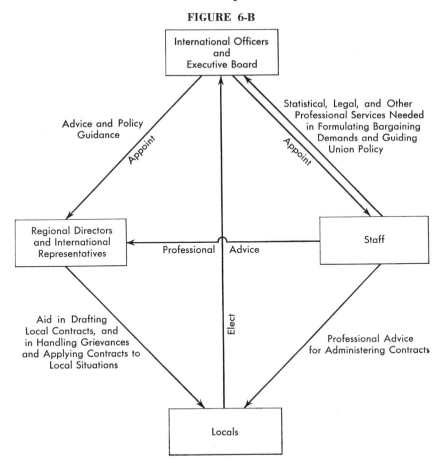

The formal government of the internationals has a number of parallels with that of the Federation. The international's chief source of authority is the convention; between convention meetings, it is the executive boards, and between meetings of the boards, the president and other officers. Conventions are held at least every two years by 114 of the internationals, and at least every four years by another 48. In general, the more frequent the convention, the more control the membership has over the actions of the officers.

In the actual operation of the governmental structures, there are real differences between the Federation and the internationals. The officers of the latter have much more power over their constituent bodies. They need not tolerate as much dissension among their junior officers, having greater freedom to dismiss them or cause them to lose the next time they stand for re-election. Moreover, they can remove the officers of a local and directly take over its administration; the Federation has no parallel power over the internationals.

THE LOCALS

The worker's first—and for the large majority of workers, the only—point of contact with unionism is through a local. In fact, to be a union member, it is necessary to belong to a local. In industrial unions, locals are usually organized on a plant basis, and in craft unions on a territorial basis, e.g., all bricklayers within a city. In 1957 there were more than 77,000 locals, with eighteen of the internationals claiming more than 1,000 each. In all, over 50 per cent of them were in 10 per cent of the internationals.

Functions of the Locals

The functions performed by the locals vary considerably from one international to another, although three functions are performed by almost all locals. First, they represent their members in grievances against management. That is, if a worker believes he has been treated unfairly, the officials of the local defend the worker in securing a fair settlement of the complaint. The second function is to provide the opportunity for union members to participate in union affairs. It is through the local—at meetings, elections, or informal conversation with the local's officers—that the individual member expresses his opinion and exerts his influence on the union.

The third function performed by almost all locals is that of collecting union dues and fees. Generally, the local keeps a portion for its own activities and forwards the per capita amounts to other union organizations, i.e., city centrals, state organizations, and internationals. In 1955 the average member paid dues of slightly more than $25 per year to his union, with some unions as low as a dollar per month and the airline pilots charging $25 per month to those whose annual income was over $19,000. The typical union member pays monthly dues equal to less than he earns in two hours of work. Unions in the United States and Canada collect over $500,000,000 annually in dues and fees, about half of which is retained by the locals.[4]

Beyond these three functions the local may formulate bargaining demands and conduct the bargaining sessions with the employer. The local may initiate and conduct strikes, including the supervision of picket lines and the distribution of strike benefits. The extent to which these functions are performed by the local depends partly on the nature of competition in the industry, as described in the discussion of the functions of the internationals. A similar distinction can be made for the division between the internationals and the locals of authority over organizing unorganized workers. Those locals which exercise control over the bargaining activities usually have charge of organizing the workers in their jurisdiction.

The nature of the organization of the local is likely to reflect that of its international, but there are many important exceptions. Locals may be organized on a craft or industrial basis or a mixture of both. For example, Local No. 600, of the United Automobile Workers, the local for the Ford plant at River Rouge, Michigan, is an industrial local in the sense that it covers all of the many different skilled and semi-skilled jobs within the plant. The craft locals are usually organized by geographical areas, as in the case of all carpenters who work on residential construction within a city or a metropolitan area. Within an international, there may be both craft and industrial locals, with carpenters, for instance, having industrial locals in woodworking factories as well as their craft locals.

Government of the Locals

For the locals the basic policy-making unit is the local meeting, usually held once each month. Most of the elected officials of the local serve on a part-time basis while continuing on their regular jobs. The primary exception is the business agent, a full-time paid official, usually

[4] National Industrial Conference Board, *Handbook of Union Government Structure and Procedures*, 1955; and Philip Taft, *The Structure and Government of Labor Unions* (Cambridge: Harvard University Press, 1954), pp. 65–96.

elected, but sometimes appointed by the president of the international or by the president of the local. Whether a local will have a business agent depends to a large extent on the types of functions performed by the locals. Business agents are most typically found in those locals which have members in several different firms, perhaps twenty or more different employers, and where jobs are of comparatively short duration. In the latter case the business agent serves as a mobile employment office. He is the connecting link between employers needing workers and members looking for jobs. Hence, the business agent is in a position to discipline employers who fail to abide by all the union working rules. He may do this by refusing to send any workers to the recalcitrant employer, or by sending only second-rate workers. Likewise, he may discipline those union members who have worked on nonunion jobs, or in other ways have violated union rules. These workers may have long waiting periods between jobs, or may be sent only to the less desirable jobs.

The business agent also supervises the local's bargaining for new contracts. Once the contracts are signed, he polices them by traveling about from employer to employer to check on whether union working conditions are being observed and to listen to and attempt to settle the grievances of the workers. He may—without further ado—call the workers out on strike if he thinks such action is necessary. The business agent, then, is an extremely powerful union officer. Unfortunately, some business agents have abused this power, accepting bribes and retaining their position by discriminating in jobs offered to opposition groups.

What is said about business agents in the above paragraphs does not apply to the locals of industrial unions, which generally do not have such officers. Where the local's members are all employed by one employer and where the jobs are more or less permanent, the local has little or no need for a business agent. A special employment office is not required, and there is only one contract and one employer to police. A business agent may be elected for such a local, but if so, his power will be far less extensive than that of the business agents, say in the construction industry.

Regardless of whether the local has a business agent, its chief administrative unit is the executive committee, consisting of the officers of the local and several elected members. It is their duty to bring policy recommendations before the membership meeting of the local and to put into effect the resolutions adopted. Another important committee of the local—in those cases where the local has some control over the bargaining—is the bargaining committee which formulates the contract demands. The business agent must work with and be responsive to the wishes of the executive committee and the bargaining committee. In many cases he serves as chairman of their meetings. Where the international controls the bargaining, the local generally elects delegates to a convention which drafts the bargaining demands.

The shop steward is the low man on the totem pole as far as union officialdom is concerned. He is usually an elected official with the primary function of being first listener to the grievances of the members: the link between the members and the officers. In any large unionized plant there are a number of stewards, each responsible for ten or twenty or more workers in a department. The stewards may exercise a substantial amount of authority in the settlement of grievances, depending on the status of union-management relations in the plant. Or they may be caught in the middle of a feud between the workers and the foremen. Customarily, there is a stewards' committee with a chief steward presiding. Since the ordinary worker is most concerned over what the union can do about his day-to-day job problems, the stewards are the union officers in whom they are most interested. In many craft unions, however, there is no steward, or else it is a position possessing very little power, with the steward's functions being performed by the business agent.

CHANGING LOCATION OF POWER

The internationals constitute the primary power center in the American labor movement. Although there are many important qualifications, it is the internationals which exercise the more decisive controls in each of the two sets of authority relationships: 1) between the Federation and the internationals and 2) between the internationals and their locals. But in a dynamic union movement, this need not remain the case. Is there any tendency for power to move away from the internationals toward the locals or the Federation? It appears that power is moving upward within both of the authority relationships; but there are persistent and strong barriers to this upward movement.

Internationals Versus Locals

The loss of power by the locals stems from changes in labor legislation and in patterns of collective bargaining. The location of control over collective bargaining is greatly influenced by the nature of competition among the organized firms. As the technology of production

changes in the direction of more automation and greater capital investment per worker, we tend to have fewer firms meeting the country's
requirements in any given line of trade, and the competition between
the remaining firms moves from a local to a regional or national level.
This makes necessary a parallel movement in the control over bargaining,
otherwise collective agreements won by some locals may be undermined
by concessions granted by other locals. The consolidation of the cross-
country trucking industry and the greater centralization of bargaining in
the teamsters' union illustrate the point.

New technology often involves more complicated machinery. The
problems of adjusting wage rates, worker-to-equipment ratios, safety
regulations, and other working rules become the job of a trained
specialist. The international is in a better position to hire the specialist;
it would be a waste of money for each local to hire its own.

The continual additions to our labor laws place a further burden on
the local. The Labor-Management Reporting and Disclosure Act of 1959
and legislation in some states impose regulations on the internal affairs
of unions. Among other things, they are required to file financial reports
and adhere to certain standards in their election procedures. Legal
advice is necessary to assure that these reports and procedures satisfy
all specifications. State and national legislation limits what can be
included in a contract and the tactics unions may use in their dealings
with employers. Again, it is the international and not the locals, with
some exceptions, which can afford to hire a staff of lawyers who will
devote full time to studying the court interpretation of the legislation.

Federation Versus Internationals

Beginning with Franklin Roosevelt's first term as President, the federal
government has been playing a continually more important role in industrial relations. And at least as important as the direct regulation of
collective bargaining are the policies followed by the government with
respect to promoting full employment, stabilizing prices, providing social
security programs, enforcing minimum wage legislation, etc. These
policies set the economic climate and thereby substantially affect what
unions are able to win in dealing with employers. It is only natural,
then, that unions should attempt to expand their influence in government
circles. The Federation is best suited of all the different levels of union
organization to carry on this type of activity in Washington. Its staff,
engaging in continual research and lobbying on matters of interest to
all unions, can do this work more effectively than the internationals.

Compared with their predecessors, the officers of the AFL-CIO are vigorous men, willing to assert the power vested in their office. They are likely, therefore, to accumulate greater power than the leaders of the old AFL. Examples of this are already visible. When Maurice Hutcheson, president of the carpenters' international union, threatened to take his union out of the AFL because Meany would not do as he dictated, Meany's response was simply to say, go ahead. Hutcheson did so, but meekly returned in a few days. Furthermore, Meany exercised more authority than Green ever had in causing the AFL to expel the International Longshoremen's Association for reasons of internal graft and corruption. The influence of the CIO leadership in the merged Federation has not altered this trend; they had always exercised more power over their internationals than had the AFL.

The revelations of graft and corruption, particularly within the teamsters' union, made by Senate investigating committees between 1956 and 1959, created an atmosphere which contributed to increasing the power of the Federation relative to the internationals. The sordid manipulation of finances and the abuse of positions of trust and authority which were brought to light demonstrated, both to the public and to union members, the need for an agency to act as a watchdog over such union affairs. Within the union structure such policing can be done only by the Federation; and if it is not done by the Federation, Congress may adopt severely restrictive legislation, as demonstrated by the Landrum-Griffin Act. Hence, many internationals have encouraged the AFL-CIO to assert more authority in these matters. The Ethical Practices Committee is the arm of the AFL-CIO designed to serve this purpose, and the Federation's prestige and power are enhanced to the extent that it can effectively deal with this problem. The point, then, is that the publicity given to the presence of racketeering in a few unions has brought about an increase in the authority of the Federation over the internationals in order to eradicate the corruption and to improve public relations of all unions.

The quelling of jurisdictional disputes is another area where the authority of the AFL-CIO is expanding. True, in the past both the AFL and the CIO attempted to assert similar authority. However, the new determination of the present leaders of the AFL-CIO—first expressed in the No-Raiding Pact—points in the direction of greater restrictions on the internationals. If jurisdictional disputes are successfully reduced, then the Federation will have prevented internationals from engaging in certain activities which previously had been their prerogative.

A potential source of pressure which may cause power to move from the internationals to the Federation stems from the relationship between wage increases and inflation. If, at some future date, the public is strongly aroused over an inflationary price rise and believes it is caused by abnormally large wage increases, the government may be forced to exercise some sort of control. There is a variety of control mechanisms which could be adopted, but in any case, the Federation would be forced to come more directly into the bargaining arena. No single international could represent all unions, hence representation in the wage-regulating procedures would have to be through the Federation. At the present time this line of reasoning is largely speculation. Nevertheless, other Western nations have taken steps in this direction and our postwar price trends have produced much concern over the wage-price relationship.[5]

Barriers to the Upward Movement of Power

There are, however, certain tendencies which are likely to delay or impede the movement of power from the local to the international and the movement of power from the international to the Federation. Among these impeding factors are, first, the fact that the locals are the immediate point of contact with the members. That is, the members express themselves through the locals and therefore will expect the locals to carry some real authority: ". . . the way in which on-the-job grievances are handled has never ceased to be the central day-to-day concern of the rank and file of the membership. . . . To the extent that local grievances continue to be as important as they are now, the centralization process in matters of consequence to the average union member will not undermine the vital position that the local organization holds in the scheme of union matters." [6]

The pace at which power moves from locals to internationals and from internationals to the Federation is influenced by the historic development of the international. Some internationals grew from the top down, that is, the internationals took the initiative in most of the organizing. In these unions the international generally exerts considerable influence over the locals. In other unions the locals appeared first,

---

[5] The studies of the Joint Economic Committee are outstanding examples of this concern. The relationship between collective bargaining and inflation is fully discussed in Chapters 23 and 24.

[6] Jack Barbash, *Labor Unions in Action* (New York: Harper & Brothers, 1948), p. 58.

with the international binding them together at a later date. Under these circumstances, the locals have retained a considerable amount of their authority. For either type of international, whether organized from the top down or from the bottom up, the traditional power centers are, naturally, reluctant to relinquish their authority.

A further barrier to the upward movement of power is the fact that the internationals always have the option of withdrawing from the Federation. Thus, if an international feels that it is suffering from too much interference in its internal affairs, it may disaffiliate. The internationals are autonomous bodies and can exist independently, as the teamsters have so clearly shown. Since the locals are more closely tied to the international than to the Federation, they would, in almost all cases, go along with their disaffiliating parent body. However, the officers of an international may be less willing to disaffiliate from the merged AFL-CIO than from the old federations. They would be opposed by a more formidable alliance and would not be able to take advantage of the old rivalries.

The balance of power within the union structure, then, is changing at two levels: between the internationals and the Federation and between the locals and the international. Whether the movement of power from the international to the Federation will be rapid or hesitant depends on a complex of economic and environmental factors. If and when the role of the government in union affairs generally, and in collective bargaining in particular, is greatly expanded, more power will gravitate to the Federation. This is not to imply that either the locals or the internationals will eventually become powerless organizational shells. The bargaining and grievance-handling functions which they perform guarantee their continuing importance in union institutionalism. In short, the internationals will continue to be the chief power centers of the American labor movement for years to come.

DEMOCRACY IN UNIONS

Unions have frequently been criticized by friends and foes for permitting undemocratic characteristics to creep into their structure. The criticism reached a high level in 1959 and became one of the many forces culminating in the Labor-Management Reporting and Disclosure Act. Why should the government be interested in the internal affairs of unions? First, because the power of unions over the day-to-day economic lives of the members is so manifest that, in keeping with our traditional philosophies, the use of this power should be responsive to its constituency. Second, leaders should be prevented from manipulating their authority for racketeering purposes. Finally, the public appears to have a pious hope that increased democratic control will mean less labor-management strife. Whether the Act will actually raise the level of union democracy is uncertain. Perhaps no significant change will be made, since it is impossible to "ram democracy down the throats" of unwilling or uninterested recipients. In other words, imposing requirements on maximum length of time between elections and setting rules for the nomination of candidates and voting procedures—as provided in the Landrum-Griffin Act—does not guarantee that union members will exercise their rights; it only gives them the opportunity.

What does democracy in unions mean? A union, be it federation, international, or local, is democratic if all its important decisions represent the wishes of the majority of the members, with the members being reasonably well informed on the issues involved and having ample opportunity to participate in making decisions, and with the minority protected in its right openly to oppose any of the majority's policies. Whether democracy is achieved depends on the methods and procedures which unions adopt. Certain barriers to a complete democracy are the natural outgrowth of their organization and goals. Furthermore, unions have acquired, over the course of their development, certain undemocratic practices.

Barriers to Democracy

In appraising democracy in unions, the following general barriers must be considered: 1) A large portion of the membership has an apathetic attitude toward the union, which is reflected in poor attendance at union meetings and, in general, nonparticipation in union activity. 2) A system of patronage has developed, making it possible for the officers in power to extend their control over the membership and to increase the likelihood of maintaining themselves in office. 3) The union, as a militant organization, must grant to the leaders considerable authority over the day-to-day activities of the unions. This is not a complete list of the reasons for imperfections in the democracy in unions. Such a list would be impossibly long, not only for unions, but also for churches, political parties, or any other similar organizations. However, these are the ones which grow out of the unique characteristics of American unions.

Membership Apathy

Although our knowledge of the operation of union locals is all too scanty, it is well known that most locals suffer from poor attendance at their meetings. A study of twenty locals, although a small sample, indicated some of the factors which contribute to membership apathy. The meetings were often very long and dull as a result of an effort to make them fully democratic and to give everybody an opportunity to say his piece. Frequently they became heavily involved in parliamentary procedure, and often the chairman of the meeting was poorly trained for dealing with these kinds of problems. It was generally necessary to hold the meetings at night after the dinner hour, hence competing with the members' family responsibilities and favorite television programs. And anyway, any important problem could be "taken care of with the steward, tomorrow." The pattern of attendance of a newly organized local varied with the importance of the meeting, as shown in Table 6-A.[7]

TABLE 6-A

Month	Attendance	Percent of membership	Significant business
July	350	20	Election of temporary officers
August	320	18	Discussion of contract demands and proposed seniority rules
Sept.	220	12	Nominations of permanent officers; some contract questions discussed
	150	8	Rejection of proposal to allow voting at more than one place; report on negotiations progress
Oct.	150	8	Report on negotiations progress; strike vote taken
Nov.	325	18	Report on completed contract
Dec.	750	42	Ratification of contract
	75	4	Selection of constitution committee
Jan.	90	5	Selection of job evaluation chairman
Feb.	80	4	Blue Cross discussion; dispute with company over contract discussed
March	85	5	Complaints about officers
April	110	6	Discussion of president's salary
May	65	4	First reading of permanent constitution
June	110	6	Adoption of constitution

How important are the local meetings as decision-making bodies? A sharp variation was found between the different locals studied.

[7] George Strauss and Leonard R. Sayles, "The Local Union Meeting," *Industrial and Labor Relations Review*, Vol. VI (January, 1953), pp. 206–10. Reproduced by permission of *Industrial and Labor Relations Review*.

In a majority, there was very little—if one defines decision-making as voting "yes" or "no." Instead of using a ballot, the members had learned to influence union policy by expressing their opinions at meetings and even through silence, just by attending and letting their "weight" be felt. Much of the discussion which revolves around officers' reports and individual grievances is irrelevant in the strict parliamentary sense. Still, the officers take these complaints into account after the meetings are over.[8]

Who are the people who actually participate in union affairs? A distinction between those who participate and those who do not seems to be unrelated to how dissatisfied the union members happen to be with their jobs. The previously cited writers found four factors which seemed to be important in affecting union participation: "1) the homogeneity of the group—its ability to unite to achieve its objectives; 2) its status or prestige in the plant community; 3) the technological importance of its job to the company; 4) the nature of the job." They found that in many locals one or two departments would dominate the local. Sometimes this depended upon the nationality factor (homogeneity of the group). Sometimes it was a result of the wage differential that was paid (status in the plant community). Sometimes it was the result of the job being particularly crucial to the employer (technological importance of the job). Some jobs gave workers free time to discuss union affairs with fellow workers, whereas other jobs left the worker too exhausted to consider active union participation (nature of the job).[9]

What is the relationship between the apathy of union members and democracy in unions? As a result of poor attendance at union meetings, decisions regarding bargaining goals, use of union funds, positions taken on political issues, and the host of other issues which the union must decide are left in the hands of an active minority. If an official with a small corps of followers usurps control of a local, he may be able to promote his political ambitions, or to line his own pockets through shady financial deals. So long as he does not arouse the inactive majority, he may continue these practices indefinitely.

Union Patronage

Once in power a union official may become more deeply entrenched through the use of patronage, which—very similarly to patronage in any other political body—acts as a barrier to democracy. The president of an international generally has the authority to select international repre-

[8] *Ibid.*, p. 217. Quoted by permission of *Industrial and Labor Relations Review*.
[9] George Strauss and Leonard R. Sayles, "Patterns of Participation in Local Unions," *Industrial and Labor Relations Review*, Vol. VI (October, 1952), pp. 35–43.

sentatives and a research and office staff. In filling these positions he will naturally give preference to those people who are loyal to him and to those people who will do a good job of enhancing his position as president. The patronage extends to control over the union newspapers and other sources of information relevant to the operation of the union. Through this control, the officers are able to dispense information about the successes which they have achieved and play down any possible shortcomings.

The officials of a local are also in a position to grant patronage. In terms of passing out political plums, they have less opportunity than the president of an international. However, with their control over grievances, they may distribute—or withhold—economic favors of considerable value, which may be judiciously administered so as to keep the officials in office. This is particularly true of business agents who control access to the job market.

A Militant Organization

Since a union must act as a fighting unit, occasionally being called out on strike and always ready to act with solidarity, it must adopt characteristics similar to those of any other fighting organization. This means that a considerable amount of authority must be granted to the leaders of the union. They must be able to make decisions on very short notice and they must have a fairly wide discretion in carrying out the functions of their office. For example, it would not be feasible to have the members decide by open meeting just how the union should bargain on each point in a contract and just what reaction should be manifested on each concession from management. This does not mean that the rank and file are ignored in drawing up bargaining demands; rather, in the heat of battle, when the final settlement is being reached, the horse-trading with management must be done by a small group with much secrecy surrounding the process. This is especially so for industrial unions where the bargaining is done by national officers far removed from the local members. Too much democracy would force the leader to expose his hand—as serious a mistake in collective bargaining as in poker.

It follows from this that the union leader must shrewdly judge management's resistance power and his members' bargaining preferences. A person with the necessary experience and know-how to be successful on both of these scores becomes exceedingly valuable to the union. For the union to capitalize best on this experience, it must grant its leader a wide range of power and a long tenure in office. This statement applies to the president of the international, in those unions where the international controls the bargaining policies and procedures, and it applies to the business agent where he exercises such authority.

A word of interpretation should be entered here. Just because a union leader holds office for many years does not mean that he has seized undemocratic authority. In most unions it is merely a reflection of the fact that he can best carry out the wishes of the members, as these wishes are democratically expressed. By holding office a number of years, he gains a real advantage over any other candidate for his position: a monopoly in the experience of dealing with employers.

Undemocratic Practices of Unions

We now consider some of the important areas in which undemocratic practices by unions are liable to occur: admission policies of the unions, procedure for disciplining members, and deprivation of self-government by international officers. Although the first two of these may represent the will of the majority, they may involve undemocratic deprivation of the rights of minorities.

Some unions enforce admission policies which exclude certain people from the membership. For example, certain unions restrict their membership on the basis of skin color. Others discriminate by establishing segregated locals, that is, two locals covering the same jurisdiction, each for a different race.[10] As well as specific admission policies of a discriminatory nature written into the union constitutions, there is an incalculable amount of subtle discrimination based upon nationality, religion, color, and sex. Such discrimination may be exhibited through the vigor with which grievances are processed. However, arbitrary discrimination is no more prevalent in unions than in many other American institutions, and a great many unions and union officials have acted as community leaders in fighting against discrimination.

Disciplinary procedure is the second area in which some unions have engaged in particularly undemocratic practices. As fighting organizations, unions need to have controls over their membership in order to proscribe anti-union actions. Some of the offenses which unions are likely to prohibit are: nonpayment of dues, strike-breaking, wildcat strikes, promoting dual unionism, supporting or joining subversive groups, and conduct unbecoming a union member. The last-named

---

[10] The AFL-CIO is pledged to eliminate racial discrimination from its affiliates. It has one vice-president who is a Negro. Lack of progress was one of the major sources of contention at the 1959 convention.

offense is, of course, all-inclusive, but it is aimed primarily at those who bring public disrespect to the name of the union through immoral or criminal behavior. Penalties for any of these offenses are usually fines, loss of right to hold union office or to attend union meetings, suspension from membership or outright expulsion.

The problem of democracy here centers around the procedures used to discipline the wayward union members. Procedures are democratic if the accused is informed of the charges against him, is given a fair hearing with ample opportunity to present his side of the case, is judged impartially under the union's constitution, and is penalized in proportion to his crime. However, these procedures sometimes suffer from the shortcoming that the accusers, the prosecutors, and the judges are all from the same group. Thus, if a union member is accused of promoting dual unionism he will be tried, judged, and sentenced by those whose self-interest he is supposedly threatening. Nevertheless, in the large majority of cases, the procedures followed in trying union members are fair and the punishment is not severe.[11]

To guard against this weakness in democratic practices, it has been suggested, by the American Civil Liberties Union and others, that a judicial procedure supervised by some outside party should be introduced into the disciplinary procedure. This would bring impartiality to the decision on whether an individual should be deprived of his union membership. Some unions have taken this step. The UAW has established a board consisting of eminent professional men with much experience in labor affairs who act as a court of appeals for union members who believe they were not tried fairly or judged impartially.

Title I, Bill of Rights of Members of Labor Organizations, of the Labor-Management Reporting and Disclosure Act of 1959 included safeguards against unwarranted disciplinary actions by requiring that the accused member be "(A) served with written specific charges; (B) given a reasonable time to prepare his defense; (C) afforded a full and fair hearing." If, in the opinion of the member, this procedure has not resulted in justice, he may take his case to court. Prior to the legislation, many union constitutions prohibited members from going to court or required them first to go through a time-consuming process of appealing to their local, international executive committee, and finally the international's convention. Under the 1959 law, a four-month limit is imposed; at the end of that time, even if the internal appeals

[11] Clyde Summers, "Disciplinary Powers of Unions," *Industrial and Labor Relations Review*, Vol. III (July, 1950), pp. 483–513; "Disciplinary Procedures of Unions," *Industrial and Labor Relations Review*, Vol. IV (October, 1950), pp. 15–32.

have not been completed, the union cannot prevent a member from going to court to stop the disciplinary action.

The third undemocratic practice grows out of the power of the international to discipline union locals and their officers for violating the constitution of the international. In some cases the internationals may remove the local officers for such offenses as misappropriating union funds, conducting strikes in violation of the bargaining agreement, or signing contracts which do not come up to the international's standards. Under such circumstances, the international appoints an administrator, often an international representative, who temporarily operates the local. Placing the union on a trusteeship basis becomes an undemocratic practice when the officers of the international abuse their power. Since they are the ones who interpret the constitution and decide when a local has violated it, they have a wide latitude for interference in local union affairs. Furthermore, administrators appointed by the international have been kept in power indefinitely. Thus, trusteeships become a technique through which the president of the international can dominate locals which rebel against his authority. It is a potent kind of patronage which goes along with his office. For example, this technique was used by both Dave Beck and Jimmy Hoffa to maintain their control over the teamsters' union.

The Landrum-Griffin Act allows an international to take control of a local only for legitimate purposes, e.g., to prevent corruption or restore democracy. The international must file a report with the Secretary of Labor specifying why the trusteeship is being established, how much control is being exercised, and complete financial details of the local. The parent body is not to raid the local's treasure. A trusteeship can last no longer than eighteen months unless clear and convincing proof is provided showing that its continuance is necessary for a legitimate purpose. The union can be compelled to provide this proof to a federal district court.

Evaluation of Union Democracy

American unions differ considerably one from another. Many of them lean over backwards to encourage participation by the membership in union decision-making. However, in a few internationals, e.g., the teamsters, the bakery workers, the textile workers affiliated with the AFL prior to the merger, and in a few locals of other internationals, the officials have wielded undemocratic authority. One of the most important factors contributing to this situation is the lethargy of the members. So many of them take the attitude that so long as their wages continually rise there is no need for them to be active in the union. And many of the union officials who exercise dictatorial power have been shrewd bargainers, winning good wages and working conditions for their members. When the members are informed of the corruption on the part of their leaders, many of them simply shrug their shoulders and say, "I am better off now than when these leaders came into power."

Basically, however, the structure permits the majority of union members to exercise typical democratic authority, and the Bill of Rights in the Labor-Management Reporting and Disclosure Act gives legal guarantees to voting rights, opportunity to run for office, and freedom of speech. There is little doubt but what the membership can, in almost all unions, control the major decisions, if it is willing to make the sacrifice of actively participating in union affairs. This is less true of internationals (representatve democracies) than of locals (direct democracies), but it is unlikely that an international will be very undemocratic if its locals are operated democratically. In unions, as in any other institution, democracy cannot be taken for granted. Unless the constituents are willing to assert themselves, their democratic rights may be lost.

American unions are highly representative American organizations. Many close analogies can be drawn between unions and local governments, and between unions and many voluntary associations. In the unions, as well as in these other institutions, the dominant political power is exercised by a small active minority. Frequently this minority acts in a fashion that appears to be quite undemocratic. Nevertheless, this minority must be responsive to the wishes of the majority in some vague long-run fashion. If the majority feels that it is not being properly "taken care of" it will rise up and unseat the minority, or else move its allegiance to some other institution.

SUMMARY

The structure of American unions represents an adjustment to the American environment. At the top is the Federation, the AFL-CIO, with the powers granted to it by the internationals. The real power rests with the internationals, which are largely independent and autonomous organizations. At the root of the union structure is the local which supervises the day-to-day activities of all union members.

Trends over the past few decades indicate that the seat of union power is moving upward. The international is exercising more and more control over the local. Also there seem to be trends in the direction of the Federation exercising more and more power over the internationals. Nevertheless, the vital functions performed by the locals and the internationals guarantee that they will continue to occupy a major position within the union hierarchy.

Unions are basically democratic, but not perfect on this score. Important barriers do exist, stemming from the nature of the unions as fighting organizations, the apathy of the membership, and the patronage system. As a consequence certain undemocratic practices tend to persist in the procedures for disciplining members, in the abuse of powers by international officers, and in discrimination on the grounds of race, religion, national origin, and sex.

DISCUSSION QUESTIONS

1. The AFL-CIO is a federation. What does this mean?
2. Why have Trade and Industrial Departments appeared within the structure of the union movement? What are their functions?
3. The AFL-CIO is really controlled by the presidents of the large internationals. To what extent is this an accurate statement?
4. Do the state and local central bodies serve any useful purpose? Explain with references to your own community.
5. Explain the nature of the forces which have caused the upward movement of power within union institutionalism.
6. If the trend toward increasing power held by the officers of the Federation continues, what, if any, powers do you expect will be retained by the internationals and locals? Why?
7. Inherent in unionism are certain barriers to democracy which can never be completely eliminated. Do you agree? Explain.
8. Would you deny unions the right to expel members? Why or why not?
9. What is meant by saying that interested parties have too much control over the appeals from disciplinary rulings?
10. Describe the different ways in which the Labor-Management Reporting and Disclosure Act of 1959 attempted to make unions more democratic.
11. Unions are about as democratic as our city governments. Explain, indicating whether you agree or disagree.

BIBLIOGRAPHY

Barbash, Jack. *Labor Unions in Action.* New York: Harper & Brothers, 1948.
Democracy in Labor Unions. New York: American Civil Liberties Union, 1952.
Directory of National and International Labor Unions in the United States, 1957. Bureau of Labor Statistics Bulletin No. 1222.

Goldberg, Arthur J. *AFL-CIO Labor United*. New York: McGraw-Hill Book Company, 1956.

Handbook of Union Government Structure and Procedures. National Industrial Conference Board, 1955.

Industrial and Labor Relations Review. "The AFL-CIO Merger," IX (April, 1956), entire issue.

Sayles, Leonard R., and Strauss, George. *The Local Union: Its Place in the Industrial Plant*. New York: Harper & Brothers, 1953.

Seidman, Joel. *Union Rights and Union Duties*. New York: Harcourt, Brace and Company, 1943.

Slichter, Sumner. *The Challenge of Industrial Relations*. Ithaca: Cornell University Press, 1947.

Taft, Philip. *The Structure and Government of Labor Unions*. Cambridge: Harvard University Press, 1954.

7 ⟩ THEORY OF UNIONS

Now that we have surveyed the history of unions, can we find some thread that ties the story together, a framework on which the disparate pieces can conveniently be hung? Can we find the general principles—theory or philosophy—by which unions guide their activities? To accomplish this task, we will review five widely recognized theories of the labor movement.

The purpose of a theory of unions is to explain the basic motivating factors behind union organization, growth, and bargaining policies. Unions engage in a wide variety of actions, ranging from conducting strikes to maintaining health clinics. It is easy to become lost in the welter of daily union activity, but a theory of unions should provide us with an intelligible map.

WHAT DOES A THEORY OF UNIONS EXPLAIN?

To serve as a useful analytical framework, a theory of unions must answer several critical questions: 1) What factors cause the original organization of a union? What conditions must be present to bring a union into existence? 2) Why do workers join unions? Why do others remain unorganized? 3) Why do unions have different patterns of growth and development in different industries and different geographical regions? 4) How do unions decide which goals to seek through collective bargaining? When a union knows it cannot win everything at a particular bargaining session, how does it decide whether to fight harder

132

for wage increases or for a better grievance procedure? 5) How do unions decide which techniques to use in accomplishing their goals? What determines whether unions will select economic or political methods? 6) What are the ultimate goals of unions? How will these affect the political, economic, and social structure of the country in the long run? [1]

These questions are not entirely independent of each other. The way in which any one is answered will partially determine the answer to one or more of the others. For example, the decisions which unions make with respect to their ultimate goals will certainly affect the techniques they chose to accomplish these goals. In attempting to devise a unified and consistent set of answers to these questions three theories of the labor movement proposed by Americans and two proposed by Europeans will be analyzed. No one of them deals with all six questions, but selecting the most pertinent parts of each theory provides us with a provocative approach to the problems we are considering.

THREE AMERICAN THEORIES

Justice cannot be done to the individual theories we are about to discuss in the few pages allotted to them. However, to help us to interpret the American labor movement, it is enough to stress the most important principles embodied in each. We will present the theories largely in the manner originally developed by their authors, before comparing and analyzing them.

Two of the three American theories suffer from having been developed prior to the 1930's, Hoxie's which was constructed in 1920 and Perlman's in 1928. Even so, much can be learned by examining them at this time. Tannenbaum's theory was originally expressed in 1921 and substantially revised in 1951.

Robert Hoxie

Hoxie believed that unions grew out of the social-psychological environment of the workers. Workers who are "similarly situated economically and socially, closely associated and not too divergent in temperament and training, will tend to develop a common interpretation of the

---

[1] The first three and the last of these questions are the same as those formulated by John T. Dunlop in his survey of theories of the union movement in "The Development of Labor Organization: A Theoretical Framework," *Insights into Labor Issues,* ed. by Richard A. Lester and Joseph Shister (New York: The Macmillian Co., 1948), pp. 164–65.

social situation and a common solution of the problem of living. This may come about gradually and spontaneously, or it may be the apparently sudden outcome of some crisis in the lives of the men concerned." [2]

Each group of "closely associated" workers develops its own group psychology which grows out of its environmental conditions and the temperamental characteristics of its members. The differences in group psychology cause different types of unions to appear. Hoxie classified these types according to their structure and according to the functional operation. Dividing unions into structural types was not unique with Hoxie, but classifying them by functional types was a major and original contribution to an understanding of the American labor movement.[3]

Functional Types of Unions

Business unionism, "perhaps the most clearly recognizable functional type . . . is essentially trade-conscious, rather than class-conscious." It stresses immediate goals: improvements in wages, hours, and working conditions, giving little attention to political and social action, unless they directly enhance the economic goals. "It is conservative in the sense that it . . . accepts as inevitable, if not as just, the existing capitalistic organization and the wage system. . . ." Its goals are accomplished primarily through collective bargaining, relying heavily on the strike weapon. It is likely to "limit its membership, by means of the apprenticeship system and high initiation fees and dues, to the more skilled workers in the craft or industry. . . ." With the rise of the AFL, this functional type became the most typical of American unions.

Friendly or uplift unionism "aspires chiefly to elevate the moral, intellectual, and social life of the worker. . . ." Although using collective bargaining, these unions prefer to rely on the weapons of political action, mutual insurance programs, and cooperative enterprises. Hoxie cited the Knights of Labor as the closest approach to this type of unionism.

Revolutionary unionism "is extremely radical both in viewpoint and in action. It is distinctly class-conscious rather than trade-conscious." It rejects private ownership of productive resources and the wage system. Its weapons are either political action or direct action in the

---

[2] Hoxie's theory is presented in his book, *Trade Unionism in the United States* (New York: D. Appleton and Co., 1917). The quotation is from the 1920 edition by the same publishers, p. 58. This and other excerpts from Hoxie's book are reprinted by permission of Mr. Allan D. Hoxie.

[3] We discussed structural types when describing the dispute between the Knights and the AFL and between the AFL and the CIO, and in detail in Chapter 6. The following discussion of functional types is from *ibid.*, pp. 45–52.

form of violence and general strikes. Unions become an economic wing to an over-all political program. Hoxie distinguished two types of revolutionary unionism, *socialistic unionism,* which concentrated on political action and looked upon a socialistic state as the end result of union activity, and *quasi anarchistic unionism,* which concentrated on direct action and sabotage and was willing to use violence frequently. An example of the former was the Western Federation of Miners, and of the latter, the Industrial Workers of the World. These two revolutionary unions, after joining forces, found that they had incompatible views on what constituted "heaven on earth" and what weapons to employ to win the millennium.

Predatory unionism has as its distinguishing characteristic the "ruthless pursuit of the thing in hand by whatever means seem most appropriate at the time, regardless of ethical and legal codes or effect upon those outside its own membership." It is generally boss-ridden and corrupt, the membership for the most part being content to follow blindly the instructions of the leaders so long as they receive occasional wage increases. It often joins with employers to squeeze out competition for the mutual benefit of both parties. The International Longshoremen's Association on the east coast and the Brotherhood of Teamsters under Beck and Hoffa are modern examples of predatory unionism.

Some of the followers of Hoxie identified a fifth union type, which they named *dependent unionism.* Dependent unionism appears in two forms, one that could be called *company unionism* and the other *union label unionism.* The former depends entirely on the employer for its support and does not really represent the interests of the workers in so far as they may be opposed to the interests of management. The second type depends upon the union label being imprinted on the products made by union members. The union label is supposed to encourage greater sales and thus make it necessary for employers to hire union workers.[4]

Hoxie believed the functional types he identified were separate and distinct, although no union would necessarily correspond exactly to any one of them. The way in which a union operates is determined by the relative strength of the contending groups and factions within its membership. Changing economic conditions or new members could bring about a new balance of power between the factions. In this manner unions might progress from one functional type to another. Hoxie argued,

[4] E. H. Downey, Introduction to Hoxie, *Trade Unionism in the United States,* p. xviii.

however, that the types persisted even though the specific aspects of union programs and tactics continued to change and develop.

Unions Are Opportunistic

To Hoxie, the success of the AFL "may be explained largely by its supremely adaptable and catholic character, made possible by its nontheoretical, opportunistic, trial method and ideals, and its loose organization. It is thus sufficiently broad and elastic to have a place within itself for every form and type of organization—structurally and functionally—that has arisen and proved itself effective in the history of American unionism." [5]

American unions have grown out of American experience rather than by imitating unions abroad. They have solved immediate problems through experimental, opportunistic, and pragmatic methods. The American workers did not have long-run revolutionary goals; they wanted more here and now. This desire was reinforced by the visible possibility of immediate improvement in the workers' economic condition.

Although it is not an essential part of his theory, Hoxie made the interesting prediction that with the rise of union power, collective bargaining would develop into a form of industrial democracy and bring an end to the profit system. Tannenbaum made a similar prophecy, which has been further developed by some modern-day economists. [6]

Frank Tannenbaum

Tannenbaum traces the rise of unions to the workers' reaction to the philosophy of individualism dominating the nineteenth and twentieth centuries. The workers are engaging in "an unconscious rebellion against the atomization of industrial society." It is inevitable that a sense of identity should develop among men laboring at a common task. The "moral fusion of men physically associated in labor" is an age-old experience. Thus, according to Tannenbaum, the "original organizer of the trade-union movement is the shop, the factory, the mine, and the industry. The agitator or the labor leader merely announces the already existing fact." [7]

Union Monopoly Power

Tannenbaum believes that unions have become exceedingly powerful organizations. By organizing all workers within its jurisdiction a union

---

[5] Hoxie, *op. cit.*, p. 132.

[6] This prediction is discussed in Chapters 23 and 24.

[7] Tannenbaum's theory is presented in his book, *A Philosophy of Labor* (New York: Alfred A. Knopf, 1951). The quotations are from pp. 14, 31, 60.

attempts to gain monopoly control over the labor supply to that trade or industry. It may then prevent nonunion workers, and even uncooperative union members, from performing the tasks covered by its jurisdiction. Tannenbaum cites the musicians' union and its closed-shop relationships with the recording, movie, and television industries as an example of one having such power. Unlike Hoxie, he does not distinguish between different types of unions.

With their monopoly power, unions are in a position to impose wage bargains on employers who must accept on penalty of going out of business. By driving out of business those firms which cannot afford to pay the wage, the union has "tended to strengthen the very power of monopoly to which it presumably is opposed." The union, "originally created by the workers to make their bargaining more effective, has now become so powerful that it has reduced both the worker (member) and the employer to a subordinate position." [8]

Union Goals

Unions are not using their power to create a socialistic or communistic state. In fact, Tannenbaum views trade unionism as the "conservative movement of our time . . . a complete repudiation of Marxism." Those people who tried to guide the American union movement in a revolutionary direction did not understand that "the quarrel between the labor unions and management has always been a family quarrel." The two protagonists are "different aspects of the same institution."

Rather than striving for socialism or communism, unions use their new-found power to absorb the functions of management. Tannenbaum argues that unions cannot afford to stand still on this subject because every activity of management affects the well-being of the workers, and the primary purpose of unions is to protect and promote this well-being. Thus, unless unions continually invade management prerogatives, they will cease to exist. Although each dispute is over a specific issue, the main drift is toward increased union participation in management functions. Hence, no line can be drawn between the prerogatives of management and of unions, except for a single moment in time and for a specific industry.

Tannenbaum believes this process will ultimately lead to unions absorbing all the functions of management. "What is presumed in this development is that the union will gradually take on the role of the modern corporation by buying into it, and the ownership will cease to

[8] *Ibid.*, pp. 130–36.

be fluid and impersonal." The unions will have the funds to buy into corporations, according to his argument, as a result of their control over the trust funds set up under the various union welfare programs. The control of the modern corporation by unions will create "as many difficulties as it will eliminate. It will re-establish a society of status, the 'estates' of an older day, with all of the restrictions upon personal mobility and personal freedom." [9] That is, the worker will be tied not only to his union, but also to the corporation which is under the control of his union.

Selig Perlman

Perlman, after analyzing the labor movements in Russia, Germany, Great Britain, and the United States came to the conclusion that there are three factors which are "basic in any modern labor situation: first, the resistance power of capitalism, determined by its own historical development; second, the degree of dominance over the labor movements by the intellectual's 'mentality,' which regularly underestimates capitalism's resistance power and overestimates labor's will to radical change; and third, the degree of maturity of a trade union 'mentality.'" [10]

Job-Conscious Unionism

Trade union mentality developed out of what Perlman called the scarcity consciousness of the worker. The worker's scarcity consciousness stems from his belief that his economic position cannot improve beyond that which is barely sufficient to cover the minimum essentials of an ordinary standard of living. There are two causes for this belief in the scarcity of economic opportunity: "The typical manualist is aware of his lack of native capacity" for coping with the complex business world. He also has the "conviction that the world has been rendered one of scarcity by an institutional order of things, which purposely reserved the best opportunity for landlords, capitalists and other privileged groups."

Out of scarcity consciousness grew a job-conscious unionism, a unionism which controls the job opportunity. The union establishes certain job "rights" which it then rations among the members through regulations applying to overtime, seniority, etc. The union does not displace

[9] *Ibid.*, pp. 3, 82, 190.

[10] Perlman's theory is presented in his book, *A Theory of the Labor Movement* (New York: The Macmillan Co., 1928). The quotation is from the edition reprinted by Augustus M. Kelley, 1949, p. x. This and other excerpts from Perlman's book are reprinted by permission of Mrs. Fannie Perlman.

the employer as the risk-taker and owner of the business, but it does become the administrator of the scarce job opportunity.

Perlman disagrees with the accusation that American unions are without an ideology. Even business unionism has an ideology, though it be thoroughly unsophisticated. It is motivated by scarcity consciousness and is expressed by sharing the job opportunity through the "common rule"—a communism of the job opportunity, rather than communism of production and distribution. Since the union "expects its members to sacrifice for the group on a scale almost commensurate with the sacrifices which patriotism evokes, [it] cannot be without its own respectable ideology." [11]

The workers' scarcity consciousness "stands out in contrast with the business men's 'abundance consciousness,' or consciousness of unlimited opportunity." The businessman's urge to "individualism shows up clearest during periods of great economic expansion. When markets are becoming rapidly extended and technology revolutionized; in other words, when opportunity is expanding by leaps and bounds, then his competitiveness approaches the ruthlessness of a Darwinian struggle for existence." [12] Under certain conditions, e.g., a depression, businessmen may be dominated by a scarcity consciousness, leading to cartel-like arrangements, such as under the National Industrial Recovery Act from 1933 to 1935.

Unions and the Intellectuals

According to Perlman, intellectuals are nonmanualists—outsiders—who attempt to impose their ideology on the labor movement. They consider the workers' economic position to be most unfortunate and claim that it can be remedied only by the acceptance of their ideology. They differ from each other in how they diagnose the ills of society and in the cure they recommend. Karl Marx and the Webbs, discussed below, would exemplify two varieties. Intellectuals have in common a desire to manipulate the unions, using them as weapons to bring about great political, social, and economic changes. These self-elected prophets of the workers are prone to refer to the "toiling masses" as being blind to their degraded condition and in need of leadership to guide their tremendous but latent power in the right direction.

Why, asks Perlman, have these intellectuals had so little appeal to American workers? To the workers, the freedom which really matters is that directly connected with their jobs. They want to be treated

[11] *Ibid.*, pp. 239–40, 274–75.
[12] *Ibid.*, pp. 6, 243–244.

without discrimination and to be able to voice their complaints freely. Compared with this tangible sort of fredom, the higher freedoms extolled by the intellectuals seem too far distant. The worker prefers to gain modest benefits here and now rather than sacrifice for long-range goals that have no meaning in his day-to-day life.

Union Goals and Tactics

Writing in 1928, Perlman believed the AFL had succeeded in adjusting its organization and policies to the American environment, capitalizing on the scarcity consciousness of the workers, recognizing the resistance power of American capitalism, and eschewing the programs of the intellectuals. The proof of the success of the AFL, to Perlman, rested in the stability of its membership. The fact that it could withstand a series of depressions indicated that it had arrived at a new degree of maturity for American labor movements.

The AFL succeeded "first, because it recognized the virtually inalterable conservatism of the American community as regards private property and private initiative in economic life . . . secondly, because it grasped the definite limitations of the political instrument under the American Constitution and under American conditions of political life . . . [and finally] because it was under no delusion as to the true psychology of the workingman in general and of the American workingman in particular." [13] Each of these cornerstones of the AFL's achievement merits further comment.

Even without the domination of an intellectual ideology and without the support of class consciousness, the labor movement is a potent attack on the institution of private property. Through strikes, boycotts, and working rules, and through securing governmental restrictions on employers, unions restrict the absolute rights of private property. How far the labor movement may go and what tactics it may use depend on how strongly the institution of private property is entrenched in the community. In America, unions cannot "afford to arouse the fears of the great middle class for the safety of private property as a basic institution." [14] The AFL satisfied itself with modifying the rights of private property, and never sought to eliminate it as a basic institution.

The union attack on private property was never an attack on the American political system. The AFL recognized the difficulty of capturing the political instrument for the exclusive benefit of labor. First, it is divided into forty-nine separate parts (now fifty-one; Alaska and

[13] *Ibid.*, pp. 201–2.
[14] *Ibid.*, pp. 155–60.

Hawaii were admitted after Perlman published his theory), comprising the federal government and the separate state governments; hence success at one point does not ensure universal success. Secondly, each of these governmental units is balanced between three competing powers, the legislative, the executive, and the judiciary. And therefore, not only is it necessary to capture fifty-one governmental units, but it is necessary to capture three branches in each. Thirdly, the nature of the American two-party system frustrates the possibility of a third party. Each of the two parties shows itself capable of adjusting to labor's demands whenever these demands are backed up by substantial voting power.

The great difficulty of keeping workers organized arose from the lack of class cohesiveness among American workers. They did not consider themselves inevitably as members of a working class; that is, they did not think and act as class-conscious workers. Therefore, American workers did not automatically join unions, nor were they willing to make extensive personal sacrifices to maintain the permanent operation of unions. The AFL, in adjusting its goals and tactics to this basic environmental factor, capitalized on the self-interest of skilled workers and concentrated its attention on their immediate economic concerns.

Without class consciousness to hold American unions together, the AFL unions were compelled to resort to overt means of preventing rebellion within their ranks. They adopted the tactics of fighting ruthlessly against dual unionism and "outlaw" strikes. Strikes not approved by the regular procedure, and especially if they were in violation of the collective bargaining contract, were often suppressed by the national officers themselves, even to the extent of recruiting out-of-town members to replace the strikers. When a new organization, or a dissident faction, attempted to raid the jurisdiction of an established AFL union, it was fought with all the power the AFL could command.

TWO EUROPEAN THEORIES

We now turn to two theories of the labor movement that were formulated outside of this country. Though less relevant for the American labor movement, they add to our understanding by way of contrast. Furthermore, they are useful interpretations of labor movements in important segments of the world.

Sidney and Beatrice Webb

The Webbs viewed the purpose of the unions as more than merely winning economic benefits for their members. Beyond this lay political goals which should be "nothing less than a reconstruction of society, by the elimination, from the nation's industries and services, of the Capitalist Profitmaker, and the consequent shrinking up of the class of functionless persons who live merely by owning." [15] Their whole interpretation of the labor movement, particularly the direction it was destined to take in the future, was colored by this belief in the need for establishing a form of socialism.

According to the Webbs, the pressure put on the workers by the "higgling of the market" caused them to organize into unions to protect their economic interests. The conditions of employment were determined by the "chain of bargains linking together the manual worker, the capitalist employer, the wholesale trader, the shopkeeper, and the customer." [16] The pressure began with the customer, the final consumer, and constantly increased with each link in the chain, until it finally gave the employer no choice but to produce as efficiently as he could, forcing him to hold wages and other labor costs to as low a level as possible. Each class of producers engaged in concerted activity (trade associations) to evade this pressure. In the case of workers, it led to union activity.

In order to improve their members' economic status, the unions sought to require each firm to pay at least a minimum rate and to provide minimum working conditions, in terms of hours, sanitation, safety, etc. The Webbs referred to this as the "Common Rules." The unions employed three different techniques to bring continual improvements in the Common Rules. At first (1700) they relied upon mutual insurance: union-financed programs for the needy, aged, and unemployed members. These programs had two objectives: to provide something tangible to bind the worker to his union and to prevent those out of work from exerting a downward competitive pressure on wages. As early as the eighteen century, unions sought protective legislation, especially regulating safety conditions in factories. After 1924, union activity being no longer outlawed, they added the technique of collective bargaining.

Up to 1900, British unions tacitly accepted the capitalistic system, aiming only at improving their living conditions within the existng economic organization. At the turn of the century the Webbs saw new ideas taking root, focused on the aspirations of the workers to gain increasing control over, and eventually to nationalize, the major indus-

---

[15] The Webbs' theory was presented in their books, *Industrial Democracy* (London: Longmans, Green and Co., Ltd., 1897), and *The History of Trade Unionism* (London: Longmans, Green and Co., Ltd., 1894). The quotation is from the 1920 edition of the latter, pp. 717–18.

[16] Sidney and Beatrice Webb, *Industrial Democracy* (1920 ed.), p. 654.

tries. According to the Webbs, the unions would accomplish these goals through political action. The Labour Party made important steps in this direction when it controlled the British government after World War II. The Webbs were the dominant intellectual leaders of the Labour Party in its beginnings during the second and third decades of this century, drafting its original socialistic platform.

Karl Marx

Although both the Webbs and Karl Marx expected that the capitalistic system would be abolished, they advocated very different paths to bring about its downfall. The Webbs, and the Fabian Society, with which they were associated, wanted a peaceful and gradual evolution to the socialistic form of government; Marx and his followers,[17] on the other hand, insisted on a rapid, revolutionary, and perhaps violent change to the new order.

According to Marx, unions are the natural result of the development of capitalism. In the *Communist Manifesto,* he and his colleague, Friedrich Engels, stated that

with the development of industry the proletariat not only increases in number, it becomes concentrated in greater masses, its strength grows, and it feels that strength more. The various interests and conditions of life within the ranks of the proletariat are more and more equalized, in proportion as machinery obliterates all distinctions of labor, and nearly everywhere reduces wages to the same low level. The growing competition among the bourgeois, and the resulting commercial crises, make the wages of the workers ever more fluctuating. The unceasing improvement of machinery, ever more rapidly developing, makes their livelihood more and more precarious; the collisions between individual workmen and individual bourgeois take more and more the character of collisions between two classes. Thereupon the workers begin to form combinations (Trades' Unions) against the bourgeois; they club together in order to keep up the rate of wages; they found permanent associations in order to make provisions beforehand for these occasional revolts.[18]

[17] Marx's theory of the labor movement was integrated with his theory of the eventual demise of the capitalistic system. In presenting his theory of the labor movement outside of this context, we are missing much of its real meaning. The primary development of his theory is presented in the three volumes of *Capital,* the first published in 1867, and the other two after his death in 1885 and 1894. The core of the argument appears in the famous *Communist Manifesto* (1848), written with Friedrich Engels. Other sources (giving more emphasis to his opinions on unions) are Marx, *Value, Price and Profit,* ed. by Eleanor Marx Aveling (New York: International Publishers, 1935); V. I. Lenin, *What is to be Done?* (New York: International Publishers, 1929); and A. Lozovsky, *Marx and the Trade Unions* (New York: International Publishers, 1942).

[18] Quoted from the text of the *Communist Manifesto,* reprinted in Harold J. Laski, *Karl Marx; An Essay* (New York: League for Industrial Democracy, 1933) pp. 68–69.

Marx believed that the trade unions did not properly represent the workers. The labor movement as it developed spontaneously from the workers was pure and simple trade unionism, with the workers remaining subordinate to the owners of industry. Unions had a necessary and useful task to perform in protecting wages and working conditions, but should not limit themselves to these narrow economic goals. Instead they should use their organized power to emancipate the working class by destroying the capitalistic system.

How were unions to become imbued with the "correct ideology" and to understand "properly" their function in the capitalistic system? "The workers can acquire class political consciousness *only from without,* that is, only outside of the economic struggle, outside of the sphere of relations between workers and employers." It is the intellectuals who must "lead the struggle of the working class not only for better terms for the sale of labour power, but also for the abolition of the social system which compels the propertyless class to sell itself to the rich. Social-Democracy represents the working class, not in its relation to a given group of employers, but in its relation to all classes in modern society, to the state as an organized political force." [19] In the words of Marx, the unions should not adopt "the *conservative* motto: '*A fair day's wages for a fair day's work!*' They ought to inscribe on their banner the *revolutionary* watchword: '*Abolition of the wages system!*'" [20]

What do all these slogans mean when implemented in a political system that is alleged to follow the dictates of Marx? This is revealed in an interchange in 1959 between Walter Reuther and Nikita Khrushchev, Premier of the Soviet government and Chairman of the Russian Communist Party, when the world's leading communist was touring the United States

REUTHER: How could the [Russian] worker . . . get justice if he would not strike or publicly protest?

KHRUSHCHEV: His trade union.

REUTHER: The union is an extension of government, the Soviet Government. Does a union ever disagree with the Government? Can you give us one single example in which one of your unions ever disagreed with Government policy?

KHRUSHCHEV: Why poke your nose into our business?

REUTHER: Freedom is everybody's business. You are always expressing a concern for the workers in Asia. There is a thing called international labor

[19] Lenin, *op. cit.,* pp. 76, 56. Italics in original.
[20] Marx, *Value, Price and Profit,* p. 61. Italics in original. See also Lozovsky, *op. cit.,* pp. 15–25.

solidarity. When I was in Russia I was a member of a union, and it was what we would call a company union.[21]

CONTRIBUTIONS OF THE THEORIES

Now that the five theories have been surveyed individually, we are ready to distill from them the elements which contribute most to an understanding of the American labor movement. A few general comments should be made first. Although the theories were divided into American and European, this does not mean they are geographically limited in their application. Each writer was attempting to set forth universal explanations of labor movements. Two of the theories, by Perlman and Tannenbaum, view worker organizations as essentially conservative, not desiring to make basic changes in the socio-economic structure; one, by the Webbs, views them as essentially radical. Marx thought unions would be radical only if they followed "enlightened" leaders. Hoxie gave a qualified answer, saying that unions would differ depending on the conditions surrounding their birth and growth.

In selecting the most useful elements from the theories, Marx can be left out of account, not because he is unimportant, but because his observations have proved to be largely incorrect, at least as far as this country is concerned. Workers have not grown increasingly poverty-stricken; on the contrary, their standard of living has continually risen, not only in absolute terms, but also relative to other groups in the economy. American unions have relied on "home-grown" leadership rather than accepting domination by intellectuals who would lead them into political or revolutionary activity. However, Marx's recommendations have been put into action in Russia, where the unions are subservient to the Communist Party.

The Webbs' description of the economic origin of unions, though oversimplified, is applicable to America. But it fails to explain why unions did not appear among the lower-paid workers until many decades after the skilled workers were organized. The Webbs' advocacy, as well as prediction, of the long-run goals which they believed unions should and would seek was partly heeded in Great Britain, but has been ignored here. From the founding of the AFL up to the present time, American unions have demonstrated almost no interest in socializing industry.

Tannenbaum's emphasis on the relationship between the unions and management prerogatives touches upon an important characteristic of

---

[21] *New York Times*, September 22, 1959. This interchange occurred at a dinner meeting of Mr. Khrushchev and a number of labor leaders. The comments are quoted from a text made public by the labor leaders.

the current labor scene. His theory suffers from an overestimate of union power relative to that of management and to other interest groups in American society. As a result, he predicted union ownership of corporations as the ultimate outcome of their growth. The evidence indicates just the opposite: unions prefer to bargain with owners rather than be the owners.

Hoxie's emphasis on social and psychological factors as the sources of unions, and in fact as the sources of five different varieties of unions, constitutes a significant contribution to an understanding of the union movement. However, he laid too much stress on the organic and permanent nature of the five functional types. As a matter of fact, they can probably be reduced, without loss of insight, to one: business unionism.[22] Revolutionary and uplift unionism no longer exists in this country. Predatory unionism is simply business unionism using undesirable tactics, or in extreme cases, a criminal organization operating under a union disguise to cover up its racketeering. Company unions are entirely dominated by the employer and can hardly be called unions in the ordinary sense. Union label unions are simply using a special technique to pursue ordinary business union goals.

Job consciousness as emphasized by Perlman is one of the basic characteristics of all American unions. Job-conscious unionism and business unionism are two different ways of saying approximately the same thing. Both in Hoxie's and Perlman's theories the American labor movement is seen as the product of the American environment, pragmatically adjusting its goals and tactics to the rapid growth and popular support of capitalism, the entrenched institution of private property, and the nature of our political system. The unique characteristics of America caused the rise of a unique brand of unionism.

Conclusion on Theories

Where does this leave us? Basically, with the theory that American unions are job-conscious business unions. Business unionism exhibits its opportunism by appearing in various forms, depending on the socio-economic environment in which it develops. Conservative in character, it does not desire to abolish the private enterprise system, but concentrates its efforts on short-run goals to be reached mainly through such nonpolitical techniques as strikes.

[22] Russell Bauder, "Three Interpretations of the American Trade Union Movement," *Social Forces,* XXII (December, 1943), pp. 220–22.

The conclusion reached here has been subjected to many criticisms. A brief consideration of three of these criticisms should enlarge our interpretation of the American labor movement. First, it has been argued that job-conscious business unionism is no longer an accurate label. The general principles were formulated more than twenty-five years ago, and since then the appearance of the CIO, the labor laws of the 1930's, and the high employment of the last fifteen years have changed the nature of the American labor movment. Included in these changes would be a 400 per cent rise in membership and in the number of workers covered by collective agreements, government protection of collective bargaining, and insurance benefits for unemployed workers. It is true that unions are not the same today as when Hoxie and Perlman developed their theories, but the CIO, even prior to the merger in 1955, was not so different from the AFL as many people had originally expected. The CIO unions were equally concerned with jurisdictional boundaries, seniority in the job, closed and union shops, and other features of job-conscious business unionism.

Secondly, it is argued that unions do engage in a rather substantial amount of political action now, far beyond that contemplated by job-conscious unionism; witness the large sums spent under union auspices in recent political campaigns. Furthermore, it is said that the unions now support social security programs, fair labor standards legislation, collective bargaining legislation, full employment fiscal policies, etc. However, all this does not mean that the unions are not job-conscious; it merely adds another dimension to protecting and expanding the scarce opportunity, implying that unions will support those political programs which promote the goals of business unionism. Unions continue to rely upon bargaining power as the primary mechanism for improving their members' welfare. The political activity is designed to enhance the bargaining power by enlarging the job opportunity, for example, laws requiring full train crews regardless of the size of the train, and advocacy of full employment policies to maintain jobs for union members and reduce the competition from unemployed workers.

As a third criticism, it is claimed that unions are pragmatic, adapting their techniques and goals, particularly their short-run goals, to the changing social, political, and economic milieu. Since unions grow out of their environment, they must change as the environment changes. This part of the argument is consistent with Perlman and Hoxie. But the further point is made that because of the increasing importance of the government and of giant industrial firms, unions have expanded their range of activities beyond those included in job consciousness. Yet, the basic aim is still job control, with a greater concern for the economy-wide aspects, but a continuing emphasis on plant-wide control.[23] In their public speeches union leaders may condemn the "grasping monopolies," but they are more than glad to sign a collective agreement with them and hope that the firms will prosper.

SUMMARY

A theory of the union movement is necessary in order to understand a social phenomenon as complicated and many-sided as the trade union movement. It must be able to tell us why unions appear, how they develop, why workers join unions, what goals, both short-run and ultimate, are chosen, and how unions decide which techniques to adopt to secure these goals.

To find answers to these questions, we have surveyed five different theories. Tannenbaum emphasized the importance of the atomization of the factory atmosphere associated with the need for the workers to return to a society of their own creation, and expected that unions would eventually control all corporations. Hoxie was impressed by the different types of unions which would grow out of different social-psychological conditions and different temperamental characteristics of the workers. Perlman saw the worker as a person with a pessimistic outlook, a feeling of scarcity of economic opportunity, and consequently in need of an organization which would control that scarce opportunity and ration it on some predetermined and fair basis. The Webbs viewed the union movement as a reaction to the competitive pressures of the capitalistic society, and believed it would eventually change the structure of society through political techniques. Marx saw unions as misguided organizations, failing to understand the real nature of the capitalist system, and therefore in need of guidance toward revolutionary activity.

In comparing these theories, we selected job-conscious business unionism as the most valid explanation for this country. The earlier chapters provided us with factual information which can be more consistently interpreted in the light of this theory. The remainder of the book is likewise more easily understood when viewed within this framework.

[23] For a discussion of these and other criticisms, as well as support for a job-conscious interpretation of unions, see Part VI, "Theory of the Labor Movement—A Reappraisal," *Proceedings of the Third Annual Meeting of the Industrial Relations Research Association* (Madison: Industrial Relations Research Association, 1951) pp. 139–183.

DISCUSSION QUESTIONS

1. What is a theory of the labor movement? Why is it useful?

2. What did Hoxie mean by his observation that unions grow out of their social-psychological environment? How does this lead to different functional types of unions?

3. What is implied by the comment: American unions are opportunistic? Cite evidence to support this contention.

4. Unions are a reaction against the individualism which has dominated the nineteenth and twentieth centuries. What does this mean?

5. Is Tannenbaum consistent when he argues that unions will absorb all the functions of management and yet are conservative?

6. What is job-conscious unionism? How does it compare with business unionism? How does it compare with Tannenbaum's notion that unions are a "moral fusion" of men working together?

7. Do you agree with Perlman that American unions made a wise choice, from their own point of view, in deciding not to use political techniques as their primary weapon? Explain.

8. Explain why American unions have conformed to the Webbs' theory much less than have the British unions.

9. According to Marx and Lenin, why is intellectual leadership necessary to the trade unions?

10. If you had to rely on only one of the five theories, which would you choose? Why?

11. Select one of the questions posed at the beginning of the chapter and compare the answer presented by each of the theories.

12. Write a brief essay elucidating the basic factors, as you understand them, which have determined the origin, growth, and goals of the American labor movement.

BIBLIOGRAPHY

Dunlop, John T. "The Development of Labor Organization: A Theoretical Framework," *Insights Into Labor Issues*. Edited by Richard A. Lester and Joseph Shister. New York: The Macmillan Co., 1948.

Hoxie, Robert F. *Trade Unionism in the United States*. New York: D. Appleton and Co., 1917.

Lenin, V. I. *What is to be Done?* New York: International Publishers, 1929.

Marx, Karl. *Value, Price and Profit*. Edited by Eleanor Marx Aveling. New York: International Publishers, 1935.

Marx, Karl, and Engels, Friedrich. *Communist Manifesto*. New York: International Publishers, 1948.

Perlman, Mark. *Labor Union Theories in America*. Evanston: Row, Peterson and Company, 1958.

Perlman, Selig. *A Theory of the Labor Movement*. New York: The Macmillan Co., 1928.

Tannenbaum, Frank. *A Philosophy of Labor*. New York: Alfred A. Knopf, 1951.

Webb, Sidney, and Webb, Beatrice. *The History of Trade Unionism*. London: Longmans, Green and Co., Ltd., 1894.

———. *Industrial Democracy*. London: Longmans, Green and Co., Ltd., 1897.

PART

2

COLLECTIVE

BARGAINING

Collective bargaining is the technique that has been adopted by unions and management for compromising their conflicting interests. What is the nature of collective bargaining? What are the major issues at dispute between the two parties? Is the conflict permanent in nature or does it represent only an imperfect and temporary stage of development?

A union, of course, is an organization of people of differing ages, backgrounds, and personalities. How do they arrive at a common set of demands satisfactory to their heterogeneous desires? What determines how vigorously a union will pursue its bargaining goals? Why do some seek a guaranteed annual wage plan while others put more emphasis on preventing employers from hiring nonunion workers?

How does management react to the union challenge to their control of plant operations? What do employers try to win through collective bargaining? What factors bring about industry-wide bargaining? Why does it appear in some industries but not in others? Although strikes and contract negotiations receive almost all of the publicity, we know that unions and management must get along on a daily basis. What are the problems that arise in day-to-day relations and how are they handled?

Where does the government fit into the picture? To what extent should it regulate the processes of collective bargaining? The American attitude of "there ought to be a law" has fostered a stream of new legislation decade after decade. What has been the pattern of development of the law, and what impact has it had on union growth and labor-management relations? What can we do and what should we do about preventing stoppages that cripple the entire economy?

8

THE NATURE OF

COLLECTIVE BARGAINING

The central focus of union activity is collective bargaining, the process of arriving at compromises which settle disputes between an employer and an organization of his employees. It is called *collective* because the employees, as a group, select representatives to meet and discuss differences with the employer. Collective bargaining is the opposite of *individual* bargaining which takes place between management and a worker, as an individual, apart from his fellow employees.

This chapter is an introduction to our analysis of collective bargaining, sketching the nature of the processes in broad terms and describing the general areas in which disagreements between management and unions may occur.

FUNCTIONS OF COLLECTIVE BARGAINING

In a dynamic society with continually changing relationships between individuals and groups, techniques must be found to control the pace of change, preventing it from being either too fast or too slow. These techniques must permit groups which are rising in power and prestige to approach their new levels of authority, and at the same time permit groups which are declining—either absolutely or relatively—to retain some degree of social respect and dignity. If these techniques are not sufficiently flexible to allow for gradual change, repressed groups, when they become powerful enough, foment revolutionary change. Safety valves must be built in, allowing the rising groups' excess steam to escape with-

153

out blowing the whole mechanism to pieces. If the declining groups are treated too harshly, they fight tenaciously and irrationally to hold their former position, creating explosive group antagonisms. Therefore, the processes of social change must provide successive compromises acceptable to all parties.

Collective bargaining is a technique of social change, sometimes performing its function smoothly and other times threatening to blow up. The performance of its functions can be viewed under three headings: Collective bargaining 1) acts as a technique of long-run social change, bringing rearrangements in the power hierarchy of competing groups, 2) serves as a peace treaty between two parties in continual conflict, and 3) establishes a system of industrial jurisprudence, defining the rights and duties of the conflicting parties.

Process of Social Change

In looking on collective bargaining as a process of long-run social change, we are going beyond the definition stated at the beginning of the chapter. Collective bargaining, in its broader aspects, is not confined solely to the economic relations between employers and employees. Perlman has defined it as "a technique whereby an inferior social class or group carries on a never slackening pressure for a bigger share in the social sovereignty as well as for more welfare, security, and liberty for its individual members." Collective bargaining "manifests itself equally in politics, legislation, court litigation, government administration, religion, education, and propaganda."[1]

When viewed as a process of social change, collective bargaining encompasses more than the direct clash between employers and unions. It refers to the rise in political and social power achieved by workers and their organizations over the course of the last century and a half. It compares with the rise of the towns in their struggle with the feudal lords during the Middle Ages. Desiring recognition as a group, the towns sought and won charters, thus preventing the lord from taxing as much as he pleased and from arbitrarily disciplining individual members of the towns. Under the charter, the lord was compelled to bargain with the guild members and townsmen as a group. In granting his loyalty to the guild and town, the individual won his freedom from the lord. By presenting a united front, the guilds and towns chipped away at the power of the feudal lord, eventually winning the incorporation of their customs and working rules into the law of the land.

[1] Selig Perlman, "The Principle of Collective Bargaining," *The Annals of the American Academy of Political and Social Science,* Vol. CLXXXIV (March, 1936), p. 154.

Collective bargaining, thus viewed, is not an abstract class struggle in a Marxian sense, but is rather pragmatic and concrete. The inferior class does not attempt to abolish the old ruling class, but merely to become equal with it. It aims to acquire a large measure of economic and political control over crucial decisions in the areas of its most immediate interest, and to be recognized in other areas of decision-making.

One lesson to be learned from this broad view is that collective bargaining has no final form. It adapts itself to the changing social, legal, and economic environment. At any point in recent history collective bargaining has varied considerably from plant to plant and industry to industry, and also between and within unions. For example, a number of industrial unions have successfully bargained for pensions and guaranteed annual wages, while many unions in the construction industry have ignored these goals. Bargaining in some plants is characterized by comparatively frequent strikes, whereas in other plants there are long records of uninterrupted industrial peace.

When looking back over many decades, one can see collective bargaining as a source of stability in a changing environment. Wage earners have enhanced their social and economic position—in absolute terms and in relation to other groups—and at the same time, management has retained a large measure of power and dignity. These gains were not registered in one great revolutionary change, but rather step by step, with each clash between the opposing parties settled with a new compromise somewhat different from the previous settlement. In short, collective bargaining accomplishes long-run stability on the basis of day-to-day adjustments in the relations between labor and management. We turn now to these more immediate concerns.

Temporary Truce

Collective bargaining may be viewed as a struggle between two opposing powers with the outcome depending on their relative strength. The inherent strength of each side is its ability to withstand a strike. This is partly an economic matter: To what extent can the union provide financial aid to the strikers? Can the workers find temporary jobs? Are unemployed workers available to serve as strike-breakers? How much will the employer's sales be reduced? Will his position in the product market be permanently impaired? The ability to withstand a strike also depends on such noneconomic factors as the loyalty of the workers to the union, their willingness to make personal sacrifices to support its goals. The degree of loyalty, of course, is affected by the presence of any factionalism within the union. For either the employer or the union, a belief that some basic principle is at stake, e.g., management rights or union security, stiffens the will power of the antagonists.

The settlement between the two parties, when finally reached with or without a strike, is a compromise. The extent to which each side is willing to accept less than its original bargaining demands depends, in part, on how strong it feels relative to its opponent.

The compromise, then, is a temporary truce with neither side being completely satisfied with the results. Each would like to modify it at the earliest opportunity. Since the contract is almost always of limited duration, each begins immediately to prepare a new list of demands, including previously unsatisfied demands, and to build up its bargaining strength in anticipation of the next power skirmish. The compromise differs from an armed truce in one important respect. Armies have as their goal the annihilation of the opponent, whereas bargaining opponents expect to coexist indefinitely.

The above paragraphs perhaps overemphasize the combative aspects of collective bargaining. The great majority of collective bargaining contracts are reached without a strike; the truce is signed before either opponent fires a shot. In many situations there is a long history of peaceful relations between the employer and the union.[2] A tranquil stability has been achieved in the process of controlling economic change. That is, the union seeks first of all to make changes and improvements in its relation with the employer. Once a truce has been signed, the union stabilizes working conditions by preserving the status defined in the contract. It generally adheres to this agreement; in fact, it might bring substantial sanctions against any portion of the membership which attempted to abrogate the agreement, such as engaging in a wildcat strike.

Industrial Jurisprudence

Collective bargaining creates a system of "industrial jurisprudence." It is "a method of introducing civil rights into industry, that is, of requiring that management be conducted by rule rather than by arbitrary decision."[3] It establishes rules which define and restrict the traditional

---

[2] An excellent documentation of peaceful union-management relations may be found in the series of case studies by the Committee on Causes of Industrial Peace Under Collective Bargaining of the National Planning Association. The Committee's final report summarizes its findings: *Fundamentals of Labor Peace* (Washington: National Planning Association, 1953).

[3] Sumner H. Slichter, *Union Policies and Industrial Management* (Washington: the Brookings Institution, 1941), p. 1.

authority exercised by employers over their employees, placing part of the authority under joint control by union and management.

A convenient but somewhat overdrawn analogy can be made between collective bargaining and a democratic government. The negotiation of a new contract is analogous to the legislative process, the making of laws or rules. The executive branch consists of shop stewards and other union officials, on the one hand, and foremen and supervisory officials on the other. They share the responsibility of enforcing the rules. The judicial function is performed by the grievance procedure, the process by which disputes concerning application of the contract to particular cases are settled. Through the grievance procedure the contracts are interpreted and applied to particular cases, and where the contract does not specifically cover the dispute, it may be settled according to the unwritten law of shop practices: the rules and traditions long accepted by union and management in the particular plant. The decisions in these cases act as precedents in a manner similar to the common law and court interpretation of legislation.

Successful collective bargaining requires that these three functions be served effectively and continuously. The contract must provide a workable system of industrial jurisprudence, and even though it is a truce, some portions of which are reluctantly accepted by one side or the other, each must be willing to make the appropriate accommodations. And finally, collective bargaining must never stagnate if it is to serve its role of adapting labor and management institutions, and their relative power positions, to the changing socio-economic environment.

NEGOTIATING AND ADMINISTERING CONTRACTS

Collective bargaining entails two separate but interrelated steps: 1) negotiating the contract and 2) administering the contract. In negotiating the contract, a union and management present their demands to each other, compromise their differences, and agree on the conditions under which the workers are to be employed for the duration of the contract. There are more than 125,000 contracts covering approximately 18,000,000 workers. The coverage of collective bargaining is very uneven; in some industries almost all workers are under agreement, while in others only a small portion of the employees are in firms which bargain with unions. (See Figure 8-A for the coverage in manufacturing industries.) Many contracts cover only a few workers, but approximately 2,000 cover 1,000 or more workers each. Some are long and filled with technical details, running to 200 or more pages. Others are brief statements of only a few

FIGURE 8-A

Labor-Management Contract Coverage in Manufacturing, 1958

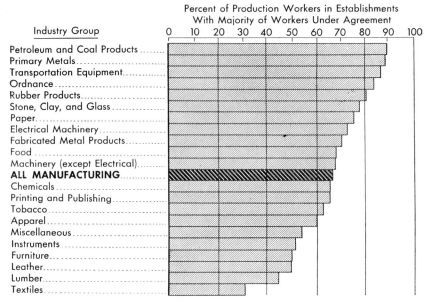

Source: *Monthly Labor Review,* Vol. LXXXIII (April, 1960), p. 346.

pages, relying on shop practices to fill in the details of labor-management relations. The negotiation process is the part of collective bargaining more likely to make headline news and attract public attention: wage increases are announced, ominous predictions about price increases and reductions in employment are made. And it is in the negotiating process that strikes and threats of strikes are most liable to occur, particularly strikes which shut down an entire industry.

The administrative process is the mundane day-to-day application of the provisions of the contract to the work situation. At the time of writing the contract it is impossible to foresee all the special problems which will arise in applying its provisions. Sometimes it is a matter of differing interpretations of a specific clause in the contract, and sometimes it is a question of whether the dispute is even covered by the contract. Nevertheless, each case must somehow be settled. The methods that managment and the union jointly adopt for this purpose constitute the administrative process.

The negotiative and administrative processes are interrelated because as new contracts are written they take into account the special problems which developed under the previous contract. Furthermore, as day-to-day problems are solved, they set precedents for handling similar problems in the future. Such precedents are almost as important as the contract in controlling the working conditions. In short, collective bargaining is *not* an on-and-off relationship that is kept in cold storage except when new contracts are drafted. Rather it is a continually growing relationship that takes on new dimensions each day.

CONTENTS OF COLLECTIVE BARGAINING AGREEMENT

Collective bargaining in its modern form is comparatively new, dating from 1891, when a major trade agreement was negotiated on a national basis in the stove foundry industry, ending many years of continuous bickering. Earlier unions had typically presented a list of demands on a take-it-or-leave-it basis. After the appearance of national unions, agreements were negotiated in some industries, but the stove foundry contract set a precedent by providing a comprehensive scheme for dealing with disputes that arose during the administration of the contract. Collective bargaining, in its present form, then spread into other industries, with its growth paralleling that of unions.

Along with the growth in number of workers covered, collective bargaining has expanded in subject matter. In this section the major topics covered by a typical collective bargaining agreement are sketched. Table 8-A[4] indicates the prevalence of key contract provisions in 1939 and 1945. Although some of the provisions are found in the majority of contracts, it can be seen in the table that there is a variation at any point in time as well as with the passage of time. The changes in the contents of collective bargaining contracts between 1939 and 1945, as shown in Table 8-A, were much more remarkable than those since 1945, except for the addition of major fringe benefits, in the form of pension plans and health and welfare plans, as discussed later in this chapter and in Chapter 21.

The subject matter covered by the contract generally varies with the maturity of the bargaining relationship between the two parties. When a union and a firm are negotiating their first agreement, they may be novices in the techniques of bargaining and drafting a contract. The union members may expect unreasonably favorable changes in working conditions, thus causing the union to take an extreme bargaining position. Management may approach the new situation with great fear and unwillingness to change old practices. The resulting contract may be awkward

[4] W. S. Woytinsky and Associates, *Employment and Wages in the United States* (New York: The Twentieth Century Fund, 1953), p. 267. Quoted by permission of the Twentieth Century Fund.

TABLE 8-A
Percentage of Union Contracts with Specified Provisions, 1939 and 1945*

Contract Provision	Percentage of Contracts 1939	1945	Contract Provision	Percentage of Contracts 1939	1945
Contract coverage			Wages		
Agreement covers:			Minimum wage		
Only union members	27	3	established	37	63
All eligible employees	73	97	Wage scale or rates		
Employees ineligible for			specified	21	38
membership:			Wage increases provided	6	32
Supervisory employees	50	64	Hours		
Salaried employees	48	61	Regular working hours		
Union security			per day:		
Type of shop:			Less than 8 hours	5	2
No union security	70	32	8 hours	74	78
Maintenance of mem-			More than 8 hours	2	2
bership	..	43	Regular working hours		
Closed or union shop	30	25	per week:		
Preferential hiring	16	6	Less than 40 hours	4	3
Checkoff	6	42	40 hours	60	73
Rights and responsibilities			More than 40 hours	15	2
Union:			Days per week:		
Union members not to			5 days	62	45
coerce or solicit mem-			6 days	10	3
bership on company			Call-in pay		
time	40	49	Time payable when no		
Strikes prohibited	38	78	work available:		
Transaction of union			Less than 4 hours	27	28
business permitted			4 hours or more	11	42
on company property	10	16	Vacations		
Management:			Vacations with pay	60	80
Company not to dis-			Grievance procedures		
criminate against			Union representative		
union or interfere			allowed time off:		
with employees'			With pay	8	31
right to join	55	80	Without pay	29	15
Lockouts prohibited	38	78	Arbitration:		
Company responsible			Provided	75	81
for industrial health			Award binding on		
and safety of			both parties	65	75
employees	40	49	Expenses shared		
Functions reserved to			jointly	50	54
management:					
Employment	33	49			
Promotion	4	36			
Transfer	29	41			
Suspension	29	41			
Discharge	38	45			
Layoff	29	42			

* Source: Based on analysis of 114 contracts in 1939 and 212 contracts in 1945 by the National Industrial Conference Board. Cf. Harold F. Browne, "A Comparison of Union Agreements," *Conference Board Management Record*, July 1939, pp. 101–09, and Abraham A. Desser, "Trends in Collective Bargaining and Union Contracts," *Conference Board Reports*, Studies in Personnel Policy No. 71, National Industrial Conference Board, New York, December, 1945, pp. 3–14.

and subject to a variety of interpretations eventually causing a large number of grievances, particularly if the workers' expectations are not realized. The truce between the antagonists is unstable and frequently violated with "quickie" strikes and employer refusal to abide by some of the provisions.

As the bargaining relationship matures and the two parties grow in mutual trust and confidence, the agreement acts as a framework for peacefully settling day-to-day disputes. And when new contracts are negotiated, additional subjects are brought under the control of collective bargaining. Of course, where a contract is being drafted for the first time between a firm and a local of a well-established union, much of this maturity is likely to be accomplished without so many growing pains.

In reading the following parts of this section, the discerning student will note that there are many provisions in the contract on which one or both of the parties is likely to be dissatisfied. It is with regard to these provisions that the contract takes on the form of a temporary truce. Also, the student will note that the manner in which these provisions are finally settled determines the nature of the system of industrial jurisprudence which evolves from the bargaining situation, as in the provisions describing the grievance procedure which spell out the nature of the judicial process.

Contract provisions may be divided into four categories: union security, worker security, economic factors, and management protection. Some provisions are relevant to more than one of these categories. This chapter, which merely sketches the contents of collective agreements, serves as an introduction to the following chapters where we analyze union and management approaches to collective bargaining.

Recognition and Union Security

The first section of the contract generally names the parties to the contract, which, in effect, recognizes the union as the representative of the employees. Usually the union is the exclusive representative; that is, the contract covers all specified employees regardless of whether they are union members.

Union security means the extent to which the contract protects the union in holding its membership. Union security clauses vary from mere recognition, at one extreme, to the closed shop at the other, with many variations between the extremes. The most notable examples are defined as follows: A *closed shop* requires the employer to hire only union members, and to discharge any employee who fails to retain his membership in good standing. The closed shop is not permitted under the Taft-Hartley Act; however, the practice is still followed in many parts of the construction industry, and elsewhere. A *union shop* differs from the closed shop only in that employees need not be members of the union when hired. But they are required to join within some specified time period, usually fifteen to thirty days. The union shop is found in many manufacturing industries where the closed shop is not feasible. The latter would be unworkable since the employer sometimes hires large numbers of untrained workers at one time. The Taft-Hartley Act permits a modified form of the union shop, allowing the employer to discharge an employee for refusal to pay his union dues. It differs from the earlier form because expulsion from the union, regardless of the reason, is not tantamount to discharge so long as the worker continues to offer to pay his union dues. A *maintenance of membership* clause requires each union member to state, within some specified time after the contract is signed, whether or not he wishes to maintain his union membership. Unless he elects to leave the union, he is required to remain a member in good standing for the duration of the contract. Failure to do so leads to discharge. Maintenance of membership is a union security compromise which was widely adopted during World War II, as may be seen in Table 8-A. It gives the union some degree of security, but less than either a closed or union shop. A *preferential hiring* clause requires the employer to give preference to union members whenever he hires new employees. This is a typical provision in the construction industry, and other places where skilled craftsmen are required. In these cases the employer hires through the union business agent. It is also frequently found in the maritime industries, where the employer hires through the union hiring hall. The elimination of preferential hiring was an objective of the Taft-Hartley Act, but hiring halls that did not discriminate between union and non-union workers were permitted. A *checkoff* clause requires the employer to deduct the union dues from the employees' pay and forward it directly to the union. This may be either on a compulsory basis, so that all people covered by the contract are required to have such deductions made, or on a voluntary basis, each employee stating whether or not he wants his dues paid in this fashion. Under the Taft-Hartley Act, only the voluntary checkoff is permissible.

It might be asked why any attention should be given to these definitions since several of the provisions are contrary to the Taft-Hartley Act. There are at least two reasons for this. First, union security, even in a modified form, continues to be a major union goal. Second, the Taft-Hartley Act has not completely eliminated these practices from collective bargaining, partly because the Act does not cover intrastate commerce and partly because of difficulties in enforcing the Act.

Why Union Security

At this point, a brief digression is necessary to inquire into why unions spend such a large portion of their bargaining energy to win union security clauses. Union security has been one of the most hotly debated issues in labor-management relations since World War II, with much of the debate taking place at the political level. The Taft-Hartley Act imposed regulations, slightly modified in the Landrum-Griffin Act, and "right-to-work" laws—prohibiting many forms of union security—are now in effect in eighteen states, and have been considered by many more. Unions and management organizations continue to contest the issue in radio and television debates, newspaper releases, and state and national elections. His support of a proposed "right-to-work" law contributed to the defeat of William Knowland in the 1958 gubernatorial election in California.

There are many reasons why unions press for security clauses in their contracts: 1) Since the union wins improved working conditions for all employees covered by the contract, it is only fair to require all workers to make equal sacrifices for its support. 2) The union's bargaining power is enhanced by 100 per cent membership. 3) The presence of fellow workers who are nonmembers leads to factional disputes and unpleasant working conditions. 4) The union's income is increased. 5) Its ability to discipline its members is much greater, i.e., if expulsion from the union is immediately followed by loss of job, the worker will, of course, be more inclined to obey union rules. Unions argue that if they are to be held responsible for living up to all provisions of the contract, they must have some effective disciplinary power over their members.

Beyond these direct and immediate reasons, there are three fundamental and long-run factors which have caused American unions to place great emphasis on union security. First, employers historically have been opposed to unions and especially considerate of workers who refuse to join unions. Special favors in job assignments and promotions have been granted to nonmembers. A union security clause makes it more difficult for the employer to undermine the union's position in the plant. Second, the union can better protect itself against jurisdictional raids from other unions and from splinter groups within its own membership if it possesses a union security clause. The employer himself may be anxious to avoid this type of labor turmoil. Third, since there is no powerful motivating ideology—no class consciousness—causing American workers automatically to join unions, special pressure must be provided.[5]

On the opposite side are the arguments that no person should be compelled to join an organization if he is in strong disagreement with its basic principles. It is claimed that all workers should have free access to any job for which they are qualified with no interference from unions. Another argument often posed is that union security clauses give the union leadership monopoly power making it possible for them to win excessive wage increases. Furthermore, this power has been abused, particularly in those unions where the officials are not subject to democratic controls. Workers who do not "play ball" with their leaders may find it impossible to secure jobs. The publicity given to these arguments is partly motivated by desires to weaken the economic and political strength of unions.

Management, in some instances, believes that it is better off to deal with the union on a closed-shop or union-shop basis. The union, feeling more secure, may not insist upon an inflexible interpretation of the contract, making special concessions to the employer when he is temporarily in a strained economic position. Thus, the employer gives in on this point and receives in return more complete cooperation. Of course, where the union is the sole source of a particular type of skilled labor, the employer has no choice but to operate on what amounts to a closed-shop basis.

Wages, Hours, and Working Conditions

Wages and hours have customarily been the center of union activity. They served as the major organizing impetus of the unions. Even though collective bargaining is far from being a purely economic phenomenon, almost every contract includes provisions for wages, hours, and working conditions.

Wage provisions generally specify methods of payment, indicating whether wages are to be paid on an hourly basis or by piece-rate. Thus, the contract may include a series of complicated and technical provisions describing each job in the plant and the quality and rate of output which applies to that job. In other cases the contracts are quite informal, merely stating the wage rates to be paid for certain types of skills. And in some instances, particularly in the printing and construction industries, the amounts actually paid may exceed what is required by the written contract. If some incentive plan is to be included in the wage payments,

[5] Jack Barbash, *Labor Unions in Action* (New York: Harper & Brothers, 1948), pp. 84–86.

it will be spelled out, e.g., a normal rate of output will be defined along with a schedule of higher rates of pay that may be earned by exceeding the normal rate of output.

Extra payments may be made for special aspects of particular jobs: travel time, clean-up time, night work, or working where it is very hot or very cold. Some of these special problems relating to wage provisions are referred to as fringe benefits. These are discussed below, but it should be recognized that they are really part of the economic gain resulting from the job. Generally, one of the more difficult aspects of bargaining is involved in determining the appropriate wage differentials and fringe benefits for the different job classifications, causing disputes not only between unions and management, but also between different factions within the union.

Limitations on hours to be worked usually come in the form of penalty rates (one and a half or two times the hourly rate) for time worked beyond some specified amount, often forty hours in the week, but an increasing number of contracts set the normal work week at less than forty hours. The Fair Labor Standards Act, adopted by the federal government in 1938 and covering many industries involved in interstate commerce, requires overtime—"time-and-a-half"—payments for hours worked beyond forty in one week. Historically, the goal of unions in charging penalty rates has not been to increase take-home pay, but rather to spread the scarce job opportunity among more members. As a practical matter, workers are generally anxious to work overtime in order to earn the extra income.

Unions attempt to control working conditions by including a statement of working rules in the collective agreement. Since materials handled, machinery used, skills and physical exertion required, etc., differ considerably from industry to industry, each bargaining situation creates its own working rules. In industries such as railroads and construction, the working rules have been a leading bone of contention between employers and unions. They cover such things as the ratio of men to machines, the number of men required to complete a certain job, the amount of time required to do a certain job, the ratio of apprentices to master craftsmen, the amount of rest time that should be permitted on a particular job, and so on. For a number of unions, working rules serve as a device for expanding the job opportunity, spreading a given amount of work among more union members, and for corralling more jobs within the union's jurisdiction. This is accomplished by making the job last longer or by requiring more men than are needed to complete the job.

Working Rules and Technological Change

Early in this chapter, we noted that collective bargaining serves the long-run function of providing stability in a changing environment. One of the severest tests of this function is adaptation to technological change. In order to examine some of the problems involved in adjusting working rules to new methods of production, we now digress from our review of the contents of collective agreements.

If an economy is to enjoy rising standards of living, it must have an unending stream of innovations, bringing increased output per man-hour. A business firm, to maintain its competitive position, must have a large measure of flexibility in introducing new methods. But workers naturally desire protection against changes which threaten their jobs and income. Finding a harmonious solution to the aspirations of the firm and the security of the employees places a heavy burden on both the negotiative and administrative aspects of collective bargaining. As new contracts are negotiated, they must spell out the ratio of men to machines, normal output per day, and so forth, in a manner which takes changing conditions into account. Conflict is almost certain to arise if technology has changed drastically since the last contract was signed, particularly if the union interprets management's demands for modified working rules as meaning harder work or fewer jobs. Even after agreement has been reached on the new contract, problems of interpretation will occur because technological change does not wait for the next period of negotiation. In fact, any major innovation sets off a chain reaction of smaller technological changes, each one testing the administration of the contract. The judicial arm of industrial jurisprudence may be under constant pressure as workers complain about new job assignments and wage rates. When old departments are closed and new ones started, considerable friction results from the wholesale shift in jobs.

Bargaining over automation—the name given to much recent technological change—illustrates some of the points we have been making. When new automated processes are introduced, the entire job structure may be changed. Old jobs cease to exist and new job descriptions are needed. There is a change in the relationship between skilled workers and apprentices and the ratio at which they should be employed. For example, it may have been previous practice to employ one apprentice for each three craftsmen and advance the apprentice to full craftsman status within four years. New conditions may permit more apprentices and allow them to advance more rapidly, particularly if they are upgraded from a semi-skilled job where they have already gained valuable experience. The United Automobile Workers won agreement from Ford to rescind the previous maximum age limit of twenty-six for new apprentices, and thereby made it possible for unskilled workers replaced by automation to move into training programs. The rule change permitted one person over twenty-six for each two under that age.

Automation frequently shifts work from one department to another. Shop practices may vary between the departments, causing confusion and misunderstanding among the men transferred; thus, methods of sharing overtime may be different, safety rules may be more strictly enforced, or time allowed to turn in worn tools for new ones may be more restricted. Automation typically reduces the amount of control the worker exercises over the rate of production. Hence, jobs formerly under piece-rate and the associated working rules are placed on time payment with a new set of working rules.

Of course, technological change has implications going far beyond working rules. Over the long run, it is improvements in productivity that make wage increases possible. Wages are often increased when technological changes are introduced in order to stimulate greater cooperation from the workers. The surge of automation may give additional impetus to the continuous trend in reducing the work week. A downward adjustment in hours would help to offset workers' fears for the security of their jobs. Training programs will have to be modified to meet the new job requirements. Finally, seniority provisions and grievance procedures will need reconsideration.[6]

Promotion and Layoff

Returning now to the main theme of this chapter, a review of the contents of the collective agreement, we look at promotion and layoff provisions. Since they stand so close to the worker's immediate security and his aspirations for the future, unions attempt to bring them under the purview of collective bargaining.

Promotion and layoff are generally controlled by the seniority provisions in the contract, which may take many different forms. Basically, they consist of granting special recognition for the amount of time a worker has been in the employ of a firm; the longer the term, the greater the protection against layoff, and the greater the likelihood of promotion.

In mass production industries, with big firms employing many workers,

[6] Robert L. Aronson, "Automation—Challenge to Collective Bargaining?" in Harold W. Davey, Howard S. Kaltenborn, and Stanley H. Ruttenberg (editors), *New Dimensions in Collective Bargaining* (New York: Harper & Brothers, 1959), pp. 47–70.

the seniority provisions constitute the heart of the security provided to the individual under the contract. They protect the employee against arbitrary discharge and discrimination in promotion or job assignment. With adequate protection, the union member is in a better position to defend his rights against his foreman; in short, he can "talk back."

A typical collective bargaining provision relating seniority to layoff is the following:

> Layoffs shall take place within each occupational classification in the following order: 1) Temporary employees shall be laid off first; 2) Employees having less than 6 months' service shall be laid off in such order as to cause the minimum disturbance to the business and when practicable in reverse order of employment; 3) Employees having more than 6 months' service shall be laid off in reverse order of seniority.[7]

The forms which seniority may take vary with its coverage, depending on whether it is department-wide, plant-wide, or company-wide. For example, when it is department-wide, an individual with less tenure than anyone else in the department is the first one to be laid off, even though he may have more seniority than employees in other departments in the same plant. Where seniority is wider than simply in a department, the problem of "bumping" may become important. An employee may be laid off by one department but, because of his length of service, may be put into another department where he displaces—bumps—some other worker with a shorter employment record, who in turn may bump another employee, etc. Or, an employee with considerable seniority may be transferred from one department to another and promoted over the top of workers with long service in that department. The opportunities of these workers for promotion and higher pay are thereby delayed. Human relations problems are usually associated with regulating promotions and layoffs. Some workers are going to feel cheated by plant-wide policies and others by department-wide policies. Plant-wide provisions may be resisted by management on the grounds that they cost more in terms of disrupted work and training for unfamiliar jobs.

Management's greatest complaint about seniority provisions is that they substitute length of service for merit. The man that management believes to be most qualified and deserving of promotion may have to wait years before his turn comes. It therefore becomes difficult to establish a sequence of progressively more responsible jobs from which new supervisory personnel may be recruited. Unions counter these arguments by claiming

---

[7] Quoted in *Analysis of Layoff, Recall and Work-Sharing Procedures in Union Contracts*, U. S. Department of Labor, Bureau of Labor Statistics, Bulletin No. 1209, 1957, p. 7.

that employers would promote favorites, often nonunion workers. Furthermore, if an outstanding worker is clearly recognized (spotting merit may be difficult where the pace of production is determined by the machine), he may be shifted into a staff job or training program not covered by the collective agreement.

To provide management with some assurance that incompetent workers will not move into important jobs, the seniority clause generally states that the employee's rights to promotion are qualified by his ability to do the job. One typical method is: the worker with the longest service is given the first opportunity to demonstrate his ability in the higher level job; if he is unable to perform satisfactorily, the worker with the next greatest seniority is given an opportunity.

Whenever technological changes are occurring rapidly, seniority becomes exceedingly important as old jobs become obsolete and new opportunities appear. Thus, the adoption of more highly automated production techniques in the automobile industry has led to the opening of new plants and closing or complete remodeling of old ones. Workers, protected by seniority, have moved into the new jobs, often receiving training in new skills. Large-scale technological changes often require new definitions of the unit covered by seniority. Automation may bring a shift toward plant-wide or company-wide coverage because old departmental divisions become meaningless.

The greatest value of seniority for the ordinary worker is the protection it affords against layoffs resulting from economy-wide depressions. Many unionized industries are subject to wide fluctuations in employment over the course of succeeding periods of prosperity and depression. After an employee has devoted a number of years of his life to a single firm, he believes he has the right to expect some security in return. When "hard times" appear, workers have good reason to worry about meeting payments on their mortgages, refrigerators, children's education, etc. Several years of seniority, recognized through collective bargaining, at least reduces these worries. No nephew of the foreman, or "bright young squirt" without a family, is going to steal his job. And when the worker does fall victim to unemployment, he knows he will be called back sooner than others with less seniority, a system he can understand and respect.

Rigid observance of seniority is not the only way of meeting the problem of depression unemployment. An alternative is sharing the limited number of jobs. One possible approach is to lay off all those with less than two years of seniority, and put the remaining work force on a three-day week. Other variations of seniority and job rotation could be used. But again, seniority plays a role in protecting the experienced employee, and his employment is controlled by procedures he can understand, which he—through his union—helped to create.

One special exception usually made in the seniority provisions is for union officials. They are granted "super-seniority," making them the last to be laid off and the first to be recalled. The reason for the exception, of course, is to provide for continuity in the union's affairs at the workplace.

Another device adopted by some unions to fend off unemployment among their members is to restrict subcontracting. Employers subcontract some of their work to other employers when their own facilities are operating at capacity or when they can get lower costs than if the work is done in their own plants. It is common practice in communications, utilities, and the apparel industries to include clauses in the collective agreement that prevent the employer from subcontracting regular work during slack periods.

Grievance Procedure

Disputes over the interpretation and application of the contract to particular cases are settled through the grievance procedure. Thus, it serves the judicial function within the system of industrial jurisprudence. A smoothly operating grievance procedure avoids strikes which might otherwise occur over misunderstandings of the exact meaning of the agreement. Workers are less likely to rely on force if they are certain of getting a fair hearing for their complaints.

Typically, the grievance procedure is set into motion when an employee, feeling that he has been denied his rights under the contract, complains to his union steward, or his foreman, or to both simultaneously. As step 1, the union steward, the foreman, and the employee discuss the grievance. The grievance may be settled at this point; if so, that ends the matter. If agreement is not reached at this stage, step 2 is taken: the supervisor of the division, the plant industrial relations manager, or perhaps the plant superintendent in smaller-sized firms confers with a shop committee or the local union president. If the grievance is not settled at this stage, the process continues. Step 3: the international representative or the business agent, or both, meet with a vice president in charge of industrial relations or the top personnel man of the firm. If a settlement is not reached at this stage, the final step 4 is taken: the grievance is submitted to arbitration. An impartial umpire or a panel of three reviews the grievance and issues a decision which is customarily binding on both sides.[8]

Once the dispute is settled, whether at step 1 or step 4, it becomes, in effect, a part of the contract. Consequently, both sides should approach the grievance procedure only after carefully studying the contract and the facts in the particular case. Unfortunately, management and unions have often neglected this responsibility, hence causing needless wrangling and poor contract administration. Contrariwise, a number of unions offer training programs to their stewards, and special classes for foremen are conducted by many firms.

One item often sharply debated by management and unions, even though it receives little general publicity, is the amount of time that stewards may take to look after grievances. It is common practice to allow stewards and other officials a number of hours each week—paid by employers at the regular hourly rate—to tend to the needs of the members. Unions claim the time is necessary to gather facts accurately, and will stoutly resist any reduction in time since that would weaken union-worker contacts. Management believes that stewards sometimes go around the shop looking for trouble: fomenting grievances on unimportant matters and disrupting regular work. In any case, management strives to keep the time to a minimum.

The grievance procedure, along with its primary function of settling disputes, serves as a form of union security. The union is likely to fight harder to win the grievance cases of union members than of non-members covered by the contract. Hence, workers have an additional reason for joining the union.

The day-to-day living under the contract, governed by the grievance procedure, is less spectacular and less newsworthy than the negotiation of new contracts, but, from the point of view of the individual union member, it is his primary contact with collective bargaining.

Fringe Benefits

Fringe benefits are economic rewards received by employees beyond their basic wage rate. Some are sponsored by the government, others by employers, and still others come through bargaining. Each fringe benefit adds to the employer's labor cost, but some of them do not become income to the worker until he is injured, retired, on vacation, working on a holiday, or in some other special category.

[8] This aspect of collective bargaining, the administration of the contract through grievance procedure and arbitration, is discussed in more detail in Chapter 11.

Fringe benefits sponsored by the government include old age, survivors, and disability insurance, unemployment compensation, etc. Those sponsored by employers, separately from collective bargaining, include free coffee at rest periods, special low prices for the purchase of the corporation's common stock, etc. Typical benefits resulting from collective bargaining are: health and welfare plans, vacation pay, special pay for travel time, and regular wages while on jury duty.[9]

To a certain extent, fringe benefits are substitutes for wage increases. They have grown particularly fast during periods when wages could not be increased, yet union bargaining power was at a maximum, for example, during war periods when wage controls were in effect. The total cost amounts to anywhere between 5 and 50 per cent of the payroll, with the most common amount being between 20 and 25 per cent. Over the past two decades the percentage has been rising: fringe benefits have been rising faster than wage rates.

Management Prerogatives

Management prerogatives mean the right to make decisions without first conferring with the union. That is, management exercises unilateral authority within the area covered by the prerogatives; whereas other decisions must be jointly made with the union. Management has been concerned over the decreasing area in which its prerogatives remain unchallenged, and has therefore attempted to write into the contract certain restrictions on the union's invasion of what it considers its rightful authority. A glance at Table 8-A indicates the increasing tendency for such provisions to appear in contracts.

In some cases the provisions state that all things not covered by the contract are reserved for management authority. In other cases the provisions spell out the areas in which decisions may be made by management without first conferring with the union. For example, the following may be specifically reserved: number of employees, nature of goods to be produced, price of final product, location of new plants, dividend policy, accounting and financial techniques, etc. In other areas management may initiate actions, but the contract grants the union the right to file a grievance if it believes the action is unjust. Typical areas in which prerogatives are exercised in this fashion are: scheduling production, introducing new production methods, and setting pay scales for new jobs.

Basically, all union activity is an invasion of management prerogatives,

---

[9] Fringe benefits resulting from collective bargaining are discussed in some detail in Chapter 21.

hence it has been one of the thorniest problems of collective bargaining. Tannenbaum's theory of the labor movement gives special emphasis to this aspect of union-management relations. All the issues covered by the collective agreement were at one time matters determined solely by the employer. It appears that over the long run unions will continue to widen the sphere of subjects which fall within the scope of collective bargaining. Also, it is probable that management will vigorously resist this whittling away of its authority. An interesting case of this occurred in 1957 when Walter Reuther suggested that the automobile firms reduce the price of their cars by $100 and in return the union would moderate its demands in the following year when the new contract was to be negotiated. The presidents of the automobile firms replied in no uncertain terms that determining the price of the product was their prerogative.

The historical development of the management prerogative issue is a good example of the application of Perlman's broad definition of collective bargaining. The inferior social group has enhanced its sovereignty as opposed to the superior group.

SUMMARY

Collective bargaining serves the long-run function of stabilizing the pace of social and economic change, allowing competing institutions to move to their new power positions. In a more immediate sense it establishes a temporary truce between opposing parties. If bargaining is successful, the truce is not violated, even though neither party is satisfied with its terms and strives to change them at the earliest opportunity. The agreement creates a system of industrial jurisprudence, which includes a legislative branch in the negotiating sessions, an executive branch in the union stewards and the foremen, and a judicial branch in the grievance machinery.

The provisions included in collective agreements may be divided into four categories: 1) union security, ranging from mere recognition to the closed shop; 2) worker security, involving seniority protection covering promotion, job assignment, and layoff; 3) economic items, including wages, hours, working rules, and fringe benefits; and 4) management protection, attempting to stem the tide of broadening the scope of collective bargaining. Once the contract is negotiated, a conflict occurring in any one of these categories may be processed through the grievance procedure, the administrative aspect of collective bargaining. The over-all view of typical contract provisions presented in this chapter serves as a framework within which we will fit the pieces in the following chapters.

DISCUSSION QUESTIONS

1. Discuss fully the meaning of Perlman's statement that collective bargaining "manifests itself equally in politics, legislation, court litigation, government administration, religion, education, and propaganda."

2. Compare and contrast collective bargaining as a process of: 1) social change, 2) a truce agreement, and 3) a system of industrial jurisprudence.

3. Describe how collective bargaining has acted as a technique of social change in this country.

4. In what sense does collective bargaining create a system of industrial jurisprudence?

5. Draw an analogy between a collective bargaining contract and an armed truce.

6. Define the following terms: recognition as exclusive bargaining agent, closed shop, union shop, Taft-Hartley Act modification of union shop, maintenance of membership, preferential hiring, checkoff.

7. Drawing on what you learned in earlier chapters, why has the closed shop been a traditional demand of American unions?

8. Under what conditions would it be to a firm's economic benefit to agree to a union security clause in its collective bargaining contract?

9. Beyond its effect on the members' income, why do unions insist on premium pay for overtime work?

10. Why do unions insist on including working rules in collective agreements? What is the relationship between working rules and technological change?

11. Why do unions place so much emphasis on seniority?

12. What function is performed by the grievance procedure? What steps are normally included in the grievance procedure?

BIBLIOGRAPHY

Barbash, Jack. *Labor Unions in Action.* New York: Harper & Brothers, 1948.

Chamberlain, Neil W. *Collective Bargaining.* New York: McGraw-Hill Book Company, 1951.

Committee on Causes of Industrial Peace Under Collective Bargaining of the National Planning Association. *Fundamentals of Labor Peace.* Washington: National Planning Association, 1953.

Davey, Harold W.; Kaltenborn, Howard S.; and Ruttenberg, Stanley H. (Editors). *New Dimensions in Collective Bargaining.* New York: Harper & Brothers, 1959.

Dunlop, John T., and Healy, James J. *Collective Bargaining.* Homewood: Richard D. Irwin, Inc., 1953.

Harbison, Frederick H., and Coleman, John R. *Goals and Strategy in Collective Bargaining*. New York: Harper & Brothers, 1951.

Slichter, Sumner. *The Challenge of Industrial Relations*. Ithaca: Cornell University Press, 1947.

U. S. Bureau of Labor Statistics. *A Guide to Labor-Management Relations in the United States*. Bulletin No. 1225. Washington: Government Printing Office, 1958.

UNION APPROACH TO COLLECTIVE BARGAINING

9

A union is an economic institution, but it is much more than just that. It is concerned not only with the economic welfare of its members, but also with their personal status and security. Beyond that, it must have regard for its own interests as an institution, protecting itself against employer opposition, raiding unions, and apathy or factionalism among members, and enhancing its growth prospects. A union without genuine survival power cannot look after the economic and personal needs of its members.

Therefore, in approaching collective bargaining, a union has a series of goals, some economic and some noneconomic, not all of which can be won from the employer at any one time. Furthermore, a number of the goals are in conflict with each other. How does a union decide which goals are to receive priority? That is, what causes a union to bargain for fifteen cents an hour instead of striving to win a union shop, or to bargain for a guaranteed annual wage as opposed to broader seniority? What tactics do unions use to achieve their goals? Unfortunately, it is impossible to give universal answers which fit all situations, since the economic environment, the personalities of the leadership, and the characteristics of the membership vary so widely from one union to another.

UNION COLLECTIVE BARGAINING GOALS

There are many ways of classifying the goals unions seek through collective bargaining. The two categories used here are economic and noneconomic; however, they may also be classified according to the members as individuals opposed to the union as an institution, according to leader versus rank and file, or according to intra-union interest groups, such as the young against the old or one group of skills against another.

It should not be inferred that one set of goals must always be in conflict with another: the objectives of the leaders often may be in complete harmony with the desires of the rank and file. However, each time a union negotiates a contract, a choice must be made as to which goals will be given priority. In making this choice, a conflict may occur on the basis of one or more of the classifications suggested above.

It follows, then, that the priority ranking of the demands by the union represents a compromise between the different pressures within the union. This compromise must, of course take into account the prevailing economic environment. The labor leader who maintains his position over a long period of time in a union where the lines of conflict are sharply drawn must necessarily be an astute politician. The union, therefore, becomes a political institution adjusting itself to the pressures behind each of the different sets of goals.

Economic Goals

The unions' major economic goal is constantly increasing wages. In general terms, this means "more, more, and more" or "as much as we can get." This could mean the maximum wage rate, or the maximum wage bill, or some variation of the two. The maximum wage rate, if the union ignores possible unemployment caused, may be much higher than the wage rate which maximizes the wage bill. The wage bill is the number of workers employed multiplied by the wage rate. The choice between these alternatives involves a conflict between those workers who are secure in their jobs and those who are not. The burden of the unemployment will be borne by those in the marginal jobs or those with little seniority. Thus, after a wage increase, a multi-plant firm might close down its less efficient plants, and marginal firms might be forced out of business. Of course, workers who are already unemployed will find it more difficult to secure employment. On the other hand, if the union seeks to maximize the total wage bill, more workers may be employed, but at a lower wage rate.

Generally, unions place greater emphasis on the wage rate than on the total amount paid out in wages by an employer. Many unions, particularly those in manufacturing industries, believe that their wage rates can have little or no direct effect on employment in the firm or the industry.[1] Therefore, the best technique to enhance the economic position of the members is through raising the wage rate. However, there are some exceptions to this, particularly in the construction and clothing industries. For example, a wage increase of house painters may have a significant effect on the do-it-yourself trend; or a wage increase in a unionized clothing firm may shift employment to unorganized firms. Hence, where the employment effect of a wage increase is substantial, affects a large share of the members, and can be predicted with a high degree of certainty, the union may moderate its wage demands. Furthermore, where there is competition between union and nonunion firms, demands will have to be adapted to this situation.

The fact that unions generally emphasize the wage rate rather than employment does not mean that unions neglect the latter. However, the approach to this goal is usually not through wage rate adjustments, but rather through regulation of hours, seniority, and working rules. Thus, wherever unemployment increases significantly, unions will propagandize and bargain for shorter work weeks rather than decreased wages. Some unions adopt share-the-work schemes in periods of reduced employment, restricting members to a three or four-day work week. There have been instances, however, in which unions agreed to wage reductions. This occurred during the postwar period in the textile industry, partly as a result of nonunion competition. The question of a wage reduction was put to a vote among the workers when high labor costs threatened the existence of the Studebaker plant at South Bend, Indiana, in 1954. The local of the United Automobile Workers urged its members to vote in favor of the reduction, which they did, even though other workers were receiving increases at the time.

Unions also attempt to enhance the employment of their members by devising and enforcing work rules. As noted in the previous chapter, these vary substantially from plant to plant and industry to industry. In many cases they are clearly restrictions on production, limiting the type of machinery used and the speed at which the machinery is to be operated, or requiring needless work to be done or unnecessary musicians or stagehands for a theatrical production. In some instances the work rules are designed to protect the life and limb of the employees or to avoid "speed-ups" (regulating the rate of flow of an assembly line) and unhealthful working conditions (how long at any one time a worker

[1] The highly controversial relationship between wages and employment is developed in later chapters, particularly Chapter 19.

should be required to be in the immediate vicinity of great heat in a steel mill, and how long the intervening rest periods should be).

Whether a particular work rule is "featherbedding," restricting production or requiring unnecessary workers, or is necessary for the safety of the workers, is often a matter of opinion over which management and unions will dispute. Sometimes the safety of customers is also involved. The locomotive firemen's union claims that one of its members should be on hand in diesel engines in case something happens to the engineer, or in case of fire. The airline pilots argue that the new large jet aircraft require a third pilot for safe operation. In some instances what was originally necessary for the workers' safety may, after a change in the methods of production, become outdated. Nevertheless, the union may still insist on the working rule in order to provide more jobs for the members. The loaded term, "featherbedding," is used by management, particularly in the railroad industry, in order to win public support for its desired changes in working rules. Sharp retorts usually come from unions, insisting that their members work hard. The railroad unions have invented an equally loaded term, "thornbedding," to make propaganda gains for their side. It stands for harsh working rules demanded by management.

In deciding which economic goals to pursue most vigorously, unions must choose, then, between wages, hours, and working rules. Furthermore, fringe benefits should be included, since they add to the employer's labor cost.

Noneconomic Goals

Through collective bargaining, unions seek to secure two types of noneconomic goals: satisfaction of the workers' social and psychological needs and satisfaction of the unions' institutional drives. Writing in 1942, Golden and Ruttenberg observed that the "dynamic quality, the militancy, and the crusading spirit of the labor movement, especially of CIO, in the last decade were nurtured by the failure of management to satisfy the noneconomic needs of workers."[2] What are these needs and how are they satisfied through collective bargaining?

The social and psychological needs center around the worker's desire to express his individuality and at the same time to be an accepted member of his social group. Workers, if they are to feel that they have some distinct personal worth, must be able to complain to their employers

[2] Clinton S. Golden and Harold J. Ruttenberg, *The Dynamics of Industrial Democracy* (New York: Harper & Brothers, 1942), p. 21.

without fear of reprisal. They want to be more than a lump of economic assets in a depersonalized enterprise. An established grievance procedure and the protection of seniority help to make this possible. For example, an employee may object to a job assignment or a wage rate as being improper, and the employer must listen to his complaint if the union supports it. The protection afforded the individual is well expressed by a glass worker:

> The boss just can't up and fire us because he doesn't like us or because some-one else tries to influence him to dislike us. He can't take us off our jobs to work somewhere else if we have the right seniority. . . . If we didn't have our union we wouldn't have our seniority nor our jobs. The boss would have us fired already because, well, maybe we're too large, too ugly, too old or maybe just anything.[3]

The worker's feelings of security, of protection against arbitrary or spiteful actions by his supervisor, are of immeasurable value to him. For this reason the union is worthwhile to many workers regardless of whether it is able to bring them higher wages than they otherwise would receive. It satisfies the need of feeling secure in their jobs and in their status as individuals.

Tannenbaum, whose theory of unions was considered in Chapter 7, provides us with a somewhat different way of saying much the same thing. The union is a reaction to the impersonalization foisted upon the workers by the shop, mine, and factory. Instead of vigorously competing with each other for the employer's favor, workers prefer to join together and present a solid front to the employer. This, of course, is not true for all employees: some prefer the competitive struggle, independently relying on their wits and ability.

The union satisfies another type of social-psychological need by providing an opportunity for the worker to become active in a social organization in association with his fellow-workers. Almost all of us have an urge to belong to one or more groups in which we are accepted as equals with other members, be it church, Rotary, Junior League, college fraternity, or union. Organizations perform a vital social function for people who feel a great need for recognition by a group. Securing this personal satisfaction is a major objective of many active unionists who serve as shop stewards, committeemen, etc.

The second variety of noneconomic goals sought through collective

[3] Quoted in Jack Barbash, *Labor Unions in Action* (New York: Harper & Brothers, 1948), p. 80.

bargaining is aimed at protection of the union as an institution. Although business unions came into being primarily to satisfy the economic desires of their membership, to achieve this goal requires their continued existence as going institutions. When an employer threatens to break a union, or when a rival union attempts to raid its membership, the fight to protect itself becomes more urgent to a union than securing an immediate wage increase. The union may accept less in the way of economic concessions in return for one of the union security clauses discussed in the previous chapter.

DETERMINATION OF GOALS

Unions have a wide range of economic and noneconomic goals. How do they decide which ones are the most important at any particular stage of collective bargaining? Obviously, they cannot win all of them at once. All goals are in conflict with each other since employers are willing to make only a limited number of concessions at any particular bargaining session. Therefore, the union must have some mechanism for determining an order of precedence. Making these decisions necessarily involves a series of political compromises which, hopefully, will maximize the satisfaction of the contending interest groups, or, perhaps more accurately, minimize the dissatisfactions.

There are a number of frequently heard explanations of how unions decide on the priority. Some say "the employer gets the kind of union he deserves." That is, if the employer distrusts the union, the latter will respond by demanding rigid union security and grievance provisions, and will attempt a wholesale invasion of management prerogatives. Others say it depends entirely on what the union leader believes will keep him in power. Still others phrase their pat answer in terms of the dominant groups within the union, claiming that a particular nationality or skill group determines all policies. Enough instances can be found where each of these explanations has a sufficient degree of truth to give it some plausibility. However, any decision involving so many dynamic relationships cannot be generalized for all unions in such a simple manner.

There are five factors which enter into a union's determination of the priority of its collective bargaining goals: 1) economic conditions relevant to the bargaining relationship, 2) precedent of recent major agreements, 3) inter-union rivalry, 4) influence of the international, and 5) intra-union influences. The relative importance of these factors varies from one bargaining situation to another.

Economic Conditions

The specific content of bargaining demands rising from the economic goals of unions is partially determined by the conditions prevailing in the economy, the industry, and the firm. For the economy, the relevant conditions are the amount of unemployment and changes in the price level. For the industry and the firm, the relevant conditions are generally the rate of profitability and the current position of the firm and industry in both the labor and product markets. In their approach to bargaining, unions frequently phrase the general economic conditions in terms of "cost-of-living" and the conditions of the firm in terms of "ability-to-pay."

The cost-of-living is used by unions as an argument for higher wages during periods of rising prices and full employment. Although unions generally give more attention to dollar wages than to real wages (purchasing power of dollar wages), a decline in real wages, resulting from an increase in the cost-of-living, is always used as a potent argument for a wage increase, partly because it wins public support. Obviously, unions do not use this argument when prices are falling.

As a firm's earning capacity improves and as this is represented in its profit position, unions demand a share of this increased ability to pay. When profits have been increasing faster than wages, this becomes powerful propaganda for a union wage demand. Furthermore, if workers believe profits are rising rapidly, their notion of what is fair may cause them to exhort their leaders to stress wage demands. Another situation in which workers are likely to believe that they deserve an increase in pay occurs when output per manhour has been rising more rapidly than wages.

A distinction needs to be made between the arguments adopted by unions for propaganda purposes and the real determinants of their goals. The propaganda may be used by the leaders to persuade the membership to approve their policies, and also to win general public support for union goals. But that does not answer the question of what really determines the emphasis a union will put on wage goals in the final critical stages of bargaining for a new contract. Under what conditions are economic considerations of overriding importance in determining union goals?

The question can best be answered in two parts: economy-wide conditions and those pertaining to an industry or firm. When consumer prices have been rising rapidly, wage demands are likely to be given highest priority. Contrariwise, when there is much unemployment, economic demands, with the possible exception of shorter hours, will be postponed in favor of other union goals. The second part of the answer focuses on the profit rate in the industry. If it differs from the average for the economy, the union may adjust its bargaining accordingly. In fact, if a single firm or group of firms has profit rates differing from the rest of the industry, the union may give these firms special consideration. Obviously, if there is nonunion competition within the industry, wage demands will have to be moderated appropriately. A rapidly growing industry—particularly if it is characterized by a high rate of technological change—may be subject to unusually high wage demands, especially if it encounters labor shortages. Finally, since nothing succeeds like success, when a union feels that the employer is vulnerable to a strike, e.g., if he is behind in filling his customers' orders, it may decide that this is the appropriate time to win maximum concessions.

Precedent of Recent Major Agreements

An important determinant of the bargaining demands of any union is the gains made by other unions. Any major bargaining agreement sets a precedent for other unions and employers. It may be a nationwide agreement, covering hundreds of thousands of employees, or it may be local in coverage, between a powerful local and employer. Examples of the former are the rounds of wage increases following World War II. For a number of years a settlement in a major industry, e.g., steel, rubber, or automobiles, served as a pattern which was followed across the nation with only modest variations. Instances of the latter occur frequently in the construction industry, where, for example, the carpenters may reach an agreement which determines the pattern for the bricklayers, metal workers, etc.

Of course, a major agreement does not guarantee that other unions will receive the same concessions; there will be variations around the precedent. Nevertheless, the employers' resistance to similar demands is lessened. Once an important employer makes a given concession, other employers are in a less advantageous position to object to it for public relations reasons. The employer may feel compelled to grant the demand in order to maintain the morale of his workers who are aware of concessions granted by other employers. This would hold true even in firms which are not unionized. Furthermore, unionized employees would be more willing to withstand a long strike after other employers have granted what their employer refuses.

The effect of recent major agreements cuts both ways. That is, it may cause some unions to accept less than they might have been able to receive had no such precedent existed. The unions would have less public sympathy in striking for amounts greater than other unions have accepted. Thus, in the bargaining at General Motors in 1946, the United Automobile Workers went on strike for a nineteen and one-half cents per hour wage increase. However, the United Electrical Workers settled with General Motors for eighteen and one-half cents per hour, only a penny less. This undermined the bargaining strength of the UAW and forced a capitulation at the lower figure.

The importance of major agreements as precedent setters goes beyond merely wages. An outstanding example is the steel settlement of 1950 which included a retirement pension plan and was followed by a wave of agreements which included similar plans. The steel pension plan had been inspired by the success of the United Mine Workers in winning a pension as a result of the (Secretary of Commerce) Krug-Lewis agreement in 1946, when the coal mines were under federal control. Likewise, the duration of the contract (whether it is to be in force for one year or more than one year), the type of seniority granted, and other matters may be affected by other settlements. Nevertheless, it is the economic matters which are most easily influenced. The noneconomic matters are more likely to be uniquely oriented to the specific industry or firm involved in the bargaining. For example, the winning of a favorable seniority provision by a union in a manufacturing industry would not serve as a useful standard for the construction industry where the jobs are typically of short duration. The working rules of the railroad unions, such as those regulating the size of crew for a freight train, are another example of what may be won by one union without serving as a precedent for others.

Inter-Union Rivalry

The ability of a union leader to gain concessions for his union at least equal to those won by other unions affects his status with his constituency, which, of course, is an important reason why major agreements affect settlements in other industries. However, inter-union rivalry has implications beyond merely following precedents. It may involve a struggle for power between leaders of two different unions, or perhaps between leaders of two different factions of the same union. An ambitious local leader or regional director who wants to rise in the union hierarchy seeks to make greater gains than his rivals. To the extent that he influences the bargaining demands of his local or region, he gives priority to those demands which will enhance his position. In some instances the leader has the support of his membership in a "patriotic" drive to make the union a leader of the entire union movement. The automobile workers' and steel workers' unions seem to be motivated by this type of rivalry.

Leadership rivalry is the lifeblood of unionism in the United States. After all, the American trade union is pragmatic to the core, neutral in ideology, and weak in political purpose. In the absence of competition for the allegiance of workers, there would be little else to ensure its militance and guarantee its role as an agency of protest. Moreover, rivalry has been the most effective stimulus to organize the unorganized.[4]

Perhaps the clearest expression of this rivalry was response of the AFL to the rise of the CIO, forcing the old federation to shed its lethargy. Unfortunately, inter-union rivalry has occasionally led to union activity severely castigated by the public, such as jurisdictional strikes.

Thus, inter-union rivalry is motivated partly by a desire to lead the American labor movement in the "right" direction, as in the competition between the UAW and USW to win the most favorable guaranteed annual wage plan. And it is motivated partly by the drive of leaders to accumulate more power and influence both within and outside of the labor movement. Whenever the rivalry is keen, the determination of union goals is influenced by a factor which is outside of the immediate union-management relationship.

Influence of the International

Recent issues in collective bargaining have brought a consolidation and expansion of the bargaining authority of the internationals relative to that of the locals. The technical complications of negotiating a sound pension plan or a guaranteed annual wage requires professional competence beyond the range of most local officials. Negotiating and administering a contract in compliance with the Taft-Hartley and Landrum-Griffin Acts extend the need for legal counsel. The local treasury generally cannot afford full-time legal services, hence this falls to the international. There appears to be no reason to expect a reversal of the trend toward increasing international authority over the determination of the priority of bargaining demands.

There are, however, many variations between unions, as illustrated

[4] Arthur M. Ross, *Trade Union Wage Policy* (Berkeley, University of California Press, 1953), p. 63. Quoted by permission of University of California Press.

in the San Francisco Bay area. The building service workers, representing one extreme, are decentralized. The locals have large independent strike funds and bargain independently. The steel workers represent the opposite extreme. The international negotiates across-the-board wage increases with the parent corporation, which, in turn, apply to the locals in each plant. The local contracts require approval by the unions' top officers and are negotiated with the international representative participating. The teamsters are between these two extremes. The negotiation is done locally, but the contract must receive the approval of the international, and permission must be granted before the local is free to strike. This device is sufficient to give the international substantial control over the bargaining of the teamsters' locals.

There are several factors which influence the degree of control exercised by the international union over the local wage bargain. Unions organized in local-market industries can, and do, permit more local autonomy than those organized in national-market industries. Unions which have grown from the top down, such as the Steelworkers, are more centralized than those which have grown from the bottom up, such as the Clothing Workers. Personal characteristics and historical accidents undoubtedly play a role.[5]

The increase in the international's control over bargaining influences the choice between various union goals, tending to give greater emphasis to union-wide goals as opposed to strictly local goals. The international officers and representatives are generally shrewder and more mature bargainers; they are the professionals. They have a better understanding of the employer's ability to pay, of the impact of any bargaining demand on the entire industry. In some cases this will cause them to bargain for larger amounts, while in other cases they may seek less than the locals desire, depending on the economic conditions affecting the industry at the time. When the international exercises a large amount of control in the bargaining, less emphasis is generally placed on such purely local issues as speed-up of the production line, discharge of a single employee, or setting the wage rate for a new job. It is not that the international is uninterested in these matters, but rather that it sees them in a broader scope. For example, the workers in one local of an industrial union may be most concerned about the speed at which the assembly line operates, claiming it causes too much fatigue. They therefore urge the international to make this a major bargaining issue. However, if the great majority of other locals in the international prefer to concentrate attention on wages, the desires of the particular local may be passed over.

[5] *Ibid.*, pp. 35–36. Quoted by permission of University of California Press.

Intra-Union Influences

Within a union, as in almost any other organization of individuals, there are special interest groups who clash over the choice of goals for the organization. Attention has been given to two areas of interest group conflicts up to this point: the union as an institution as opposed to the rank and file, and the international as opposed to the local. Since there are so many areas of potential conflict, only the more typical ones are outlined here, with no attempt at a careful analysis of each one.

Different skill groups within the union are liable to disagree over pay differentials; they may take different views of technological changes within the plant, since each group is likely to be affected differently by such changes. A conflict may develop between the more productive and the less productive workers, the former favoring an incentive pay plan which would increase their earnings, the latter favoring straight time payment. Conflicts between the day shift and night shift over the amount of the differential are not uncommon; since the employer will grant only a limited total amount of monetary concessions, a larger night differential may mean a lower average wage for the day shift. Different age groups are likely to have different bargaining goals; the older workers would favor pension plans, whereas younger workers have little interest in these. The younger workers with less seniority would favor a guaranteed annual wage plan, whereas those with considerable seniority would have little to gain from such a plan. The United Automobile Workers engaged in an extensive educational campaign among its members in order to overcome opposition to its proposed guaranteed annual wage plan. Younger workers may want seniority to play a lesser role in wage increases and promotion opportunities, whereas older workers may give greater emphasis to seniority. A conflict may develop within a union over whether to seek plant-wide or department-wide seniority, when one or two departments in a firm are contracting while others are expanding. In some unions nationality differences play an important role: Community religious and social differences are likely to be carried over to the work environment. Where one nationality holds many of the union offices, claims of favoritism on the part of other nationality groups may appear. Finally, splinter groups within a union may develop over the control of political power, fostered by ambitious workers who are anxious to unseat the present union leadership.

The different forces impinging upon the union's choice of bargaining goals may be summarized as follows:

Union leaders are not free to consider the problem of wages purely as an exercise in economics. They are leaders of a mass movement, subject to a variety of pressures and cross pressures, who meet the needs of their membership or risk replacement at the next election. If wage pressures are mounting, then an increase must be sought, even though the leaders are more fearful than the membership that a lower volume of employment might result. Similarly, in dividing the gains that can be won at any particular time, the leaders must balance somehow the rival claims of workers at different levels of skill. The less skilled workers in an industrial union may keep the gains equal to all because of their numbers and voting strength, or the skilled minority may obtain a larger share by a threat to bolt the union and join a rival craft group. A factional conflict within the union may compel the officers to seek wage gains at an inauspicious time, lest the failure to act vigorously become the source of attack during an impending election campaign. . . .

Although wages are important, workers may be more disturbed over a non-wage matter that directly affects them and makes life in the plant unpleasant. Sometimes working conditions are at fault, sometimes the lack of lockers or the condition of the rest room is the issue, sometimes it is the way in which supervisors address workers, sometimes it is the laying off or promotion of workers by favoritism rather than by seniority or ability. Members of minority racial or national groups, similarly, are alert to any evidence of discrimination, not only against themselves but against any members of their minority. These are immediate issues that all workers understand and to which many react emotionally . . .[6]

Since most union members are apathetic, the active minority may have little or no difficulty in securing the priority of goals it desires. However, the apathetic members may rise up and unseat the leadership, or revolt and form a new union if they feel cheated out of their fair share of collective bargaining rewards. The leader must be an astute politician in satisfying all competing groups.

UNION BARGAINING: WEAPONS AND STRATEGY

In order to win concessions from an employer, a union must be able to exert pressure effectively. Collective bargaining would be an empty institution if the union did not have the capacity to place some degree of financial strain on the employer. There are many ways in which this can be done, directly, as by striking or threatening to strike, or indirectly, by fostering dissatisfactions which lead to low morale, and hence lower production. The direct techniques are generally most important during the negotiation of a new contract; the indirect techniques apply to contract administration. The chief direct techniques are strikes, boycotts,

[6] Joel Seidman, "The Labor Union as an Organization." By permission from *Industrial Conflict,* edited by Kornhauser, Dubin & Ross. Copyright, 1954. McGraw-Hill Book Co., Inc., p. 116.

and picketing. They may be used separately or in conjunction with one another.

A slowdown—a group of workers holding production to less than normal rates of output—is another direct technique, but it differs from a strike in that it grows out of spontaneous reactions of employees, and is generally not organized by the union. In fact, it sometimes occurs among nonunion workers; however, it does require a cohesive group acting with a high degree of solidarity. Its most frequent cause is dissatisfaction with the piece-rates which the employer has set for the job. The slowdown has been used as a technique for compelling the employer to go around the union and deal directly with the workers involved.[7] Since it is generally not a part of union bargaining strategy, no further attention will be given to it here.

The Strike

A strike is a collective cessation of work on the part of a group of employees with the intent of bringing the employer's production to a halt and forcing him to grant specified concessions. (In relatively few instances, the concessions desired are not made clear.) Strikes may be classified according to their purposes: 1) economic goals, to compel the employer to make a bargaining concession; 2) organizing, to compel the employer to recognize and bargain with the union; 3) a protest against an unfair labor practice, to compel the employer to stop some specific action which is, in the mind of the union, an unfair labor practice under the Taft-Hartley Act; 4) political aims (often involving what is called a general strike because its success depends on the cooperation of many unions; however, it is rarely used in this country), to win some concession from a governmental agency; and 5) jurisdictional rivalry, to compel the employer to assign a particular job to one union as opposed to another union.

A "wildcat strike" may be for any one of the above purposes. It is distinguished from other strikes by being called in opposition to the top union authorities, typically occurring when management has taken some action which is violently opposed by the members, such as discharging one of the employees. Under such circumstances, rather than taking the complaint through the grievance procedure and patiently waiting for this to remedy the wrong—if the employer was wrong—the workers rush off their jobs, hoping to compel the employer to rehire the discharged employee immediately.

[7] Richard S. Hammett, Joel Seidman, and Jack London, "The Slowdown as a Union Tactic," *The Journal of Political Economy*, LXV (April, 1957), pp. 126–34.

The higher union officials object to wildcat strikes for a number of reasons: 1) Such strikes frustrate one purpose of the contract, peacefully settling grievances. In order to abide by the agreement, the international or the local, whichever signed the contract, must attempt to persuade the strikers to return to work. This pits one group in the union against another and undermines the power and influence of the leaders. 2) Wildcat strikes are an open invitation to internal union warfare. The faction which is out of power may use the dispute to embarrass its opponents, e.g., accuse them of "selling out" to management by refusing to support the strikers. 3) The union officers generally prefer to conserve the members' strike potential for periods of negotiating new contracts. Union members have only a limited endurance for undergoing the sacrifices entailed in a strike, and wildcat strikes fritter away this endurance on goals which are not the choice of the leaders.

A sympathy strike is a strike by one union in support of another. Like a wildcat strike, it may occur for any of the five purposes described above. The objective is to place additional pressure on an employer from whom concessions are sought by a sister union. It may involve two or more craft unions which have organized the same employer, or two locals of the same union dealing with employers who are in a customer-supplier relationship to each other. The teamsters are much sought after allies because of their control over delivery of raw materials and pick-up of finished goods. Their sympathetic support may make the difference between stopping and not stopping the employer's production. The union striking in sympathy does not expect to win improvements in its contract. However, it expects the other union will return the favor at some future date. Sympathy strikes are restricted by the Taft-Hartley Act, as we shall see in Chapter 13.

A strike is an eruption of the truce between the two opponents. To win the battle, the union must employ sound strategy and tactics. From the union point of view, the best timing depends on when it will cause a loss in production which will hurt the employer most. This may be at the seasonal peak of the industry, when production is scheduled at a maximum, when inventories are very low, or when the employer is engaged in a competitive battle with rival employers. The attitudes of the government and the general public also play an important part in the strategy of timing. For example, the strikes in the late thirties occurred in a favorable political atmosphere. Other factors affecting the timing are the attitudes of the workers, whether they are economically and psychologically prepared to make the sacrifices necessary for a successful strike. If many of the workers are able to obtain temporary employment elsewhere, their ability to withstand loss of their regular income is greatly enhanced. Of course, the status of the strike fund is of considerable consequence to those unions which pay benefits. About half give some support to members engaging in an authorized strike. But payments are usually very modest because a strike fund of $20,000,000 would be entirely depleted in four weeks if payments of only $10 weekly are disbursed to 500,000 strikers. The Air Line Pilots' Association is an exception, generously granting up to $650 per month to its highly paid high-flying members.

For the union, successful tactics mean—above all else—preventing the employer from resuming production. The union must daily buoy the spirit of the workers. This includes frequent press releases concerning the justification of the union's demands and the obstinacy of the employer. The support of other unions is enlisted in a display of fraternal effort against the common enemy. And in a major strike this support is freely granted because of the precedent-setting effects of the ultimate agreement.

Strike Statistics

Since work stoppages make news and peaceful bargaining settlements generally do not, it is only natural that the media of public communication should emphasize the former. This contributes to the general misconception that they cause union members to lose a large amount of income and the economy to lose a great deal of production. Table 9-A presents the statistics for 1930 through 1958.[8] In 1958, with less than 4,000 strikes and about two million workers involved, man-days idle were barely more than two-tenths of one per cent of total working time. The number of workers involved equaled less than 5 per cent of all employed persons, and this relatively small group gave up an average of only twelve work days in the year. The number of stoppages reached a high level in 1937. That was the year when the National Labor Relations Act was declared constitutional by the Supreme Court. The attitude of the public, the rising level of economic activity, and the crusading spirit of the early CIO all contributed to this increased number. The high point in man-days idle occurred in 1946. Workers were anxious to raise their money wages to keep pace with a rising price level and to counteract their loss of overtime pay. Furthermore,

[8] U. S. Department of Labor, Bureau of Labor Statistics, *Analysis of Work Stoppages 1958*, Bulletin No. 1258 (July, 1959), p. 9.

TABLE 9-A

Work Stoppages in the United States, 1930-58*

Year	Work stoppages		Workers involved [a]		Man-days idle during year		
	Number	Average duration (calendar days)[b]	Number (thousands)	Per cent of total employed	Number (thousands)	Per cent of estimated working time of all workers	Per worker involved
1930	637	22.3	183	.8	3,320	0.05	18.1
1931	810	18.8	342	1.6	6,890	.11	20.2
1932	841	19.6	324	1.8	10,500	.23	32.4
1933	1,695	16.9	1,170	6.3	16,900	.36	14.4
1934	1,856	19.5	1,470	7.2	19,600	.38	13.4
1935	2,014	23.8	1,120	5.2	15,500	.29	13.8
1936	2,172	23.3	789	3.1	13,900	.21	17.6
1937	4,740	20.3	1,860	7.2	28,400	.43	15.3
1938	2,772	23.6	688	2.8	9,150	.15	13.3
1939	2,613	23.4	1,170	4.7	17,800	.28	15.2
1940	2,508	20.9	577	2.3	6,700	.10	11.6
1941	4,288	18.3	2,360	8.4	23,000	.32	9.8
1942	2,968	11.7	840	2.8	4,180	.05	5.0
1943	3,752	5.0	1,980	6.9	13,500	.15	6.8
1944	4,956	5.6	2,120	7.0	8,720	.09	4.1
1945	4,750	9.9	3,470	12.2	38,000	.47	11.0
1946	4,985	24.2	4,600	14.5	116,000	1.43	25.2
1947	3,693	25.6	2,170	6.5	34,600	.41	15.9
1948	3,419	21.8	1,960	5.5	34,100	.37	17.4
1949	3,606	22.5	3,030	9.0	50,500	.59	16.7
1950	4,843	19.2	2,410	6.9	38,800	.44	16.1
1951	4,737	17.4	2,220	5.5	22,900	.23	10.3
1952	5,117	19.6	3,540	8.8	59,100	.57	16.7
1953	5,091	20.3	2,400	5.6	28,300	.26	11.8
1954	3,468	22.5	1,530	3.7	22,600	.21	14.7
1955	4,320	18.5	2,650	6.2	28,200	.26	10.7
1956	3,825	18.9	1,900	4.3	33,100	.29	17.4
1957	3,673	19.2	1,390	3.1	16,500	.14	11.4
1958	3,694	19.7	2,060	4.8	23,900	.22	11.6

* The number of stoppages and workers relate to those beginning in the year; average duration to those ending in the year. Man-days of idleness include all stoppages in effect. For a discussion of the procedures involved in the collection and compilation of work stoppage statistics, see BLS Bull. 1168, Techniques of Preparing Major BLS Statistical Series, Chapter 12.

[a] Workers are counted more than once in these figures if they were involved in more than one stoppage during the year.

[b] Figures are simple averages; each stoppage is given equal weight regardless of its size.

the unsettled economy created by the rapid conversion to peacetime production contributed to the increased number of strikes.

During 1958 about three-fourths of the idleness resulted from strikes concerning only monetary considerations, and another 8 per cent of the time lost occurred over union organization and money matters. Disputes which were entirely concerned with working conditions accounted for more than a fifth of the strikes and about 15 per cent of the idleness. The question of union organization and security played an important role in approximately one-sixth of the stoppages but involved only 3.5 per cent of the workers. Although the percentage of strikes and of idleness caused by the various issues changes from year to year, the pattern for 1958 is typical.

Strike statistics presented in this fashion are somewhat misleading. Although an almost insignificant proportion of the total working time is involved, an entire firm or industry may be closed down. The workers' regular income is completely cut off. In some cases a whole community may come to a standstill for a brief period. Many nonparticipants suffer inconveniences, including the firm's customers and suppliers, and the merchants whose sales depend on the workers' income.[9] Yet, viewed in the long run, only a very few big strikes in the basic industries cause more than a ripple on the flow of production.

Worker Attitude Toward Strikes

There would be far fewer strikes, it is often argued, if workers themselves made the decision. That is, union leaders cause more strikes, ignoring the real desires of the workers. Although perhaps true in some instances, the argument misses the basic nature of the forces in operation. A proposal sometimes made, based on this misunderstanding, would require a secret ballot among the members to accept or reject the employer's last offer before a union be permitted to walk off the job. The experience under the War Labor Disputes Act, adopted in 1943, would indicate, however, that strike votes, at best, bring only a negligible reduction in the amount of time lost. Furthermore, in some cases they may actually instigate stoppages which could otherwise be avoided. The workers will generally overwhelmingly favor rejection of the employer's last offer because an opposite vote would undermine the bargaining power of their representatives. To favor rejection does not mean that

[9] For a careful and complete analysis of the effects of strikes on the community, see Neil W. Chamberlain and Jane Metzger Schilling, *The Impact of Strikes* (New York: Harper & Brothers, 1954).

a stoppage must follow, but rather that the union bargainers can exert pressure and therefore are in a position to win greater concessions.

A major reason for arguing that workers object to strikes is the loss in income which they suffer. If employees who earn $80 per week are out of work for two weeks, and as a result, win five cents per hour more than the employer would otherwise have granted, it will require eighty weeks at forty hours per week, to regain the lost pay, leaving out of account the effect of income taxes. However, when workers "hit the bricks," they never know how long the strike is going to last. Therefore, even the most rational worker cannot make this type of calculation before the walkout starts.

Even after returning to work, it is extremely difficult to compute the loss of income suffered by the workers. Much of the income may be recovered through overtime work as the employer tries to catch up on back orders. Or it is possible that the work time would have been lost anyway as a result of a slack period in the employer's business. This is particularly true when the goods produced may be stored over a period of time, thus making it possible for the employer to halt production and sell from his inventory of finished goods.

Another factor which makes it difficult to compute the wage loss associated with a strike is the uncertain effect it has on future negotiating sessions. A demonstration of militant solidarity may cause the employer to be willing to make greater concessions later. Certainly if the employer has the impression that the workers are very reluctant to support their union, he will take a more adamant approach in future negotiating periods. Therefore, since the worker cannot compute his wage loss either before or after a strike, it usually only vaguely affects his willingness to make the sacrifice.

Furthermore, the workers' attitude is conditioned by more than just economic considerations. There may be a latent hostility toward the employer, a general feeling that the workers have not been treated fairly or as well as workers in other firms. Such an attitude is often very important in wildcat strikes. In such a case the walkout may serve the useful function of blowing off steam and thereby clear the air for more rational negotiations.

Secondary Boycott

A secondary boycott is an attempt to bring pressure on one employer by acting against another. The typical strike is a primary boycott; the employer who is to be influenced is the direct recipient of the union action. The secondary boycott is frequently used for approaching a plant when the employees do not join through a normal organizing campaign. For example, a union finds that it cannot organize the employees of firm A. This may be the result of employer interference with organizing tactics, or the workers' lack of interest in the union, or fear that the employer will leave town if the plant becomes unionized. Firm A's best customer is firm B, which is organized by the union. A strike is called, or threatened, against firm B unless it ceases to buy from firm A. Thus, on penalty of losing its sales, firm A is forced to sign a contract covering its employees. The secondary boycott may also be used as a device for winning a jurisdictional dispute, wage increase, or other goal.

The employer who is caught in the middle, firm B in the above example, is frequently referred to as the neutral and innocent victim. This is one reason the secondary boycott was declared to be an unfair labor practice by the Taft-Hartley Act. The organized firm, however, may be glad to cooperate in order to force nonunion firms to pay higher wages, and thus restrict price competition in the product market. In that sense firm A is the "innocent" victim, and perhaps consumers as well.

Secondary boycotts may be either of two types—labor or commodity. The union may threaten to withhold labor from a neutral employer, or it may encourage its friends to cease patronizing the neutral employer's products. As an illustration, one union may attempt to convince the members of all unions to cease buying in stores which sell the product of the employer from which it is seeking a concession. The "we-do-not-patronize" or "unfair-to-labor" lists published by unions are examples of commodity boycotts.

Picketing

Picketing is the marching back and forth of one or more persons carrying placards, or signs of some sort, which announce a dispute between a union and management. The picketing is supposed to discourage anyone from crossing the line of march. One of the most common purposes of picketing is to support a strike. The picket, whose placard announces the plant is closed, attempts to discourage employees from going to work and truckers from carrying supplies in or finished goods out. If the employer does not try to produce, there is no problem. If he does, the union may resort to mass picketing, a large number of union members milling around each entrance to the plant, threatening, or appearing to threaten, violence to anyone who passes through.

Naturally, under such circumstances emotions run high. Each group of workers, those striking and those crossing the picket line, feel that the other group is attempting to steal their jobs. It is under these circumstances that American labor disputes have produced the considerable amount of bloodshed that has appeared over the last hundred or so years; and violence still erupts when non-strikers try to cross picket lines.

Picketing may also serve an important role in an organizing campaign. The objective is to notify workers of the union's efforts and where they may go to sign membership cards. The signs will usually have some unkind things to say about the employer and the wages he pays. The picketing may also prevent customers from patronizing the firm and truckers from providing their services. Even persons who have no sympathy with unions may be afraid of crossing the picket line, recalling that they are often the source of violence. Under these circumstances, the employer may be compelled to sign an agreement even though the majority of his employees prefer not to join the union. The Landrum-Griffin Act included regulations designed to minimize these effects of organizational picketing.

SUMMARY

Through collective bargaining, unions attempt to secure a wide variety of economic and noneconomic goals. The economic goals include wages, hours, working conditions, and fringe benefits. The noneconomic goals center around the worker's satisfaction with his job and the protection of the union as a growing institution.

One of the most difficult problems confronting unions is deciding which goals deserve priority. Within the union there are many actual and potential areas of conflict between different interest groups. In approaching any particular bargaining session, it must make some political compromise between the competing goals. The choice of pressing hard for one objective is liable to mean that some other must be neglected or put off to some future bargaining session. The important factors in determining which goals are to receive priority are: economic conditions affecting the firm, the industry, and the economy, the precedent of recent major agreements, rivalry between different unions and union leaders, the growing influence of the international with its concern for the over-all industry problems, and the dominant groups within the union.

The major bargaining tactics of unions are strikes, secondary boycotts, and picketing. Although successful strikes exert a considerable amount of pressure and create some hardships for employers, workers, and the general public, the amount of production lost through strikes is relatively small. Contrary to a generally held belief, the workers customarily are sympathetic to any strike in which they participate, partly because it is very difficult to compute the real amount of wage loss resulting from a strike.

DISCUSSION QUESTIONS

1. In what sense is a union a political institution? Explain.
2. Under what circumstances do the noneconomic goals of unions take precedence over their economic goals? Why?
3. The union is an institution apart from its membership. What does this mean?
4. Distinguish between union-oriented bargaining goals and worker-oriented bargaining goals.
5. Under what economic circumstances are union bargaining goals likely to place little or no emphasis on a wage increase? Explain why.
6. Explain the effects of a recent major agreement on the collective bargaining in your community.
7. Cite a recent example of inter-union rivalry. Explain how it has affected the strategy and goals of the unions involved.
8. What factors have caused internationals to exercise greater influence in collective bargaining? What effect has this had on bargaining goals?
9. What special interest groups are liable to appear in a union? What sorts of conflicts over union goals are liable to arise as a consequence?
10. Since idle man-days caused by strikes are such a small fraction of total man-days worked, there is no reason for the public to show concern over strikes. Comment.
11. Discuss a recent strike with which you are familiar. What did the workers lose and what did they gain? How accurate do you think your answer is?
12. What are secondary boycotts? Give an example of one. Why do you think they should, or should not, be subject to government regulation?

BIBLIOGRAPHY

Barbash, Jack. *Labor Unions in Action.* New York: Harper & Brothers, 1948.
Chamberlain, Neil W. *Social Responsibility and Strikes.* New York: Harper & Brothers, 1953.
Chamberlain, Neil W., and Schilling, Jane Metzger. *The Impact of Strikes.* New York: Harper & Brothers, 1954.

Golden, Clinton S., and Ruttenberg, Harold J. *The Dynamics of Industrial Democracy*. New York: Harper & Brothers, 1942.

Gouldner, Alvin W. *Wildcat Strike*. Yellow Springs: The Antioch Press, 1954.

Kornhauser, Arthur; Dubin, Robert; and Ross, Arthur M. (Editors). *Industrial Conflict*. New York: McGraw-Hill Book Company, 1954.

Ross, Arthur M. *Trade Union Wage Policy*. Berkeley: University of California Press, 1953.

10

MANAGEMENT APPROACH TO COLLECTIVE BARGAINING

It has frequently been alleged that we live in a managerial society, that management is the dominant institution in determining the direction of our social, economic, and political affairs. Without arguing the merits of this assertion, it can be agreed that management enjoys a high degree of public prestige and exercises a wide range of authority in many fields, including collective bargaining.

What do we mean by management? Each business firm, each government agency, and each nonprofit institution must have a group of people, or a single person, with final authority for making the decisions which control the operations of that institution. This is true for the smallest of business firms and for the largest of corporations. The management personnel must make decisions concerning not only labor relations but also all other aspects of the organization.

Even if this is a managerial society, management, with respect to collective bargaining, has been on the defensive. Over the last few decades, unions have increased their power relative to management by making a wider range of labor-management issues subject to collective bargaining. However, management is not enthusiastically abdicating its responsibilities. It, too, has goals which it attempts to achieve through collective bargaining.

MANAGEMENT COLLECTIVE BARGAINING GOALS

In performing its functions, management must satisfy several interest groups. 1) The owners and their representatives, the board of directors,

199

must be convinced that the profits and the growth of the firm are the best that can be achieved. 2) The customers must be satisfied with the price and the quality of the product. 3) The suppliers must be willing to provide a continuing source of raw materials at reasonable prices. 4) The banks and other sources of funds must be satisfied with the financial condition of the firm. 5) The workers must be stimulated to produce with maximum efficiency. 6) Finally, management, since it is a group of individuals, has its own personal objectives to fulfill, including personal economic security, social prestige, satisfaction in a job well done, the respect of other managers, and the preservation of their authority status within the firm. In many respects these claims against management conflict with each other, yet some workable and harmonious solution must be found for each claim.

Although dealing with employees is only one of management's problem areas, improper handling of employee relations can halt production of the entire firm, in the case of a strike, or it can cause the firm to operate so inefficiently that it will eventually cease to exist. But it is also true that unsatisfactory relations with the other interest groups can bring about the demise of the firm. Thus, in attempting to achieve its collective bargaining objectives, management cannot forget that the broad framework within which it operates includes more than labor relations.

In approaching collective bargaining within this framework, management has two primary goals: 1) retaining control of the enterprise and 2) maintaining efficiency in its operation. Although these two goals overlap in many respects, they are sufficiently distinct to be analyzed separately.

Control of the Enterprise

In order to perform its functions, management must have a wide range of flexibility in making its decisions. As more restrictions are placed on its freedom of action, whether by unions, government, or whatever the source, management's ability to satisfy these diverse interest groups is reduced. Maintaining control of the enterprise, keeping the widest possible range of flexibility in decision-making, therefore becomes a major management goal.

Loss of some of its control over decision-making means that management is no longer managing in the full sense of the word. On a personal basis, a manager, finding that his employees have just unionized, suffers the frustrations of a reduction in his authority. His predicament may be compared to that of workers when faced with a technological change in methods of production. The job is no longer what it was previously. For the manager, the employees are no longer "my workers." They now belong to the union. Successful operation of the firm now requires the cooperation of the union leaders, an outside group over whom management has no disciplinary power and no influence in selecting who they are to be. The personal frustrations growing out of this new situation may lead to emotional reactions on the part of management, so that it may grant no concessions to the union without a show-down battle, or may manipulate all its weapons with the purpose of winning the workers away from the union.

The union threatens management's control position by reducing its freedom in many areas. After conferring with sixty leading representatives of management, studying management periodicals and the proceedings of meetings of their associations, E. W. Bakke summarized their attitude as follows:

A large part of management irritation with this development [reduction in freedom of action] arises from specific restrictions on such items as discipline, hiring, transfers, work assignments, promotions and demotions, layoffs, the establishment and administration of work schedules and production quotas, organizational and technological innovations, the setting up and administration of wage systems, and like matters. Particularly irritating to many managements is the denial of their freedom to reward or punish individual workers in accordance with management's estimate of their individual merit and promise. Even in cases in which satisfactory working agreements have been made on such issues, management is disturbed by delays and restrictions upon quick decisions considered essential in the operations of the company. Beyond the specific restrictions involved, however, is the anxiety felt by many managers about the future; uncertainty as to where this process will end; a fear that it will eventually culminate in such stringent impairment of management's freedom that it will not be able to do its job satisfactorily.[1]

Thus, the issue of management prerogatives has become important in collective bargaining. Management feels that unions have interfered with its institutional right to manage. In order to preserve its control of the enterprise—its freedom of action—management is anxious to insert clauses in the collective agreement which clearly spell out its prerogatives or which restrict the subjects which are open to joint negotiation.

Improved Efficiency

Management's ultimate responsibility is to the owners of the firm. To carry out this responsibility means earning the maximum return on

[1] E. Wight Bakke, *Mutual Survival* (New York: Harper & Brothers, 1946), pp. 6–7.

the owners' investment, which is partially determined by the degree of efficiency at which the firm operates.

In many respects collective bargaining frustrates the efficiency aspirations of management. Since efficiency is measured by costs in dollar terms, the most obvious interference is union pressure to raise wages and fringe benefits. But costs are raised in other ways as well. Seniority restrictions on promotion, work assignments, layoffs, etc. interfere with management's ability to reward workers considered most productive or most loyal and its ability to discipline less productive workers. Union work rules reduce flexibility in adjusting work schedules. The need to explain and receive approval from the union for many of its actions likewise hampers its ability to manipulate the workers quickly and efficiently.

Hence, management, with its cost-conscious concern for efficiency, finds that the union erects many roadblocks. Management objects as vigorously, often more vigorously, to interference with worker assignments and production schedules than it does to wage increases. For example, during a recession when demand for a product is declining, employers often attempt to "tighten up," to get the same output at a lower labor cost. Jobs are redesigned so that lower-paid workers can handle them, and the speed of production lines is increased, raising the amount of output required from each worker. If there were no union present, the workers, fearing discharge, would have to submit to the new regimen without complaint. However, with the protection of seniority, unionized workers can file grievances which may block management's efforts to reduce costs.

How is it possible that the two goals of management might be in conflict? The drive for efficiency may be viewed as ownership-oriented and the desire for control as management-oriented. In small enterprises the owner, or group of owners, may also serve as the manager, or at least maintain close supervision over the person in charge of day-to-day operations. A conflict between the goals would be unlikely in these circumstances. In large corporations, however, it is difficult to identify the owning group. The stockholders include investment companies, mutual funds, pension funds, estates administered by banks and other trustees, as well as thousands of individuals, some of whom may be employees eligible for special stock-purchase plans. And no single individual or organization owns as much as 5 per cent of the stock. Under these circumstances, the managers often become a self-perpetuating body, and control of the enterprise may take precedence over profit maximization. Of course, profits are not neglected. Stockholders must be satisfied by regular dividend payments or growth in the market value of their stock. But they are usually in no position to judge whether the board of directors is achieving the highest return possible on their investment.

A conflict between the goals may appear in a number of forms. It may develop over the question of expansion. Perhaps the existing size of the firm is best as measured by profit per dollar invested, but a larger firm will command more attention when the president attends the country club. A thirty-story office building in downtown Manhattan may add little to profits but considerable to the officers' prestige. The conflict may also appear in labor relations. Cooperation with the union may be the most profitable course, but management may resist because of the reduction in its freedom of action. Or management may be generous in wage concessions in return for less interference in its decision-making.

In spite of the possibilities for conflict, efficiency usually becomes the chief goal when profits are low or declining. That is, management is not able to give special regard to its own distinct interests until the profit position is secure. In that sense, profit maximization is the ultimate goal of the firm.

FACTORS DETERMINING MANAGEMENT APPROACH
TO COLLECTIVE BARGAINING

How does management compromise between the different groups exerting pressures on its decisions? What factors determine the approach it will use to retain control of the enterprise and to improve efficiency? "Despite management's professed responsibility to multiple interest groups, its continued acceptance of profit positions as reflecting the competency of its performance suggests the strength still remaining in the link to ownership interests. Even where pride in high wages and low prices exists, as evidence of other responsibilities met, these carry less weight than the profit record *within the management fraternity* as indications of ability, as the source of prestige, and as command over income." [2] This does not mean that pressures from the non-owner interest groups go unheeded, but rather that they take a lower order of priority. The bargains concluded with them must be the best possible compromise aimed toward maximizing the profit position and protecting the special interests of the managers.

The degree of conflict between these pressures on management is of

[2] Neil W. Chamberlain, *Collective Bargaining* (New York: McGraw-Hill Book Company, 1951), p. 266; italics in the original.

a different order than the conflicting pressures on union bargaining goals. For management the resolution of each of the pressures is directed toward two interlocking goals, profit maximization and control of the enterprise; whereas unions do not have a comparable degree of unity in their goals, except where the organization itself is threatened. The resolution of pressures on management is generally in the form of contractual relationships with customers, suppliers, etc., involving specified monetary amounts, while the resolution of conflicts between interest groups within a union may emphasize union or worker security. In other words, management's collective bargaining goals are more unified, while union goals are to a greater extent in conflict with each other.

Even though management goals can be unified under the heading of profit maximization, this goal becomes complicated when considered in the light of collective bargaining. Should the firm maximize profits in the short run or long run? This question may be crucial in deciding whether to concede a particular union demand. To do so may mean continued production now, but at a higher cost level. Contrariwise, to endure a strike means no production and no profit for the time being, but a show of resistance may lead to more moderate union demands in future negotiations. Or, strictly enforcing disciplinary rules may cause a wildcat strike or a slowdown, whereas lax enforcement may encourage flagrant violation of management's rules with dire results for profits in the long run. In other cases to grant a union concession may entail an immediate reduction in profits, but at the same time improve worker morale and union cooperativeness with beneficial effects on profits for the long haul. The goal of maximum profits, then, is not so simple and straightforward as it at first appears. The union compels management to make difficult choices, with an impact on profits which is not clearly predictable.

How does management resolve these conflicting pressures? What determines the compromises managers will make in seeking their goals? In resolving the conflicts with employees and their organization, the controlling factors are: 1) management's view of the future demand for its product, qualified by the inventory it has on hand, 2) the precedent of recent major collective bargaining agreements, 3) the cost structure within the firm, and 4) the competitive forces within the industry.

Economic Outlook and Size of Inventory

Since the ultimate goal of management is measured in terms of profits, it follows that the attitude toward a strike will be tempered by the expected impact of that strike on profits. To illustrate, assume that profits will be reduced by some given amount over the long run if a certain concession is granted to the union. The resistance the employer will put up before granting that concession will depend on the estimated cost of that resistance. This estimated cost is likely to be very low if the expected sales of the company's product are low and the inventory of finished goods is high; the cost of a strike is likely to be high when the opposite situation holds. In deciding how much resistance to put up to a strike, management compares the long-run cost of the concessions with both the short-run and long-run cost of the strike; immediate loss of sales and permanent loss of customers.

Some unions try to manipulate the conditions which make the strike more expensive relative to the concession. For example, the United Mine Workers, during the 1940's, frequently conducted so-called memorial periods as a preliminary to their bargaining, closing the mines, perhaps in memory of a fatal mine accident, thus reducing the inventory of coal above ground, and increasing the pressure on management to make an early settlement. Furthermore, the United Mine Workers frequently conducted their negotiations during the winter, when the demand for coal is at its peak.

Just as the union and its members are unable to predict the length of a strike, so management is unable to guess accurately this relevant information. And just as the union considers more than economic factors in deciding whether or not to strike, so management considers non-economic factors in deciding how much resistance to put up. Thus, it may be decided to make a show of strength against a particular concession even at a considerable cost, in order to reduce the union's desire to strike in future bargaining relations. Or a particular issue may be contested as a matter of principle, e.g., protection of management prerogatives, rather than as a fight strictly on the grounds of maximizing profits. Fighting over broad principles is more likely to occur in the early years after the union has entered the scene, when, for example, the employer is very reluctant to give up the notion that the employees are "my workers," and is attempting to maintain unqualified control of job assignments or work loads.

Management's bargaining power relative to that of the union tends to be less during periods of full employment. The employer is under greater pressure to make concessions when the number of job-seekers is relatively low, because of the fear of losing some of his more competent workers. Furthermore, during prosperity the demand for his product is likely to be greater and he is more able to shift the cost increase to the consumers in the form of a price increase.

Precedent of Recent Major Agreements

Management's willingness to make concessions is usually affected by the concessions recently granted by other firms. It may be a local agreement that sets the pattern for a community, or an entire industry may follow a leading firm. In fact, an agreement made by a large firm may act as a precedent beyond geographical and industrial lines. It was more than sheer coincidence that the steel workers and the automobile workers won guaranteed annual wage plans in the same year.

Since cost and profit conditions vary from firm to firm, why should wage patterns set in one firm, or group of firms, affect the wage rate paid in other firms? A major reason is that the firm is no longer going against the current of the management fraternity once other members have made a similar concession. For a manager to make a concession too different from that of his fellow managers may entail the disapprobation of his colleagues. Just as a worker's attitude toward unionization is affected by that of his fellow workers, so one management's attitude toward concessions is affected by that of other managements.

A recent major agreement may act as a precedent for other reasons. A reluctant management, by refusing to grant a similar demand, may be at a disadvantage in the eyes of the public. Furthermore, since dissatisfaction among the workers may cause low productivity in the long run, management must make at least enough concessions to give them the feeling that they are getting a "square deal." The firm, in order to attract the most competent workers, or to avoid losing workers in periods of high employment, must pay amounts which are approximately equal to the workers' notion of what is being paid elsewhere.

There are numerous instances where unions and managements negotiate contracts which do not follow recent major agreements. If an employer can convince the union that his costs and competitive conditions do not warrant a wage increase equal to that of the major agreement, they may reach a settlement for a lesser amount. For example, smaller and less efficient firms in the steel fabricating industry are permitted by the United Steel Workers to pay less than the large firms in basic steel. The unions in the textile and clothing industries have frequently settled for less than major agreements in other industries because of inadequate demand for the final product and the presence of competition from nonunion firms and imported goods.

Employers of unorganized workers are affected by bargaining settlements made by organized firms. Management in an unorganized firm, if it wants to continue on a nonunion basis, must make concessions quite similar to those made to organized workers. It is not at all unusual for an unorganized firm to advertise that it offers wages and working conditions equal to or better than those secured through collective bargaining. Eastman Kodak in Rochester, New York, is a good example. The unorganized firm must also be concerned with the morale of its workers lest it lead to slowdowns and low productivity, and hence must also give the workers a feeling of having a "square deal."

Cost Structure Within the Firm

The employer's attitude toward making concessions to the union is affected by the cost structure within his firm. If labor costs are a large fraction of total costs, a given wage increase or fringe benefit substantially reduces his profits. Where labor costs are a small fraction of total costs, as in the oil industry, the resistance of the employer is likely to be less, other things being equal.

The possibility of substituting a new production process incurring lower labor costs affects management's approach to bargaining. As labor costs rise, the employer may find it more efficient to use labor-saving machinery. If this opportunity is open to him, his bargaining power is enhanced. The union, fearing the employment effect of a wage increase, may moderate its demands.

In some industries costs and revenues are determined by maintaining a fixed time schedule. For example, in the newspaper publishing industry and in the theatre industry, if the printers or the operators of moving picture projectors do not perform their services on a certain day, that day's revenue is permanently lost to the employer. Obviously, the employer's bargaining power is affected by the possibility of a complete loss on his substantial fixed investment for that period of time. In the construction industry the employer is frequently required to finish the job by a certain date specified in the construction contract, or else make a penalty payment equal to a considerable fraction of total cost. His willingness to make concessions and avoid a strike is obviously affected.

Competitive Forces Within the Industry

Employers who feel the pressure of competition may find themselves in a poor bargaining position. The employer who loses production because of a strike may find that his unsatisfied customers permanently attach themselves to his competitors. Fearing such consequences, he may be willing to make substantial concessions to the union.

In some industries the union provides a degree of stability in the face of competitive pressures. By organizing all firms in the industry and imposing similar wage and working conditions, the union removes a major cost from the area of competition. Thus, employers may price their products with the knowledge that their competitors will not undersell them because of lower labor costs. Furthermore, the union may prevent cut-throat competitors from entering the industry and temporarily stealing the customers of the "legitimate" employers. This is sometimes accomplished with the cooperation of the teamsters' union, so that if the truck drivers refuse to deliver supplies to a "noncooperating" contractor, he is soon out of business. Or it may be accomplished by controlling the supply of skilled labor. Under these circumstances stable industrial relations may be maintained over a long period of time, as in the clothing industry in the metropolitan New York area.

Competitive pressures which exert a significant impact on management's approach to collective bargaining may appear in an industry characterized by many small firms all producing approximately the same product. Examples are the residential construction industry or the cleaning industry in large cities. For their individual protection, these firms may be forced to bargain jointly with the union, which has more resources than any one of them singly. In an oligopolistic industry, where there are a few giant firms which dominate the industry and engage in sharp competition with each other, competitive pressures of a different order are in operation. A long strike suffered by one of these firms, while its rivals are producing, would cause it to lose its relative position in the market. This would be true in the steel, automobile, or electrical machinery industries. Hence, the bargaining position of each firm is substantially affected by that of its rivals.

The opposite kinds of competitive pressures are present when a large portion of the firms in an industry can operate successfully on a nonunion basis, as in residential construction in smaller cities. With the union having so little bargaining power, management has a wide range of freedom in determining and winning its bargaining goals.

MANAGEMENT BARGAINING: WEAPONS AND STRATEGY

Although it appears that in achieving its bargaining goals, management has been largely on the defensive for the last twenty-five years, this has not always been true. The traditional controls over its work force—hiring, promoting, discharging, and setting wages—which were largely unrestricted prior to collective bargaining, constituted a potent offensive weapon for dealing with the threat of unionization. By withholding promotions or the better job assignments from those who did not demonstrate pro-management sentiments, unionization could be convincingly discouraged. By simply discharging any employee who exhibited any interest in unions, employers could halt organization in its infancy. Or management could grant a wage increase just as the union organizers were approaching his employees, thus reducing their dissatisfaction with the firm and decreasing their inclination to join a union.

Although federal legislation and the growth of unions have modified management's freedom in manipulating its employees, they have by no means eliminated it. However, this is only one of the weapons available to management for achieving its goals. The entire arsenal of weapons includes: 1) lockouts, 2) traditional controls over the work force, 3) management associations, 4) appeals to public opinion designed to exert pressure on the union, and 5) personnel techniques designed to win the loyalty of the workers to the firm and thereby reduce their proclivities to union activity.

How management will manipulate its weapons depends on whether it believes it can best achieve its goals by trying to destroy the union, or by granting the minimum degree of recognition and minimum amount of concessions, or by trying to secure the cooperation of the union in accomplishing common objectives of efficiency of production. Since collective bargaining is a process of mutual accommodation, and since learning to accommodate takes time, management's strategy in manipulating its weapons will depend partly on how many years it has been dealing with a union. With the passage of time, both parties learn to know each other, and if this leads to mutual trust and confidence, it will certainly influence management's use of its weapons.

Of course, bargaining strategy also varies with the conception of the type of union encountered. For example, if management believes there is unreasonable interference with efficiency of production and challenge to its prerogatives, it may attempt to undermine the union's relationship with the employees. Or if it believes the union has failed to abide by the contract, management may become less willing to make compromises in bargaining. If the conception of the union, however, is that of a business-like organization which keeps its word and strives to build stable relations, management is more likely to adjust its techniques and procedures to secure mutual accommodations. Such business-like relations, after all, are what management is accustomed to in dealing with bankers, suppliers, and customers.

The methods of implementing bargaining strategy and manipulating weapons vary with the size of the firm. In a small owner-managed establishment, problems can be settled by straightforward, uncomplicated negotiation. The owner and union local president or business agent can quickly reach final and binding agreements. In large corporations, however, no one person can look after all details; the president or chairman of the board of directors delegates responsibilities to other supervisors. Labor relations are assigned to a vice president in charge of personnel or to an industrial relations department. In a multi-plant firm the supervisor in charge of employee relations has a large staff with representatives at each plant location. In order to achieve consistency, every important labor dispute is cleared through his office. A large complicated network, occasionally entangled in red tape, assumes responsibility for negotiating new agreements and settling grievances under the existing contract. With several layers of supervisors between the actual dispute and the decision on how to solve it, the pronouncements of the personnel department may sometimes confuse rather than settle the problem.

Lockouts

The most obvious employer weapon, the counterpart to the unions' strike, is the lockout. A lockout is a cessation of work initiated by the employer: closing his plant in order to make some bargaining gain. Lockouts are comparatively infrequent in this country, since the employer has the initiative in setting wages and working conditions and can therefore set those which he desires. It is the union which then raises objections and goes on a strike in order to compel a change.

If forced to choose between a strike and a lockout, management usually prefers the former since it has public relations advantages. It can set the conditions which push the union into a strike and therefore does not need to lock out its employees. The side which is the aggressor in bringing about a work stoppage is the one which is at the initial disadvantage in explaining its position to the public. In nine states (Arkansas, Connecticut, Kentucky, Minnesota, Mississippi, New Hampshire, Ohio, Pennsylvania, and West Virginia) there is a special reason for employers to prefer strikes to lockouts, if they have to choose between them: employees receive unemployment compensation benefits in case of a lockout. But in only two states (New York and Rhode Island) do they receive benefits in case of a strike, and then only after an extended waiting period. The payment of benefits causes the employer's tax rates to rise, and increases the workers' ability to withstand a long strike.

Control of Hiring, Promotion, Discharge, and Layoff

For management, its traditional control over rewarding and punishing workers is obviously more than a bargaining weapon. The number of workers employed by the firm at any point in time is largely controlled by economic conditions. Nevertheless, management has a degree of flexibility in deciding whom it will hire or discharge whenever it is expanding or contracting its scale of operations, including control over timing the change in employment. Thus, the employer may lay off a large number of workers prior to negotiating a new contract in order to convince his employees that a sizable wage increase is out of the question and that a strike would be unsuccessful. In large multi-plant firms management may decide which divisions or plants are to be affected by the reduction or expansion of the work force. The choice might reflect the strength and cooperativeness of the union in different divisions and plants. Where one or more plants of a firm are nonunion, shifting the work to the latter can be held as a threat against the union. Some firms have built new plants in the South and Southwest in order to put themselves in this position.

Management Associations

Managers often find that they can better accomplish their collective bargaining goals through association with other managers. Management associations are most typical of those industries where there are many small employers, usually confronting one large union, or a group of cooperating unions, as in the building trades. Under these circumstances the union may achieve a dominant bargaining position, picking off the employers one at a time with what is known as a "whipsaw" technique. By striking one employer and allowing his competitors to produce, the union brings tremendous pressure on the struck employer. He sees his customers taking their business elsewhere and fears that he may suffer a permanent loss in sales. Consequently, he is likely to capitulate, granting extreme concessions. The union then uses this favorable agreement as a precedent in challenging the other employers one at a time. The employers are compelled to join forces and form an association which then becomes a major management weapon in collective bargaining.[3]

Management associations may be established for reasons other than response to whipsaw tactics. Employers, particularly in small firms, often find that it is more efficient to bargain through an association. Competent professional bargainers may be hired on a full-time basis. By having an agreement which covers a large number of employers, an industry may be stabilized in terms of one of the major cost items, wages. Furthermore, it is often possible to hire one arbitrator who handles all grievances, thus making it easier to maintain peaceful and consistent bargaining relations throughout the market area of the industry.

Management associations assume a variety of forms, some of them being very tightly organized, and others quite informal, doing no more than exchanging information on wages and productivity. The closely knit management associations exercise a significant influence over collective bargaining, particularly the types that have been labeled combative, negotiatory, or administrative.

The combative management association has as its major purpose the prevention of unionization. This type reached the peak of its influence during the 1920's. Many of the techniques formerly used by such associations are now illegal, e.g., the use of blacklists and strike-breakers. Such associations now exist on an informal, extralegal basis. They are of some consequence in parts of the South and the mountain states where unions have had little success with large-scale invasions.

A negotiatory association meets jointly with the union for the purpose of writing a new contract. The agreement when reached is signed by all employers and covers the employees of each of them. Its purpose is to offer common resistance to the union and thereby win a more favorable contract than could be won singly. The philosophy of a negotiatory association is that a strike against one is a strike against all. Its success depends on the willingness of all employers to cease operating when any one is closed by the union, even though it means giving up a substantial temporary increase in revenues. Six major airlines have devised a unique variation of joint negotiating. When one is struck the others continue to operate but share profits with their less fortunate competitor, pledging an amount equal to their increase in profits. Strike insurance, a new technique which appears to be gaining popularity among railroads, newspaper publishers, and others, pays benefits to a struck employer. The insurance

---

[3] Clark Kerr and Lloyd H. Fisher, "Multi-Employer Bargaining: The San Francisco Experience," in Richard A. Lester and Joseph Shister, Ed., *Insights into Labor Issues* (New York: The Macmillan Company, 1948), pp. 30–32.

is sold to an industry when a sufficiently large percentage of the firms are ready to pay the annual premium. Similarly to the airlines arrangement, all insured firms would continue to operate while one or two were shut down by labor disputes.

An administrative association administers the agreement for its duration. It settles any disputes which arise under the contract and acts for the several managements in interpreting the contract to meet new situations. The administrative association usually involves all the aspects of the negotiatory association as well. Its methods of operation are discussed in some detail in the following chapter.

Appeals to Public Opinion

Management, like labor, must pay heed to the potential effects of public opinion; failure to do so invites public interference and regulation. For example, the strike wave of 1946 undoubtedly played a large role in bringing about many provisions in the Taft-Hartley Act which unions considered restrictive. Management was able to channel the aroused public opinion into legislation approaching its desires. To cite another example, the conditions of the docks in the New York City harbor led to joint legislation by New York and New Jersey to control hiring and working conditions, imposing regulations on both management and unions. A public reaction can appear in the form of comprehensive or direct interference in a particular strike. A much less overt form of public reaction can also be decisive, particularly in a small or one-industry town.

Management has special advantages in winning public support for its point of view. All the major media of public communication, press, radio, and television, are largely supported by advertising revenues. Obviously, these agencies must not be too unsympathetic to their customers. The support to employers is sometimes in the form of articles and editorials on the inflationary consequences of a wage increase sought by a major union. This is not to argue that all communication media are always partial to management, for there are many outstanding exceptions. But one cannot deny the economic pressure in that direction.

Often management attempts to manipulate public opinion with the objective of bringing substantial pressures to bear on its employees. One extreme form of this has been labeled the Mohawk Valley Formula.

Mohawk Valley Formula

The Mohawk Valley Formula is included here not because it is typical of the weapons management now uses to achieve its goals through collective bargaining, but rather because it illustrates the importance of public opinion and because some aspects of the Formula continue to appear, particularly where a union is organizing a plant for the first time and the community is largely nonunion. The technique was originated in 1936 by the Remington Rand Corporation for the purpose of combating union organization in its plants. It was so successful at that time that the company had it published for the use of other employers.[4]

The first step calls for labeling the union leaders as agitators representing only a small clique of the employees, and advocating demands not worthy of bargaining. All channels of public communication are used to carry this message. If the strike is called in spite of the public opinion created, management then begins to spread information about the losses to the workers and the business community. The employer threatens to move his plant to a distant city rather than recognize the union. A citizens' committee is organized, supposedly independent of the employer, consisting only of people with the "right" attitude toward the strike, including representatives of the press, radio, clergy, etc. If the strike continues, the employer begins a back-to-work movement with letters sent to the homes of the employees specifying a date for the beginning of full-scale production, and repeating the charges that the union leaders are agitators with unreasonable demands not representing the wishes of the majority of workers. "Missionaries," employees who are anti-union, are sent to the workers' homes to convince them that the strike will be a failure. Those workers who show no desire to return are threatened with the permanent loss of their jobs. On the day the plant is opened, the workers loyal to the company march through the gates with abundant police protection, accompanied by sirens, bands, flag-raising, and patriotic speeches. Regardless of the number of people who return to work, the plant must be made to appear to be in full operation, trucks moving in with supplies and out with finished goods, smokestacks belching a full quota of smoke. The sheriff is informed of these proceedings and is aided in deputizing the proper number of the "right"-minded people to make sure that pickets do not interfere with the rights of private property. The employer may hire a private detective agency to provide the "right"-minded people for the sheriff to deputize. This is done in a manner which impresses the general public that the

[4] Reproduced in Fred Witney, *Government and Collective Bargaining* (New York: J. B. Lippincott Company, 1951), pp. 633–35.

employer is on the side of law and order and that the strikers are not. A barrage of press releases is maintained, claiming that the union leaders are agitators representing a minority and are seeking selfish gains which are contrary to the best interests of the majority of the employees.

This process may run on for a number of weeks, depending on the timing that seems most appropriate. If by this time the strike is not broken and the union thoroughly defeated, the Mohawk Valley Formula has not proved effective in the particular case.

Personnel Techniques to Win Loyalty of Workers

No firm can operate efficiently unless its employees have sufficient respect for it to be willing to work effectively. Stating the point in reverse, if workers believe they are overworked, underpaid, and treated like a herd of cattle, this will be reflected in their rate and quality of output. In dealing with its employees, management adopts personnel techniques designed to win employee respect, perhaps by giving promotions and economic benefits to those who are most productive. It may involve a large financial bonus to a worker for a suggestion that increases efficiency, or it may be as simple as a personal pat on the back.

Personnel techniques may be used as a bargaining weapon in either organized or unorganized plants. In some cases they prevent organization or cause an independent union to decide not to affiliate with an international. In organized plants some of them are incorporated into the collective agreement. When a union suspects the techniques are designed to undermine its position in the plant, it attempts to make them subject to collective bargaining.

We will briefly survey three systems of personnel techniques: scientific management and incentive wage systems, welfare capitalism, and human relations.

Scientific Management and Incentive Wage Systems

Scientific management was originally developed at the beginning of this century and widely used during and after World War I. Frederick Taylor, a firm believer in the engineering approach to labor relations, was its leading proponent. Scientific management "sought to apply scientific methods to industrial relations problems—to simplify and clearly define jobs, to improve the physical conditions of work, to set up operations in such a way as to minimize waste time and lost motions, and to provide an incentive to increased production through methods of pay based on worker productivity." [5]

An incentive wage system is based on payment for the amount of work done rather than the amount of time spent on the job. A production standard is set, based on some measurement of what is deemed to be a standard rate of output. The measurement requires a detailed time and motion study of each job, minutely dividing the job into its fundamental and necessary operations. A bonus is then paid for exceeding the daily production quota.

The techniques of scientific management have been modified and incorporated in modern personnel programs. Emphasis on accident prevention and the rationalization of jobs has contributed significantly to the modern industrial scene. Our main interest is emphasis on an incentive wage system, since this becomes a major issue in collective bargaining.

An incentive wage system continually encounters the problem of adjusting the wage rates as the techniques of production change. From management's point of view, when production becomes more efficient owing to improved equipment, the standard rate of output should be increased. At the same time, management wants to give workers the impression that they are being properly rewarded for improvements in output. Hence, adjustments of the pay rate and production standards require delicate manipulation, if a lowering of employee morale is to be avoided. In organized firms these adjustments are subject to bargaining and are sometimes the source of a large number of grievances.

Many unions consider an incentive wage system as a technique for bringing about a "speed-up," and therefore argue for having the pay rates set high enough so that the production line does not have to run at an "unreasonable" speed in order for employees to earn "fair" weekly incomes. Of course, the definition of a fair income is never satisfactorily resolved. In some cases unions absolutely refuse to accept an incentive wage system. In other cases, of which outstanding examples are the clothing and steel industries, unions fully accept the principles involved in time and motion study of the jobs, and the basic rates are set through collective bargaining. In fact, in the clothing industry, the best time study and incentive wage technicians are on the unions' professional staffs. They often provide valuable advice to management in establishing and adjusting their incentive wage plans.

[5] Edwin E. Witte, *The Evolution of Managerial Ideas in Industrial Relations*, Bulletin 27, New York State School of Industrial and Labor Relations, November, 1954, p. 6.

In unorganized as well as organized plants, an incentive wage system does not necessarily prevent soldiering on the job. Even nonunion workers know that if they work too fast, they may work themselves out of a job; or if they earn too much on a piece-rate basis, their pay rate per unit of output may be reduced. A group attitude develops as to what is an appropriate amount of output. A worker who exceeds this norm is liable to lose status in the group.

Welfare Capitalism

During the 1920's it was the fashion among many firms vigorously to oppose unions, a reaction to the growth of unions during and immediately after World War I. An outstanding aspect of the campaign was the development of "welfare capitalism," which usually included establishing company unions, or employee representation plans. It frequently entailed special recreational programs, company picnics, etc., with the intention of picturing the employer as the benefactor of all the workers, both at work and play, and thereby win their allegiance to the firm as opposed to the union.

Many ingredients of welfare capitalism have carried over to the present day. In one form it appears as the paternalistic approach of some nonunion firms which grant pension plans, health and welfare plans, Christmas bonuses, sponsor bowling leagues, etc. In another form, welfare capitalism has been modified, or replaced, by collective bargaining. Firms which at one time voluntarily offered these special inducements were required, after the employees became organized, to submit the plans to the scrutiny of collective bargaining.

Human Relations Approach to Employees

The emphasis on human relations in management's approach to workers grew out of the studies directed by Elton Mayo at the Hawthorne Plant of Western Electric.[6] They demonstrated that a worker's rate of output was determined by more variables than just quality of materials, working conditions, and wage rates. His attitude toward the job and the team spirit of his immediate fellow workers were extremely important variables. The research indicated that workers tended to form into small informal groups which set their own production norms. As a consequence of the Hawthorne and other studies, the new approach was adopted as part of the standard equipment of management's personnel techniques.

[6] F. J. Roethlisberger and William J. Dickson, *Management and the Worker* (Cambridge: Harvard University Press, 1947), especially pp. 551–604.

The main emphasis in the human relations approach is on making the worker feel that he and his job are significant—giving him the impression that he is personally necessary for the successful operation of the plant. The firm portrays an interest in him as an individual, with a regard for his own personal rights, interests, and problems. Thus, attention is given to some of the non-monetary motivations of the employee, his desires to be recognized and to feel important.

Emphasis on human relations generally involves a much greater burden on the foreman, since he is the representative of management who comes into daily contact with the employees. It is up to him to make the worker feel that he is being treated as an equal individual. A permissive type of supervision is required, with the foreman doing as little direct order-giving as possible. Instead, he encourages the worker to understand the work and to see the necessary tasks to be performed, inviting participation of the worker in making decisions on how the jobs should be set up and in what order they should be done.

A personnel program which emphasizes human relations must include a system of communications for channeling information upward from workers through foremen to the top supervisors and channeling instructions downward. If the firm is genuinely interested in its employees' personal aspirations and their suggestions for improving production, a method must be established, which they clearly understand, for bringing their views to the attention of appropriate company officials. Likewise, directions issued by top management must be filtered downward in a manner showing respect for individual workers. For example, if a new production technique is about to be initiated, it should be thoroughly explained to the employees and their suggestions for its implementation solicited. Of course, if their suggestions are ignored, the communication system—in fact, the entire human relations approach—would be only a sham. But when information and instructions are flowing effectively, both up and down, a real spirit of teamwork may develop.

In some cases management has used a human relations approach in an effort to hold the loyalty of the worker to the firm in opposition to the union. The impression is created that the "team" includes the employees and all levels of the supervisory force, but no outside party, especially no union. In a less extreme form, human relations may serve as a management bargaining weapon to persuade union members to be less militant in support of extreme demands.

The human relations approach has brought about, in a great number of cases, substantial improvements in employee-employer relations. This has been true of both unionized and nonunionized plants. Certainly, treatment of a worker, or anyone else for that matter, as a significant individual, is a desirable characteristic of a democratic society.

Perhaps one of the most famous experiments in the human relations approach is what has come to be known as the Scanlon plan, named for its originator, a member of the United Steel Workers who became a college professor. The Scanlon plan is an incentive wage system which emphasizes worker participation in production planning. A production committeeman, one selected for each department, meets regularly with the foreman to discuss suggestions for improving production; however, the discussions may include all workers who would be involved in any proposed change. If management is proposing an innovation, it is also considered by the production committees before being put into operation. The essential idea is to win the cooperation of all workers and all levels of management. The worker with shop experience, the foreman, and the engineer combine their know-how to launch a new production technique. Under the Scanlon plan, the incentive bonus is paid on a group rather than an individual basis. Any reduction in labor cost relative to total sales is shared among all those participating in the plan. The payment plan is designed to promote the goal of cooperation.[7]

The three sets of personnel techniques which have been described may be considered as three stages in the evolution of personnel administration. Scientific management and incentive wage systems emphasized the mechanical process of simplifying work and increasing output through bonus payments. Welfare capitalism showed concern for the workers' welfare outside the shop or factory. The additional benefits were to be considered as pouring from the generosity and kindness of the employer. The human relations approach stresses the individual worker and his work group, and attempts to elicit his participation in production planning. It goes beyond the other two by recognizing that employees have non-monetary needs which must be satisfied in the work environment.

IS THERE A BASIC CONFLICT BETWEEN UNIONS AND MANAGEMENT?

Now that we have discussed the collective bargaining goals of unions and management, we are ready to ask: To what extent are these goals in conflict with each other? To what extent are they in harmony? And where there is conflict, can it be expected that well-intentioned and reasonable men will find an effective way of resolving the conflict?

[7] William F. Whyte, *Money and Motivation* (New York: Harper & Brothers, 1955), pp. 166–88.

It is sometimes argued that the interests of employers and employees are really the same. In support of this argument it is reasoned that both gain from greater productivity, more efficiency, and larger output. The incomes of both groups are enhanced by such improvements. Others argue that there is a basic conflict of interests which can never be permanently resolved. This is evidenced by the persistence of strikes and threats of strikes. Even under conditions of peaceful industrial relations, new contracts must continually be negotiated.

Community of Interests

Since the two sides are cutting a single pie, anything that increases its size can be to the benefit of both parties simultaneously. The pie to be shared consists of the total revenue of the firm minus all nonlabor costs, and must be divided into wages, salaries, and profits. It may be increased by increasing total revenue at a rate faster than nonlabor costs, or by producing the same revenue at lower nonlabor costs. In either case the amount left over for division between the owners and employees is greater. It is therefore argued that both sides should bend all efforts to increase the size of the pie, to expand output and reduce wastage. Cooperation toward this goal should be the primary aim of employer-employee relations, since the monetary incentive is obvious.

The two sides have a second common goal—mutual survival.[8] Each wishes to adjust its position, relatively to the other and relatively to all pressures to which it is subject, so as to maintain its institutional existence indefinitely. Each, by compromising its most extreme demands, can gain a survival value beyond that which would ordinarily be accomplished by "fighting it out." The survival of management depends on the continual cooperation of the workers. The survival of the union local may in turn depend on the survival of the firm. Both management and the union leaders gain in stature over the long run if the firm expands, satisfying the employment needs of the members and increasing the size of the union.

Conflict of Interests

Even though it is true that there is a broad area in which the interests of unions and management are the same, there are at least two areas in which conflict is likely, in fact, almost certain to occur.

[8] Bakke, *op. cit.*, pp. 79–82.

Division of Total Product

The fact that both sides gain by an increase in output does not settle the all-important question of dividing the increase. There is no clear and acceptable formula for attributing a certain portion of the output to the efficiency of labor or to the efficiency of management. The slogan, "a fair day's wage for a fair day's work," defies precise definition. The decision on dividing the output, therefore, must be one of relative bargaining power, which, on the subject of wages, is largely a matter of economic conditions and willingness to fight. Each side will naturally want to receive as large a share as possible, and hence there is a basic conflict which would seem to continue indefinitely within a private enterprise system.

Developments in production technology lead to the need to reconsider the division of the total product. As technology changes, the size of the pie changes. Furthermore, labor and capital change in proportion to each other. For example, output may be increasing while the number of employees is decreasing. Because of increasing output and changing ratios of labor to capital, then, the question of redividing the new pie is continually brought to the surface. Any solution to the question can only be temporary.

Efficiency Versus Security

There will also be a continuing conflict between the efficiency aspirations of management and the security aspirations of the workers. Management is constantly seeking ways to reduce costs, including labor costs. As efficiency increases, the cost per unit of output decreases and generally the amount of labor per unit of output also decreases. In other words, technology, perhaps in the form of new machinery, displaces labor. Since this means lower costs of production, management will be anxious to adopt improvements in technology in all haste.

On the other hand, workers, fearing less employment, may object to the changes. However, since the march of progress is inevitable, the most that unions can hope to do is affect the methods of introducing new technology. Since their members' jobs are at stake, unions insist on seniority provisions and working rules which limit management's flexibility in manipulating the employees to make the most efficient adjustments for the new technology. For example, management may want to transfer young workers to higher-paying jobs on new machines, but may be prevented from doing so because of seniority provisions in the contract.

Therefore, the workers' continued insistence on the protection of seniority and working rules remains in conflict with management's drive for efficiency.[9]

Thus, the presence of a union brings about a conflict of loyalties on the part of workers. They have a loyalty to the firm, the source of their income. Its continued efficient operation is necessary to their economic welfare. Hence, workers have strong motives for cooperating with management. Yet, to protect their job rights and prevent the employer from discriminating against them, workers support their union. As long as the institution of collective bargaining continues, unions and management will be in conflict to win the loyalty of the workers.

It is true that unions in some instances cooperate with management to achieve higher levels of efficiency. However, such action generally occurs only when it can be demonstrated that greater efficiency is necessary to protect the workers' security in their income and jobs, or when a technological change such as automation in a mass production industry, is inevitable.

SUMMARY

Management's collective bargaining goals are: 1) the control of the enterprise, maintaining its ability to manage with a high degree of flexibility, and 2) efficiency of operation, being able to make whatever adjustments seem desirable to increase efficiency in a changing economy. Striving for these goals is accomplished within a framework of pressures exerted by workers, owners, customers, suppliers, and bankers as well as management's personal aspirations.

The basic factors determining management's approach to collective bargaining are its views on the economic outlook, conditioned by the size of inventory on hand, precedents from recent major agreements, cost structure of the firm, and competitive conditions in the industry. These factors interact with each other, their relative importance varying with different economic conditions.

The bargaining techniques of management consist, first, of its control of hiring, promotion, discharge, and layoff. This weapon has been in management's arsenal from the beginning, however its usefulness as a weapon in collective bargaining has diminished as the unions have become stronger. Second, management, in some instances, finds that its

[9] For an interesting discussion of this point, see Clinton S. Golden and Harold J. Ruttenberg, *The Dynamics of Industrial Democracy* (New York: Harper & Brothers, 1942), pp. 128-31.

bargaining power is enhanced and its ability to achieve its goals increased if it joins a management association. The third bargaining technique results from its influence over public opinion. Its close connections with the media of communications lead to a bargaining advantage in many situations. Fourth, management's lockout weapon corresponds to the unions' strike weapons, but is used rarely. A final weapon is personnel techniques, consisting of incentive wage systems, special benefits provided voluntarily by the employer, and a human relations approach to the employees. Management, through these personnel techniques, attempts to win the loyalty of its workers quite apart from the status of collective bargaining in the firm, and perhaps erect a barrier to the unionization of the plant, or to the effectiveness of the union if it is present.

These goals and techniques of management place it in conflict with labor in certain basic aspects of collective bargaining. Although the two sides have broad areas of common interest in terms of increasing total output, efficiency of operations, and mutual survival, there are basic questions of dispute which seem incapable of permanent solution: the appropriate division of the total product and the resolution of the efficiency desires of management and the security desires of workers.

DISCUSSION QUESTIONS

1. Management is the dominant institution in our society today. What does this mean and what are its implications with respect to collective bargaining?

2. Management, in making its decisions, must satisfy a variety of interest groups. Explain how these interest groups might be in conflict with each other concerning management decisions.

3. "The very existence of organized action among the employees is a threat to management's control of the enterprise." Explain the meaning of this statement and indicate the areas in which management's control is threatened.

4. "Management's approach to collective bargaining is determined largely by economic forces." Comment, showing to what extent this is an accurate statement.

5. Why should a bargaining settlement made by one firm have any effect on another firm's bargaining, when the cost structures and the goods produced are substantially different?

6. What cost factors, internal to the firm, are likely to have a major effect on bargaining? Explain why in each case.

7. Cite two unionized industries with substantially different degrees of competition. Compare the effects of the competition on the collective bargaining in the two industries.

8. Why are some managers willing to join management associations, thus giving up their bargaining freedom?

9. Study the reporting on a recent strike in your local newspaper and other media of communications and determine whether the facts seem to have been reported fully and impartially.

10. How may personnel techniques be used to increase the workers' loyalty to the firm and reduce their loyalty to the union? Do you think these are wise policies for management to follow for its own interests? Explain.

11. What is an incentive wage system? Why might a union be opposed to this method of wage payment?

12. What is meant by the human relations approach to collective bargaining? Do you think this is an improvement in employer personnel techniques? Explain.

13. "The interests of workers and managers will always be opposed to each other." Comment, showing how you agree or disagree.

BIBLIOGRAPHY

Arensberg, Conrad M. et al. *Research in Industrial Human Relations: A Critical Appraisal.* New York: Harper & Brothers, 1957.

Bakke, E. Wight. "The Goals of Management," in Bakke, E. Wight, and Kerr, Clark (editors). *Unions, Management and the Public.* New York: Harcourt, Brace & Company, 1948, pp. 241–53.

————. *Mutual Survival.* New York: Harper & Brothers, 1946.

Bendix, Reinhard. *Work and Authority in Industry.* New York: John Wiley & Sons, 1956.

Chamberlain, Neil W. *Collective Bargaining.* New York: McGraw-Hill Book Company, 1951.

————. *The Union Challenge to Management Control.* New York: Harper & Brothers, 1948.

Golden, Clinton S., and Ruttenberg, Harold J. *The Dynamics of Industrial Democracy.* New York: Harper & Brothers, 1942.

Hill, Lee H., and Hook, Charles R., Jr. *Management at the Bargaining Table.* New York: McGraw-Hill Book Company, 1945.

Kennedy, Van Dusen. *Union Policy and Incentive Wage Methods.* New York: Columbia University Press, 1945.

Roethlisberger, F. J., and Dickson, William J. *Management and the Worker.* Cambridge: Harvard University Press, 1947.

Strauss, George, and Sayles, Leonard. *Personnel: The Human Problems of Management.* Englewood Cliffs: Prentice-Hall, Inc., 1960.

Whyte, William F. *Money and Motivation.* New York: Harper & Brothers, 1955.

11 ADMINISTRATION OF COLLECTIVE BARGAINING AGREEMENTS

The three preceding chapters dealt primarily with problems which arise in the negotiation of agreements and with the contents of agreements. Now our attention is directed to the problems of administering contracts. Effective administration requires the continued and patient efforts of both union and management personnel. Even the most carefully negotiated contract, constructed of model provisions precisely drafted, can be the source of confusion and bickering if it is poorly administered.

THE DISTINCTION BETWEEN NEGOTIATION AND ADMINISTRATION

The distinction between negotiation and administration within the framework of Slichter's definition of collective bargaining, although described earlier, is worthy of restatement here. Negotiating a contract is a legislative process involving the adoption of new rules and laws, binding on both parties. Administration corresponds to the judicial and executive processes, the interpretation and application of the contract to the day-to-day operation of employer-employee relations. By way of illustration, assume a foreman disciplines an employee with a three-day layoff for failing to complete his work assignment properly. This would be an executive action in the system of industrial jurisprudence. If the union objects on the grounds that this is in violation of the contract, it may file a grievance—the first step in a judicial process which would determine whether the foreman's executive action conformed to the contract.

In negotiating a new agreement, the union and management clearly sit on opposite sides of the table. Their goals are in conflict. But in administering the contract, there may appear to be no conflict in interests. Both parties want the contract to serve as an instrument of peace; both want its provisions obeyed and enforced until they are changed. They may join forces to punish violators of the contract. Negotiation entails a militant union ready to strike, whereas administration implies a cooperative union willing to abide by the contract.

Assuming that both parties are exerting all efforts to cooperate and always fully agree in interpreting the contract is, however, an oversimplified view of administration. At the opposite extreme the union may use the grievance procedure to bring constant pressure on the employer to change working conditions, to gain concessions it could not win when the contract was negotiated. Or management may take advantage of the fact that it holds the initial authority in setting working conditions and introduce a series of changes which do not comply with the spirit of the contract. Under these circumstances, of course, a serious conflict of interests occurs in the administration of the contract.

During the course of the administrative process the contract expands through settling specific cases which arise under its various clauses, becoming a living document stretched to cover all possible incidents of labor-management disagreement. The contract includes not only what is written down and signed by each party; it also includes shop practices and traditions, informal understandings between union officers and company supervisors, and the accumulation of grievance settlements. If there is a dispute over how these various phases of the contract apply to a particular incident, it is settled through the grievance procedure.

GRIEVANCE PROCEDURE

Since the grievance procedure is the heart of the administrative process, we must elaborate considerably on our earlier skeleton description. The grievance procedure serves three functions: 1) protecting the rights of both the employees and management, 2) acting as a system of communication, and 3) providing a procedure for solving new problems as they arise.

The contract defines the rights of the workers and the union and establishes the grievance procedure as the mechanism for protecting these rights. It is less widely recognized that the grievance procedure also protects management. Since it is an orderly system for settling disagreements that might otherwise lead to strikes, it assures the employer of greater stability of production. Furthermore, when an employee has a gripe against the company, he may file a grievance, and even though he loses his case, he is less likely to hold a grudge because he has had his "day in court." His steam has been blown off in an innocuous fashion without interfering with daily work or management policies.

The grievance procedure, being more than a simple mechanical process, serves as a system of communication between workers and their union and all levels of management, informing management of potential trouble spots in its personnel relations, and informing the union and the workers of management's attitudes toward various provisions of the contract.[1] For example, a large number of grievances from a particular department may indicate to management where improvements in supervision could be made or where policies need clearer explanation to employees. Or it may indicate to the union that the stewards are in need of more training, or serious factional troubles are brewing.

When technological changes occur or new products are introduced, individual workers or the union may feel that their rights have been transgressed. The grievance procedure then becomes a mechanism for adjusting to the new job assignments and wage rates. The contract must be interpreted to fit the new conditions. Hence, through the settlement of grievances the contractual relationship is continuously growing even though new contracts are written only periodically.

In serving these three functions, the grievance procedure does not operate automatically. We turn now to the techniques by which a particular grievance is handled and observe some of the problems which may be encountered in the process.

Processing a Grievance

As the provisions of the contract are applied to varied work situations in the plant—the executive process, in Slichter's terminology—it is inevitable that there will be differences of opinion, that some workers will feel the contract is not being properly applied to their jobs. The grievance machinery—the judicial process—is set into motion by the registration of a complaint by a worker. Immediately, the problem appears: Should he go first to his union steward or to his foreman? He will probably decide on the basis of the one to whom he feels

[1] See Leonard R. Sayles and George Strauss, *The Local Union: Its Place in the Industrial Plant* (New York: Harper & Brothers, 1953), especially pp. 27–29.

he owes the greater loyalty, or the one who will solve his problem more quickly and favorably. Thus, a conflict of loyalties between union and management appears as soon as the grievance appears. The steward and the foreman may openly compete for the loyalty of the worker, thus causing the grievance procedure to be a source of conflict rather than cooperation.

If the grievance is not settled between the foreman, steward, and worker, it goes on to the next step. Customarily, grievance handling is not conducted as formally as a reading of the contract might indicate. The workers soon learn the limitations on the powers of the foremen and the stewards. Management may give the foreman very little real authority to settle grievances for fear that different foremen may grant conflicting settlements. Under these circumstances the stewards, who deal with the foremen, would likewise have little power. In such cases the workers may go directly to higher officials in the union or management hierarchy. Quick and efficient settling of disputes depends on the amount of authority granted to the foremen and the stewards. If they trust and respect each other, grievances can be settled quickly and with a minimum of conflict. Clashing personalities at the foreman-steward level can soon cause a breakdown in the grievance machinery. Generally, where the collective bargaining relationship is characterized by mutual trust and confidence, grievances are settled at the foreman-steward level; otherwise decisions are centralized at the top union and management levels.

The important thing from the point of view of healthy industrial relations is not the precise order in which the steps are followed, but rather the way in which the grievances are settled: Are unimportant and ill-founded complaints dropped by the union? Are major grievances freely and openly aired and brought to a rapid and satisfactory conclusion? Or is the grievance machinery used as a mechanism for each party to make nuisance attacks on the other? To illustrate, if the union leaders have effectively won the respect of their membership, they will be able to tell disgruntled workers to drop their gripes when they are only imagined rather than real violations of the contract. On the other hand, when the leadership is uncertain of the support of the members, it may have to make a big fuss over every minor complaint.

When the grievance machinery has been working harmoniously and with mutual confidence over a period of time, the union exercises a portion of the decision-making power with respect to determining job assignments, wage incentives, promotion, overtime, layoffs, etc. By participating in these decisions, the union officers may find that they can satisfy some members only by antagonizing others. Just as conflicts of interest appear between various categories of union members in negotiating a contract, so they appear in administering a contract. Each worker is a member of one or more special groups, determined by his shift, his skill level, his seniority, etc. In numerous instances these special groups will be in conflict over what grievances are and how they should be settled. For example, a job may be assigned to lower-paid class "B" workers. The higher-paid and higher-skilled class "A" workers, claiming that it is properly their job, insist that the union press a grievance. The leadership is thus on the spot in deciding whom it should favor. Or, workers paid by the piece may claim that materials provided by the stockroom should be in better condition so they can process them more quickly, and file a grievance to that effect. But if this increases the work load of the stockroom employees, the union will have to make a choice between the conflicting groups.

The union officers therefore must act as politicians in finding compromises between feuding members. In order to satisfy a particular group, the officers may push grievances they have no hope of winning, perhaps even no desire to win. To protect themselves against the different factions, they may insist on rigid formality, requiring that grievances be presented in writing and signed, and they may "pass the buck" —the task of denying unfounded grievances—to the international representative or to the arbitrator.

Processing grievances may also bring about internal conflicts on the management side. Admitting that a foreman has too strictly interpreted a contract provision may undermine his authority over his workers. Or settling a seniority grievance in a manner satisfactory to department A may cause serious problems for management when used as a precedent in department B. Management may shift the burden of making the decision to the arbitrator.

Functions of the Arbitrator

If the grievance is not settled at any of its intermediate steps, it is sent to an arbitrator. Although not all collective agreements provide for arbitration as the final step, there has been an increasing tendency for this to be the case. About 90 per cent of the contracts now include arbitration. An outsider then decides the issue, perhaps with less knowledge of the real causes of the disagreement. The function of the arbitrator is to decide a dispute which the union and management have not been able to settle between themselves. He is impartial, having no economic interest in either the company or the union. His decision is binding: both parties must abide by it.

It is likely that a more satisfactory settlement would be made if the two parties were willing to compromise and reach an agreement among themselves. Therefore, arbitration is a last resort in a grievance procedure. The number of grievances pressed into arbitration is an indication of the success of the grievance procedure. Where a small proportion of the grievances go to arbitration, it is a sign that the union and management trust each other sufficiently to settle their disputes among themselves.

Arbitration should be distinguished from mediation. In both, a third party aids in settling the disagreement between the union and the management. However, in mediation the neutral party simply suggests possible settlements of the dispute. The mediator attempts to get the two opponents to reach their own solution, whereas the arbitrator pronounces a final verdict.

Arbitration may be used in writing a new contract, e.g., determining the new wage rate or seniority provisions, as well as serving as the final step in the grievance procedure. In this country the latter is much more common than the former and is the subject of our interest in this chapter.

The practice of arbitration is comparatively new. The standards of conduct and methods of procedure are not as yet clearly defined. Arbitrators themselves are frequently university professors, attorneys, clergymen, and judges. However, a growing group of professional personnel is bearing a larger portion of the load and is often preferred to the nonprofessionals by both unions and management. Increased professionalization has been accompanied by a rising cost of arbitration, often $100 or $150 per day, and twice that much or more is not unusual where traveling expenses are necessary. Since the cost is shared by management and the union, the high price acts as an incentive for the two sides to reach a settlement before arbitration is required.

The arbitrator may serve on a permanent basis, handling all grievances under a given contract. Or he may serve on an *ad hoc* basis; an arbitrator is selected for each dispute. Management and unions appear to have a slight preference for an *ad hoc* arrangement. Since the arbitrator wields tremendous authority over management and labor, both parties are extremely cautious in selecting him. If he is not a permanent arbitrator named in the contract, the typical method is for each side to submit a list of names for the other's consideration; otherwise the Federal Mediation and Conciliation Service (a governmental agency) or the American Arbitration Association (a private nonprofit organization) may be asked to submit a list. The names deemed unsatisfactory to either side are stricken, and the arbitrator is chosen from those remaining. The contract may state that if all names are eliminated, the FMCS or AAA is empowered to name the arbitrator. An arbitrator may have sole responsibility, or he may serve on a tripartite board with one member from management and one from labor who join in writing the decision, usually reached by a two-to-one vote. Generally, both management and the union prefer the single arbitrator.[2]

Should there be any limitation on the kinds of issues brought to arbitration? The study conducted by Warren and Bernstein found significant disagreement between management and labor on this issue, with unions favoring a wide-open field and management preferring some limitation. Management's preference for limitations reflects the desire to protect its prerogatives. As the range of issues pushed through the grievance procedure and into arbitration widens, the scope of collective bargaining is expanded and the area over which management has unchallenged jurisdiction is reduced. A company will sometimes refuse to concede on a grievance, pleading that the question up for decision is solely its prerogative and not a bargainable matter. When faced with such an issue, the arbitrator, before disposing of the grievance, must determine whether the contract gives him authority even to deal with it. In making his decision, the arbitrator, of course, relies primarily on the contract, but he may also give some weight to what he believes will contribute most to a stable relationship between the parties. When the decision goes against management, the range of prerogatives is less than what it was previously believed to be.

Many criticisms have been made of arbitration by unions, management, and the arbitrators themselves. Among management's criticisms are that arbitrators tend to be too favorable to unions, supposedly on the grounds that this will promote more stable collective bargaining relationships, and too lenient in disciplinary cases, particularly in not ordering discharge, the capital punishment of industrial relations. Management also argues that arbitrators tend to give the contract an interpretation which is much too broad, thus encroaching upon management prerogatives. The criticisms made by labor include the charge that

[2] Edgar L. Warren and Irving Bernstein, "A Profile of Labor Arbitration," *Industrial and Labor Relations Review,* Vol. IV (January, 1951), pp. 205–9.

arbitrators are too legalistic in their interpretation, writing long and wordy opinions to support their decision which have the effect of making it subject to different interpretations. The arbitrators claim that both sides are too critical: after granting a large amount of authority they complain when the authority is exercised. The arbitrators also observe that many of the cases brought to them should be settled directly by the two parties rather than be submitted to an outside party. And in some instances cases are brought just to save face for one side or the other.[3]

These are partisan criticisms. If they were universally true, the arbitration of grievances would soon be replaced by some other device. Since the decisions cover disputes which the two parties were unable to settle between themselves, it is not surprising that one or the other—and sometimes both—is dissatisfied. In defense of arbitration it must be remembered that the alternative is an unsettled dispute, often leading to a strike. At any time, even prior to its expiration date, management and the union, if they agree, may rewrite the contract so as to abrogate the effects of an arbitrator's decision.

What are the limits on the authority of the arbitrator? These are largely determined by the nature of the question which is submitted for his decision and by the provisions of the contract. However, arbitrators are frequently called upon to decide cases which are not precisely covered by the terms of the contract. When this happens, they rely on the customs and shop practices—the unwritten laws—which have been followed in the plant. Once a decision is rendered, refusal to abide by it on the part of either management or the union constitutes a violation of the contract. Either party may go to court to compel the other to obey the decision. Although legislation on this subject varies from state to state, courts will generally issue an order compelling obedience where it is appropriate. However, if the arbitrator renders a decision which goes beyond the question submitted to him or which is contrary to the contract, it may be set aside by the courts.

Long-Term Contracts

A new collective bargaining problem has developed in the years since World War II: administering long-term contracts. The trend toward two and three-year contracts was inaugurated by the 1948 agreement between General Motors Corporation and the United Automobile

[3] Tracy H. Ferguson, Herman Cooper, and Aaron Horvitz, "An Appraisal of Labor Arbitration," *Industrial and Labor Relations Review,* Vol. VIII (October, 1954), pp. 79–89.

Workers. Management's attitude toward the duration of the agreement is affected by the desirability of long periods without strikes. In industries having large investments in plant and equipment, the opportunity to compute labor costs with greater accuracy is a real advantage in developing long-run capital spending plans. However, more favorable concessions may have to be granted to the union in order to overcome its reluctance to commit itself far into the future.

The most hotly disputed issue in negotiating long-term contracts is providing for periodic adjustment of wage rates. The issue may be settled by allowing for contract reopening each year to renegotiate wages or by drafting formulas which make automatic adjustments. The formulas typically have two parts: an improvement factor, allowing for increases roughly matching productivity gains, and an escalator clause, involving adjustments for changes in the cost of living. For example, once each year wage rates may rise by six cents per hour (improvement factor), and every three months they may be raised or lowered two cents per hour for every one-point change in the Consumers' Price Index.

A long-term contract is feasible only if each side trusts the other's willingness to abide by the contract and administer it fairly. Hence, it is necessary to have a grievance procedure which permits introduction of new technology in a manner acceptable to both parties. Several years' experience is usually required to bring the collective bargaining to this mature stage. The security of a long-term contract aids the union in controlling internal factions; thus, their disruptive effect on grievances is reduced. Another prerequisite is an arbitrator, or group of arbitrators, whose wisdom and impartiality is mutually respected by management and the union.

THE LEGAL VERSUS THE HUMAN RELATIONS APPROACH TO GRIEVANCES

After a grievance procedure has been in operation for a few years, it adopts the coloring and personality of the shop. As disputes are settled, the evolving experience gives the grievance procedure a new complexion. This experience can develop in many ways, which can be divided into two categories: the legal and the human relations approach.

The two different approaches to grievances are paralleled by two different approaches to arbitration. There has been a continual controversy over the role that the arbitrator should play. Should he act as a judge, deciding which disputant should win and which lose in each case? Taking this legalistic approach, the arbitrator's decisions must strictly follow the letter of the contract and the precedents of previous decisions. Or is a broader interpretation of his function more realistic? Should he structure his decisions so as to promote harmonious industrial relations between the firm and the union? If he follows this approach, the arbitrator tends to broaden the meaning of the contract and existing shop practices. Though remaining impartial, he takes an active interest in helping to eliminate the sources of disagreement. If successful, the need for his services will be sharply reduced.

One purpose in examining the two approaches to grievance procedures and arbitration is to expand the understanding of the administrative aspects of collective bargaining. It should become clear that the same problem may be handled differently in different bargaining situations.

The Legal Approach

The legal approach emphasizes a strict application of the written contract to each grievance that arises. As grievances are settled, a body of precedents is built up which clarifies the interpretation of the contract. Each grievance is "reduced" to a written form and classified as a dispute over discharge, seniority, wage rates, job assignments, etc. Any grievance which is not distinct and which does not fit into a prescribed category is disallowed. Hence, all intangible elements are squeezed out of consideration.[4]

The strictly legalistic approach has a number of advantages. Is is simple and precise. Both parties know where they stand at each step in the grievance procedure and are better able to predict the arbitrator's decision. Complaints which are not valid grievances are not allowed to clutter the machinery. The precision of the legal approach may be necessary to the newly organized plant when the day-to-day relationships are first being established. In a large bargaining unit, particularly one covering many plants and many locals, uniformity in handling grievances can be more easily achieved through this approach.

When factional rivalry within the union threatens to become disruptive, a strict legalistic interpretation of the contract may be the most effective. Rigid adherence to the contract may be the only way of maintaining some semblance of shop order. Otherwise, each faction in the union will enter into competition to demonstrate which can make the most gains for its partisans through pushing grievances, regardless of how petty the complaint. Also, the legalistic approach may offer the

---

[4] Benjamin M. Selekman, *Labor Relations and Human Relations* (New York: Mc-Graw-Hill Book Company, 1947, pp. 75–110.

best protection against an extremely militant unionism which is taking advantage of the hostilities which are always present in employer-employee relationships. After all, it is the rare person who believes that his employer recognizes the full extent of his abilities and pays him accordingly. If the union promotes such hostilities and files a multitude of grievances, the employer will be compelled to follow strict interpretation of the contract.

A legalistic approach, however, has a number of disadvantages. Often, a grievance does not fit into any of the defined categories, but nevertheless it is a sign that something is wrong. For example, a group of workers may file a grievance, claiming that they have been unjustly disciplined by their foreman. If the rule infraction which they committed calls for that type of discipline, it would appear that their grievance is without foundation. According to the legalistic approach, it would be denied and the matter ended then and there. However, the grievance may really be the result of rules which do not fit the work situation, and therefore are not understood by the workers. It may be the result of the foreman showing favoritism for some workers over others, or a sudden "cracking down"—perhaps because of pressure from higher levels of management—and strictly enforcing rules which were previously administered laxly.

Under the legal approach, a poorly drawn contract provision can lead to a grievance settlement which is extremely unsatisfactory to one of the parties, and with which it must live until a new contract is negotiated. Poorly drawn contract provisions occasionally occur, since it is impossible to foresee all eventualities in union-management relations. What seemed like a harmless provision when the contract was negotiated may, when legalistically interpreted, cause an unnecessary and long-festering dissatisfaction preventing the development of a harmonious relationship.

The Human Relations Approach

In the previous chapter we discussed human relations as a personnel technique and management weapon in collective bargaining. The early practitioners of human relations tended to be authoritarian or paternalistic in their views of how to deal with individuals and groups of workers. The common attitude was that management knew what was best and the employees could be made to think the same way if they were manipulated properly. Further research in human relations revealed that industrial democracy—cooperation with unions—could, in many situ-

ations, more effectively increase production and satisfy other management
goals. As a result, a new approach to handling grievances appeared.

In the human relations approach the existence of grievances is viewed
as an indication that readjustments should be made in the union-
management relationship. Keeping in mind that one of the functions of
the grievance procedure is to serve as a system of communication, dismissing a complaint simply because it has no precise legal foundation
amounts to passing up an opportunity to gage the quality of worker-
management relationships. Instead, the complaint should be considered—
regardless of whether it is eventually granted or denied—and the background within which the incident occurred should be studied, even
if the grievance appears to have no valid basis. Both union and management officials should then take the proper action to eliminate the basic
cause of the grievance. The grievance, as formally presented, may be
only a symptom of the real difficulty.

To illustrate this point, suppose a worker is discharged for being tardy
more than five times in one month. Merely dismissing his complaint
on the grounds that his discharge is according to the shop rules over-
looks the opportunity to obtain valuable information. An investigation
may show that his work is never ready for him to start and therefore he
just stands idly by for the first hour each day. An improvement in work
scheduling may solve the problem and increase output at the same time.

Both the legal and the human relations approach stress the need for
gathering all facts pertinent to the grievance, but the approaches diverge
on the question of what is a pertinent fact. The human relations approach
includes personalities and emotions as worthy of study, whereas the
legal approach would tend to ignore them.

Both observance of the agreement and efficient production rest ultimately
upon the relationships of the men working together in the shop. Each grievance,
even as it mirrors those relationships, must also be handled through them. In
human relations the distinctions between cause and effect are seldom clean cut;
the ties that link the sequence in which one experience proceeds from another
are those of interacting influence. That is why grievances can be instruments
for promoting sound relations; while sound relations certainly are the best means
for dealing adequately with grievances.[5]

Thus, the grievance procedure becomes the mechanism by which
union-management relations continually expand and adjust to new situations. New problems, not specifically covered by the agreement, are
handled as they arise rather than being postponed to the next contract

[5] *Ibid.*, p. 110.

negotiations. In the human relations approach the sharp distinction between negotiation and administration is blurred. The status of union management relations is not changed abruptly at each contract renegotiation, but rather it is ceaselessly changing.

A warning should be introduced at this point. Even when management and labor make the most genuine efforts to follow a human relations approach to administering the contract, collective bargaining is not all milk and honey. The basic conflicts continue over dividing the output and balancing efficiency against worker security. Temporary solutions are reached with less acrimony and perhaps with greater advantage to employer and employees.

To restate the difference between the two approaches: the legalistic emphasizes correct and strict contract interpretation, with one side or the other scoring a victory in each dispute; the human relations approach emphasizes finding out what is wrong and what might be done to correct the situation in order to help both sides gain.

Integration of the Two Approaches

The differences between the two approaches have been emphasized so as to distinguish them clearly. The grievance settlements, even under the human relations approach, cannot be in violation of the contract. Using this approach

will not affect the basic aim of grievance procedure, which remains always, of course, the effective administration of the agreement. It will not even transform in any fundamental way the steps by which treatment is initiated. Instead, it will modify and expand prevailing procedures until orderly handling utilizes not only the law of the agreement but every instrument of control that psychological and social insights make available.[6]

The human relations approach may be carried on through the final step of the grievance procedure—arbitration. Where this is the case, the arbitrator also relies upon social and psychological insights. David Cole, one of the nation's foremost arbitrators, believes "it to be unwise to think of arbitration as litigation in the conventional sense. In litigation victory is the great objective, facts are withheld when they are detrimental to the search for victory, and there is no concern for the future relationship of the parties."[7] In either case the arbitrator is bound to

---

[6] *Ibid.*, pp. 87–88.
[7] David L. Cole, "Arbitration—Whose Responsibility?" *Proceedings of the Fourth Annual Meeting of the Industrial Relations Research Association,* December, 1951, ed. by L. Reed Tripp, p. 153.

abide by the contract, even if, in his opinion, the parties have made a poor agreement. The best he can do is give a reasonable and intelligent interpretation of the contract; one that is designed to promote healthy bargaining relations.

What is the attitude of management and unions with respect to the two approaches? This depends on the nature and history of the bargaining relationship. Where management is jealously guarding its prerogatives, it prefers the legal approach since it is more certain of just what decision-making power has been reserved as its right. In large firms with plants in many cities, a legal approach is preferred since this leads to greater consistency. Otherwise, the union may try to compel all plants to match the conditions in the plant most favorable to it. Unions show a greater preference than management for the human relations approach. However, where the international dominates the bargaining, there may be a tendency to be more legalistic. Since the human relations approach emphasizes direct settlement of grievances between foremen and stewards, it leaves the international with somewhat less control over the administrative aspects of collective bargaining.

Is it possible to integrate the two approaches? Yes, in the sense that the human relations approach, in order to have the necessary degree of consistency, must remain within the spirit of the agreement. In either case the written contract is supreme—it must not be violated—from the first step, formulating the grievance, to the final step, arbitration. Hence, the human relations approach is an amendment to the legal approach, not a replacement. It widens the horizons, adding greater flexibility and a broader point of view to the legal approach.

In general, management, concerned with maintaining its prerogatives, prefers not to broaden the coverage of the grievance machinery. Unions, seeking a larger sphere of participation in decision-making, favor an expansion of the application of the grievance machinery. The long-run trend has moved in the direction of the unions' preference, but the rate of change in the 1950's was small.

AREA COVERED BY THE CONTRACT

One factor which has a major impact on both the administration and the negotiation of collective agreements is the area covered by the contract. The two phases of collective bargaining are affected by whether the contract applies to only one firm, or to several firms. A collective agreement may cover a single firm having only one plant, or, at the opposite extreme, it may cover all employers in an industry and many locals of one or more internationals. Between these two extremes are many forms of multi-employer bargaining. One rather loose form is pattern bargaining, as in the basic steel industry. The union presents common demands to each of the large firms, and the resulting agreements are basically the same. In another form, groups of employers may join together and bargain with the union, concluding separate agreements for different geographical areas, as in the coal-mining and maritime industries. Finally, all the employers in the industry may bargain on a nation-wide basis, as in the flint-glass industry.

It is difficult, if not impossible, to estimate with any degree of accuracy the number of workers who are covered by multi-employer agreements. The primary reason stems from the difficulty in defining multi-employer bargaining. In many industries, e.g., construction and trucking, an association reaches an agreement with a union which is then followed by other employers in the same industry, even though they are not members of the association. These informal arrangements make it difficult to draw the line between what is and what is not multi-employer bargaining. In spite of these difficulties, it has been estimated that one-sixth of all contracts are multi-employer, covering one-third of all workers under collective agreements.[8]

Industry-wide or market-wide stabilization of wages and working conditions may develop even without unionization. In the steel industry uniformity in wage rate increases became apparent as early as 1904 in labor markets widely separated geographically. In short, some of the pressures for broadening the bargaining unit arise from sources other than unions.

What forces lead companies and unions to bargaining on a multi-employer basis? No neat, clear-cut answer can be given to this question; the forces are different in different industries, but a few cases may illustrate the nature of these forces.

In some industries, competition in the product market compels employers to insist that they all be treated equally by the union. In highly competitive industries, as in clothing, multi-employer bargaining standardizes a major cost item—labor costs. Without uniform piece-rates enforced on all producers, those paying union rates would be undersold by the other firms. It therefore becomes a major goal of the union to sign all employers to the same basic contract, and equally important to

[8] Van Dusen Kennedy, "Association Bargaining," *Monthly Labor Review*, LXXXII (May, 1959), p. 539.

enforce uniform administration of the contract. One of the primary issues in the strike of the International Ladies' Garment Workers' Union in 1958 arose out of the fact that some firms were making special deals with their locals. The employers who were abiding by the contract demanded that the union demonstrate that it could effectively police the laggard employers. In industries, then, that are characterized by many small firms with relatively low capital requirements for entering the business, the union must enforce uniform wage rates and working conditions if it is to preserve its existence. At the same time, companies with a long record of dealing with the union insist that marginal firms incur the same labor costs in order to eliminate one important basis for cutthroat competition.

In some industries employers desire to bargain jointly in order to avoid whipsaw tactics by the union; this is particularly characteristic of the construction trades, printing firms, and cleaning and laundry employers. In some cities associations of building contractors have a rather checkered history. They are liable to become inactive for a period of time, with little support from the member employers. After the building trades unions have made gains through whipsaw tactics, the association will again appear—perhaps only temporarily—as a major factor in collective bargaining.

In industries where the firms are very large, internal politics may compel the union to make similar bargains with each employer. To do otherwise would generate pressures against the leadership from the locals which have suffered by the discrimination. In some cases the union's policies, consciously or unconsciously, lead to an increased degree of concentration in the industry. The less efficient firms, unable to meet union standards for wages and working conditions and still sell at competitive prices, are driven out of business. However, unions may grant some concessions to the marginal firms located outside of the geographic centers of the industry if this does not undermine union wage rates in the main segments of the industry.

Hence, multi-employer bargaining—either through associations or pattern bargaining—may develop for a wide variety of causes. Furthermore, there appears to be a tendency for its influence to spread over a larger portion of the economy. Multi-employer bargaining has important consequences from the point of view of both the negotiation and the administration of collective agreements, and we now direct our attention to these.

Multi-Employer Bargaining—Negotiation

Multi-employer bargaining leads to fewer strikes since all companies are making the same concessions at the same time. Firms which otherwise might be reluctant to grant the concessions are under pressure from their fellow managers to join the united front. Thus, it is unnecessary for the union to strike laggard firms individually in order to bring them into line.

Strikes, when they do occur, however, have more far-reaching effects. Since all employers in the association are struck at once, an entire industry may be closed down. For this reason some public pressure has developed to pass laws restricting the area covered by the collective agreement. Such proposals have won the support of anti-union groups who believe this will reduce union strength generally.[9]

Although the first impression might be otherwise, it appears that small firms actually have more voice in the contents of the agreements when they bargain jointly than when they bargain individually. If no management association is present, the union is free to select the most profitable, or the most vulnerable, firm and use it as a leader to set wages and working conditions to be forced on the other firms within its bargaining orbit. Contrariwise, within the management bargaining association, the smaller firms are able to express themselves on the nature of the joint concessions to be made to the union. Thus, over the course of many years of bargaining, the small firms are better able to continue to compete with the large firms rather than being driven out of business. This, however, is not true in pattern bargaining, where the smaller firms may have little or nothing to say about the final agreement.

Multi-employer bargaining may be divided into two types: 1) one taking place within a metropolitan area and 2) the other extending beyond metropolitan areas. The geographical limits of competition in the product market generally determine which type will prevail in a particular industry. Typical of the first type is that between construction contractors and the building trades unions, or the printers' association and the International Typographical Union. In this type of bargaining the local and the business agent play a dominant role, with the opposite side being an employers' association of either the negotiatory or the administrative type.

In multi-employer bargaining extending beyond the metropolitan area, the employers may be represented by an association or they may bargain

[9] The subject of industry-wide strikes and public policy is discussed in Chapter 14.

on a pattern basis. In either case the international generally plays a much more important role than the locals because the final agreement is more likely to be precedent-setting, affecting many other locals. The international's negotiators are likely to take a broader point of view toward the bargaining and to exhibit a greater understanding of the problems of the industry than are the local's negotiators. The participation by the international does not necessarily lead to greater concessions from employers. More than the local's officials, the international's negotiators are likely to adjust the demands to the long-run economic needs of the industry. Not being responsible to the workers on a day-by-day basis, they are better able to take this attitude. Consequently, multi-employer bargaining may contribute to more stable union-management relations during the negotiatory stages.

Multi-Employer Bargaining—Administration

An administrative employers' association, wherever it represents management in the bargaining relationship, plays an important role in the daily application of the collective agreement. In the San Francisco Bay area study it was found that three-quarters of all employees covered by collective agreements were under contracts involving administrative employers' associations. Such bargaining involves the shifting of decision-making power from the individual employers to the associations.

> The effect of centralizing decisions, at least in San Francisco, generally seems to have turned collective bargaining, in a particularly pronounced way, into a political and legal institution, with formal procedures replacing informal ones and institutional relationships replacing personal relationships. Flexible personnel policies are supplanted by a legally defined system of rights and duties. Grievance procedure is vested in professional personnel. Differences of opinion are referred to the final authority of the contract, regardless of other considerations of equity.[10]

The employers' associations become institutionalized with their professional personnel having a vested interest in the continued operation of complicated administrative procedures. Similarly to the unions, they become very concerned over any threats to their continued survival.

In handling grievances, the association replaces the employer. That is, any grievance brought by the union is against the association as much as it is against any particular company. Just as the union insists on having all workers' grievances handled by the union in order to secure

[10] Clark Kerr and Lloyd H. Fisher, "Multi-Employer Bargaining: The San Francisco Experience," *Insights Into Labor Issues*, ed. by Richard A. Lester and Joseph Shister (New York: The Macmillan Company, 1948), p. 33.

uniformity, the association insists that all employers grant grievance handling powers to the association in order to secure uniformity. Either a common arbitrator or a common system of arbitration is adopted. In some cases the association goes so far as to standardize personnel techniques among all the employers. For example, all job descriptions and job evaluations are standardized, and thus wage rates are equalized in all of the firms.

The human relations approach to grievances may be used very successfully within the framework of an administrative employers' association. This is amply demonstrated by the nature of union-management relations in the clothing industry in a number of eastern metropolitan areas. During the long history of harmonious relations in both the men's and women's clothing industry, the International Ladies' Garment Workers and the Amalgamated Clothing Workers have demonstrated a reasonable concern for the employers' economic problems, while management, in turn, has accepted the union as a permanent partner in production. This allows for a give-and-take within the individual plant with very little emphasis on legalism. Furthermore, the permanent arbitrators who have served in the clothing industry have been men of much wisdom and experience, stressing the settlement of problems rather than declaring a winner and a loser in each dispute.

The legalistic approach to grievance handling is adopted by some management associations, particularly when the firms have joined forces in response to whipsaw tactics by a militant union. An absolutely solid front may be the only way of preventing the union from continuing its practice of winning special grievance settlements with the companies one at a time. Legalism will also be emphasized by a management association when its professional staff is ambitious to expand its authority. Centralizing control over every little decision becomes a technique for enhancing its prestige.

SUMMARY

Though less spectacular than the forces at play in negotiation, the administrative aspects of collective bargaining are no less important. The heart of the administrative process is the grievance machinery. To be effective in protecting the rights of the parties, the grievance procedure establishes arbitration as the final step for settling disagreements on how the contract applies to a particular case. In handling grievances, a union must resolve conflicting interests among its own members, and at the same time promote workable relationships with management. The grievance procedure communicates much valuable information, which, when intelligently interpreted by management and the union, contributes significantly to maintaining harmonious relations.

There are two approaches to the grievance machinery and arbitration, legal and human relations. The legal approach puts its emphasis on strict interpretation of the contract and confining all grievances to the scope of the contract. The human relations approach attempts to go beyond this, applying broad social and psychological insights to the operation of the grievance machinery. The contract is still supreme, but it is given a broader interpretation, and a greater willingness is shown to hear complaints which may not have been envisioned at the negotiation of the contract. The two aproaches are not inconsistent, since the contract is basic to both; the human relations approach builds on the legal approach. The tendency, over a period of time, has been to expand the strict legal approach in the direction of the human relations approach as the collective bargaining relationship between management and the union matures. However, this is not a universal tendency. In some cases, e.g., the automobile industry, the union and management have continued to deal with each other on a strictly legal basis over long periods of time.

The administration of the contract, as well as the negotiation, is affected by the area covered by the contract. There is a trend toward larger and larger geographical and economic coverage for the collective agreement. This leads to fewer but larger strikes, and tends to increase the bargaining role played by the international. When multi-employer bargaining is carried out by an administrative employers' association, the control of the grievance handling may rest with the association. Authority on these matters passes from the individual management to the collective group.

DISCUSSION QUESTIONS

1. Collective bargaining is more than the fireworks of writing a new contract; it includes the day-to-day relations between management and the union. Explain.

2. The grievance procedure is the heart of the administrative process in collective bargaining. Illustrate this statement with two or three examples.

3. Explain how the grievance procedure makes the contract a living, growing document.

4. In what sense is the grievance procedure a system of communications?

5. What information would you try to secure if you had to judge how well a grievance procedure is operating? What standards of good operation would you set? Why?

6. What are the probable conflicting pressures on management in the settlement of grievances? What are the probable conflicting pressures on unions in the settlement of grievances?

7. "Arbitration should be used sparingly and only as a last resort." Comment, showing to what extent you agree.

8. What special pressures are put on the administrative process when contracts are written to cover a three-year period?

9. Compare and contrast the legal and human relations approaches to the grievance procedure. Under what conditions would the former be more suitable? Explain your answer.

10. What are the advantages of the human relations approach over the legal approach to grievance handling?

11. Are the legal and human relations approaches inconsistent with each other? Explain your answer.

12. From the point of view of negotiating new contracts, what differences are liable to result from the employers bargaining jointly rather than individually?

13. Compare the position of the small employer in pattern bargaining with his position in association bargaining.

14. "The professional personnel in an administrative employers' association may become institutionalized in its position." Explain. What effects will this possibly have on the administration of the contract?

BIBLIOGRAPHY

Arensberg, Conrad M.; Barkin, Solomon; Chalmers, W. Ellison; Wilensky, Harold L.; Worthy, James C.; and Dennis, Barbara D. (editors). *Research in Industrial Human Relations.* New York: Harper & Brothers, 1957.

Davey, Harold W.; Kaltenborn, Howard S.; and Ruttenberg, Stanley H. (editors). *New Dimensions in Collective Bargaining.* New York: Harper & Brothers, 1959.

Kornhauser, Arthur; Dubin, Robert; and Ross, Arthur M. (editors). *Industrial Conflict.* New York: McGraw-Hill Book Company, 1954.

Proceedings of the Conference on Industry-Wide Collective Bargaining, May, 1948. Philadelphia: University of Pennsylvania Press, 1949.

Sayles, Leonard R., and Strauss, George. *The Local Union: Its Place in the Industrial Plant.* New York: Harper & Brothers, 1953.

Selekman, Benjamin M. *Labor Relations and Human Relations.* New York: McGraw-Hill Book Company, 1947.

Warne, Colston E. (editor). *Industry-Wide Collective Bargaining, Promise or Menace?* Boston: D. C. Heath and Company, 1950.

Warren, Edgar L., and Bernstein, Irving. "A Profile of Labor Arbitration," *Industrial and Labor Relations Review,* Vol. IV (January, 1951), pp. 200–22.

Whyte, William F. *Money and Motivation.* New York: Harper & Brothers, 1955.

12

ANTITRUST REGULATION

OF UNIONS

The government has played an important role in union-employer relations since the days worker organizations first appeared in this country. With the growth of collective bargaining, there has been a continuing, though uneven, trend toward an increasing amount of government participation, influencing the goals and tactics of management and the goals, tactics, and growth of unions. This trend will probably continue as the public attempts to shape the institutions of collective bargaining into patterns of behavior which conform to standards of fairness and economic efficiency.

Our discussion of government regulation of collective bargaining, covering this and the following two chapters, begins with an analysis of court suppression of union activity.[1] But first we want to consider the policy goals which the public may seek through its efforts to control labor-management relations and briefly survey the history of government interference.

POLICY OBJECTIVES OF PUBLIC REGULATION

What do we hope to accomplish by restricting the freedom of unions and companies in their dealings with each other? One answer frequently offered is: equality of bargaining power. But bargaining power defies accurate measurement; and certainly it is impossible to predict precisely

[1] The examination of government regulation of labor affairs is not completed in these three chapters. We will later look into other important matters such as minimum wage and social security legislation.

how a particular law will affect the relative strength of each side. Even while laws remain unchanged, the bargaining power of both labor and management fluctuates widely with varying economic conditions, internal changes in leadership and members' loyalty, or modifications of company personnel techniques. These comments do not imply that the public should tolerate grossly uneven bargaining power, but rather that the goals of policy cannot usefully be stated in terms of *equality* of bargaining power.

Another goal frequently suggested for public policy is to strengthen and spread collective bargaining as a technique for settling disputes. This can be achieved only by encouraging the growth of unions. Of course, there are many persons, both inside and outside of unions, who believe democracy would be more vigorous and better equipped to protect the rights of all citizens, regardless of economic status, if the great majority of workers belonged to strong organizations. But the goal, when stated in these terms, arouses antagonism among large segments of the population, particularly since the increase in union political and economic power in the 'thirties and 'forties. And the proposal does have the ring of favoring one side as opposed to the other.

The objectives of government interference in collective bargaining can perhaps best be stated in neutral terms: 1) to encourage a continuous flow of production, especially preventing the cessation of production of vital goods and services; 2) to prescribe and enforce a code of fair conduct to be observed by the two parties in their relations with each other—in other words, to prevent either side from taking unfair advantage of the other in collective bargaining; and 3) to prevent the two parties from reaching agreements which abrogate the rights of other groups of workers or which restrict the flow of production and unduly burden the price system. The third objective must be included because the agreements determine the incomes and working conditions of millions of workers and affect the prices paid by all consumers; therefore, the government must protect the public against the possibility of collusion between the two powerful interest groups.

A fourth objective, somewhat different in nature, should be added: prevention of undemocratic practices and fiscal malpractices in unions. Since they exercise so much influence over the economic affairs of their members, unions and their leaders should be required to carry out their responsibilities in the best interests of their constituency.

In regulating labor-management relations, as much freedom as possible should be allowed to the two parties. A minimum of government interference is in keeping with our traditions, or at least, our alleged traditions. Defining what constitutes **too** much interference will always be controversial—as we shall soon **see**—and no answer satisfactory in all conditions can be found. But as a general policy the two sides should have sufficient freedom to experiment with new contract clauses and to adjust to the ever-changing economic environment.

SURVEY OF GOVERNMENT REGULATION

In its collective bargaining policies, the government has never clearly pursued the objectives listed, or any other clearly defined set of goals. Rather, executive action, court decisions, and legislation have evolved pragmatically as situations developed which attracted the attention of the public. Naturally, both labor and management have sought to influence all branches of government, each hoping to bring about interference in its own behalf.

Chronologically, the government has passed through three stages in its control of labor-management relations. The first stage, restriction of unions with no attempt to define and protect legitimate activity, started at the beginning of the last century and lasted until 1935. The second stage, dominated by the Wagner Act, was characterized by encouraging the spread of organization through placing a number of restrictions on management and few or no restrictions on unions. The third and current stage, beginning in 1947 with the enactment of the Taft-Hartley Act and including the Labor-Management Reporting and Disclosure Act of 1959, features both regulation and protection of each of the parties.

Labor-management relations have been—and are now—regulated by all three branches of government, at the state level as well as the federal level. Historically, the judicial branch was the first on the scene, interpreting the common law to restrict union activity. The state and federal courts continue to apply common law, and now also legislation, in exercising their controls over labor-management relations. The legislative branch exerts its influence by enacting laws designed to change the whole scope of collective bargaining in one stroke. Congress and the state legislatures have established administrative boards for enforcement of such legislation. These boards, in turn, adopt rules and regulations which must be observed by both parties, thus adding further to our labor law. The executive branch of the government enters the picture through enforcement of the laws and through interference in disputes which affect the national health and welfare.

These areas of direct regulation refer only to the obvious influences. Behind the scenes the political push and pull between and within both major political parties and the lobbying before legislative committees and executive agencies likewise play an important role. In short, public regulation of labor-management relations includes more than legislation and administrative agencies. The legal aspects of labor-management relations range from legislative halls to county courthouses to smoke-filled rooms.

THE CONSPIRACY DOCTRINE

The courts played the leading role during the first stage of government control of labor-management relations. Their early decisions were based on the common law—the accumulated precedents of previous court decisions—rather than on specific statutes passed by legislative bodies. The American courts followed the English common law doctrine of conspiracy, applying it to unions throughout most of the nineteenth century.

During much of this period, the judges—drawn largely from the middle and upper socio-economic groups—were very sympathetic to the needs and interests of the owners of industry. Their attitude was often characterized by a lack of sympathy, and often outright antagonism, for the organizations of workers which interfered with "normal" business relations. The judges were merely reflecting the prevailing social attitudes: allow the private owners of industry to develop the country as rapidly as possible and with a minimum amount of interference.

The first important instance of court regulation was the Philadelphia cordwainers' case of 1806. The case grew out of the changing nature of shoe manufacturing in Philadelphia and other urban centers. With the growth of the contract system in place of personal orders for shoes—the "bespoke" system—and the development of improved transportation facilities, the shoe manufacturers in Philadelphia were in competition with those in other cities. To meet the competition, the master cordwainers reduced wages, acting through an early form of an employers' association. The cordwainers' union struck to regain their previous wage rates and to prevent the masters from employing anyone not a member of their union. Their purpose in seeking the closed shop was to prevent non-members from undercutting union wage rates.

The employers, anxious to increase their sales in the expanding settlements in the West and the South, took their case to court. A grand jury indicted the journeymen cordwainers on the charge of engaging in a criminal conspiracy. After hearing the case, the judge charged the trial jury as follows: "A combination of workmen to raise their wages may be considered in a two-fold point of view: one is to benefit themselves . . . the other is to injure those who do not join their society. The rule of law condemns both." The real concern of the judge is found in his rhetorical question: "Is there any man who can calculate (if this is tolerated) at what price he may safely contract to deliver articles, for which he may receive orders, if he is to be regulated by the journeymen in an arbitrary jump from one price to another?"[2] This was the statement of a supposedly impartial defender of the law. The jury, consisting exclusively of merchants and employers, found the defendants guilty of criminal conspiracy to raise wages. The court fined the defendants $8.00 each. According to this interpretation of the conspiracy doctrine it was permissible for a single worker to threaten to leave his employment unless he received specified wages and working conditions, but it was a criminal conspiracy for two or more workers to join together and jointly refuse to work unless granted specified concessions.

The charge to the jury represented the opinion of the "substantial" citizens of the community. At that time in our history only property owners had the right to vote, and the common law was interpreted to uphold their interests. The judge argued that supply and demand should regulate prices and wages, and accused the union of imposing artificial barriers to the operation of economic law, thus taking undue advantage of the public. The doctrines of the classical economists held sway in the courtrooms as well as the classrooms.

The decision rendered in the cordwainers' case became a precedent enforced in the courts of most states. Obviously, wherever this doctrine was employed, it closed off the major areas of union activity. If it was a criminal act to join together to raise wages and to bargain for a closed shop, the main functions of unions were eliminated. It is little wonder that the unions attempted to improve their lot through political action. The reactions of the workers to the criminal conspiracy doctrine included waves of strikes and mob violence. In a few instances the unfairness of the decisions was condemned by newspapers and public leaders. But in the main the most influential segments of public opinion were against unions on the grounds that they threatened the "rights" of employers to conduct their businesses and impeded the economic development of the country. What was perhaps the most extreme position of the courts

---

[2] Quoted from Charles O. Gregory, *Labor and the Law* (revised edition), (New York: W. W. Norton & Co., Inc., 1949), p. 24.

appeared in another Pennsylvania case, decided in 1821. The court ruled that the criminal conspiracy doctrine did not apply to a combination of employers to combat union efforts to raise wages. If the workers joined together to raise wages, it was a criminal conspiracy, but it was perfectly legal for employers to join together to depress wages. This could hardly be called even-handed justice.

The precedent of the cordwainers' case was modified in the decision in the *Commonwealth* v. *Hunt* case in 1842. In the factual background to this case, a group of workers had organized to raise their wages and to prevent others from working for less than the agreed rates. Chief Justice Shaw, of the Supreme Court of Massachusetts, ruled that union organization in and of itself is not necessarily a conspiracy, that the goals of the union may be harmonious with the goals of society. That is, in each case, the goals sought by the union must be examined to determine whether there had been a criminal conspiracy. Shaw's opinion was undoubtedly influenced by the likelihood of a severe strike wave if he decided against the union. The rise of the factories in Massachusetts had changed the relationships between employers and employees, and the latter had won some public support for improvements in their condition.

Although the *Commonwealth* v. *Hunt* case seemed to make union activity legal under many circumstances, it did not end the application of the conspiracy doctrine to unions. In fact there were more cases after 1842 than before. Only some of the states accepted the Massachusetts case as a precedent. It was not until after 1880 that the early form of the conspiracy doctrine ceased to be applied to union activity. By the end of the nineteenth century the courts dressed the doctrine in new clothing and continued to use it to regulate union activity.

ANTITRUST ACTIONS AGAINST UNIONS

In 1890 Congress passed the Sherman Act, whose purpose was to eliminate all monopolies and all conspiracies in restraint of trade. The primary objective was to restrict the growth of large corporations which were monopolizing many branches of industry. Within a short time, however, it was applied to unions. There are three techniques for enforcing the Act: 1) civil suits for triple damages, permitting the party who is damaged as a result of monopolistic activities to go to court and sue the monopolist for three times the amount of loss he (the plaintiff) suffered; 2) criminal suits, providing for fines and imprisonment for those engaging in monopolistic activities or in conspiracies to restrain trade (by amendment to the original Act, the fines range up to $50,000 and imprisonment up to five years for each criminal offense); and 3) the Attorney General may seek an injunction in the federal courts to stop any attempt to monopolize or restrain trade. An injunction is a court order directing someone to cease or perform a certain action. The penalty for disobeying an injunction is contempt of court, entailing a fine or imprisonment to whatever extent the judge deems appropriate.

In the Danbury Hatters' case, decided by the United States Supreme Court in 1908, the Sherman Act was interpreted to cover any union activity that was monopolizing or a conspiracy in restraint of trade. The case grew out of a nation-wide organizing campaign by the United Hatters of North America. As part of the campaign the union had attempted to organize the hat shop operated by Dietrich Loewe and Martin Fuchs in Danbury, Connecticut. When the company refused to recognize the union, a secondary boycott was put into effect by having all union members refuse to patronize any store selling the company's hats. Retail hat stores were visited by union members and were requested not to handle Loewe hats, on penalty of losing all union customers. Since the AFL cooperated in the United Hatters' campaign, Loewe's sales began to decline.

As a consequence of its losses, the company decided to sue the union for triple damages under the Sherman Act. In the long and expensive lawsuits which followed, the company was encouraged and financially assisted by the American Anti-Boycott Association, an organization sponsored by employers anxious to eliminate the boycott as a union bargaining weapon. The company won the decision, and in a later case (1915), the Supreme Court ruled that since the union had inadequate funds, the members were individually responsible for paying the damages awarded. The AFL, however, took up a special collection; otherwise many hatters would have been forced to sell their homes or go into personal bankruptcy. The company itself was forced into bankruptcy and Loewe lived out his last years on charity. To complete the irony, his grandson, an employee in a hat factory, became a member of the union.[3]

The consumer boycott, a favorite union weapon, was thus made illegal by the Danbury Hatters' case. The old conspiracy doctrine was back again, now in the form of a conspiracy in restraint of trade. The unions naturally marshaled their political power toward amending the

[3] Elias Lieberman, *Unions before the Bar* (New York: Harper & Brothers, 1950), pp. 56–70.

Sherman Act so that it would not apply to union activity. They believed their objective had been won in the Clayton Act, passed by Congress in 1914, which included provisions interpreted by Samuel Gompers and other labor leaders as excluding unions from the coverage of the Sherman Act. The Clayton Act stated (in Section 6) that labor was not an article of commerce, and (in Section 20) that unions engaging in legitimate and lawful activities were not to be considered illegal combinations in violation of the Sherman Act.

The joy of the unions was dispelled within a few years. In the Duplex Printing Company decision issued by the Supreme Court in 1921, the Clayton Act was interpreted in a manner which caused it to be of no benefit to the unions, leaving their position under the Sherman Act unchanged. In fact, the new statute provided management with an additional legal weapon to use against unions. Whereas the Sherman Act had allowed only the Attorney General to seek injunctions, employers were now permitted to go directly to the federal courts to seek injunctions against unions.

The Duplex Printing case involved an injunction against the International Association of Machinists which was sustained by the Supreme Court on the grounds that the union was restraining trade by conducting a secondary boycott. The IAM had organized all manufacturers of printing presses except the Duplex Company. The organized firms, as a consequence of the competitive pressures from Duplex, threatened to end their agreements unless the union could organize the company and force it to provide comparable wages and working conditions. An organizing strike at the Duplex plant in Battle Creek, Michigan, was completely unsuccessful. The union then boycotted all Duplex printing presses in New York City by refusing to install or service them, thus effectively driving the company out of one of its major markets. This secondary boycott was adjudged to be in restraint of trade. The Supreme Court ruled that it was not a legitimate and lawful union activity to be protected by Section 20 of the Clayton Act. It argued that there was no legitimate labor dispute since the union had not organized Duplex Printing Company employees. To be a labor dispute in the eyes of the law, it was necessary for the striking or boycotting workers to be employees of the company against which pressure was aimed. In effect, the Court said it would continue to decide, on the same basis as before the Clayton Act, what was legitimate and lawful union activity. Unions were no better off than in the previous century under the old common law.

The Duplex Printing case made the secondary boycott an illegal weapon. During the 1920's the bulk of the union movement consisted of craft unions, many of which relied on this weapon to expand their membership and eliminate nonunion competition. Without the secondary boycott, pockets of nonunionism could often resist organization, and even though small, relative to the whole market area, might create enough competitive pressure to undermine the union's bargaining power and keep wages down.

In the Coronado Coal case (1925) the Supreme Court's decision went even further than in the Duplex case. A number of mining companies in Arkansas and Oklahoma attempted to dislodge the union. In response the United Mine Workers conducted a number of strikes closing the nonunion mines. The strikes featured considerable damage to the mining properties, and the loss of several lives in gun battles between the strikers and the plant guards and imported strike-breakers. The companies sued for triple damages. After many years of litigation, twice before the Supreme Court, the case was settled out of court. However, the doctrine was established that when a union strikes with the *intent* of preventing goods from flowing into interstate commerce, the union is engaging in a conspiracy in restraint of trade. Henceforth, any time a union attempted to raise wages in any company engaged in interstate commerce, the courts might declare it to be in violation of the antitrust laws. Striking a nonunion company to compel it to agree to union wages and working conditions would be in conflict with the law as long as it could be proved that the purpose of the union was to prevent the company's goods from flowing into interstate commerce. And this could be proved with very little difficulty when the union dealt with employers whose goods were sold across state lines. It is no wonder that the unions sought relief from the antitrust laws.

Injunctions

The technique used by the Court to halt the secondary boycott of the International Association of Machinists in the Duplex Printing Company case was an injunction. Injunctions are issued by equity courts, which differ from ordinary courts in that their purpose is to do justice where the ordinary procedures of law would not be adequate. An injunction in a labor dispute immediately stops a union from engaging in illegal actions which might permanently impair the employer's business, e.g., by causing a permanent loss of sales. By the usual civil court procedures, even if the firm could eventually win money payments through suing the union for damages, this would be too late to restore business to its normal levels. Seeking damages through a civil suit involves very lengthy litigation, particularly when the case is appealed to a higher level court. Without a speedy court procedure, employers may find it less costly to capitulate to the union's illegal attack, rather than offer resistance and engage in long, tedious litigation. In fact, for small employers, bankruptcy may occur before the courts are able to determine whether the union has been acting illegally. Hence, equity courts should be prepared to enter labor-management relations whenever quick action is required.

The injunction, by restricting the aggressor from taking any action, preserves the status quo—the existing situation—the logic being that if everything is held in its original condition, neither party will suffer while the court is making its judgment. If the strike or boycott is deemed to be legal, the union may then go ahead. However, the delay may put the union at serious disadvantage in terms of timing its strike, perhaps because the employer has built up a large inventory of finished goods or the members' enthusiasm cannot be aroused to the strike level. In other words, the injunction may be—and has been—used as a technique to defeat a perfectly legitimate strike.

Typically, the following steps are taken during the course of injunction proceedings. An employer, believing that the actions of a union are illegal and damaging, or are threatening to damage his business, brings to court sworn affidavits to that effect. If the judge agrees that quick action is necessary and that adequate remedies are not available through other court procedures, he issues a temporary restraining order directing the union to cease engaging in specified activities. A temporary restraining order has the same effect as an injunction. It remains in effect a few days until the court has given the union the opportunity to present its side of the case. If the judge is still of the opinion that the union's actions should be stopped, he then issues a temporary injunction, which will last a few more days. This is designed to hold the union in check until a careful examination can be made of whether it should be allowed to proceed or be permanently prevented from following its original course of action. This decision is made at another hearing, at which both sides present their evidence and cross-examine witnesses. If the judge is convinced by the employer's evidence and reasoning, a permanent injunction is then issued.

If the union or its leaders violate the injunction, they are in contempt of court and subject to a fine and imprisonment. Before the enactment

of the Norris-LaGuardia Act in 1932, the trial to determine whether
the union leaders were actually in contempt was conducted without
a jury and was often before the same judge who issued the injunction.
Frequently these injunctions were written in very broad language,
completely restricting any union action, and even preventing discussion
of the case. The injunction procedure left much room for abuse by
judges who were not impartial.

An employer with a strike or other union pressure on his hands went to a
judge, regardless of whether or not he was actually sitting on the bench at the
time, submitted to him affidavits made out by his own agents to the effect that
the strikers or other union folk were about to commit or were committing,
and would continue to commit, alleged unlawful acts at his plant, all of which
would cause irreparable damage to his property, and prayed for a restraining
order pending suit for a permanent injunction. Judges usually issued such
orders on request, frequently in the absence of anyone representing the persons
to be enjoined. Sometimes these orders were directed at named individuals, but
frequently they were not. And in any event they all purported to restrain
everyone "whomsoever," in a vague but grand manner. Obviously not much
care was devoted in these transactions to legal theory or even to what was
actually transpiring around the plant. And by the time the matter was set for
the trial which was to determine whether or not the employer was justified in
securing protection of this sort, the strike was broken up, either through the
obedience of the union leaders or because they were in jail for disobedience.[4]

Injunctions were used in labor disputes prior to the Sherman Act,
and increased in number after the passage of that Act and particularly
after the Debs case in 1894. An injunction was secured by the United
States Attorney General and federal troops were used to crush a strike
by Debs' American Railway Union. There was a further increase in the
number of injunctions issued after the Clayton Act was passed. Witte
found records of nearly 2,000 injunctions between 1880 and 1931, and
estimated that there were many more for which no records were kept.[5]
During the railroad shopmen's strike of 1922, several hundred injunctions were issued, with nearly every federal district court becoming
involved.

One of the most famous injunctions enforced the yellow dog contract.
A yellow dog contract is an agreement which the employer compels an
employee to sign in order to continue to hold his job, promising never
to join a union while in the employ of the company. The Hitchman Coal
and Coke Company had such contracts with its employees. The United

    [4] Gregory, *op. cit.*, p. 100.
    [5] Edwin E. Witte, *The Government in Labor Disputes* (New York: McGraw-Hill
Book Company, Inc., 1932), p. 84.

Mine Workers' organizers attempted to persuade the employees to promise to join the union, not actually to join it, in spite of these contracts. The company sought and was granted an injunction to stop the union from encouraging the workers to violate the intent of their yellow dog contracts. The United States Supreme Court in 1917 upheld the injunction on the grounds that the union was inducing breach of contract. The yellow dog contract was thus raised to the status of legal enforceability.

For unions the American legal environment was extremely hostile until 1932. The courts, with their injunctions and restraint of trade decisions, impeded union growth and set narrow limits on the range of legitimate activity. Generally, the legal environment reflected the attitudes of the groups most influential in forming public opinion. To them, unions constituted a barrier to the full development of the free enterprise system by interfering with the rights of individual workers and employers to contract for labor as they saw fit. But the advent of the great depression changed public attitudes and brought legislation more favorable to union growth.

THE NORRIS-LAGUARDIA ACT

Unions were naturally disappointed with the course of events during the 1920's. They blamed their declining membership partly on the adverse court decisions. Their political activities finally bore fruit with the Norris-LaGuardia Act in 1932, passed before the New Deal came to power. The primary purpose of the new law was to restrict the authority of the federal courts in issuing injunctions in labor disputes. It listed a number of union techniques which were to be free of injunctive interference, including striking, inducing others to strike, picketing, paying strike benefits, and by other means giving aid to workers in a labor dispute.

Although the Norris-LaGuardia Act does not completely prohibit federal courts from issuing injunctions in labor disputes, the eventual interpretation caused it to have this effect for most practical purposes. It established a number of procedural barriers making it more difficult for employers to secure injunctions and more difficult for federal courts to grant them. The employer is not eligible for injunctive protection unless he enters the courts with "clean hands;" that is, he must have made reasonable efforts to settle the dispute, including a demonstration of willingness to bargain with the union. He also must have obeyed all relevant laws, and must prove that the damage he will suffer if no injunctive relief is granted will be greater than the damages the union will suffer as a consequence of an injunction. Furthermore, if union leaders are brought to trial on contempt of court charges for allegedly violating an injunction, they may ask for a judge other than the one who granted the injunction, and they are also given the right to have a jury trial.

The Norris-LaGuardia Act gave a broad definition to the term "labor dispute." The definition includes secondary boycotts within the allowable area of economic conflict, thus giving anti-injunction protection to this union activity. The statute also made yellow dog contracts unenforceable in the courts. Many states followed the leadership of the federal government by adopting "little Norris-LaGuardia Acts."

Since the passage of the Act, unions have fared much better before the courts, partly because of the law and partly because of changes in the personnel of the federal courts. An important step was taken in this direction with the decision in the Apex Hosiery Company case in 1940. The Supreme Court in effect reversed its Coronado decision. The essential facts in the case closely paralleled those in the Coronado case, including damage to company property and interfering with the shipment of goods in interstate commerce. It was a civil case, a suit for triple damages. The Court ruled that the union activity in this instance was not covered by the Sherman Act. This interpretation of the law greatly expanded the freedom of unions to strike companies which sold goods across state lines.

In 1941 the Supreme Court issued a decision that went much further than the Apex decision in freeing unions from antitrust prosecution. The case grew out of a jurisdictional dispute. The carpenters, objecting to a contract awarded to the machinists to erect wooden platforms for installation of machinery, picketed new construction work being done at the Anheuser-Busch Company in St. Louis, Missouri. When the construction company continued to refuse to award the contract to the carpenters, the union decided to apply a secondary boycott. It urged all carpenters and their friends to cease purchasing Anheuser-Busch beer, hoping that this would cause the brewery to direct the construction company to hire carpenters and discharge machinists.

Anheuser-Busch retaliated by urging the United States Attorney General to bring criminal charges under the Sherman Act against William Hutcheson, president of the carpenters' union. The indictment charged Hutcheson and other officers of the union with criminal conspiracy in restraint of trade. The defendants argued that the Norris-

LaGuardia Act included jurisdictional disputes within the allowable area of economic conflict, and thus protected them from antitrust prosecution. In its decision, freeing Hutcheson of the charges, the Supreme Court reinterpreted Section 20 of the Clayton Act in the light of the Norris-LaGuardia Act. The effect of this decision was to relieve unions of all antitrust prosecution in the federal courts as long as their actions could be construed as pursuing their self-interest as a union. As a consequence, unions were left almost entirely outside the scope of civil cases (suits for damages), criminal cases, and injunctions under the antitrust laws.

The importance of the Hutcheson decision was spelled out by the Allen Bradley case, decided by the Supreme Court in 1945. The International Brotherhood of Electrical Workers, Local No. 3, held a tight grip on the electrical equipment market in New York City. Local No. 3 had organized both the production workers in the companies which manufactured electrical equipment and the highly skilled electricians who installed the equipment in construction projects. The union permitted only installation of equipment manufactured by New York City firms, hence manufacturers located outside of the area were denied access to this lucrative market. The same equipment was sold in New York City at one price and outside of New York City at a much lower price; as a consequence, the local manufacturers made large profits in the guaranteed market. The electrical contractors were willing to pay high prices for the equipment they installed, since their profits were determined on the basis of cost plus a percentage mark-up set by the contractors' association. The more they paid for labor and equipment, the more profits they earned on any single construction project. The contractors had no fear of being underbid by nonunion contractors—the powerful Local No. 3 took care of that. In return, the union was able to secure high wages both from the manufacturing firms and from the construction industry. In order to increase the employment of its members, the union insisted that all electrical panels, signs, etc. be assembled at the construction site. If such equipment arrived already assembled, it was dismantled and reassembled by union members, usually in its exact original form.

The monopolistic aspects of this arrangement naturally aroused the wrath of the firms outside New York City, and of the international officers of the Brotherhood who were concerned about the loss of employment for its members outside Local No. 3. Several of the firms damaged by this monopolistic arrangement, including the Allen Bradley

Company, brought charges against the union for violation of the anti-trust laws and sought an injunction in the federal courts. The Supreme Court decided, in the light of the Hutcheson decision, that the union action was permissible as long as it was not in collusion with the employers. An injunction was granted, but it applied only to those actions involving collusion between the employers and the union to conspire to raise prices and restrict competition in the construction industry. The Court pointed out that if the union had brought about the same results entirely on its own, it would be acting within the law.[6]

Present Status of the Unions under the Antitrust Laws

The Sherman and Clayton Acts were designed to prevent monopolies and combinations in restraint of trade. The Norris-LaGuardia and Clayton Acts, as interpreted in the Hutcheson and Allen Bradley cases, largely free the unions from antitrust prosecution. "As a result organized labor is now free to create and maintain the most flagrant of market controls . . . as long as it relies on its own resources and does not connive with employers. And apparently it is now a matter of indifference to the Supreme Court that unions may effect market controls in an area with no intention of organizing the employees in outside plants, the normal objective of any nationally affiliated labor unions."[7] Thus a dilemma has risen. Since the Court has ruled that the Clayton and Sherman Acts must be interpreted in the light of the Norris-LaGuardia Act, unions are permitted to engage in activities which do, as a matter of fact, have the effect of restraining trade. As long as unions are pursuing their own self-interest and are not acting in collusion with their employers, they are free to establish market controls which would be illegal if established by business firms. However, unions are not quite so free to do this since the passage of the Taft-Hartley Act, which restricts the use of the secondary boycott.

The conclusion is not to be drawn that injunctions can never be issued against unions. Injunctions may be imposed to prevent mass picketing or violence in connection with a strike. If unions picket or strike for purposes illegal under state legislation or the common law, state courts may enjoin the unions. Furthermore, the Taft-Hartley and Landrum-Griffin Acts specified a number of circumstances in which federal courts may issue injunctions in labor disputes. These are discussed in the following chapter. The injunction performs the function of

[6] Lieberman, *op. cit.,* pp. 272–86.
[7] Gregory, *op. cit.,* p. 284.

immediately stopping an action prohibited by law when the usual court processes would be too slow to act as a genuine deterrent. Since *immediate* action is necessary if certain union techniques such as jurisdictional strikes are to be effectively prevented, they are probably a permanent part of the legal machinery for handling labor disputes.

CURRENT ISSUES IN ANTITRUST REGULATION OF UNIONS

The relation between unions and antitrust legislation is by no means a closed issue. Many believe it was an unfortunate mistake ever to have excluded labor organizations from the anti-monopoly laws. Others believe that the power acquired by unions since the Norris-LaGuardia Act demands antitrust legislation in order to preserve competition and to treat labor and management equally.

These attitudes have led to the introduction of bills into Congress that would repeal Sections 6 and 20 of the Clayton Act, thus giving back to the federal courts the authority to issue injunctions in labor disputes. Legislation of this type is widely supported by management organizations and objected to strongly by unions, and up to the present time has made very little headway in Congress. The National Association of Manufacturers believes the "labor monopoly problem" cannot be effectively handled unless we outlaw all union security clauses and all types of secondary boycotts.[8]

In support of a return to earlier forms of antitrust regulation, it is argued that since business monopolies are outlawed, union monopolies should receive the same treatment. In opposition to this argument, it is pointed out that the purpose of antitrust legislation is to regulate business profit-making activities in the product market. Unions are not profit-oriented institutions, hence should not be subject to the same regulations. Furthermore, employers are permitted to form organizations for the purposes of collective bargaining; in effect, they are permitted to conspire to hold down wages just as workers may conspire to raise wages.[9]

Another argument advanced for including unions within the coverage of antitrust laws is that industry-wide organization has given them power to raise wages to monopoly levels, and hence causes inflationary price

[8] See *Monopoly Power as Exercised by Labor Unions*, published by the National Association of Manufacturers, 1957.

[9] For a survey of the opinions of experts drawn from the ranks of labor, management, and the government, see Julius Rezler and Gerald Caraher, *Labor Experts on Pending Labor Legislation: An Opinion Survey*, Research Bulletin of the Institute of Social and Industrial Relations, Loyola University, Chicago, Illinois, 1958.

rises. But this power, if it exists at all, occurs primarily in industries dominated by a few firms which have plants located all across the county. It would be nearly impossible to force bargaining patterns to break up into several genuinely independent regions. For example, wages and working conditions in the Chicago steel-producing area could not differ substantially from other areas of the country; competitive forces would compel a substantial degree of equality. Otherwise, rivalries between union leaders and between firms would create chaotic labor conditions. It may well be that nation-wide bargaining, based on nation-wide union and employer organization, leads to wage rates higher than would otherwise obtain, i.e., higher than would result from pure competition. But it seems most unlikely that antitrust regulation is a feasible means of attack on this alleged problem.[10]

The above comments are not presented as an argument that unions should be free from all legal restrictions, nor even free from all anti-trust regulation. Perhaps special antitrust legislation should be adopted to prevent unions from accomplishing monopolies in the product market, but such laws, unless carefully drafted and interpreted, would tend to restrict normal labor market operations. Since the 1930's the government's approach has removed emphasis from monopoly laws and placed emphasis on comprehensive labor relations legislation. Probably this is the most feasible way of regulating union activity. The reader may judge better after completing the next chapter.

SUMMARY

The first stage of government regulation of labor-management relations may be called the period of restriction of unions without protection for legitimate union practices. From the beginning of the nineteenth century until the 1930's, unions fought a long and eventually successful fight to free themselves from extreme court restriction. The original court restriction came through the application of the criminal conspiracy doctrine. Unions were condemned for conspiring to raise wages, which was held to interfere with the property rights of employers—the right of free access to the labor and product market and the right to pay wages and charge prices as they thought proper—as interpreted by the judges. The judges, along with the jury members, came from the upper middle class and reflected the spirit of this group, dominant in society at that time.

[10] The impact of unions on wages is discussed in Chapter 17 and their effect on inflation in Part 4.

The Sherman Act, primarily designed to prohibit monopolies and combinations in restraint of trade by large business firms, was held to apply to unions in the Danbury Hatters' case. The Clayton Act, at first believed to limit the coverage of the Sherman Act, turned out to make the situation even worse for unions by permitting employers to go directly to court to seek injunctions. In the Coronado case the Supreme Court interpreted the antitrust laws to mean that unions were in restraint of trade if they struck for higher wages against a firm engaged in interstate commerce, when the union's intent was to prevent the shipment of goods across state lines. The injunction, one of the courts' techniques for enforcing the antitrust laws, was most obnoxious to the unions, since it was often written in very broad terms restraining any and all union activity and since the union often had no opportunity to present its own case.

The tide began to turn with the passage of the Norris-LaGuardia Act in 1932. As interpreted in the Hutcheson and Allen Bradley cases, the law substantially freed the unions from antitrust prosecution. Unions may now establish substantial restrictions to the free flow of commerce without violating the Sherman and Clayton Acts, as long as they are acting in their own self-interest and are not in collusion with employers.

DISCUSSION QUESTIONS

1. What different types of governmental agencies exercise some control over labor-management relations? Give an example of each.
2. What was the early conspiracy doctrine? How did it restrict union activity?
3. Why would you expect it to be unusual for the unions to get a sympathetic trial in the courts in the nineteenth century?
4. Why were unions at first elated and then discouraged by the Clayton Act?
5. Of what significance to the development of labor law is the Danbury Hatters' case? The Duplex Printing case? The Coronado Coal case? Briefly state the factual background and the decision in each case.
6. How was this situation (Question 5) changed by the Apex and the Hutcheson cases?
7. What is an injunction? How was it used in labor disputes? Give an example.
8. What are the key provisions of the Norris-LaGuardia Act?
9. Using the Allen Bradley case as an illustration, explain the present position of the unions with respect to the antitrust laws.

10. Write an essay in support of putting unions back under the coverage of antitrust regulation.

BIBLIOGRAPHY

Gregory, Charles O. *Labor and the Law* (revised edition). New York: W. W. Norton & Co., Inc., 1949.

Lieberman, Elias. *Unions before the Bar.* New York: Harper & Brothers, 1950.

Sufrin, Sidney C., and Sedgwick, Robert C. *Labor Law.* New York: Thomas Y. Crowell Company, 1954.

Witney, Fred. *Government and Collective Bargaining.* New York: J. B. Lippincott Company, 1951.

Witte, Edwin E. *The Government in Labor Disputes.* New York: McGraw-Hill Book Company, Inc., 1932.

13

GOVERNMENT AND
COLLECTIVE BARGAINING

The previous chapter carried us chronologically beyond the beginning point of this chapter. At about the same time that the Norris-LaGuardia Act was being subjected to its first test cases in the courts and before its broad interpretation became completely evident, Congress adopted regulations of collective bargaining of an altogether different type. With the passage of the Wagner Act in 1935, the first comprehensive labor relations law, the federal government entered the second stage of its control of labor-management relations, which lasted until 1947, when Congress adopted the Taft-Hartley Act.

THE WAGNER ACT

The Wagner Act represented the culmination of union efforts to secure legislation favorable to their growth. The government took a clear stand advocating collective bargaining and supported this with effective enforcement procedures. During the twelve years of the benevolent reign of the Wagner Act, union membership increased from three and a half million to more than fourteen million. The Wagner Act was not the only factor, but it was an important part of the environment favorable to rapid union growth.

The Wagner Act was not created out of a legislative vacuum; there were a number of precedents which deserve our attention since they shaped its content and interpretation.

Precursors of the Wagner Act

The first outright support of collective bargaining by the federal government came in World War I. In 1918 President Wilson established a National War Labor Board to deal with disputes which arose in defense production. The Board's policy statement advocated collective bargaining in strong, clear terms. Employees were to have complete freedom to select representatives of their own choosing and employers were directed to bargain with these representatives. President Wilson supported the policy of his Board, placing under government control plants which refused to abide by the Board's suggested solution to their labor disputes.

In 1926 Congress passed legislation dealing with collective bargaining on the railroads. The Railway Labor Act permitted employees to choose their own representatives and required employers to bargain with them. For the first time, Congress enunciated a policy in favor of collective bargaining, even though it was for only one segment of industry. The Act also established procedures for government agencies to enter into the settlement of disputes—which the Wagner Act did *not* do—providing for mediation and voluntary arbitration on the railroads. Railway labor legislation, which also covers the airlines, is discussed in the next chapter.

In 1933 Congress passed the National Industrial Recovery Act: depression legislation designed to change the whole fabric of the economy. Business firms were urged to agree to a code of operations for their industry. The codes were collusive agreements, sponsored and enforced by the government, for regulating prices, amount of output, hours of work, and other production variables; in short, employers were permitted to cartelize their industries. Each code was required to include Section 7(a), whose purpose was to promote collective bargaining and which expressed the fundamental aim later incorporated in the Wagner Act. Section 7(a) stated: "(1) that employees shall have the right to organize and bargain collectively through representatives of their own choosing, and shall be free from the interference, restraint, or coercion of employers of labor, or their agents, in the designation of such representatives or in self-organization or in other concerted activities for the purpose of collective bargaining or other mutual aid or protection; (2) that no employee and no one seeking employment shall be required as a condition of employment to join any company union or to refrain from joining, organizing, or assisting a labor organization of his own choosing."

President Roosevelt created the National Labor Board, and later the National Labor Relations Board, to enforce the principles enunciated in Section 7(a). Their powers of enforcement were very weak and consequently the Boards eventually degenerated into impotence. There is no doubt, however, that Section 7(a) and the Boards did encourage the growth of unions and collective bargaining from 1933 until 1935, when the NIRA was declared unconstitutional by the Supreme Court. The procedures and decisions of these Boards set important precedents for the National Labor Relations Board established by the Wagner Act. The framers of the 1935 law also had the advantages of observing some of the weaknesses in Section 7(a), particularly the lack of a clear statement of what employers were not permitted to do. This is one reason why a list of unfair labor practices was included in the Wagner Act. Thus, although the two Boards and Section 7(a) had only a short existence, they played a major role for the new labor legislation by exploring uncharted territory.

General Policy of the Wagner Act

In Section 1 of the Wagner Act, Congress stated that the refusal of employers to accept collective bargaining caused "strikes and other forms of industrial strife or unrest, which have the intent or the necessary effect of burdening or obstructing commerce. . . ." Congress further stated that the inequality of bargaining power between employers and employees caused low wages, which in turn led to depressions because of inadequate purchasing power of the workers. Since the Constitution grants Congress the power to regulate interstate commerce, these statements were designed to indicate its constitutional authority for labor relations legislation. Despite the fact that many influential members of the American Bar Association advised their business clients to the contrary, the Supreme Court in 1937 agreed with Congress and upheld the constitutionality of the Wagner Act by the narrow margin of five to four.

In order to eliminate the obstructions to commerce, Congress established as its policy: "encouraging the practice and procedure of collective bargaining and . . . protecting the exercise by workers of full freedom of association, self-organization, and designation of representatives of their own choosing, for the purpose of negotiating the terms and conditions of their employment or other mutual aid or protection." In proclaiming this policy, earlier stated in Section 7(a) of the National Industrial Recovery Act, Congress permanently entered the collective bargaining arena. During this second stage of the relationship between law and collective bargaining, the government acted as a partisan on the side of the workers, aiding and protecting them in selecting representatives of their own choice.

THE TAFT-HARTLEY ACT

The Taft-Hartley Act, properly cited as the Labor Management Relations Act of 1947, is technically an amendment to the Wagner Act. In many respects it merely makes small changes in the wording of the Wagner Act. Much more important, however, are the substantial additions made to the original legislation, and in that sense the Taft-Hartley Act creates an entirely new law. The policy statement of the Taft-Hartley Act is a repetition of that of the Wagner Act, except that it makes two significant additions reflecting the spirit of the new law. It states that certain union practices are undesirable and therefore should be eliminated, and that workers should not only be protected in their right to join unions, but they should also be protected against unions. These two additions to the policy statement were designed to overcome the one-sidedness of the Wagner Act. The Wagner Act put restrictions on employers with practically no restriction placed on unions; this one-sidedness was one of the major criticisms made against the Act. The Taft-Hartley Act places restrictions on unions as well as on employers, and for that reason was widely heralded by employers as bringing the proper balance into labor law.

The economic environment in which the Taft-Hartley Act was passed differed significantly from that of the Wagner Act. The first came in the midst of the great depression, the second in the early postwar boom period. Immediately following World War II the United States experienced its worst strike wave. Even during the war there had been a number of strikes which aroused the public's antipathy, particularly those of the coal miners led by John L. Lewis. Furthermore, the twelve preceding years had witnessed a marked rise in the status of unions. Unions had grown significantly in membership and in political, economic, and social power, and were no longer generally viewed as underdogs in need of protection. When any institution becomes powerful and influential in public affairs, and at the same time is involved in partisan disputes, it is almost inevitable that it will become subject to government regulation.

The consumer at the end of the war found himself in the anomalous position of earning a high income and possessing an accumulation of savings but finding too few goods to buy, particularly consumers' durable goods. Scapegoats had to be found to carry the blame, and these included rationing and price controls, unions, and the Democratic administration in Washington. Hence, the Republican-controlled Congress, elected in 1946, expressed much hostility to union activities. For these reasons, then, it was argued that there was a need for a new law which would restrict unions as well as employers.

The coverage of the Taft-Hartley Act follows that of the Wagner Act. All workers in plants whose products are sold in interstate commerce are covered, with the exception of employees of government agencies, railway and airline employees (covered by the Railway Labor Act), agricultural workers, and domestic workers. Those workers whose employers are in intrastate commerce are not covered by the legislation. The Taft-Hartley Act also excludes foremen from its coverage. The National Labor Relations Board has discretionary power in deciding how far to extend its jurisdiction within the limits of interstate commerce. It specifies a minimum amount of business which must be done across state lines (purchases or sales of goods) in order for a firm and its employees to be within the jurisdiction of the Board. How this discretionary power may be exercised to restrict the jurisdiction of the Act is discussed in a later section.

The Landrum-Griffin Act

As noted earlier, the McClellan Committee hearings precipitated a demand for regulating internal union affairs and culminated in the Labor-Management Reporting and Disclosure Act of 1959, commonly called the Landrum-Griffin Act. Pressures for changing the Taft-Hartley Act, coming from a variety of sources, had been building up for many years. Management was dissatisfied with loopholes in the secondary boycott provisions as well as other "weak spots." Unions were urging changes in the law with regard to treatment of economic strikers (discussed in the section on decertification elections), and hoping to have many "harsh" provisions rescinded. President Eisenhower had frequently called for new labor-management relations laws, including proposals acceptable to both labor and management. In 1958 the Senate passed the Kennedy-Ives Bill incorporating many of the proposals, particularly those favored by the AFL-CIO, but it was killed in the House of Representatives. The Kennedy-Ervin Bill, a modified version of the earlier bill, passed the Senate in 1959, but lost out to legislation proposed by Representatives Phil Landrum (Democrat from Georgia) and Robert

Griffin (Republican from Michigan), which was much less favorable to unions. The Senate and House Conference Committee reported out a bill quite similar to that of the lower chamber; and, with the support of the President, it was overwhelmingly adopted by Congress.

The Landrum-Griffin Act has seven Titles (divisions of the law) and each has its own collection of provisions. This mass of legal detail can be viewed under three general headings: 1) promotion of democracy in union affairs, 2) elimination of racketeering and dishonest practices, including compulsory reports by unions and management to the Secretary of Labor, and 3) amendments to the Taft-Hartley Act. In Chapter 6 we discussed the democracy sections and some of the provisions dealing with racketeering. We will complete our discussion of the 1959 law in this chapter, along with the major parts of other labor-relations legislation.

Unfair Labor Practices

The Wagner Act, as amended by the Taft-Hartley and Landrum-Griffin Acts, contains two lists of unfair labor practices, one enumerating restrictions on employers and the other restrictions on unions. An employer or a union is in violation of the law if found to have committed one or more of the designated unfair labor practices. The purpose of the restrictions is to prescribe a set of rules for the game of collective bargaining. They restrict the ability of both unions and management to interfere with the legitimate operations of the other, at the same time leaving a considerable amount of latitude for the two parties to make their own rules of the game. These unfair labor practices are also designed to protect third parties, employers and employees not involved in the particular labor disputes, and to protect the general public.

The unfair labor practices are—and must be—written in very broad language, since they deal with such a dynamic area of human activity. Congress left considerable discretion to the National Labor Relations Board to interpret them to fit the detail of bargaining situations. Similar to other regulatory legislation administered by specially created boards, e.g., the Federal Trade Commission and the Securities and Exchange Commission, the law must grant the board sufficient latitude to apply broadly stated policies to the great variety of individual situations and to develop procedures in the light of changing economic problems and institutional relationships.

Employer Unfair Labor Practices

The employer unfair labor practices constitute the heart of the protection of the right of employees to choose representatives without employer interference. The list in the Taft-Hartley Act is the same as that in the Wagner Act, with the important modification that employers cannot agree to a closed shop and only a limited form of the union shop is permitted. The Landrum-Griffin Act makes no changes in employer unfair labor practices, except for special cases which are discussed in the next section.

The actions which employers are not to commit are: 1) They are not to interfere in any way with the right of the employees to select representatives of their own choosing. This is a catch-all provision designed to cover the whole range of possible employer interference. 2) They are not to establish company unions or attempt to dominate any union. 3) They are not to discriminate "in regard to hire or tenure of employment or any term or condition of employment to encourage or discourage membership in any labor organization." The one exception to this occurs when the employer and the union have signed a union shop contract. Under the Wagner Act a closed shop contract was permitted; the Taft-Hartley Act allows only the union shop, and that only to a limited extent. An employer is permitted to agree with the union to discharge workers for refusal to pay union dues; under the Act, the union shop extends no further than that. 4) Employers are not to discriminate against anyone for testifying under the Act. 5) Finally, they are obligated to bargain collectively over wages, hours, and other terms and conditions of employment.

In the application of these broadly worded provisions, there are many borderline cases. For example, how is it possible to delineate clearly just what is good faith bargaining by an employer? Obviously, it cannot mean that he must sign a contract regardless of what the union demands and how uncompromising the union may be. Contrariwise, the employer himself cannot take an uncompromising attitude. Good faith bargaining is somewhere between these two extremes. How far must the employer be willing to go beyond his original offer in order to satisfy his obligation to bargain? It is probably impossible to find a generalized answer to this question applicable to all situations. But he must at least be willing to listen to the union's demands and make reasonable counter-proposals. Furthermore, he cannot make rigid demands on the union, with respect to what is to be included in the contract, if they fall outside the realm of wages, hours, and working conditions. For example, an employer cannot insist that the contract include a requirement for a vote among all employees before the union is free to strike.

The Taft-Hartley Act includes special provisions, which did not appear in the Wagner Act, guaranteeing freedom of speech to the employer. The interpretation given to these provisions by the National Labor Relations Board has substantially expanded employers' opportunities to oppose unions without committing unfair labor practices. They may make whatever statements they wish concerning the union and the possible consequences it will bring to their employees, with the exceptions that the employer must not threaten those who support the union nor make promises of benefits for nonsupport of the union. That is, the employer is not to threaten to discharge employees who favor organization, he is not to threaten to move his plant to another area if he is forced to recognize the union, and he is not to promise a wage increase to the workers for renouncing the union. He may, however, state that the economic forces involved in demands for higher wages may make it imperative for him to close his plant. This is approximately the position that the National Labor Relations Board took under the Wagner Act, although that law contained no specific employer free speech provisions.

Following the adoption of the Taft-Hartley Act, the Board has widened the latitude permitted to employers in exercising their right to freedom of speech. A general meeting of all employees may be convened on plant property during working hours with the agenda devoted exclusively to anti-union speeches. And there is no requirement that the union be granted equal time to rebut the allegations. In short, the Board has interpreted the Act to permit employers to express themselves strongly against unions and still not be in violation of the proscriptions in the first unfair labor practice.

In deciding whether or not a specific act constitutes an unfair labor practice, the Board takes into account the whole pattern of the employer's approach to his employees and their efforts to organize. For example, if an employer calls all his employees into his office one at a time to question each as to whether he has joined the union, this may or may not be construed as an unfair labor practice. If the employer is only attempting to learn whether a majority favor the union and whether he should therefore bargain with the union, the questioning may be innocent. Although this is an extreme situation, there have been a few cases where the Board has so decided. However, if the employer uses the information as the basis for threatening discharges or withholding promotions, or in some other discriminatory manner, the Board would certainly condemn the action as an unfair labor practice.

Union Unfair Labor Practices

The list of unfair labor practices that unions are not to commit is entirely new with the Taft-Hartley Act and additions were made in the Landrum-Griffin Act. Six were listed in the 1947 law: 1) Unions are not to coerce workers into joining, or to coerce employers into selecting bargaining representatives they do not want. 2) No union may attempt to force an employer to put into effect a closed shop contract, or any other type of union security clause which violates the third unfair labor practice listed for employers. 3) Unions must bargain collectively. 4) Unions are prohibited from engaging in certain types of secondary boycotts, striking against a certification of bargaining representative by the Board, or engaging in jurisdictional strikes. Striking against certification by the Board occurs when a union strikes in order to bring pressure on an employer to recognize it rather than recognizing the union which has won a collective bargaining representation election (described below). 5) Excessive or discriminatory initiation dues or fees may not be charged if the contract includes a union security provision. 6) Unions may not compel employers to make payments for services not rendered. 7) The final unfair labor practice, added by the 1959 law, restricts organizational picketing—picketing designed to organize the employees and compel the employer to recognize the union, where the firm does not now have a contract with the union.

Except for the secondary boycotts, jurisdictional disputes, and national emergencies,[1] the unions' right to strike remains intact. However, work stoppages by federal government employees are prohibited. And employers may sue for damages in federal courts if a union strikes in violation of the collective agreement.

Of the union unfair labor practices, it is the second and fourth which have required the most attention of the Board. Unions rarely violate the third, since collective bargaining is one of their chief goals. The Board has interpreted the fifth in the light of customary practice, recognizing that a union's fees may appropriately be related to the members' expected earnings. A typical case under this unfair labor practice involves charges of discrimination against members who have been slow to join the union,

---

[1] The Taft-Hartley Act provisions for dealing with national emergency strikes are discussed in the next chapter.

such as increasing the initiation fee just after a union shop contract has been signed. The sixth unfair labor practice was aimed primarily at the musicians' union, which responded to the law by requiring employers to have unwanted musicians actually play rather than just "stand by."

A typical violation of the first unfair labor practice occurs during strikes when employers continue to operate their firms. Picket-line leaders may not engage in physical violence to coerce non-members into joining the union and staying away from work. This unfair labor practice also prevents unions from denying benefits to non-members under a collectively bargained health and welfare plan on the grounds that this is coercing them into joining the union.

The Landrum-Griffin Amendments placed limitations on organizational picketing because some unions had used this technique to harass employers into signing contracts even when their employees were indifferent or opposed to unionization. The picketed employer may be forced to capitulate because customers refuse to cross in front of the marching sign-carriers or because teamsters refuse to service the company. It becomes an unfair labor practice when a union 1) pickets an employer who has recognized another union, 2) pickets within twelve months after losing a National Labor Relations Board election to determine bargaining representation at the firm, or 3) continues the picketing for more than thirty days and does not petition for a representation election. In the third instance the picketing is permissible for more than thirty days if it does not disrupt services at the employer's place of business.

The Landrum-Griffin Act is still too young to say whether this section will be successful in preventing union harassment while at the same time preserving the rights of unions to engage in legitimate picketing when organizing nonunion firms. Although innocent persons may be protected against illegitimate union actions, anti-union employers can more easily resist organization. When a legitimate union begins a campaign for new members, an employer may retaliate by signing a "sweetheart contract" with a bogus union. A sweetheart contract specifies low wages and substandard working conditions, and frequently includes a union shop clause. Some racketeering union locals specialize in granting them in exchange for periodic "protection" payments, pocketed by the corrupt union officials. The Landrum-Griffin unfair labor practice prevents a legitimate union from picketing companies which have agreed to sweetheart contracts.

Unions, particularly those of skilled workers, have complained most about the prohibition of the closed shop. The evidence which has been gathered since the passage of the Act indicates that the closed shop is still widely used.[2] When a hiring practice is firmly imbedded in an industry and when both employers and employees are anxious to continue that practice, it is well-nigh impossible to eliminate it, even under threat of punishment from the federal government. Furthermore, it is usually very difficult for a worker to prove that he was not hired for a job as a consequence of an unwritten closed shop agreement.

Before the Taft-Hartley Act, hiring halls were widely used in the construction and maritime trades as well as a few other industries. The employer would notify the union-operated hiring hall of how many workers he needed each day. Generally the halls gave preference to union members, often being available exclusively to union members. Under the second unfair labor practice, hiring halls are permitted only if they are equally available to all job applicants. This restriction is often circumvented, e.g., by registering only "experienced" (union) seamen.

The restrictions on union security clauses were particularly difficult to administer in the building and construction industry because of the short duration of so many of the jobs. To be in compliance with the Taft-Hartley Act, a union shop agreement must allow workers thirty days to join and the union must be selected as representative by a majority of the employees. Both of these requirements were too time-consuming to be suitable to the unique problems of the construction industry. Therefore the Landrum-Griffin Act makes a special exception, allowing union security contracts to be signed without a proof of majority status of the union, in fact, even before any workers are hired. Employees can be required to join in seven days. And employers may agree to notify the business agent whenever there is a job vacancy. In other words, something closely approximating the closed shop is now permissible in the building and construction industry. However, the union membership rolls must be open to all qualified applicants.

The fourth unfair labor practice attacks two of the major organizing tactics of the skilled trades unions, secondary boycotts and jurisdictional strikes, techniques not commonly used by the industrial unions. Craft unions are thus returned approximately to the same condition which prevailed after the Duplex Printing case. The Taft-Hartley secondary boycott provisions prohibit unions from inducing employees of any employer to strike or refuse to handle goods for the purpose of compelling an employer

[2] Horace E. Sheldon, *Union Security and the Taft-Hartley Act in the Buffalo Area,* Research Bulletin No. 4 (Ithaca: New York State School of Industrial and Labor Relations, 1949).

to cease doing business with any other company or forcing another company to recognize a union. Many borderline cases and loopholes appeared in the application of this section. The Landrum-Griffin amendments make some additions designed to tighten the proscription against secondary boycotts: preventing unions from 1) bringing pressure directly on a secondary employer for any purpose prohibited in the Taft-Hartley Act, 2) inducing a single employee of a secondary employer to cease handling materials, and 3) inducing employees of employers not covered by the Taft-Hartley Act (e.g., railroads or government agencies) to bring pressure on other firms.

The Landrum-Griffin Act gives special treatment to a device perfected by the teamsters to circumvent the Taft-Hartley restrictions on secondary boycotts. The truckers' union signed contracts including "hot cargo" clauses, an agreement not to handle or transport unfair goods. Thus, any trucking firm which refused to recognize the union and abide by its rules found that it could not transport goods to union firms to continue their journey. Companies licensed to haul in Texas and Oklahoma, for example, might be denied all shipping that traveled through their territory with destinations or points of origin in other states. The Supreme Court declared hot cargo clauses legal, on the grounds that employers signed them voluntarily, but ruled that if unions enforced them by strikes, they were engaging in unfair labor practices. Nevertheless, trucking firms, desiring the long-run cooperation of the teamsters, generally lived up to their contracts without additional union pressure. The Landrum-Griffin Act makes it an unfair labor practice for either an employer or union to enter into a hot cargo agreement, and declares it to be a secondary boycott for a union to bring pressure on a company to include it in a contract.

Again, unique problems in particular industries make it very difficult to administer legislation written for all industries. The drafters of the Landrum-Griffin Act allowed the secondary boycott and hot cargo provisions to be modified in their application to the apparel and clothing industry and the building and construction industries. When employers are in close relation to each other, such as contractor and subcontractor, jobber and manufacturer, or a number of employers on a single construction site, and are working on parts of an integrated process, unions in the two exceptional industries are permitted to bring pressure on one employer to compel another to abide by union working conditions.

Both unions and employers are obligated to bargain collectively, or else be subject to unfair labor practice charges. The Taft-Hartley Act specifies certain steps which must be included in the negotiating procedure in all cases where a collective bargaining contract is already in existence. If either party desires a change in the contract, it must give a sixty-day notice to the other party. The two parties are then obligated to meet, make their demands on each other, and confer. To be in full compliance with the Board interpretation of this section of the Act, the two parties must at least make the pretense of being willing to compromise. If, at the end of the first thirty days, no agreement has been reached, the Federal Mediation and Conciliation Service is to be notified. If this agency believes it can be of service, it assigns a mediator to help the two parties settle their dispute. If, at the end of the second thirty days no agreement has been reached, either party is free to use whatever economic force it deems appropriate. To engage in a strike or lockout before this time would be to commit an unfair labor practice.

Enforcement of Unfair Labor Practice Provisions

The Taft-Hartley Act established two administrative offices which divide the responsibility for enforcing unfair labor practices: the National Labor Relations Board and the General Counsel. The Board acts in the capacity of a judge and the General Counsel acts both as a prosecuting attorney and a grand jury. When an unfair labor practice is alleged to have been committed, the aggrieved employee, employer, or union files a charge with the regional office of the NLRB. The regional representative of the General Counsel conducts an investigation of the charge. During the course of his investigation he generally attempts to bring about an informal settlement between the two parties. The overwhelming majority of cases are terminated at this point. However, if a settlement is not reached and the General Counsel's representative believes the charge has merit, he files a formal complaint with the NLRB.

After the formal complaint has been issued the case is heard by a trial examiner. Trial examiners are full-time employees of the Board and bear a similar relation to the NLRB that a lower federal court bears to the Supreme Court. The representative of the General Counsel argues the complaint and the offending party is permitted to explain why he believes he has not committed an unfair labor practice. The trial examiner then issues his decision, and if within ten days no exception is filed to his ruling, it becomes binding on the parties. Either party may appeal the decision, and likewise the General Counsel's office may take the case to the NLRB. The Board then studies the evidence and issues its decision, reversing, modifying, or affirming the trial examiner's decision. If the party which is deemed to have committed an unfair labor practice does not appeal to the federal courts, the decision is then binding. If he feels that the Board has exceeded its jurisdiction or has decided incorrectly on the basis of the preponderance of evidence, he may appeal the case in the Federal Court of Appeals. If, after the trial examiner's decision becomes binding, or the Board's decision becomes binding, one or both parties continue the unfair labor practice, the Board itself may go to the Federal Court of Appeals.

If the court decides that the Board's decision is correct, it issues a court order directing the parties to comply. Failure to obey the court order makes the offender subject to action for contempt of court. It is not until this point that the commission of the unfair labor practice makes the party subject to a fine or imprisonment. The decisions of the Board are directed to the party who has committed the unfair labor practice and orders him to cease and desist from the action and to take the appropriate remedy, e.g., to hire the person discharged for union activity and pay back wages, or to cease coercing employees. The party which committed the unfair labor practice must display prominently, for sixty days, a notice that it will cease engaging in such activity. This can be most humiliating.

There are special enforcement procedures for secondary boycotts, strikes against certification, jurisdictional strikes, and organizational picketing. When a charge is brought against a union for any one of these offenses, it must be given immediate attention by the General Counsel's representatives. If the charge has merit the General Counsel is required to seek an injunction immediately, except in the case of a jurisdictional strike, where he may seek an injunction if he thinks it appropriate. The reason for injunctions in this type of case is that Congress believes that speedy action is necessary. So much time elapses during the usual procedures of the Board that they would be ineffective for stopping secondary boycotts, jurisdictional disputes, and organizational picketing before it is too late. A union would be able to win its economic battle even though it later lost a relatively meaningless legal case.

If the parties in a jurisdictional strike cannot settle the dispute among themselves, the Board is empowered to enter the dispute and award the work assignments in accordance with its own standards of fairness. The Board has made almost no use of this power, except as an implied threat. One objective of Congress in adopting this approach to jurisdictional disputes was to put more pressure on the parties to arrive at a settlement among themselves, without strikes. The NLRB, in using these provisions of the Act, has always remained outside of the dispute if the parties had established machinery to settle it themselves. The threat of interference by the federal government caused the Building and Construction Trades Department of the AFL-CIO to join with a number of contractors' associations to establish the National Joint Board for the Settlement of Jurisdictional Disputes. Although the National Joint Board has not eliminated jurisdictional disputes, it at least provides a method for settlement when they arise and has made it unnecessary for the NLRB to enter such disputes covered by the authority of the National Joint Board.[3]

One of the most difficult parts of the law to enforce is the prohibition against closed shops. After a worker has applied for a job and been refused, it is not easy to prove that he was refused because he did not belong to the union, or to the right local of an international. He may have been turned down because he lacked the proper skills or did not make a good appearance. But if the NLRB is convinced that closed shop practices are being followed, it will order the company to offer employment to the worker and pay full wages from the date he was refused a job, less any amount he has earned in the meantime. The union may be required to share in paying the back wages. The NLRB may also apply the Brown-Olds remedy, requiring the union to refund dues and fees collected in the preceding six months to *all* employees. This severe penalty is assessed on the grounds that the funds were extracted from the workers under an illegal union security clause. If hiring the worker and paying back wages were the only penalties, the prohibition against the closed shop would have no real teeth. The Brown-Olds remedy was first enunciated by the Board in 1956 in a case involving the plumbers' union and the Brown-Olds Company.

The National Labor Relations Board

Under the Wagner Act the National Labor Relations Board had three members. This was replaced by the Taft-Hartley Board of five members, each appointed by the President for five-year terms. The interpretation given to many provisions of the law has changed substantially as new Board members take office. When a President has made three new appointments to the Board, it tends to reflect his attitudes on labor-management relations. Tracing its decisions over a period of time indicates that the Board has changed its interpretation of many sections of the laws.

It should be recalled that the legislation leaves a wide range of dis-

---

[3] William Haber and Harold M. Levinson, *Labor Relations and Productivity in the Building Trades* (Ann Arbor: Bureau of Industrial Relations, University of Michigan, 1956), pp. 233–41.

cretion with the Board in setting its jurisdiction and its operating procedures, and in determining just what constitutes an unfair labor practice. This discretion may be exercised to bring about differing results from the same piece of legislation. To illustrate: In 1954 the Board announced new rules determining its jurisdictional boundaries, eliminating many smaller firms from the coverage of the Taft-Hartley Act. Two members of the Board strongly objected to the change, charging that it would reduce jurisdiction by more than 25 per cent. One writer claimed that this represented "the most drastic change in labor-management regulations since the passage of the Taft-Hartley Act in 1947." [4] In short, the membership of the Board is crucial to the real meaning of the Act.

Independent Functions of the General Counsel

The General Counsel, appointed by the President for a four-year term, exercises substantial administrative powers independently of the NLRB. Under the Wagner Act there was no corresponding position; the powers were exercised by the Board. The General Counsel's decision is final on whether or not a complaint will be issued in an unfair labor practice case. Like a grand jury, he decides what charges should be brought. If he believes no formal complaint should be brought, the complaining party has no avenue of appeal. Even if the Board is of the opinion that a formal complaint should be issued, it cannot compel the General Counsel's office to issue it.

With this much responsibility it is essential that the General Counsel be nonpartisan in the conflicts between unions and management. The first person to hold this office, Robert Denham, frequently disagreed with the Board. He issued complaints which were not warranted according to previous decisions of the Board, and refused to issue complaints where the Board believed they would be appropriate. His actions were severely condemned by unions as being partisan in favor of management. In 1950, after a number of widely publicized speeches criticizing decisions of the NLRB, President Truman asked for and received Denham's resignation.

The succeeding General Counsels have cooperated somewhat more effectively with the Board, although there have been occasional disputes over administrative and personnel matters. Regardless of the degree of cooperation, partiality in the General Counsel's office may cause the labor laws to be administered either in a strongly pro-union or strongly pro-management manner. A conclusion following from this and the previous

[4] John P. Henderson, "The Impact of the NLRB upon Union Growth." *Labor Law Journal*, May, 1956, p. 277.

section is that the labor laws are what the NLRB and the General Counsel make of them, subject, of course, to review by the federal courts. In fact, the real meaning of any law is determined by what administrators and courts do with it.

Representation Elections

The Taft-Hartley Act, through representation elections, provides a mechanism enabling employees to select their bargaining representatives freely. In the election the employees indicate whether or not they wish to be represented by a union, and if so, which union. Prior to the establishment of this procedure, which first appeared in the Wagner Act, the only way a union could convince a reluctant employer was through an organizational strike. The issue can now be settled peacefully.

Typically, a union, after conducting a successful organizing campaign, notifies the employer that it is prepared to bargain. If the employer refuses to recognize the union, it may petition the regional office of the Board. An investigation is conducted in the course of which the employer may become convinced; thus the issue of representation is settled. If, after the investigation, the employer is still doubtful, a representation election is held. The first step is to determine the appropriate bargaining unit, which workers are to be included in the election.

Sometimes employers frustrate a union's organizing strategy by calling for an election before the union is ready. If the union loses in a "premature" election, it must ordinarily wait at least a year before seeking another. This is one reason unions opposed restrictions on organizational picketing. More than thirty days may be needed to convince employees they should join. An election which occurs too soon and is lost as a consequence, bars the union from picketing for the next twelve months.

Determination of the Appropriate Bargaining Unit

Determining the appropriate bargaining unit is a matter of deciding which workers are eligible to be represented by the union. The Board has the responsibility for making the decision, taking into account the wishes of the two parties. Frequently there is disagreement, in which case the Board groups together workers with substantially common work interests. Sometimes it is a matter of size of the bargaining unit. Should it include only those segments of the company where the union has made progress in its organizing campaign? Or should it include all employees, thus reducing the union's chances of winning the election? Sometimes the disagreement is over including small groups of skilled workers in an all-inclusive bargaining unit. Should it be an industrial unit, including all production and maintenance workers, or should it be divided into a number of units according to each craft in the firm? If there is a previous bargaining history, the Board will take this into consideration in making its decision. If not, it decides on the basis of what will promote the most stable bargaining relations.

The bargaining unit decisions of the Board under the Wagner Act brought many complaints. Therefore, in the Taft-Hartley Act, Congress gave new instructions for determining who should be included. The AFL had objected bitterly over the treatment of craft workers, believing that they were too frequently included in larger industrial units, and were thus represented by CIO unions. As a consequence of the AFL complaints, the Act gives the Board authority to conduct special elections among clearly defined craft groups to determine whether they wish to be included in an over-all industrial unit or to be represented as an independent unit. The Board still has discretion to determine what is a clearly defined craft unit within a manufacturing plant. Professional employees are not to be included in the bargaining unit unless they so indicate through a special election. Plant guards cannot be included in the same unit with other employees. If they are to be represented in collective bargaining, it must be as a special unit of their own and by a union not affiliated directly or indirectly with the organization representing the production workers. Supervisors and foremen may not be included in the bargaining unit since they are not employees within the definition of the Act. However, the employer may bargain with them if he so desires.

Certification of the Bargaining Representative

After the appropriate unit is determined, an election is held by secret ballot. The ballot includes the name of the union, or of each union if more than one is in the contest for representation, and provides the opportunity to vote for no union. When there are more than two choices on the ballot, and no one of the choices receives a majority, a run-off election is conducted between the two receiving the most votes. If a union wins the election, the Board certifies it as the bargaining representative. The certified bargaining representative becomes the *exclusive* representative of the employees in that bargaining unit. The only exception to its exclusiveness is the right of each employee to take his grievances individually to the employer if he so chooses. However, even in this instance, the union has the right to be present to protect its interests and to prevent any special agreements contrary to the contract.

The election may be nullified by the Board if it has evidence that the results were prejudiced by the actions of either party. That is, if the Board feels that the workers have been unduly influenced by improper or coercive campaigning tactics, it will void the election and conduct a new one at a later date. Or if the employer has made improper promises or threats, the election may be voided.

Decertification Elections

The Taft-Hartley Act allows for decertification elections, giving workers an opportunity to vote against a previously certified bargaining representative. If the union loses the election, it is decertified by the Board, and hence loses its bargaining status. An employee, or a group of employees, or another union may petition for a decertification election. The procedure followed by the Board is the same as for representation elections.

Unless there are special circumstances, the Board will conduct an election in a given bargaining unit only once a year. If an employer and a certified bargaining representative have signed a two-year contract, the Board will not entertain a petition for a decertification election during that period except under special circumstances, e.g., a contract signed with a union which did not represent a majority of the employees. In setting such restrictions, the Board endeavors to resolve two partly conflicting purposes of the Act. It attempts to achieve stability in collective bargaining by restricting the opportunity of an outside union, or of the employer, to upset the bargaining relationship. At the same time it wants to provide the employees with adequate opportunity to designate their representative freely.

The Taft-Hartley Act provided that "employees on strike who are not entitled to reinstatement shall not be eligible to vote." Hence, in an economic strike, if the employer had permanently replaced an employee, the replaced employee was not eligible to vote in a representation or decertification election. If an unfair labor practice by the employer was involved, the strikers were eligible to vote, but when only wages and working conditions were at issue, the replaced strikers lost their status as employees. Unions argued that decertification elections in combination with the treatment of economic strikers provided employers with a powerful union-breaking weapon. Their argument was that employers are always able to provoke a strike and often able to hire permanent replacements, especially during a period of substantial unemployment. The employer could then convince an employee, or group of employees, to petition for a decertification election. Since the strikers—the union members—would not be eligible to vote, the union would lose its bargaining status. Although this was one of the primary union objections to the Taft-Hartley Act, the evidence indicates that employers did not make widespread use of the tactic.[5]

There were, however, a few outstanding cases where unions lost decertification elections after long economic strikes. Perhaps the most famous was at the O'Sullivan Rubber Company, manufacturing what it calls "America's No. 1 Heel." The company, located in Winchester, Virginia, had no paid holidays, not even Christmas, and paid wages that were comparatively low for the rubber industry. In April, 1956, the employees voted 343 to 2 in favor of the United Rubber Workers. Negotiations immediately bogged down over wage increases, and the union was on strike one month after becoming the certified bargaining representative. Strike-breakers were hired, many coming from the surrounding rural community where wages for apple-picking were even lower. The company continued full operations, selling much of its output to the nonunion General Shoe Company of Nashville. In October, 1957, the employees voted to decertify the union by 288 to 5, with the replaced strikers being ineligible to vote.[6]

The President and Congressmen from both parties favored a change in the voting rights of replaced economic strikers. The Landrum-Griffin Act permits them to vote in any election held twelve months after the beginning of the strike, even though they are not entitled to eventual reinstatement in their jobs. The period was limited to twelve months because by that time most replaced strikers have lost economic interest in the company and the union is likely to be broken. Whether this amendment to the Taft-Hartley Act will have any real effect on the willingness and ability of some employers to provoke economic strikes in order to decertify a union cannot be predicted at the present time. It should be noted that the election in the O'Sullivan case occurred seventeen months after the strike commenced.

Filing Requirements

In order to make use of the Board's facilities, i.e., to file charges of unfair labor practices or to petition for representation elections, a union had to be in compliance with the Taft-Hartley Act by satisfying certain

[5] Joseph Krislov, "Union Decertification," *Industrial and Labor Relations Review,* IX (July, 1956), pp. 589–94.

[6] William L. Abbott, "Three Years of the O'Sullivan Formula," *The Reporter,* May 14, 1959, pp. 25–27.

filing requirements, sending a financial statement, and furnishing a copy of its constitution, by-laws, and other organizational information to the Secretary of Labor. The purpose was to place pressure on unions to maintain honest finances. Each officer of each local and international was also required to file with the Board an affidavit "that he is not a member of the Communist Party or affiliated with such party, and that he does not believe in, and is not a member of or supports, any organization that believes in or teaches the overthrow of the United States Government by force or by any illegal or unconstitutional methods" (Section 9[h]).

Most union leaders viewed the requirement to file a noncommunist affidavit as an insult and contrary to American traditions. A few, clearly noncommunist in their political beliefs, refused to sign as a matter of principle, e.g., John L. Lewis of the United Mine Workers. A union could continue to operate even though it had not met these filing requirements: it could strike, bargain, and sign collective agreements. However, it could not bring unfair labor practice charges against employers or have its name included in an election except where it was already the certified representative.

The purpose of the noncommunist affidavit requirement is obvious. The influence of communists in unions has decreased substantially since the passage of the Taft-Hartley Act, but the filing requirement has had no consequential effect on this decline. The primary causes have been the vigorous anticommunist campaigns of a number of union leaders and the changed attitude of the public since the end of World War II.

Except for the noncommunist affidavit, the Landrum-Griffin Act kept substantially the same list of filing requirements, and added several more to it. Any loans by a union to its officers aggregating more than $250 in a year must be reported. All the foregoing reports must be made available to the members. Officers must also file reports on any financial dealings, other than ordinary union business, which they have with firms with which the union bargains, including any direct payments they may receive from employers. The law requires employers to file parallel reports on their dealings with union officers and also payments made to labor relations consultants. The latter are included because they have often served as intermediaries in racketeering connections between employers and unions. All reports filed with the Secretary of Labor are public information.

Instead of the Taft-Hartley type of enforcement, denying a noncomplying union access to the Board, the Landrum-Griffin Act relies on criminal penalties for false information and empowers the Secretary of Labor to go into the federal courts to seek injunctions or to sue to force compliance with the filing requirements.

In place of the noncommunist affidavit, the Landrum-Griffin Act forbids persons who are, or in the five preceding years have been, members of the Communist Party from holding union office. It also forbids office to anyone who, in the last five years, "has been convicted of, or served any part of a prison term resulting from his conviction of, robbery, bribery, extortion, embezzlement, grand larceny, burglary, arson, violation of narcotics laws, murder, rape, assault with intent to kill, assault which inflicts grievous bodily injury, or a violation of title II or III of this Act, or conspiracy to commit any such crimes. . . ." (Sec. 504[a]).

Suits for Damages

Congress, hoping to compel both parties to abide by their collective bargaining agreements, made it possible for either one to go into the federal courts to sue the other in case of violation of the contract. Although the Congressional debates centered around "making arrogant union leaders more responsible," encouraging suits for damages to enforce contract compliance tends to work mainly to the disadvantage of employers. The collective bargaining contract is primarily a series of promises made by the employer, with very few promises, if any, made by the union. The majority of collective agreements contain a no-strike provision, which is about the only thing the union can violate.

Providing easy access to the courts opens a loophole through which collective bargaining may be thrown into continual litigation. Either side may use it as a bargaining weapon by fabricating a suit against the other, particularly while a strike is in progress. These suits, then, become part of the pressure—both public relations and financial—put on the opponent, and at the same time they become some of the thorniest issues to be bargained at the negotiating sessions. This technique of contract enforcement has one serious drawback. The parties must continue to live together after the new contract is written, and settling issues by court decree rather than joint negotiation does not contribute to amicable relations under the new contract. The goal of collective bargaining should be to settle disputes, not to win court cases. Suits for damages have not been widely used as a bargaining technique, but these provisions of the Act make them potentially dangerous to effective union-management relations. It is not being argued that violations of the contract should be ignored, but rather that the parties should not be encouraged to run frequently to the courts.

Suits for damages may also be brought to federal court by anyone injured as a consequence of secondary boycotts, strikes against Board certification, and jurisdictional strikes. Since a great amount of time is required to settle such cases, this is an ineffective technique for stopping them. However, the threat of being sued for damages may deter unions from engaging in the prohibited strikes. In general, unions object to these provisions since they tend to take collective bargaining into the courts from whence it was rescued by the Norris-LaGuardia Act.

The Taft-Hartley Act—An Appraisal

At the time of its passage the Taft-Hartley Act was extremely controversial, with Congress adopting it over the veto of President Truman. In the next presidential election, 1948, the law became a major campaign issue. Unions labeled it a "slave labor" act, while many management leaders looked forward to a new era of labor peace and an end to undesirable union practices. As is usually the case, both extreme positions were exaggerations. Wages and working conditions continued to improve, unions were not driven out of their strongholds, and some union leaders continued to abuse their positions of trust.

Controversy also surrounded the passage of the Landrum-Griffin Act, but not to the extent of its predecessor. In fact, labor relations legislation will always generate fireworks. Unions again made dire predictions about the consequences, and management claimed the law did not go far enough. Many of the fond hopes of those advocating stronger legislation were not realized, e.g., union security clauses have not been eliminated and industry-wide strikes are not outlawed.

Although unions continue to oppose the Taft-Hartley Act and the 1959 amendments, they do not make as much of an issue of it politically as they did originally. Opposition is now in the form of lobbying for changes in particular provisions rather than trying to eliminate the entire law. Unions still fear certain possibilities, especially regarding potential effects during a depression when employers are under great pressure to reduce wages. Decertification elections, with economic strikers denied the right to vote after a year, could become a powerful anti-union weapon during periods of substantial unemployment. So far the Act has not been tested under such conditions. The possible impact of power wielded by an anti-union General Counsel is another source of concern. Unions further claim that the Taft-Hartley and Landrum-Griffin Acts have created a climate of opinion which stifles their organization drives, particularly in the South.

On balance, it appears that the laws have had no substantial effect on collective bargaining. The outward form of union security provisions has been changed, and perhaps the number of jurisdictional strikes and secondary boycotts has been somewhat reduced. An analysis of over-all strike statistics and the general trend of bargaining agreements does not indicate any clearly defined impact of the legislation. Certainly, the Wagner Act wrought far greater changes in industrial relations than did the Taft-Hartley Act.

STATE LABOR RELATIONS LEGISLATION

State labor relations legislation is much more important than commonly recognized because so many workers are employed by small firms not engaged in interstate commerce. And some of the state laws, such as those relating to picketing, cover all workers regardless of how extensive their employers' business. In some cases the states have paralleled federal legislation. Eleven states have labor relations acts, more or less similar to the Taft-Hartley Act. All of these contain a list of unfair labor practices which employers are not to commit and eight of them have lists of unfair labor practices which unions are not to commit. The states were the first to pioneer in union unfair labor practices, predating the Taft-Hartley Act.

The borderline between the jurisdiction of the NLRB and of the state boards and state courts has never been clear, and after the NLRB reduced its jurisdiction, the issue became even more cloudy, creating a "no-man's-land" between the federal and state laws. Firms engaging in interstate commerce, but not to a sufficient extent to fall within the federal jurisdiction, were beyond the regulation of both the federal and state laws. Hence, neither unions nor management were protected from the unfair labor practices of the other, e.g., employers could discharge workers merely for being interested in joining a union. The Landrum-Griffin Amendments attempt to remedy this situation by granting authority to state agencies, including courts and labor relations boards, to take jurisdiction over any cases declined by the National Labor Relations Board. Thus a small firm, even though involved in interstate commerce, is no longer left in a "no-man's-land."

Eighteen states now have "right-to-work" laws which declare union shops, closed shops, and other types of union security to be illegal. Section 14(b) of the Taft-Hartley Act permits such state laws, if they are stricter than the federal law, giving them precedence over the latter on matters of union security. In other words, a firm in a state which has a "right-to-work" law would be governed by the state legislation with respect to union security clauses even though the firm is clearly in interstate commerce. In almost all cases of conflict between federal and state legislation, the federal law governs; nevertheless, the Taft-Hartley Act has this unique provision. Three states have taken a somewhat different approach to restricting union security clauses. They require the workers to vote in favor of such clauses before they may be included in contracts. The Taft-Hartley Act had a similar requirement, but this was eliminated in 1951, since the votes were almost always overwhelmingly in favor of the union security clauses.

Unions vigorously oppose "right-to-work" laws, calling them "right-to-wreck" laws, not only because they eliminate union security clauses, but also because, in the public mind, they constitute a stamp of disapproval on union growth. Proponents of the laws argue that workers should not be compelled to join, that unions should be voluntary associations having as members only those who really want to belong. Of course, part of the support comes from anti-union management organizations. Perhaps the most clear-cut effect—revealed in a study of the Texas "right-to-work" law —is to reduce the hold of unions on their membership. As a consequence, more attention must be given to dissident minorities and their special collective bargaining desires. In other words, unions are less free to follow stable long-run policies. Therefore, employers may find that union demands are more extreme and backed up by a greater show of militancy.[7]

The "agency shop" has been developed as a compromise: all employees in the bargaining unit must pay dues or lose their jobs, but need not become members. The logic of this arrangement is that workers may hold whatever beliefs they choose about joining unions and subscribing to their programs, but should, in any case, pay a proportionate share of the cost of being represented in negotiations over wages and working conditions.

The national debate over "right-to-work" laws and other limitations on union security clauses will probably continue for many years. The Taft-Hartley Act banned the closed shop and allowed states to restrict other forms of union security. The Landrum-Griffin Act took a step in the opposite direction, but only for the construction industry. In 1958 "right-to-work" legislation was voted on in six state-wide elections, with only

---

[7] Frederic Meyers, *Right to Work in Practice* (New York: Fund for the Republic, 1959). For a good background discussion, see Paul Sultan, "Historical Antecedents to the Right to Work Controversy," *Southern California Law Review*, Vol. 31 (April, 1958), pp. 221–45.

one favoring it. Almost every year, proposals are made in states currently not having the laws. Aside from Indiana, the laws are in the southern and mountain states, the less industrialized areas.

THE FUNCTION OF LEGISLATION
IN COLLECTIVE BARGAINING

After considering this broad mass of legislation dealing with labor-management relations, the question naturally rises: What is the proper role of the government in collective bargaining? Should it act as a football referee, allowing the two sides a wide range of freedom as long as they play the game according to the rules, thus permitting the stronger side to make the biggest gains? Or should the government take a partisan position protecting the weak against the strong? Or do the interests of the public demand severe restrictions on both antagonists? Certainly the government cannot take a completely hands-off attitude; too much is at stake.

As a minimum, the government should grant to workers the opportunity to choose their bargaining representatives without employer interference or union coercion. Each side should be prevented from taking unfair advantage of its bargaining power—although what is generally accepted as unfair will change with differing political conditions. However, a dynamic field such as industrial relations needs a wide range of freedom in order to develop. New techniques and procedures of bargaining should be explored. New subjects are continually entering into the bargaining arena, and therefore too frequent government interference, or legislation which is too rigid, would inhibit its freedom of growth. Furthermore, the two parties must live together from one negotiating session to the next. To drag the government into each minor dispute is to endanger the ability of collective bargaining to function smoothly over the long run. This does not mean that the legislation must be absolutely neutral. The list of unfair labor practices may shift with changing bargaining relationships, occasionally adjusting to the new balance of power. The government may manipulate the balance of power, as it did with both the Wagner and Taft-Hartley Acts, in order to promote bargaining relationships designed to achieve collective agreements acceptable to the public.

When labor-management disputes create national emergencies, the government must step in to protect the public interest. This second area of government interference is discussed in the next chapter.

A third area in which government interference may be desirable is that of wages and employment, particularly during a period of inflation or of depression and unemployment. What the government does, and may do, is the subject matter of later chapters and is not discussed here.

The government, then, should enter labor-management relations to 1) set the broad rules within which the game of collective bargaining is to be played, 2) restrict those rare disputes which create real—not imaginary —national emergencies, and 3) exercise some indirect controls over wages and employment. Just what the government should do in each of these areas is a matter of controversy, and always will be in a democratic society. What may appear to be appropriate legislation at one time may become inappropriate—even disastrous—under different economic, political, and social conditions.

SUMMARY

With the Railway Labor Act and later the Wagner Act, the federal government plunged into the substantive regulation of collective bargaining. The purpose of this legislation was to promote collective bargaining by eliminating employer unfair labor practices and by providing a mechanism for employees to select their own representatives freely. The Taft-Hartley Act made many important additions to the Wagner Act, and at the same time retained many of the principles of its predecessor. By listing unfair labor practices for both employers and unions, it sets the rules for the game of collective bargaining. The Taft-Hartley Act brings injunctions back into labor disputes for handling secondary boycotts, jurisdictional disputes, and national emergency disputes. The Landrum-Griffin Act, as well as enlarging the list of union unfair labor practices, added many regulations of internal union affairs.

Although universal standards of government regulation of collective bargaining are subject to much controversy, it might at least be agreed that the public should establish rules of fair conduct in collective bargaining, restrain national emergency disputes, and promote desirable levels of wages and employment. This will entail occasional changes in our labor laws in order to keep them current with changing economic and political conditions. Furthermore, broad discretionary powers will always have to be granted to the government administrative agencies in charge of applying the law to the facts of individual situations.

DISCUSSION QUESTIONS

1. The Wagner Act inaugurated the second stage in the growth in labor law: protection of unions without restrictions on unions. Explain the differences between the government approaches of the first and second stages.

2. Although the Wagner Act represented a major change in national labor policy, there was a substantial legal history leading up to it. What was this legal history?

3. Compare the general policy set forth in the Wagner Act with that of the Taft-Hartley Act.

4. What is an unfair labor practice? Why is a list of these written into the Taft-Hartley Act?

5. What is meant by employer freedom of speech? What limitations should be placed on it? Why?

6. How does the Taft-Hartley Act deal with secondary boycotts and jurisdictional disputes?

7. The economic and political attitudes of the members of the National Labor Relations Board have a significant effect on the meaning of the Taft-Hartley Act. Explain.

8. A strongly pro-union or pro-management General Counsel could cause a partisan application of the Taft-Hartley Act. Explain.

9. What functions are served by having the government conduct representation elections?

10. Why do unions fear the potential effect of decertification elections during depressions?

11. What are the arguments for and against regulating organizational picketing?

12. Critically evaluate suits for damages as a technique of enforcing collective bargaining contracts.

13. Write an essay portraying the "proper" role of government in collective bargaining. Support the positions which you take.

BIBLIOGRAPHY

Annual Reports of the National Labor Relations Board.

Derber, Milton, and Young, Edwin. *Labor and the New Deal.* Madison: The University of Wisconsin Press, 1957.

Gregory, Charles O. *Labor and the Law.* New York: W. W. Norton & Company, 1949.

Mathews, Robert E. (editor). *Labor Relations and the Law.* Boston: Little, Brown and Company, 1953.

McNaughton, Wayne L., and Lazar, Joseph. *Industrial Relations and the Government.* New York: McGraw-Hill Book Company, 1954.

Millis, Harry A., and Brown, Emily Clark. *From the Wagner Act to Taft-Hartley*. Chicago: the University of Chicago Press, 1950.

Mueller, Stephen J. *Labor Law and Legislation*. Cincinnati: Southwestern Publishing Company, 1956.

Taylor, George W. *Government Regulation of Industrial Relations*. New York: Prentice-Hall, Inc., 1948.

Witney, Fred. *Government and Collective Bargaining*. New York: J. B. Lippincott Company, 1951.

14 { DEALING WITH NATIONAL EMERGENCY DISPUTES

A special kind of government interference is needed for some labor management disputes: strikes which cut off the flow of goods essential to the operation of the economy, usually referred to as national emergency disputes. A work stoppage by the producers of electricity in New York City, for example, could not be tolerated for more than a few days at most. The inconvenience of no heat or light for homeowners and shop-keepers and the lack of power for factories, compelling them to lay off workers, not to mention the needs of hospitals, fire departments, etc., would soon cause public insistence for remedial action to rise to an irresistible pitch. Speedy and direct methods for handling national emergency disputes have therefore become a permanent element in our labor relations legislation.

National emergency disputes can be divided into two categories. The first includes those occurring in basic industries essential to carrying on the normal affairs of society—even such mundane activities as garbage collection have been classified under this heading—or essential to several other industries which employ large numbers of workers. The proper definition of what constitutes an essential industry is always a matter of disagreement. Every strike causes some hardship. How great must the inconvenience be before extreme measures need to be adopted? Also, a work stoppage in coal mining, for example, becomes more burdensome, closer to being a catastrophe, the longer it lasts. How much unemployment in steel, railroads, automobiles, etc. and how many cold schoolrooms must we tolerate before declaring a state of emergency?

The second category consists of disputes in defense industries. No argument need be made for adopting effective regulations for maintaining full production when the country is at war. Almost all large employers, and most small ones, are then engaged in essential production. It is argued by many that even peace-time strikes should be prohibited in some defense industries, e.g., atomic energy. And government employment is often put in this category, particularly strategic departments.

We have a long history of direct government interference in national emergency disputes, beginning with the injunction, enforced by federal troops, to stop Eugene Debs' American Railway Union strike in 1894. The first legislation to establish a permanent set of procedures was the Railway Labor Act of 1926, and the Taft-Hartley Act has special sections dealing with national emergency strikes. These laws have proved to be less than completely satisfactory, and proposals for new legislation are frequently debated.

Many of the major work stoppages are complicated by the fact that the settlement, when it is reached, will act as a precedent for many other contracts, and perhaps have potential inflationary implications. Hence, unions and employers attempt to attract much attention to the "reasonableness" of the position of the partisans in the dispute. Supposedly impartial persons, academic economists, government officials and news commentators make conflicting pronouncements on the "inevitable" consequences of various proposals for ending the strike. The net result of the glare of publicity may be to prolong the stoppage as each protagonist comes to believe he is waging the battle of the century involving great principles of justice and sound economic policy.

MEDIATION AND ARBITRATION

The time-honored techniques for heading off emergency strikes are mediation and arbitration. Of course, these may be, and are, used for ordinary disputes as well as those which cause national crises. Congress created the United States Department of Labor in 1913, vesting it with the function of mediating labor disputes. Four years later the United States Conciliation Service was set up. This agency was divorced from the Department by the Taft-Hartley Act on the grounds that it would be more impartial if separated from the government body designed to represent labor's interest, and given a new title, Federal Mediation and Conciliation Service. Most states have similar agencies.

The FMCS offers both mediation and arbitration services. Although we described mediation and arbitration earlier,[1] it will be useful to repeat the distinction here. A mediator brings the contending union and management together and suggests possible solutions of their differences, with no compulsion to accept his proposals. An arbitrator, however, after listening to the arguments of each side, announces a settlement which is binding on both parties.

Federal mediators are ready and willing to provide expert advice and conciliation services in the drafting of all major contracts. In fact, the Taft-Hartley Act requires unions and employers to notify the FMCS thirty days before striking or locking out in order to win a change in contract provisions. Hence, any dispute which is, or threatens to be, a national emergency comes to the agency's attention and receives the help of its most experienced mediators. Often their most important contribution is to keep unions and management in the mood to talk over the areas of disagreement, changing the subject when negotiations have arrived at a temporary stalemate, and suggesting novel methods for compromising the differences. When the two parties take adamant positions and refuse to talk to each other until a substantial concession is made, the mediators act as go-betweens, seeking to isolate the real causes of the impasse and reach a successful compromise. Behind-the-scenes maneuvering is sometimes necessary when unions and management have issued strong public statements in support of their positions. Shrewdness and experience must be combined to work out the proper face-saving formula.

Arthur S. Meyer, chairman of the New York State Board of Mediation from 1940 to 1950, describes the role of the mediator as follows:

> The mediator is a catalytic agent. The mere presence of an outsider, aside from anything he may do or say, will cause a change, and almost certainly a change for the better, in the behavior of the disputing parties. The importance of such a change will be clear when we recognize that the economic aspects of a dispute never account entirely for the asperities that accompany it. Rudeness, irritation, and the habit of not listening—these are as vexing as the untenable arguments that accompany them. Progress has been made through the mediator's presence, though that presence has brought nothing more than temperate speech.[2]

Mediation may be used to settle grievance disputes under existing contracts; however, arbitration is the technique predominantly employed for this purpose. American collective bargaining traditions have reserved mediation primarily for drafting new contracts. It should be noted that

---

[1] Chapter 11.

[2] Arthur S. Meyer, "Function of the Mediator in Collective Bargaining," *Industrial and Labor Relations Review*, Vol. XIII (January, 1960), p. 161.

unions and management are not required to accept the mediator's suggestions, or to do any more than acknowledge his presence. Whatever reliance is placed on his aid is strictly voluntary.

Whenever a union or management wishes to use arbitration to settle a disagreement, it may request help from the FMCS which maintains a list of qualified arbitrators in all important industrial centers. The agency will select several names for consideration by the two parties, and when they cannot decide whom to name, the FMCS will, if asked, designate a particular individual to hear the dispute. Arbitrators are used almost entirely for settling grievances under existing contracts, but are also available for ruling on wage rates and other provisions of new agreements.

It is frequently suggested that arbitration be made compulsory for disputes affecting the national health and safety, but except for a few state laws covering public utilities, the proposal has not won the support of legislative bodies, even while the country has been at war.

RAILWAY LABOR ACT

Legislation dealing with labor relations on the railroads dates from as early as 1888, when a law, which proved to be ineffective, was adopted to provide for investigating commissions and voluntary arbitration. During World War I the railroads were seized by the federal government in order to settle a dispute. The government, in contrast to employer practices, did not discriminate against the workers on the basis of union membership, but instead bargained over wages and working conditions. After the railroads were returned to private ownership in 1920, there was a period of unsettled, and occasionally violent, labor relations as the unions attempted to maintain the advantages they had won under government control. Eventually, both labor and management supported legislation to provide for collective bargaining on the railroads, and thus in 1926 the Railway Labor Act was passed.

The Railway Labor Act drew from the experiences of war-time control of the railroads by the government and from the earlier legislation. It was substantially amended in 1934, and the airlines were brought within its jurisdiction in 1936. The law provides for free choice of bargaining representatives, with no employer interference, and obligates both sides to bargain collectively.

The National Mediation Board, one of the agencies created to administer the Railway Labor Act, supervises elections for the choice of bargaining representatives. In addition to this function, which parallels that of the National Labor Relations Board, it also has a power beyond that of the NLRB; it intervenes in the writing of new contracts. If the two parties are not successful in reaching an agreement through collective bargaining, the Board enters the dispute to mediate the differences. If mediation is unsuccessful, voluntary arbitration is proposed. If this is refused by the railroads or the unions, the Board may certify the dispute to the President. In this case no strike or lockout is permitted and the railroad may not make unilateral changes in working conditions. The President then appoints an emergency investigation board which studies the dispute for thirty days. The emergency board is an *ad hoc* board— especially appointed for the particular dispute—which has the power to make recommendations for settlement. These recommendations are not binding on either side, although there is substantial public pressure to abide by them. Regardless of whether they are accepted, neither party is free to strike or lock out for an additional thirty days. At the end of this time, as far as the legislation is concerned, either side is free to take whatever action it wishes.

The Railway Labor Act, at one time considered an excellent model for labor relations legislation, has had a comparatively poor record since the end of World War II. This is partly the result of the deterioration of the financial position of the railroads and the substantial decrease in the differential of railway workers' pay over that of other workers. As a consequence, the President has entered a number of disputes, in some cases seizing the railroads after all the legislative machinery has been exhausted and the recommendations of emergency boards have been refused.

The National Railroad Adjustment Board, the other administrative agency under the Railway Labor Act, deals with the interpretation of existing contracts. It consists of thirty-six members, half of them appointed by the railroads and half by the unions. It arbitrates grievances which the two parties cannot settle by direct negotiation, relying on neutral referees if necessary to get a majority decision. The parties are obliged to take their unsettled disputes to the Adjustment Board and are compelled to accept its decisions. Its effectiveness is reduced by the large backlog of undecided cases and the continuing conflict over the complicated working rules. The unions want to extend these working rules in order to maintain the job territory, and the railroads want to reduce them in order to decrease costs; hence they are a never-ending source of grievances.[3]

[3] Jacob J. Kaufman, *Collective Bargaining in the Railroad Industry* (New York: King's Crown Press, 1954).

TAFT-HARTLEY ACT NATIONAL EMERGENCY PROVISIONS

Since the Taft-Hartley Act was written in the atmosphere of reaction to the strike wave of 1946, it is not surprising that it includes provisions limiting strikes of nation-wide consequence. Congress established a step-by-step procedure to be set in motion if a strike or lockout threatens the national health or safety. The initiative for using this national emergency procedure rests with the President. If he believes that the dispute is not of sufficient magnitude to warrant special attention, the national emergency provisions remain dormant.

When the President is of the opinion that an actual or threatened strike or lockout does endanger the national health or safety, he appoints an *ad hoc* board which investigates the dispute and reports to him its analysis of the facts. The board is not empowered to make an effort to settle the dispute. If, after receiving the board's report, the President still believes that the dispute threatens the national health or safety, he directs the Attorney General to seek an injunction in the federal courts. If the judge agrees that the dispute affects the national health or safety he may then issue an eighty-day injunction. During the first sixty days of this injunction the board reconvenes and restudies the dispute and again sends the President a report of its findings. In the meantime the Federal Mediation and Conciliation Service attempts to bring about agreement between the two parties.

If, at the end of the first sixty days, no agreement is reached, the National Labor Relations Board enters the picture for the first time. The NLRB conducts an election among the employees to determine whether they are willing to accept the employer's last offer. Within the last five days of the injunction, the NLRB certifies the results of this election to the President. In every instance the workers have voted in favor of striking in preference to accepting the employer's last offer. At the end of the eighty days the parties are free to strike or lock out. The President then reports his analysis of the dispute to Congress which may take whatever action it deems appropriate.

Experience under the National Emergency Provisions

Presidents Truman and Eisenhower used the emergency dispute procedure fourteen times, with injunctions issued in eleven of the cases. There were strikes in ten instances, three long strikes occurring after the injunctions had run their full course. In only four instances were agreements reached during the eighty-day cooling-off period. In one case, the 1950 bituminous coal strike, the strikers refused to return to work in spite of the injunction and the government was unable to prove in court that the union was responsible for their demonstration of solidarity.

The record of the national emergency dispute provisions of the Taft-Hartley Act is far from impressive. It is much too inflexible, once the injunction has been issued, both parties know what will happen, and when, and can plan for the exact day when the strike may be resumed. The rigidity of the procedure causes the government to show its hand in an atmosphere that closely parallels a bluff in a poker game. The two parties merely adjust the timing of their strategy to take into account the extra waiting period. Hence, the eighty days are more likely to be used for making propaganda blasts against the opponent than for cooling off and giving calm and mature consideration to settling the differences. The actual bargaining results would probably have been about the same even without the government interference. Perhaps the best that can be said for the national emergency provisions is that they have not unduly burdened collective bargaining.[4] The Landrum-Griffin Amendments made no changes in this part of the Taft-Hartley Act.

The 1959 Steel Strike

To illustrate the peculiar difficulties of collective bargaining in national emergency disputes and how the Taft-Hartley Act attempts to deal with these, we will look into the steel strike of 1959. As in any other strike, the economic and political conditions in the months before the actual stoppage influenced the bargaining positions. During most of 1958 the country was struggling through a recession with up to 8 per cent of the labor force unemployed. In this depressing atmosphere, the United Automobile Workers decided against striking when their contracts expired in the summer of 1958. The withholding power of the companies was too great because of the low demand for cars and the large inventories not yet sold. The UAW finally settled for modest improvements when the new models were being introduced in the fall. David McDonald wanted to demonstrate that he could win a better package than Walter Reuther had won; at the same time, the steel companies hoped to fare as well as the automobile employers.

Even though working far below full capacity during the recession, the steel companies were able to register profits, and with the return to high

---

[4] Frank C. Pierson, "An Evaluation of the National Emergency Provisions," *Emergency Disputes and National Policy*, ed. by. Irving Bernstein, Harold L. Enarson, and R. W. Fleming, Industrial Relations Research Association Publication No. 15 (New York: Harper & Brothers, 1955), pp. 129–46

levels of operation in early 1959, their earnings zoomed to record levels. Part of the abnormal demand for steel represented efforts of customers to stockpile in anticipation of a possible shutdown. The strike began on July 15, when the USW and management could not agree on the amount by which wages and fringe benefits should be increased. The union claimed the workers should receive a larger share of the rising revenues, and management replied that the profits were necessary for investment in expanding output and more efficient machinery. President Eisenhower adopted a "hands-off" policy, exhorting the contestants to pursue good-faith bargaining to find a compromise that would be fair but not inflationary.

The companies, in keeping with a current trend among many employers, insisted on changes in working rules that would give them greater flexibility in reassigning workers when new production techniques were introduced. This developed into an argument over local work practices, including the number of men required to perform certain jobs, time off for rest periods, who has first choice in overtime work, etc. Management proposed that studies be conducted in each plant, followed by arbitration of any disagreements over changes to be made. The union argued it had won the working rules over long years of bargaining and would agree to changes only through negotiation. The workers, fearing that the companies' demand would mean fewer jobs, became more solidly entrenched behind the leadership. What had begun as a not very popular strike among the steel workers was converted into emotional solidarity to retain daily job amenities of great personal value. A number of industry executives later admitted that it was a mistake to raise the work practices question at that time. The two issues, wages plus fringes and working rules, continued to divide the parties for nearly half a year.

The first government interference, other than mediation by the FMCS, came when the Secretary of Labor, James Mitchell, published, in mid-August, the findings of his study of steel wages, prices, and profits. Both sides found material in the report to support their expensive propaganda campaigns.

In October, after the strike had set a record as the longest in the steel industry, President Eisenhower put the Taft-Hartley machinery into motion, appointing a three-man fact-finding board headed by George Taylor, an experienced mediator and arbitrator and professor of labor economics at the University of Pennsylvania. Following the board's report, an injunction was sought by the Attorney General and granted by the Federal District Court in Pittsburgh. However, a stay of the injunction was also granted so that the USW could appeal to a higher court to determine the constitutionality of that part of the Taft-Hartley Act and to determine whether a national emergency really existed. The injunction was sustained in both the Court of Appeals and the Supreme Court, and on November 9 the workers returned to the steel mills 116 days after the strike began. And for two months they continued to work under the uncertainty of being called out again at the end of the eighty-day injunction.

In the meantime the USW scored some genuine bargaining victories, setting precedents which severely weakened management's position. Kaiser Steel, operating mainly on the West Coast, broke the solid front and signed a contract at the end of October, providing economic benefits beyond what had been offered and not requiring arbitration of working rules. Within a few days Detroit Steel and Granite City Steel followed the Kaiser formula. In early December the USW won favorable contracts from the manufacturers of tin cans, and the aluminum companies came to terms before Christmas. Agreements between the USW and copper companies also reduced steel managements' resistance power.

During the injunction the fact-finding board was reconvened to continue its studies. George Taylor, operating outside the authority of the Taft-Hartley Act, strived to mediate the dispute, but without success. At the end of its sixty-day period, the board reported to the President that the two parties were farther apart than before the injunction was issued. As the final days of the court order approached, the union conducted a straw vote among its members and reported 95 per cent favored rejecting the companies' last offer.

Vice President Nixon and Secretary Mitchell instituted behind-the-scenes conferences with top executives of steel and the USW. The mediation was successful, with the Vice President receiving much of the credit and thereby advancing his chances of winning the Republican Party's nomination for President in 1960. The industry calculated the cost of the settlement at 41 cents per hour, 80 per cent more than the union estimated it gained in the Kaiser contract, which was for only twenty months as compared to thirty months for the rest of the industry. Roger Blough, Chairman of the Board of Directors of United States Steel, predicted the cumulative cost would be $1,000,000,000 during the life of the contract. Nevertheless, it was the smallest percentage increase in wages won by the USW since the end of World War II. The union also won its point on working rules; any changes would be made only through negotiation. It was generally expected that steel prices would rise within a few months.

It is impossible to know how the steel strike would have been settled if there had been no Taft-Hartley emergency provisions. But it is clear that the final negotiations, promoted by the Vice President, involved a procedure not contemplated by the Act. And unquestionably, the bargaining power of the union increased during the course of the injunction. One cannot generalize from the steel strike, however; each national emergency dispute occurs in its own unique economic and political environment.

Comparison of the Taft-Hartley and Railway Labor Acts

The provisions for emergencies in the Taft-Hartley and Railway Labor Acts have some important similarities, but differ basically on the flexibility allowed for investigating boards. The first step under each Act is mediation, which is always available regardless of the potential impact of the dispute. Emergency measures are taken only when the President so decides. For the railroads and airlines, a threatened strike or lockout is officially brought to his attention by the National Mediation Board, whereas Taft-Hartley disputes require his own initiative for taking notice of crisis conditions. Both laws require about three months of stalling under the surveillance of mediators, in the hope that the extra time will be sufficient to arrive at a peaceful settlement.

The laws are also parallel in providing for the appointment of an *ad hoc* board to investigate a particular dispute. But the railway emergency board has much wider power, because it is charged with the duty to negotiate differences, and if unsuccessful, to publish a recommended settlement. Hence, it can probe more deeply into the real position of each antagonist by observing reactions to various proposals. Furthermore, diplomatic threats—in terms of what will be included in the published recommendations—can be employed to pressure one or both parties into a greater willingness to compromise. The Taft-Hartley investigators, however, are mere fact-finders. Any mediation or recommendations given to the President are strictly unofficial.

After the eighty-day injunction has expired or after thirty days have elapsed following the publication of the emergency board's recommendations, the disputants under either law are free to strike or lock out. The official procedures have been completed, and it is up to the President to decide what further action, if any, should be taken. As far as the laws are concerned, he is on his own, and his powers are restricted except under war-time conditions. Whether he can seize facilities or seek additional injunctions is not clear. The President can, however, rely on the enormous prestige of his office to persuade recalcitrant parties to act more patriotically.

SETTLEMENT OF DISPUTES DURING WORLD WAR II

In a war period the federal government faces unusual labor problems and at the same time an urgency to have these problems settled quickly and peacefully. During World War II—and what follows would hold true in any other national emergency—the government had to deal with three major labor problems: 1) speedy settlement of disputes which threatened to interrupt essential production, 2) stabilization of wages so as to avoid inflation, and 3) allocation of labor to the most vital industries.

Unfortunately, any solution that might have appeared to be the most appropriate for any one of these problems was liable to be in conflict with one of the other problems. For example, a wage increase might encourage the best allocation of labor from the point of view of the third task, but at the same time be inflationary and therefore undesirable from the point of view of the second. Or a wage increase granted quickly in order to solve the first problem might lead to a bad allocation of labor with respect to the third.

The policies generally followed with respect to settlement of labor-management disputes were based on voluntarism. That is, it was assumed that the parties would settle their disputes by direct negotiation, or at least voluntarily accept National War Labor Board recommendations for settlement. Only as a last resort and only on comparatively rare occasions were the parties compelled to accept a government-dictated settlement. The negotiated agreements, however, were required to conform to the "Little Steel formula," maximum wage increases of 15 per cent over May, 1941. Immediately after the entrance of the United States into World War II, management and labor issued their no-strike, no-lockout pledge. Voluntarism was largely successful, even though there were some strikes and some firms were seized by the federal government. In the light of the problems of defense production with many workers shifting to new jobs and employers, complete elimination of work stoppages would have been impossible.[5]

The National War Labor Board was the administrative agency charged with the responsibility of avoiding strikes and lockouts during World

[5] W. Ellison Chalmers, Milton Derber, and William H. McPherson, *Problems and Policies of Dispute Settlement and Wage Stabilization during World War II*, Bulletin No. 1009, United States Department of Labor, Bureau of Labor Statistics, 1950.

War II. It was tripartite in membership with twelve members, four each from labor, management, and the public. The advantages of a tripartite board are: 1) more willing acceptance of a decision, since each party knows it is represented in the making of the decision, and 2) more realistic decisions, since they are made by participating parties. The decisions of the Board were not binding; however, the Board could certify the dispute to the President who then could seize the facilities and operate them under government authority. The President made forty seizures during the conflict, nineteen of them for employer non-compliance with decisions of the Board, and twenty-one for labor noncompliance. Following seizure, production was immediately resumed in almost all cases. The American record on labor disputes during World War II was a remarkable tribute to the cooperative spirit of both management and unions. Reference to Table 9-A indicates that the amount of time lost due to strikes averaged less than 0.1 per cent of total man-hours for the war years 1942–1944.

ALTERNATIVE PROPOSALS

Whenever a national emergency dispute causes widespread inconvenience and figures prominently in the daily headlines, public orators make demands for new and more vigorous legislation. For example, one month after the injunction had gone into effect in the 1959 steel strike and while only dim hopes were held for a settlement without a renewal of the walkout, Adlai E. Stevenson delivered a plea for changing the labor laws. "Where private groups—like big business and big labor—are performing public functions, they must be held to public responsibility. . . . But it is now apparent that the emergency disputes provisions in the Taft-Hartley Act do not work and that a new and reasonable law is needed." [6] The law Stevenson wanted changed is itself an example of legislative response to crisis pressures, and perhaps, some time in the future, we will adopt more restrictive laws, again hoping to prevent "abuses" of collective bargaining. A greater degree of direct government interference in drafting new labor-management contracts may also be stimulated by a fear of the effect of wage increases on price inflation.

Compulsory Investigation

One proposal involving less government control than many of the often heard and more radical suggestions is compulsory investigation, somewhat like the role of the emergency board in the railroad industry.

---

[6] Quoted from a speech delivered on December 8, 1959, to the Institute of Life Insurance, and partially reprinted in the *New York Times*, December 9, 1959.

The primary difference would be more emphasis on publication, well before the strike deadline, of all the facts relating to the dispute. Supposedly, the public would then be able to form reasonable opinions about the justice of the positions of management and the union. Unfortunately, the statistics will almost always give some support to diametrically opposing views. Publication of the facts in the 1959 steel strike, motivated by the philosophy of the proposal for compulsory investigation, had no perceptible impact on the outcome.

Even an expert and impartial analysis of the statistics, such as one would expect to find in the final recommendations of an investigating board, has an imprecise and often only negligible influence on public opinion. And, at best, public opinion has an indeterminate effect on the willingness of reluctant parties to make concessions. A union or company will sometimes disregard it in battling for contract improvements or the preservation of prerogatives. A union leader may be forced in some instances to support a position which is unpopular with the general public, or else lose his office in the next membership election.

Perhaps the main advantage of an investigation board is that it forces the contestants to express their stands in more reasonable terms, convincing to a group of disinterested experts. And by a shrewd judgment of what is being put forward only for purposes of trading, the experts may be able to make the right suggestion for mediation at the opportune time. Even when compulsory investigation is accompanied by mediation and publicized recommendations for settlement, it will not be enough to prevent stoppages when strong and determined parties are separated on major issues.

Compulsory Arbitration

A proposal which represents about the maximum public interference in labor-management relations consistent with a free enterprise society is compulsory arbitration, which would put the government in the business of writing contract provisions. Strikes and lockouts would be prohibited and the contestants compelled to submit disagreements to a third party for final adjudication. The public arbitrator or labor court would listen to all arguments for and against changes in the contract and then issue a decision that would be legally binding on both sides. National emergency disputes have frequently inspired proposals for compulsory arbitration, particularly during a war. It is argued that this would not only avoid work stoppages, but also guarantee settlements in harmony with the public interest. The handling of war-time disputes in this country has always allowed greater freedom to labor and management than that envisioned by compulsory arbitration. Nevertheless, Australia and New Zealand and also a number of states in this country have used the technique for labor-management disputes in peace as well as war. The existing state laws deal only with public utility industries.

Even aside from the fact that compulsory arbitration laws have not completely eliminated strikes, there are shortcomings which would make similar federal legislation of dubious value in this country at the present time. Any labor-management contract involving a basic industry and a major union, if the terms were to be dictated by a government agency, would certainly be strongly affected by political considerations. Both sides would fight to control the government arbitration machinery, probably with unions actively supporting a labor party. Hence, collective bargaining would be thrown into the political arena.

Apart from these political overtones, compulsory arbitration distorts collective bargaining because, with the threat of an outsider's decision hanging over their heads, neither party would be willing to assume the necessary compromising attitude. Since the arbitrator, in search of a solution reasonably acceptable to both sides, is likely to make his decision fall somewhere between the union's final demand and the employer's last offer, neither side would be willing to make concessions prior to the arbitration.

If the settlement is not accepted, how is the compulsory award to be enforced? Are large masses of strikers to be thrown into jail? This is not a feasible technique of enforcement. Should just the strike leaders be thrown into jail? They become martyrs and the strike may be converted into a political class war. Assessing large fines may be politically unworkable, because of fear of consequences at the next election. The alternative is not to enforce the law which makes mockery of the whole government. Hence, compulsory arbitration has a tendency to break down, and therefore is inappropriate government interference in labor relations.

Government Seizure

Another extreme proposal, again involving prohibition against strikes and lockouts, is government seizure. If the union and management cannot amicably reach an agreement, the government takes possession of and operates the facilities until a contract is signed. Seizure is generally proposed only for vital industries or war-time disputes; it is quite possible, however, that a union will strike against the government, and therefore special enforcement techniques may be necessary. Some have argued that the office of the President, or a state governor, includes the power to take control of private property when necessary in an emergency. In 1952 President Truman seized the steel mills without any specific legislative authority, although he requested it from Congress. The Supreme Court ruled he had exceeded his executive powers as granted by the Constitution. But it is not clear whether this decision means he can never seize private property except under express legislative authority.

The essence of seizure is maintenance of the status quo until a new agreement is signed. Hence no changes in wages or working conditions are made, and for that reason unions may be reluctant to force the impasse into the final stage. Once the government has assumed control, a knotty problem arises: What should be done about profits? Is it fair to hold wage rates stagnant but allow the company to earn its normal profits? Or should the government seize the profits or a fraction of them? What should be done about the company's research and development programs, new products, or competitive price reductions? A possible solution would be requiring that the final settlement be made retroactive to the date of seizure. In the railroad case of 1950 and 1951, when government control lasted for twenty-one months, all operating decisions were actually made by management and the profits were retained by the company.

Pragmatic Combination

Because of the shortcomings of any one of these methods taken separately, more recent proposals have suggested a package of tools to be used in varying proportions depending on the special conditions of each national emergency dispute. The objective is to equip the chief executive with a wide range of flexibility in weapons and timing as opposed to rigid procedures like those included in the Taft-Hartley Act. Neither union nor management would be able to know ahead of time just what action the government would take or when. Therefore, they would have to keep all avenues open for sincere collective bargaining between themselves.

The Atomic Energy Labor-Management Relations Panel has been able to exploit a combination of weapons in dealing with disputes in the defense industry, and is a good example of the advantages of this approach. Congress created the Panel immediately after the first use of the Taft-Hartley emergency provisions, which occurred in 1948. The injunction lasted the full eighty days and was soon followed by an agreement without a strike. The President, in his required post-injunction report to Congress, asked for a permanent agency to deal with the peculiar labor problems in the atomic energy industry.

Since the government owns the facilities that are operated by private contractors and since the Atomic Energy Commission is always anxious to maintain continual production and research, the Panel has been able to employ an ill-disguised threat of compulsory arbitration, backed up by seizure, as an ultimate weapon. It has authority to enter into any dispute when it believes the parties, with the aid of the FMCS, are not making adequate progress. By being specialists in atomic energy labor problems, the Panel members can do an efficient job of fact-finding. They are always prepared to mediate the differences and to make recommendations. Their recommendations for settlement have always enjoyed the full support of the Atomic Energy Commission and have been accepted by the parties, sometimes grudgingly, with one or the other voicing objections. The Panel's over-all record rates quite high;[7] however, atomic energy is a unique industry, and the techniques should not and could not be copied without substantial modification.

The so-called Slichter law, named for its leading proponent, the late Sumner Slichter of Harvard University, and adopted by Massachusetts in 1947, provides the governor with a choice of procedures to follow. The law covers only public utilities and medical facilities. The governor may take action well before the strike deadline, conducting an investigation over the immediacy of the disruption of services. Preliminary mediation can be conducted at this stage. The parties are then directed to appear before a moderator and explain why the dispute should not be submitted to arbitration, if indeed there is any objection. The moderator can also attempt mediation. If unsuccessful in his efforts, he announces who has refused arbitration, thereby applying some public pressure to withdraw the refusal. The parties must then appear before a three-man emergency board which has power to recommend settlement. During this time work continues under the old contract. The governor may next declare a state of emergency and seize part or all of the facilities. A special arbitration board may be selected to suggest changes in wages and working conditions which may be instituted. Furthermore, there is always the possibility that the governor will step down at any stage in the process, leaving the parties to reach agreement by their own devices. The Slichter law, although a little short of compulsory arbitration, arms the governor with substantial power, and at the same time provides an appropriate amount of flexibility to adjust the weapons to the unique facts in each dispute.

During its first twelve years the law was invoked six times. Each of the procedures has been used, but not all of them in any one dispute. Both labor and management in Massachusetts believe the state law is preferable to the Taft-Hartley emergency provision.[8]

A Word in Conclusion

The public generally tends to become impatient during a national emergency work stoppage, demanding some airtight legislation so that "it can never happen again." Every politician running for office is obliged to outline and defend his pet scheme for protecting consumers, innocent workers, and shopkeepers. But this is a vain hope! We can never have a labor law that will eliminate all strikes, unless we are willing to destroy collective bargaining, and perhaps some of our other freedoms as well. Work stoppages can be completely avoided only if all contract terms are dictated by an all-powerful central agency.

In the United States we rely on collective bargaining to reconcile the conditions of work to the changing economic forces. Variations in the patterns of development in different industries require that labor-management relationships be given the broadest possible opportunity to adjust efficiently and in a manner mutually satisfactory. Therefore, our laws, even those covering national emergencies, should minimize direct interference in contract writing, particularly because we are often too quick to accuse a strike of creating a crisis.

We should, nevertheless, continue to try to reduce the number of strikes in vital industries, and to shorten the duration of those that do occur. As collective bargaining changes, new legislation will be needed. In fact, any law, after it has been on the books for a decade or so, begins to expose its loopholes. Each party continually looks for the weak spots and will certainly take advantage of them. If unions and management succeed in making collective bargaining work, the laws will be of small consequence. But if freedoms are constantly abused, they will inevitably be restricted.

[8] *Business Week,* October 31, 1959, p. 105.

DISCUSSION QUESTIONS

1. What role does the Federal Mediation and Conciliation Service play in national emergency strikes? in ordinary strikes?

2. Compare and contrast the procedures for handling national emergency disputes under the Taft-Hartley Act and the Railway Labor Act.

3. Explain the chief shortcomings of the Taft-Hartley Act for avoiding crises resulting from strikes. Use the 1959 steel strike to illustrate your points.

4. What special problems complicate the settlement of war-time labor disputes? What techniques did we rely on to solve these problems during World War II? Explain.

5. What is compulsory arbitration? Would you favor its adoption for all major disputes? Explain your position.

6. What are the advantages of granting an emergency investigating board the power to make public recommendations for the settlement of a dispute? Explain.

7. Why must government seizure be supplemented by some other techniques if it is to be a generally effective weapon for quelling national emergency disputes?

8. Describe the Slichter law (Massachusetts) for dealing with emergency disputes. Use your imagination to explain how a similar law, if it had existed at the national level, could have been applied to the 1959 steel strike.

BIBLIOGRAPHY

Bernstein, Irving: Enarson, Harold L.; and Fleming, R. W. (ed.). *Emergency Disputes and National Policy*. Industrial Relations Research Association Publication No. 15. New York: Harper & Brothers, 1955.

Kaufman, Jacob J. *Collective Bargaining in the Railroad Industry*. New York: King's Crown Press, 1954.

Taylor, George W. *Government Regulation of Industrial Relations*. New York: Prentice-Hall, Inc., 1948.

U. S. Department of Labor, Bureau of Labor Statistics. *Problems and Policies of Disputes Settlement and Wage Stabilization during World War II*. Bulletin No. 1009. Washington: Government Printing Office, 1950.

Witte, Edwin E. "Industrial Conflict in Periods of National Emergency," *Industrial Conflict*. Edited by Arthur Kornhauser, Robert Dubin, and Arthur M. Ross. New York: McGraw-Hill Book Company, 1954, pp. 428–41.

PART

3

WAGES

A wage rate is a price, and like other prices it is determined by conditions of demand and supply. Employers hire workers to increase their profits, hence the *demand* for labor depends on how much workers are able to produce and the price for which the output can be sold.

Since his income depends on how much he can receive in selling his labor time, the worker will strive for the best bargain obtainable. However, "best bargain" is not measured solely in dollar terms; his personal interest, often in conflict with his pecuniary interest as a wage earner, affects his labor market activities, hence the *supply* of labor is affected by unique institutional conditions not applicable to the supply of commodities.

Why do some workers receive more than others? Are the variations accounted for entirely by differences in ability to produce? How can we explain changing patterns of industrial, occupational, and geographical wage differentials?

One of the primary objectives of unions is to raise their members' wages. How successful are they on this score? What conditions are most favorable for union wage increases? What effect do unions have on the wages of non-union workers? What is the impact on the distribution of income as between wages, interest, rent, and profits?

What role does the government play in wage determination? As the representative of the general public, what should it strive to accomplish? In its position as employer, accounting for a large portion of all wage and salary earners, it cannot avoid having a significant influence on the labor market. And of course, with the minimum wage law, it sets a floor below which the wages of covered workers cannot fall.

15 | THEORY OF WAGES

The workers' primary and perennial objective is higher wages. What factors determine the amount of wages a worker will receive? Under what conditions are they likely to change? To give a generalized answer to these questions, a theoretical framework is needed, hence a theory of wages. However, we are not primarily striving to fashion a universally acceptable theory of wages; nobody has yet succeeded in doing that. We are concerned with establishing a broad framework within which we may analyze the impact of unions and collective bargaining, and of the government, on wages.

This chapter is restricted to wage theory as it applies to the individual business firm. No attempt is made here to describe the determinants of the general level of wages for the entire economy; obesrvations on that subject are made in later chapters. In constructing a theory of wages, an economist attempts to depict how prices and other economic variables are related to wages. The theory explains how a change in any one variable or set of variables, e.g., cost of raw materials, technological conditions, etc. affects all other variables.

In approaching wage theory, we begin by constructing a model, based on a number of simplifying assumptions. This model is applied to hypothetical situations in order to see how the essential variables act on each other. The model described in this chapter is known as the marginal productivity wage theory. It suggests, in the simplified form we will use, a much higher degree of precision than actually exists in the labor market, neglecting, among other things, the fact that adjustments to such economic changes as wage rates and the number of persons employed generally require an extended period of time. Furthermore, many possible offsetting economic activities may interfere with the adjustments as depicted by the model.

In the later sections of the chapter the rigid assumptions of the marginal productivity theory are relaxed. The model is made both more complicated and more realistic, and therefore somewhat better able to explain the actual operations of the labor market.

MARGINAL PRODUCTIVITY WAGE THEORY

The marginal productivity wage theory is one aspect of the marginal analysis used by economists to explain how a firm combines factors of production and decides on its level of output. The variables which are relevant to its application are: the employer's expectations with respect to the amounts of his output which can be sold at each of a series of possible selling prices, the anticipated costs associated with each possible method of combining the factors of production to secure different quantities of output, and the conditions under which labor is supplied to the firm. Assumptions—simplified generalizations which abstract from reality but at the same time emphasize basic underlying forces—will be made with regard to each of these variables in order to construct our model.

Basic Assumptions

As the first simplifying generalization, we will assume that each employer is in business for one purpose only: to maximize profits. He is not motivated by a desire to be the biggest employer, or the most generous employer, or by any other nonpecuniary consideration. All his decisions are made in the light of whether or not they will increase his profits. Is the employer concerned with maximizing profits in the short run or long run? This depends on how far into the future he can make reasonably accurate estimates of his sales. Obviously, he would not jump for a quick increase in his profits this month if he were certain it would reduce his total profits for the year. Conversely, if it is impossible for him to estimate his sales beyond a few months, he might very well take the quick increase in profits.

On the basis of this assumption it is possible to construct an employer's demand-for-labor curve, if additional information is provided on the costs of the other factors of production and on the demand for the product. The employer's demand for labor depends on what he expects an additional worker will add to his total revenue, less the cost he incurs for the additional factors necessary for employing this worker, called complementary factors. For the first part of our analysis we will assume that the costs of the complementary factors are equal for each employee, i.e., complementary costs are directly proportional to the size of the work force. The amount which the additional worker adds to the total revenue is referred to as the *marginal revenue product*. The marginal revenue product of the added employee will be greater the more he increases the physical output of the firm, this being determined by the technology of the firm. As more workers are hired, the increments to physical output decrease, in accordance with the principle of diminishing returns. If, because of the nature of the demand for his product, the employer has to reduce the selling price in order to sell the additional output, the marginal revenue product of the worker is reduced more sharply as the total output increases.

Thus, the employer's demand-for-labor curve—the marginal-revenue-product curve—is determined by the demand for the final product, the technology of production, and the costs of the other factors used by the firm. A change in any one of these variables alters the marginal-revenue-product curve. In the latter part of this chapter, when the model is made a little more realistic, typical possibilities of change are considered.

On the side of the supply of labor, it is assumed that the workers are homogeneous, equal to each other in ability as far as the employer is concerned. Furthermore, the workers have knowledge of all job openings and wage rates and shift about freely from company to company in accordance with the economic opportunities available.

With these assumptions we may now develop a model depicting the labor market activities of a firm and apply it to a number of hypothetical situations.

Competitive Demand and Supply

In our first hypothetical situation we assume the employer is a competitor in the labor market; that is, he is one of many employers all hiring the same type of labor. We also assume that the workers compete for their jobs individually; they are not unionized. The employer will find that he must offer the prevailing wage in order to attract and hold his workers. He would not offer more since this would reduce his profit, and he would not offer less, since the workers, according to our assumptions, would move elsewhere. The prevailing wage would be equal to the amount necessary to bring about an equilibrium between the total demand of all employers for a particular kind of labor and the supply of all workers of that type. The employer would hire workers up to, but not beyond, the point where the marginal revenue product of the last worker just equaled the prevailing wage. If the employer failed to hire additional workers whose marginal revenue product exceeded the prevailing wage, he would be missing an opportunity to increase his profits. And if he continued to hire workers after their marginal revenue product has fallen below the prevailing wage, he would pay to these workers more than they add to his total revenue, and therefore he would be reducing his profits. When employment has reached the point where marginal revenue product equals the prevailing wage, the employer will be maximizing profits and the firm will be in equilibrium; that is, there will be no tendency to change the number of workers hired unless there is some change in the technology of production, costs of other factors, or demand for the final product or a change in the conditions under which workers offer their services.

This situation is depicted in Figure 15-A. Wages and the marginal revenue product are measured in dollar terms on the vertical axis. The number of units of labor is measured on the horizontal axis. The supply of labor to the firm (S_1) is a horizontal line in this case; the workers offer their services at the prevailing wage (W_1) and are not willing to offer them for less since they could secure that amount of pay from other employers. The marginal-revenue-product curve (MRP_1) slopes downward and to the right in accordance with the principle of diminishing returns. The slope of the MRP curve would be steeper for those employers who are not competitors in the market for the final product, since they have to reduce prices in order to sell additional amounts of output. A vertical line dropped from the intersection of S_1 and MRP_1 shows the number of workers the employer hires (H_1). To hire more than this, or less than this, would cause profits to be less than the maximum that could be secured, given this wage rate and this demand for his product.[1]

[1] A supplementary numerical example may help to make the diagram easier to understand:

Total number of workers hired	MRP_1 (per week)	Wage (W_1) (per week)	MRP_2 (per week)	Wage (W_2) (per week)
15	$110	$80	$130	$100
$H_3 = 16$	100	80	120	100
17	90	80	110	100
$H_1 = 18$	80	80	100	100
19	70	80	90	100
$H_2 = 20$	60	80	80	100
21	50	80	70	100

A shift in either of the curves would lead to a new equilibrium number of workers hired. Thus, a shift in the employer's expectations with respect to the demand for his product, e.g., a shift from MRP_1 to MRP_2, would lead the employer to hire a larger number of people, H_2. Or, if all the other employers competing for this type of labor should demand a larger number of workers, thus causing an increase in the prevailing wage, the supply curve of labor to this firm—and to all firms in the labor market—would move from S_1 to S_2 and the employer would have to pay wage W_2. If his demand remains at MRP_1, he would reduce employment to H_3.

FIGURE 15-A

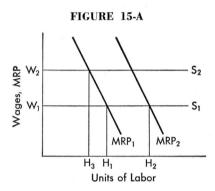

Units of Labor

Monopsonistic Demand and Competitive Supply

Our second hypothetical situation differs from the first in that the employer has monopoly power in the labor market. The employer is a monopsonist: the only one, or one of a few, hiring this type of labor. If he reduces his labor force, the competition between the employed and the unemployed workers drives the wage down. On the other hand, if he wishes to hire more workers, he must offer a higher wage in order to draw them from other economic pursuits, or from leisure.

The nature of the equilibrium is depicted in Figure 15-B. The supply curve slopes upward and to the right, reflecting the fact that the employer must pay higher wages when he wishes to induce more workers to work for him. The curve labeled *MLC*, marginal labor cost, indicates the additional labor cost the employer incurs for each additional worker hired. The *MLC* curve is above and steeper than the supply curve because the employer's wage bill is increased by both the wages paid to each new

According to the MRP_1 demand schedule and the W_1 supply schedule, the equilibrium number of workers hired would be eighteen, H_1. A rise in the demand schedule to MRP_2 would lead to a new equilibrium, twenty workers hired, H_2. If the supply schedule shifts to W_2 while the employer's demand for labor remains at MRP_1, sixteen workers would be hired, H_3.

worker and the higher wages paid to those already in his employment, assuming that he cannot discriminate between the old and new employees. The equilibrium point is at the intersection of the *MLC* and the *MRP* curves. At this point the last worker causes an increase in the employer's total costs just equal to the increase in total revenue resulting from the sales of the amount produced by the additional worker. Dropping a vertical line from the intersection, we determine the number of workers hired, *H*. A horizontal line is drawn to the vertical axis from the point where the vertical line intersects the supply curve indicating that the wage *W* must be offered in order to attract the most profitable number of employees. Notice that in this situation the workers are being exploited in the sense that their wage rate is less than their marginal revenue product.

Any change in the conditions under which the workers supply their services brings about a change in the S curve, and hence in the *MLC* curve. And any change in the employer's estimate of the demand for his product or his estimate of his costs of production leads to a new *MRP* curve. Either of these changes would lead to a new equilibrium.

FIGURE 15-B

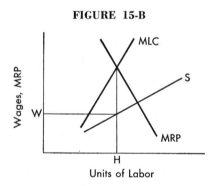

Monopolistic Supply and Competitive Demand

The supply of labor to the firm becomes monopolized if the employer is obliged to bargain with a union, rather than with his employees individually. The union insists upon a standard wage paid to all workers in the bargaining unit. It is an all-or-none proposition: either the employer pays to all workers in the bargaining unit the rate agreed upon or else no union members will work for him. Hence the supply curve becomes horizontal. The equilibrium position can then be diagrammatically portrayed in the same manner as that for competitive demand and competitive supply, as in Figure 15-A, with W_1 being equal to the wage collectively agreed upon. An increase in the union's demands for wages is comparable to an increase from S_1 to S_2 in Figure A, thus leading to a reduction in the number of workers employed, assuming no change in the employer's demand for labor.

Bilateral Monopoly

When a monopsonistic employer faces a union, he finds that the union bargain covers all employees in the bargaining unit, regardless of the number of workers hired, hence the supply curve becomes horizontal. Figure 15-C represents the equilibrium position after the appearance of the union. S_1 and MLC_1, which apply before the workers are organized, are both replaced by S_2. (MLC_2 is identical with S_2 since the latter is horizontal.) The equilibrium number of workers hired shifts from H_1 to H_2 and the wage from W_1 to W_2. In this situation the union increases both wages and employment, because the employer's profits are maximized when he hires at the point H_2. Hiring fewer workers would mean

FIGURE 15-C

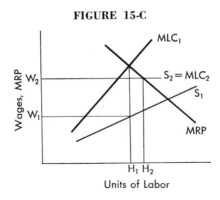

Units of Labor

giving up the opportunity to receive increases in revenue (MRP) greater than the increases in cost (MLC), and hence passing up the opportunity to raise his profits. Of course, if the union forces the wage rate to a level higher than the intersection of the MLC_1 and MRP curves, the employer's profits would be maximized at a level of employment lower than that which existed before the appearance of the union.

FACTORS AFFECTING ELASTICITY OF DEMAND FOR LABOR

In this section we will relax the assumptions concerning the employer's demand for labor and make it somewhat more applicable to real labor markets. Our purpose is to shed more light on the real meaning of the

MRP curve. Since the employer's demand for labor is determined by his expectations concerning the demand for the product and by the technological and cost conditions in the firm, it is these which must be examined in order to appraise the elasticity of his demand.

The second purpose of this section is to argue that under many typical circumstances the employer's demand for labor is very inelastic. *An inelastic demand for labor means the employer will respond to a change in wages by making a proportionately smaller change in the number of workers employed.* If the employer's demand for labor is extremely inelastic, a change in wages will have very little effect on the number of workers employed. Any particular degree of inelasticity of demand for labor applies only within a given wage range, not for the full length of the demand curve. In the hypothetical situations the *MRP* curves were all drawn sloping down and to the right, indicating some degree of elasticity. As pointed out at the end of this chapter, the conclusions reached by applying our model would be substantially altered if we assumed a perfectly inelastic demand for labor.

The discussion turns now to five conditions which may cause the employer to view his demand for labor as quite inelastic over the relevant wage range. The reverse of these five conditions would cause the demand to be elastic. The following analysis is couched in terms of inelasticity, not only because this better represents the conditions frequently found in collective bargaining, but also because it provides a unifying theme to the discussion. It should be noted that there are parallels between these five conditions and the determinants of the employer's resistance to the demands of the union in collective bargaining.

Elasticity of Demand for Final Product

The employer's demand for labor is derived from the demand for the final product. Hence the elasticity of the latter will condition the elasticity of the former. If the product demand is inelastic, the employer can pass a wage increase on to the consumer by raising his price, suffering only a small reduction in the number of units sold. Under such conditions the employer's response to wage changes is likely to be inelastic. Of course, an elastic demand for the product would tend to cause an elastic demand for labor.

The nature of the competition in the industry affects the elasticity of demand for the product of the individual firms. When there are many sellers competing in the same product market, with each seller providing only a small fraction of the total production, the employer is likely to view the demand for his output as being very responsive to price changes, which would tend to cause his demand for labor to be more elastic.

In an industry with only a few sellers, each of whom produces a sizable fraction of the total output, the employer is likely to view his demand quite differently. If he decreases his price, he may expect his rivals to retaliate with price reductions, particularly if his price reduction threatens their volume of sales. Their retaliatory price cuts would sharply reduce the potential gain in sales he might secure from the original price decrease. Hence, at prices below the existing price, his demand would tend to be inelastic; therefore he would gain little by forcing down wages and reducing his prices. If he raises his price, he may or may not be followed by his rivals. If each of the firms in the industry grants approximately the same concessions to the union, they may all raise their prices by the same amount and at the same time. That is, if one employer is the recognized price leader and if he raises his price in response to an industry-wide wage increase, the others are likely to follow. A price increase under these circumstances would cause the sales of the individual firm to diminish by no more, relatively, than those of his rivals. Hence, the effect on his demand for labor would be relatively the same as that of his rivals, assuming they produce under approximately the same technological conditions.

Thus, an oligopolist is likely to view the demand for his product as inelastic, compared to that of an employer selling in a competitive market, for any price below the existing price, and is likely not to consider any price above the existing price except when he believes that all his rivals will raise their price along with him; in which case he is likely again to view the demand for the product as relatively inelastic. This, of course, tends to make the oligopolist's demand for labor more inelastic. The inelasticity is of considerable importance to wage determination and collective bargaining because many segments of American industry are oligopolistic, particularly in manufacturing where unions are strong, e.g., steel, rubber, and automobiles. Conditions such as these put pressure on employers to bargain jointly, or at least to adopt the practice of pattern bargaining. Not all oligopolistic firms view their demand curves in the manner described; nevertheless, this is a typical characteristic.

In oligopolistic industries where the firms are in a fierce battle for market position, an additional reason for inelasticity in demand for labor appears. If only one of the firms is organized and it is seeking to maintain or increase its percentage of the total industry sales, it may pay the union rates and make substantial sacrifices in labor costs—that is, operate with lower profits per unit of output—rather than lay off a part of its work force, assuming that a given amount of labor is required in order to maintain the amount of production necessary to preserve its market position. Believing that his profits in the long run depend on maintaining his relative share of the industry's total output, this employer would retain the same number of employees even after being forced to pay union wage rates. This firm's demand for labor, then, would be inelastic in response to a wage increase. It would urge the union to organize the rest of the industry in order to equalize labor cost.

Availability of Substitutes

The employer's demand for labor is affected by the possibility of substituting other techniques of production which require lower expenditures for labor for an equal level of output. The demand for labor tends to be elastic if substitute techniques are available that would permit production at slightly higher costs than the present methods of operation. Under these circumstances a wage increase, raising the cost of the present process above the substitute process, may cause the adoption of the labor-saving technique. If no alternate technique of production is available, or if its cost is much greater than the technique currently used, the firm's demand for labor is more likely to be inelastic.

To adopt a new technique often requires a considerable amount of time, hence the change in employment may not appear immediately. In fact, an increase in wages may induce a firm to search more diligently for a substitute process; thus, the effect of the wage change may be quite different in the long run than in the short run. A wage increase is not the only stimulant to the adoption of labor-saving techniques. A substantial increase in the demand for the product may make it possible to use mass production techniques which would not be economical at lower levels of output. And of course the sudden appearance of a labor-saving and cost-reducing innovation, previously unknown, could lead to the adoption of a substitute technique, independent of a change in wages.

Availability of Complements

The elasticity of demand for labor is partly determined by the elasticity of supply of products complementary to labor. Complementary products are those goods and services which must be used in conjunction with the workers, e.g., tools, raw materials, etc. As more workers are hired, more complementary products must be purchased, and as workers are discharged, smaller amounts are needed. The elasticity of supply of complementary goods affects the demand for labor in the following manner. A decrease in wages encourages an increase in the number of workers employed. However, if complementary goods are inelastic in supply, higher prices must be paid for the increased amounts of goods used along with the additional workers, and therefore fewer additional workers are hired. Contrariwise, the employment effect of a wage increase would also be partly offset as a result of the decreased cost per unit of the complementary products as fewer workers are employed. Hence, an inelastic supply of complementary products contributes to an inelastic demand for labor because the effect of the wage change is partly offset by an opposite change in the cost of goods used along with the workers.

Cost of Labor as a Proportion of Total Cost

When the labor cost represents a very small portion of the total cost of a product, the employer is less likely to reduce his employment as wages increase. On the other hand, his demand for labor would tend to be more elastic if labor costs represent a high proportion of total costs. For example, if the wages of workers of a certain skill represent only 2 per cent of the total cost of production, a 10 per cent wage increase would raise the total cost by only 0.2 per cent. If the employer does not react to this small increase in costs, his demand for labor is inelastic. This type of situation prevails in many branches of the oil and chemical industries, and some work in atomic energy is of this nature.

Ratio of Men to Machines

In certain kinds of productive processes the type of equipment determines the number of men who must be employed, with little or no range of freedom. For purposes of illustration, imagine an assembly line process which is engineered to operate with 200 workers. Slightly fewer men would cause the assembly line to break down and output to drop precipitously, and additional workers would add practically nothing to total output. In such a situation the employer's demand for labor is very inelastic over a fairly wide range. An increase in wages would have to be great enough to cause him to close down the whole assembly line, and adopt a substitute technique of production, before it would bring a reduction in the number of workers employed. Likewise, a reduction in wages would have to be great enough to make it profitable to open a new assembly line or to run this one overtime before it would affect employment. Therefore, unless the firm can find an alternative method of production, its demand for labor for this productive process is inelastic. On the other hand, when the employer has a wide range of freedom in his mixture of men and machines, his demand for labor is likely to be more elastic.

Summary of Elasticity of Demand for Labor

Unfortunately, it is not possible to rank these five factors in the order of their importance in determining the firm's elasticity of demand for labor. Nor is it possible to state that the presence of one, two, three, or even four of them will cause the demand for labor to be elastic or inelastic. In each case it is a matter of degree. There is one possible exception. If a substitute process is readily available and easily installed and only slightly more expensive than the present method of production at the prevailing wage, this may be sufficient to cause the employer's demand for labor to be elastic to a wage increase in spite of whatever may hold for the other four factors affecting the elasticity of demand for labor.

The argument which is being made here, and will be applied later in the chapter, is that it frequently works out that the combination of these five factors causes the employer's demand for labor to be inelastic over a significant range of the *MRP* curve. This is particularly true in oligopolistic industries because of both market conditions and technological conditions, and, as noted earlier, these are frequently highly unionized. The supply of complementary goods is often inelastic, especially when it involves new work space and equipment during a period of expanding employment, thus contributing toward an inelastic demand for labor. The cost of labor is, in many instances, a small portion of the total cost; this is particularly true for highly skilled craftsmen who are working in industrial plants where the great bulk of the labor costs are for semi-skilled workers, frequently in a separate bargaining unit. Again, in many of our large manufacturing industries the number of men is largely determined by the type of equipment used, and in any short period of time this equipment cannot be readily changed. The firm must decide whether or not to operate the whole process or to close it down entirely, either temporarily or permanently. It should be emphasized that we are talking about elasticity to wage changes, not changes in national income. Many firms with highly inelastic demands for labor are very responsive to shifting levels of national income, and hence suffer wide fluctuations in employment.

Our discussion of the factors which determine the elasticity of the employer's demand for labor amplifies the meaning of the demand for labor as developed in the model. Although this still leaves the model as basically an abstract concept, its application to actual labor market conditions should now be clearer. Before making further applications, the meaning of the supply side must be amplified.

FACTORS AFFECTING ELASTICITY OF
SUPPLY OF LABOR

The discussion turns now to a reconsideration of the assumptions on the supply of labor, offering a more realistic appraisal of the way in which workers offer their services to employers. In our model we made the supply of labor depend on the wage rate offered, which has an unclear meaning. Is it the rate for new workers or for experienced workers, time-rates or piece-rates, hourly rates or weekly rates? Secondly, how are non-wage benefits (pension plans, regularity of work, opportunity for promotion, pleasant working conditions, etc.) to be taken into account in the supply curve? A gross simplification can be made, although it involves a number of technical difficulties in actual application. We take wages to mean the average weekly earnings inclusive of nonwage benefits which are economically measurable. (Which noneconomic benefits are economically measurable and the extent of their importance to the supply of labor are extremely complicated problems. In this section only suggestive comments are made concerning the difficulties.)

If we had a labor market which satisfied the conditions required for perfect competition, there would be sufficient movement of workers from job to job to bring about approximately equal wages for similar types of work throughout all firms in the labor market. A centralized employment agency would be necessary for registering all workers and all jobs, including all relevant information on skills and experience of workers and wages and working conditions for each job. We have no agency in this country which comes even close to this. The public employment service, as it is now established in each state, is not designed to perform this type of function.

The following paragraphs set forth the qualifications on the freedom of movement of workers, or what is generally called mobility of labor. We first consider the changing participation of different groups in the labor force, a major factor influencing the reallocation of our labor supply over the long run. Second, we turn to mobility of workers already in the labor force and the barriers restricting their movement from job to job.

Labor Force Participation

In Chapter 1, the factors determining labor force participation were outlined. At this point it is necessary to recall that young people each year enter the labor market in large numbers, and that other groups, e.g., housewives, each year move in and out of the labor force. The expansion of metropolitan areas at the expense of rural areas has made additional workers available to nonagricultural industries. As these workers find their way into the expanding industries, a reallocation of resources takes place. Since there are substantial barriers to mobility among workers already in the labor force, as described in the following paragraphs, new entrants into the labor force constitute the major element in bringing about a change in distribution of labor as new industries rise and old ones decline.

Perhaps as important as new entrants in bringing about a reallocation of labor is another group, the secondary labor force. These are workers who join the labor force only when jobs are easily and conveniently available, and often have no intention of working continuously until their normal retirement age. The secondary labor force consists largely of housewives and others who are not the family's primary breadwinners. As new industries develop and spread into new geographical areas, the secondary labor force supplements the total labor supply. Contrariwise, as plants are closed down, these workers retire from the labor market.[2]

Thus, important sources of labor supply for a firm which is expanding its employment are the secondary labor force and the new entrants to the labor market. A firm which has the reputation of paying well and of providing secure employment with opportunities of advancement should be able to attract more than its share of the new entrants who intend to remain in the labor market permanently. Hence it is in a position to take the "cream of the crop" as a reward for its reputation.

Mobility

By mobility of labor is meant the movement of workers from job to job in response to changing economic opportunities. Mobility may involve changing employers, industries, occupations, or geographical areas, or any combination of the four. The most common type of mobility is from plant to plant, or employer to employer. The next most common is movement from one industry to another industry. Movement from occu-

[2] Richard C. Wilcock and Irvin Sobel, "Secondary Labor Force Mobility in Four Midwestern Shoe Towns," *Industrial and Labor Relations Review*, Vol. VIII (July, 1955), pp. 520–40.

pation to occupation is less frequent, and the most infrequent is movement between geographical areas.

It has been found that mobility is characterized by the following factors:

1. Most labor turnover occurs within a small segment of the labor force. Only a minority of the labor force changes jobs in a given year; and it is a minority of this minority—those who move two or more times during the year —which accounts for most of the movement. . . .

2. Unskilled workers change jobs more frequently than the semi-skilled, and these in turn move more frequently than skilled workers. . . .

3. The propensity to change employers diminishes rapidly with increasing length of service. . . .

4. The propensity to change employers decreases also with increasing age (which is correlated, of course, with increasing length of service). In most cases this indicates that the worker, after a certain amount of "shopping around" in early life, has arrived at a satisfactory occupational adjustment and has settled down to piling up seniority, pension rights, and other forms of security for his later years. . . .[3]

Our model has been devised to apply to an individual firm and our examination of mobility is primarily concerned with the supply of labor to the individual firm. However, the mobility of labor at any point in time is affected by the level of employment in the economy as a whole. Unemployed workers are under much greater pressure to look for new jobs. Furthermore, by going from plant gate to plant gate, the unemployed worker has the advantage of being on the spot as job openings occur. Conversely, when the economy is operating at its peak and job opportunities are widely available, employed workers are more likely to shift. Latent hostilities toward the job may then be safely expressed in the form of quitting and finding a new job.

How can it be that only a small segment of the labor force is mobile in an economy which has exhibited as much growth and dynamism as ours? Four major barriers to mobility are surveyed in approaching the answer to this question.

Seniority

Length of service is the greatest single barrier to voluntary job movement. The longer a worker has held his job, the less likely he is to leave it for another. In the case of a unionized firm the seniority provisions protect the worker from layoffs and demotions and enhance his opportunity for promotion. These factors are also important for a nonunion firm.

[3] Lloyd G. Reynolds, *The Structure of Labor Markets* (New York: Harper & Brothers, 1951), pp. 39–40. Quoted by permission of Harper & Brothers.

That is, the employer emphasizes length of service in making layoff and promotion decisions, since this improves the workers' morale. Furthermore, those with considerable experience are likely to be the most efficient workers. Seniority affects the mobility of unemployed workers as well as the employed, since the amount of seniority is usually the most important factor in determining how soon a worker is likely to be called back. Thus, seniority makes the employed worker reluctant to leave his job in spite of higher wages paid elsewhere, and it reduces the range of job searching by the unemployed worker.

In some firms, when unemployment threatens, work-sharing programs are devised. All workers with a given amount of seniority work fewer hours per week, and pass the limited economic opportunity around. This technique, often promoted by unions, has the effect of further tying the worker to his employer.

Job Market Ignorance

In general, workers have very little knowledge about the labor market. There is no centralized source of information where workers can learn what wages are being paid in other plants for jobs comparable to theirs. A high wage in one plant often does not attract large numbers of workers from other plants, partly because they do not know about it. Employed workers generally feel that their wage is fair. In the plants in the lower half of the wage scale in Reynolds' study, 80 per cent of the workers believed that their company's wages were higher than wages elsewhere.[4] Hence, workers lack sufficient knowledge to be constantly shifting from job to job in response to changing economic opportunities, contrary to what we assumed earlier with respect to the supply curve used in the simplified model.

The union contributes to the lack of job information on the part of the workers by giving the unionized workers the impression that their wage rates are as good as those found in other plants. The worker feels that the union is bringing him the best wage that is available and does not bother to learn about pay rates elsewhere. On the other hand, the union may contribute to an increased amount of job knowledge. This is particularly true when employers do their hiring through a business agent or a hiring hall.

The public employment service is only modestly helpful in improving the workers' information about the labor market. This is partly because employers generally do not list their best jobs with the employment

[4] *Ibid.*, p. 214.

service, but rather promote from within the plant. Employers likewise do a large amount of their hiring from people who appear at the plant gate, since such persons are on the spot and can take the job immediately whereas hiring through the employment service may entail two or three days' delay.

One might expect the unemployed or new worker carefully to study the job market. On the contrary, the typical pattern of behavior appears to be:

> . . . the worker seeks word of vacancies from friends and relatives, and by dropping into the employment offices of a few companies. He also registers at the State Employment Service, but does not usually rely mainly on the Service to find him a job. As soon as he finds a job which meets his minimum standards as regards income and type of work, he takes it. This is a tentative decision; the worker takes the job "on probation," just as the employer considers the worker on probation for a certain period. After he has worked at the job for a few months, he is able to tell whether it meets his original expectations concerning income and type of work, and also how it measures up as regards supervision, fellow employees, chance for advancement, and other factors which could not be gauged in advance. If it measures up to his standards of a satisfactory job on all counts, he gradually makes a firmer mental commitment to stay with it. If it does not measure up, he begins to cast around for other possibilities . . ., and perhaps eventually quits the job and starts looking again.[5]

In other words, the typical worker does not have an organized method of looking for the best job opportunities and is unable to know many important things about the job until he has worked at it for a few weeks.

Individual Inertia

One of the sources of immobility of workers, perhaps the primary source, stems from the individual's own inertia. Movement from one geographical area to another presents the hazards of the unknown as well as the expense of moving. It means breaking off ties with family, friends, and the accustomed community facilities, such as schools, churches, etc. Transferring from one industry to another, or even from one employer to another within the same industry, requires breaking old ties and forming new habit patterns, even if no geographical movement is involved. The inertia even extends to an unwillingness to expend the efforts necessary to learn more about the job market.

The individual's age is an important determinant of his mobility. Younger persons have fewer ties to the community and are more willing to experiment with new jobs and new vocations. The insecurity of income

---

[5] *Ibid.*, p. 111. Quoted by permission of Harper & Brothers, New York.

associated with leaving one job to look for another may usually be borne more easily by the young worker who does not yet have family and home responsibilities. Furthermore, he does not have children who would be forced to change from one school environment to another.

To overcome the inertia which holds him to his present job, the worker must become dissatisfied with the job requirements, working conditions, opportunity for advancement, treatment from supervisors, or whatever. He may then look for another job. If he is extremely dissatisfied, he may quit even before learning of another job opportunity.

In a depression the inertia of the employed worker is likely to be more of a barrier. The generally prevailing belief that jobs are scarce will be strengthened by the knowledge that relatives, friends, and fellow union members are without employment. The worker will be much more willing to endure wage cuts and poor working conditions without registering a complaint, or at least without quitting. Even irregular employment may be viewed as preferable to accepting a new job with no seniority rights.

A depression has just the opposite effect on the inertia of unemployed persons, who are forced to widen their horizon of job search. The mobility of an unemployed worker may not increase immediately upon losing his job since he may have hope that his experience and seniority will make it possible for him to return to his former position. After his financial reserves run low and he has been turned away by his old employer a number of times, the search for jobs elsewhere will become more urgent. He will become more receptive to wages below his previous rate of pay and will consider working at a less skilled occupation. He may very well become discouraged with his home community and entertain thoughts of geographical mobility. For many of the unemployed, however, this is financially impossible; though people with no family responsibility are more likely to act on this motivation.

Barriers Created by Employers

The personnel policies of employers frequently affect the mobility of their employees. To the employer, turnover is undesirable because it raises the cost of production. Replacing departed employees requires expenditures for recruiting, selecting, and training new workers. Hence, employers through their personnel programs attempt to instil a loyalty to the firm. In some cases the employee may recognize that the training in which he has invested time and effort may be useful only in the firm in which he is employed, thus reducing his desire to look for other jobs.

Pension plans, frequently a major segment of a personnel program, undoubtedly have some negative effect on the mobility of workers. Many of the plans require the employee to complete a minimum of fifteen years of continuous service and still be with the company at the time of retirement in order to secure even minimum benefits. To be eligible for maximum benefits often requires a much longer period of service. This acts as a powerful restraint on the mobility of workers who have accumulated a number of years of seniority, but these are workers whose mobility would be low in any case. Those plants which give the worker a vested right to a fraction or all of the equities the employer has paid into the pension fund allow for a greater freedom of movement away from the firm. Since vacation rights usually increase with years of service in the same firm, they have approximately the same effect on mobility as pension plans.

Employers who have pension plans are deterred from hiring workers over forty or forty-five years of age. To hire older workers means proportionately higher costs of providing a pension, or it means retiring the man with an inadequate annuity. Faced with such a choice, the employer is likely to refrain from hiring older workers. Since they realize that it is more difficult for them to find jobs, this hurdle acts as an additional barrier to the mobility of those currently employed.

An employer policy, supplemental to the personnel program, which reduces the mobility of workers is the avoidance of pirating workers. Each employer is anxious to prevent other employers from hiring workers away from him, hence they may cooperate in an anti-pirating arrangement. When an employed worker applies for a job at another firm, the personnel director calls the firm at which the person is employed in order to get clearance before hiring him. Employers who refuse to cooperate in the anti-pirating policy become subject to widespread retaliatory pirating. The obvious consequence is to restrict the worker's economic opportunity and further bind him to his present employer.

Summary of Elasticity of Supply of Labor

The supply of labor to the individual firm, as measured in terms of current employees, is frequently quite inelastic in the short run. Those employees with many years of seniority generally ignore opportunities to earn higher wages elsewhere. Those with fewer years of seniority are also immobile, owing to their lack of job market information. The workers' inertia with respect to breaking established habit patterns further contributes to their resistance to change. The employer augments this inelasticity through his personnel program. For these reasons the employer finds that his wages may decline relatively to other firms and cause no substantial exodus of workers, at least in the short run.

This does not mean that the employer can make an absolute reduction in wages without suffering a loss of workers. Such a reduction, if made at a time of full employment and when other firms are not reducing wages, may induce a degree of elasticity in the supply curve. Under such circumstances workers may become sufficiently dissatisfied with their jobs to cast aside their seniority, overcome their inertia, and set about looking for a "fair" employer. In other words, the firm's short-run supply of labor may be inelastic to wage increases in other firms—a relative wage decline for the firm in question—but quite elastic to direct wage decreases.

The previous two paragraphs describe the labor supply in terms of the possibilities of workers leaving the firm. What economic inducements must the firm offer in order to attract new workers? Is the supply curve elastic or inelastic beyond the point of present employment? Generally, a firm needs only to announce that it is taking on more workers and it finds that an adequate number of workers appears at its gates. Since a wage increase is usually not necessary to attract the additional workers, the supply curve is elastic. There are three important exceptions: 1) If there is full employment in the labor market, the employer may have to raise wages to pirate workers from other firms. 2) If the firm is new and needs to hire an entire labor force, or is making a very substantial addition to its present labor force, it may need to advertise higher wages in order to attract an adequate number of workers. 3) If the firm is the only employer in the community and there is no appropriate secondary labor force, he may have to offer higher wages to attract workers from the surrounding rural areas.

The supply of labor is more elastic in the long run than in the short run. The new entrants to the labor market are more likely to gravitate toward the better opportunities than toward the poor ones. The same holds true for the unemployed. For this reason a firm may desire to earn the reputation of being a high-paying employer and thus be able to apply rigid employment standards to a large number of job applicants instead of taking just anyone who appears at the plant gate.

RANGE OF WAGES

The simplified model used at the beginning of this chapter has been re-examined with respect to the elasticity of demand for and supply of labor. The argument states that the demand for labor under many typical circumstances is quite inelastic. This implies that there is a range over which wages may change with the employer making little or no change in employment. The supply of labor to the firm is inelastic to a relative decline in wages, but elastic to a direct wage decrease if general employment conditions in the surrounding labor market are good. Ordinarily, additional workers may be hired with little or no increase in wages, except in a very tight labor market or when a very large number of workers is being added. Since the vertical axis in our diagram is calibrated for the wages of the firm in question, and not its wages relative to those of other firms, the supply curve is quite elastic.

In the hypothetical situations the range and amount of employment were uniquely determined by the point of intersection of two lines. More realistically, there is a range of wage rates, rather than a single rate, at which a firm may operate. This may be represented graphically as lines *MRP* and *S* in Figure 15-D, with *S* intersecting *MRP* anywhere between points *A* and *B*. Any wage rate between point *A* and point *B* would be associated with approximately the same amount of employment. If the firm in question is unionized, the difference between points *A* and *B* provides a bargaining range. In Figure 15-D, the effect of unionization on the supply curve is represented by replacing line *S* with line *U*. The union naturally attempts to push line *U* (wages) up toward point *A*.

FIGURE 15-D

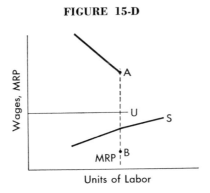

What are the determinants of the upper and lower limits of this range? What factors would cause a firm to pay wages toward the upper or lower points within the range? In the following paragraphs our model is extended to provide a first approximation of the answers to these questions. The three chapters following provide a more realistic understanding of the factors involved.

Upper Point

Over the long run the upper point of the inelastic section of the employer's demand for labor is determined by the availability of substitute processes; in the shorter run it is determined by his ability to pay, i.e., the demand for his product and his other (nonlabor) costs of production. However, for the nonunion firm, this must be qualified by the informal restraints exercised by the management fraternity. The upper point is determined "not by the highest wage which the most prosperous firm in the area could afford to pay, but rather by the maximum which it can pay without being considered 'unethical' by other employers." [6] That is, if a firm attempts to raise its wage rate substantially above that of other firms hiring in the same labor market, it runs the risk of being "expelled" from the management fraternity. Whether a nonunion firm will pay wages near the upper point depends on the quality of labor it wishes to recruit. If the firm insists on rigid hiring requirements, it will have to pay higher wages in order to maintain high quality workers over a period of time.

The upper point will change over a period of time. A change in the demand for the product will lead to a change in the location of the upper point. For example, a general improvement in economic conditions leading to an increased amount of sales on the part of the firm will shift the MRP curve to the right and perhaps cause the upper point to move higher. On the other hand, if competing firms are underselling the firm in question, its MRP curve will be forced downward and to the left and the firm will adjust by attempting to reduce labor costs or employment. The appearance of substitute processes may cause the firm to shift from one level of employment to another. If the new process is labor-saving, it will cause the upper point and the whole MRP curve to shift to the left. A reduction in the price of raw materials may enable the firm to lower its price and consequently sell a larger number of units. This would mean a movement of the MRP curve to the right. These are simply suggestions of what might bring about a shift in the MRP curve and hence in the upper bargaining point. In an industry growing at the average rate for the economy, or growing faster, point A would shift up and to the right.

It must be remembered that the MRP curve and the upper point depend on the employer's *estimate* of demand conditions and cost conditions. He makes this estimate in the light of existing conditions in the product, labor, and raw materials markets. Hence, union activity, through bargain-

[6] *Ibid.*, p. 233. Quoted by permission of Harper & Brothers, New York.

ing with other firms, especially if they are in the same industry or the same geographical area, may affect the employer's estimate of his demand for labor. For example, he is affected by such psychological factors as his notion as to what the prevailing wage is. Furthermore, under oligopolistic conditions, industry-wide bargaining may cause all firms in the industry to raise their product prices at the same time. In this situation the union induces a change in the firm's own estimate of the demand for its product and therefore brings about a change in the upper bargaining point.

What does all this mean for collective bargaining? For a unionized firm the upper point represents the maximum the employer is willing to concede. If wages are forced above this point, he will sharply reduce his employment, perhaps go out of business or relocate his firm. However, since the upper point is partly determined by psychological factors, it is subject to change as a result of union pressure. A long strike may have this effect, at least in the short run. From the point of view of bargaining strategy, an employer would never reveal the location of his maximum possible wage level.

Lower Point

The lower point of the range within which a firm may set its wages is determined by the conditions under which labor is supplied to the firm. It is the minimum price at which an adequate number of workers will offer their services to the firm. Unless the firm offered at least this much in wages, it would be unable to operate. Since workers prefer employment and income to unemployment, even at a low wage if that is the best they can do, under severe depression conditions point B could be extremely low. However, prevailing notions of an adequate standard of living, strongly influenced by the current standard of living, prevent point B from approaching zero. Furthermore, the worker's notion of a minimum price for his labor is certainly affected by the minimum wage set by the government and by levels of unemployment compensation.

The location of point B also depends upon the historic path followed in arriving at a wage rate. It is one thing for a firm to be at the bottom of the range as the result of wage increases lagging behind those of other firms and another thing for it to be there as the result of a wage decrease. In the former case the workers are liable to accept their lot, particularly if they are older than forty or forty-five or cannot meet more rigid hiring requirements set by other employers. In the second case the workers are likely to take positive action in the form of seeking other employment or organizing a union.

The location of point B changes over a period of time. As the community develops changing notions with respect to adequate living standards, the minimum labor supply price to each firm will tend to rise. As the levels of government-enforced minimum wages, unemployment compensation, and other types of social security payments increase, the minimum supply price will likewise rise.

SUMMARY

In this chapter we have developed a framework for analyzing the manner in which wages are determined for the firm. No attempt has been made to determine what is a natural, proper, or fair wage. Nor has any attempt been made to explain the general level of wages for the economy. This is the subject of later chapters.

We devised a simple model of a firm operating in the labor market, indicating that the demand for labor depends on the demand for the final product and on the costs and technical conditions of production. The supply of labor depends on the willingness of workers to shift from job to job in response to changing economic opportunities. This simplified model was applied to four hypothetical situations: a labor market which was competitive both in demand and supply, a monopsonistic employer facing a competitive supply, a union facing an employer competing with other employers in the labor market, and finally a monopsonistic employer facing a union. These four hypothetical situations were designed to be suggestive, in an abstract sense, of possible labor market conditions.

The firm's demand for labor was then subjected to a more complete analysis by investigating its relation to the demand for the final product, the availability of substitute processes, the availability of complementary goods, the cost of labor as a proportion of total cost, and finally the ratio of men to machines. It was argued that these factors are frequently arrayed in such a manner that the demand for labor becomes inelastic, so that the employer will hire approximately the same number of workers even though wages may be shifted upward or downward within a given range.

The supply curve of labor was likewise subjected to a more complete analysis. New entrants into the labor market and the secondary labor force constitute the primary factors in the reallocation of labor between different industries and occupations. However, there are substantial barriers to the mobility of workers already in the labor market, barriers sufficient to cause the supply of labor to a particular firm to be tied to that firm even in the face of a relative decline in wages. The factors which lead to the immobility of labor are seniority, the general ignorance of workers with respect to job market opportunities, the inertia of the individual, and a number of barriers erected by employers as a part of their personnel programs.

Since the demand for labor is inelastic in many typical labor markets, there is a range of wage rates which may be paid to any given type of labor. For unionized firms this provides an area within which bargaining may take place. The upper point of this wage range is determined by the employer's estimate of the demand for his product and his estimate of production conditions and costs of factors other than labor. The lower point is determined by the worker's minimum supply price.

DISCUSSION QUESTIONS

1. With the aid of a diagram explain, within the framework of the marginal productivity theory of wages, how the equilibrium wage and number of workers hired is determined when a monopsonistic employer is hiring in a competitive labor market. Show how and explain why the diagram is changed by the appearance of a union.

2. How is the employer's demand for labor affected by the consumers' demand for the final product?

3. What would be the impact on a firm's demand for labor if an innovation were developed permitting the substitution of machinery for labor at a cost much below previously available substitutes? Explain.

4. How is the demand for labor affected by an inelastic supply of goods complementary with labor?

5. Construct a diagram showing the *MRP* curve of a firm with a fixed ratio of men to the equipment used in its major production process. Explain why you gave the curve the shape you did.

6. Why is it that new entrants to the labor force account for a relatively larger share of the reallocation of resources than do those already in the labor market?

7. It is almost unbelievable that the workers, in a country which places so much emphasis on education, should know so little about the job market. Comment.

8. How is it that the personnel programs of employers can affect the elasticity of the supply of labor?

9. How is it possible that the supply of labor to a firm can be inelastic to a relative wage decline, but elastic to a direct wage reduction?

10. What is meant by bargaining range? What determines the upper point? The lower point?

11. Select a business firm in your community and explain how you believe it would react to a 5 percent increase in wages, assuming its competitors

must increase wages by a like amount. Use the type of analysis developed in this chapter.

BIBLIOGRAPHY

Cartter, Allan M. *Theory of Wages and Employment.* Homewood, Illinois: Richard D. Irwin, 1959.

Dobb, Maurice. *Wages.* New York: Pitman Publishing Corporation, revised 1946.

Douglas, Paul H. *The Theory of Wages.* New York: The Macmillan Company, 1934.

Dunlop, John T. (editor). *The Theory of Wage Determination.* New York: St. Martin's Press, 1957.

Hicks, John R. *The Theory of Wages.* London: The Macmillan Company, 1932.

Reynolds, Lloyd G. *The Structure of Labor Markets.* New York: Harper & Brothers, 1951.

Rothschild, K. W. *The Theory of Wages.* Oxford: Basil Blackwell, 1954.

Taylor, George W., and Pierson, Frank C. (editors). *New Concepts in Wage Determination.* New York: McGraw-Hill Book Company, 1957.

16 { APPLICATIONS OF

WAGE THEORY

The model developed in the previous chapter pointed to a range of possible wage rates, allowing for variations in wages from firm to firm. There is, as a matter of fact, a considerable amount of variation of wages in this country, even for workers doing the same type of work in the same locality. The purpose of this chapter is to use the model to help explain the causes of these wage differentials and their shifting patterns over a course of time.

There have been a great many labor market studies in recent years, providing us with much information. Some of these were intensive studies of single markets; some have been extensive, covering industries and occupations over a series of labor markets; and some have combined extensive and intensive studies. Although far from giving complete knowledge on the operation of the labor market, they indicate patterns of interaction of the forces of demand and supply. In this chapter our model will be applied as a technique for explaining these patterns of interaction.

The first and largest part of this chapter is devoted to a discussion of three types of wage differentials: 1) industrial, 2) occupational, and 3) geographical. In each case the primary causative factors, to the extent that they are discernible, are integrated into our model in order to analyze the causes and lines of development of wage differentials. This gives us an understanding of the determinants of the wage structure and its shifting patterns. The final pages of the chapter comment on the relationship of the wage structure to the general level of wages.

RESTRICTIONS ON THE APPLICATION OF THE MODEL

Before calling on our model to explain the real world, we should again emphasize that it is a theoretical construct and recognize its severe limitations. The degree of precision implied in our diagrams does not exist in day-to-day labor market operations. The workers' inertia and lack of job information, discussed in the previous chapter, prevent the labor supply from adjusting rapidly to changing economic opportunities. Likewise, the inability of employers to calculate accurately the costs associated with different levels of output and different methods of production prevents them from reacting quickly to changing labor market conditions. Furthermore, the ordinary businessman is not the sharp, penny-pinching entrepreneur envisaged by our model. He may prefer to follow old established practices rather than engage in a hectic daily manipulation of his labor force. Afternoons at the country club and a month in Florida may be more appealing than a 10 per cent increase in profits, particularly if it means the pain and effort involved in continually adding to and subtracting from his work force.

When it is further recognized that much of today's employment is accounted for by large corporations, the model acquires additional complications. The managers of giant firms are only indirectly tied to the goal of profit maximization. When there are thousands of stock-holders with no one of them holding more than a small fraction of the outstanding stock, the ability of the owners to exercise control in order to maximize profits is very limited. Real control may well rest with management. Even when a large share of the ownership is held by a pension or trust fund, the managers may retain a free hand because the fund trustees generally are reluctant to interfere in internal policies. In these circumstances it is not unusual for the corporation executives, who generally own only a negligible portion of the stock, to look on themselves as trustees of wealth with responsibilities to the public as well as the stockholders. The officials compromise the conflicts between employees, customers, suppliers, and owners.[1]

Are we then forced to admit our model is useless for practical problems? No, it simply does not explain every immediate detail of the labor market. It focuses on basic long-run tendencies. The model is accurate in a practical sense when it tells us employment will expand

[1] For a thorough and penetrating study of the difficulties of fitting the modern corporation into marginal productivity theory, see A. A. Berle, Jr., *The Fictions of American Capitalism: Power Without Property* (New York: Harcourt, Brace and Company, 1959).

in those situations where the marginal revenue product has a continuing tendency to exceed the wage rate, and will decline in opposite situations. And wages will tend to rise when workers cannot be found at existing wage levels which are substantially below the *MRP*. For example, an expanding industry like electronics with a rising *MRP* for engineers is characterized by increasing employment and higher earnings.

Even though employed workers do not rush from one job to a higher-paying one, there are long-run movements of employment which correspond to the principles of our model. Young persons, the unemployed, and secondary workers, and also the minority of the regular labor force that is very mobile, do drift toward the occupations and industries that are economically more attractive. It is not necessary for all workers to be continually on the move in order to approximate, in the long run, the supply curve which has been postulated.

The theory is not designed to explain why Mr. Jones wants to be a "good guy," employing many surplus workers and paying them the best wages in town. But unless his father endowed him with a large inheritance, or he is selling in a protected monopolistic market, he cannot long avoid bankruptcy if his wage payments continue to exceed the *MRP*. The theory does attempt to explain why competitive pressures would have a disciplinary effect on his economic profligacy.

In the real world, then, when changes occur in labor market conditions, employers make adjustments not only in wages and size of the work force, but also in hiring standards, qualifications for promotion, job assignments, price of the final product, and other related variables. When the shifting conditions are as extreme as those associated with mass unemployment or severe labor shortages, companies vary the degree of strictness in enforcing working rules and assessing penalties. These adjustments do not take place immediately. Time is required to appraise the significance of new forces in the labor market and to investigate alternative methods of operation under the new conditions.[2]

WAGE DIFFERENTIALS

Wage differentials are supposed to perform the important economic function of allocating labor. High wages should attract more workers into a particular line of endeavor and low wages should cause workers

[2] For a more complete discussion of the limitations on the applications of the marginal productivity theory to practical labor market problems, see Melvin W. Reder, "Wage Determination in Theory and Practice," in Neil W. Chamberlain, Frank C. Pierson, and Theresa Wolfson (editors), *A Decade of Industrial Relations Research, 1946–1956* (New York: Harper & Brothers, 1958), pp. 64–97.

to leave less favored kinds of work. Over the long run, then, there should be a continuing tendency for wage differentials to become smaller as workers shift jobs in response to improving economic opportunities. However, there are substantial barriers to this type of mobility. These were described in the previous chapter. Furthermore, in a dynamic economy, new causes for wage differentials continually appear, e.g., an innovation in production technology or a change in consumers' tastes which could cause a sharp increase in the demand for a particular type of labor.

Even in an economy where wages and prices were administered by an all-powerful central authority, wage differentials would not disappear. They would be necessary to bring about the allocation of labor desired by the planning agency. It is not at all surprising, then, that a largely individualistic economy should have continuing variations in pay rates. The original source of differentials is in the individual firm, which makes its own wage decisions in response to its interpretation of its economic environment. This does not mean that wages vary in a completely irrational fashion; rather, there are patterns of differentials. These patterns are the concern of our investigation.

Although wage differentials will be discussed in this chapter in terms of money payments, it must be remembered that there are other economic differences between jobs: pensions, sickness benefits, regularity of employment, etc. The money value of these additional benefits tends to be greater where wages are higher. If they were included in our presentation of wage differentials, the patterns of differentials, by and large, would not be changed, but rather would be amplified. It should also be noted that differences between jobs are not purely economic, varying in terms of supervision, pleasantness of surroundings, and the degree to which they personally satisfy the employees. These non-economic factors will be left out of account in our discussion.

Interindustrial

In May, 1958, the average straight-time hourly wage of the more than 11 million workers in manufacturing industries was $1.97. There were wide variations, with 15.6 per cent receiving less than $1.25 and 2.25 million earning more than $2.50.[3] Table 16-A portrays these variations by industry; however, the statistics are undoubtedly affected by the date of the survey, which coincided with the lowest employment level

[3] U. S. Department of Labor, Bureau of Labor Statistics, *Factory Workers' Earnings, May, 1958* (Washington: Government Printing Office, 1959).

in the 1957–1958 recession. The industries with the higher rankings tended to suffer most in employment and perhaps also in pay rates, thus causing the wage range to be narrower than it otherwise would have been. Nevertheless, Table 16-A indicates the diversity in hourly earnings in manufacturing industries. If other sectors of the economy had been included, e.g., agricultural, service, trade, and construction industries, the range would have been even wider.

TABLE 16-A

Number and Average Straight-Time Hourly Earnings [a] of Production Workers in Manufacturing Industries, May, 1958

Industry	Number of workers (in thousands)	Average hourly earnings
All manufacturing	11,245	1.97
Ordnance and accessories	68	2.28
Food and kindred products	978	1.78
Tobacco manufactures	70	1.58
Textile mill products	831	1.42
Apparel and other finished textile products	985	1.50
Lumber and wood products (except furniture)	542	1.61
Furniture and fixtures	283	1.74
Paper and allied products	432	1.84
Printing, publishing, and allied industries	540	2.31
Chemicals and allied products	510	2.17
Products of petroleum and coal	157	2.58
Rubber products	172	2.17
Leather and leather products	302	1.52
Stone, clay, and glass products	405	1.93
Primary metal industries	840	2.44
Fabricated metal products	756	2.07
Machinery (except electrical)	1,029	2.21
Electrical machinery, equipment, and supplies	715	2.00
Transportation equipment	1,081	2.38
Instruments and related products	200	2.05
Miscellaneous manufacturing industries	348	1.68

[a] Excludes premium pay for overtime and for work on weekends, holidays, and late shifts.

Source: U. S. Department of Labor, Bureau of Labor Statistics, *Factory Workers' Earnings, May, 1958* (Washington: Government Printing Office, 1959), p. 19. Adapted from material presented in Table 1.

To highlight the data in Table 16-A, the following facts are worth noting: "Nearly 70 per cent of the production workers earning less than $1.15 an hour were employed in establishments manufacturing food, textile, apparel, and lumber products. At the upper end of the wage scale, more than two-fifths of the workers earning $2.50 or more an hour were employed in the primary metals, machinery (except electrical), and transportation equipment industries."[4]

Why are wages so much higher in some industries than in others? The most obvious reason is varying skill requirements. Two industries may pay exactly the same rates for each type of work but have quite different averages for total employment because of the skill mix, one requiring many highly trained workers and the other a large proportion of common laborers. Variation in the pay to workers of different skills—occupational differentials—is discussed in the next section.

Another obvious cause of wage differentials is differences in productivity, output per worker. In those industries where workers, in combination with capital, produce the most, employers are more likely to be able to afford higher wages. Dunlop, in a study of thirty-five industries, covering the period between 1923 and 1940, found a correlation between increases in productivity and increases in wages. That is, wage increases were larger in industries making greater gains in output per manhour and smaller in industries which exhibited less gain in productivity. The correlation was not perfect; a number of industries were exceptions to the general rule.[5] In fact, in a later study, covering a longer period of time, very little correlation was found between percentage wage increases and productivity changes.[6] It may be tentatively concluded that improvements in productivity tend to push wages upward, but too many other forces are at play at the same time for a clear pattern to emerge.

What are these other factors which prevent productivity from being the sole determinant of the interindustrial wage structure? Dunlop suggested the following reasons for a less than perfect correlation between increases in productivity and increases in wage rates: 1) A pattern of wage relationships between industries, once established, does not change easily, regardless of differing rates of change in productivity. That is, certain industries tend to follow other industries, perhaps because of tradition, or because of union pressure. 2) The method of wage payment may affect how fast productivity increases are passed on to the worker, with piece-rate workers tending to make gains consistent with productivity sooner than time-paid workers. 3) The nature of competition in the product market may affect the ability of the employer to retain

[4] *Ibid.,* p. 1.

[5] John T. Dunlop, "Productivity and the Wage Structure," *Income, Employment and Public Policy,* Essays in Honor of Alvin H. Hansen (New York: W. W. Norton & Co., 1948), pp. 341–62.

[6] Frederic Myers and Roger L. Bowlby, "The Interindustry Wage Structure and Productivity," *Industrial and Labor Relations Review,* Vol. VII (October, 1953), pp. 93–102.

the benefits of the productivity increase within the firm, sharing a portion of the benefits with the workers. In highly competitive markets, the employer may be compelled to reduce his prices rather than raise profits and wage rates. 4) The differing bargaining power of unions in different industries may have some effect on how quickly and to what extent the productivity increase is passed on to the workers in the form of a wage increase.

The interindustrial wage structure, when measured by average annual earnings within manufacturing industries, has been remarkably constant; most of the high-paying industries at the turn of the century are still in that category and most of the low-paying industries have likewise maintained their position. Furthermore, the percentage differential between the earnings in the high-paying and the low-paying industries has shown only a slight tendency to decrease.[7]

Although the over-all pattern of the wage structure in manufacturing industries appears to be one of little change, there have been a few significant shifts in the interindustrial wage structure. Cork products and domestic laundry equipment were among the industries which made substantial improvements in average annual earnings relative to other manufacturing industries, whereas saddlery, harness, and whips declined markedly. Industries particularly sensitive to the business cycle, such as locomotives, motor vehicles, and steel, moved up and down the scale at different times.

Although the relative ranking of manufacturing industries exhibited a high degree of stability in terms of average *annual* earnings, there was much less stability in average *hourly* earnings. When hourly rates for 1940 are compared with those for 1923, considerable variation in the pattern of change may be seen, ranging from a decrease of 3.7 per cent in the boot and shoe industry to an increase of 64.1 per cent in the chemical industry. For the most part, the industries which made the greatest productivity gains were the ones which made relatively the greatest gains in average hourly earnings. Dunlop attributes this variation to the following factors:

. . . change in productivity, change in output, proportion of labor costs to total outlays, competitive conditions in the product market, and the changing skill and occupational content of the industry. Wage and salary rates would be expected to increase most where productivity and output increase most, where labor costs are a small percentage of total costs, where the enterprises are in strong bargaining power with the purchasers of their output, and

[7] Donald E. Cullen, "The Interindustry Wage Structure, 1899–1950," *American Economic Review*, Vol. XLVI (June, 1956), pp. 353–69.

where technical change operates to increase the skill and raise the occupational rating of employees.[8]

Industries which most closely approximate this collection of characteristics would, over the long run, increase wages more than other industries. Workers in industries having the opposite characteristics would find their wages lagging behind.

Each of these factors affects the employer's demand for labor, his *MRP* curve. A change in the productivity of the workers would affect the marginal revenue product through its effect on the marginal physical product. A change in the output of the industry would be associated with a changing demand for the product. That is, as consumers demanded more of the product, the output of the industry would increase. The proportion of labor costs to total costs would affect the degree of elasticity of the employer's demand for labor. If the employer had some monopoly position in the product market, the demand curve for his product being less than perfectly elastic, he would be better able to retain a portion of the gain from the productivity increase within the firm and thereby share it with the workers. If the change in productivity changes the skill requirements of the firm, this would mean a new *MRP* curve for each of the different types of labor, and changes in the relative amounts of each kind hired.

In terms of our model, then, interindustrial wage differentials arise primarily for reasons on the demand side, the factors which determine the *MRP* curve. These stem partly from the nature of the demand for the final product, both in terms of quantity demanded at the moment and the rate of increase in the quantity demanded, and in terms of the degree of competition in the product market. As indicated in the previous chapter, the *MRP* is also affected by the technological conditions of production within the firm, i.e., the existing productive technology and changes in it over a period of time. Both sets of factors cited by Dunlop —those explaining why wage changes are not perfectly correlated with productivity changes and those explaining the long-run variations in the interindustrial wage structure—arise out of the demand side of our model.

Two exceptional situations may cause interindustrial wage differentials to arise from the supply side. When a new industry is forced to recruit its workers in a tight labor market, it may then occupy an unusually high position in the national wage ranking. The initial differential may

[8] Dunlop, *loc. cit.*, p. 360.

continue for a long period because of the slowness with which the market adjusts. The other exception is union bargaining power which we leave undiscussed until the next chapter.

Interoccupational

It is well known that different occupations have different pay rates, that skilled workers earn more than unskilled, that physicians earn more than schoolteachers. What causes the appearance of occupational wage differentials and how are they changing over periods of time? The cause of the differentials is to be found on both the demand and supply side of the labor market. On the demand side, there are 1) the differences in productivity between the workers of the different occupations, and 2) varying consumers' demands for the output of the different occupations.

On the supply side, education, training, and experience play an important role. That is, the supply of labor for some employments, such as unskilled labor, is unrestricted except for minimal physical requirements, whereas for others the prerequisite qualifications in terms of training and education restrict the supply. These qualifications may be enforced by government through licensing requirements, or by private associations through apprenticeship requirements or entrance examinations, e.g., bar examinations in order to practice law. The supply may be sufficiently restricted, relative to the demand, to bring a high price to those possessing the qualifications. Complicating these restrictions on supply, the barriers to mobility operate so as to reduce the movement of workers from one occupation to another. Thus, noncompeting groups appear within the labor market, e.g., semi-skilled operatives who do not compete with lawyers, and consequently do not exert a downward pressure on the fees for legal services.

With the passage of time, the percentage differentials between skilled and unskilled workers have decreased. For example, a study of different occupational categories in the nonelectrical machinery industry showed marked decreases in the percentage differentials between 1945 and 1953. The reduction in percentage differentials came about despite the fact that absolute differences, measured in cents per hour, increased somewhat over the same time interval. This study noted that "wage adjustments had the effect of reducing the differential in the average pay of tool and die makers, as compared with hand truckers, from 63 per cent in 1945 to 39 per cent by the winter of 1952–1953; for machinists, the reduction was from 51 per cent to 30 per cent during the same period." [9]

This narrowing differential between skilled and unskilled workers is typical of most other industries and, in fact, is a continuation of a trend which has been in operation since the beginning of the century. In 1907 skilled workers were receiving twice as much as unskilled workers, whereas, by 1947, the differential was only 50 per cent. Most of the narrowing of the differential occurred during World Wars I and II and the immediate postwar periods. [10]

What has been the cause of this narrowing of the differential between skilled and unskilled workers? The fact that much of the narrowing has occurred during periods of peak labor demand indicates the importance of the competitive pressure exerted by unemployed workers and by the secondary labor force. In a tight labor market, employers find that they cannot fill all their needs for additional workers and at the same time maintain their former hiring standards. Therefore, the hiring standards are reduced and less qualified workers are attracted away from the lowest-paying jobs. Employers who previously satisfied all their needs by hiring unemployed casual workers and members of the secondary labor force at low wages, now find that even this segment of the labor supply is drained of all surplus workers. They must either raise wages or reduce output.

In most factories the more desirable jobs are filled by promotion from within rather than by hiring from the outside. When employment is expanding and relatively few workers are available, standards for promotion are reduced, again having the effect of raising the wage rates of the lower-paid workers. That is, unskilled and semi-skilled workers who would otherwise have to remain in lower-paying jobs are able to secure higher wages, while those at the top of the scale—near the end of the promotion ladder—make relatively smaller gains.

Competition in the hiring of lowest-paid workers accounts for the narrowing of the differential during periods of very high employment, but why does the old differential not return in a later period? This is the result of a number of long-run factors which are in operation. The extension of educational opportunities to broader segments of the population and the sharp reduction in immigration lead to a more homogeneous labor supply. The advance of productivity has diluted many skilled jobs and upgraded other jobs previously performed by common laborers.

[9] Toivo P. Kanninen, "Job Pay Differentials in Machinery Plants," *Monthly Labor Review*, Vol. LXXVII (April, 1954), p. 373.

[10] Harry Ober, "Occupational Wage Differentials, 1907–1947," *Monthly Labor Review*, Vol. LXVII (August, 1948), pp. 129–31.

Furthermore, on-the-job training provides opportunities to workers who might otherwise be stranded at the bottom of the wage ladder.[11]

Unions have had their effect on the narrowing of the occupational wage differential with their comparatively recent organization of the semi-skilled and unskilled. Unions, generally with the willing cooperation of employers, have sought across-the-board wage increases rather than percentage wage increases. These have had the effect of narrowing the percentage differential between low and high-paid jobs.

Whether or not the narrowing of the interoccupational wage differentials has unduly restricted the supply of skilled labor is an unsettled question. Management appears to be becoming more concerned with this narrowed differential and its ability to recruit skilled labor in the future. Unions which include workers at a number of different skill levels may encounter internal dissension as the more highly skilled workers find their pay differentials decreasing. For example, after the 1955 bargaining with the automobile manufacturers, dissatisfied skilled workers engaged in brief wildcat strikes and threatened to leave the United Automobile Workers and form an independent union. This has caused the union to give more attention to the problems of its skilled members. After a considerable narrowing of occupational differentials in the steel industry, extending over a period of forty years, the relative differences have remained fairly constant since 1947.[12] Perhaps the occupational wage pattern has entered into a quiescent stage, maintaining the existing skill differentials, at least as far as production workers are concerned. It is interesting to note that other countries have gone much further than the United States in narrowing the differential between skilled and unskilled workers.

In terms of our model, occupational wage differentials first appear as a result of shifts in the demand for workers having special productive talents. Since, in the short run, only a limited number of these workers are available, the supply curve slopes sharply upward beyond a certain point determined by the number of workers able and willing to fill this demand. Over a long period of time, the pay differentials tend to become smaller as more workers are induced by the higher incomes to undergo the education and training necessary to enter the more lucrative employ-

[11] M. W. Reder, "The Theory of Occupational Wage Differentials," *American Economic Review*, Vol. XLV (December, 1955), pp. 833–52; and Richard A. Lester, "A Range Theory of Wage Differentials," *Industrial and Labor Relations Review*, Vol. V (July, 1952), pp. 494–97.

[12] Jack Stieber, "Occupational Wage Differentials in the Basic Steel Industry," *Industrial and Labor Relations Review*, Vol. XII (January, 1959), pp. 167–81.

ments. Competitive forces during periods of high employment shift the demand for labor sufficiently to make it worthwhile for expanding firms to hire less qualified workers, causing a narrowing of pay differentials. As the population becomes more homogeneous, supply curves of the cheapest labor tend to be eliminated and the reduced differentials become engrained into the wage structure. Of course, new causes of occupational wage differentials, particularly on the demand side, continually appear in a dynamic economy.

Geographical

There are a number of geographical wage patterns. Metropolitan areas fall into a wage hierarchy which tends to remain relatively fixed over long periods of time. There are also continuing differentials between large regions of the country and between urban and rural labor markets.

Table 16-B

Indexes of Wage Rates in Selected Nonmanufacturing Industries, Twenty Urban Areas, April, 1943, to April, 1948

Urban Area	Index Number [a]		
	April, 1943	April, 1945	April, 1948
Seattle	136	122	187
San Francisco	135	123	202
Detroit	116	124	189
Buffalo	115	106	165
Los Angeles	114	109	191
Chicago	112	117	188
Cleveland	110	109	161
Milwaukee	106	108	175
Pittsburgh	105	98	167
Philadelphia	103	105	169
Providence	102	95	158
Boston	100	97	155
Minneapolis	100	94	152
Baltimore	93	92	145
Denver	90	87	143
St. Louis	88	89	147
Kansas City	88	89	148
Louisville	86	90	142
Houston	83	87	135
New Orleans	73	77	117

[a] 1943 average wage rate index for thirty-one urban areas = 100.
Source: Frank C. Pierson, *Community Wage Patterns* (Berkeley: University of California Press, 1953), p. 174. Adapted from Ruth Macfarlan, *Wage Rate Differentials: Comparative Data For Los Angeles and Other Urban Areas* (Los Angeles: 1946). The Indexes are based on figures published by the U. S. Bureau of Labor Statistics. Table 16-B is quoted by permission of University of California Press.

A study of the Los Angeles labor market illustrates the persistence of these geographical wage patterns. It was found that over long periods of time, Los Angeles maintained its wage position relative to other metropolitan areas with only minor modifications. This was true in spite of the fact that it was growing from a sparsely populated frontier community to a highly industrialized metropolitan area.[13] The constancy of the metropolitan areas, relative to each other, as measured by non-manufacturing wage rates is illustrated in Table 16-B. (The relationship between the metropolitan areas is equally constant when they are ranked according to wage rates in manufacturing industries.) The high-paying and low-paying cities tend to maintain their relative position, even while the whole wage structure is moving upward.

What causes the original appearance of these geographical differentials? Pierson cited nine factors which, in varying combinations, lead to different wage levels in different geographical areas. The presence of all these factors would lead to high wages; the absence of several of them would lead to lower wages. The nine factors are: "(1) rich, readily accessible natural resources, (2) cheap, efficient transportation facilities, (3) a large, well-trained labor force, (4) plentiful supplies of savings and credit, (5) a rapid and sustained growth in investment in new plant and machinery, (6) prevalence of industries with high labor skill mix and large amounts of capital equipment per worker, (7) continued rapid expansion in markets for consumers' and producers' goods, (8) a strong, enlightened trade union movement, and (9) large-scale business enterprises under skilled, forward-looking managements." [14]

Several of these factors fall within the demand side of our model. The availability of natural resources, cheap transportation, and adequate credit lead to a substantial amount of investment in new plant and machinery, which would cause the productivity of labor to be high and hence the employer's demand for labor to be high. The expansion of the product market, both for producers' and consumers' goods, and a skilled, forward-looking management would further induce a substantial demand for labor. A large well-trained labor force would increase both the demand and supply. That is, as the labor force grows, the number of consumers increases, leading to an increased demand for labor in consumers' goods industries. On the supply side, the abundance of labor would tend to hold wages down.

[13] Frank C. Pierson, *Community Wage Patterns* (Berkeley: University of California Press, 1953), p. 157.
[14] *Ibid.*, p. 20. Quoted by permission of University of California Press.

New York City is an interesting example of the interplay of these forces. Because so much of its manufacturing is concentrated in the clothing industry, factory wages are low compared to other metropolitan areas. The pay in nondurable goods production typically is less than that in durable goods. A large proportion of the labor force is Negro and Puerto Rican, whose continuing influx has provided a cheap and easily exploited supply of workers. The latter group, being the late-comers, are offered the lowest-paying jobs, e.g., in unskilled labor in costume jewelry and cheap clothing.

Geographical wage differentials are largely the result of the clustering of different industries in different metropolitan areas. Nevertheless, wages for the same type of work in the same industry do vary from one part of the country to another. To a large extent, this is the result of com-petitive forces in the labor market and can be traced to one or a few industries which dominate the community, e.g., steel in Pittsburgh. That is, wages paid in steel influence those of workers in other Pittsburgh firms whose jobs are similar. This by no means accounts for all the differences between geographical areas. Some of the peculiarities in geographical wage patterns result from acute shortages of certain skills in the local labor market, or from the recruiting policies of a few business firms, or from the successful bargaining of a shrewd business agent.

Why do these differentials continue to exist over long periods of time? Once established by the different industries which settle a particu-lar metropolitan area, they tend to persist because of the immobility of both labor and capital. Thus, workers are reluctant to make the sacrifice involved in moving from low-wage to high-wage areas, and management frequently finds it more economical to expand in areas already possessing a skilled labor force than to move to low-wage areas and train a new labor force.

We turn now to two special cases of geographical wage differentials: the one between the North and South, and that between urban and rural areas.

North-South

The North-South wage differential is one of the most obvious and persistent of regional differentials. At the same time, the amount of the differential has not been constant and in many respects appears to be irrational. Lester found that "the average North-South differential (a) is wide for some industries (like rubber tires, furniture, and full-fashioned hosiery which averaged 20 to 30 per cent below Northern scales for comparable jobs) but is extremely narrow or nonexistent in related industries (like automobiles and aircraft, pulp and paper, and seamless hosiery); (b) has narrowed considerably during recent decades in such industries as pulp and paper, cotton textiles, and seamless hosiery but has not been reduced in neighboring industries like lumber, furniture, and agriculture; and (c) has moved in opposite directions for considerable periods of time in industries that compete for labor, like cotton textiles and agriculture." [15] There are also differences between firms in the same industry. In some cases firms will pay the same rates in both the North and the South, whereas competing firms in the same industry will have wage differentials of as much as 25 to 40 per cent.

There are many reasons for the development of the North-South differential. Manufacturing industries have been slow to develop in the South, with only 2.4 million employees in May, 1958, while the Northeast had 4 million and the North Central states had 3.8 million. Average straight-time earnings were, respectively, $1.63, $1.94, and $2.13.[16] Transportation costs have been relatively higher in the South, partly because of discriminatory rates established by the railroads. The South, being more rural, has supplied abundant labor to expanding manufacturing industries, thereby holding wages down.

The odd pattern of the differential is the result of a number of different factors. In the first place, some managements deliberately pay the same rates in all geographical areas, while others historically began with a wage differential which they have continued over a course of time. Where industrial unions have achieved high levels of organization, they have sometimes, but not always, attempted to reduce or eliminate the wage differential. Certain industries are much more mobile from the point of view of capital movement and can therefore take advantage of the lower wage in the South. The effect of this uneven mobility of capital is to contribute toward the inconsistency of the wage differential between different industries, while at the same time narrowing the gap between the average of all wages in the North and South. Furthermore, certain industries such as cotton textiles and wood products are favored in the South by an abundance of natural resources. Other things being equal, this would tend to push up wages. The minimum wage has also exerted a greater effect in the South than in the North, reducing the percentage wage differential which otherwise would have existed.

Another oddity of the North-South differential has been discovered

[15] Lester, *loc. cit.*, p. 498.
[16] U. S. Department of Labor, *op. cit.*, p. 19.

by Henderson in a study of wages in thirty-five cities in 1951 and 1952. Although the earnings of production workers in the South are significantly below those in the North, the same does not hold for office workers. The latter group is paid at rates comparable with many cities in the North. Although, in most parts of the country, the differential of white-collar pay over blue-collar pay has been substantially reduced in recent decades, this has not been the case in the South. The primary reason, Henderson believes, is racial discrimination. This institutional barrier prevents Negroes—approximately half of the Southern labor supply—from competing for white-collar jobs. A second cause of this peculiar wage pattern, probably of somewhat less importance, is the comparative weakness of unions in the South.[17]

How is the North-South wage pattern explainable in terms of our model? There are crucial factors on both the demand and supply side which differentiate the two regions. The demand for labor in the South has been somewhat repressed by the slow growth of manufacturing industries below the Mason-Dixon Line, which has been caused by the distance from markets for both producers' and consumers' goods, complicated by the discriminatory railroad rates. Partial compensation for these barriers to capital development is the proximity to certain raw materials and special tax advantages offered by state and local governments to new firms entering the South since the end of World War II.

On the supply side the South has been able to offer a relatively abundant backlog of labor from depressed farm areas where incomes and marginal productivity are extremely low. The comparatively low percentage of unionization in the South also affects the conditions under which labor is supplied. The fact that the supply curve for certain occupations consists largely of Negroes, while other occupations are closed to them, further distorts the nature of the North-South differential. The comparative cheapness of labor has induced some firms to expand in the South, thus increasing the demand for labor. However, one labor supply characteristic, shortage of many kinds of skilled labor, has inhibited this expansion.

Urban-Rural

Another wage differential which has persisted over a period of time is that between urban and rural areas. For manufacturing industries in 1958, working within or near a city of 50,000 or more, provided a

[17] John P. Henderson, "A Deviation in the Pattern of Relative Earnings for Production Workers and Office Personnel," *The Journal of Business*, Vol. XXVIII (July, 1955), pp. 195–205.

premium of nearly $.40 per hour over nonmetropolitan areas—$2.08 versus $1.70. Including other industries in the comparison would have widened the differential considerably.[18] There are a number of reasons for the spread between rural and urban pay: 1) Productivity in manufacturing and other urban industries is substantially higher than in agriculture, partly because, with rising incomes, a larger proportion of our spending is on goods emanating from metropolitan areas. 2) The supply of labor to agriculture has not decreased at a rate commensurate with its gains in productivity. The average productivity has risen substantially, but the marginal productivity for the existing supply has fallen sharply. Thus, there is an oversupply of labor on farms, particularly family-sized farms, leading to much underemployment of labor— workers whose skills and labor time are not being efficiently utilized. 3) Although there has been a considerable amount of mobility from rural to urban areas over the past decades, special barriers to this mobility continue to exist, and therefore the pools of surplus labor have not moved to the industries with higher marginal productivity. Many people remain in agricultural pursuits because of the tradition of their families and their way of life. They enjoy working in the fresh air, and like the feeling of accomplishment when the crops are harvested. Furthermore, the government, through its farm price-support programs, encourages people to remain in farming. 4) Capital has not moved into rural areas because of the distance from markets, transportation costs, and lack of an appropriate labor supply concentrated in a single area. 5) Finally, the lack of unionization in rural areas has contributed to the amount of the differential.

Summarizing in terms of our model, the demand for labor in rural areas is low relative to urban areas because of distance from product markets and the immobility of capital. The supply of labor is abundant relative to the demand, and is characterized by under-employment, inadequate mobility, and practically no unionization. As long as the barriers to mobility of labor continue to exist, there is likely to remain a wage differential between urban and rural areas. However, if the trend toward decentralizing manufacturing industries continues—that is, if capital moves into small towns at an increasing rate—the differential may decrease. This capital movement would need to absorb a large portion of the secondary labor force before it would have a marked effect on relative wage rates.

[18] U. S. Department of Labor, *op. cit.*, p. 2.

Causes of Wage Differentials

This review of wage differentials has indicated a variety of interactions between demand and supply in different labor markets. It appears that the following factors play an important role on the demand side: 1) productivity, as it is affected by the presence of natural resources, cheap transportation, sufficient credit, and investment in capital equipment; 2) the demand for the product; 3) the nature of competition in the product market; 4) the ratio of labor costs to total cost; and 5) the skill and efficiency of management. The important factors on the supply side are: 1) the manner in which new entrants to the labor force enter the labor market; 2) the mobility of workers, including the movement from rural to urban areas; 3) the training and education of the labor force; 4) the degree to which the labor force is unionized; and 5) the willingness of workers to respond to the monetary stimulus of the private enterprise system. Institutional factors mold these interactions of demand and supply. For example, our attitudes toward the proper role of women in the labor market—whether or not it is socially acceptable for married women to accept gainful employment—affect the supply of labor. Especially important is the institutional role played by government through minimum wage and social security legislation.

The patterns of wage differentials are superimposed upon each other. The pattern of wages in a given locality depends on the industrial, occupational, and regional characteristics of its labor market. That is, the natural resources in a locality, along with market and financial characteristics, attract the industries which are most productive with these resources. The industries in turn attract workers with the corresponding occupational skills. The growth of a competent skilled labor force encourages further industrial growth. Suggestive of these types of interactions is Pierson's comment on the Los Angeles labor market:

Productive soil, favorable climate, and a few outstanding resources such as crude oil have made higher rates and earnings possible not only in industries immediately concerned but throughout the area as well. On the other hand, certain deficiencies, notably in water and basic minerals, have militated against the growth of heavy manufacturing and related fields, so that this customary source of wage gains has been generally precluded. Similarly, the factor of geographical location has had mixed wage effects. Since Los Angeles is the center of a new and relatively undeveloped region, its wages reflect the community's increasing importance in commerce and trade, but its remoteness from major consumption and industrial markets has exerted a serious counteracting influence on local wage levels.[19]

[19] Pierson, *op. cit.*, pp. 159–60. Quoted by permission of University of California Press.

THE WAGE STRUCTURE AND THE
GENERAL LEVEL OF WAGES

The previous chapter outlined wage determination for a particular firm. This chapter has taken a broader view, looking at wage patterns between industries, occupations, and geographical areas. This still leaves untouched the question of the determination of the level of wages for the economy as a whole. Our model, even as expanded in this chapter, is not designed to answer this question; rather, it describes the determinants of the wage structure. The general level of wages, discussed in later sections of this book, is determined by the total amount of spending in the economy—consumption spending, investment spending, and government spending—and the distribution of income between wages and other types of income payments.

Although, for purposes of analysis, we have treated the wage structure —wage determination in the firm and patterns of wage differentials—as independent of the general level of wages, these two do interact. For example, the rise of a new, highly productive industry, bringing with it a changed pattern of wage differentials, would tend to lift the general level of wages. Contrariwise, a shift in the general level of wages tends to disrupt the existing wage structure. An example of the latter occurred during the tremendously high demand for labor during World War II when employers were forced to lower their hiring standards, thus causing low wages to increase at a faster rate than high wages. This was partly the result of increased mobility of labor, as a result of which low-paying employers had to raise their wages in order to hold their work force. The changed wage structure was also partly the result of the policies of the National War Labor Board which permitted special wage adjustments to compensate for inequitably low pay and at the same time held a ceiling on wages generally.

Furthermore, the wage structure plays an important role in the nature of the expansion of the economy, giving certain industries and geographical areas a special stimulus. The relatively low wages in the South have attracted much capital spending in the area since World War II. The rapid expansion of the labor supply in southern California, holding wages lower than they otherwise would have been, contributed to the industrial growth of the Los Angeles area. Of course, relatively high wages have the opposite effect, as in the New England states, where they appear to have been one factor, among many others, in discouraging industrial growth, and have contributed toward the decision of some firms to relocate in other regions. High wages in the

Detroit area were undoubtedly one reason why the automobile industry spread into other areas of the country.

Not only does the wage structure play an important role in giving direction to the dynamic growth of an economy, but the manner in which it interacts with the general level of wages affects the total amount of economic growth and also the price level. An improper balance between the level of wages and the wage structure may lead to either unemployment or to inflation. This subject is discussed at length in Chapters 22, 23, and 24.

It was noted above that the general level of wages depends on the total amount of spending and on the distribution of income between wages and other types of income payments. Both total spending and the distribution of income are affected by union and government activities. Moreover, each of these institutions has a significant impact on the wage structure and on the nature of its interaction with the wage level. The next chapter extends our analysis of wages to include the impact of unions, and the following chapter the impact of the government.

SUMMARY

Wage differentials serve the economic function of allocating workers toward those positions where the demand for labor is greatest and away from those positions where the demand is least. Although workers are somewhat responsive to these wage differentials, particularly new entrants to the labor market, the differentials continue to exist over long periods of time because of the barriers to labor mobility and because of dynamic changes in the economy. Wage differentials also serve the economic function of encouraging the allocation of capital into those areas—geographical and industrial—where wages are relatively low and away from those areas where they are relatively high.

Interindustrial wage differentials appear largely for reasons on the demand side of our model, such as skill mix needed, productivity of labor, demand for the final product, competitive conditions in the product market, and the ratio of labor costs to total costs. The interindustrial wage structure appears to be fairly constant over the long run when measured in terms of average hourly earnings. Interoccupational wage differentials appear for both demand and supply reasons. Important on the demand side are the varying levels of productivity of the different occupations and the differing demands for their products. On the supply side are the educational and training barriers to the entrance into many occupations. With the passage of time interoccupational wage differentials have been narrowing, but the process seems to have ended, at least for the time being. Geographical wage differentials also appear for both demand and supply reasons. The availability of natural resources and capital equipment and the characteristics of the region's economic growth are important on the demand side. One of the major factors on the supply side is whether an abundant pool of labor from nearby rural areas is available. This is particularly important in the case of the North-South differential.

The wage structure is also affected by the general level of wages. During a period of high labor demand, low wages tend to rise relatively more rapidly than high wages. The wage structure, in turn, affects the general level of wages through its impact on the direction and amount of economic growth.

DISCUSSION QUESTIONS

1. What useful economic functions do wage differentials play? Briefly explain.

2. What are the primary causes of interindustrial wage differentials? Briefly explain each one.

3. What factors might prevent the wage increases in an industry from being directly proportional to the productivity increases in that industry?

4. How do you explain the fact that interoccupational wage differentials are narrowing but interindustrial wage differentials are not?

5. Explain the causes of different wage rates for different occupations.

6. Why have occupational wage differentials narrowed more rapidly during war periods than at other times?

7. How do you account for the fact that wage rates in certain cities remain higher than those in other cities for long periods of time?

8. What are some of the peculiarities in the North-South wage differential? What are their causes?

9. Why is there an urban-rural wage differential? How has this been affected by rising productivity in agriculture?

10. Describe an example of the interaction between the wage structure and the wage level.

11. How do the wages in your community compare with those for the country as a whole? Write an essay explaining why your community is in this position in the national wage structure.

BIBLIOGRAPHY

Cullen, Donald E. "The Interindustry Wage Structure, 1899–1950," *American Economic Review*, Vol. XLVI (June, 1956), pp. 353–69.

Dunlop, John T. "Productivity and the Wage Structure," *Income, Employment and Public Policy*, Essays in Honor of Alvin H. Hansen. New York: W. W. Norton & Co., 1948, pp. 341–62.

——— (Editor). *The Theory of Wage Determination*. New York: St. Martin's Press, 1957.

Pierson, Frank C. *Community Wage Patterns*. Berkeley: University of California Press, 1953.

Reder, M. W. "The Theory of Occupational Wage Differentials," *American Economic Review*, Vol. XLV (December, 1955), pp. 833–52.

Reynolds, Lloyd G. *The Structure of Labor Markets*. New York: Harper & Brothers, 1951.

Reynolds, Lloyd G., and Taft, Cynthia. *The Evolution of Wage Structure*. New Haven: Yale University Press, 1956.

Taylor, George W., and Pierson, Frank C. (Editors). *New Concepts in Wage Determination*. New York: McGraw-Hill Book Company, 1957.

Woytinsky, W. S., and Associates. *Employment and Wages in the United States*. New York: The Twentieth Century Fund, 1953.

17 { UNIONS AND WAGES

After a union wins a wage increase, it typically advertises its success far and wide. It is only natural that the union would claim the credit for the higher wages, since it wishes to retain the members' allegiance and to win respect for the leadership. But is it the union which is really responsible for the improved earnings of its members? Are wages really higher than they would otherwise be if the unions were not present? Or are wages determined by basic economic forces over which unions have little control?

Although positive sounding answers have been given on both sides of these questions, definitely proven answers are not available. The present status of knowledge of the labor market can give us only theoretical propositions and statistical relationships possessing uncertain meaning. If it were possible to compare one series of firms with another series of firms exactly the same in all respects except that the first series was unionized and the second not, then some degree of proof could be given. But even then, the findings would apply only to the time period studied and would not be clear proof for firms not included in the study.

Nevertheless, in attempting to answer these questions, we can achieve a better understanding of the impact of unions on our economy. It is worth our effort if we do no more than replace a few prejudices with an inquiring and skeptical attitude. Therefore, we will consider the theoretical possibilities of unions having a significant effect on wages and evaluate the available statistical evidence.

363

In the previous chapter we hinted at the role of unions in changing the pattern of wage differentials. Although a given wage differential may change for a variety of reasons (and it is often difficult to determine which is the major reason), it is quite possible that union bargaining pressure plays a major role. In this sense, this chapter is a consideration of a special case of the subject which was treated more generally in the previous chapter. One reservation which must be kept in mind throughout this chapter is that unions are many-sided institutions; increasing wages is only one of their goals. If, after evaluating the evidence, the conclusion is reached that they gain no real wage advantage, one should not decide, solely on that basis, that workers are foolish to join unions. Other types of advantages may be sufficient to convince the members to support their union.

Beyond the effects unions have on the wages of their members, what effects do they have on the general level of wages and on the distribution of income? Again, these are questions for which definitely proven answers cannot be given. Certainly, the level of wages and the distribution of income are different now from what they were when unions were comparatively poorly organized in this country. But there have been many economic and institutional changes, other than the growth of unions, which may have been more important causative factors. Nevertheless, some interesting statistical evidence has been uncovered and is evaluated in the last sections of this chapter.

DO UNIONS RAISE WAGES?

There is no doubt that in the typical situation, wage rates are higher after the union has signed a new contract than they were before. But are the new pay scales the same as those which would be dictated by economic forces or has the union given them an extra upward push? And if wages are higher, is employment reduced as a consequence? Even though proven answers cannot be given to those questions, our model may be extended to suggest some of the theoretical possibilities.

Theoretical Possibilities

It is often argued that wages are determined by economic forces over which unions have no control. The argument runs as follows: The demand for any particular type of labor is derived from the demand for its product, which depends on the tastes and purchasing power of the consumers and is entirely unrelated to union activity. Further, the nature of the derived demand for labor depends on the technical conditions of production: the existing state of the industrial arts, the cost and availability of credit and capital equipment, and the natural resources available. These are factors which unions are not able to alter in their favor. The presence of the union simply formalizes the wage-determining process and affects the timing of the wage increase.

Those who argue in this fashion usually grant that there are exceptions which, they claim, are comparatively unimportant. If the employer has a significant amount of monopoly power in the product market and the union is able to restrict the entry of workers into the trade, wages can be pushed higher than they would be without a union. But, it is argued, these high wages are at the expense of employment; fewer workers will be hired.

The argument that unions can have little effect on wages generally assumes a high degree of competition both in the product market and in the labor market. It further assumes a substantial amount of mobility on the part of workers. Wage differentials are considered to be the consequence of "frictions" or "time-lags" in the labor market. Wages for the same type of labor would be equalized between firms if employers gave more care to maximizing profits and if workers were more responsive to changing job opportunities.

Theoretical arguments may be made in the other direction as well—that unions are able to raise pay rates higher than would otherwise be possible. If the effect of the wage increase on employment is ignored, few would deny that it is theoretically possible for unions to have a positive wage effect. But the crucial question is: Can unions win the wage increase with little or no effect on employment? In the terminology of our model, unions, through their ability to withdraw the supply of labor, are able to raise earnings with very little effect on employment under four conditions.

1) If the employer's demand for labor is highly inelastic, unions may increase wages with little or no decrease in employment. This would follow from the discussion of the bargaining range in Chapter 15. Of the four conditions, this is the one which is most relevant to existing labor market conditions, particularly in oligopolistic industries.

2) If there is a substantial difference between the employer's marginal labor cost and the wage being paid prior to the organization of the workers, the appearance of the union could bring an increase in wages with no decrease in employment. This would correspond to the fourth hypothetical example described in Chapter 15, a comparatively rare case applying only to small one-employer towns or similar special

conditions in which the employer has monopsonistic power in the labor market.

3) If the union control of the job opportunity is sufficient to restrict entrance to the trade, and thereby effectively limit the supply of workers, the union might be able to push wages above what they would otherwise be. Some of the craft unions in the larger cities wield such influence and the American Medical Association provides similar protection for its membership. In this type of situation, however, the wage rate is being maintained at the expense of employment. Since the unemployed are not members, the union may ignore the employment effect. The union may be cautious and avoid pushing wages so high that they cause unemployment among the members.

4) The union wage demands may exert a *shock effect* on the employer. The shock effect can appear only where the firm has been lethargic in adopting new production methods and in efficiently organizing plant operations. A wage increase forced on the firm by union bargaining pressure alters the employer's cost structure: the higher wages plus the inefficiency may push his costs above the competitive level. Thus, the employer is forced to reconsider his entire operation—he is shocked out of his lethargy. His reaction to the shock may be to replace worn-out equipment with new machinery, or to improve the flow of work through the plant, or to expand his sales promotion, or to buy his raw materials from suppliers who charge lower prices. It is quite possible that changes of this type may be put into effect without altering the size of his work force. If this is the net result of the firm's reaction to the shock, its demand for labor has increased; higher wages are paid to the same number of workers. However, the shock effect may induce the lethargic company to adopt labor-saving machinery, causing its demand for labor to diminish, with the result that considerably fewer workers will be hired at the union wage rate. The shock effect may be favorable from the union point of view, then, 1) if the employer has previously been sheltered from competition in the product market and therefore has not been forced by competition to become an efficient producer, and 2) if there is no reasonable substitute for the type of workers whose wages increase.

Up to this point the examination of the theoretical possibilities of unions raising wages has been primarily a single market analysis, focusing on the labor market with extensions to the product market only to interpret the nature of the employer's *MRP* curve. More realistically, the labor market should be considered as one of a series of interconnected markets, including the product market, the money market, the raw materials market, and other markets which would have a bearing on the employment relationship. In short, the wage rate is not the result of bargaining solely between a single buyer and a single group of sellers; rather, it is the result of the interaction of the forces of demand and supply in a cluster of markets.

Within this cluster of markets, the strong bargainers exact tribute from the weak. For example, in the construction industry, the firms currently competing with each other are faced with a potentially large amount of new competition from persons who could enter the industry. Going into business as a new firm in residential construction requires very little capital investment. The union has a stake in preventing "too much competition" in the industry, since that would tend to create additional downward pressure on wages. In order to prevent this increased degree of price competition in the product market, the union supports the management association, and sometimes selected groups of suppliers. In some instances the union has not allowed its members to work for employers who are not members of the association. The union may control the price of the product by specifying standards which the employers must observe in bidding on jobs. In the residential construction industry the weak bargainers in the cluster of markets are the buyers of housing and the potential contractors prevented from entering the industry.[1]

The Allen Bradley case, described in Chapter 12, provides an extreme example of this type of union interference in the product market. Local No. 3 recognized that the wages of its members were determined in a cluster of market relationships rather than solely through direct negotiation with the employer. The weakest links in this chain of markets, the suppliers of electrical equipment located outside New York City and the buyers of electrical construction, absorbed the burden of the restrictive agreements promoted by Local No. 3. Here again, total employment in the industry was perhaps adversely affected by the union action, but as long as Local No. 3 did not push wages so high as to cause unemployment among its current members, their income was maximized.

Other techniques which unions may use to raise wages through direct interference in the product market include joining forces with the employer to finance an advertising program, typical of various branches

[1] John T. Dunlop, *Wage Determination Under Trade Unions* (New York: Augustus M. Kelley, Inc., 1950), pp. 95–117.

of the clothing industry. The use of the union label is an age-old tactic for affecting the demand for the product. Furthermore, unions may influence the product market through political pressures by lobbying for tariff barriers or subsidies for their industries. Examples have occurred in coal mining and elsewhere. In slack periods in the automobile industry, the union supports its employers in efforts to secure government contracts for defense work. Manipulating economic factors outside the labor market has certainly affected union wages in specific instances. Even if the effect is no more than maintaining employment at existing wages, it reduces downward pressure on union pay scales.

One can argue within the framework of our theory either that unions have practically no influence on wages or that they can raise wages significantly higher than they would be in the absence of unions. This does not mean that the theory is worthless or confused; just how the argument turns out depends on the assumptions one makes. The problem, then, becomes one of learning enough about the labor market to know which set of assumptions best approximates actual conditions. Although an examination of the statistics does not settle the argument, it does provide some interesting evidence.

Statistical Evidence

The simple question: do unions exert a positive impact on wages? becomes especially complicated when a statistical answer is sought. The decisive question: would nonunionized workers receive more income if they were unionized? cannot be answered since it is not possible to hold everything else constant while unionism is introduced. Time and economic forces will not stand still. Therefore, it is necessary to design the statistical analysis so that it eliminates the wage impact of differing occupations, industries, plant sizes, geographical areas, methods of payment (time rates versus incentive rates), special characteristics of product markets and raw materials markets, etc. In short, the mere phrasing of the question to be statistically analyzed may determine the answer which is found.

Positive Evidence

A direct comparison of wages by occupation and industry might at first seem sufficient to settle the argument over the unions' impact on wages. It is true that union members generally receive higher wages than nonunion workers in the same type of job in the same industry. But the differentials vary in no consistent pattern and are the result of so many causes that a simple direct comparison is not adequate to isolate the unions' effect. For example, statistics gathered in the full-fashioned hosiery industry in 1946 and 1947 showed that union wages exceeded nonunion on a nation-wide basis, but that was partly the result of greater union strength in the higher-paying regions. The hourly wages of nonunion workers in the Middle Atlantic region were substantially higher than those of union workers in the Southeast. Other studies also made in 1946 and 1947 showed that nonunion workers, paid on an incentive basis, in most cases received more than union time-paid workers in the same types of jobs. However, union incentive workers generally received more than nonunion incentive workers. Finally, nonunion workers in large firms usually received more than union workers in the same occupation in small firms. These statistics suggest that union workers were earning more than similar nonunion workers but that there were many exceptions and that the differentials were complicated by the operation of many factors unrelated to unionism.[2]

In his pioneering study of wages Paul Douglas found that unions, under some circumstances, did have a positive effect on wages. His evidence showed that the wages of union members rose by more than the average increase for all workers in the period immediately after unionization. Following this early period, the wages of union members increased at approximately the same rate as other workers. Union members in the building trades were an exception; they continued to gain at a more than average rate. Douglas noted that during the period of his study, the greatest nation-wide gain in real wages occurred while total union membership was declining.[3]

Douglas presented his results in terms of percentage changes in wages rather than in absolute terms, which obscured the fact that union members gained more in cents per hour than did nonunion workers. Since percentage wage differentials tend to be compressed as the wage level rises over long periods of time, his statistics should be rearranged to eliminate this effect. Comparing those industries, four nonunion and three unionized, which began with approximately the same absolute wages, between $.15 and $.30 per hour in 1890, it was found that wages in the unionized industries had increased 61 per cent by 1926 whereas nonunion wages increased only 18 per cent. In the last third

---

[2] H. M. Douty, "Union and Nonunion Wages," W. S. Woytinsky and Associates, *Employment and Wages in the United States* (New York: The Twentieth Century Fund, 1953), pp. 493–97.

[3] Paul H. Douglas, *Real Wages in the United States, 1890–1926* (Boston: Houghton Mifflin Company, 1930), pp. 562–64.

of the time period, 1914 to 1926, after the early effects of unionization were supposed to have worn off, the unionized industries continued to gain in wage rates at a pace twice that of the nonunion.[4]

More adequate statistics are available now than when Douglas made his study. Arthur M. Ross analyzed the impact of unions between 1933 and 1945, using hourly earnings for sixty-five manufacturing and extractive industries. His study included 8.5 million production workers out of a total of 10.5 million production workers in all manufacturing and extractive industries. A few industries were excluded for lack of adequate data, but with more than 80 per cent coverage, his findings may be taken as representative of manufacturing and extractive industries and are summarized in Table 17-A.[5]

TABLE 17-A

Percentage Increase in Real Hourly Earnings, 1933–1945

Wage class (*average hourly earnings,* *Jan., 1933*)	*Group I*	*Group II*	*Group III*	*Group IV*
$0.250–$0.399	Not tab.[a]	72.7	69.8	63.2
.400– .499	61.4	52.4	43.2	Not tab.[a]
.500– .650	50.6	34.0	Not tab.[a]	28.9

[a] Not tabulated; less than two industries.

The industries are divided into three classes according to wages paid in 1933. This makes it possible to compare wages which are more nearly equal in cents per hour and prevents small percentage changes from obscuring large absolute changes in wages. Each of the three classes is divided into four groups according to the percentage of workers covered by collective bargaining agreements in 1945: Group I, 80 to 100 per cent; Group II, 60 to 80 per cent; Group III, 40 to 60 per cent; and Group IV, 0 to 40 per cent.

The data show a consistent relationship between the degree of unionization and the amount of wage increase between 1933 and 1945. Ross concludes that the relationship could not be so consistent unless unions had a positive effect on wages. He grants that other factors played a role in the pattern of wage change. "There are a higher proportion of skilled workers, a greater concentration in urban areas,

[4] Arthur M. Ross, *Trade Union Wage Policy* (Berkeley: University of California Press, 1953), pp. 128–32.

[5] *Ibid.*, p. 122. Quoted by permission of University of California Press.

a smaller proportion of women, a higher degree of monopoly, and a greater sensitivity to cyclical influences among the industries in the first two groups." [6] Nevertheless, he feels that the effect of unionization cannot be explained away by these other factors.

The most comprehensive study of the impact of unions on wages is that of Harold Levinson, covering the period from 1914 to 1947. For 1914 to 1933 his sample includes between 7,000,000 and 11,000,000 workers, depending on the level of employment. During the 1933 to 1947 period his sample is the same as that of Ross, plus the addition of several service and trade industries. In order to observe the unions' effect on wages under different economic conditions, Levinson divided his statistics into a number of time periods. Following Ross's approach, he established four wage classes for 1914 to 1933 and three for 1933 to 1947, with wage class I including the highest-paid workers.

Levinson's data, summarized in Tables 17-B and 17-C,[7] show that unionized workers won a significant wage advantage over nonunion workers between 1920 and 1933, while by 1947 much of this wage advantage had been gained back by the nonunion workers. Within this over-all pattern, Levinson noted a number of special cases where substantial changes in a union's bargaining power were associated with

TABLE 17-B

Percentage Changes in Union and Nonunion Wages for Selected Periods, 1914–1933

Period	Wage class I		Wage class II		Wage class III		Wage class IV	
	Union	Non-union	Union	Non-union	Union	Non-union	Union	Non-union
1914–1920	+ 93	+137	+129	+128	+151	+144	+118	+180
1920–1923	+ 3	− 24	0	− 10	+ 5	− 10	+ 18	− 19
1914–1923	+ 99	+ 81	+129	+105	+163	+119	+157	+128
1923–1929	+ 22	+ 6	+ 13	+ 10	+ 13	+ 7	+ 5	− 2
1914–1929	+143	+ 92	+161	+125	+197	+134	+169	+123
1929–1933	− 10	− 36	− 8	− 14	− 12	− 17	− 6	− 17
1914–1933	+118	+ 23	+139	+ 94	+162	+ 95	+154	+ 85

clear-cut wage effects. For example, between 1914 and 1920 the newly organized railroad shopcraft workers made gains beyond those of other unionized, and also nonunion, workers. When the railroad shopcraft

[6] *Ibid.*, p. 128. Quoted by permission of University of California Press.

[7] Harold M. Levinson, *Unionism, Wage Trends, and Income Distribution, 1914–1947* (Ann Arbor: University of Michigan Press, 1951), pp. 47, 60–61. Quoted by permission of University of Michigan Press.

union collapsed after a three-month strike in 1922, their wages dropped, losing all the advantage and more that they had gained in the 1914 to 1920 period. During the 1920's the United Mine Workers' bargaining power declined sharply because of the existence of many nonunion mines and an unsuccessful strike. Between 1923 and 1929 their wages dropped 22 per cent as contrasted to a 22 per cent rise for unionized workers and a 6 per cent rise for unorganized workers.

The full-fashioned hosiery workers represent the opposite side of the same story. Their union became very effective after 1922, and by 1928 was able to secure wage increases that raised their pay scale from 14 per cent below the nonunion level to 47 per cent above it. A final example of a union whose degree of organization changed during the course of Levinson's first period is provided by the men's clothing workers. Their wages increased much more rapidly than the wages of unorganized workers and of those who had long been organized, so that by 1923 they exceeded the former by 35 per cent and the latter by 13 per cent, even though they had started at approximately the same absolute level in 1914. These special cases do not prove that unions were the cause of the increase in wages—certainly other economic factors were important in each case—but they at least indicate that the growth of unions may be associated with a more than average rise in wages. Of course, it may be that the same factors which made the union growth possible caused the rise in wages, e.g., an increase in the demand for labor in those particular industries.

Why is it that unions appeared to have the power to win wage advantages during some time periods but not in others? Levinson explains this by the interaction of three factors: *Level of employment, government policy,* and *sympathetic pressure.* When the *level of employment* is exceedingly high, nonunion workers are likely to make gains on a par with union workers, as in 1914 to 1920 and 1940 to 1947. Employers find it necessary to raise wages in order to hold their employees, because workers are more willing to be mobile, leaving lower-paying jobs in favor of higher wages in other firms. In other words, the narrowing of wage differentials that usually occurs under these circumstances gives the lower-paid nonunion workers a special advantage. From 1920 to 1933, however, there were two depressions, 1920 to 1922 and 1929 to 1933; between these depressions employment was high, but always with the supply of labor able to satisfy the demand without putting great upward pressure on wages. Under these circumstances nonunion earnings suffered comparatively, perhaps because unions had the power to

TABLE 17-C

Indexes of Weighted Averages of the Increase in Straight-Time Hourly Earnings in Manufacturing and Extractive Industries, 1933–1947 (1933 = 100) *

		Proportion Under Collective Bargaining Agreements			
Wage class	Year	Large proportion	About half	Medium proportion	Almost none
I	1933	100	100	No Data	100
	1938	145	145		129
II	1933	100	100	100	100
	1938	146	128	137	134
III	1933	No Data	100	100	100
	1938		135	140	128
I	1938	144	140	130	No Data
	1941	158	153	143	
II	1938	143	134	133	No Data
	1941	161	150	146	
III	1938	No Data	140	137	No Data
	1941		151	160	
		80–100 Per cent	60–80 Per cent	40–60 Per cent	Below 40 Per cent
I	1941	160	144	150	142
	1947	244	235	238	219
II	1941	158	150	143	147
	1947	259	261	239	256
III	1941	No Data	154	161	156
	1947		289	292	322

* The first third of the table includes thirty-four industries classified according to the proportion of workers under collective bargaining agreements in 1938. The second third of the table includes thirty-seven industries classified according to the proportion of workers under collective bargaining agreements in 1941. The last third of the table includes forty-four industries classified according to the proportion of workers under collective bargaining agreements in 1946.

raise rates or at least prevent declines, whereas unorganized workers, without the sharp competitive bidding for their services, were unable to push up their wages as much or suffered declines in pay.

The level of employment helps to explain the pattern of wage changes for 1914 to 1933 and 1940 to 1947, but it does not explain the intervening years. Levinson's second factor, *government policy*, provides a partial explanation of this period. Strange as it may seem, when government policy is favorable to them, unions seem less able to win comparative wage advantages than when it is unfavorable. From 1920 to 1933 the government actively discouraged union organization through its court decisions and in many respects aided employers in anti-union activities, yet unions did comparatively well during this period, as measured by relative wage rates. (This was probably because of the absence of sympathetic pressure, explained in the following paragraph.) From 1933 to 1940 the government actively supported unions in extending their organizations with the passage of the National Industrial Recovery Act and the Wagner Act. Even though unions gained rapidly in membership, they barely kept pace with the wage gains of the unorganized. The same story holds true for the two war periods when the very high level of employment was of greater importance in affecting wage patterns than were the policies of the government. Of course, this does not prove that unions were powerless between 1933 and 1940; their inability to raise wages above those of unorganized workers may have been the result of sympathetic pressure.

The third factor, *sympathetic pressure,* applies only to nonunion employers. It does not operate independently, but relies on one or both of the other two for its effectiveness. When unionized workers receive wage increases and improvements in working conditions, nonunion employers are under pressure to grant similar concessions, particularly if there is a threat that the firms will be unionized or that their workers will go elsewhere to seek employment. Sympathetic pressure, then, is particularly strong when the government is actively supporting union expansion or when employment is sufficiently high that employees may attempt to organize their nonunion shop even on the threat of losing their jobs. The degree of sympathetic pressure varies from one nonunion employer to another. Thus, regardless of the levels of employment, and regardless of labor relations legislation, a typical small town bank is likely to experience comparatively little sympathetic pressure, while the pressure might be substantial for a nonunion machine shop in a large city.[8]

Negative Evidence

The statistical evidence which has been presented up to this point lends weight to the belief that unions may have a positive effect on wages. However, there is sufficient negative evidence to cause one at least to qualify this conclusion. Albert Rees examined wage changes in the basic steel industry from 1945 to 1948, and concluded that the

[8] *Ibid.,* pp. 67–73.

increases can be attributed entirely to factors other than collective bargaining, chiefly the tremendous demand for steel and the consequent demand for labor. Even after wage increases had been negotiated, shortages of labor plagued important steel producing centers. With the rising cost of living and the rapidly advancing output per manhour, wages would have certainly increased regardless of unionization. The increase in real average hourly earnings, however, was only half of what it was in a comparable period of rising demand for steel, 1914 to 1920, when steel workers were almost entirely unorganized. For these reasons it may be argued that the wages secured by the highly organized steel workers between 1945 and 1948 were perhaps no more than what they would have received if they had not been organized.

It is even possible that wages would have risen faster and higher in the steel industry without the presence of the union. With wages fixed until the expiration of the contract, a temporary ceiling was placed on union wages while unorganized workers probably would have received increases more frequently. Furthermore, the employers were probably not willing to grant as large money concessions as they would have to unorganized workers because it would be more difficult to reduce union wages in a future period of declining demand for steel.[9]

Further reason to question the wage advantages which unions are able to gain was uncovered in a study of seven manufacturing industries by John Maher. In order to isolate the union effect from other causes of differentials, he used 1950 wage statistics for union and nonunion firms of equal size and in the same geographical areas. His statistics showed that unions held a significant wage advantage in only one industry, furniture, while nonunion workers appeared to have a significant wage advantage in one of the other industries, footwear.

An analysis of the timing of the wage changes in each of the industries studied by Maher indicated that the date the statistics were collected affected the results. In the furniture industry the wage survey was taken just after union contracts had been negotiated, and perhaps the nonunion workers later reached equality with the union workers. In the footwear industry the nonunion workers had been granted wage increases prior to the survey and union bargaining was completed in the months immediately following the survey. Since the nonunion employers had not sufficiently anticipated the bargaining pattern, they later granted increases bringing their wages up to the union level. Maher's study,

[9] Albert Rees, "The Economic Impact of Collective Bargaining in the Steel and Coal Industries During the Post-War Period," Industrial Relations Research Association, *Proceedings of the Third Annual Meeting*, 1950, pp. 204–5.

then, showed that union and nonunion wages were approximately the same in the industries he examined, although the timing of the wage changes varied, with the organized workers sometimes leading and sometimes lagging behind the unorganized.[10]

There is one important reservation to be made with respect to Maher's study. The average hourly earnings in the seven industries were below the average for all manufacturing industries together. Therefore, the wage characteristics of these industries may not be typical. Furthermore, it is not at all clear that nonunion wages would have been as high if part of the industry had not been organized. In other words, nonunion employers may have been raising wages to avoid unionization or to avoid losing workers, particularly in the last six months of 1950, the early stages of the Korean War. If sympathetic pressure, as defined by Levinson, was bearing heavily on the nonunion employers, this would help to explain the wage patterns found by Maher.

The negative evidence which has been presented conflicts only partly with the positive evidence. Taking both stands of evidence into account, it appears that unions do not win comparative wage advantages during periods when sympathetic pressure is strong. However, both union and nonunion money wages may be higher because of the effect of union bargaining power. When sympathetic pressure is weak, unions may be able to win a wage advantage over nonunion workers. The negative evidence is not inconsistent with this possibility.

Impact on Wage Structure

Up to this point the analysis of the statistical evidence has been centered on whether unions push wages higher than they otherwise would be. However, union wage bargaining has other goals as well: rational wage structure within the firm, elimination of gross differentials between firms in the same industry, and, in many instances, the reduction of occupational differentials. Regardless of whether unions are able to push up the absolute wage level, they may have a substantial impact on wages by eliminating what they consider to be inequities in the wage structure.

An example of this type of union impact is found in the evolution of wage structure in the basic steel industry. Prior to the rise of the United Steelworkers of America, wage rates varied substantially within

[10] John E. Maher, "Union, Nonunion Wage Differentials," *American Economic Review*, Vol. XLVI (June, 1956), pp. 336–52.

and between firms for approximately the same type of work. The chaotic situation was described by an official of one of the companies as follows:

There was no central department or authority responsible for fixing rates of pay. Such rates were fixed largely by supervisors of departments without relation to the rates in effect in other departments. There was no centralized control over the fixing of work standards which formed the basis of the employee's pay. Rates of pay were fixed largely on the basis of the opinion of individual foremen. . . . In consequence of the foregoing, many inequities in rates of pay developed and much inefficiency existed in the use of both labor and machines, causing gross wage inequalities within the plant.[11]

By 1940, having become well enough entrenched in the industry so that a smaller portion of its energies was required for organizing purposes, the union directed its attention toward reducing and eliminating these differentials. The differentials had generated considerable unrest among the membership, and hence there was much pressure on union officials to take some action. Working primarily with the United States Steel Corporation, typically the pattern setter in the industry, but also with the Cooperative Wage Survey, established by twelve of the leading producers in 1943, the USW reached agreement on a manual which divided all jobs into thirty-two labor grades. Each labor grade was assigned a pay rate equal to a specified amount above the plant minimum. These rates were incorporated in the contract signed with United States Steel in 1947 and followed by firms employing 80 per cent of the workers in the industry.

The union next aimed at eliminating the differentials in the plant minimums. Except for the Duluth and Birmingham plants, this was accomplished for United States Steel in the 1947 agreement. Again, most of the larger firms included this equalization of plant minimums in their agreements. By 1954 the Southern differential was eliminated and most of the companies were paying the same minimum, which, along with the established labor grades, meant that the industry's wage structure had been equalized. The exceptions were the smaller, nonintegrated firms, many of which were comparatively inefficient. Although contrary to the union's general policy, contracts were signed with these inefficient firms at less than the standard rates where the only alternative was closing the plant. However, since these firms account for only a small fraction of the industry's employees, they do not constitute a significant exception to the standardization of wages.[12]

[11] Quoted in Lloyd G. Reynolds and Cynthia H. Taft, *The Evolution of Wage Structure* (New Haven: Yale University Press, 1956), pp. 45–46.
[12] *Ibid.*, pp. 45–55.

Further examples could be cited but are not necessary to make the point. Union wage bargaining affects the wage structure as well as the wage level. In fact, its impact on the former is much more discernible than on the latter. Interpersonal wage differentials—between persons doing the same type of work in a common industry within a single geographical area—have been substantially reduced, particularly those occurring within a single firm. Unions have played an important role in narrowing interpersonal differentials, but, in many instances, management has also been anxious to reduce these wage inequities.

The impact of unions on occupational and industrial differentials is not nearly so clear. These two differentials were discussed in the previous chapter. Since the interindustrial wage structure has remained relatively stable, it is difficult to estimate the unions' impact. It may be concluded either that unions were unable to change the structure, or that they prevented changes from occurring that would have been unfavorable to them. It is not possible to demonstrate that either of these opposing propositions is accurate.

There are some grounds for arguing that unions have contributed to the narrowing of occupational differentials. Union wage bargaining tends to promote equal cents-per-hour wage increases. Nevertheless, the economic forces described in the previous chapter may have been strong enough to accomplish the narrowing of the differential regardless of the pressure from unions. Perhaps the most that can be said is that unions rode along with the economic tide. Occupational differentials had narrowed considerably in many industries before unions had any membership in those industries.[13]

Conclusions

As a first step in summarizing this mass of confusing statistics, the conclusions of four students of the labor market are set side by side. According to Ross: "Real hourly earnings have advanced more sharply in highly organized industries than in less unionized industries, in periods of stable or declining union membership as well as periods of rapid organization."[14] Levinson states his position along similar lines but in more moderate terms: ". . . at least during certain periods, union workers obtained a considerable wage advantage over nonunion laborers, and

[13] Clark Kerr, "Wage Relationships—The Comparative Impact of Market and Power Forces," in *The Theory of Wage Determination*, edited by John T. Dunlop (New York: St. Martin's Press, 1957), pp. 173–93. See also M. W. Reder, "The Theory of Occupational Wage Differentials," *American Economic Review*, Vol. XLV (December, 1955), pp. 833–52.

[14] Ross, *op. cit.*, p. 132. Quoted by permission of University of California Press.

that, even when this was not the case, union pressure may have been a factor causing both union and nonunion wages to rise more rapidly than otherwise." [15] Dunlop is more dubious of the effect of union bargaining power. After studying wage variation over a wide cyclical pattern, he concluded that the "differential wage movements could not possibly be attributed to union activity, since if anything the degree of union organization was relatively greater in those industries in which declines occurred first and increased last." He believed that much more significant influences were exerted by "the proportion of total costs that are wages and the character of competition in the product market . . ." [16] Finally, Rees believes that for the rise of wages in the basic steel industry "collective bargaining was not a significant factor. Its effects on wages were largely confined to altering the timing of increases, the form in which they were paid, and their distribution among workers in the industry." [17]

How can such divergent opinions be held by impartial observers of the same phenomena? In the first place, the phenomena are not exactly the same; each observer phrased the question he studied differently. The results were affected by the time periods selected, the industries selected, and the refinements introduced into the statistical procedure. In spite of this divergence, it may be reasonably argued that in some industries and during certain time periods unions have raised wages to higher levels than otherwise would have obtained. Conversely, it is also clear that the mere existence of a union, even a strongly organized union, does not guarantee wage increases greater than the average for the economy. In other words, unions occasionally, perhaps only infrequently, are able to make an economic gain for their members over and above what they would receive as unorganized workers.

How does the very modest conclusion based on the statistical evidence —that unions under some conditions appear to be able to raise wages— relate to the earlier theoretical discussion? Each union functions in an economic framework which is ceaselessly changing. The determinants of this framework—the economic forces operating in the labor, product, and raw materials markets—have greater influence than union bargaining power in setting wage rates. These economic forces determine the boundaries within which unions may exercise their influence over wages. By shrewdly judging these economic forces and finding those which will

[15] Levinson, *op. cit.*, pp. 112–13. Quoted by permission of University of Michigan Press.

[16] Dunlop, *op. cit.*, pp. 148 and 145.

[17] Albert Rees, "Postwar Wage Determination in the Basic Steel Industry," *American Economic Review*, Vol. XLI (June, 1951), pp. 401–2.

yield to pressure, a union may be more able than individual workers to take advantage of the economic framework. Within Dunlop's cluster-of-markets concept, the function of the union is to prevent the workers from being the weak link in the chain of interrelated prices. In this sense a union may raise wages; or it may prevent wage decreases which might otherwise occur in periods of unemployment and declining economic activity. In terms of our model, organization of the workers not only affects supply, but the power may be deployed to influence demand factors, the determinants of the marginal revenue product.

UNIONS AND THE GENERAL LEVEL OF WAGES

In the preceding sections we examined the question of whether union members gained a wage advantage over nonunion workers. An equally important question with an equally elusive answer is whether unions exert an upward pressure on the level of wages of all workers. Are total money wage payments higher than they otherwise would be because a portion of the labor force is organized? Or is the union wage advantage—if it exists—offset by lower wages for nonunion workers, thus leaving total wages unchanged? It should be emphasized that the question with which we are concerned here is the general level of *money* wages and not *real* gains in the purchasing power of workers' incomes.

The answer depends on 1) whether unions gain a wage advantage and 2) the impact of this wage advantage on nonunion firms. A moderately positive answer has been hazarded on the first point. The second depends on the operation of what Levinson called sympathetic pressure. He believed that his evidence demonstrated that unions do influence the general level of wages. Under conditions of very high employment or government support of labor, gains that unions make may be transferred through sympathetic pressures to increases in the wages for unorganized workers. Levinson argues that under conditions varying between substantial unemployment and nearly full employment, unions counteract the downward pressures at least on the wages of their members, if not on other wages. His conclusion, then, is that in "periods of recovery and prosperity, wages and prices rise more than they would in the absence of unionism, while during periods of recession and depression, they are prevented from dropping as much as they would otherwise." [18] If this is correct, unions have a positive effect on the general level of money wages. However, Rees's findings in the steel industry suggest that this conclusion must be taken with some reservation. When

[18] Levinson, *op. cit.*, p. 116. Quoted by permission of University of Michigan Press.

the demand for labor is very high relative to the supply, the effect of collective bargaining, with its fixed time periods, may be to retard wage increases.

Another way of viewing the impact of unions on the general level of wages is through the patterns of wage leadership. The wage structure in our economy is affected by a follow-the-leader influence. The growth of pattern bargaining means that the wages of many employees are influenced by a key bargaining agreement. If this key bargain is concluded with an expanding industry having a high labor demand, it will tend to push other wages higher than if it occurs in a contracting industry. What determines whether the wage leader will be in an expanding or contracting industry? In some cases it is determined by political power maneuvers among union leaders, in other cases by accidents of extraordinarily profitable firms jumping into the lead, or by the chance timing of a contract expiration.[19] Under certain circumstances, then, when the wage leader happens to be in an expanding industry, the effect of collective bargaining will be to push the general level of wages higher than it otherwise would be.

The key bargain tends to influence other bargains because it sets a standard which is convenient to follow. It may become a face-saving solution in a difficult bargaining situation. But beyond this the key wage settlement has especially great influence within what has been called its orbit of coercive comparison. That is, the key settlement would be a particularly compelling pattern for other bargaining situations which are closely related. A variety of factors determines which firms would be included in the orbit of coercive comparison. In some cases it would be all firms competing in the same product market. In other cases the efforts of the union to centralize bargaining would determine the orbit, e.g., seeking the same basic wage for all plants owned by one giant firm such as General Motors. Rivalries between union leaders may extend the orbit across industry and union lines. Finally, when the government plays an important role in wage setting, it is necessarily affected—for political reasons—by a widely publicized bargain. Thus, a key bargain spreads its influence over a large portion of the economy, but it is most closely followed by the bargaining agreements within its orbit of coercive comparison.[20]

The argument made in terms of coercive comparison can also be

[19] John T. Dunlop, "Productivity and the Wage Structure," Essays in Honor of Alvin Hansen, *Income, Employment and Public Policy* (New York: W. W. Norton & Company, 1948), pp. 354–56.

[20] Ross, *op. cit.*, pp. 49–64.

made in terms of sympathetic pressure. Employers free from the threat of unionization and located in isolated labor markets may safely ignore bargains concluded elsewhere, at least in the short run. Furthermore, when the government's labor policy is neutral or opposed to union growth and when there is some unemployment, the sympathetic pressure would be negligible for almost all employers.

Therefore, if it is granted that unions gain a wage advantage for their members, then it follows that they exercise some influence over the general level of wages. Nevertheless, the effects of unions on the general level of wages are diffused and impossible to isolate and measure. The factors which determine the national income are of much greater consequence than the special effects of union bargaining power. The determinants of the general level of wages are considered in Part 4 along with the related subjects of unemployment and inflation.

UNIONS AND THE DISTRIBUTION OF INCOME

Up to this point the chapter has been concerned with money wages with no attention given to changes in the earnings of nonlabor groups. The trend in money wages has been generally upward, and perhaps this can be partly attributed to unions, but has the rise in money wages been associated with a redistribution of income in favor of labor? Or have other income payments—rent, interest, and profits—risen proportionately? In other words, what has happened to labor's share of the national income? And to what extent are any changes in labor's share of the national income attributable to unions?

This question involves the real significance of any wage advantage that unions are able to win. If all nonwage income payments rise as much as or more than union wages, the union wage gain would amount only to keeping up with the rest of the society while leaving unorganized workers behind. It is possible that unions do not win a wage advantage over nonunion workers but do cause total wage payments to rise relative to other income payments. Finally, in the situation which would indicate the most economic power for unions, it is possible that their wage gains outstrip all other income payments. If this occurs in a growing economy, the standard of living of union members will rise faster than that of other groups.

The share of national income paid out as employee compensation has changed very little since 1919, remaining in the neighborhood of 55 per cent, except during severe depressions when it was temporarily higher. However, such statistics obscure important changes which may take place within the over-all totals. For example, workers may gain a larger share of the income payments originating in certain industries, but this would be obscured in the over-all data if the nation's production were shifting toward industries which pay a comparatively small fraction of total income payments to workers. The two shifts would tend to offset each other. In other words, a change in labor's share of the national income may be the result of 1) intraindustrial shifts, namely, changes in the proportion of income being paid to labor within one or more industries; or it may be the result of 2) interindustrial shifts, a change in the portion of the total national income accounted for by industries with differing fractions of income paid in wages.

Between 1919 and 1929, employee compensation rose from 53.3 to 59.3 per cent of private national income, excluding government payments. Nearly one-half of this increase was the result of interindustrial shifts, largely away from agriculture where a low portion of total income is in the form of wage payments. The other half of the increase, the result of intraindustrial shifts, was the consequence of a rising portion of income paid to workers in agriculture, retail and wholesale trade, and service industries. Since these industries are almost entirely nonunion, the increase in labor's share of the national income does not appear to be the result of collective bargaining. The most that can be said for the union impact on the distribution of income during this period is that it may have prevented the share of organized labor from being lower than it might otherwise have been. Levinson's analysis of three industries—men's clothing, anthracite mining, and railroads—showed that organized workers maintained their relative position while unorganized workers in these industries suffered a decline.

A different picture is presented by the period between 1929 and 1947. Employee compensation, excluding that of corporation executives, rose from 51.9 to 56.1 per cent of private national income,[21] an increase of 4.2 percentage points. The entire increase occurred among highly unionized industries, with workers in nonunion industries just maintaining their relative position. The gains of organized workers were at the expense of interest and rent receivers whose shares declined substantially. On the basis of this evidence Levinson concluded that the unions were instrumental in bringing about some redistribution in favor of organized workers. However, other factors were probably more important than

[21] The discrepancy between the figures for 1919 to 1929 and those for 1929 to 1947 is the consequence of using Simon Kuznets' data for the earlier period and Department of Commerce data for the later period.

union bargaining pressure. The high demand for goods following World War II, much of it concentrated in organized industries, brought a great demand for workers who happened to be unionized. The fact that inflationary rises in prices and wages occurred at the same time that the government was controlling interest and rents also contributed to a redistribution of income in favor of labor.[22]

If Levinson had selected a terminal year other than 1947, however, his results would have been quite different. When 1929 is compared with 1950 or 1951, employees in unionized sectors of the economy are found to have gained less than other employees. But the picture is again reversed if the terminal year selected is 1952, 1953, or 1954. In years when profits were high in unionized industries, labor's share was a smaller fraction of the total income created by those industries. Contrariwise, when profits are low, employee compensation tends to be a larger fraction of the income created. It would therefore appear that labor's share of the total income is affected more by cyclical fluctuations in the economy than by unionization.[23]

It may be concluded, then, that the union impact on the distribution of income is not clearly discernible. Under economic and political conditions which were favorable to union growth, the share of national income going to union members increased. However, under less favorable conditions, organized workers barely held their own. And in years of prosperity their share of total income declined. Taken all together, this is certainly not decisive evidence that unions are capable of altering the distribution of income in favor of their members.

SUMMARY

The analysis of the union impact on wages and income has provided only inconclusive answers. It may be argued theoretically that unions can have no effect on wages, except under very unusual conditions. Or, with different assumptions, it may be argued that unions in many situations are able to raise wages. A union, by preventing the workers from being the weak link in the cluster of markets within which they operate, may transfer competitive pressures to other groups.

The statistical evidence clearly does not prove that unions gain a wage

[22] Levinson, *op. cit.*, pp. 80–110.

[23] Clark Kerr, "Labor's Income Share and the Labor Movement," in *New Concepts in Wage Determination*, edited by George W. Taylor and Frank C. Pierson (New York: McGraw-Hill Book Company, 1957), pp. 260–98. Allen Cartter arrived at similar results after studying the relative share of income received by workers in a number of organized and unorganized industries. See his *Theory of Wages and Employment* (Homewood, Illinois: Richard D. Irwin, 1959), pp. 161–71.

advantage for their members. When the economy's total demand for labor is very great, unions have gained little or no wage advantage over unorganized workers. Wage increases won by unions are quickly passed to unorganized workers through sympathetic pressure, particularly if the unorganized workers are potentially unionizable. Under conditions of nearly, but not quite, full employment, as in the twenties, it appears that unions, at least those with dynamic leadership, have been able to capitalize on their bargaining power. During periods of substantial unemployment, the most that unions seem to be able to do is prevent the wages of their members from falling as far as they otherwise would.

Even though it is not certain that unions gain a wage advantage for their members, there is one impact on wages which they certainly have —the reduction of interpersonal wage differentials. Their impact on interindustrial and interoccupational differentials has been obscured by the variety of other—and more important—economic variables operating on the wage structure. In other words, unions bargain in an arena which is determined largely by economic forces over which they exercise little control. Whatever unique wage gains they achieve are the consequence of shrewdly judging and taking advantage of those economic forces which favor collective bargaining techniques.

The union effect on the general level of wages depends on the wage advantage that unions gain for their members and the extent to which this is transferred to unorganized workers through sympathetic pressures. This, in turn, depends on which union has acted as wage leader in setting the wage pattern and the amount of the wage increase it has won.

Even though unions may push up the general level of money wages, it does not necessarily follow that they bring about a redistribution of income in favor of labor. The rising money wages may be offset by rising income payments to other productive factors. The statistical evidence indicates that unions, at least between 1929 and 1947, did improve their share of the national income. However, when other terminal dates are selected—particularly years of prosperity and high profits—the results show union members' share of income to be largely unchanged.

DISCUSSION QUESTIONS

1. Why is it so difficult to give a conclusive answer to the question: Do unions raise the wages of their members higher than they otherwise would be?
2. Devise a theoretical situation, making the necessary assumptions, in

which a union would have little or no success in winning a wage advantage for its members.

3. Using the cluster-of-markets concept, devise a theoretical situation in which unions are able to gain a wage advantage for their members without suffering a loss in employment.

4. What is the "shock effect"? Under what circumstances would a collectively bargained wage increase produce a shock effect that would leave employment unchanged?

5. The average wage of union members exceeds that of unorganized workers. Explain why this fact is not convincing proof that unions are able to increase the wages of their members.

6. Explain the role of each of the following in determining the union impact on wages: level of employment, government labor policy, and sympathetic pressure.

7. Evaluate the negative evidence relative to the union impact on wages. To what extent is it inconsistent with the positive evidence?

8. Using the steel industry as an example, describe the changes which unions may cause in an industry's wage structure.

9. Write an essay elucidating your own conclusion on the union impact on wages.

10. Under what economic circumstances are unions likely to be able to push up the general level of wages? Explain.

11. Define "key bargain" and "coercive comparison." Explain how they are related to sympathetic pressure and to the union impact on the general level of wages.

12. The redistribution of income in favor of labor from 1929 to 1947 was largely the result of union bargaining power. Comment, showing to what extent you agree or disagree.

BIBLIOGRAPHY

Cartter, Allen M. *Theory of Wages and Employment.* Homewood, Illinois: Richard D. Irwin, 1959.

Douglas, Paul H. *Real Wages in the United States, 1890–1926.* Boston: Houghton Mifflin Company, 1930.

Douty, H. M. "Union and Nonunion Wages" in Woytinsky, W. S., and Associates. *Employment and Wages in the United States.* New York: The Twentieth Century Fund, 1953, pp. 493–501.

Dunlop, John T. *Wage Determination Under Trade Unions.* New York: Augustus M. Kelley, Inc., 1950.

Kerr, Clark. "Labor's Income Share and the Labor Movement," in Taylor, George W., and Pierson, Frank C. (Editors). *New Concepts in Wage Determination.* New York: McGraw-Hill Book Company, 1957, pp. 260–98.

————. "Wage Relationships—The Comparative Impact of Market and Power Forces," in Dunlop, John T. (Editor). *The Theory of Wage Determination.* New York: St. Martin's Press, 1957, pp. 173–93.

Levinson, Harold M. *Unionism, Wage Trends, and Income Distribution, 1914–1947.* Ann Arbor: University of Michigan Press, 1951.

Maher, John E. "Union, Nonunion Wage Differentials," *American Economic Review*, Vol XLVI (June, 1956), pp. 338–52.

Rees, Albert. "Postwar Wage Determination in the Basic Steel Industry," *American Economic Review*, Vol. XLI (June, 1951), pp. 389-404.

Reynolds, Lloyd G., and Taft, Cynthia. *The Evolution of Wage Structure.* New Haven: Yale University Press, 1956.

Ross, Arthur. *Trade Union Wage Policy.* Berkeley: University of California Press, 1953.

18 GOVERNMENT AND WAGES

No analysis of wages can be complete without consideration of the role of the government. Because of the broad scope of its penetration into our economy, the government cannot avoid having a significant impact on the labor market. Furthermore, as a matter of public policy, it may deliberately attempt to change either the wage level, or the wage structure, or both. As the representative of the general public, it may seek to effectuate certain policies in the labor market: full employment, a wage structure encouraging the development of certain occupations and industries, or a wage level which promotes high consumption spending. In order to pursue such policies it would have to manipulate the labor market deliberately so as to create conditions differing from those which would result from the interplay of free market forces and collective bargaining.

There are many avenues which the government may follow to affect either particular wage rates, or the general level of wages, or both. The most direct entry of the government into wage determination—aside from war-time wage stabilization—is through minimum wage legislation. Another important, often overlooked, role of the government is its position as an employer: hiring millions of workers and bargaining with a variety of unions. It further influences wages through labor relations legislation affecting the organization and bargaining power of unions, through social security legislation, and through its monetary and fiscal policies.

MINIMUM WAGE LEGISLATION

Originally, minimum wage legislation was advocated as a technique for relieving poverty and for preventing "unscrupulous" employers from exploiting women and children. Those who supported the minimum wage before World War I pointed to statistics such as the following: It required $8.00 a week to maintain a female worker in ordinary decency, yet 75 per cent of women workers earned less than $8.00, 50 per cent earned less than $6.00, and 15 per cent earned less than $4.00 weekly. Although $15.00 to $20.00 per week was required as a minimum to support a man with a wife and three children, at least 6,000,000 men were earning less than $12.00 per week in 1912.[1]

The arguments used today in support of minimum wage legislation reflect the current higher standard of living, showing concern over the possibility that competition in the product market may be based on depressing wages to "abnormally" low levels. It is argued that if a firm cannot pay a "decent" wage, it should not be allowed the privilege of remaining in business. Unions advocate higher minimum wages as a device to push up the whole wage scale. A rise in the minimum raises their members' pay if unions can compel employers to maintain traditional differentials. The older arguments, in terms of poverty, have not been abandoned. For example, the City Council of New York, on March 8, 1960, asked Congress to increase the minimum to $1.25, stating in its resolution that many thousands of families "are subsisting under substandard living conditions primarily because of the low wages paid to the wage earners of the families, . . ." and therefore requiring "many millions of dollars annually" in relief grants. The Council added that "these vast expenditures constitute subsidies by the taxpayers and contributions to business and industry, which are neither morally nor economically justifiable. . . ."

To what extent has minimum wage legislation accomplished the goals of its proponents? Or has this interference brought distortions into the labor market which lead to higher prices and less employment? Before analyzing these problems, it is necessary to review briefly the federal and state legislation.

Fair Labor Standards Act

As in many fields of social legislation, the United States lagged behind other democracies in placing a floor under wages. There were

[1] John R. Commons and John B. Andrews, *Principles of Labor Legislation*, Fourth Edition (New York: Harper & Brothers, 1936), p. 44.

minimum wage laws in Australia and New Zealand before 1900, and in England in 1909. The first law in the United States, covering only women and children, was passed in Massachusetts in 1912. The first federal legislation with general coverage was included in the National Industrial Recovery Act of 1933, which provided for establishing industry codes allowing member firms a great deal of freedom from competitive pressures. In order to be approved, these codes were required to set a minimum wage for adult males employed in the industry, as well as for women and children, the groups most typically protected by state minimum wage legislation.

After the National Industrial Recovery Act was declared unconstitutional, the federal government adopted a different approach to minimum wage regulation, passing the Fair Labor Standards Act in 1938, setting a minimum wage of $.25 per hour, with $.30 becoming effective in the following year, and $.40 per hour in 1944. It was amended in 1949, raising the minimum to $.75 per hour, and again in 1955, raising the minimum to $1.00 per hour, effective in 1956. The Act provides for a standard work week, requiring employers to pay time-and-a-half for hours in excess of forty per week. It was passed during a depression, and part of the purpose of the maximum hours regulation was to spread the limited amount of employment over a wider number of workers. Restrictions on employment of children under the age of sixteen are also included.

The Fair Labor Standards Act covers approximately 24,000,000 workers employed in the production of goods going into interstate commerce. Notice that this coverage is much narrower than the Taft-Hartley Act which covers all workers in firms whose production *affects* interstate commerce. The coverage is further reduced by excluding a number of industries, e.g., retail and service trades, agriculture, and laundries. Some of the excluded industries have wage scales which are comparatively very low. The extent of the coverage has caused almost as much controversy as setting the level of the minimum wage.

A violation of the Act makes an employer liable to fines up to $10,000 and imprisonment up to six months. The Administrator of the Wages and Hours Division of the Department of Labor is empowered to set lower minima for minors, learners, and handicapped workers. The purpose of the exceptions is to prevent the Act from serving as a barrier to the employment of these persons.

Walsh-Healey and Davis-Bacon Acts

There are two federal laws dealing with minimum wages for workers employed by firms doing contract work for the federal government. The Walsh-Healey Public Contracts Act, adopted in 1936, gives the Secretary of Labor the power to set minimum wages, maximum hours, and health and safety conditions for workers on government contracts in excess of $10,000. Unlike the Fair Labor Standards Act which sets a flat rate for all covered employees, the Walsh-Healey Act provides for separate minima for each industry, to be determined with the aid of public hearings. The Secretary of Labor, after the hearings, generally sets the minimum at the prevailing wage for the industry. The purpose is to prevent employers from securing government contracts by underbidding their competitors as a consequence of maintaining substandard working conditions. When contracts are awarded to firms in highly unionized industries, the union seeks to have its standards adopted as the minima. Thus, the Walsh-Healey Act can be used for enforcing union standards.

The Davis-Bacon Act, adopted in 1931, gives the Secretary of Labor power to set minimum wages for workers on government construction contracts in excess of $2,000. The rate generally corresponds to the prevailing minimum for each of the crafts involved. Under this Act, just as in the Walsh-Healey Act, collectively bargained wages tend to exert a substantial influence in setting the minimum.

State Minimum Wage Legislation

State governments started experimenting with minimum wage legislation long before the federal government. State efforts were curtailed by the Supreme Court when, in 1923, it declared the District of Columbia law unconstitutional in the famous Adkins case, which involved a law setting minimum wages only for women. Similar legislation for Arkansas and Arizona was also declared unconstitutional. The Supreme Court declared that these laws represented undue interference with the individual's freedom of contract. Nevertheless, by the time the federal government adopted the Fair Labor Standards Act in 1938, fifteen states, Puerto Rico, and the District of Columbia had minimum wage legislation. Except for Oklahoma, these laws covered only women and children.[2]

Twenty-nine of the states and territories now have minimum wage

[2] Sidney C. Sufrin and Robert C. Sedgwick, *Labor Law* (New York: Thomas Y. Crowell Company, 1954), pp. 120–28, 136–45.

laws, with the majority applying only to women and children. Unlike the Fair Labor Standards Act, the state laws generally set different minima for different industries rather than a flat rate for all covered industries.

Economic Effects of Minimum Wage Legislation

The economic effects of minimum wage legislation vary depending on how high the minimum is set relative to the existing wage structure. A low minimum, affecting only a small number of the lowest-paying firms, is quite different from one which is higher than the current wage for five or ten million employees. Between these extremes an effective minimum is likely to have an impact not only on particular wage rates, but also on the wage structure, employment, production techniques, and the allocation of resources.

Economists are far from agreement in evaluating the economic effects of minimum wage legislation. Some argue that, in the main, its only effect is to raise substandard wages and thus reduce abnormal profits based on worker exploitation. At the opposite end of the scale, other economists hold that the existing wage structure is the consequence of competitive forces in the labor market, and to upset it with a minimum wage would cause unemployment, higher product prices, and a decline in output. In attempting to determine which of these two arguments more correctly describes the economic effects of minimum wage legislation, we turn first to a theoretical analysis and then to a survey of the statistical evidence available.

Theoretical Effects

To analyze the economic effects of minimum wage legislation, it is convenient to divide employers into two categories: those who hire in a competitive labor market and those who exercise some degree of monopsony. Employers in the first category would be required by economic forces to pay a wage equal to the marginal revenue product of the workers. A minimum wage set above this amount would cause the employers to discharge enough workers to bring the marginal revenue product into equality with the minimum wage. There would also be a shift to substitute production processes which had previously been somewhat too expensive but now would be cheaper than employing higher-priced labor. Furthermore, employers, as a consequence of the increased production cost, would be forced to raise their prices and hence would sell fewer units of output. As a result of lower sales at the higher price and of using different production techniques, the employer's *MRP* curve would shift to the left and the number of workers employed would decline.

In making this argument concerning competing employers, George Stigler conceded only one possible qualification: the "shock effect," similar to the shock effect of unionization in an unorganized firm, described in the previous chapter. An increase in wages brought about by government legislation might force an employer to eliminate inefficiency or adopt improved methods of production and thereby make it possible to pay the higher wages and still sell his product at the same price and continue to operate at a profitable level. Stigler pointed out that the low-wage industries, those which would be most affected by the minimum wage, are highly competitive and have a high ratio of labor costs to total costs. Hence, he argued, these employers are not likely to be lethargic; in other words, they are likely to have been fully shocked into maximum efficiency by the competitive forces under which they operate.

Where the employer has some monopsony control over wages, the effect of the law depends on whether the minimum wage exceeds the marginal revenue product. If it does, employment will decline for the same reasons which apply to competing employers. If, however, the legal minimum falls between the existing wage and the marginal revenue product, employment will be increased. This corresponds to the second hypothetical example in Chapter 15, with the government changing the nature of the labor supply curve. Stigler believes that the latter case is very unusual and certainly one which could not be secured by a public administrative agency, since the minimum wage must cover a large number of firms in many industries, each of which has different wage rates and different marginal revenue product schedules. Therefore, considering both competing employers and monopsonists, Stigler concludes that imposing a minimum wage leads to a reduction in employment and aggregate output, and that the workers whose wage rates had been less than the minimum actually receive less in annual earnings because of fewer hours worked.[3]

Richard Lester has found evidence which he believes contradicts the reasoning of Stigler. Taking note of the great variation in wages among competing firms hiring the same types of labor in the same labor market, Lester argues that it is unlikely that the rate is precisely equal to the

[3] George J. Stigler, "The Economics of Minimum Wage Legislation," *American Economic Review,* Vol. XXXVI (June, 1946), pp. 358–65.

marginal revenue product. In the firms he studied, the demand for labor appeared to be quite inelastic, at least in the short run. Moreover, substitute processes were not easily available, again, at least in the short run. After discussing the effects of wage increases with a large number of low-paying Southern firms, he concluded that the shock effect is of some consequence. In other words, employers reacted to increased wages, to some extent, by improving efficiency in the plant and by engaging in increased sales efforts.[4]

The short-run effects of the minimum wage are likely to be substantially different from the long-run effects. In the short run the adjustments may be in the form of increased prices to consumers, lower profits to the business firm, or shocked increases in efficiency. In the long run the employer may shift to labor-saving techniques, if they are available. Consumers may shift to other products, or at least reduce their purchases of the higher-priced product. Low-paying firms may go out of business or shift to another line of production. To analyze the long-run effects of a minimum wage requires holding all other variables constant. In reality, this is, of course, impossible. For example, if consumers, because of higher incomes, increase their demand for a product, the higher wages may be passed on through higher prices with no apparent effect on employment or method of operation of the firm. The short-run and long-run effects of the minimum wage, then, depend on the assumptions one makes on the elasticity of the employer's demand for labor and changes in this demand, e.g., the possibilities of a shock effect, or consumer reaction to high prices.

With one important exception, these conclusions apply in the same manner to employers who must compete in hiring workers as they do to employers who have monopsonistic power in the labor market. The important exception stems from the divergence between the wage rate paid by the monopsonist and the marginal revenue product of his last unit of labor. As a consequence of this divergence, the employer who can maintain his monopsony power over the long run is better able to absorb a wage increase without reducing employment. That is, for employers alike in all respects except that one competes in the labor market and the other does not, the latter is less likely to discharge workers as a consequence of an increase in the legal minimum wage.

In the long run the minimum wage undoubtedly has the effect of driving some firms out of business and causing others to reduce the

[4] Richard A. Lester, "Marginalism, Minimum Wages, and Labor Markets," *American Economic Review*, Vol. XXXVII (March, 1947), pp. 142–46.

size of their operations. The law tells the employer he will be denied the privilege of hiring workers if he is unable to pay a wage at least equal to a "minimum level of decency." Thus, a reallocation of labor is brought about, forcing workers out of submarginal firms. It may be that in the long run, society is better off to eliminate the inefficient firms and encourage the workers to move into more productive pursuits. Supposedly, the forces of competition would accomplish the same result, but the minimum wage may do so more quickly. Furthermore, in some small communities, competitive forces are weak, allowing employers over a course of many years to exploit workers or operate inefficiently.

So far the analysis has dealt with employment effects in individual firms with the conclusion depending on the assumptions made with respect to the employer's demand for labor. The conclusion to be drawn concerning the impact of the minimum wage on the level of employment for the entire economy likewise depends on the assumptions made. If the minimum wage increases the total wage bill of the economy, total consumption spending will probably increase. Thus, employment would increase, unless the economy is already operating at maximum capacity, assuming that no significant amount of substitution of capital for labor takes place. If, however, the wage bill decreases, then, in all likelihood, employment would also decrease.

The impact of the minimum wage on the wage bill depends upon the elasticity of demand for the workers whose wage rates are increased. It further depends on whether wage differentials are maintained, that is, whether the entire wage structure moves upward causing an increase in the general level of wages. The impact of these wage changes on total spending depends on the expectations of consumers with respect to prices and their income, and the expectations of businessmen with respect to wages, other costs, and their sales. The impact of the minimum wage on these expectations might be in any direction, depending on economic and social conditions at the time. For example, if the rise in wage rates causes consumers to be optimistic about their future incomes, they may increase their spending, particularly if they anticipate a rise in prices. This would lead to increased sales, causing businessmen to hire more workers in spite of the higher wage rates. Contrariwise, if employers anticipate rising raw material costs and no increase in sales, they may reduce employment. This might induce consumers to take a pessimistic outlook on their income, causing them to decrease their expenditures, thus leading to further decreases in employment. Or businessmen may reduce their investment if they believe the higher wages will not be offset by increased sales. Lower investment spending would contribute to a lower level of total spending and hence to a decline in employment. At any given point in time, so many dynamic relationships are in operation that it would be impossible to predict the effect of a change in the minimum wage on the expectations of consumers and businessmen.

Statistical Evidence

The most recent change in the federal minimum wage, an increase from $.75 to $1.00 per hour, went into effect in March, 1956. Of the twenty-four million workers covered by the Act, approximately two million were receiving less than $1.00 per hour just prior to the change, averaging $.15 less than the new requirement.[5] The effect of conforming to the law, neglecting any possible reduction in employment, would have been to raise the total wage bill by $560,000,000, less than 1.0 per cent of the earnings of all covered workers. Hence, the direct effect on the over-all economy could not be very great. However, some workers received significant pay increases and others lost their jobs.

The Department of Labor has conducted a number of studies designed to measure the impact on employment and the wage structure of changes in the minimum wage from $.40 to $.75 in January, 1950 (which directly raised the wages of 1.3 million workers), and from $.75 to $1.00 in 1956. Within six months after the first of the two increases went into effect, the nation was engaged in the Korean War. The long-run effects, therefore, became rapidly diffused as a result of other economic pressures.

The initial impact was greatest in low-wage industries, low-wage regions, and low-wage firms, reducing the differentials between high-paid and low-paid workers. Surveys conducted several months later indicated that the wage structure had a tendency to spread apart again. The initial impact of the 1950 increase in the minimum was counteracted by the effects of the rapidly rising level of economic activity and the consequent increased demand for labor. Wage differentials following the 1956 increase, under circumstances less extreme than the Korean War, also tended to return to their normal spread.

It was found that the wages of workers not covered by the Act also increased under special circumstances. In Southern sawmills with fewer

[5] U. S. Department of Labor, Wage and Hour and Public Contracts Divisions, *Results of the Minimum Wage Increase of 1950* (Washington: Government Printing Office, 1954); *Studies of the Economic Effects of the $1.00 Minimum Wage* (Interim Report) (Washington: Government Printing Office, 1957); and *Studies of the Economic Effects of the $1.00 Minimum Wage; Effects in Selected Low Wage Industries and Localities* (Washington: Government Printing Office, 1959).

than twelve logging employees, the wages of the loggers are exempt from coverage. Nevertheless, their wages were increased along with the covered employees in other divisions of the firm. A similar effect was found among fertilizer firms producing only for intrastate commerce, and therefore not covered by the Act. These firms raised their wages almost as much as the firms producing for interstate commerce which were compelled to pay the minimum. To a limited extent, then, the rise in the minimum forced wage rate increases even for non-covered employees. Of course, it is possible that some other factor, e.g., an increased demand for labor, was the real cause.

The 1950 increase appeared to have only a minor impact on factors other than wages in the low-paying industries. That is, the level of employment did not materially change, prices to consumers remained largely unchanged, and employers continued to operate their firms in much the same manner. There appeared to be no increase in the rate of adoption of labor-saving machinery. The one major exception occurred in the men's dress shirt and night wear industry where employers switched to hiring policies which discriminated against older and inexperienced workers. The employers, being forced to pay increased wage rates, decided to raise their hiring standards, consequently excluding marginal members of the labor force.[6]

The rise to a $1.00 minimum, however, appeared to cause some decline in employment in low-paying industries. Those firms forced to raise wages most made the adjustment partly through reducing work forces. But the pattern was not perfectly clear: in some of the industries the percentage change in employment was closely related to the required percentage change in wages; in others there was no evident correlation. In some cases the adjustments involved raising product prices, reducing overtime, stepping up the production rate, or substituting more experienced labor.

The effects of the 1950 rise in the minimum were investigated for firms which paid low wages and had comparatively high ratios of labor costs to total costs: oyster canning in the Gulf area, hand-manufacturing of

[6] After making a detailed study of these data, and also data relating to the 1938–1940 increases in the minimum wage, John M. Peterson concluded that there was a negative employment effect. He concentrated his attention on geographical regions where the higher minimum caused the greatest wage increases and on industrial groups whose final products were very similar. See his "Employment Effects of Minimum Wages, 1938–50," *Journal of Political Economy*, Vol. LXV (October, 1957), pp. 412–30. See also Richard A. Lester, "Employment Effects of Minimum Wages: Comment," and John M. Peterson, "Reply," *Industrial and Labor Relations Review*, Vol. XIII (January, 1960), pp. 254–73.

cigars, raw sugar production in Louisiana, and forty-one additional firms which claimed to have substantial difficulty in adjusting to the increased minimum, covering all the firms with special adjustment problems brought to the attention of the Department of Labor. These firms employed a total of 38,000 workers, a very small percentage of all employees whose wages were raised by the new minimum. Their adjustments were similar to the often predicted consequences of an increase in the minimum wage, including increased product prices, reductions in rate of output, and, in some cases, completely ceasing business operations. However, the minimum wage was only one of the difficulties confronting these firms, and its impact was impossible to isolate from the other factors which may have forced the firms to make the same adjustments even if the minimum had not been increased. For all the firms, only two or three thousand workers became unemployed during the period of the study. All in all, it appeared that even these most seriously affected firms did not suffer too grievously from the 1950 minimum wage increase. Perhaps those which left the business world only had their departure hastened by the compulsion to pay higher wages.

An interesting part of the Department of Labor studies consisted of an investigation of the wages of seventeen industries from 1938, when the Fair Labor Standards Act went into effect, to 1956, after the minimum was raised to $1.00. The industries were divided into three groups, and wage rate increases compared: 235 per cent for low-paying industries covered by the Act, 182 per cent for high-paying, and 167 per cent for low-paying. The first group gained on the other two whenever the minimum was raised and the second group outpaced the others in the intervening periods. According to these statistics changes in the minimum probably had a substantial effect on the wage pattern. An important qualification of this conclusion must be made because the majority of the covered workers were in manufacturing industries, and the non-covered workers were primarily in retail and service industries. It may be that the special economic forces pressing on the different industries were more responsible for the differential changes than was raising the minimum. The possible consequence of a minimum wage change during a time of declining economic activity cannot be determined from this study.

THE GOVERNMENT AS EMPLOYER

As the largest employer in the nation, the government has almost unlimited possibilities for affecting wages and working conditions. By increasing or decreasing the number of their employees, public agencies change the supply of labor available to private employers. The government can act as a model employer setting precedents in wages and working conditions that would have an upward pressure on those in private industry, and it may follow labor relations policies that would encourage the growth of unions and the development of collective bargaining.

Growth of Government Employment

The government, including all federal, state, and local agencies, employs approximately eight million persons, more than 12 per cent of total employment, and there is a long-run trend toward increasing both the absolute amount and the percentage. During both wars and depressions, government employment increases and then, after the emergency has passed, there is a reduction, but by an amount less than the increase, as illustrated in Table 18-A.[7]

Government employment includes almost all occupations found in other industries, as well as some occupations not found elsewhere, and is not predominantly white collar, as is commonly believed. In 1947 less than half of the federal government workers employed in the continental United States were in white-collar jobs. Even in public education, the largest single group of government employees, a large portion of the workers are in custodial and maintenance work and other blue-collar jobs.[8] The government, then, competes with private employers for all the important types of labor.

In periods of depression the government may use its power as an employer to bring about more favorable labor market conditions. The purpose of such a policy would be to provide jobs for the unemployed and at the same time to reduce the downward pressure on wage rates and the level of income. Although some areas of government employment are not so easily expanded as others, the fact that the government includes so many occupations gives it an opportunity to exercise wide influence over all labor market forces during a depression.

Wages and Working Conditions

The power to determine wages of government employees rests with the legislative authority. This power may be used directly, setting wages by statute, or indirectly, by an administrative agency exercising power

[7] U. S. Department of Commerce, Office of Business Economics, *Business Statistics, 1959 Biennial Edition* (Washington: Government Printing Office, 1959) pp. 59, 62.

[8] Sterling D. Spero, *Government as Employer* (New York: Remsen Press, 1948), pp. 71–76.

TABLE 18-A

Government Employment

	Number of employees (thousands)	Per cent of total employment
1929	3,066	6.4
1933	3,167	8.2
1940	4,202	8.8
1945	5,944	11.3
1947	5,474	9.4
1948	5,650	9.5
1949	5,856	10.0
1950	6,026	10.1
1951	6,389	10.5
1952	6,609	10.8
1953	6,645	10.7
1954	6,751	11.0
1955	6,914	10.9
1956	7,277	11.2
1957	7,626	11.7
1958	7,893	12.3

granted to it by a legislative body. In general, the government attempts to pay the prevailing rate rather than to act as a pace-setter by setting abnormally high wages.

The application of the principle of the prevailing rate has met with the fewest complications in the industrial services where the work is directly comparable with that outside. The employees of these services belong to the regular unions of their trades or industries and are generally better organized than other government workers. Their wages are usually fixed by administrative action rather than by law. This has made it possible for these "blue collar" workers to exert such strong pressure on the wage fixing authorities that their right to a voice in the determination of their wages is now generally recognized. The part they play in the fixing of their pay ranges from the right to hearings before wage boards to collective bargaining.[9]

The wages of government employees are generally less responsive to changes in economic conditions than are the wages of other workmen. The relative position of the government employee improves when the price level declines, assuming that he is able to maintain his job; and he usually has more security than the typical nongovernment employee because his job does not depend on profits. Moreover, the laws and

[9] *Ibid.*, p. 425.

regulations applying to civil service employees generally protect them from arbitrary discharge by their supervisors, thus providing a form of job tenure similar to that provided by seniority to the private employee. During a period of rapidly rising prices government employees tend to suffer relative to other workers, as was especially true in both World War I and World War II.

Labor Relations of Government Employees

There are approximately one million government employees in unions, less than 20 per cent of the total number, with the federal workers more than a third organized and state and local workers only a little more than 10 per cent.[10] About 60 per cent of these were affiliated with the AFL-CIO. Unionized government workers do not bargain in the same manner as their fellow workers in private industry, primarily because they are generally deprived of the use of the strike weapon. Nevertheless, strikes have occurred among government employees in surprisingly large numbers. David Ziskind chronicled well over one thousand among government employees up to 1940. More than half of these were among workers in the various depression employment programs, but strikes had also occurred among policemen and firemen, teachers, public health and sanitation workers, and employees in publicly owned utilities.[11]

Fear of the growth of unionism and strikes among public employees led to legislative restrictions. The Taft-Hartley Act (Sec. 305) prohibits strikes by federal employees on penalty of immediate discharge and forfeiture of civil service status. Strikers are ineligible for re-employment for a period of three years. As well as the legal barriers, there is a general lack of public sympathy—in fact, usually outright antagonism—for strikes against the government.

What is to be done in case government workers do go out on strike? Legal restrictions and public opinion notwithstanding, such strikes do occasionally occur. The problem is illustrated by a strike of 500 garbage collectors in Yonkers, contrary to a New York State law prohibiting strikes among state and local government employees. After eight days the accumulation of garbage caused the olfactory and political stench to become unbearable. The city, unable to recruit strike-breakers, reinstated the strikers without prejudice. In general, if work is to be continued successfully after a strike, it is not feasible to discharge all

[10] *Ibid.*, p. 76; and Charles C. Killingsworth, "Grievance Adjudication in Public Employment," *American Arbitration Journal*, Vol. XIII (1958), pp. 3–15.

[11] David Ziskind, *One Thousand Strikes of Government Employees* (New York: Columbia University Press, 1940).

the public employees involved. In other words, a no-strike prohibition is very difficult to enforce even against public employees. It is much more effective to provide flexible machinery for dealing with grievances as they arise and before they foment strikes. This is at least as true in public employment, where strikes are restricted, as it is in private employment.

There is a great deal of variation in the collective bargaining of public employees. At one extreme is the Transit Authority in New York City which bargains with the Transport Workers' Union in a manner very similar to bargaining in private employment. There is a collectively bargained contract covering the 32,000 employees which provides for an impartial umpire to arbitrate grievances. At the other extreme are the governmental units which prohibit unionism and compel employees to sign yellow dog contracts, not unusual for policemen and school teachers.

The public employees who are most susceptible to legal pressure against unionization, and particularly against striking, are the policemen and firemen. Nevertheless, unionism has spread into these occupations in a number of cities as a consequence of inadequate pay and working conditions. Some of the policemen's locals are affiliated with the American Federation of State, County, and Municipal Employees, others are independent associations. The firemen's union is the International Association of Fire Fighters, affiliated with the AFL-CIO. Although these unions do attempt to engage in a form of bargaining, their right to strike is severely limited. In fact, the constitution of the American Federation of State, County, and Municipal Employees forbids strikes by policemen, and the Fire Fighters have a similar prohibition. Therefore, their bargaining must take the form of presenting their grievances publicly in the hope that this will generate adequate pressure on local political officials.

The postal employees, the largest group of workers under a single public agency, are the most completely organized of all government employees. There are a dozen different unions involved, five of them having long been affiliated with the AFL. Some of the unions have fought vigorously for wage increases and improvements in working conditions, while others act very much like company unions. They have frequently been successful in bringing enough pressure on Congress to win significant advancements. The postal employees serve as an interesting contrast to the policemen and firemen. Strikes are prohibited weapons for both groups, yet one group, the postal workers, has been able to cope with the situation much more advantageously than the other, partly because of more widespread unionism and partly because it is easier to deal with Congress than with individual city councils.[12]

In the largest field of public employment, education, unions have made very little headway. The American Federation of Teachers has approximately 100,000 members. Recruiting new members is made difficult by the attitude that unionism is unbecoming to the profession. Although strikes have been called on rare occasions, union activity is primarily in the form of propaganda designed to put pressure on legislative bodies. The largest organization of public school teachers is the National Education Association. The NEA has long held that teachers should not soil their professional standards nor prejudice their educational impartiality by direct association with organized labor, contrary to the AFT which exhibited its willingness to use union tactics and to accept the support of organized labor by affiliation with the AFL-CIO. However, in the post-World War II inflation, when teachers' salaries lagged far behind other pay scales, the NEA modified its attitude and in a number of areas adopted tactics closely paralleling the bargaining approach of government employees' unions. It recognized that professional standards could not be maintained with inadequate salaries and therefore lobbied and propagandized for higher salary scales much as the AFT had done, but at the same time continued its policy of independence with regard to unionism. The development of the AFT and the NEA parallels that of unionism and professional organization among nurses and engineers in private employment.

The Tennessee Valley Authority workers have probably gone the greatest distance of any group of public employees in securing ordinary collective bargaining as it is known in private industry. The Authority has bargained with the unions representing the various crafts involved in the construction and maintenance of its facilities and has signed contracts paralleling those of private employers. The TVA is an illustration of how an independent authority, which does not have to run to a legislative body for approval of each of its actions and therefore has a greater flexibility of operation, is in a position to promote peaceful and normal relations with its employees.

Recently, the cities of New York and Philadelphia stated that they are willing to bargain with representatives of their employees. If a union wins the majority of the employees in a municipal department, the city will recognize and sign an agreement with it covering all

[12] Spero, *op. cit.*, pp. 105–67, 228–94.

employees in the department. This may become a precedent leading to pressure on other cities to deal with unions.

In the past the AFL and the CIO frequently adopted resolutions favoring government ownership of electric utilities. However, those workers most directly involved, the utility workers, have been strongly opposed to public ownership. The problems of the policemen, firemen, postal employees, and teachers indicate why they take this attitude. They are certain they will have greater bargaining flexibility if they deal with a private employer rather than with a public employer. Hence, there is little reason to expect increases in government employment resulting from nationalization of already existing businesses.

Collective bargaining in government employment, with a number of important exceptions, is largely an unexplored frontier to the unions. If unions are to secure nearly complete organization of the labor force, they will obviously have to make greater inroads among government employees. However, the avenue is partly blocked by law, public opinion, and the attitude of the unions themselves. They generally regard government employees as their poor cousins, since the latter do not have the unrestricted right to strike.

Ordinarily, as an employer, the major role played by the government in the labor market is that of being another hirer of labor, following the prevailing wages and working conditions. But since its work force is so large, a relatively small change in its total employment has a substantial effect on the prevailing wage. When private employees are making rapid improvements in wages and working conditions, government employees tend to lag behind. Under these circumstances a greater interest is shown in organizing and exerting collective pressure. However, the government has not used its position as an employer to stay abreast of the latest collective bargaining developments, much less to set new precedents. Not only has it lagged behind the organized sector of the labor market, but it has also erected legal barriers to many phases of collective bargaining, particularly the use of the strike weapon. Those phases of collective bargaining not prohibited are adopted only with much reluctance, important exceptions occurring among authority-type agencies and a few cities and among some classes of blue-collar workers.

WAGE EFFECTS OF LABOR RELATIONS LEGISLATION

Labor relations legislation and the impact of unions on wages have been discussed in previous chapters. An extensive review of these chapters is not needed here. However, it should be recalled that the nature of the law and its administration by the National Labor Relations Board, the General Counsel, and the state and federal courts modify the operation of collective bargaining. It should further be recalled that the nature of the wage impact of the unions is not at all clear, apparently changing in a peculiar manner with changes in the government's attitude toward unions and collective bargaining. As the legal environment becomes more favorable to unions, they appear to be less able to win a wage advantage over nonunion employees. Finally, through the operation of sympathetic pressure, legislation which favors unions tends to raise the wages of nonunion employees. In short, labor relations law is another avenue through which the government may affect wages.

During a national defense period the labor relations legislation becomes more directly involved in wage-setting. In order to combat inflationary pressures, the government establishes ceilings on wages and prices. If successfully enforced, the ceilings obviously exert a downward pressure on the general wage level. However, a stabilization program must allow for adjustment of inequities and of especially depressed wages, thus altering the wage structure. For example, during World War II, low wages tended to increase faster than high wages, with the blessing of the Wage Stabilization Board. The wage structure was further modified by techniques devised by employers and unions to circumvent the ceilings. One typical technique was upgrading workers, giving them new job titles with higher pay but with the same work assignments.

One of the major consequences of wage stabilization was improvement of the economic position of the worker without changing his take-home pay, through adding various fringe benefits. The most outstanding examples were pension and health and welfare plans, discussed in a later chapter. The widespread adoption of these plans permanently affected the bargaining goals of unions. Unions have continued to accept a portion of their gains in the form of delayed-payment schemes as opposed to immediate increases in take-home pay.

WAGE EFFECTS OF SOCIAL SECURITY

The government further influences wages through its social security programs: old age, survivors, and disability insurance, unemployment compensation, and workmen's compensation. The benefits paid under these programs (discussed at length in Chapter 20) tend to enhance the bargaining power of old persons, widows, injured workers, and unemployed workers, provided they satisfy the eligibility requirements of the relevant legislation. One requirement, common to most benefit payments, is loss of income through unemployment. Because of the benefit payments, the unemployed worker is in a position to refuse very low-paying or undesirable jobs. He becomes less desperate in his job-searching. A man over 65, or a widow, may stay out of the labor market unless job opportunities are quite tempting. Granted that benefit payments are substantially less than average income from employment, they at least help the recipient to stand aside from the labor market for a period of time and wait for a desirable job to come along. The same is true, perhaps to a lesser extent due to age and family responsibilities, for the person receiving unemployment compensation. He at least has a period of weeks during which he may attempt to find a job fitting his skills and ability.

The benefit rates under the various social security programs undoubtedly have an effect upon the prevailing notions as to what is an acceptable wage. That is, any worker approaching the labor market has a reservation price below which he would refuse to consider a job, except under the most trying circumstances. This applies to new entrants to the labor market as well as beneficiaries of the programs. Thus, the amounts paid through the social security programs affect the supply of labor to the extent that they affect this reservation price.

The social security programs are financed by payroll taxes (unemployment compensation and old age, survivors, and disability insurance) or by premiums to insurance companies (workmen's compensation). Thus, the cost of labor to the firm is increased by the amount of these taxes and premiums, and thereby the programs undoubtedly have an effect on an employer's hiring policies. To some extent he may shift these payments to the workers by paying lower wages than he otherwise would; if so, the social security programs have a negative effect on the workers' take-home pay. Although it cannot be proven, it appears that the positive effect of greater labor market bargaining power outweighs this negative effect, and hence the social security programs tend to increase wage rates.

WAGE EFFECTS OF MONETARY AND FISCAL OPERATIONS

The government exerts its most comprehensive influence over the wage level through its monetary and fiscal operations. The demand for labor is affected by both the taxing and spending sides of fiscal operations. The taxes collected limit the amount of incomes left over for spending by private consumers and businessmen. Furthermore, the nature of these taxes affects the incentives for consumer and investment spending. The amount of private spending plus the amount which the government spends determine the total demand for labor. The monetary policies of the government determine the total amount of money available and hence have a major impact on the money demand for labor. These government controls over total money spending—primarily exercised by the federal government—make it the final arbiter of the general level of wages.

Through monetary and fiscal policies, the government not only determines the general wage level, but also substantially influences the wage structure. The incidence of particular taxes may encourage or discourage certain industries. For example, an excise tax on liquor tends to reduce the amount of production, and demand for labor, in this industry. The government spending programs also affect the wage structure; e.g., public works projects increase the demand for construction workers. As well as the wage impact, the government's monetary and fiscal policies have a substantial effect on the amount of unemployment, discussed in Chapter 22, and on the relationship between wages and prices, discussed in Chapter 23. Although not fully elaborated here, the point is that monetary and fiscal policies constitute a fifth avenue through which the government exercises a substantial wage effect.

SUMMARY

The government has five major devices by which it influences the wage level and the wage structure. By the nature and magnitude of its operations, it cannot avoid having some impact on the labor market; but far beyond that, it can deliberately put into operation policies designed to secure certain wage goals deemed desirable for general economic welfare.

The most direct avenue of government interference in the determination of wages is through minimum wage legislation. Preventing employers from hiring workers except at wage rates at least equal to the minimum has effects both on employment and the wage structure. Under conditions of declining employment, the enforcement of a minimum wage may cause further unemployment and misallocation of resources. However, it is not possible to examine this statistically since increases in the minimum wage in the United States have always occurred during periods of rising employment. The short-run effects of these increases have been to cause the wages of low-paid, covered workers to rise more than the wages of high-paid, covered workers and of non-covered workers. Even after the initial impact has worn off, the low-paid covered workers have maintained the wage advantage over low-paid, non-covered workers.

Acting as an employer, the government exercises considerable influence over both the wage level and the wage structure. Considering only the size of its work force, it exerts a substantial impact on labor demand, since approximately 12 per cent of all employment is directly involved. The government tends to pay the prevailing wage rates rather than attempting to become a precedent setter for private industry. Government wages and working conditions often lag behind those of unionized employment. Typically, labor-management relations in the government are not handled through collective bargaining, although there are numerous exceptions. Wages are generally set directly by legislative authority, or indirectly through administrators with little or no direct participation by the employees.

The government also influences the wage structure and wage level through legislation regulating collective bargaining. By encouraging or discouraging the growth of unions, it qualifies their bargaining power. Through the social security programs, the government gives workers a greater degree of bargaining power in the labor market and probably influences the minimum amount which workers are willing to accept for any given job. The government's greatest impact on the general level of wages stems from its monetary and fiscal policies. Its control over taxing, public expenditures, and the money supply gives it the power to exert a substantial impact on the total demand for labor.

DISCUSSION QUESTIONS

1. Why do comparatively high-paid union workers support minimum wage legislation? Explain.

2. Compare the Fair Labor Standards Act with the Walsh-Healey and Davis-Bacon Acts in terms of coverage and approach.

3. What are the primary differences between the Fair Labor Standards Act and state minimum wage legislation?

4. Assuming no change in the demand for labor, an increase in the minimum wage must lead to a decrease in employment. Critically appraise this statement.

5. What is the "shock effect" and how might it be induced by an increase in the minimum wage?

6. How does the minimum wage affect the wage structure? Base your answer on the statistical evidence presented in this chapter.

7. The statistical evidence proves that the minimum wage does not cause unemployment. Critically appraise this statement.

8. Acting as an employer, the government may bring about substantial changes in the wage structure. Explain.

9. Compare the collective bargaining of unionized teachers and policemen with that of steel workers and auto workers.

10. Write an essay on this subject: The general level of wages and the wage structure are ultimately determined by government policy.

BIBLIOGRAPHY

Commons, John R., and Andrews, John B. *Principles of Labor Legislation.* New York: Harper & Brothers, 1936.

Spero, Sterling D. *Government as Employer.* New York: Remsen Press, 1948.

Stigler, George J. "The Economics of Minimum Wage Legislation," *American Economic Review,* Vol. XXXVI (June, 1946), pp. 358–65.

Sufrin, Sidney C., and Sedgwick, Robert C. *Labor Law.* New York: Thomas Y. Crowell Company, 1954.

Ziskind, David. *One Thousand Strikes by Government Employees.* New York: Columbia University Press, 1940.

PART

4

UNEMPLOYMENT AND

ECONOMIC INSECURITY

Unemployment, the plague of a free enterprise economy, continues to be a threat in the postwar world. What are its causes? Why is it sometimes much greater than at other times? Which industries and occupations are most seriously affected?

One aspect of the government's attempt to meet the problem consists of various social security programs, providing partial income protection for most workers who become unemployed for specified reasons, e.g., retirement and on-the-job injury. What are the trends in the development of social security? Are the costs becoming too staggering for the economy to bear? Are we becoming a welfare state like many of the Western European countries, or are we niggardly in helping those in need?

With the government spending tens of billions of dollars for social security, why do unions enter the field? What are the deficiencies in the public programs that lead to the tremendous and costly private programs? Do the two types of programs supplement or compete with each other?

Of course, the best remedy for unemployment is another job. In a free labor market some workers will always be "between jobs"; unemployment becomes a national problem only where there are not enough new jobs. But government action to create a full employment demand for labor may cause powerful inflationary pressure to develop.

Since modern western economies have a strong bias favoring full employment, and since we have only crude tools for providing these conditions, the recent environment of collective bargaining has been—and probably will continue to be—very different from that of its developmental period. What changes will this cause in labor management relations? Will unions be blamed for inflationary pressures which may appear in a full employment economy, and if so, what types of legislative restrictions will be adopted?

19 { UNEMPLOYMENT:

NATURE AND CAUSES

Many of the most vexing problems confronted by workers and unions stem from inadequate job opportunities. The fear of unemployment, often made vivid by a previous grim experience, causes what may seem to be irrational union demands and irrational worker reactions to new methods of production. For example, in the 1956 East Coast dock strike, the International Longshoremen's Association insisted upon maintaining the traditional twenty-man work gangs even though mechanized loading and unloading had changed the work processes and even though the New York Shipping Association offered a special fifteen-cents-per-hour wage premium to those who worked in smaller-sized gangs.

The American economy has been debilitated too often by excessive unemployment, at times by exceedingly large numbers of persons vainly searching for work. How can we explain the inability to eliminate this economic plague with its devastating personal consequences and its inefficiency in the use of valuable resources? What are the causes of unemployment? The shifting levels of business activity constitute the most important disrupting factor. The seasonal, cyclical, and secular changes in activity lead to corresponding variations in the total demand for labor. Loss of jobs may also result from changes in technology or from the inevitable inperfections in the operation of a free labor market. These various causes interact on each other, e.g., technological unemployment tends to be greater during periods of cyclical decline in business activity.

DEFINITION OF UNEMPLOYMENT

In order to describe and measure unemployment, a definition is necessary. The most widely used, that of the United States Department of Commerce, includes everyone actively seeking work, but not gainfully employed for even an hour during the week the census-taker knocked on the door to ask questions about labor market activity. Persons without jobs and *not seeking* work, i.e., persons outside the labor market, are not counted as unemployed. Basically, we are estimating the number of job applicants, but not how many manhours or man-days are being involuntarily lost. Someone temporarily laid off, even though expecting to be called back soon, is listed with those out of work. People who work part-time but prefer full-time jobs are excluded, and so are underemployed persons, that is, those working at a level of skill below their maximum abilities. The self-employed or those working in a family enterprise are counted as working, regardless of how small their net earnings may be. Anyone who has left the labor market because he has given up hope of finding a job is not included in the statistics. Thus, the definition of unemployment has arbitrary boundaries, but this is necessary in order to be specific and to provide a measurable standard.

Since the amount of unemployment serves as one of the primary criteria for determining government fiscal and monetary policies, it will always be sharply debated. Union leaders, demanding more public spending, will point to one figure and those favoring conservative policies will point to a smaller total, with the disagreement growing out of how to define the term properly. However, a *precise* definition, though not entirely satisfactory from all points of view, at least gives us a picture of the direction in which the economy is currently moving. And this may be adequate for deciding on what changes in policy are needed.

In interpreting labor force statistics, the arbitrariness of the definition should be remembered. Although any other definition would also have limitations, this one seriously underestimates one important aspect of unemployment. That is, in most periods other than war-time, there are many persons outside the labor market—those in the secondary labor force—who would enter if jobs were conveniently available. What is the significance of leaving them out of account in our measure of unemployment? It means we are underestimating the amount of production being lost through less than full utilization of those who are willing to work, and, at the same time, underestimating the amount of income being lost to family groups.

We have just outlined a statistical definition of unemployment, useful for gauging the economy's state of health, but containing human meaning only by implication. What really happens to the typical person who is laid off or discharged? How does he adjust to the lack of income? Of course, there are no "typical unemployed persons." Some of them are young and single or want only part-time work, while others are the sole means of support for their families. The construction worker expects intermittent periods of idleness, but the office worker may have held his job without interruption for years. The skilled man of twenty-five can count on finding a job somewhere reasonably soon, but the semi-skilled man of fifty may never again find a dependable source of income. And certainly the adjustment to a two-week layoff is not as staggering as learning to get by after six months without work. In spite of all these differences, some generalizations can be made: savings are depleted, bills go unpaid, money is borrowed, a humiliating appeal is made to relatives, cheaper housing is found, food and clothing decline in quality, and in extreme cases the family admits poverty and accepts relief. Unemployment insurance is a valuable help, but not all persons are eligible, and it is only a limited substitute for regular income. In some instances wives reluctantly decide to search for full-time jobs, and young people delay plans for marriage and children. All in all, unemployment of more than a few weeks erodes family goals and aspirations.

The decline of a major industry, where it is the chief employer, may depress whole metropolitan areas such as happened to a number of New England cities as the textile industry moved to the South. Under these circumstances unemployment takes on its grimmest aspects; loss of a job is unfortunate, but inability to find a new one is the real problem. In the New England situation mentioned above, periods of joblessness stretched into years for many workers, impelling those with the most to offer a potential employer to leave for states with more promising opportunities. Trade and service industries experienced a fall in demand, leading to secondary unemployment and wage rates lagging behind the national average. Schools, parks, city streets, and other social capital fell into neglect, providing an unattractive prospect to ambitious workers and new enterprises. It is a long road back to prosperity, if it is ever achieved.[1]

[1] For an extensive description of the labor market problems of a depressed area, see "New England Labor and Labor Problems," eight articles in *Monthly Labor Review*, Vol. LXXX (March, 1957).

SEASONAL CHANGES IN EMPLOYMENT

Seasonal variations in employment and unemployment stem from the annual weather cycle and from customs and traditions. Some industries require certain kinds of weather conditions in order to operate at or near full capacity, the most outstanding examples being agriculture and construction. Other industries are very responsive to holidays, to the vacation seasons, or to style and model changes which appear at the same time each year.

Seasonal changes in employment are to be distinguished from seasonal changes in the labor force (discussed in Chapter 1), although the two are closely related. It is typical for seasonal increases to occur simultaneously in employment and unemployment, particularly in June and July when many young people enter the labor market during school vacations. Seasonal increases in the labor force, then, are the result of 1) people seeking temporary jobs and 2) seasonal increases in the demand for labor.

The seasonal pattern of unemployment is the consequence of these two factors not being in perfect harmony. Hence, the number of people without jobs is normally at a peak in January, February, and March, when the seasonal demand for labor declines more rapidly than does the labor force. In June and July there is another peak when the labor force expands more rapidly than the demand for labor. The troughs occur in April and in November and December. In an ordinary year 50 per cent more people are out of work at the seasonal low point as compared to the peak.

The seasonal pattern of unemployment is subject to change with the passage of time. New technology and changing customs and traditions alter the timing of the peaks and troughs. For example, improvements in the materials used in cement has made it possible to continue construction in temperatures which were previously considered to be too cold. For the economy as a whole, the amount of employment which is seasonal in nature appears to have declined over the past few decades. Prior to World War II it was about 6 per cent of all work performed and in the postwar period it was about 4 per cent. This is partly attributable to the very high demand for labor, partly to technological changes, and perhaps partly to the unemployment compensation tax system (discussed in the next chapter). Nevertheless, seasonal fluctuations continue to be the cause of about 20 per cent, perhaps more, of our total unemployment.

A large part of the seasonal variation in jobs is concentrated in a select group of industries: agriculture, building construction, food industries, iron and steel, machinery, the automobile industry, textiles, clothing, leather products, lumber, coal mining, wholesale and retail trade, service industries, and stone, clay, and glass. The seasonal and nonseasonal components of unemployment are shown, classified by major industry categories, in Diagram 19-A. In agriculture alone, between

FIGURE 19-A

Industry Unemployment Rates by Seasonal and Nonseasonal Components, 1957

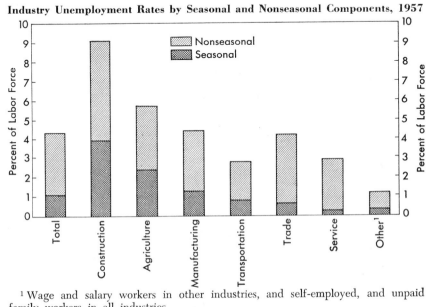

[1] Wage and salary workers in other industries, and self-employed, and unpaid family workers in all industries.

Note: Rates are based on old definition of unemployment. Only wage and salary workers are included except for "Total" and "Other."

Source: U. S. Department of Labor, Bureau of Labor Statistics.

1948 and 1951, the difference between the January-February trough in employment and the June-July peak averaged more than 2.4 million workers. For the construction industry, between 1946 and 1950, there was an average variation of more than 400,000 between the February trough and the August peak. At the Christmas rush the wholesale and retail trade industry employs between 800,000 and 1,000,000 more than in the February slack season.[2]

[2] W. S. Woytinsky, "Demand for Labor," W. S. Woytinsky and Associates. *Employment and Wages in the United States* (New York: The Twentieth Century Fund, 1953), pp. 337–40; U. S. Congress, Joint Economic Committee, *The Extent and Nature of Frictional Unemployment,* Study Paper No. 6, prepared by the Bureau of Labor Statistics, U. S. Department of Labor (Washington: Government Printing Office: 1959). Diagram 19-A appears on p. 53 of Study Paper No. 6.

Some of the industries subject to wide seasonal variations are unionized, others are not. It should not be surprising that some unions exert their bargaining power toward alleviating the burden of seasonal unemployment.

Attempts to Alleviate Seasonal Unemployment through Collective Bargaining

Union approaches to seasonal unemployment are so varied that they defy easy generalization. Some unions appear to accept it as an inevitable hazard and do not attempt to secure any special adjustments in work assignments. Others have devised elaborate schemes for passing out the scarce job opportunity. Historically, the clothing industry has adopted a work-sharing program to spread the unemployment equally among the members. To retain full-time jobs only for those members with the greatest seniority would tend to split the organization into rival factions. Those members without jobs might attempt to underbid union working conditions, perhaps by working for nonunion firms. Hence, to protect themselves, the clothing unions bargain for work-sharing programs, a technique which may work well for short seasonal periods of unemployment but has severe disadvantages for time periods of unpredictable length. Workers with greater seniority will put pressure on the union to secure full-time employment; hence, some unions, e.g., flint glass workers and ladies' garment workers, apply work-sharing only to short periods of unemployment.[3] Other unions insist upon layoffs in preference to work-sharing, on the grounds that laid-off workers receive unemployment compensation benefits. When these are supplemented by payments under a guaranteed annual wage plan, the unemployed workers may receive more than they would earn by working three days a week.

The construction workers compensate for seasonal joblessness with higher wages and work restrictions. The purpose of the former is to provide sufficient income to tide them over the periods of irregular employment, and the latter is demanded so as to make the job last as long as possible. Work-sharing is not well adapted to the construction industry, since most jobs are for a short duration and there is much shifting between employers.

Currently, unions are showing interest in variations of the guaranteed annual wage and have made significant gains along this line in collective

[3] Sumner H. Slichter, *Union Policies and Industrial Management* (Washington: The Brookings Institution, 1941), pp. 112–15.

bargaining. Historically, these plans have developed in industries subject to wide seasonal swings in employment, but the more recent plans have been designed to alleviate technological and cyclical as well as seasonal unemployment. Guaranteed annual wage plans are discussed in Chapter 21 along with other collective security plans promoted by unions.

Of course, individual firms, quite independently of union pressure, may attempt to eliminate seasonal unemployment, although there are limitations on how successful they can be. However, if the firm can predict its annual sales with a high degree of accuracy and can also warehouse its goods over a period of months, it may be able to reduce the fluctuations in production even though its sales continue to follow a seasonal pattern. If the firm can add a new line of production with a seasonal pattern just the opposite of its original line of production, e.g., adding Christmas toys to summer playground equipment, the firm may be able to regularize its employment. Not only do these measures provide the firm with more complete utilization of its capital equipment, they also help to retain a stable labor force, thus reducing problems of recruitment and training. In short, firms are motivated by higher profits to eliminate seasonal fluctuations wherever possible. Nevertheless, in many industries this is impossible with the present technology.

CYCLICAL CHANGES IN EMPLOYMENT

The most severe swings in unemployment are those associated with business cycles. In the depths of the great depression of the 1930's more than 13,000,000 workers were without jobs, while at the peak of the postwar prosperity, less than 2,000,000 were unemployed. Such drastic fluctuations constitute a grave social problem as well as severe hardship for individual workers who are anxious but unable to find work. Cyclical declines in jobs are more devastating than seasonal because the number of unemployed is much greater and because workers cannot count on being called back in a few weeks. Although the marginal members of the labor force—young people, housewives, non-whites—tend to be out of work longest, a depression also reduces or eliminates the income of adult male workers, in spite of their many years of seniority and experience. And many of those over the ages of forty-five or fifty will never again approach their former earning levels.

Economists have isolated a number of different types of business cycles: forty-month, nine-year, eighteen-year cycles unique to the construction industry, and long waves lasting from forty to fifty years in some other areas. These are *average* lengths for the different cycles identified. A particular "nine-year" cycle may last for seven and a half years followed by one which is ten years in duration. The shorter cycles are superimposed on top of the longer ones, e.g., there will be two or three forty-month fluctuations within each nine-year cycle.

No cycle is exactly like its predecessor; each has its own unique characteristics. Hence, it is difficult to formulate successful policies to counteract the effects, and also difficult to judge the interaction between unions and economic fluctuations. However, common to each cycle is the recurring rise and decline in business activity, affecting almost all industries, and an associated rise and decline in the demand for labor. During depressions, profits typically decline and unemployment increases, and the opposite holds true for periods of prosperity.

Business cycle patterns have changed considerably since World War II, being a succession of short fluctuations with none of the longer types of cycles evident. The amount of unemployment in absolute terms, and relative to the size of the labor force, has been substantially less than prewar. Also, the duration of the depression phase has been shortened. It is too early to tell whether this is a permanent change in our economy, although there is good reason to believe it is. This point is discussed more completely in Chapters 22 and 23. Although the postwar experience indicates that business cycles have been substantially modified, swings in employment have not been completely eliminated.

Attempts to Alleviate Cyclical Unemployment through Collective Bargaining

Cyclical, even more than seasonal, unemployment imposes a severe strain on collective bargaining as unions strive to find satisfactory means for alleviating the distress. A cyclical decline in jobs, unlike a slack seasonal period, is a nation-wide malady. True, certain industries suffer more than others, but most are affected in the same direction and at the same time. Hence, any successful remedy must go beyond patchwork in particular industries; it must be in the form of an economy-wide rise in the total demand for goods and services, and hence an increase in the derived demand for labor.

Although collective bargaining affects both wage income and labor costs and thereby affects total demand for goods and services, it is certainly not the sole determinant of total demand. In order to cure depressions by manipulating wages and labor costs through collective bargaining, it would be necessary to have a single master bargain covering all employers and all workers, or at least something which had the same kind of nation-wide effect. Therefore, collective bargaining as it is presently conducted is not adequate for the task of counteracting cyclical fluctuations. Nevertheless, proposals are frequently made that wage reductions—or wage increases—should be put into effect in order to reduce unemployment. In describing the weaknesses of these proposals, we may, at the same time, shed some light on what collective bargaining cannot do.

Wage Reductions

Before the publication of John Maynard Keynes' *General Theory of Employment, Interest, and Money* in 1936, many economists argued that a widespread decrease in wages was the most effective way of eliminating unemployment. Such proposals are still occasionally heard from some economists, and frequently from management circles.

The wage reduction argument runs as follows: A general decrease in wages makes possible a general reduction in prices. As a consequence of the lower prices, consumers increase the number of units which they purchase, thus leading to an increase in the demand for labor. The number of workers demanded would also be increased as employers substitute lower-priced labor for other factors of production. The lowered wages and increased sales lead to greater profit anticipations for employers, who would therefore expand their production, further increasing employment. The greater profit anticipations would stimulate businessmen to expand investment spending, thus giving another upward boost to the demand for labor. In short, a transfer of income from wage-earners to employers causes an increase in employment and eventually an increase in wage-earners' real income.

Buried in this argument are many assumptions which may inaccurately characterize reactions to wage reductions during depressions. If they are to lead to an increase in employment, the total demand for goods must not decrease. This means that non-wage-earners (salaried people, landlords, stockholders, etc.) must increase their spending, since wage-earners, whose income initially decreases, will be compelled to reduce their purchases. Some of the increased spending by the non-wage-earners may be in the form of rising purchases of consumer goods now selling at lower prices. Possessors of liquid assets, such as bonds, savings accounts, life insurance policies, etc., will feel wealthier since a decline in the price level raises the value of their holdings. As a consequence, these people may spend a larger fraction of their income for consumption goods. But a decline in the price level will occur only if business firms pass on their cost reduction to their customers. However, employers may attempt to hold the price line in order to restore profit margins which have been severely reduced because of previous price decreases forced upon them by the depression. If that is the case, consumers will have no reason to increase their purchases. If there is no increase in the amount of consumer goods purchased, total demand would have to rise, if it rises at all, as a consequence of increased investment spending; otherwise the wage decrease will not bring greater employment. For investment spending to rise requires businessmen to feel that the lower labor cost has materially improved the profit outlook. Finally, as noted previously, the wage reductions must be economy-wide—or at least their influence on labor costs must be economy-wide—something which is practically impossible to secure with our system of many separate wage bargains. These represent very formidable barriers to increasing employment through wage reductions.

Keynes and most other economists since the publication of his *General Theory* have argued that wage reductions may backfire and lead instead to a decrease in employment. Decreasing the money income of workers may cause a decrease in the total demand for goods and services, if income is transferred to other groups who spend a low portion of their new income on consumption. And a decrease in demand for consumption goods may set up expectations of further decreases in spending. The decline in consumption spending would discourage investment spending, causing it to fall to still lower levels.

The decline in wages is also liable to set up expectations of additional reductions in pay scales. Employers then are likely to postpone any hiring they may have intended until the new wage reductions occur. Hence, both consumption spending and investment spending are liable to decrease, unless non-wage-earners increase their consumption spending and unless the wage decline is viewed as a once-and-for-all reduction. With the prevailing atmosphere during a depression one of pessimism about future prices, profits, and income, the increases in consumption and investment spending are not likely to materialize. In fact, the wage reduction is more likely to increase the degree of pessimism.[4]

The impact of general wage reductions on unemployment during depressions, then, depends on how it affects the expectations of con-

[4] John Maynard Keynes, *The General Theory of Employment, Interest, and Money* (New York: Harcourt, Brace and Company, 1936), pp. 257–71; and Arthur Butler, "Wages, Prices, and Employment," *Current Economic Comment,* Vol. XX (February, 1958), pp. 3–16.

sumers and investors. Since the effect is more likely to be one of depressing these expectations than of expanding them, it must be concluded that a wage decrease would be inadvisable public policy except in very unusual circumstances. This is not to say that particular wage rates should never be reduced in a depression. It is possible that certain workers, because of a previous severe shortage of their type of labor or because of extreme immobility in certain portions of the labor market, have been able to push their pay scales significantly above those for other types of skills. Lowering such wages may lead to increased purchases of the final product and increased investment in the specific industries. This, however, applies only to particular wage rates, not to the general wage level.

Wage Increases

If wage decreases are likely to decrease employment, why not increase wages? Would this increase the demand for labor? If one is not cautious in reversing the previous argument, it might seem to follow directly that a wage increase would produce this salutary result. Unions often make such proposals during depression periods.

To be successful in counteracting unemployment, a general wage rise must be translated into greater consumption spending, thus raising total money demand for goods. A wage increase would transfer income from non-wage-earners to wage-earners. The wage-earners, with their propensity to spend a large portion of new income on consumption, would perhaps bring about a rise in total consumption spending, particularly if they anticipated that the higher wages represented a permanent increase in income or were the forerunner of further improvements in income. What if prices rise as much as or more than wages? Will this prevent consumption spending from going up in real terms? Not if workers' spending habits are dominated by a money illusion, causing them to have a blind belief that they are better off, a belief held so tenaciously that they would actually spend enough to shift to higher living standards. After all, when the husband comes home with the joyful news that he is earning more money, the wife and children tend to greet the good tidings with anticipations of "better things in life."

The rise in consumption spending, if it materializes, must not be offset by a fall in investment spending. If the new pay rates set up expectations of further increases in labor costs, they would tend to encourage businessmen to invest and to increase employment now rather than to postpone expansion until wages are higher.

The wage increase, of course, raises the labor cost per unit of output. However, if sales increase because of the transfer of income to workers, and if this makes it possible for businessmen to use idle machinery and plant capacity, thus reducing fixed costs per unit of output, the over-all effect may not be too great. That is, the cost effect of the wage increase may not be sufficient to discourage an increase in employment.

One of the major drawbacks to achieving greater employment by this method is that widespread wage increases during a period of declining business activity are difficult to secure. With large-scale unemployment, union bargaining power would be extremely low. Even if wages could be pushed up, increases in consumer spending would not occur unless they brought about a rearrangement of consumers' expectations with respect to incomes and prices in the future. Until it is widely believed that the bottom of the depression has been reached, expectations of consumers are more likely to be in the direction of waiting for lower prices than buying now from fear of higher prices. However, if the general public is convinced that government fiscal and monetary policies have reversed the decline in business activity, then the wage increase might favorably affect consumer attitudes toward spending.

In short, the effects of a wage increase are not the direct reverse of the effects of a wage decrease. Each is an independent case which must be considered within the framework of the economic conditions existing at the moment. Each generates its own set of expectations with respect to consumption and investment spending and breeds its own type of uncertainty among consumers and investors.

During depressions, unions frequently demand a shorter work-week with no reduction in weekly wages. Basically, this is the same as a demand for increased wages and would have similar consequences. If the same level of output is maintained, employment would rise. But again, it is extremely difficult to judge the impact of such a change on the expectations of consumers and investors, particularly of the latter since their costs have been pushed up, and therefore difficult to predict what the impact on employment would be. Again, with the low level of union bargaining power, it is not likely that unions could secure such a goal outside of government enforcement—and the government has more effective weapons for dealing with unemployment.

The conclusion for our discussion of wage increases or decreases as a technique for combating a depression, then, is that wage policy is not the proper avenue for curing cyclical unemployment, especially if it is relied upon as the sole remedy. Rather, the government must bring its prowerful weapons, monetary and fiscal policy, into use.

SECULAR CHANGES IN EMPLOYMENT

The possibility of long-run stagnation for the entire economy is another potential source of unemployment. This would come about if the long-run inducements to private investment decline and if, as a consequence, the total demand for goods and services becomes inadequate to maintain full employment. The line of reasoning which predicts this dim future is known as the secular stagnation, or mature economy, thesis. Depressions will be longer and more severe and periods of prosperity will be comparatively rare. Unless the government takes some action to offset the decline in private investment, national income and employment will be low in most years.

Experience since World War II has caused a number of economists to suggest a parallel argument with an opposite conclusion: secular inflation. The high levels of consumption and investment spending have been more than the economy could digest without a substantial inflationary rise in prices. Furthermore, any potential slowing of the pace of spending, which threatens to raise unemployment above some minimum level, is likely to be offset by prompt government action. Thus, demand for labor will always be at a high level and prices will generally move upward.

Which of these two opposing views of the secular outlook is more accurate? Although dealing with this question takes us into the realm of uncertain forecasting, the amount of unemployment is so crucial in determining workers' welfare and the nature of union goals and tactics that the opposing arguments must be at least briefly considered.

Secular Stagnation

The secular stagnation thesis was developed at the end of the 1930's, under the influence of the great depression of that decade. The long-run outlook for private investment was described as very dim because of the pessimistic predictions made on each of its determinants: population growth, new frontiers and resources, and innovations. In the decades leading up to the end of the 1930's, our population clearly showed a tendency to grow at a *decreasing* rate. Hence, it was argued that there would be a declining rate of increase in spending for consumption goods and residential construction. Our frontier areas had been fully explored and settled and our most easily accessible natural resources had been exploited. The remaining natural resources and comparatively undeveloped areas offered less profitable opportunities for investment. Finally, it was argued that the nature of the inventions which were pouring forth from research laboratories were not of the type that would lead to innovating investments requiring heavy capital expenditures, such as we had at the end of the last century and the beginning of this, e.g., for railroads, electrification, and automobiles.

A second strand of the secular stagnation thesis grew out of the changing patterns in the nation's savings habits. People were generally becoming more security-conscious and therefore were saving more, and were holding their savings in the form of very secure assets, such as government bonds, savings accounts, pension funds, and life insurance. There was a trend away from the more risky type of investments, like starting a new personally owned business. Consequently, personal savings were not going directly back into the spending stream, but were required to follow a roundabout route if they were to end up as new investment. At the same time, corporations were financing much of their expansion internally, out of retained earnings and depreciation allowances, and were therefore not absorbing the increased savings of individuals. The higher levels of saving, which meant lower consumption spending out of any given level of income, required a higher level of investment spending to provide a full employment level of total spending.

With the long-run inducements to investment appearing to be very poor, with higher levels of saving, and with the flow of funds into investment inhibited by many barriers, the secular stagnationists predicted that the level of private investment in most years would be too low to provide an adequate number of jobs. Consequently, the economy would be characterized by chronic unemployment unless the government took counteracting measures. The economists supporting this thesis proposed that the government commit itself to a program of continuous deficit spending, making up for the shortages in the total demand for goods and services.

Those who disagree with the secular stagnation thesis take a more optimistic view on the outlook for the three long-run determinants of private investment. First, more recent statistics indicate that our population is expanding at a rate much faster than it was prior to 1940. Furthermore, even if the population returns to a slower rate of growth, the important question is how rapidly the level of consumption spending increases. If per-capita consumption spending rises at a sufficient rate, that would compensate for any possible decline in the rate of growth of the population. In other words, there will be no falling off in the rate of increase of consumption spending if we raise our standard of living fast enough. Hence, consumption spending in the future could work in favor of, rather than discourage, greater investment. Secondly, even if it is true that frontier areas are no longer available to the extent that they were fifty years ago, new techniques of exploitation are now available. As a consequence, what formerly appeared to be infertile land and unexploitable resources are now easily accessible, and more such techniques are constantly being discovered. Also, resources previously unknown or considered worthless are now recognized as having great value, one outstanding example being uranium. Thirdly, with respect to the outlook for innovations, it is very difficult to say what the future holds in the way of inventions, whether or not they will require large amounts of capital. It is still too early to know what the effects of atomic energy or automation will be, to cite only two examples.

The prospect of long-run unemployment, then, is far less pessimistic than that proposed by the secular stagnation thesis. The three long-run determinants seem to favor high levels of income. This is not to say that the thesis was wrong on the basis of the information then available, or that it is wrong with respect to some future period in our economy. The war and postwar periods significantly changed the nature of our economy. Furthermore, the thesis called this potential weak spot in the operation of our economy to the attention of those who influence public policy.

Secular Inflation

Those who predict secular inflation argue that there will be no long-range unemployment problems. They expect our economy to alternate between periods of rising prices and periods of relative price stability. During the latter, if there is a deflationary movement in prices that threatens to cause large-scale loss of jobs, the government will be forced either to reduce taxes or to raise its spending, or both. To allow workers to remain idle would constitute political suicide for the party in power. During the periods of rising prices, the government will be too meek to take vigorous counteracting measures, since these would entail restraints on money wages and profits. Again, the reason would be fear of the loss of power by the political party currently dominant. With the government guaranteeing permanent prosperity, the argument goes, businessmen will tend to expand investment too rapidly, and with full employment guaranteed, consumption spending will also rise too rapidly. If this prediction proves to be accurate, the problems of workers and unions will be very different from what they have been in the past. Since this chapter is concerned with the sources of unemployment, the possibility of secular inflation is mentioned here only as a counterbalance to secular stagnation. The argument will be more carefully explored in Chapters 23 and 24.

TECHNOLOGICAL CHANGES AND EMPLOYMENT

There are two broad categories of technological change: new products and new methods of producing old products. A new product may be a substitute for an already existing product, such as synthetic rubber, or it may be something entirely new, such as television. Within either category, the technological change may be of modest proportions, perhaps only a revision in materials handling, or it may initiate cataclysmic changes in the entire economy, similar to the introduction of railroads.

Technological change is the primary cause of our continuously increasing efficiency—our continuously rising output per manhour—but it is not an unmixed blessing. More efficient production methods mean that fewer workers are necessary to produce a given amount of output; hence, the immediate consequence may be unemployment. A new product, while establishing a new industry, may wipe out a previously prosperous industry, as in the case of the impact of automobiles on blacksmith shops, or the effect of natural gas and petroleum on anthracite coal mining. Thus, any given technological change, or series of technological changes, may produce unemployment for some workers and new job opportunities for others.

The Impact on Individual Workers and Union Policies

The effects of technological change on individual workers who become unemployed are too easy to overlook when concentrating on the operation of the economy as a whole. The suffering attendant upon the loss of a job and income means more than simply a decline in consumption spending. The worker may lose a lifetime investment in a skill and be forced to start his career over again in substantially poorer circumstances. Or the economic life of an entire community may be wiped out, as in some anthracite mining towns, or railroad towns which had been devoted to servicing the coal-burning locomotives. It is very pleasant for all of us collectively to bask in the glory of the remarkable efficiency of recently adopted innovations, but it is a very different matter for the fifty-year-old auto worker displaced by automation or the white-collar worker whose office is closed because of the rise of a new industry. They and their families have their dreams shattered and may face the bleak prospect of living on relief.

Workers individually are usually in no position to affect the rate of technological change and its impact on their jobs. However, collectively, through their unions, they may exert a significant influence. With a matter so crucial as the number of jobs for their members at stake, and indirectly the size of their membership, it is not unnatural for unions to do so. Their actions may take any one of three directions: to obstruct, compete, or control.[5]

A union may obstruct the introduction of a technological improvement by refusing to permit its members to use the new machinery, a technique which can be successful only if the union has organized nearly 100 per cent of the craft and if the new production process does not completely replace the craft workers, i.e., if the members of the union are still necessary at some point in the production process. Otherwise, the employers could completely replace their labor force with workers of a different skill, or, what amounts to the same thing, new employers could enter the trade using the new production process and employing workers other than members of this union. The International Typographical Union has been successful in avoiding some unemployment among its members which would have resulted from modern printing processes. It requires resetting of all electrotype plates or mats for local advertisements which come into the newspaper publishing plant from the outside. That is, the work must be done all over again for each newspaper. In return, the union has ceased to oppose other production methods the employers wanted to adopt.

If employers find it profitable to adopt the innovation, it is only a question of time before the union's obstruction must crumble before the economic pressure. The attacks on the union's position come from too many sides: nonunion workers, nonunion employers, discontented union members, an extension of the new technology making it possible completely to dispense with the union, declines in the prices of substitute products, and potential public investigations and legislation. Conversely, if the employers also gain through restricting output, obstruction may persist indefinitely. The construction industry offers several examples, e.g., the objection to prefabrication of parts of buildings or entire residences. In short, without the collusion—or at least

[5] Slichter, *op. cit.*, pp. 201–81.

tacit approval—of employers, unions cannot prevent the eventual adoption of technological improvements.

Competition with the new methods of production is the second technique which unions may adopt. This may be accomplished by lowering wage rates, making the old production method as efficient (inexpensive) as the new. Since obstruction is generally impossible for semi-skilled or unskilled workers—they are too easily replaced—they may delay technological change by competitive wage reductions. It is not unusual for a union to allow a firm to pay wages lower than the industry standards when the firm would otherwise be forced to discharge its workers and go out of business because it is less efficient than its competitors. The International Ladies' Garment Workers' Union grants special concessions to inefficient firms located away from the major markets, and the United Automobile Workers allow wage differentials for some automobile parts manufacturers. In short, the union encourages employees of these firms to compete with more efficient companies rather than to accept unemployment. Obviously, there are limits on how far a union will go in using this competitive approach, and its success is generally only for a limited time.

The avenue most frequently taken by unions in response to technological change is control, although the degree of success varies widely between different bargaining situations. Unions customarily seek some control over rates of pay for the new jobs, workers to be assigned to the new jobs, the speed at which the machines operate, and the number of workers per machine. Any workers who are discharged are generally given priority in rehiring. Collective bargaining may also influence the timing of the introduction of new production methods. The controls may be exercised through grievance procedures—worker complaints over changes in incentive rates or in amount of output required per day— even though there was no direct negotiation on the subject before the introduction of the technological improvement.[6]

Technological changes which bring new job assignments often present formidable human relations problems. Much patience and foresight must go into proper planning for the change. It requires the best efforts of personnel managers and union leaders to make changes in job assignments and work loads with a minimal amount of worker dissension. The burdens which fall on individual workers as a consequence of technological change are so severe that it is not surprising if they push

[6] Solomon Barkin, "Trade Union Attitudes and Their Effect Upon Productivity," L. Reed Tripp (ed.), *Industrial Productivity* (Madison: Industrial Relations Research Association, 1951), pp. 110–29.

their unions into adopting what might otherwise appear to be irrational actions.

The Impact on Total Employment

To consider the economic impact of technological changes on the economy as a whole requires taking a broader view than that of an individual worker or a union. The improvement is adopted because it reduces the cost of production, making it possible to decrease the price of the product, or to sell a better quality product at approximately the same price. Assuming that the employer passes on at least a fractional part of this reduction in cost to the consumer, the total number of units sold should increase; and since the demand for labor is derived from the demand for the product, the rise in sales should partly offset the fall in employment. (There are other types of technological improvement, of course, but we are interested in the labor-saving type since that is the type associated with unemployment.)

Furthermore, the investment required to produce and install the new equipment may become an additional source of employment. The adoption of some innovations entails less investment than previously used methods, but historically, technological improvements have replaced labor with more capitalistic methods of production. Hence, innovations generally require increases in capital spending, and in this respect they have a favorable effect on jobs available.

On balance, is total employment increased or decreased by technological improvements? The employment effects of innovations tend to counteract each other, therefore no simple universal answer can be given. There is a downward pressure on employment since manhours per unit of output decrease, but this is partly counterbalanced, or perhaps more than counterbalanced, by upward pressures caused by increased sales of the final product, depending on the elasticity of demand for the product, and by investment in new equipment.

The effect of an innovation on employment cannot be analyzed in isolation, particularly when considering the appropriate policy to adopt in counteracting unemployment. The currently prevailing status of secular and cyclical business conditions determines the over-all impact of a new production method. For example, in a period of cyclical decline, businessmen may replace worn-out equipment with labor-saving machinery, thus further complicating the job problem. However, it is during periods of full employment that the greatest number of technological changes is made. The expected rate of profit on the proposed investments would be higher because of the favorable market conditions. The crucial question in determining the economy-wide employment effect of a technological change is whether or not the total demand for goods and services will be high enough to provide an adequate number of jobs after the innovation has been adopted. During a period of secular and cyclical rise, with the optimistic outlook of businessmen and consumers, this may very well be the case.

Technological unemployment, then, from the point of view of the entire economy, is not independent of job declines for secular and cyclical reasons. It may be of substantial proportions in localized areas, occupations, or industries, but it is negligible relative to the total labor force unless there are other reasons for a substantial fall in the demand for labor. In other words, technological unemployment is not a unique public policy problem, whereas the other two are. Job loss itself is not a serious social and economic problem, *if* new positions at reasonable pay can be found quickly. If not, the wastage of resources and the personal hardships are a major cause of general concern.

This does not mean that individual workers or unions can, or should, pretend that technological unemployment does not exist. The worker who loses his source of income—if only temporarily—and the union which sees part of its job territory melt away are naturally going to use whatever power they have to regulate the impact of technological change. An outstanding example is the insistence by firemen that they are necessary to the operation of diesel engines on the railroads. The public should not ignore the social costs of technological change which take the form of ghost towns and uprooted workers whose skills are no longer useful. These are only partly ameliorated through training programs, unemployment compensation, and termination allowances.

FRICTIONAL UNEMPLOYMENT

Frictional unemployment, caused by the imperfections in the daily operations of the labor market, is a catch-all term covering all types of unemployment not included in the previous classifications. It may be divided into two types: the short run, growing out of normal labor turnover, and the long run, resulting from structural maladjustments. We always have some workers without jobs, even in periods of highest employment, which could be avoided only by conscription of labor or compelling employers to hire anyone who applies. For example, in 1957— a reasonably normal year with unemployment characteristics similar to the two previous years, even though a recession started in the later months—unemployment averaged nearly three million (4.3 per cent of the labor force) and more than ten million people suffered some loss of working time. Half of them were back at work in less than ten weeks, but a third of them went fifteen weeks or more without success in their job seeking.[7]

Short-Run Frictions

About 20 per cent of those out of work were in the process of coming into the labor market for the first time or returning after a period of absence. They are at a disadvantage in experience and completely without seniority, and therefore constitute a major source of frictional unemployment. Some housewives enter the labor force only when they know of a job opening and hence never join the ranks of the unsatisfied job seekers. However, many others, particularly young people who have just completed their schooling, may have to search for a few weeks before finding a remunerative use for their skills. Hence, some people will always be out of work simply because new people are entering the labor force.

Voluntary job shifting, the source of about 10 per cent of the unemployment in 1957, is a perennial characteristic of a labor market where workers are free to leave their present employers out of sheer disgust, to go to a different part of the country, or for a better position. A few weeks may elapse between quitting the less desirable job and starting the new one. Voluntary job shifting is necessary, of course, for a dynamic economy to adjust to changing consumer tastes and improvements in production technology.

Furthermore, there are always temporary dislocations leading to brief periods of layoff. A few examples will suffice to illustrate the point. A shortage of materials, perhaps caused by transportation failures or strikes, may close a plant for a week or two. An overestimate of consumer demand causing an abnormally large inventory of unsold goods may lead to temporary job losses. Remodeling the shop, installing new equipment, or introducing new styles or models may bring a brief shutdown of operations. Unexpected weather developments—from hurricanes to bad harvest weather—may cause disruptions in production.

Long-Run Frictions

Certain industries and areas fall victim to long periods of job decline, usually resulting from technological change or the exhaustion of local natural resources. Included in this category of long-run frictional unem-

[7] U. S. Congress, Joint Economic Committee, Study Paper No. 6, *op. cit.*, p. 14.

ployment are workers who have vainly searched for new jobs for many months. Some of them become so discouraged that they leave the labor force, retiring at an early age on minimum financial resources. Long-run unemployment is most prevalent in depressed areas, such as Michigan's upper peninsula, where copper mines and forested areas have been fully worked over. It is only when prices of copper and wood products are unusually high that these industries can return to previous levels of employment. Since new businesses have been slow to move into the area, a chronic surplus of labor exists. Much the same could be said about the textile towns of New England, the coal towns of southern Illinois, and other depressed areas. The initiating factor may be technological change, such as diesel engines causing the decline of railroad towns, or it may be shifts in consumer taste, such as a lower fraction of our income being spent on automobiles and hence the longer periods of idleness for auto workers in Detroit, Flint, and Toledo. But the seriousness of the problem results from the failure of new opportunities to appear.

Secular unemployment, economy-wide in its impact, differs from long-run frictional unemployment which refers to the tendency for a comparatively few industries and areas to stagnate while the rest of the economy is growing. The time dimension is the same, but the proportion of the total labor force involved differs considerably. During the 1950's the amount of job losses from long-run frictions showed a slight trend toward rising, with the main cause appearing to be the shift in consumer spending from goods-producing to services-producing industries. Of course, if this trend should accelerate, it would eventually amount to secular unemployment; but for reasons discussed earlier, this does not seem likely.

Unions, in industries afflicted with long-run declines, are forced to adjust their bargaining to economic realities, including a retarded rate of increase in wages. But even relatively lower labor costs may not be enough to prevent the creeping paralysis; more imaginative schemes may be required. The clothing unions in New England and New York have made substantial loans to faltering employers, and have bought entire factories that were going out of business, thus setting themselves up as employers in order to prevent wholesale job losses among their members. The United Hatters, Cap, and Millinery Workers invested $3,000,000 of their welfare and pension funds in two loft buildings in the New York City garment area when the landlords raised the rent and threatened to expel the millinery manufacturers preparatory to renovating the building for use as office space. The union froze the rents and allowed the employers to continue manufacturing, avoiding further unemployment among its ranks, and at the same time earning a fair income on its investment.

Incidence of Frictional Unemployment

Certain groups in the labor market fall victim to a disproportionate share of the frictional unemployment. Young persons, with no seniority, are likely to feel the effects of even a modest decline in employment. Old workers, once out of a job, find it very difficult to regain permanent positions, and often take marginal jobs which are the first to be squeezed when frictions appear. Females are affected more than males; unmarried, widowed, and divorced men more than the heads of typical families; and blue-collar workers more than white-collar. Migrant workers, who follow the agricultural industry and some parts of the construction industry, are subject to the whims of the weather and delays in raw material deliveries. Non-whites have a much higher unemployment rate than white workers because discrimination confines a large portion of them to marginal jobs. Generally, they are the newest members—with the least seniority—in the industrial work force. The wastage of resources and unfairness associated with discrimination have been the basis for sixteen states to adopt fair employment practice laws, prohibiting employers from discriminating against employees or job applicants on the grounds of race, religion, or national origin. Seven states even prohibit discrimination based on age, hoping to give older workers a better break in the job market.

Frictional unemployment is concentrated in a relatively small group, because some workers become unemployed several times during a year while most remain constantly employed. In 1957 more than 40 per cent of those who lost some working time had two or more spells of unemployment. The outstanding offender was the construction industry.[8] Of course, there are workers who prefer the type of job that has occasional one or two-week interruptions, and use the time hunting, fishing, painting the house, or tending a small farm, rather than immediately launching a diligent search for a new job. Self-employed workers suffer very little frictional unemployment, but temporary dislocations may have a drastic effect on their incomes.

[8] *Ibid.*, p. 32; Thomas C. Fichandler, "The Distribution of Unemployment," W. S. Woytinsky and Associates, *op. cit.*, pp. 403–7; and U. S. Congress, Joint Economic Committee, *The Structure of Unemployment in Areas of Substantial Labor Surplus*, Study Paper No. 23 (Washington: Government Printing Office, 1960).

If these workers, many of whom are on the fringe of the labor force, could immediately find new jobs, frictional unemployment would be negligible. Their immobility is one factor preventing them from moving quickly into new employment. Those residing in rapidly expanding sections of the country will suffer shorter periods of unemployment; whereas many of those in the relatively declining sections of the economy, particularly older persons who have been long-time residents of the community, are reluctant to set out for new territory. As the more skilled and experienced workers leave a depressed area, its labor force becomes dominated by older persons, housewives, and the very young, and thus the community is less capable of attracting new businesses. Hence, even when the over-all demand for labor is very high, time is required to match the unemployed worker with a suitable job opening. The public employment service aids this matching process, but is in no position to eliminate the time lapse. And of course, in a period of cyclical unemployment, the time lapse may extend to months or years. Thus there will always be some unemployment in a free economy. If all forms of unemployment except the frictional were eliminated, what would be the minimum amount in a free labor market?

The Minimum Level of Unemployment

The answer to this question is a major policy matter because full employment is a widely desired objective, but it must be interpreted in the light of real labor market conditions. If there is some quantity of unemployment which cannot be avoided in a free society, the real meaning of the goal must be expressed accordingly. That is, to push the total of consumption, investment, and government spending up high enough to eliminate *all* joblessness would undoubtedly entail wage and price inflation. Furthermore, the minimum amount will vary with the number of new entrants to the labor force, the pace of technological change, the nature and number of strikes in effect, and other temporary dislocations.[9]

In attempting to find a realistic measure of the minimum amount of unemployment, we divide our approach into two parts: war-time and peace-time conditions. During a war the demand for labor is insatiable, particularly after the economy has made the initial adjustments to defense production, and patriotism impels unemployed workers to be

[9] For an excellent discussion of the meaning of full employment and minimum unemployment, see Albert Rees, "The Meaning and Measurement of Full Employment," in National Bureau of Economic Research, *The Measurement and Behavior of Unemployment*, a conference of the Universities—National Bureau Committee for Economic Research (Princeton: Princeton University Press, 1957), pp. 13–60.

more active in their job seeking. Even during World War II the number of job seekers never fell below 400,000, at a time when employers were offering all manner of inducements for new workers. Setting this as our goal would probably be shooting too high, creating substantial inflationary pressures.

In the years since World War II, our economy has enjoyed its highest levels of peace-time business activity. Even at the seasonal peaks of employment, however, the level of unemployment has always been above 1,200,000. The lowest annual average (eliminating seasonal influences) was more than 2,000,000. On the basis of our recent history this would appear to be the irreducible minimum of unemployment.

SUMMARY

Although we have described five separate classifications for unemployment, it should be recognized that the categories are artificial in the sense that it is impossible to take the existing unemployment at any point in time and precisely divide it according to the different sources. There is a considerable amount of overlapping; e.g., technological and frictional unemployment are much greater in times of substantial cyclical unemployment. Measuring unemployment is further complicated by the varying amounts of partial unemployment and underemployment.

Three of our categories, seasonal, cyclical, and secular, are directly related to time sequence. There are two peaks in seasonal joblessness, mid-winter and late spring. The former is caused by a decline in the demand for labor, the latter by an increase in the supply of labor. The seasonal demands for labor vary considerably from one industry to another and shift with the passage of time. Cyclical unemployment is undoubtedly the most severe of the five types: certainly this has been true of the last three or four decades. It exceeded 13,000,000 in the depths of the great depression of the 1930's. A secular decline may have complicated the problem of the great depression, but it is questionable whether it is a problem for the foreseeable future.

Technological and frictional unemployment are characteristics of our economy even in its most prosperous stages. Technological change is a serious problem for those workers directly affected; but for the economy as a whole, it is not a unique phenomenon except when accompanied by a general depression. Frictional job loss, resulting from imperfections and structural maladjustments in the labor market, is the source of an irreducible minimum of unemployment which the economy must suffer even in its most prosperous periods.

Unions have attempted to prevent or regulate unemployment among their members, especially that arising from seasonal and technological sources. At best, their efforts have met only with modest or temporary success. As a substitute for fighting unemployment head-on through job control, unions have supported government social security programs, and have devised collective bargaining plans, designed to provide some income to workers while they are without regular jobs. We will examine these programs for alleviating individual and family distress before going on to the problems of government policy to promote full employment.

DISCUSSION QUESTIONS

1. Seasonal unemployment is an inevitable characteristic of an unregimented economy. Comment.

2. The impact of cyclical unemployment on seasonal unemployment will depend on which industries are most affected by the cyclical downswing. Explain.

3. Explain how seasonal unemployment could divide a union into warring factions.

4. If workers would accept lower wage rates, their total wage income would increase during periods of cyclical unemployment. What does this statement mean? Have you any reservations? Explain.

5. Since a wage increase would lead to greater consumption spending, it is a wise policy to follow for alleviating cyclical unemployment. Explain why you agree or disagree with this statement.

6. The nature of collective bargaining in this country makes it advisable to use wage policy as a technique for counteracting cyclical unemployment. Critically appraise this statement. To what extent do you agree with it? Why?

7. The amount of cyclical unemployment is unrelated to wage rates. Comment.

8. Of the five types of unemployment described, technological unemployment is the only one which cannot exist independently. What does this mean? Explain the reasoning which supports this statement.

9. Cite an example of actual or potential technological unemployment and describe the union's reaction to it.

10. Describe the general nature of frictional unemployment. What groups are hardest hit? Why?

11. Why is it that a free labor market must always have some unemployment, even aside from seasonal unemployment?

BIBLIOGRAPHY

Fellner, William. *Trends and Cycles in Economic Activity.* New York: Henry Holt & Company, 1956.

Hansen, Alvin H. *Fiscal Policy and Business Cycles.* New York: W. W. Norton & Co., 1944.

Keynes, John Maynard. *The General Theory of Employment, Interest, and Money.* New York: Harcourt, Brace and Company, 1936.

McKelvey, Jean Trepp. *AFL Attitudes toward Production, 1900–1932.* Ithaca: New York State School of Industrial and Labor Relations, 1952.

National Bureau of Economic Research. *The Measurement and Behavior of Unemployment.* A Conference of the Universities–National Bureau Committee for Economic Research. Princeton: Princeton University Press, 1957.

Slichter, Sumner H. *Union Policies and Industrial Management.* Washington: The Brookings Institution, 1941.

Tripp, L. Reed (Editor). *Industrial Productivity.* Madison: Industrial Relations Research Association, 1951.

U. S. Congress, Joint Economic Committee. *The Extent and Nature of Frictional Unemployment,* Study Paper No. 6, prepared by U. S. Department of Labor, Bureau of Labor Statistics. Washington: Government Printing Office, 1959.

————. *The Structure of Unemployment in Areas of Substantial Labor Surplus,* Study Paper No. 23, prepared by U. S. Department of Labor, Bureau of Labor Statistics. Washington: Government Printing Office, 1960.

Woytinsky, W. S., and Associates. *Employment and Wages in the United States.* New York: The Twentieth Century Fund, 1953.

20

GOVERNMENT AND

ECONOMIC INSECURITY

We have observed that some unemployment is always present in a free labor market and that the number of jobless sometimes grows to excessive proportions. One consequence is personal economic insecurity: the loss—or fear of loss—of the means of financially supporting the family unit. It has been, and continues to be, one of the major problems confronting the American worker. What will he do if he becomes sick, is discharged from his job, or is retired? Regular employment is the best protection against economic insecurity; conversely, unemployment is its chief cause.

What can be done to alleviate the hardship brought on by loss of income caused by unemployment, or by old age, or whatever the cause? In this chapter we examine the public programs that have this goal. Just as there are a variety of causes of economic insecurity, there are a variety of approaches the government may take to protect against it. In the United States, major emphasis is placed on the social insurance approach, partly because it tends to maintain the dignity of the individual.

ECONOMIC INSECURITY: CAUSES AND CONSEQUENCES

The chief cause of economic insecurity is discharge from employment for any of the reasons described in the previous chapter. As noted, millions of individuals may suffer from unemployment even when the economy is operating at the most prosperous levels. Additional causes of loss of income are: retirement due to old age, inability to work owing to sickness or injury, death of the family's breadwinner, or unexpected expenses (e.g., medical) beyond the limit of the family's capacity to pay.

Hiding behind these broad classifications of the causes of economic insecurity are a multitude of individual hardships. A worker discharged from a job which he believed to have a bright future may become so discouraged he never again develops into an effective worker. A young woman widowed by an industrial accident may not be able to face up to the trial of being both a mother and an economic provider. The point is that regardless of the cause of the loss of income, if the victims do not have a substitute source of income, the consequences may be personally disastrous.

These consequences take the form of loss of personal savings, delay in necessary medical care, curtailment of educational plans, loss of status in the social group, and in some cases, crime and juvenile delinquency. If widespread, they may lead to an embittered attitude toward society, a willingness to overthrow the established social institutions. Destitute persons are susceptible to lending their support to ill-conceived social reforms.

The hardships of economic insecurity are personalized, falling on the individual, even when the cause is a social malady such as cyclical unemployment. One aspect of the remedy, then, properly should be protection of the individual and the family unit, one of the basic principles of our social insurance programs.

SOCIAL SECURITY: THREE DIFFERENT APPROACHES

The best protection against economic insecurity is an abundance of job opportunities, but even when this is provided (discussed in Chapter 22), many persons will be without income. Should the government assume the responsibility of caring for them? If so, how and to what extent?

One extreme answer is to refuse any type of government aid, to allow each to prosper according to his individual ability and initiative with no public program designed to help those who are unfortunately not able to care for themselves. A slight deviation from this extreme is the provision of a relief dole to the "worthy poor," largely those physically unable to work. This is the philosophy we inherited from the English poor laws and followed well into this century. At the opposite extreme is the theoretical communist philosophy: from each according to his ability, to each according to his needs. This would require the collection and distribution of the entire production of the nation through some elaborate government administrative agency, and probably would have disastrous effects on production incentives. At present, no communist government adheres to this philosophy.

Between these extremes are social security programs which provide a limited amount of protection against certain specified risks. This is the pattern followed in the United States, through relief and social insurance, and, in periods of considerable unemployment, public works.

Relief

A relief program makes payments to people in order to add just enough to their own limited resources to make it possible to provide for certain legally defined minimum needs. The first step is to administer a means test, an investigation of the person's financial support from all sources—employment, insurance, savings, value of his house and other assets, and frequently the ability of his close relatives to support him. For many people, revealing such personal information to even the most tactful of public officials is a humiliating experience. To add to the humiliation, in some states the names of all persons on relief rolls are made public information. After the person's means are determined, he receives a payment based on whatever formula prevails in the state. The general notion is that the payments should provide a very minimum standard of living. Thus, it is reasoned, individuals are prevented from starving, but strong economic inducements to secure gainful employment are maintained.

The recipient is impressed with the notion that the amount of his dole depends on his poverty, a sign of his own weakness. It is a gift toward which he has made no specific tax contribution, and is not given to him because he has a right to it. In short, the relief recipient suffers a demoralizing experience and is forced to the lowest rung of the social ladder.

Allowances

The allowance type of social security program, widely adopted in other countries but not used here, involves a fixed payment to individuals who qualify under specified categories, e.g., family allowances based on the number of children in the family, or old age pensions paid to individuals attaining a certain age. The allowances differ radically from relief, since they are paid regardless of economic status. They do not carry the stigma of the dole, and no means test is connected with them. However, they parallel relief in that the recipient has not made any specific tax contributions earmarked for the funds from which the payments are made. That is, he has not "earned" the right to the allowances by paying a tax which is adjusted to his income. Relief payments and allowances are usually paid out of the general revenues of the government.

Social Insurance

The keystone in America's approach to combating economic insecurity is the social insurance program. The individual, his employer, or both make contributions to a reserve fund, the size of the contributions being scaled to his income. The beneficiary receives his payments as a right, with the amount depending upon how much he has previously contributed. The major social insurance programs in this country are old age, survivors, and disability insurance, unemployment compensation, and workmen's compensation, each of which is described in the following sections. They are insurance programs in the sense that a premium is paid for each covered person, buying a certain amount of protection against loss of income for specified reasons. They differ from private insurance because the contributions are required by law and, with only minor exceptions, the individual cannot choose to be covered or not covered. Furthermore, the relationship between tax contributions and benefit payments is designed to favor the lower income groups.

Public Works

In periods of substantial unemployment, the government has engaged in public works programs for the purpose of providing direct wage payments through employment. These have encompassed both make-work activities and useful public projects, and may be considered as an aspect of social security to the extent that they were tailored to meet the needs of the unemployed. For example, during the great depression workers were hired on the basis of the length of their unemployment, size of their families, etc. Although much of the public works spending of the 1930's would fall into this category, very little interest since 1940 has been shown in make-work projects, except for chronically depressed areas. When the spending is designed to bring forth end-products of economic value by the most efficient methods, the public works should more properly be considered as part of the government's over-all fiscal policy.

OLD AGE, SURVIVORS, AND
DISABILITY INSURANCE

In 1935 the federal government adopted the Social Security Act, the basic legislation for old age, survivors, and disability insurance, unemployment compensation, and a number of public assistance programs, such as aid to blind persons and needy aged persons. Up to this time we had required individuals to adjust to economic hardships through their personal initiative and savings, relying on relatives and public relief in extreme cases to provide whatever supplementation was necessary. The cataclysm of prolonged mass unemployment caused a re-evaluation of our individualistic approach, which was then replaced by comprehensive social insurance. Although many other countries had similar programs, the Social Security Act represented a major break with our past traditions. The law was motivated by the economic and political conditions at that time, and many of its clauses still bear the imprint of the depression. Each successive Congress has amended the original legislation, most frequently the old age, survivors, and disability insurance sections, and as a result social security has not yet attained its final form.[1]

Although it has been in effect for more than twenty-five years, OASDI is still young and growing; no retired person has been covered throughout his working life. Measured in terms of dollar amounts and number of persons covered, it is the largest social security program. In 1959 more than 13.5 million beneficiaries received benefit payments of more than $10 billion, and tax collections exceeded $9.5 billion for the year. Total taxes collected from 1937 through 1958 exceeded $55 billion and the reserve in the trust fund was nearly $22 billion.[2] All these figures will continue to rise in the coming years as the number of aged persons increases at a rate faster than the total population and as the proportion of the aged who are eligible for OASDI increases. For these reasons, OASDI has not as yet assumed its final form, and perhaps it never will since Congress has shown a tendency to change it frequently.

[1] For a brief factual summary of the experience under the Social Security Act, see *Social Security Bulletin,* Vol. XVIII, August, 1955, entire issue, and U. S. Department of Health, Education, and Welfare, Social Security Administration, *Social Security in the United States* (Washington: Government Printing Office, 1959).

[2] U. S. Department of Health, Education, and Welfare, Social Security Administration, *Social Security Bulletin, Annual Statistical Supplement, 1958* (Washington: Government Printing Office, 1960).

Coverage

The Act initially limited coverage to employees of firms engaged in mining, manufacturing, construction, and commerce. With the accumulated experience in keeping accurate wage records and in other aspects of administering the program, it became possible to expand the coverage, which is now nearly universal, including self-employed persons. The railroad retirement programs are largely integrated with OASDI, and federal employees, both civilian and military, at present excluded from coverage, will soon have their old age benefit plans made a part of the over-all program. Self-employed physicians are excluded because the American Medical Association has fought vigorously to remain outside of the Act; also outside are domestic workers and farm employees unless they earn at least $50 within a calendar quarter from one employer. All persons not excluded are subject to compulsory coverage, except clergymen, employees of nonprofit organizations, and state and local government employees, who may elect to be included in the program if they so desire. The extent of the coverage may be observed from the fact that the number of persons who have at least some taxable earnings over the course of a year are always greater than the average size of the labor force.

Benefits

The three types of benefits—retirement, survivors, and disability—are related to the worker's average earnings during all the years he is covered, with the privilege of dropping out the five years with least earnings. The *primary benefit* (from which all other benefits are determined) is related to the average wage as shown in the top line of Table 20-A.[3] The formula for computing benefits is designed to award greater amounts to lower wage employees, with the maximum primary benefit currently set at $127 per month. Almost no retired person will be eligible to receive that much until about 1997, because of the limitations on the amount of income that may be included in determining the average earnings, as is discussed below in the paragraphs on the tax base. The formula for computing the primary benefit has been changed frequently, beginning with the amendments of 1950; the maximum at that time was $45.60, considerably less than half what it is now. And it is safe to predict that Congress will continue to liberalize the payments, for political reasons as well as for staying abreast of rising living standards.

[3] *Social Security in the United States, op. cit.,* p. 21.

TABLE 20-A

Old Age, Survivors, and Disability Insurance: Examples of Monthly Payments Beginning after 1958

Average monthly earnings after 1950 [a]	$50 or less	$75	$100	$150	$200	$250	$300	$350 [b]	$400 [c]
Retirement at 65, or Disability at 50	$ 33.00	$ 45.00	$ 59.00	$ 73.00	$ 84.00	$ 95.00	$105.00	$116.00	$127.00
Retired woman worker starting at 62 [d]	26.40	36.00	47.20	58.40	67.20	76.00	84.00	92.80	101.60
63	28.60	39.00	51.20	63.30	72.80	82.40	91.00	100.60	110.10
64	30.80	42.00	55.10	68.20	78.40	88.70	98.00	108.30	118.60
Retired couple, wife starting at 62 [d]	45.40	61.90	81.20	100.40	115.50	130.70	144.40	159.50	174.70
63	46.80	63.80	83.60	103.50	119.00	134.60	148.80	164.40	180.00
64	48.20	65.70	86.10	106.50	122.50	138.60	153.20	169.20	185.30
65	49.50	67.50	88.50	109.50	126.00	142.50	157.50	174.00	190.50
Widow, surviving child, or dependent parent	33.00	33.80	44.30	54.80	63.00	71.30	78.80	87.00	95.30
Widow and one child, or two dependent parents	49.60	67.60	88.60	109.60	126.00	142.60	157.60	174.00	190.60
Widow and two children	53.10	67.60	88.60	120.00	161.60	190.10	210.20	232.00	254.10
Usual maximum family payment [e]	53.00	67.50	88.50	120.00	161.60	202.40	240.00	254.00	254.00
Single lump-sum death payment	99.00	135.00	177.00	219.00	252.00	255.00	255.00	255.00	255.00

[a] In figuring your average, you may omit up to five years of lowest earnings and any period your record was frozen because you were disabled.

[b] Average monthly earnings over $350 will not be possible before 1960 in most cases.

[c] A $400 monthly average will generally not be possible for anyone who has reached the age of twenty-seven before 1959.

[d] Retirement payments to women are permanently reduced if started before age 65.

[e] In some cases payments to a family will be a few cents higher than the amounts shown in this line because each person's benefit is rounded to the next higher ten cents.

To be eligible for *retirement* benefits the recipient must be over sixty-five and retired, or at least not earning more than $1,200 in the benefit year. But no matter how much he has earned during the year, no deduction will be made in a month during which he earns $100 or less. The retired person receives the full primary benefit; if he has a wife who is also over sixty-five and is retired, she is entitled to one-half of the primary amount in addition to his payment. If she is over sixty-two but less than sixty-five, and wishes to begin drawing benefits immediately, she is entitled to a somewhat smaller amount. After the age of seventy-two the person is eligible to receive full benefits regardless of his earnings. In 1958 the average payment to a man and his wife, both over sixty-five, was about $125 monthly.

To illustrate how the formula works, suppose a man has retired with average earnings of $300 per month after dropping out the five years with lowest earnings. He would be entitled to a retirement benefit of $105 per month. If his wife is over sixty-five, she would be entitled to $52.50 per month. If she is sixty-two and elects to begin collecting benefits immediately, she would receive $39.40 per month.

The payments are made as a right without a means test. That is, regardless of the amount of stocks, bonds, or real estate owned, the individual will receive his payments as long as his earnings from employment or self-employment do not exceed the specified amount. In 1960 more than 10,000,000 people, two-thirds of those over sixty-five, were receiving retirement benefits. The proportion of those eligible will rise until it is 85 or 90 per cent of all old people.

Survivors benefits are paid to widows if they are caring for children under eighteen. A widow is eligible to receive three-fourths of the primary benefit, the first child also receives three-fourths of the primary benefit, and each additional child receives one-half. The maximum which will be paid to any one family is $254 or 80 per cent of the average wage, whichever is less. In 1958 the average monthly payment to a widowed mother with two children was about $175. The widow, upon reaching the age of sixty-two, is again eligible to receive three-fourths of the primary benefit, but loses her rights if she remarries. If the deceased worker leaves no widow, his surviving parents, if over sixty-five, become eligible for benefits. Upon death of a covered person, a lump sum payment equal to three times the primary benefit, up to a maximum of $255, is paid to the survivors. It should be noted that both the retirement and the survivors benefits are paid on a family basis. One major aspect of the philosophy supporting the Social Security Act has been to help the family face disaster collectively rather than individually.

The 1956 amendments provided for *disability* benefits to be paid to covered workers and their dependents who become *permanently and totally disabled*. To be eligible, the worker must be over *fifty* years old, meet specified disability standards, and serve a waiting period of six months. The benefits, the same as for a retired worker, are designed solely to replace a portion of the lost wages, with no special payments to cover medical and hospital expenses. A surviving dependent child who becomes totally disabled before reaching eighteen years of age also is entitled, for the rest of its life, to a monthly disability benefit equal to the monthly amount received by a surviving child. The widowed mother caring for the disabled dependent is also entitled to a mother's benefit.

Financing

OASDI is designed to be a self-supporting program, with its tax and interest income sufficient to pay benefits indefinitely into the future and to cover the relatively small administrative costs. That is, it is anticipated that the government will not have to make grants from general revenues to support OASDI. The tax contributions are paid into a trust fund and are invested in bonds issued by the federal government, and along with the interest earned, they are expected to provide for all benefits even though the number of eligible retired persons is increasing more rapidly than the population.

The taxes are assessed against payrolls, with equal rates applying to employee and employer. As set forth in the 1958 amendments, the tax rate is to be 3 per cent until 1962, and then move up 0.5 per cent in 1963, in 1966, and in 1969, and remain at 4.5 per cent thereafter. Self-employed persons pay one-and-one-half times the rate assessed against employees. Judging by the tendencies of Congress in the past, as benefit payments are liberalized and new types of benefits added, the tax rates will rise in order to maintain OASDI on a self-supporting basis.

The tax is assessed against only a certain portion of the earnings, known as the tax base. In the original legislation this was $3,000, raised to $3,600 in 1950, to $4,200 by the amendments of 1954, and to $4,800 in 1959. Raising the tax base has three important consequences: First, the tax becomes less regressive, but as long as the base is less than an individual's total income, proportionally more will be extracted from low earners than from high. And since dividend, rent, and interest income is generally excluded, the tax will always be somewhat regressive. Second, a higher tax base increases the contributions to the program even though the rates remain constant, thus making it possible to raise the benefits and still operate on a self-supporting basis. Third, since benefits are computed from average annual earnings, a higher tax base means that the amount of income to be figured into the average is greater, hence automatically providing more generous benefits. For example, under the 1958 amendments a worker receiving $6,000 in 1960 has only 80 per cent of that counted as earnings for purposes of calculating his benefits.

Controversial Issues

Since OASDI directly affects almost everyone and since so many billions of dollars are involved, some controversy over its scope and operation is only to be expected. Private insurance companies fear that if the benefits are increased, they will interfere with their sales of life insurance and annuity plans. However, the experience with the present levels of benefits appears not to support this fear. In fact, OASDI has aroused an interest in protection against the economic risks of old age, and at the same time has brought the possibility of making modestly adequate provisions for their retirement within the reach of many workers by converting what was formerly a hopeless view of retirement into something with reasonable opportunities. An individual can now purchase a small amount of private insurance, as icing on the cake, rather than expecting his own efforts to be dissipated as a deduction against inevitable relief payments in his old age. In this respect, public insurance has induced an increase in the sales of private life insurance companies. Whether higher benefits would cause people to buy still more life insurance, or to buy less, cannot be determined.

Regardless of the impact on life insurance companies, the present level of benefits is not overly generous and many claim that it is too niggardly. The average old age benefit for a person without a spouse eligible to receive benefits is about 20 per cent of average earnings in manufacturing. Some supplementation from savings, life insurance, or a private pension plan is obviously necessary if retired persons are to continue at former living standards, particularly when it is recognized that their medical costs will rise. And the great majority have little or no income beyond their benefits and only a minimal amount of assets.

Another area of controversy grows out of the methods of financing the program. Should it be financed through a payroll tax segregated from all other taxes for this special purpose, or should it be financed out of the general revenues of the government? Arguments supporting the payroll tax include: 1) the general public knows just how much it is necessary to pay in order to support any suggested increase in benefits, thus reducing the temptation to be overgenerous; and 2) it is more unlikely that Congress would ever eliminate the program since the tax contributions are set aside in a special trust fund and are "owed" to the potential recipients. The chief arguments against the payroll tax are that it is regressive and that it is difficult to manipulate the tax for the purpose of adjusting the government's fiscal policy to cyclical variations in the economy. Manipulating the tax rate, of course, would entail abandoning the principle of a self-supporting program.

The tax base of $4,800 falls far below the standards of the original Social Security Act. In order to include the same proportion of total payrolls as the $3,000 did in 1935, the figure would have to be approximately $10,000 now. At present we exempt part of the income of those most able to pay, and also allow employers to pay the tax on only a fraction of their payrolls. Many therefore argue that the tax base should be increased substantially, providing more generous benefits and permitting the addition of new types of benefits.

At present all OASDI benefits are direct cash payments to replace lost income; none are service benefits to reimburse hospitals, nursing homes, pharmacies, or doctors for services performed for the aged or disabled. It is assumed that each recipient pays his own bills out of his benefits and other resources. However, the incidence of medical bills is not evenly distributed among the retired; some are put under no additional economic strain, but others are forced into destitution by prolonged illness. Hence, it is argued that several kinds of service benefits —varying with needs but not involving a means test—be added to OASDI. More will be said on this point in the section on health insurance.

The disability insurance provisions added in 1956 were only a small step in the direction of aiding the large number of people who are unable to care for themselves because of illness or accident. The comparatively low monthly benefit is paid only after the age of fifty is reached regardless of the age at which disability occurred, and no extra amount is paid for hospital and doctors' bills. This is one of many areas in which our social security system differs from that of most other industrial nations.

UNEMPLOYMENT COMPENSATION

Unemployment compensation is a form of social insurance which provides a limited protection against loss of income to eligible unemployed persons who are willing and able to work. It is jointly administered by the federal and state governments, unlike OASDI, which is strictly a national program. Each state has its own law, which has been the source of some confusion and discord between Washington and state authorities. The federal government pays all the administrative costs of the program and sets minimum requirements, both with respect to civil service standards for personnel and with respect to coverage, benefits, and taxing provisions, allowing each state to go as far beyond the minima as it likes. The states operate the employment offices and the unemployment compensation offices, collect the taxes, and pay the benefits.[4]

One of the most difficult problems to confront unemployment compensation was the conversion from defense production to peace-time production following World War II, and at the same time the entry into the labor force of those discharged from the armed services. The Servicemen's Readjustment Act of 1944, administered by the unemployment compensation offices, provided a necessary helping hand. During the five years of its existence, it made payments to 9.5 million beneficiaries.

Coverage

The unemployment compensation law of each state must provide for coverage at least as broad as that prescribed by the federal law. The Social Security Act, as amended in 1954, requires that all firms employing four or more persons for twenty or more weeks in a year be subject to the tax. The principal exclusions are state and local employees (federal employees are covered), workers in firms with less than four employees, domestic and farm workers, self-employed workers, and the personnel of nonprofit institutions. There is a separate program for railroad employees, administered by the federal government. The states may go beyond the required minimum coverage; however, they have generally covered only the occupations required by the federal law, except

[4] For a descriptive history of the operation of the unemployment compensation program, see *Employment Security Review*, Vol. XXII, August, 1955, entire issue. For a detailed analysis of the state laws, see U. S. Department of Labor, Bureau of Employment Security, *Comparison of State Unemployment Insurance Laws as of January 1, 1958* (Washington: Government Printing Office, 1958).

that Hawaii includes agricultural workers. Twenty-three states, containing one-third of the civilian labor force, have extended coverage to firms with less than four employees.

The original Act of 1935 left nearly two-thirds of the labor force outside of unemployment insurance. In 1955, 39.3 million workers were covered, 55 per cent of all employees. With the amendments which became effective in January, 1956, 80 per cent of all wage earners are now included.

Benefits

To be eligible to receive benefits the unemployed person must register at a public employment office. He must have previously worked in covered employment earning a minimum of between $90 and $800, depending on the state law, during a specified time period. Partial or complete disqualification from benefits will occur if the worker was discharged for cause, if he quit voluntarily, if he is unemployed as a result of being on strike, or if he refused to accept a reasonable job offer. He must report regularly to the employment office and take other actions to prove that he is willing and able to work, such as inquiring about employment at plants in his community. However, he is not disqualified from benefits if he refuses a job which would require giving up his union membership, where he would be replacing a striker, or which has substandard wages and working conditions. In most states, after registration at the employment office the worker is required to wait one week before receiving benefits.

The benefits are determined by a formula—each state has its own— which relates the benefit to the amount earned in the base period prior to unemployment, with each state setting a maximum benefit amount, presented in Figure 20-A. In 1941 the average benefit payments was $11 per week, in 1950, $20, and in 1958, $32, considerably more than the primary benefit under OASDI, and about equal to the amount received by a retired couple. In 1939 the average benefit was 41 per cent of the average wage in manufacturing, but at the present time it has fallen to approximately one-third. The liberalizations of the benefit formulas have not kept pace with the increases in wages, primarily because the maxima have not been raised sufficiently. In 1954, 61 per cent of the benefits paid were at the maximum permitted, and in only seven states was the maximum equal to 50 per cent or more of the average weekly wage in that state. The inadequate liberalization of the benefits has been one of the primary causes for unions to press for the so-called

FIGURE 20-A

Unemployment Benefits

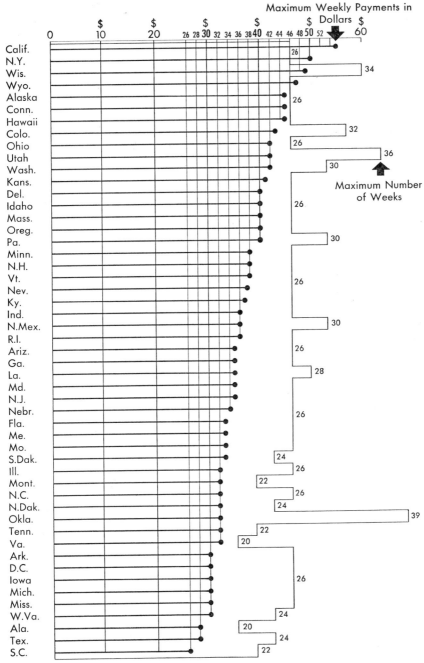

Source: Bureau of Employment Security, as presented by The Conference Board, as of July, 1960.

453

guaranteed annual wage, which in recent times has been in the form of unemployment compensation supplements.

The widespread unemployment of 1958 caused many states to liberalize their laws. (As is typical of so many of the changes in our social security legislation, we waited until overwhelmed by a desperate condition and then made hasty patchwork changes.) The maximum is now $40 or more in a third of the states, including about half of all covered workers. And in fourteen, the maximum equals at least 50 per cent of the average wage of all insured workers, but these states include less than 25 per cent of the covered labor force.

Dependents' allowances are added to the unemployment benefit in eleven states, with each having its own formula for computing the amounts. They have the effect of raising benefits for those eligible by 19 per cent. Payments are also made for partial unemploymnt, but these are of little significance, amounting to only 4 per cent of total benefits.

The duration of benefits varies between states, as shown in Figure 20-A, with four-fifths of them having a maximum duration of twenty-six or more weeks; railroad workers may collect for twelve months if they have fifteen or more years of service. During recessions many workers continue to be unemployed even after collecting benefits for the maximum number of weeks. In 1958, for example, more than two million exhausted their benefit rights, but it is generally less than half of this number in prosperous years. The federal government, in response to the 1958 recession, offered loans to states that temporarily extended duration by 50 per cent. This was a strictly voluntary program, although many inside and outside of Congress favored a permanent and compulsory extension. Seventeen states accepted the loans, and six have adopted permanent plans to increase duration whenever unemployment rises above a specified level.

Financing

The federal government taxes payrolls at the rate of 3 per cent on the first $3,000 for each employee. The tax is levied on employers and is not to be deducted from wages. The federal law permits employers to receive a credit for 90 per cent of this tax (2.7 per cent of the payroll) if that amount is paid to the state under an approved unemployment compensation law. This tax offset provision, of course, puts considerable pressure on all states to pass acceptable unemployment compensation laws. Any state that did not pass an approved law would be giving up tax revenue, and also giving up the opportunity to have an unemployment compensation program, without saving any tax payment for employers located in its borders. The remaining part of the tax, 0.3 per cent of the first $3,000 for each employee, is collected by the federal government to cover the cost of administering the state and federal unemployment compensation agencies and the employment service. All funds are collected by the states, then deposited with the federal government, segregated according to the states, and invested in interest-bearing bonds. By the end of 1958 more than $23 billion had been collected in taxes and nearly $20 billion had been paid out in benefits. Including interest payments of more than $3 billion, the trust fund totaled about $7 billion. In the recession year of 1958, employers contributed nearly $1.5 billion, but $4 billion were paid out in benefits, draining the trust fund to its lowest level since World War II.

Unemployment compensation tax laws in all states include experience rating provisions which allow employers to be excused from part or all of their taxes depending on their employment records. That is, an employer pays a lower rate if he has only a few laid-off employees drawing unemployment compensation. Conversely, a firm which lays off a large number of employees who draw benefits will be taxed at the maximum rate. In short, firms with the greatest fluctuation in employment pay the highest tax rates. The net effect of the experience rating provisions has been to reduce the tax collections to a level more comparable with the costs of the existing benefit levels, and perhaps somewhat below in several states. Currently, the tax rates average approximately half of the original 2.7 per cent of covered payrolls, as a consequence of experience rating.

Controversial Issues

The introduction of experience rating caused one of the most serious controversies in the development of unemployment compensation. Those who favored it claimed that it gave employers a financial incentive to stabilize their employment, pointing out that experience rating in workmen's compensation had had the effect of encouraging employers to adopt safety measures in order to avoid high premium payments, and an analogous result could be expected with unemployment compensation. Furthermore, those industries in which employment could not easily be stabilized, e.g., construction and clothing, would be forced to pass on a part of the cost increase to consumers; and, they argued, consumers should be required to pay these higher prices if they insist upon purchasing the products of industries with irregular employment.

Those who opposed the adoption of experience rating believe that employers have little or no control over the amount of unemployment from their firms. Rather, unemployment is determined by broader economic forces. Furthermore, experience rating causes tax rates to be higher during periods of unemployment and lower during periods of prosperity, and hence operates in a manner to discourage business spending in depressions and encourage it during inflations. Finally, it gives employers an economic incentive to do all in their power to prevent their unemployed workers from collecting benefits, such as finding some excuse to discharge a worker for cause instead of laying him off, or terminating employment before a worker has had an opportunity to earn enough to become eligible for benefits.

In attempting to decide on an appropriate benefit level, a conflict develops. If the weekly benefit is too high, it may destroy the incentive to produce, causing workers to prefer unemployment, and if payments are too low, they do little to alleviate the hardship of those out of work. Moreover, low benefits mean a drastic reduction in the purchasing power of the jobless, which contributes to spreading the economic decline. Unemployment compensation is one of our most important automatic stabilizers: without any special Congressional action, it pays out more than it collects in depressions and does the opposite in boom periods. To serve this function effectively requires benefit amounts that are a reasonable fraction of past earnings, since otherwise laid-off workers will make drastic cuts in their consumption spending, leading to unemployment in other sectors of the economy. It should be noted that the arguments for an increase in the number of weeks of payments are similar to those regarding a rise in benefit amounts. Extending the duration is particularly important for longer recessions and for the victims of structural unemployment.

An extremely controversial issue which receives little attention now is the question of federalizing unemployment compensation—making the federal government responsible for all aspects of the program as in OASDI. This would have the effect of equalizing the benefit amounts and duration in all states, and make it easier for unemployed workers to collect benefits while crossing state lines in their job search. Since the federal government would probably be more generous than the states, employers' organizations strongly oppose the ending of state controls. Rivalry between the states has caused benefit amounts to lag behind rising wage levels and has also retarded extension of duration and expansion of coverage. State legislatures fear that liberalization would put their local employers at a disadvantage and prevent new firms from locating within their borders, because tax rates would have to rise in order to keep the program self-supporting. In fact, the desire to adopt experience rating favorable to employers has caused some of the reserve funds to fall to dangerously low levels, particularly in six states, three of which had to borrow from the federal government to pay regular benefits during 1958. Nothing would bring on federalization faster than a threat of widespread bankruptcy to the reserve funds.

Those favoring federalization often add to their proposal 1) the elimination of experience rating, 2) raising the tax base to a much higher amount than $3,000, which would help support higher benefits, and 3) expanding the coverage so that it will more nearly parallel that of OASDI, thereby including marginal workers whose living standards are low even without the protection of unemployment insurance. Short of outright federalization, much of the content of the proposal could be accomplished by higher federal standards. Washington could refuse to give tax credits to employers in states that do not adequately liberalize their unemployment compensation legislation.

WORKMEN'S COMPENSATION

Workmen's compensation was the first social insurance program in this country. Before its development, workers who were injured on the job had to sue their employers in order to recover medical costs and wages lost while unable to work. Employers were free from liability if they could successfully plead any one of the following: 1) that the employee's negligence had contributed to the accident; 2) that a fellow servant's negligence had contributed to the accident; or 3) that the worker had knowledge of the dangerous conditions and knowingly assumed the risk when he took the job. As the economy became more industrialized, states passed employer liability acts, denying employers one or more of these common law pleas, thus making it somewhat easier for the worker to recover damages through a court case. Even so, there were always long delays and a great deal of uncertainty as to whether the injured worker would be awarded anything, and when he was, the amount seemed to bear little relationship to his injury and financial loss, depending more on his lawyer's ability to arouse the sympathy of the jury.

With the passage of the workmen's compensation laws, the chaotic system of fixing liability on the employer has been replaced, although not completely, by the principle of insuring the risk. The expense involved in caring for the injured worker is to be treated as a cost of production rather than as a penalty for the employer's negligence. The employer pays a premium based on the risk of injury in his firm, with the insuring agent becoming liable to the injured worker for a portion of his wage loss and medical costs.

The first workmen's compensation law in this country was passed by the federal government in 1908 to cover its civilian employees. Ten states adopted legislation in 1911, and by 1920 an additional thirty-two, and all the territories, had followed. The remaining states were not all in the fold until 1948. There are fifty-four separate programs, counting those of the federal and territorial governments, each operating in complete independence of the others. Special agencies were established for the administration of workmen's compensation; however, five states provide for administration through the courts, which are ill-suited to handle the specialized problems in an efficient and consistent manner. In general, the function of the administrative agencies is to guarantee that the insurance carriers settle quickly and fairly with the beneficiaries. The federal government does not set minimum standards as in unemployment compensation.[5]

Workmen's compensation costs American employers about $1.3 billion a year. It is a major source of support for the families of about 16,000 workers who are killed at work each year and a large proportion of the 2 million who are injured—compensating nearly 400,000 beneficiaries each week. It is a source of livelihood for thousands of lawyers, doctors, insurance officials and brokers, safety engineers, and a variety of other professional groups. In addition to the daily operations of 54 administrative jurisdictions, the program is a subject of public policy debate at almost every session of the forty-eight State legislatures and of prodigious litigation at every judicial level.[6]

The purpose of workmen's compensation, as well as reimbursing the injured employee, is to provide an economic incentive to the employer to reduce and eliminate all safety hazards. Since safety hazards have been included as a cost of production, there has been a phenomenal decline—in the neighborhood of 90 per cent—in the number of disabling accidents per amount of work time. Not all of this was the consequence of workmen's compensation, of course, but it did play an instrumental role in initiating safety programs. Beyond prevention and insurance comes

[5] For a review and summary of workmen's compensation laws and a comparison on a state-by-state basis, see U. S. Department of Labor, Bureau of Labor Standards, *State Workmen's Compensation Laws, August, 1957* (Washington: Government Printing Office, 1957).

[6] Herman M. and Anne R. Somers, *Workmen's Compensation* (New York: John Wiley & Sons, 1954), p. ix.

rehabilitation of the injured. Although progress has been made in this direction, the state laws, insurance carriers, and employers still leave much to be desired. In spite of the decreased rate of injury there continues to be a large number of workers injured and killed while on their jobs. "The yearly average . . . for the seven years 1946 to 1952, inclusive, was 17,529 killed or totally disabled for life, 86,243 partially disabled for life, and 1,911,800 more temporarily disabled—a yearly average of 2,015,557 injuries and deaths." [7] Unfortunately, many of these accidents are among workers who are unprotected by the state laws.

Coverage

At the present time approximately forty million workers are covered by the fifty-four different laws. The largest excluded groups are hired farm workers (even though modern mechanized agriculture is a hazardous occupation), domestic service workers, and casual workers. Many states do not cover employers with less than a specified number of employees, and many exclude religious and charitable institutions. Most government employees are covered. The coverage from state to state is very uneven: in three urban states 90 per cent of the employees are included, whereas in twenty-one states coverage is less than 65 per cent. The coverage is about equal to unemployment compensation, but much less than old age, survivors, and disability insurance.

One important qualification in the coverage in twenty-five states results from the elective provisions of the laws, leaving employers free to decide whether they wish to be covered. In general, refusing coverage entails loss of the right to plead any of the three common law defenses if injured employees sue for damages, and this can be very expensive when a badly crippled worker, along with three or four hungry children, makes an appearance before the jury.

Benefits

Three types of benefits are possible for workers whose injuries grow out of or occur in the course of their employment: payments for wages lost, medical costs, and rehabilitation expenses. In 1956 all benefits together totaled one billion dollars. The amount for rehabilitation was small and medical benefits constituted about one-third of the total. Thirty-five of the laws provide for full coverage of medical costs, and only two of the states do not provide at least some protection for occupational disease.

[7] Bureau of Labor Standards, *op. cit.*, p. 2.

Wage-loss benefits depend on the nature of the injury. The majority of the cases are temporary total disability, the worker receiving a fraction of his wages until he returns to work. Those who are permanently partially disabled receive a fixed amount, either in weekly payments for a specified period, or in a lump sum, depending on the extent of the disability, e.g., loss of a finger, a leg, sight of an eye, etc. The weekly benefits are computed as a fraction of the average wage, usually two-thirds. Since each law sets a maximum weekly amount, and since these have lagged far behind rising wages, only one-third of lost wages are actually compensated, on the average. In twenty-two states the maxima are $32 or less, including payments for dependents, with past history indicating that improvements will occur at a slower rate than the rise in general wage levels. All but one of the laws require a waiting period of up to seven days before benefits are payable.

Were it not for second-injury funds, workmen's compensation would tend to discriminate against handicapped persons because employers would be cautious about hiring them for fear that a new injury would leave them totally disabled, thus leading to very substantial benefit payments. The second-injury fund makes it possible for an employer to hire partially disabled workers without becoming liable for total disability payments in case of another accident. The employer is liable only for the last injury, namely, that suffered in the employer's firm. The rest of the amount which is due to the worker, based on his total disability, is paid from the second-injury fund. All but six of the states have such funds, and five of these make other special provisions for handicapped persons.

Financing

Workmen's compensation is financed by premiums paid by the employer. Depending on the state law, the employer may buy his insurance from a private insurance company, from a state fund, or insure himself. Nearly two-thirds use the first method and about one-fourth use the second. State funds are available in eighteen of the states, and are the only method permitted in eight of these.

In 1952, when the total cost to employers amounted to $1.3 billion or approximately 1 per cent of covered payrolls, $787 million were paid out as compensation benefits, including medical payments. That is, the benefits were only 59 per cent of employers' premiums.[8] The

[8] Dorothy McCamman and Alfred M. Skolnik, "Workmen's Compensation: Measures of Accomplishment," *Social Security Bulletin*, Vol. XVII (March, 1954), pp. 10–11.

remainder went for the various costs of administering workmen's compensation, mainly for overhead, such as the expenses of sales promotion by the insurance companies and their agents. The companies provide many useful but expensive services to the employers, in the form of advising them on efficient insurance planning, safety devices, and adjusting and policing claims. Furthermore, outlays for legal services are very substantial even though the bulk of the cases are unprotested.

As well as the direct costs of insurance premiums or self-insurance, employers have a variety of other expenses associated with injuries on the job. Many of these injuries, of course, are not sufficiently serious to result in workmen's compensation benefits. Although the data are inadequate, it appears that injuries on the job cost employers somewhere between $3 and $5 billion in 1952.[9]

Controversial Issues

Probably the most controversial issue in workmen's compensation is the adequacy of the benefits. They certainly do not provide any more than a minimum level of income, particularly when the long time periods involved in permanent disability and death cases are considered. And in some states the weekly benefits end after only a few years. In general, the workers or survivors who suffer the most are, proportionately, least adequately protected. The major improvement needed is to raise the maximum weekly payment so that it equals two-thirds of the average wage, but even then many claimants would receive benefits less than two-thirds of their previous earnings.

Other unsettled issues are those of coverage and administrative complexity. Too many workers must rely on time-consuming and uncertain court procedures in order to win any compensation for their injuries. And too large a fraction of the premium payments are dissipated in the costs of administering the program. Requiring employers to insure through state funds is one suggested answer to this problem, but it is vigorously fought by the private companies on the grounds that they provide better services in arranging programs to meet special needs and are more helpful in eliminating safety hazards.

One promising area for making significant gains is in rehabilitating injured workers. If some of those classified as permanently disabled become re-employed, large savings in benefit payments could be realized. Furthermore, the worker's dignity would be restored as he again assumes a normal status in our industrial society. A few private insurance

[9] Somers and Somers, *op. cit.,* p. 14.

companies have had notable success in their efforts to rehabilitate compensation claimants, finding it profitable as well as humanitarian. One problem involved is to assure the worker that he is not jeopardizing his rights by attempting to return to work. It would be desirable to promise him a return to benefit status if he cannot perform the job satisfactorily.

TEMPORARY DISABILITY INSURANCE

What happens to those workers who become sick or injured in a manner unconnected with their employment and are therefore ineligible for workmen's compensation benefits? They are unable to work and therefore are ineligible for unemployment compensation. The social security program designed to meet this problem, temporary disability insurance, pays wage-loss benefits for a limited number of weeks. There are only four state laws and one federal law: Rhode Island (1942), California (1946), New Jersey (1948), New York (1949), and the federal plan for railroads (1947). By 1950 it appeared that many more states were going to adopt disability insurance legislation, but for a number of reasons interest has declined, perhaps the most important being the advances made along this line in collective bargaining (discussed in the following chapter), thus reducing the pressures from one of the more powerful interest groups striving for such legislation.

The programs are financed either like workmen's compensation, with employers compelled to purchase insurance, or by payroll taxes collected by the state governments. Temporary disability insurance should be distinguished from the permanent disability sections of OASDI, which make payments for life and to dependents, and require beneficiaries to be at least fifty years old. The fact that so few states have adopted temporary disability insurance has caused some to advocate extending the federal programs into this area.

The coverage of the four state laws providing cash sickness benefits are roughly the same as the unemployment compensation laws in those states, and the benefit amounts and duration are approximately the same. In California, hospitalization and medical care benefits are also paid, making it the one social insurance plan that specifically includes service benefits. In New Jersey, California, and New York the programs are partly or entirely financed by employees through payroll taxes. They are administered by the state unemployment compensation agencies, except in New York, where the program is under workmen's compensation. All but Rhode Island, which requires insurance through a state fund, allow employers to cover through private plans, either with private insurance companies or self-insurance. In 1958 workers lost approximately $7.5 billion in income as a result of nonoccupational illness or accident, with about one-fourth of this compensated through insurance and paid sick leave. However, the $325 million paid to workers under the five disability insurance laws represented 48 per cent of all cash sickness benefits (excluding paid sick leave), even though the covered workers incurred only 28 per cent of the total wage loss. That is, the voluntary programs fall considerably short of the compulsory laws in terms of benefits and coverage.[10]

Although more than a quarter of a billion dollars were paid out under these programs in 1954, they still leave much to be desired. The coverage is restricted to a small fraction of the total labor force. Most workers are not covered by these laws and have no protection other than relief or their personal savings.

HEALTH AND MEDICAL CARE

The loss of wages, with a fractional part returned to the worker under workmen's compensation or disability insurance laws, is only one of the risks connected with injury or disease, accounting for about 40 per cent of the cost of illness. There are also hospital and medical expenses, accounting for the remaining 60 per cent, which came to more than $16 billion in 1958, including the cost of various insurance plans which helped to pay the staggering bill. Some of these plans were the consequence of workmen's compensation and disability insurance laws, but individuals had to pay any additional costs out-of-pocket, or relied upon insurance arranged through their firm. Lack of protection against the costs of health and medical care constitutes the largest gap in our public social security program. Practically all other industrialized countries have compulsory health insurance or publicly supported health care.

Hospital and medical care insurance may be purchased from private insurance companies or through the Blue Cross, Blue Shield, or similar nonprofit plans. The private insurance companies generally make a straight cash payment to the beneficiary, while the Blue Cross and Blue Shield type plans make payments directly to the hospital or physician. In 1958 insurance plans covered more than 50 per cent of hospital costs and more than 24 per cent of physicians' costs. Both of these

[10] Alfred M. Skolnik, "Income-Loss Protection Against Short-Term Sickness: 1948–1958," *Social Security Bulletin,* Vol. XXIII (January, 1960), pp. 3–10.

percentages have been rising over the past decade, being approximately 27 per cent and 8 per cent respectively in 1948.[11] But this indicates that a large part of the population has no health care insurance, and for those who have, only a fraction of their bills are paid. In 1958 only one-fourth of the total health bill was covered by insurance.

Compulsory Health Insurance

Since the cost of adequate hospital and medical care is so great and since such expenses may strike anyone without warning, regardless of financial resources and insurance protection, many have advocated legislation to provide some form of compulsory universal health insurance. Such plans have attracted the attention of Congress for several decades. The more recent proposals suggest financing through a payroll tax such as OASDI. It is also argued that some public program is necessary in order to finance medical education adequately and to overcome the shortage and unequal geographical distribution of physicians.

The administration of such a program has been the center of much controversy. The government would be required to approve hospitals and physicians and to regulate, at least to some extent, their fees. It would be quite possible for a compulsory health insurance program to operate without public regulation of the fees of physicians and hospitals, but since it would be paying the bills the government would be likely to take more than a casual interest in what is being charged. This has led to objections, particularly by the American Medical Association, and caused the program to be stigmatized as "socialized medicine," or "political medicine." However, a completely socialized medical program would involve government ownership and operation of hospitals and direct employment of physicians on a salary or fixed fee basis. The rapid spread of the Blue Cross, Blue Shield, and other health insurance plans, often paid for by employers under arrangements made through collective bargaining, has reduced the agitation for compulsory health insurance.

Nevertheless, there is still much popular support for public health insurance, at least for older persons, many of whom are not covered by private plans after they retire. The Forand Bill, named for its sponsor, Representative Aime Forand of Rhode Island, has been before Congress in various forms for a number of years. It would provide a limited amount of hospital and nursing home care and pay surgical costs for

[11] Agnes W. Brewster, "Voluntary Health Insurance and Medical Care Expenditures, 1948–1958," *Social Security Bulletin*, Vol. XXII (December, 1959), pp. 3–9.

those receiving retirement benefits under OASDI. If this legislation is adopted, it will be the first step toward adding service benefits to the federal program, and would perhaps serve as the prelude to a variety of innovations covering a wider range of age groups. The Forand Bill anticipates that the costs would be covered by an increase in payroll taxes of 0.25 per cent each, levied on employers and employees.

Of course, paying for health care through compulsory insurance does not automatically improve the health of our population. With only a limited number of doctors and hospital beds, assuming they are being used to capacity, a new method of handling the costs does not increase the medical output. In short, insurance only eases the pain of paying the bills, but a long-run program of financing hospital construction and medical education and research would be required to expand the availability of health facilities.[12]

OLD AGE ASSISTANCE AND OTHER RELIEF PROGRAMS

It should be clear by this time that the social insurance programs provide far less than complete coverage for all economic risks; probably no social insurance system could be that comprehensive. Many kinds of economic crises are met out of personal resources or from privately arranged insurance. This still leaves a large number of people, incapable of solving their economic problems, who must rely on relief. In the United States there are five major types of relief programs, all administered by the state and local governments, even though four involve federal financial participation. There are approximately 2.5 million old age assistance recipients receiving more than $1.8 billion annually, more than 2.8 million recipients of aid to dependent children receiving almost $900 million annually, approximately 100,000 receiving aid to the blind totaling more than $85 million annually, and more than 325,000 receiving aid to the permanently and totally disabled, amounting to $225 million annually. These are the four programs to which the federal government contributes, financing approximately half of the benefits and administrative costs. The general assistance program, financed entirely by the state and local governments, carried 435,000 cases in 1958 and paid out more than $300 million in relief grants.[13] The number of recipients and the amount paid out varies with the level of unemployment, particularly for

[12] For a good discussion of this point, see Joseph W. Garbarino, "Price Behavior and Productivity in the Medical Market," *Industrial and Labor Relations Review,* Vol. XIII (October, 1959), pp. 3–15.

[13] *Social Security Bulletin,* Annual Statistical Supplement, 1958, p. 74.

general assistance and aid to dependent children. Since 1958 was a recession year, the figures presented above are substantially larger than for previous years. As our standards of a "decent" minimum rise, the average allotment increases, causing a general upward drift in total relief payments.

Many of the people receiving relief are also receiving income under other social security programs. The fact that payments must come from both sources indicates that the social insurance payments are in many cases inadequate to meet the financial needs of beneficiaries.

ECONOMIC ASPECTS OF SOCIAL INSURANCE AND RELIEF

The programs described here obviously have tremendous economic effects, involving, in total, more than $20 billion annually, both in benefits received and costs incurred. And the amounts are increasing each year. They have a tremendous impact on the economy, particularly on wages, distribution of income, and consumption spending. Hence, the programs must be evaluated in terms of their over-all impact on the economy, as well as in terms of their impact on an individual's income and his social and psychological well-being.

Effects on Wages

The social security programs tend to exert an upward effect on the wage level by increasing the withholding power of an unemployed person. He is able to hold out for better wages and working conditions; he need not accept the first job that comes along if it is highly unsatisfactory. He has an opportunity to look around for a job that fully employs his skills and pays a commensurate wage.

The social security programs also affect the prevailing notion as to what is a minimum acceptable wage, particularly for jobs that are customarily low-paying. The general attitude is that the job must pay at least somewhat more than unemployment compensation benefits or relief allotments.

Effects on Distribution of Income

Except for a portion of the costs of OASDI and temporary disability insurance, the employer is the direct carrier of the financial burden of the social security programs. Part of these costs he shifts to the employees by paying lower wages than he might otherwise pay. That is, since his labor costs per worker are increased through paying OASDI, unemployment compensation, and workmen's compensation premiums, he will adjust his hiring policies in accordance with these extra labor costs. The employer, furthermore, shifts a part of these costs to consumers through higher prices. Even after taking into account this shifting of the burden of social security costs, at least a portion of it is finally carried by the employers. In other words, some of the burden is carried by the upper income groups.

The benefits go almost entirely to the lower income groups, those whose incomes have been curtailed through lack of employment because of old age, no jobs available, or sickness or injury. Therefore, the social security programs bring about a shift of income in favor of the lower income groups.

Effects on Consumption Spending

Social security programs tend to raise the level of consumption spending. People whose low incomes would otherwise be substantially less (if they did not receive the social security payments) are inclined to spend the full amounts received on consumption. For example, the recipients of OASDI, by and large, have no other source of income and little in the way of financial reserves; hence, their benefits are completely spent, being hardly adequate to provide a minimum level of living.

The effect of social security benefits on consumption spending is perhaps best illustrated by unemployment compensation. Workers whose incomes are suddenly cut off for lack of jobs customarily have very little in the way of financial reserves to tide them over to the beginning of new employment. Therefore, they tend to spend for consumption practically all the income received from unemployment compensation. The impact of this on the local economy is well illustrated by the experience in recent recessions. Although employment and income decline, consumption spending has generally shown a greater degree of stability. Unemployment compensation was certainly not the only reason—the expectation that the recession would be short was probably more important—but by restoring 25 to 30 per cent of lost income to jobless workers, it undoubtedly played an important role.

The social security programs, therefore, have a distinctly counter-cyclical effect with regard to consumption spending. That is, they contribute only modest amounts to increased consumption spending during periods of high prosperity, and when total tax collections exceed benefit payments—when the reserve funds are increasing in size—they may actually reduce consumption spending. However, they contribute very substantial amounts to consumption spending during periods of recession or depression when total benefit payments exceed tax collections. This is true of old age, survivors, and disability insurance as well as unemployment compensation, since older workers are more inclined to retire, or be forced into retirement, when jobs are difficult to find. It should be noted, however, that the experience rating provisions in the unemployment compensation program have a destabilizing influence on cyclical fluctuations in the economy.

SUMMARY

In our survey of publicly sponsored social security, we found that it is impossible to provide social insurance programs which are sufficiently comprehensive to give complete protection against all of the various types of economic insecurity. However, certain risks are reasonably predictable and can be conveniently handled on a state-wide or nation-wide basis. Primary among these are loss of income through old age, unemployment, sickness, injury, and death.

Of all the social security programs, old age, survivors, and disability insurance is by far the largest in size, covering approximately 90 per cent of the labor force when the special programs for governmental employees and railroad workers are included. It involves the largest amount of dollars in both taxes and benefits and is the only program that is entirely federally administered. Every state has its own unemployment compensation and workmen's compensation legislation with coverage, benefits, and administration varying considerably. In general, benefit levels are approximately a third of the prevailing wages. The financing of the unemployment compensation is based on a payroll tax and workmen's compensation is based on insurance premiums, with the costs paid by employers.

In the area of protection against injury and accident not connected with the job, little has been done in this country. A few states have attempted to provide for loss of income through temporary disability insurance, and OASDI includes a limited program for the permanently and totally disabled. Very little has been done in the case of making up for health and medical care payments, although compulsory health insurance has been considered by Congress on a number of occasions.

Since the social security programs do not cover all possible contingencies and since many people are unable to meet emergencies out of their own income and assets, it is necessary to have a variety of relief programs. These are administered by the states with approximately 50 per cent financial participation by the federal government.

The economic impact of the social security programs is very substantial, tending to raise wages and consumption spending and to redistribute income in favor of the lower income groups. Whether these are desirable effects depends on one's value system.

DISCUSSION QUESTIONS

1. What are the major causes of economic insecurity?

2. The government should set as its goal the complete elimination of economic insecurity for all individuals. Comment showing to what extent you agree or disagree.

3. The consequences of economic insecurity go beyond the suffering of the persons directly involved. Explain.

4. Distinguish between relief, allowances, and public works as different approaches to alleviating economic insecurity.

5. In general terms, without referring to a specific program, describe the major characteristics of social insurance.

6. Old age, survivors, and disability insurance is a young and maturing program. Explain the meaning of this statement.

7. What changes would you propose in the unemployment compensation program? Why?

8. Explain how workmen's compensation has contributed toward safer working conditions.

9. Disability insurance fills the gap between unemployment compensation and workmen's compensation. Explain.

10. What are the major differences between the Blue Cross and Blue Shield plans and compulsory health insurance?

11. If our social insurance programs were more comprehensive, relief would be unnecessary. Explain to what extent you agree or disagree with this statement.

12. What are the most important controversial issues in our public social security programs? Explain your position on each issue.

13. Write a short essay on the economic impact of social insurance.

BIBLIOGRAPHY

Burns, Eveline M. *Social Security and Public Policy.* New York: McGraw-Hill Book Company, 1956.

Douglas, Paul H. *Social Security in the United States.* New York: McGraw-Hill Book Company, 1939.

Gagliardo, Domenico. *American Social Insurance*. New York: Harper & Brothers, 1955.

Haber, William, and Cohen, Wilbur J. (editors). *Readings in Social Security*. New York: Prentice-Hall, 1948.

Peacock, Alan T. *The Economics of National Insurance*. London: William Hodge and Company, 1952.

Somers, Herman Miles, and Somers, Anne Ramsay. *Workmen's Compensation*. New York: John Wiley & Sons, 1954.

Turnbull, John G.; Williams, C. Arthur, Jr.; and Chiet, Earl F. *Economic and Social Security*. New York: Ronald Press, 1957.

U. S. Department of Health, Education, and Welfare. Social Security Administration. *Social Security Bulletin*. Monthly publication.

21

UNIONS AND

ECONOMIC INSECURITY

In the discussion of public social security programs in the previous chapter, many inadequacies in benefits and coverage were noted. In the 1930's and 1940's unions directed their political power toward expanding and liberalizing the government programs, but had only a very modest degree of success after 1950. It is not surprising, then, that they called their traditional economic weapon into play, and collective bargaining demonstrated an amazing flexibility in embracing a new range of goals. A system of private social security was thus erected, the size of which compares favorably with the public system. As a consequence of this remarkable growth, one of the most powerful interest groups has lost some of its verve in promoting greater government responsibility for economic security.

Unions have been successful in winning benefits to cover retirement, health and welfare, and unemployment, with employers paying most or all of the costs. In some instances employers have unilaterally established economic security schemes for their employees, and unions have also unilaterally devised and financed programs for their members outside of collective bargaining arrangements.

The programs of unions and employers, separately and jointly, long preceded governmentally sponsored social security. In fact, the private measures served as models for the public programs, and in some countries the basic administrative framework of the private plans was taken over and integrated into the government plans. In this country

471

social security is now about equally divided between public and private endeavors. In 1959 employer contributions to both government and nongovernment plans came to nearly $15.5 billion, almost 7 per cent of wages and salaries, and about three times the amount paid in 1949 when it was 4 per cent of wages and salaries. Employees contributed about half that amount.

EARLY UNION AND MANAGEMENT APPROACHES TO ECONOMIC INSECURITY

Privately supported social security can be traced back to the medieval English guilds, which provided burial benefits and took care of members in need. In seventeenth century England, "friendly societies," small community groups, extended similar types of benefits. During the first quarter of the nineteenth century, while labor unions were illegal in England, these friendly societies in some instances became "front" organizations for typical union activity. English unions, after being declared legal, maintained and expanded many of these benefit programs.[1]

The first employer-sponsored old age benefit program in this country was inaugurated by the American Express Company in 1875. Within the next fifty years more than 400 companies followed suit, agriculture being the only industry not represented. These plans were financed and administered entirely by employers, but because of inadequate reserve funds many were curtailed or abandoned during the depression of the 1930's. Why did employers voluntarily assume the expense of retirement benefits? Their chief motivation came from the need to retire older and less efficient personnel without destroying employee morale and arousing public antipathy. These early pension schemes, similar to their present-day successors, held an additional advantage for employers: they stimulated the employees to be more loyal to the firm and to be less likely to leave for other employment.

American unions entered the pension field with their own plans at the beginning of this century, with the Pattern Makers' League of North America leading the way in 1900. By 1930 at least thirteen internationals and a number of locals had established plans, most of them financed by members' contributions. The early union activities were an expression of the brotherhood of the workers in the face of ordinary human risks—disability, death, old age—and they were adopted

[1] Karl de Schweinitz, "Social Security," in W. S. Woytinsky and Associates, *Employment and Wages in the United States* (New York: The Twentieth Century Fund, 1953), pp. 157–58.

as techniques for maintaining and increasing membership. A few of the union programs were in retaliation against employers who had instituted pensions in the hope of forestalling union growth.[2]

Many of the union plans suffered from inadequate financial safeguards. Although the reserves were generally segregated from other union funds, in numerous instances they could be appropriated for any purpose, such as supporting a strike rather than retirement benefits. Some of the plans which were formerly supported entirely by members' contributions have now been replaced by arrangements financed solely or partly by employers. All the major forms of private social security today involve substantial, if not exclusive, employer contributions. The major exceptions are in the building trades, but the construction unions are beginning to follow the trend of providing for economic security through collective bargaining.

One conclusion which may be drawn is that workers universally desire some organized method of sharing the risks associated with old age, sickness, unemployment, and death. If adequate provisions are not made through governmentally sponsored programs, workers will devise their own means of meeting the problem. The persistence of such programs through medieval guilds, the early English and American unions, and present-day collective bargaining testifies to this characteristic of security consciousness on the part of workers.

PENSION PLANS

Since 1940 there has been a great burst of activity in establishing pension plans through collective bargaining. Recounting the reasons for this growth demonstrates that collective bargaining adjusts to pressures originating from a variety of sources.

Perhaps the foremost reason for the recent rapid expansion of pension plans has been the inadequacy of the government's old age, survivors, and disability insurance. Throughout the period of rising prices and incomes in the 1940's, the average benefit under OASDI was about $40 per month for a retired worker and his wife, just enough to stimulate an interest in monetary provision for retirement, but without satisfying the need.

During World War II two factors worked together to cause employers to be much less resistant to financing employee pensions: wage stabilization and high taxes on profits. With labor scarce and wages controlled by

[2] Charles L. Dearing, *Industrial Pensions* (Washington: The Brookings Institution, 1954), pp. 30–40.

government, employers used fringe benefits, including pensions, as a means of attracting and holding employees. Likewise, unions, unable to gain large wage concessions, turned their bargaining efforts to fringe issues. Since the tax laws permitted employers to treat their pension contributions as ordinary business expenses, a large portion of the money put into the pension funds would otherwise have been paid to the government in the form of corporate profits taxes. In effect, the government was—and still is—bearing much of the cost of these pension plans.

A further push to pension plans resulted from a decision issued by the National Labor Relations Board in 1948, when it ruled that an employers' refusal to bargain over retirement benefits constituted an unfair labor practice. This issue came before the Board as a consequence of the demands made in 1945 by the United Steelworkers, one of the unions that led the fight for pension plans established through collective bargaining.

In the summer of 1949 President Truman appointed a fact-finding board to investigate a threatened strike in the steel industry. In its report the board recommended an employer-financed pension plan instead of a wage increase, arguing that employers had a social obligation to provide for the retirement of their employees. Obviously, these government endorsements of pensions substantially aided their growth.

Coverage

By the end of 1955 more than 7.5 million employees were covered by collectively bargained pension plans.[3] However, it is not certain how many of these will actually qualify for benefits upon retirement, because minimum qualifications must be met before a retired person may collect benefits, e.g., he must have at least a minimum number of years of service under the plan. It is still too soon to make reliable estimates on the number of persons who will eventually collect benefits, but probably the great majority of people now covered will qualify when they retire. As changes have occurred in price and income levels, OASDI benefits, and union bargaining power, the pension plans have been liberalized in terms of benefits, financing, and coverage.

At the time of establishing a collective bargaining pension plan, employers frequently put into effect a similar arrangement for their salaried employees and others outside of the bargaining unit. For this

[3] *Older Workers Under Collective Bargaining, Part II: Health and Insurance Plans; Pension Plans*, Bulletin No. 1199-2 (October, 1956), Bureau of Labor Statistics, U. S. Department of Labor, p. 15.

reason, plus the fact that many employers have unilaterally established and financed pensions, coverage of all private programs greatly exceeds that of just the collective bargaining plans. All told, at the end of 1957, 17,700,000 employees were covered, and the annual increase in coverage had averaged more than 1,000,000 persons since 1950.[4]

Financing

Collective bargaining pensions may be financed either on a contributory or noncontributory basis. Under the former the employee shares the burden with the employer; under the latter the employer pays all the costs. Unions strongly favor the latter, arguing that the employer's contributions are tax-free, whereas the employees' contribution, coming out of his wage, is subject to the personal income tax. The majority of the large plans are of the noncontributory type.

To make certain that funds are available for the payment of pension benefits, the typical procedure requires that a specified amount be regularly set aside for each worker over the course of his employment. Although most of the plans are arranged through insurance companies, particularly those of small firms, about three-quarters of all covered employees are in schemes financed in some other manner, primarily through trust funds administered by banks or professional fund administrators. Upon retirement, benefits are then paid from the reserve fund. Some employers, however, have followed a pay-as-you-go principle, which eventually runs into very high costs.

One of the difficult financial problems of a new plan, or any substantial increase in one already in operation, is finding a satisfactory manner for handling past service credits. Employees with many years of service and near the retirement age want the same benefit rights as younger persons who will accumulate credits over the years. This means that employers must make large lump-sum payments into the reserve fund upon the initiation of the plan or a major change, or devise some method of funding these costs over a period of time. Hence, costs to the employer vary with the age, sex, and racial distribution of his employees, since these factors affect longevity and therefore the total amount of benefits eventually paid.

The patterns of financing pensions are still in the process of evolution. Even the laws regulating the plans, both state and federal, are far

[4] Alfred M. Skolnik and Joseph Zisman, "Growth in Employee-Benefit Plans, 1954–57," *Social Security Bulletin,* Vol. XXII (March, 1959), p. 12.

from being fully developed. Investigations by Congressional committees and state insurance commissioners have turned up numerous cases of fraud, although the overwhelming majority are honestly operated. There will probably be additional legislation to regulate financial procedures and to prevent abuses by union officers and insurance brokers. This same general point is discussed more fully in connection with fraud in the administration of health and welfare programs.

Except for the comparatively small number which are financed on a pay-as-you-go basis, the plans require the accumulation of funds, leading to the problem of how to invest the funds so as to provide a substantial but safe income to help defray the costs of the benefits. What is to be done if an unusually large surplus is accumulated? Will benefits be increased or employers' costs reduced? The tendency has been to use any potential surplus to help finance the liberalization of benefits. Since these are long-range plans for which perfectly accurate predictions are impossible, they will be a continuing subject for collective bargaining. What is the impact of these reserve funds on the money and securities markets? Will these funds eventually own controlling interests in many corporations? It is still too early to give definitive answers to these questions, but some comments on them are made in later portions of this chapter.

Benefits

In order to be eligible to collect benefits, an employee ordinarily must have at least a minimum number of years of coverage under the plan, some requiring fifteen to twenty years, others much less. In many cases, particularly in the large noncontributory plans, the employee loses his benefit privileges if he leaves his employer, voluntarily or otherwise, prior to the age of retirement. In others the employee has a vested interest in his accumulated credits, which means he retains a partial or complete right to the amount in his account even if he leaves that employer before reaching retirement age. Vesting appears in many forms and degrees. At one extreme the employee, who leaves his job at an age younger than that named in the contract, retains his right to a benefit, although reduced in amount, which is paid to him when he reaches the specified age, usually sixty-five. At the other extreme he may withdraw the full amount deposited in his account, plus interest, upon leaving his employment. The latter is a form of severance pay. The typical provision, in those plans which include vesting, gives the employee a benefit right if he has a minimum number of service credits, e.g., ten years, and has attained a minimum age, forty-five years. The tendency has been, after plans have been in existence a few years, for later bargaining sessions to liberalize the employees' vested rights as well as increasing the benefit amounts.

Generally, the level of benefits is related to past earnings; however, in some of the larger plans (as in automobile and coal) there is no relation between compensation and benefits and in others (e.g., steel) the relation is obscured by the relatively high minimum and low maximum benefit. The general pattern, as the plans mature, is in the direction of granting higher benefits to those with higher earnings and longer service. In many of those financed through insurance companies, pension benefits are based directly on the amount of the contributions for each covered person, which automatically relates them to past earnings.

The plans negotiated in the last decade are designed to be supplementary to OASDI benefits. In some cases the maximum total benefit to be paid includes the federal pension, so that the greater the OASDI benefit, the less will be paid out of the private pension fund. As a consequence, many employers have taken a new position, similar to that held by unions for many years: favoring liberalization of OASDI benefits. Workers covered by both private and public plans may receive reasonably adequate pensions. A worker with full coverage under both OASDI and a collectively bargained pension plan can expect to receive between a half and three-fourths of his employment income when he retires, if he has a retired wife who is over sixty-five.[5] To illustrate, the 1960 steel contract liberalized pension benefits, allowing $2.60 per month for each year of service after January 1, 1960, and $2.50 per month for earlier years. Assuming no changes are made—a most unlikely assumption—a worker retiring in 1995 after thirty-five years of service (the maximum number of years which may be counted) would receive $91.00 and his OASDI check each month. Workers whose wages are above average are eligible for more generous amounts. In the same negotiations, benefits for those already retired from the steel industry were raised by $5.00 per month. The private benefit alone would be insufficient, but along with OASDI, it provides a modest but livable income to a retired couple, unless they have unfortunately large medical expenses.

[5] Robert M. Ball, *Pensions in the United States* (a study prepared for the Joint Committee on the Economic Report, by the National Planning Association) (Washington: Government Printing Office, 1952), pp. 12–15.

HEALTH AND WELFARE PLANS

The phrase, "health and welfare plans," is used here to include all forms of social security negotiated through collective bargaining except pensions and supplementary unemployment benefits. Thus, the phrase includes provisions for medical and hospital benefits, life insurance, direct cash benefits for wage loss due to sickness, and many other special benefits. In recent years the range of benefits has been continually expanded through collective bargaining.

Historically, health and welfare plans date back at least as far as pensions and the two programs had parallel reasons for rapid expansion since 1940. The pressures of a tight labor market during World War II and the Korean War, the rulings of the wage stabilization boards, and the high corporate profits taxes all contributed to their explosive growth. Also, the gaps in public social insurance caused workers to seek remedies through collective bargaining.

Coverage and Financing

The number of workers covered by collectively bargained health and welfare schemes far exceeds that of pension plans. By 1954 more than eleven million workers were covered. These figures exclude government workers and railroad workers, for whom there is special legislation. The coverage has been growing at a phenomenal rate, increasing 55 per cent in the four years ending in 1954. Of the more than 1,200 collective bargaining settlements reached in 1954, each of which covered more than 1,000 workers, nearly 40 per cent included provisions establishing new health and welfare plans, or liberalizing those already in existence.[6] This is an indication of the importance which unions attach to welfare bargaining, accepting gains of this type in exchange for a somewhat smaller direct wage increase.

The financing may be either contributory or noncontributory, with nearly two-thirds of the workers covered by the latter method in 1954. Under the contributory plans, as they have developed with the passage of time, there is a strong tendency for the employers to bear a larger and larger portion of the costs.

Unfortunately, instances of misuse and fraudulent handling of funds have been found in the health and welfare plans as well as the pensions. Although the great bulk of the plans are administered honestly, the

[6] Evan Keith Rowe, *Health, Insurance, and Pension Plans in Union Contracts*, Bulletin No. 1187 (October, 1955), Bureau of Labor Statistics, U. S. Department of Labor, pp. 2–3.

large sums of money involved have tempted unscrupulous operators to "muscle" into the field. Often these are criminals looking for new lucrative rackets who assume a peripheral connection with a union.

How is it possible to reap an illicit profit in operating a health and welfare fund? They are generally financed through an insurance company whose agents earn a commission—often a very substantial amount —for selling the insurance. The agent may "bribe" a union official to favor his company by offering to split the commission, or by "giving" the union official's wife a Cadillac and a mink coat. There is even a more direct route for profiteering at the expense of the members. The union official may establish his own insurance company, perhaps in the name of a relative, and charge outrageous fees for the amount of protection actually provided. The frauds and embezzlements are comparatively rare, although they have attracted much public attention. They are generally found in the smaller plans which are jointly operated by management and the union and where management has neglected its share of the responsibility for scrutinizing the administration of the funds.

The widespread growth of private social security has been so recent that regulation of the financing is just beginning to catch up. Several states and Congress have adopted laws requiring the filing of plan descriptions and annual reports on receipts and disbursements, making it possible for covered employees, and the public generally, to observe the operations. The Welfare and Pension Plan Disclosure Act of 1958 requires reports to be filed with the Secretary of Labor for all plans covering more than twenty-five persons.

Benefits

A great variety of benefits are provided through collective bargaining health and welfare plans. A study of plans reported by 173 unions covering 8.7 million workers showed life insurance "to be the most commonly provided benefit in terms of the proportion of workers covered (93 per cent). Ranked in descending order of importance, the other benefits were hospitalization (88 per cent), surgical (83 per cent), accident and sickness (73 per cent), accidental death and dismemberment (54 per cent), and medical benefits (47 per cent)." [7]

To illustrate the nature of health and welfare benefits we may refer

[7] *Ibid.*, p. 3. A more detailed study of health and welfare plans may be found in Dorothy Kittner Greene, *Digest of One Hundred Selected Health and Insurance Plans under Collective Bargaining, Early 1958,* Bulletin No. 1236 (October, 1958), Bureau of Labor Statistics, U. S. Department of Labor.

to the 1960 contract in basic steel, which converted a previously contributory plan to a noncontributory basis. Wage-loss benefits of $53 to $60 per week are paid for time lost as a result of sickness or accident. Life insurance of $4,000 to $6,500 is provided and an employee's hospital and surgical costs are paid. A worker with two years of service is eligible for benefits, and he continues to be covered for six months after a layoff.

A new benefit recently appearing in health and welfare plans is payment of supplementary benefits to workmen's compensation. When workers receive more income through benefits resulting from accidents off the job than from accidents on the job, pressures naturally build up to provide supplements to the public program. An increasing number of health and welfare plans have been taking this into account in recent years.

Another significant trend in health and welfare plans is the extension of benefits to persons outside the bargaining unit. Most plans provide benefits of some variety for the dependents of employees, e.g., hospitalization, medical, maternity care. Also, most plans continue at least part of the coverage for retired employees; life insurance is the benefit most typically continued. In a few plans even the dependents of retired workers receive coverage.[8]

It is interesting to observe the impact of the collectively bargained health and welfare plans on Blue Shield and similar insurance plans. Unions, along with organized consumer groups, have successfully sought the widespread adoption of service contracts. Under these contracts, for those whose incomes are below a specified maximum, e.g., $6,000 per year, the full cost of covered medical care is paid through the insurance program. Before the introduction of service contracts, physicians were permitted to charge a fee greater than the amount paid by the insurance program, with workers paying the difference out of their own pockets. This would often come as a rude shock to workers who had not read the fine print in their insurance contracts. An unexpected bill for a few hundred dollars after a period of prolonged recovery from an operation naturally aroused intense feelings, particularly since the worker had been living at less than normal earnings. As a consequence, many unions threatened to cancel their arrangements with the local Blue Shield organizations. Service contracts are now available throughout most of the country even though some local medical associations fought against their adoption.

[8] Rowe, *op. cit.*, pp. 3–4.

The health care programs of all Americans are being influenced by collective bargaining provisions in this field. Union and employer administrators, looking for high quality at the most reasonable cost, have become a major force in determining how hospitals and physicians offer their services to the public. Unions must not only negotiate with employers over the scope and financing of the plan, but also with insurance companies over the quality of services which may be purchased with a given amount of funds. New technical skills are necessary for union bargainers to deal with the special cost problems and traditional pricing policies of the purveyors of health and medical care. And there can be no doubt that commercial companies and Blue Cross and Blue Shield have made adjustments to meet collective bargaining demands, partly as a result of threats of political actions if private programs are not available to fill the gaps in public social insurance, and partly as a result of unions establishing their own hospitals, clinics, and health insurance. For example, the American Medical Association has rescinded its strong objections to closed panels of physicians, a system, followed in some of the most outstanding union plans, which requires covered persons to accept medical care from a limited list of doctors. The A.M.A. had claimed that closed panels restricted the patients' free choice of a doctor.[9]

In summary, the health and welfare plans are moving in the direction of caring for the worker and his family from the date of his employment till his death, and with life insurance benefits paid to his survivors. Although current plans generally fall short of this extreme, successive bargaining agreements show a marked tendency toward extending the coverage and liberalizing the benefits, thus raising an important policy question. Would it be economically more efficient to make these benefits available to all workers through a greatly expanded public social insurance program? Comments on the relative merits of public and private programs are made toward the end of the chapter.

GUARANTEED ANNUAL WAGE PLANS

The term, "guaranteed annual wage," which has come into prominence in collective bargaining in recent years, is confusing since the modern plans are neither guaranteed nor annual. Rather, they provide limited supplements to unemployment compensation. Historically, the

[9] For a discussion of the union impact on health care, see Jack Barbash, "The Unions and Negotiated Health and Welfare Plans," in Harold W. Davey, Howard S. Kaltenborn, and Stanley H. Ruttenberg (editors), *New Dimensions in Collective Bargaining* (New York: Harper & Brothers, 1959), pp. 91–116.

term was generally taken to mean a guarantee to specified employees of at least a certain number of hours of work per year, or a minimum income per year. This type of plan is probably impractical for most firms, hence the trend toward unemployment compensation supplements.

The first GAW plans were introduced in the 1890's. By 1945 about 350 had been put into operation, mostly in small firms, but half of them had been discontinued.[10] In our modern production system where most workers have no guarantee of continued employment, the fear of unemployment creates real anxiety, particularly during recessions. The urge for greater security has led to an increased demand for some form of a guaranteed annual wage plan. The United Automobile Workers and the United Steel Workers dramatized this desire of their members, and after extensive bargaining the UAW won a supplementary unemployment benefit plan in 1955. After a month-long strike in the following year, USW also won a SUB plan, but since then only a few unions have been able to win this type of economic security.

Early Plans

There were wide variations among the early guaranteed annual wage plans and no one of them can be taken as typical. A description of the program established at the Hormel meatpacking company in 1931 will serve to illustrate one of the most successful approaches. It guarantees, to all full-time employees, fifty-two weeks of employment per year, with the average work week varying between thirty-four and forty hours per week. Although Hormel has found that its week-to-week level of work varies with the rate at which cattle is brought to the firm, its annual rate of output remains rather steady and predictable. On this basis, then, the firm felt it could guarantee an annual rate of pay, even though weekly working hours fluctuated.

In return for the guarantee, management is given a considerable amount of flexibility in assigning workers to their jobs, being able to shift workers from department to department without regard to seniority. An extra-help crew was established, constituting about 7 per cent of total employment, from which workers could be drawn by any department whose work assignments exhausted its regular labor force. Another factor of considerable importance has been an aggressive

---

[10] U. S. Office of War Mobilization and Reconversion, Office of Temporary Controls, *Guaranteed Wages: Report to the President by the Advisory Board* (Washington: Government Printing Office, 1947), pp. 289–305. This book came to be known as the Latimer Report, named for the research director of the study, Murray Latimer.

management which has brought in a variety of new products, thus giving a longer-run stability to the firm. At one Hormel packing house a livestock shortage occurred in the drought year of 1935. Employees, selected on a seniority basis, were put to work building houses, thirty-four of which were erected before the livestock shortage ended. In 1954 the firm paid out $650,000 for unworked time.

The guaranteed annual wage plans at Procter and Gamble and at the Nunn-Bush Shoe Company are as famous as the one at Hormel. Each was introduced at the initiative of management, and is presently integrated into the collective bargaining agreements. Since all three companies insist that the plans have saved them considerable sums of money, why is it that more firms do not adopt GAW schemes similar to these? The savings brought about appear in the form of reduced rates of labor turnover and hence reduced training costs, higher morale among workers contributing to greater rates of productivity, reduced need for maintaining large amounts of capital equipment which stand idle during certain slack seasons, and a number of other benefits including the opportunity to work employees for more than forty hours in any given week without paying overtime rates (permitted under the Fair Labor Standards Act which includes special provisions for guaranteed annual wage plans).

In spite of these advantages, it seems doubtful whether the majority of firms are able to predict their annual sales at a sufficiently accurate rate to put into effect a guaranteed annual wage plan of the type described. Both management and union representatives in numerous manufacturing industries have stated that they do not believe that it is practical for their particular employments. As a consequence, much interest has recently been given to supplementation to unemployment compensation.

Supplementary Unemployment Benefit Plans

The recent upsurge of interest in guaranteed annual wage plans results largely from the continued inadequacy of unemployment compensation benefits. In the previous chapter it was noted that the average benefit under unemployment compensation is equal to approximately one-third of the average wage. Naturally, workers, in the light of their success in other welfare plans, seek to supplement this comparatively low benefit.

However, not all union members were anxious to give SUB plans a high priority as a bargaining goal. Workers with long seniority and little likelihood of being laid off preferred straight wage increases. The unions, in their educational drive to win membership support for SUB, argued that it protected not only the low seniority workers, but also those whose jobs would be eliminated through automation and other advances in technology—and this could happen to anyone.

Employers strongly objected to the original guaranteed annual wage proposals on the grounds that their costs would be extremely high whenever demand for labor declined, and this would be the time when high fixed costs could be least afforded. As a compromise, unions offered to limit employers' liability to a maximum of some specified amount per hour of work. Some employer groups also objected on the grounds that supplementary payments to unemployed workers would cause them to spend their time fishing rather than looking for a new job. To meet this objection, it was agreed no one would collect SUB payments unless he satisfied the state unemployment compensation office that he was willing and able to work. Finally, employers claimed that the plans would be too costly even with these modifications. Hence, in order to get a foot in the door, the UAW—the first union to win a SUB plan—accepted benefits lower than originally demanded and duration for twenty-six weeks instead of a full year.

The typical SUB plan operates in the following manner: A worker, upon becoming unemployed, makes application for his unemployment compensation benefits. The difference between this public insurance payment and 65 per cent of his weekly take-home pay is granted to him under the SUB plan. That is, the total of the unemployment compensation check and SUB check must equal 65 per cent or some other agreed upon fraction of his take-home pay—regular earnings minus income and OASDI taxes. In addition, special allotments may be granted for dependents. SUB payments continue for a maximum of twenty-six weeks in the automobile industry. The union goal is a full year, and this has been won in the steel and can industries. In those states where unemployment compensation payments run for less than twenty-six weeks, the employer generally pays the full amount up to 65 per cent of the take-home pay after the public benefits are exhausted.

The steel worker receives a supplement up to $25.00 per week plus $2.00 for each of his first four dependents. Thus, in Pennsylvania, where the unemployment compensation maximum is $35.00 per week, a USW member out of work could receive $68.00 for thirty weeks. After the unemployment compensation benefits end, he may collect $47.50 for each of the next twenty-two weeks, plus $8.00 for dependents. In one plan—

between the United Automobile Workers and the automotive manu-facturers' tool and die association—the worker has a vested interest in the amounts accumulated in his account. Upon dismissal from the firm, or retirement, the worker is entitled to a payment equal to one-half the amount accumulated in his account.

The eligibility of the worker to receive benefits depends on how long he has been with the employer, usually two years in order to receive the maximum supplement. Furthermore, the employee must be eligible to collect unemployment compensation. If it is determined that he has been discharged for cause, has refused a reasonable job offer, or is disqualified from receiving unemployment compensation for any other reason, he also becomes disqualified for the supplementary pay. Unions prefer more liberal eligibility requirements than those set by the unemployment compensation offices, e.g., they object to the standards which the government agencies establish for determining what is a reasonable job offer. If higher standards were applied, it would be possible for workers to refuse a wider range of jobs without losing the right to collect benefits.

The typical method of financing these programs calls for the employer to make a flat payment into a fund, usually five cents per-hour-per-employee, until it builds up to a specified percentage of the annual payroll. As long as the fund remains at this level, the employer's con-tribution is zero. Whenever it declines as a result of payments to unemployed workers, employer contributions are resumed. It is not at all certain at this stage whether these contemplated funds will be adequate to cover the potential charges against them. If it turns out that the funds are inadequate, they will become the subject of future collective bargaining. Conversely, the existence of excess funds would give the union grounds to argue for more liberal payments. The UAW experience has been reasonably favorable. During the first three years of SUB, employers contributed $265 million and unemployed workers collected $108 million in supplements, leaving reserves of $180 million. (The extra $23 million resulted from earnings on investments.) The USW plans did not fare quite so well during the 1958 recession, being caught unprepared because they had only one year to build up reserves. When the recession struck just as benefits were first becoming payable, the unfortunate timing forced a number of the smaller companies to reduce or discontinue the supplements. The SUB funds of the large companies were able to weather the storm, adding significantly to purchasing power in hard-hit steel towns. It should be emphasized that the benefits are guaranteed only to the extent that there is money in the SUB fund. In case of a substantial drain on the fund, SUB payments are reduced according to a sliding scale.

Coverage of guaranteed annual wage plans, approximately 2,000,000 workers, is far less than that of the other kinds of welfare plans. In January, 1958, when about 3.3 million persons were out of work, only 125,000 were receiving SUB payments, at the rate of about $2,000,000 per week. Since SUB plans cause labor costs to rise as a result of unemployment coming from erratic work scheduling, there may be a tendency toward greater stability in production planning.

The National Association of Manufacturers, a leader of the opposition to SUB plans, has offered a counter-proposal. The NAM plan, called the Individual Income Security Plan, involves setting up a separate account for each employee, financed by employer contributions. When a worker becomes unemployed, benefits are paid directly from his account, thereby reducing what he personally owns, separately from his fellow workers. The NAM argues, therefore, that the plan has the advantage of placing greater pressure on the worker to return to work—a greater incentive to productivity. However, workers generally go back to work in any case as soon as they are recalled. If a worker leaves the company for any reason, he receives the full amount in his account.

A plan of this type has been signed by the United Glass and Ceramic Workers and the two biggest firms in the glass industry, Pittsburgh Plate Glass and Libbey-Owens-Ford. The employers contribute to special funds, one for each employee. The first $600 in a worker's account is set aside for supplementing unemployment compensation, the worker being permitted to make withdrawals at the rate of $15 to $30 a week. Any amount in his account over and above the $600 becomes available to him as vacation benefits. This is basically "saving for a rainy day," not an insurance plan in the sense of spreading the risk of unemployment over the total group of workers covered by the bargaining agreement.

Collective bargaining over SUB plans is only in its initial stages, with many unions giving it high priority in their demands. Those plans currently in existence are not fully satisfactory to the unions which negotiated them. There will undoubtedly be further bargaining over the amount of the benefit, duration of the benefit payments, vested rights in the funds, standards for determining eligibility, and systems of financing. Techniques need to be worked out for collective coverage of small firms under a single fund. It will take many years for SUB to reach even the incomplete state of maturity now enjoyed by pension and welfare plans.

ECONOMIC ASPECTS OF PRIVATE SECURITY PLANS

What are the economic consequences of private economic security plans established through collective bargaining? With the billions of dollars which employers incur in costs each year and the billions of dollars paid out in benefits, clearly the impact on the economy is substantial. With the tens of billions of dollars to be accumulated in reserve funds, and then invested to provide an additional income for the funds, the money market is materially affected. All in all, what is the effect on wages and employment? What is the impact on the individual worker? How do these plans affect his attitude toward his employer, his job, and his union? How should they be related to public social security programs? These private security plans are still too young to permit giving unqualified answers on their economic effects, but a few tentative comments may be made.

Effects on Wages and Employment

Private security plans have been severely castigated by their antagonists on the grounds that they reduce profits and thereby reduce employment and income. The proponents of these plans argue that they tend to stabilize employment and income. Unfortunately, it is impossible to prove that either side has the truth.

The chief determinant of the general level of wages and employment is the gross national product—the level of spending by consumers, investors, the government, and by foreigners in this country. Therefore, the effects of the private security plans on employment and wages must be through their influence on consumption and investment spending. Government and foreign spending are determined, by and large, separately from any effects of these plans.

Effects Resulting from Fund Accumulation

One major aspect of the economic impact stems from the fact that pension, insurance, and SUB plans require the building of large reserve funds. For the next fifteen to twenty-five years, perhaps longer, the amounts paid into these reserve funds will exceed the amounts paid out as benefits. In other words, they constitute a forced savings program. As more new plans are adopted and those existing are liberalized, the time period during which deposits in the funds exceed payments from the funds is lengthened. For the SUB plans the time period during which the fund is growing is somewhat shorter than it is for pensions and insurance. How much shorter depends on the level of unemployment and how it fluctuates. In a full employment economy, if maintained over a number of years, the fund would reach its maximum rather quickly and then deposits into the fund would no longer exceed benefit payments. For health and welfare plans, exclusive of life insurance, the accumulation of a reserve fund is comparatively unimportant.

The economic impact of fund accumulation varies with different levels of economic activity. Under conditions of full employment with inflationary pressures on the price level, the growth of the reserve funds tends to counteract the inflation. That is, it takes money out of the immediate income stream, which probably would have been largely spent for consumption, and puts it aside in a comparatively idle pool. The extent to which this is deflationary depends partly on what investment policies are followed by the insurance companies and by the fund trustees. In order to earn an income, the accumulated funds would be placed on the money market. Thus, they would finance a portion of the current investment spending, and thereby reduce the tendency to expand the money supply through the extension of bank credit to businessmen. The reserve funds will probably be invested heavily in long-term securities and will thus have the effect of lowering the interest rate for mortgages, corporate bonds, etc. During inflationary periods, then, while the funds are growing, the private security plans tend to reduce consumption spending and to limit the rate of increase of the money supply.

During periods of depression the fund accumulation process would still tend to have a deflationary effect. However, this deflationary effect, undesirable during a depression, would be partly offset by the following factors. During a period of depression, older persons, who might prefer to work but are unable to find jobs, retire and begin to draw benefits. This decreases the rate of growth of the funds and provides additional income and spending power to people who would otherwise have to rely mainly on OASDI benefits. The SUB plans are the most counter-cyclical of all the private security programs. Benefits are paid out of them only when workers are unemployed, thereby providing spending power in much larger amounts during periods of depression than during periods of prosperity. Hence, SUB reserve funds would decline in rough proportion to the degree of the depression. Offsetting this, of course, would be the added deflationary impact of employers' new contributions to the reserve funds. In general, beneficiaries under all the programs would be receiving income which would be depression-proof. With benefit payments, particularly the retirement and unemployment benefits, increasing during periods of depression, the decline in the level of consumption spending would probably be less and hence the depression less severe.

Effects on Wage Rates and Consumption Spending

The bargaining for security plans also has its impact on wage rates. Taking it for granted that there is an upper limit to the economic concessions an employer will make at any given bargaining session, the more a union receives in the way of welfare benefits the less it receives in the way of wage increases. This has an important anti-inflationary effect. Since union bargaining power is generally much greater during periods of full employment with inflationary price pressures, the willingness of unions to take a part of their economic gains in the form of deferred income has the effect of reducing the immediate increase in consumption spending, thus tending to reduce the inflationary pressures in the economy.

The fact that the workers covered by these programs enjoy a greater level of economic security is likely to affect their consumption. It becomes safer for them to engage in long-term spending programs, e.g., the purchase of a home or expensive consumers' durable goods on a long-term payment basis. The recent rapid expansion in consumer credit stands on a somewhat firmer base because of the protection individuals have secured through public and private welfare and pension plans.

Effects on Investment Spending

The impact of private economic security plans on investment spending depends on how they influence profit expectations. If, because of the costs of financing, employers expect less in the way of profits, they may inhibit the rate of investment spending and economic growth. However, since employers' liabilities are limited, the plans should not reduce profits any more than a wage increase. In fact, they tend to put a floor under a decline in investment spending during periods of depressed economic activity because of their effect on consumption spending. The fact that the decline of consumption spending has been held in check acts as an inducement to investment, preventing it from falling to lower levels.

The effect of the private security plans on the interest rate and the money market is in the direction of making loanable funds more easily available, thus tending to encourage investment. This is the consequence of reducing current consumption spending during periods of full employment in order to accumulate reserve funds. The extent of the impact on the money market depends on the size of the funds and on the investment policies of the administrators of the funds. For example, part of the funds are going into the mortgage market, thus reducing the interest rates on mortgages and stimulating construction. Some of the New York clothing unions have invested their pension reserves in apartment buildings, offering housing to members at rentals that bring a fair return on the money, and at the same time providing an indirect benefit before retirement. Part of the funds are going into common stocks, thus reducing the cost of equity capital. Since the funds tend to be invested in comparatively safe stocks and bonds, they tend to favor the large established corporations over the small new ventures.

If the recent trend toward investing larger amounts in common stocks continues, it may influence the nature of control over our major corporations. At the present time, the percentage of ownership is very modest, but pension funds are growing fast enough to absorb a significant portion of new equity issues coming into the market. Corporate managers in search of new financing are increasingly knocking on the doors of the trustees of the funds. The trustees, in turn, look over the companies' policies and officers before making investment decisions. In short, corporations are being forced to meet standards set by the administrators of the pension funds. To complicate the picture still more, it is impossible to identify the owners of the funds—the persons who should have ultimate control over the voting rights inherent in the common stocks. The employer who made the contributions has no legal claim to the reserves; the contributions are a cost which he has deducted in estimating his corporate profits tax. The potential beneficiaries can only claim limited payments under specified conditions, and have no rights to the money until they have retired. Therefore, corporations are becoming responsive to owners who cannot be clearly recognized, a trend away from capitalism, but not toward socialism as it is usually defined. The government, or the public collectively, does not have any increased control over corporate policies. And certainly the prediction of Frank Tannenbaum [11] that unions would be able to use the funds to become owners of all big corporations is not being borne out.[12]

[11] See Chapter 7.

[12] For a very interesting and thorough discussion of pension funds and corporate control, see Paul P. Harbrecht, S.J., *Pension Funds and Economic Power* (New York: The Twentieth Century Fund, 1959).

Employment of Older Workers

The programs, particularly the pension plans, act as a barrier to the employment of older workers. Employers are more hesitant about hiring older workers because their employment period would be too short to accumulate adequate funds to provide them with a reasonable pension. Whenever the pension plans require certain minimum benefit amounts to be paid for anyone who has worked, say, for a period of five to ten years, the employer would find that hiring workers from the ages of forty-five to fifty would raise the total cost of his pensions.

Furthermore, employment of older people is reduced through compulsory retirement. Once an employee has reached the age of sixty-five, the availability of pension benefits makes it easier for the employer to discharge him, forcing the employee to retire regardless of whether he wants to.

Consequences of Variation in Plans

Since workers in each firm and each industry have economic security problems unique to themselves, variation in the private security plans is to be expected. It is often stated that public programs should provide the basic protection against risks which are more or less common to all workers while the private programs should provide a frosting on the cake, adding protection for the special problems of a particular group of workers. But the gaps in public social security have caused the private plans to develop into more than just frosting; they now carry about half of the total load. Furthermore, the private plans have perhaps reached a degree of variation which is undesirable from the point of view of broad public policy.

In considering any of the economic effects described in this section, this unequal coverage among individuals must be borne in mind. Many workers are not covered by any of the private welfare plans, and the great majority have only Blue Cross, Blue Shield, or life insurance coverage. Furthermore, even for those who are covered, the benefits are unequal in amounts and in the conditions of eligibility for payment. The cost incurred in financing the plans varies among employers and among industries. Hence, their economic impact necessarily varies among industries and among geographical regions as well as from one time period to another. This makes it difficult to predict the economic impact and to gear public policy to counteract any undesirable effects of the plans on wages, employment, and the general level of business activity. Moreover, the great variety in the private plans makes it difficult to develop public programs which mesh with the private plans.

These disadvantages are sufficiently important to cause further consideration to be given to a substantial broadening and liberalizing of the public plans, OASDI, unemployment compensation, disability insurance, workmen's compensation, etc. If these public programs provided a higher level of benefits, the private plans would have a more reasonable base from which to build. Under such conditions the great variation in the private programs would be of less serious consequence.

Effects on Mobility of Labor

It has frequently been alleged that private economic security, especially the pension and SUB plans, inhibits the mobility of labor. In fact, employers hope that the plans will have exactly this effect and thereby relieve them of expenses for hiring and training new workers. It is certainly true that an employee who has acquired benefit rights under these plans would incur substantial losses if he left his job. Pension rights alone could be worth well over $15,000. In short, a job now provides an employee with much more than his weekly income; it is the source of his and his family's protection against the ordinary hazards of life, therefore more completely tying him to his place of employment. He is not a free agent to roam from job to job, ever seeking better wages and working conditions. Has he returned to the status of the feudal serf, only with a higher living standard? Is he now bound to a job which he cannot leave except at prohibitive cost? This, of course, is an overstatement of the situation, but it does indicate the direction in which we are moving.

Before taking alarm at the situation and advocating the elimination of all private security plans, certain reservations to this argument must be considered. The effects of the plans must not be examined in a vacuum, but within the framework in which they operate. One important factor in this framework—publicly financed social security—qualifies the effects on the mobility of labor. A worker takes his public benefit rights with him as he moves from one employer to another, as long as he stays in covered employment. If a sufficiently high portion of his protection depends on the public plans, the supplementary benefits will not act as a severe deterrent to his mobility. Unfortunately—from this point of view—the private plans have been growing at a relatively more rapid rate than the public plans.

The most mobile segment of the labor force consists of the new entrants to the labor market. Their mobility is largely unaffected by collective bargaining security plans, since they have accumulated comparatively little in the way of benefit rights in their early years of employment. Unemployed workers who have little hope of being recalled, another highly mobile segment of the labor force, also do not have their mobility reduced by the private plans—having already lost most of their benefit rights except for those covered by SUB plans. The point, then, is that workers who have shown the greatest amount of mobility are the ones who have the least to lose under the private plans; those employees who in the past have been comparatively immobile anyway are the ones most affected.

Although the plans, as presently established, have little effect on the most mobile segments of the labor force, their eventual development over the future may cause them to have a much greater impact. This will be the case if the plans are extended to cover workers with little seniority, or if they provide a majority of the total protection, both public and private, against economic risks, or if they cover a variety of risks not contemplated by the public plans. It is at this point that vesting in private plans becomes exceedingly important. To the extent that a worker carries his benefit rights from one employer to another, the plans should not inhibit his mobility. Furthermore, the development of multi-employer plans tends to reduce the negative effect on mobility. If a skilled tool and die maker, for example, can shift about among a number of employers but still remain within the same welfare and pension coverage, the effect on his mobility is much less than if each of his potential employers has an independent plan. The International Ladies' Garment Workers' Union is moving in the direction of pooling all its pension funds in the garment industry, thus making it possible for members to change employers with no loss in benefit rights.

The effect on mobility is a matter of major public concern because a flexible and mobile labor force is necessary to a dynamic and expanding economy. It would indeed be unfortunate if the desire for protection against economic risk is satisfied in a manner that causes rigid labor markets. For this reason it may be wise public policy to expand the public plans, broadening their coverage and liberalizing their benefits, so as to prevent the private plans from severely inhibiting the mobility of labor.

Private Social Security Versus Public Social Security

In the past ten years, private social security has been growing at a far more rapid rate than public social security. A continuation of this trend is undesirable for a number of reasons: the effect on the mobility of labor has just been noted, the great variation in the private plans in terms of the coverage and benefits was discussed earlier, and the coverage of private plans discriminates against the most insecure workers, leaving them with little or no protection.

There are other disadvantages inherent in relying primarily on a private social security system. The relative cost for the same amount of benefits is much higher than in government plans with broad compulsory coverage. Much of social security is based on the insurance principle of pooling the risk, hence the more people covered the less the costs per person. The public program has the added financial advantage of a guaranteed source of revenue—the government's taxing power—making it possible to adjust benefits to its future income as well as current revenues.

Furthermore, in a public program, it is possible to adjust financing so that the cost burden is heavier in periods of inflation and lighter in periods of recession. Similarly, it is possible to raise the benefits of the public program whenever an increase in consumer purchasing power is desired to counteract widespread unemployment. It is not likely that similar flexibility could be achieved through a private program.

The opinion being expressed here is that social security should be provided largely through public programs. At the present time, private programs occupy too large a portion of our total protection against economic risks. Nevertheless, there will always be an appropriate role for private social security: to cover special industrial and occupational situations and to give greater rewards to the more productive workers.

PRIVATE SECURITY PLANS AND UNION CONTROL OVER MEMBERSHIP

Unions first became interested in pension, unemployment, and welfare plans as a means of controlling membership, a technique for maintaining the loyalty of the worker, and modern plans still retain some of this flavor. For example, the health and welfare funds of the United Mine Workers were administered so that nonunion miners gained little or no benefits. The miner who wished to receive low cost medical care and the comparatively generous pension benefits was required to maintain his membership in good standing. Hence, the plans acted as union security techniques, effective even with miners who were unemployed or retired. If the employer takes an active interest in the administration of the plan, union control over the funds, and hence the ability to use them as membership loyalty devices, is reduced. Nevertheless, the union remains as the protector of the individual's benefit rights. A worker who feels that he has not been accorded his full rights under the benefit plan may process his grievance through his organization.

The benefit plans are certainly not the most decisive control which the union has over its membership. It is less important than other factors such as the union shop, protection of seniority rights, winning wage improvements, etc. However, over the long run, the benefit plans may become more important in this respect.

SUMMARY

Even though their purposes were quite different, both unions and management have long been interested in plans to provide economic security to workers. Management is anxious to find orderly ways of retiring workers, and techniques for reducing turnover and keeping the more experienced workers. Union interest stems from a desire to provide greater security for union members. The modern pension plans have been written so as to provide amounts over and above the OASDI benefit. The health and welfare plans have been designed to fill a gap in those states where disability benefit laws do not exist, and in many cases to provide supplements to the inadequate workmen's compensation benefits. The modern type of guaranteed annual wage plan has been designed to supplement the inadequate payments under unemployment compensation.

The coverage of the collective bargaining plans has been increasing rapidly in the past decade, with nearly twenty million workers now included in at least one type of plan. The benefit payments have been increasingly liberalized, and even though they do not allow for sumptuous levels of living, they are at least a step in the direction of providing more adequate income to workers in distress. The financing of the plans is primarily the responsibility of employers, although a number of the plans, particularly health and welfare, involve contributions from the employees.

It is still too early to assess the economic consequences of collective bargaining over economic security issues. It is clear that large funds are being accumulated and will continue to be accumulated for at least two or three decades. The impact of accumulating these funds is likely to be in the direction of reducing inflationary pressures whenever such exist. During periods of deflation and unemployment, the plans have offsetting effects: the fund accumulation is deflationary but the increased benefit payments, notably supplementary unemployment payments and pension payments, will contribute toward maintaining a higher level of consumption spending than would otherwise exist. The plans therefore help to maintain a floor under the level of spending.

At the present time the plans seem to have only a minimal effect on the mobility of labor, but it is possible that in the future this will be considerably greater. They tend to have an undesirable effect on the employment opportunities of older workers. These consequences of private security programs could be partly ameliorated by expanding the public programs, which also have the advantages of more even coverage and benefits, lower cost per benefit amount, and the possibility of manipulating the financing and benefits to counteract cyclical swings in unemployment.

DISCUSSION QUESTIONS

1. What might an employer expect to gain by unilaterally instituting a pension plan?

2. What have been the major causes of the rapid increase in collective bargaining security plans since World War II?

3. The collective bargaining security plans are a type of deferred wage payment. Explain how this is so.

4. If you were a union negotiator in a bargaining session, what arguments would you make in favor of a noncontributory pension plan as opposed to a contributory one?

5. What kinds of benefits are provided through health and welfare plans? As existing plans are broadened, what new kinds of benefits might be expected to appear?

6. How is it possible that a guaranteed annual wage plan can save money for a corporation? Why is it that more corporations do not adopt such plans?

7. A supplementary unemployment benefit plan has a counter-cyclical effect. Explain how this is so.

8. Explain how the accumulation of a pension reserve fund is anti-inflationary in a period of rising prices.

9. "Collective bargaining security plans encourage a higher level of consumption spending for any given level of take-home pay." Explain the logic of this statement.

10. How do collective bargaining security plans inhibit the employment of older people?

11. What are the disadvantages of having such a great variety of private security plans which differ from one industry to another?

12. To what extent do the collective bargaining security plans reduce the mobility of labor?

13. What advantages accrue as a consequence of a social security program which is largely governmentally operated, as opposed to private social security?

14. In what way can collective bargaining security plans be devices for promoting union security?

BIBLIOGRAPHY

Ball, Robert M. *Pensions in the United States.* Washington: Government Printing Office, 1952. A study prepared for the Joint Committee on the Economic Report, by the National Planning Association.

Bureau of National Affairs. *Pensions and Profit Sharing.* Washington: Bureau of National Affairs, 1956.

Corson, John J., and McConnell, John W. *Economic Needs of Older People.* New York: The Twentieth Century Fund, 1956.

Dearing, Charles L. *Industrial Pensions.* Washington: The Brookings Institution, 1954.

de Schweinitz, Karl. "Social Security," in W. S. Woytinsky and Associates, *Employment and Wages in the United States.* New York: The Twentieth Century Fund, 1953.

Garbarino, Joseph W. *Guaranteed Wages.* Berkeley: University of California Press, 1954.

Harbrecht, Paul P., S.J. *Pension Funds and Economic Power.* New York: The Twentieth Century Fund, 1959.

Skolnik, Alfred M., and Zisman, Joseph. "Growth in Employee Benefit Plans, 1954–57," *Social Security Bulletin,* Vol. XXII (March, 1959), pp. 4–14.

Strong, Jay V. *Employee Benefit Plans in Operation.* Washington: Bureau of National Affairs, 1951.

U. S. Office of War Mobilization and Reconversion, Office of Temporary Controls. *Guaranteed Wages: Report to the President by the Advisory Board.* Washington: Government Printing Office, 1947. (The Latimer Report.)

Unterberger, S. Herbert. *Guaranteed Wage and Supplementary Unemployment Pay Plans.* Chicago: Commerce Clearing House, 1956.

22	# GOVERNMENT AND
	# EMPLOYMENT

In the two previous chapters we discussed government and union programs designed to alleviate economic insecurity for individual workers and their families. Although these programs are indispensable, the first line of defense against economic insecurity must always be an adequate number of remunerative jobs. Under full employment conditions, the great majority of those willing and able to work provide their own economic security. The crucial questions, then, are: How can we create and maintain the conditions which will provide jobs for all those who want jobs? What can the government do to influence the levels of employment and unemployment? How can we promote a rate of economic growth that fully utilizes all our human resources? At what stage should the government actively interfere in the operation of the economy? If full employment is guaranteed, how does this affect the role of unions in our economy? How does it affect worker-employer relationships?

The scope of this book does not permit a thorough analysis of the determinants of the level of employment and the rate of economic growth.[1] However, the nature of many of the labor relations problems discussed in earlier chapters changes at different levels of employment; therefore, some attention to these questions is necessary.

[1] Among the many worthy references are William Fellner, *Trends and Cycles in Economic Activity* (New York: Henry Holt & Company, 1956); Daniel Hamberg, *Economic Growth and Instability* (New York: W. W. Norton & Company, 1956); and Alvin Hansen, *Business Cycles and National Income* (New York: W. W. Norton & Company, 1951).

498

Full employment may be secured by a variety of combinations of economic conditions. The labor relations problems differ depending on which avenue is chosen to pursue our goal. This chapter briefly considers some of the different avenues which may be followed and the next two deal with labor relations problems in a full employment economy, particularly those growing out of wage-price relationships.

AVENUES TO FULL EMPLOYMENT

The level of employment varies with the level of spending for currently produced goods and services, defined as the gross national product, the summation of all production in a given year valued at current market prices. As the spending increases, more production is demanded and hence more workers are employed. However, an increase in spending does not necessarily bring a proportionate increase in employment because the goods and services demanded may have either a high or low labor content (i.e., a large or small number of workers per dollar amount produced) or require high or low wage workers. Furthermore, after reaching full employment, a rise in spending can bring only higher prices, not further additions to employment. As our economy grows and our population increases, the gross national product should increase— the level of total spending required to maintain an adequate demand for labor is continually rising.

Gross national product may be divided into four types of spending: consumption, investment, net foreign, and government. Included in the consumption component is all spending by consumers for the purchase of goods and services to satisfy their desires. Investment spending includes factory construction, equipment, and expansion of inventories; and spending for residential housing is generally included in this category. Net foreign spending is the difference between what we sell abroad and what we buy from abroad, being a positive addition to gross national product if we sell more than we buy, and negative if we sell less than we buy. Government spending is the summation of its purchases of goods and services, including highways, military equipment, educational services etc. Thus, the determinants of total spending (demand for labor) are the determinants of each of these four types of spending.

In this chapter we discuss three different avenues which may be followed toward the goal of full employment: increases in spending by consumers, investors, or the government. Although our discussion treats these as three separate possibilities, no one avenue need be followed exclusive of the others. For example, our goal may be achieved by increasing both consumption and investment spending. However, for analytical purposes, it is useful to discuss each avenue independently. The possibility of increasing net foreign spending in order to create more job openings is ignored because it is probably unwise, for reasons of international political and economic relations, to manipulate trade with other countries for the primary purpose of directly improving the domestic labor market; that is, a "Buy America" policy should not be enforced for the purpose of augmenting the number of jobs.

High Consumption Spending

In exploring the possibility of pursuing high consumption spending as the avenue to full employment, we must first consider its determinants. Although there is a wide variety of relevant factors, the chief determinant, and the most consistent over a period of time, is disposable income, which consists of the cash receipts of individuals after personal income taxes have been deducted; it is the income which consumers may dispose of as they see fit. As disposable income increases, consumption spending increases, usually by some fraction, e.g., three-fourths or four-fifths of the increase in income.[2] Among the other determinants are: expectations with regard to the price level, expectations concerning future income, reactions to new products on the market, availability of credit, the amount of assets they currently hold, and such social institutions as the urge to "keep up with the Joneses."

Generally, consumer spending is passive: it usually does not initiate increases in total spending, but rather tags along after disposable income has risen as a result of changes in investment or government spending. Thus, consumption spending is typically not the motivating factor in changes in the levels of income and employment, in spite of the fact that it is the largest component of gross national product. But it is capable of rousing from its lethargy and leading the way toward a major change in over-all economic activity. For example, in the last half of 1950, consumers sharply increased their purchases in anticipation of a scarcity of goods because of the Korean War, and thereby actively contributed to an inflationary rise in total spending.

In spite of the fact that consumption spending is usually not an initiating cause of changes in the level of employment, it may be

[2] It will be clear to those that have read other books in economics that we are describing the consumption function. For a thorough discussion see Milton Friedman, *A Theory of the Consumption Function* (Princeton: Princeton University Press, 1957), and James Duesenberry, *Income, Saving and the Theory of Consumer Behavior* (Cambridge: Harvard University Press, 1949).

influenced through public policy, independently of the levels of government and investment spending. One method of stimulating an increase is to alter drastically the distribution of income in favor of those at the bottom end of the scale. Greater equality in income distribution may be achieved through collective bargaining—not too much should be expected on this score—or by manipulating government taxing and spending. But even if greater equality is somehow achieved, it is not certain whether this will cause a larger fraction of disposable income to be spent for consumption. If shifting income in favor of lower income receivers raises their consumption spending more than it reduces the consumption spending of the upper income receivers, then an increase in total spending will result. Unfortunately, economists are uncertain about how consumption spending actually does change when incomes are made more equal, but the evidence appears to indicate very little effect.[3] However, it seems plausible to expect that a drastic redistribution, particularly if income is transferred from the very wealthy to the very poor, will have a positive influence on consumption spending.

Direct increases in consumption spending may be promoted by broader and more generous public and private economic security programs, because they give individuals a greater certainty in the permanence of the flow of their income. And of course, increasing disposable income by lowering personal income taxes would lead to greater expenditures on consumer goods.

Although consumption spending is usually passive and does not initiate changes in gross national product, it may be used as the avenue for securing and maintaining full employment. The policies of unions and government, through redistributing income and broadening economic security plans, may encourage full employment spending with a very high level of consumption spending. Whether this is wise public policy, however, depends on the rate at which we want our productive capacity to expand—the rate at which we are willing to give up current consumption in order to produce a greater output in the future. If we skimp on the resources we allocate to research and investment, our national output will grow at a snail's pace, causing us to lose bargaining power in the international market for economic ideologies.

Consequences for Unions

If high consumption spending is taken as the avenue to full employment, what are the possible consequences for unions and labor relations?

[3] Harold Lubell, "Effects of Redistribution of Income on Consumer's Expenditures," *American Economic Review*, Vol. XXXVII (March, 1947), pp. 157–70.

Except for durable goods, industries catering directly to the consumer are less well organized than those producing investment goods. This is particularly true for the wholesale and retail trades, constituting a large segment of the consumption goods industries. As disposable income rises, if current trends continue, a large portion of total spending will be for services—again a sector of the economy where unionization is comparatively low. Thus, a full employment economy achieved with relatively greater emphasis on consumption would tend to bring about a decrease in the percentage of the labor force organized.

Furthermore, if high consumption is promoted through greater equality of income, one of the major motivations for unionization is reduced. As differences between levels of income become narrowed, union and non-union employees enjoy a standard of living which gives all outward appearances, such as the possession and enjoyment of automobiles, household appliances, vacations, etc., of being nearly the same as that of managerial and professional persons. The old rallying cry of the organizer, that workers suffer from economic discrimination, loses much of its appeal. Even beyond the difficulties of organizing new members, greater equality of income may cause present members to feel less strongly tied to their union. They may turn more of their time and interests to "typical middle-class" pursuits: care and upkeep of a personally owned home, parent-teachers' associations, etc.

There is one condition under which union growth may be favorably affected even though full employment is achieved through high consumption spending. If that avenue is selected because of union political activity and collective bargaining, and if it is widely recognized that union policies were responsible for the selection, their prestige may be enhanced sufficiently to win new members to their ranks. But it is not likely that unions would be able to gain this type of recognition unless the rise in spending and income occurs immediately after a long, severe depression. Otherwise, the influence of unions will be obscured by other economic forces, e.g., technological improvements, new products, and the growth of the economy. The conclusion, then, is that high consumption spending is the avenue to full employment least favorable to union growth.

High Investment Spending

Investment spending, along with government spending, acts as the dynamic component in the level of gross national product. Investment spending depends on the profit outlook and the cost and availability of equity capital and loanable funds. The profit outlook is determined by businessmen's expectations with respect to future sales, their expectations on costs of labor and raw materials, the degree of excess capacity in the existing stock of capital equipment, and inventories of raw materials, semifinished and finished goods, new techniques of production, and the general psychological view of entrepreneurs concerning the well-being of the economy.[4] The cost and availability of the funds to be used for investment is determined by the community's willingness to save out of current income and willingness to part with liquidity, and by the monetary policies of the Federal Reserve System and the Treasury.

Investment spending is considered to be dynamic because it is affected by factors other than the current level of income, whereas consumption spending generally changes only after income has changed. That is, the former may act independently, autonomously, while the latter usually does not. Thus, an innovation in production technology may induce businessmen to raise their investment spending, with no prior change in gross national product. Or, a new product discovered through industrial research may lead to expansions of plant and equipment in order to reap the profits from the anticipated sales. The change in investment spending may be negative as well as positive. For example, if, after a period of expansion in the sales of consumption goods, businessmen anticipate a leveling off at the existing rate of sales, this would lead to a reduction in their rate of investment in new plant and equipment.

In each of these examples the change in investment spending acted as a leader in changes in total spending. Moreover, those firms which sold the machinery and new construction to the expanding businesses experienced a rise in income; therefore they and their employees probably increased their consumption spending. Thus, investment spending is a dynamic component of gross national product.

If it is deemed wise public policy to expand the production capacity of the economy rapidly, high investment spending may be chosen as the avenue for securing and maintaining full employment. The investment component, as well as the consumption component, may be influenced by the policies of unions and the government. To encourage high investment spending, the government could grant special tax concessions to firms which build new plants and add new equipment. Or the bargaining power of unions could be restricted in order to bring about more favorable labor costs.

[4] This will be recognized as a list of determinants of the marginal efficiency of capital. A useful reference is Lester V. Chandler, *The Economics of Money and Banking* (second edition) (New York: Harper & Brothers, 1953).

There are two special considerations which should be kept in mind when deciding whether high investment spending is an advisable policy. First, it leads to wider fluctuations in the level of income and employment, because some of its determinants are erratic and independent of the current level of income, and because when it changes, total spending tends to fluctuate by an even greater amount. Thus, a high investment economy would be characterized by wide swings in the demand for labor. Secondly, this avenue would emphasize a faster rate of growth in national output. If we encourage research and the speedy adoption of innovations, associated with a substantial portion of income saved rather than consumed, and if we can avoid extreme year-to-year variations in the level of investment, our gross national product should increase at a comparatively rapid rate. As long as we consider ourselves in a race with the communist nations in terms of economic growth, this avenue to full employment has a unique appeal. Of course, we would be paying a price in terms of restricting our standard of living as measured by per capita consumption, but over the long run we could each acquire a reasonable quantity of shiny new gadgets.

Consequences for Unions

What is the impact on unions and industrial relations if high investment spending is selected as the avenue to full employment? Since investment goods industries are relatively highly organized, the growth of unions would be stimulated. For example, large expenditures on the construction of new factories would entail increased membership in the steel and building trades unions. Equipping the factories would aid the electrical workers' and machinists' unions. Therefore, taking this approach to full employment would probably enhance the power of unions, particularly in the basic industries.

Unions in the basic industries are likely to be the ones that set the pattern for collective bargaining for any given round of wage increases. If high investment spending tends to increase their bargaining power, a higher wage level for unionized workers would result; and with full employment, nonunion workers would also gain higher earnings because of sympathetic pressures. But whether workers' hourly rates would keep pace with rising profits cannot be predicted. If wages increase more than profits, then investment might be restricted by labor costs. Therefore, selecting this avenue probably involves preventing wages from going up, percentage-wise, as much as profits. Nevertheless, both may rise at the expense of other income shares, rent and interest.

Government Fiscal Policy

In a free economy with consumption and investment decisions made independently by individual consumers and businessmen, there is no guarantee that these two types of spending will at all times be sufficient to provide an adequate demand for labor. If full employment is the desired goal for the economy, then it becomes necessary for the federal government now and again to manipulate the level of total spending. By changing its fiscal policy, it may promote a rise or a fall in either consumption or investment spending, or both. The federal government's fiscal policy may also involve a change in its own level of spending. The latter is a potent weapon for influencing the level of employment, since it constitutes between 15 and 20 per cent of the gross national product.

The point, then, is that the government may select the avenue to be followed to full employment. By changing its taxes so that the burden falls on different groups in the economy, or by granting subsidies, it may choose either the high consumption or high investment avenue. Or it may plunge ahead on its own, engaging directly in a large-scale spending program, constructing a great variety of public works projects.

Although full employment is not an officially stated goal of public policy in the United States, ever since the great depression of the 1930's it has been taken for granted that the federal government would actively interfere in the operation of the economy in the event of a serious depression. In fact, it would be political suicide for the party in power not to do so. Strong action would certainly be taken long before a threatening depression reached the proportions of that of the 1930's, probably before unemployment exceeded 8 to 10 per cent of the labor force for more than a few months.

The Employment Act of 1946 requires Congress and the President to gather statistics on the trends in employment and spending, and indirectly requires them to consider possible adjustments in fiscal policy in the light of this information. The Act establishes the President's Council of Economic Advisors, which makes a report to the President each year, giving a detailed picture of the operation of the economy in the recent past and the Council's expectations on employment and income in the coming years. The President forwards this report to Congress along with recommendations for what he believes to be appropriate legislation.

The Act provides no guarantee of full employment, nor does it require Congress to take action designed to achieve that goal. It requires only that consideration be given to adjusting appropriations and government programs in the light of the level of employment. Nevertheless, it is reasonable to expect Congress to adopt some type of legislation designed to improve labor market conditions if the economy is threatened with an even moderately severe depression.

These brief comments may lead to the wrong impression that it is easy to know when remedial action is necessary and how strong the medicine should be. Competent observers—economists and policy-makers —will never be in complete agreement on when and how much. For example, the Joint Economic Committee, the Congressional body charged with the duty of appraising the President's Economic Report, and his supplementary recommendations, has frequently criticized the chief executive's proposals. The 1960 *Joint Economic Report,* presenting the views of the Committee's Democratic majority, stated: "The programs outlined in the President's budget and Economic Report will not achieve the objectives of the Employment Act in 1960. Moreover, they do not call for the actions which, as a result of its studies, this committee believes are necessary to raise the rate of economic growth while achieving a high and steady rate of employment and a stable price level." [5] The Republican minority vigorously dissented, and gave its support to President Eisenhower. In spite of the fact that unanimous opinion will never prevail, federal fiscal policy will always exercise a powerful influence over the economy, and Congress will continually be forced to choose between policies and programs which have varied effects on consumption and investment. [6]

Impact on Consumption Spending

The government may, through its fiscal policy, promote full employment levels of spending by encouraging more consumption. Aspects of this approach were suggested earlier in terms of redistributing income, subsidies to consumption goods industries, and economic security programs. More specifically, on the revenue side of the government's fiscal policy, the personal income tax could be reduced, particularly for lower income groups. Or excise taxes on consumption goods could be curtailed, as in the case of cigarettes, automobiles, gasoline, and telephone service. Hence, by maintaining a constant level of taxes, but redistributing the burden, a high consumption economy may be secured.

[5] U. S. Congress, Joint Economic Committee, *1960 Joint Economic Report* (Washington: Government Printing Office, 1960), p. 2.

[6] At this stage we are noting only the inevitable presence of disagreement. In the next two chapters, some of the aspects of the controversy are explored.

An even greater boost to consumption would result from reducing tax collections while holding government outlays constant, engaging in deficit financing with expenditures exceeding revenues. The deficit acts as a form of government investment in the economy, and the actual increase in gross national product will be some multiple of the investment, depending on the marginal propensity to consume. If the marginal propensity to consume is, for example, two-thirds, the initial increase in consumption spending would be two-thirds of the deficit. This added spending represents an increase in income for those businessmen and their employees who sold the consumption goods. They in turn raise their consumption spending by two-thirds of their added income, leading to still further increases in income. These successive waves of spending cause the total rise in consumption spending to be twice the amount of the government's deficit. The fraction of increased income spent by consumers—their marginal propensity to consume—determines how much total spending will increase; the greater their marginal propensity to consume, the greater the increase in consumption spending and in gross national product.

Before leaving this point, it should be noted that a government deficit which resulted from an increase in its spending, with taxes held constant, would also have a buoyant effect on the economy. This would cause an increase in consumption spending and hence a multiplier effect, in a manner similar to the deficit just described. Changes in private investment spending likewise have a multiplier effect through a similar process. Hence, these two components, public and private investment, are the ones primarily responsible for initiating changes in gross national product. But the multiplier effect applies to decreases as well as to increases: a budgetary surplus resulting from either a decrease in government spending or an increase in taxes would cause reductions in consumption spending and in gross national product greater than the amount of the surplus.

Impact on Investment Spending

The government may deliberately manipulate its fiscal policy to influence profit expectations and thereby induce changes in private investment spending. One possibility is to permit fast depreciation write-offs for investment in new plant and equipment, thus allowing firms, in the early years after an investment, to charge a higher portion of the expenditure as a cost deductible from their corporate income tax liability. The risk of obsolescence before the cost of the plant and equipment had been recovered would thereby be reduced, and since business firms would be able to retain a greater portion of their gross revenues, the cost of capital would be reduced. Another approach open to the government would be to tax reinvested profits at a lower rate than other profits. Or the government could offer loans at low interest rates, perhaps to firms having difficulties making financial arrangements, as it did through the Reconstruction Finance Corporation in the 1930's. It could also guarantee loans for capital investment similar to its program in veterans' housing.

Perhaps the most obvious method of influencing profit expectations is direct government purchases from business firms. The profit outlook is improved not only for the firms selling to the government, but for other firms as well, since they may anticipate increases in their sales as a consequence of rising incomes and consumption spending. Hence, spending may rise generally for all firms. For example, defense production is an important direct source of jobs for workers in aircraft and missile companies, naval yards, etc., and at the same time leads to consumption spending which supports further employment. To be more specific, it is government orders, rather than the expenditures as they appear in the budget, that provide the stimulus to business activity. The spending actually takes place when bills are submitted, often after a government-sponsored project has been completed. By proper spacing of orders, much can be done to promote stable business spending and employment.[7]

The amount of additional investment induced by government purchases depends on the ratio between inventories and sales, and on the amount of idle capacity in plant and equipment. If inventories of retailers, wholesalers, and manufacturers are high relative to sales, the additional sales can be made with very little addition to the current rate of production. And if there are substantial amounts of unused machines and factory space, any additional production can be consummated with little additional investment. But if inventories are low relative to the new level of consumption spending and if there is little or no idle capacity, new investment spending will be forthcoming when the government increases its orders for goods.

Government purchases from business firms, as a technique for promoting full employment, involve a special advantage for unions, at least for those in the favored industries. Under provisions of the Walsh-Healey

---

[7] For a critical analysis of the employment impact of defense orders during the 1950's see U. S. Congress, Joint Economic Committee, *Staff Report on Employment, Growth, and Price Levels* (Washington: Government Printing Office, 1959), pp. 213–55.

and Davis-Bacon Acts, the Secretary of Labor sets minimum wages and working conditions for those firms producing under government contract. Since the minima tend to be the prevailing union standards, these unions are protected against potential competition from nonunion firms, thus strengthening their bargaining position.

Up to this point we have investigated high consumption and high investment as avenues to full employment, and have indicated that the government, without changing its share of the nation's total spending, could manipulate its fiscal policy so as to push us in either direction. But there are two reservations which must be recognized. First, private spending, even with special encouragement, may not increase at a rate rapid enough to provide jobs for everyone in a growing labor force. Public spending may have to rise relatively to consumption and private investment in order to create an adequate demand for labor.

The second reservation stems from the question of what kind of economic growth we really want. In recent years many people have been wondering whether we have been concentrating on material welfare to the neglect of other vital aspects of the "good life." They accuse our society of piling up huge quantities of chrome-plated durable goods while our educational system, public libraries, museums, and parks, and our government servants—from ambassador to page boy—have stagnated or even deteriorated. According to this argument, our affluence in consumer goods is sufficient to support a good living standard for everyone with tremendous productive capacity to spare. Therefore, more resources should be devoted to the public sectors of the economy.[8]

If we decide that government spending should absorb a larger share of gross national product, either because private spending grows too slowly or because we want our rising standard of living to consist of a greater share of public services, then public works spending will become our avenue to full employment.

PUBLIC WORKS SPENDING

The third avenue to full employment involves the direct employment of workers in projects deemed to be of public value. It contrasts with other government spending in that the government plans and supervises all production on the project rather than purchasing already finished goods. The government may act as the direct employer, placing the workers on public payrolls, or it may contract for the work to be done

[8] One of the most outstanding proponents of this argument is the Harvard professor of economics, John Kenneth Galbraith. His book, *The Affluent Society* (Boston: Houghton Mifflin, 1958), attracted wide attention, even outside of academic circles,

according to its specifications. The latter approach is the more usual in this country.

Public works projects include public construction (highways, schools, hospitals, dams), development of natural resources (land reclamation, national forests, river and harbor development, basic research in utilization of natural resources), and development of national parks and recreational facilities. Generally, these are projects which do not offer a sufficiently high rate of profit to attract private investment. In other cases the projects are publicly owned and operated in order to avoid a nuisance, as in separate toll payments for all streets and highways, or in order to promote more equal opportunity, e.g., free education. The choice of projects should not depend on which provides the greatest monetary return, but rather on which provides the greatest social value, a concept not easily measured by the price system. Further, in selecting the projects, the potential income and employment effects may influence the decision. More is said on this subject in a subsequent section, "Tailoring Public Works to the Existing Unemployment." Public works need not involve useless make-work projects, or inefficient allocation of labor, even though this has been the case during widespread unemployment in the past.

If the avenue to full employment is that of public works spending, an increase in unionization would probably follow, because large construction projects would be built mainly by unionized firms under union wage rates and working conditions established according to the Davis-Bacon Act. To the extent that these projects are built in previously nonunion geographical areas, the influence of unionism would spread across new frontiers.

Whenever the government increases its spending with the primary purpose of raising income and employment, public works projects are given much consideration because they provide jobs directly for unemployed workers. The increase in government spending, of course, has a multiplier effect on total spending. The projects have the political advantage of being tangible and providing lasting benefits to a legislator's constituents, and a dedicatory ceremony can be the happy occasion for campaign oratory. However, there are a number of disadvantages inherent in using public works spending as the avenue to full employment.

Difficulties in Planning

Many of the difficulties associated with public works projects as a technique for increasing government spending are the result of the time required for planning and preparation before the spending can actually take place. It is not possible to begin the large-scale spending with its consequent increase in employment until these early stages have been completed. Most projects involve some type of construction. As a minimum the following steps would be necessary before the construction could actually begin: A decision must be made as to what to build and where to build, the architect's plans must be prepared, the geographical location must be surveyed, the land must be purchased, which may involve condemnation proceedings running through the courts, and then finally all is ready for the actual construction—the actual spending of money. The preliminary steps may involve two or three years, and in some cases even longer. By the time construction workers are actually employed, the depression may have become worse—because of the delay in spending—and thus require much more substantial kinds of projects to eliminate unemployment. Or the depression which the public works were designed to counteract may be a thing of the past, and the economy may be faced with an inflationary level of spending. Furthermore, many public works projects cannot be stopped half-way through: a highway cannot be stopped in the middle of a corn field, and a hospital cannot be left standing as a mere steel skeleton. Hence, the timing of public works spending—both its beginning and its termination—is not easily adjusted to variations in employment.

The remedy for these difficulties may seem obvious: make all the plans in advance and put them into operation at the time of substantial unemployment. However, this is not so simple as it may seem. It is true that construction plans can be kept on file; however, it is necessary that these plans be up-to-date. That is, an architect's plans for a hospital may be adequate for one point in time but may not take into account recent medical research if the same plans are used five years later. The plans must be up-to-date politically as well as economically; they must be satisfactory to the legislators currently in office. Nevertheless, a revolving file of plans, architect's specifications, and surveying information would aid in shortening the preliminary time period.

Our discussion of public works as a technique for counteracting unemployment has overemphasized its clumsiness. As a matter of fact, the time-lag problem can be met effectively, even though it cannot be completely overcome. Billions of dollars are spent by federal, state, and local governments for major construction projects every year, regardless of the level of employment. Continual additions and improvements are necessary, in prosperity as well as depression, if our highways, schools, post offices, etc. are to keep pace with our increasing population and its movement to new geographical areas and with our rising standard of living. The problem, then, is not that of starting and stopping projects, but rather of varying the stream of spending and the consequent additions to employment. When unemployment rises, the target dates for completion of dams, hospitals, research facilities, and other construction already under way may be advanced. Payments to the contractors can be used to induce them to purchase steel, electrical equipment, etc. sooner than had been planned, and generally to acquire inventories of building supplies immediately, while many workers are out of jobs.

An indirect effect of public works which partly counteracts the timing difficulty results from businessmen's reaction to the announcement of a major spending program. In anticipation of the increased sales to the government or to the contractors who are in charge of the construction, many firms are induced to increase their rate of investment. For example, a cement maker may increase his producing facilities when he learns that a cross-state highway is to be built, or a steel warehousing firm may increase its inventories when a public housing project is announced for its community.

Even though there are genuine possibilities for varying the stream of spending on public works, some important reservations should be noted: 1) State and local agencies are responsible for the majority of government construction, and they do not—and cannot—assume the role of smoothing out economic fluctuations. If the federal government participates in the financing, it may exercise some influence over the rate at which projects are inaugurated and completed. 2) It is extremely difficult to distinguish between a small rise in unemployment which is merely a temporary dislocation in the labor market and one which is the beginning of a substantial recession. In order to be sure, it is usually necessary to wait a few months, by which time much greater efforts will be needed to counteract what turns out to be a real downward movement. 3) If projects are planned and production schedules are set in order to achieve maximum efficiency, making changes designed to bring about a favorable employment effect may lead to higher total costs—poor use of the taxpayers' money.

Tailoring Public Works to Existing Unemployment

If public works are to be most effective in increasing consumption, they should be tailored for the existing economic conditions, perhaps giving special attention to those areas where unemployment is greatest and involving those industries which are hardest hit by the depression. Detailed, up-to-date information, by geographical area, on the number of unemployed workers and their skills is available through the public employment service offices. However, since public works are mainly in the form of construction, tailoring the projects to the existing unemployment is not easily done. Construction workers may be fully employed while the rest of the economy is sagging, as was the case in 1954. When this is the situation, public works spending leads to more intensive bidding for already employed workers and is less effective in reducing joblessness. The wages of construction employees increase while those of other workers remain constant or even decline. The multiplier associated with this spending is less than it would otherwise be, since the new income is in the form of higher wages to already employed workers whose marginal propensity to consume is probably less than that of the unemployed. This may prove to be a serious barrier to the use of public works as a counter-depression measure.

If enough money is spent on public works, full employment can be secured even in the face of a severe depression. However, it may require a disproportionate expansion of the construction industry, thus upsetting the existing wage and price structure. After once securing full employment, reducing public works expenditures could then lead to unemployment in the construction industry with many overexpanded contractors going bankrupt. Thus, although public works at first appear to be a forthright and simple method of securing full employment, there is a danger of permanent distortions developing in the economy as the result of following this avenue exclusively.

Nevertheless, variations in public works spending constitute an important weapon in the arsenal for fighting unemployment. The first line of defense should be the automatic stabilizers, particularly unemployment compensation and the personal income tax, which tend to bring about deficits in depressions and surpluses in prosperity without any new legislation. The objective is accomplished with no time lag and no waiting to see if the decline in economic activity is only for a few weeks or is a real recession. But automatic stabilizers only moderate the swings in employment; they do not have the extra kick necessary to lift us out of a depression. Unemployment compensation could be improved on this score (as described in Chapter 20), but the point would still hold. Therefore, as a second line of defense, discretionary changes in fiscal policy are likely to be needed from time to time, including Congressional and Presidential action to speed up orders for military equipment and public works. If we want our over-all pattern of economic growth to give relatively more emphasis to the public sectors, then government construction projects become the appropriate avenue for boosting us out of recessions.

SUMMARY

The level of employment depends on the amount of total spending, which may be divided into four components: consumption, investment, government, and net foreign spending. Thus a number of avenues may be followed toward a full employment level of spending. Through the appropriate public policy, increases may be encouraged in any one of these components, or a combination of them.

If the avenue of high consumption spending is selected, it may be indirectly encouraged by broadening and liberalizing economic security programs or directly promoted through a fiscal policy which includes reducing the personal income tax and reducing excise taxes on consumption goods. High investment spending may be chosen as the avenue to full employment and promoted through tax concessions to business or by government purchases of finished goods.

The government may directly expand total spending by engaging in public works projects. But since they require much planning and preparation, it is difficult to time them exactly to counteract variations in employment. Furthermore, since they involve mainly the construction industry, if there is relatively little unemployment in that industry, expanding public works spending may bring distortions in the wage and price structure. In spite of these difficulties, public works remain as a popular remedy for substantial unemployment, particularly if it continues after automatic stabilizers have done all they can do.

If private consumption and investment expenditures are not sufficient to provide a full employment level of spending, the government, primarily through its fiscal policy, can stimulate higher levels of spending. In accordance with what is deemed to be appropriate policy, which is, of course, a political decision, the government may promote greater consumption or investment spending, or engage in public works projects, or it may combine these different approaches. However, even after full employment is achieved, not all economic problems are solved. Although full employment is one of the most important social goals, there are others, including, near the top of the list, a stable economy. Some of the tensions which may develop under full employment and threaten the stability of the economic system grow out of collective bargaining.

Hence, political pressures may arise demanding modifications in the institution of collective bargainng. These problems constitute our next topic.

DISCUSSION QUESTIONS

1. A 10 per cent rise in total spending would lead to a 10 per cent increase in employment. What is the reasoning behind this statement? What reservations do you have concerning its accuracy?

2. What is the relationship between changes in investment spending and changes in employment?

3. "Our economy need never again suffer any large amount of unemployment, since it is possible to avoid this catastrophe through wise fiscal policies." Critically appraise this statement.

4. Compare a fiscal policy designed to encourage full employment through high consumption spending with one emphasizing high investment.

5. Compare the effects on union growth of achieving full employment through high consumption spending with the effects through high investment spending.

6. What is public works spending? In what sense are its employment effects similar to those of private investment?

7. Explain why public works spending is an awkward and sometimes dangerous technique to use for securing full employment.

8. If you had the responsibility for designing a public works program to eliminate unemployment, what factors would you take into consideration? What is the significance of each of these factors to the proper design of a public works program?

BIBLIOGRAPHY

Annual Economic Reports of the President.

Beveridge, William H. *Full Employment in a Free Society*. New York: W. W. Norton & Co., 1945.

Dillard, Dudley. *The Economics of John Maynard Keynes*. New York: Prentice-Hall, 1948.

Hansen, Alvin H. *Economic Policy and Full Employment*. New York: McGraw-Hill Book Co., 1947.

————. *Fiscal Policy and Business Cycles*. New York: W. W. Norton & Co., 1941.

Hearings, Reports, and Study Papers of the Joint Economic Committee.

Lerner, Abba P. *Economics of Employment*. New York: McGraw-Hill Book Co., 1951.

Musgrave, Richard. *Theory of Public Finance.* New York: McGraw-Hill Book Co., 1959.

Oxford University Institute of Statistics. *The Economics of Full Employment.* (Six Studies.) Oxford: Basil Blackwell, 1944.

23

COLLECTIVE BARGAINING IN
A FULL EMPLOYMENT ECONOMY

In the previous chapter it was argued that full employment can be maintained in a free enterprise economy, with the aid of the taxing and spending powers of the government. Thus, one of the major sources of economic insecurity can be largely eliminated for the majority of workers. However, a full employment economy is not necessarily the best of all possible worlds. There may be excessive inequality in the distribution of income. The price system may not be allocating resources in accordance with consumers' preferences. The economy may be growing too slowly or too rapidly. It may suffer from erratic movements of the price level, or from continual inflation. Any one or a number of these conditions could exist along with full employment.

What might cause these undesirable characteristics to develop in a full employment economy? Some of the potential causes are: inappropriate spending or taxing by the government, a misguided monetary policy, substantial and unchallenged monopoly power in the hands of a small number of firms, immobility of labor or capital, the drying up of important natural resources, a sudden shift in the balance of international trade, or unwise union policies with respect to wages and/or restriction of output.

In this chapter our attention is focused on union operations under full employment conditions. Do unions create pressures leading to instability in a full employment economy? Do they press for bargaining advantages that make the guarantee of full employment untenable? Or

517

does our economic system possess safeguards against the possibility that collective bargaining will create instability? If not, can such safeguards be found?

The answers to these questions depend on the bargaining pressures that unions are willing and able to exert, and the wage and non-wage goals which they seek. The extent of their bargaining power is partly determined by whether full employment means never more than two million unemployed, or never more than six million unemployed, or is given some other definition. Likewise, the counter-pressures stemming from employers and government depend on the employment goal sought through public policy. Therefore, in considering the role of unions in a full employment economy, we begin with an examination of possible government policies with respect to full employment.

PUBLIC POLICY AND FULL EMPLOYMENT

Of all public policy goals in the field of economics, full employment is probably the one with the greatest political appeal, but as a policy goal it is a vague concept that requires clarification. Recalling our discussion of Chapter 19, there will always be some irreducible minimum of unemployment because seasonal and frictional factors will never be completely eliminated and because consumers constantly change their tastes.

The crucial policy question thus becomes: What is the level of unemployment at which the federal government should institute vigorous expansionary policies? Although neither the executive nor legislative branches of the governemnt has ever authoritatively answered this question, possibilities are found in the full employment goals proposed by two eminent economists who have had some influence on government policy. Professor Alvin Hansen's proposed goal, after making allowances for imperfections in the labor market, is 95 to 96 per cent of the labor force employed.[1] Full employment with a labor force of 70 million could mean as many as 3.5 million unemployed at any one time. If the average duration of unemployment is five weeks, 35 million workers would be moving into and out of unemployment in one year. This would provide a substantial amount of mobility in a growing and changing economy, even though much of this unemployment would be concentrated among a relatively small number of workers.

Another full employment goal, suggested by Sir William Beveridge,

[1] Alvin H. Hansen, *Economic Policy and Full Employment* (New York: McGraw-Hill Book Company, 1947), pp. 107–8.

is "more vacant jobs than unemployed men . . ." with the jobs "at fair wages, of such a kind, and so located that the unemployed men can reasonably be expected to take them. . . ." [2] Again, this proposed goal includes some unemployment, but of very short duration and with very little pressure on the worker to move to a new occupation or to a geographical area which is expanding economically. Thus, the labor market would always be a seller's market.

Probably neither of these goals will be adopted as public policy, but much more likely is some sort of sliding concept of full employment. For example, four million may be tentatively taken as the maximum permissible amount of unemployment. However, if upward pressures on the price level are too great, partly as a result of union bargaining power, a less ambitious goal may be sought. The goal will probably not be set according to some complex formula based on the interplay between employment, income, and the price level, but will be primarily a political decision. Nevertheless, this economic interplay will be an important determinant of the politics of the decision.

The purpose of this section is to provide us with a basis for discussing the operation of a full employment economy. If the most politically acceptable goal is a sliding concept, how do we have anything specific to discuss? In order to meet this difficulty, we will adopt alternative goals: one approaching that of Beveridge and arbitrarily calling that a maximum of two million unemployed, and the second, somewhat less rigorous than Hansen's, allowing as many as six million unemployed before vigorous government action is taken.[3]

Six million unemployed may seem too high to be given the title of a full employment goal. It is suggested only as an extreme position with no recommendation that it be accepted as an appropriately low full employment goal. The reader may prefer to set the goal at five million or four million. However, in the recession of 1958, unemployment exceeded five million, yet the federal government did not reduce income taxes in spite of recommendations by many prominent economists and legislators. Hence, it may be argued that unemployment of six million is considered a tolerable level by some government officials, particularly if it is expected to last only a few months and if it is believed that inflationary pressures are lurking in the background.

Within the meaning of the concept of high full employment in a

[2] William H. Beveridge, *Full Employment in a Free Society* (New York: W. W. Norton & Company, 1945), p. 18.

[3] For a similar proposal, see Abba P. Lerner, *Economics of Employment* (New York: McGraw-Hill Book Company, 1951), pp. 191–208.

dynamic economy, there would still be some firms reducing their work force and others going out of business entirely. The difference between the two goals can be expressed in terms of the length of time required for an unemployed worker to find a new job. High full employment is more desirable for the economy since it means less hardship for individual workers, greater total production, and probably more rapid economic growth, *unless* high full employment breeds intolerable inflationary pressures.

As social customs change with the passage of time, we may substantially alter our notions of an appropriate full employment goal. Changes in the public's attitude toward female participation in the labor force or toward the socially acceptable ages for entering and leaving the labor force would affect the full employment goal, since much of the unemployment is concentrated among the youngest and oldest workers.

COMPATIBILITY OF FULL EMPLOYMENT, FREE COLLECTIVE BARGAINING, AND A STABLE PRICE LEVEL

Some economists have argued that full employment, unrestricted collective bargaining, and a stable price level are incompatible.[4] According to this argument, it is possible to obtain any two of them at one time, but not all three. Unrestricted collective bargaining means an absence of government control over the agreements reached by unions and management. The two parties are free to exercise their bargaining power as they see fit, to set whatever wages and working conditions they find mutually satisfactory. A stable price level means that the average of all prices, as measured by an index number, such as the Consumers' Price Index, changes very little and within a narrow range, showing no persistent tendency to change in the same direction. It does not mean that all prices are absolutely rigid; individual prices might vary considerably. However, there should be no continuing inflationary or deflationary trends in the general price level.

The question is this: With full employment and no restrictions on collective bargaining, will unions, through their bargaining pressure, create an irresistible inflationary bias in the price system? Will wage increases be greater than the economy can absorb without a continually

[4] To cite just a few examples: Charles E. Lindblom, *Unions and Capitalism* (New Haven: Yale University Press, 1949); David McCord Wright (editor), *The Impact of the Union* (New York: Harcourt, Brace and Company, 1951); Henry Simons, "Some Reflections on Syndicalism," *Journal of Political Economy*, LII (March, 1944), pp. 1–25.

rising price level? Will we be forced to give up free collective bargaining or full employment in order to have price stability? Perhaps we will have to settle for the less desirable of the two definitions of full employment. The first step in answering this question is to consider the inflationary pressures exerted by unions.

Inflationary Pressures of Unions

For many reasons the bargaining power of unions is greater under conditions of full employment. With rising consumer incomes, there is a growing demand for the employer's product. Therefore, he offers less resistance to demands for wage increases since he can raise his prices with little reduction in the number of units sold. Strikes are more likely to be successful because they will entail permanent loss of sales for the employer and because strike-breakers cannot be recruited from the ranks of the unemployed. Furthermore, the employer may voluntarily increase wages in order to be in a better competitive position to attract workers in a tight labor market.

With this increased bargaining power, unions are able to push up wages. In fact, the members may exert unusually great pressure on their leaders to push for higher wages since they are aware of the employer's increased profits and are likely to have a grandiose view of their future living standards. Thus, the employer's cost of production rises. Unions might also use their greater power to enforce more rigid working rules and to resist technological changes, and thereby further increase costs. To the extent that collective bargaining covers the entire product market, these tactics of unions are more likely to be successful. Since each firm in the industry is making roughly the same concessions, no single firm suffers a competitive disadvantage. An important qualification must be made on this argument. With their employment security at a high level, unions may be less likely to insist on featherbedding practices or to hinder technological change.

The increased wage would mean increased income to union members and hence greater purchasing power exerting an upward pressure on prices. Furthermore, nonunion employers would then be subject to sympathetic pressure to raise wages from fear of losing employees or having their plants unionized. As soon as these forces culminate in an increase in the price level, unions have new ammunition for the next bargaining sessions. Thus, union wage pressures introduce an inflationary bias into the price system, both by raising the cost of production and by increasing the demand for goods and services.

The argument up to this point has been stated in strong terms. It does not follow that price increases will be directly proportional to wage increases. If the wage increases are granted only to union members, less than half of all workers will be receiving larger money earnings. Or, if all workers receive some increase in pay, as is more likely under conditions of full employment, this does not mean an equal rise in income for everyone else in the economy. Incomes from rents may not increase as much as wages and salaries, particularly in the short run. Incomes from interest and annuities almost certainly would not enjoy commensurate improvements. Hence, the total increase in income would not be proportionately as large as the increase in wages—there would be a redistribution of income in favor of labor. Profit incomes would probably increase, perhaps proportionately as much as or more than wage income. This is generally the case in periods of rising prices. Thus, it is quite possible that wages and profits would gain at the expense of interest payments and rents, with prices rising proportionately less than wages.

In an earlier discussion, concerning the impact of unions on wage rates, we concluded that it is not clear whether organized workers receive higher wages than unorganized as a consequence of union bargaining power. The question receiving our attention here is somewhat different. Even if it is true that union members do not gain a wage advantage, collective bargaining may introduce an upward bias in the general level of wages. That is, if sympathetic pressures on nonunion employers are very strong, they may push up their wage rates to correspond with those of organized firms. If the high full employment goal is the one sought through public policy, then these sympathetic pressures may be irresistible. Even at the lower goal, nonunion employers would probably be subject to some degree of sympathetic pressure. Therefore, even though the wages of union members were rising no faster than those of nonunion workers, the entire wage level may be rising faster than it otherwise would, because of the influence of collective bargaining.

The argument has been unfolded in terms of unions as they are now constituted, with their present aims and tactics. The consequences of collective bargaining would be different—perhaps less inflationary—if wages were determined by one grand national wage agreement, as is done in Sweden. Or greater restraint might be exhibited with a labor government and the unions more directly responsible for the operation of the entire economy, as in England following World War II. Under the prevailing collective bargaining conditions in the United States, restraint on the part of unions is not to be expected. The success of the labor leader—even his very position—depends on his ability to deliver benefits to the workers, not stability to the entire economy. Each union is free to pursue its own wage and bargaining policies, even to the point of competing with other unions over which can win the largest wage increase. No one union leader can afford to appear to be doing less well than other union leaders, on penalty of losing his job at the next election.

One leading analyst of the impact of unions on the economy, Charles Lindblom, believes that with full employment, the wage policies of unions constitute "the great labor problem of our time. Unionism is destroying the competitive price system." Lindblom argues that union policies and union power are a source of inflationary pressure which cannot be restrained without substantially altering the institution of collective bargaining. The American economy "cannot produce high output and employment at union wage rates. Nor can the economy survive the unions' systematic disorganization of markets and its persistent undercutting of managerial authority." [5] Although this is certainly one of the great labor problems of our time, there are many reasons for being less pessimistic about its resolution. Unions are not all-powerful. There are many pressures in opposition to their upward pressure on wages, some of these growing out of the union movement itself.

Counteracting Pressures

The pressures which counteract union bargaining power in a full employment economy come from many sources. The most obvious is employer resistance to union demands. Not only is this the initial source of counteracting pressure, it is also the vehicle through which the others are exerted. Downward pressure may also be applied by the government with the use of its fiscal and monetary powers. The most desirable approach to counteracting a rising wage level is through increasing productivity equally fast. Finally, the unions themselves provide some of the counteracting pressure by dissipating part of their bargaining power through non-wage demands. This, of course, is not a complete list of all potential deflationary pressures, but it includes those most likely to counteract directly the inflationary potential of union wage demands in a full employment economy.

Employer Resistance

The key to an employer's resistance to union wage demands is their impact on his anticipated profits. Full employment not only provides greater security to the workers but also higher profits to the employer.

[5] Lindblom, *op. cit.*, pp. 4–5.

Hence, he need not fear the elimination of his profits as wages increase, since generally rising purchasing power will be sufficient to absorb his price increases. In fact, the wage increase gives him an excuse to raise his prices and "profiteer" in a favorable market. With the spread of industry-wide and pattern bargaining, the employer no longer has to fear that his competitors will be able to undersell him. Thus, in a full employment economy, the resistance of most employers tends to be modest, in some cases only a sham.

Those firms which are well entrenched in their industries may actually encourage a high wage rate, since it may improve their competitive position. The high wages may drive the marginal firms, often those with less capital equipment and less efficiency as producing units, into bankruptcy. Since they are often tempted to engage in price wars, particularly in industries where marginal costs are low relative to average costs, or may threaten the dominant position of the leading firms, the latter may be more than happy to use the union and its wage demands as a device for driving the marginal firms from the industry. The same technique prevents potential competitors from entering the industry. This device may be developed to the stage of outright collusion between the employer and the union in an effort to maintain high wages and high prices with the union acting as a policeman to prevent "cut-throat competitive practices."

One possible restriction on the bargaining power of a union is inter-industrial competition. If the union attempts to push up wages in an industry whose product is being displaced by that of another industry, the increased cost of production may be enough to tip the scales against the industry under union pressure. As an illustration, higher wages in the coal industry may increase the pace at which oil and natural gas are substituted for coal. However, the impact of this counteracting pressure is sharply reduced when key bargaining agreements exert their effect across industry lines. For example, a bargain reached in the steel industry may be more or less duplicated in the aluminum industry and in other industries competitive with steel, thus causing little or no loss in employment or profits in the steel industry. It should be noted, however, that if labor costs are a much lower fraction of total costs in one industry than the other, interindustrial competition will exert a coercive effect in spite of pattern bargaining. Even where it is of some consequence, interindustrial competition is often too remote to be observed by the union and taken into account in its bargaining policies.

The resistance of employers to union wage demands, then, varies from firm to firm and from industry to industry; in some instances it is very strong and in others almost zero. Where employers are weak or prefer not to resist union demands, wages may be pushed too high; where employers are strong, two monopolies are facing each other. And two monopolies are not necessarily better than one; they may not counteract each other's power.

Deliberate collusion may take place between the two monopoly groups to exploit the public. Industry-wide bargaining, however, itself is sufficient for this purpose. The employers simply pass increased wage rates on in the form of higher prices, their own monopoly power being strengthened by the union's having taken wage rates out of competition.[6]

The above paragraphs imply that employers are largely unable or unwilling to resist union demands in a full employment economy. They feel that with continued high profit anticipations, resistance would be foolish if it meant a strike with its consequent dislocations in the product market. Although this may be true for the majority of employers, there will be many who must either effectively resist the unions or be forced into bankruptcy. Declining industries or less efficient firms fall into this category, such as the New England textile firms during the 1950's. In fact, any industry which is expanding at a rate slower than the general economy may be compelled to be more resistant to the union demands. In a dynamic economy, workers should be moving away from such firms. Wage differentials would perform a useful function if they encouraged a desirable degree of mobility, even though they might cause some instability in the price system at the same time.

Fiscal Policy

If employers refuse to resist union wage demands because their profit anticipations are so favorable, what can the government do, through its fiscal policy, to counteract the inflationary pressure? There is no doubt that fiscal policy is a sufficiently potent weapon to do the trick. Taxes can be sharply increased and expenditures drastically reduced, thus withdrawing enough purchasing power from the market to prevent the price level from rising. But will the government be willing to exercise such powerful restrictions? Will it be willing to cause some unemployment with its political consequences, in order to counteract inflationary pressure?

There will certainly be powerful interest groups opposed to the use of such restrictions. Unions will not be anxious for the government to

[6] *Ibid.*, p. 224.

exert pressure aimed at reducing their ability to win wage increases, especially when the consequence might be unemployment. Employers, anxious to maintain favorable markets for their products, will likewise lobby against restrictive fiscal policy. At this point the full employment goal adopted by the government is decisive. If the government should decide, for example, to consider any unemployment beyond two million to be serious and require an increase in spending and/or a reduction in taxes until such unemployment is eliminated, the inflationary pressures may be irrresistible. On the other hand, if the less ambitious full employment goal is adopted, the inflationary pressures would be substantially less, perhaps negligible.

One possible result of a government guarantee of full employment, maintained together with protection of free collective bargaining, is an upward movement of the price level accomplished not by equal percentage amounts each year, but rather by irregular fits and starts. That is, during periods of what might otherwise be a recession, the price level would remain stable while the government was increasing its spending relative to its taxing. In the intervening boom periods, the price level would move up. The end result would be a long-run inflationary bias in the price level, but in any given year the price level might be temporarily stable, or at least not sufficiently predictable as to cause people to count on cheap money in making their spending and savings plans. This type of price rise tends to corrode savings, annuities, and pensions over the long run, but is less likely to lead to a devastating runaway inflation than a steady, predictable upward movement in the price level. The latter type, although at first appearing to be only a few percentage points each year, leads to anticipatory spending by both consumers and businessmen and hence builds up to a crescendo, eventually getting out of control.

To avoid either of these types of inflation, the government may attack the problem through squeezing profit anticipations. By withdrawing sufficient purchasing power through borrowing (without spending) or taxing—perhaps even through a sales tax—the sales and profits of business firms would be reduced. This would make it more difficult for business firms to increase prices and would therefore stiffen their resistance to union wage demands. Union leaders, sensing this greater resistance, would be forced to moderate their demands, or else face long—and perhaps unsuccessful—strikes.

The crux of the wage-price problem in a full employment economy, then, centers on adequate employer resistance, and the union response to it; but it should be emphasized that promoting employer resistance involves running the risk of a larger amount of unemployment. If the federal budget-makers insist on full employment, but are unwilling to squeeze profits, assuming the risk of a possible increase in unemployment when necessary, then some degree of inflation is inevitable. If the profit squeeze does not produce adequate employer resistance, then, again, inflation is inevitable. But if employer resistance prevents the key bargaining agreements—the precedent setters—from rising to inflationary proportions, price stability may be achieved.

Since collective bargaining is at the center of the stage in preserving price stability in a full employment economy, should not pressure be put on unions as well as on profit expectations? Why not attach some importance to the role of responsible union leaders voluntarily following statesman-like policies and moderating their wage demands for the sake of a stable economy? After all, there is no gain in real wages when money wage increases lead to proportional price increases. A reiteration of a point made earlier is necessary here. Since collective bargaining takes place on a piecemeal basis, union leaders cannot individually engage in this type of statesmanship, laudable as it may be. If a union leader appeared to his constituents to be doing less well than leaders of rival unions, his tenure in office would be brought to an abrupt end. Thus, the pressure of fiscal policy must be aimed at squeezing profits— not at unions directly—if it is to counteract inflation. This argument is based on the assumption that free collective bargaining is to be maintained and that the government is not going to exercise price and wage controls. Although it is difficult to regulate union wage demands, given the nature of collective bargaining, the government could attack the problem by directly entering the bargaining processes. This is discussed in the next chapter.

The route followed to full employment is important in determining the specific techniques to be used to put the squeeze on profits. If consumption spending has been increasing at a rate which is considered to be too rapid, sales taxes or less progressive income tax rates may be the appropriate remedy. If investment spending appears to be the culprit, then reliance on more progressive income taxes or corporate profits taxes may be the correct prescription. If government spending has been rising too rapidly, perhaps to offset a previous tendency toward unemployment, then reduce that. However, no matter which road is deemed to be proper for counteracting inflationary pressures, it will require courageous political decisions. At this stage of the analysis, we are not prepared to say whether this type of fiscal policy is capable of providing stability with the more ambitious of the two definitions of full employment.

Monetary Policy

In our economy the Treasury and the Federal Reserve System act as the monetary authorities, controlling the supply of money. By causing money to be scarce and expensive, they erect a significant barrier to an inflationary rise in prices. Conversely, an inflation feeds on abundant and cheap money. Notice that again the squeeze is initially placed on profit expectations. Reducing the money supply and thereby reducing purchasing power would tend to cause employers to resist union wage demands that compel price increases. Sole reliance on monetary policy for restricting inflationary movements in the price level would probably not be effective—except at excessively high interest rates—particularly after the inflation has gathered much momentum. However, used in harmony with fiscal policy, changes in money and credit conditions have a substantial impact on profit expectations. Since its objective and approach parallel that of fiscal policy, monetary policy need not be discussed further.

Increased Productivity

The crucial question with respect to a potential inflation is: Will the output of goods and services rise as rapidly as spending? Expressing the question differently, will new technology and expansion of production facilities be forthcoming at a rate that matches the growth of money incomes? The most desirable offset to increases in spending, induced by continued full employment, is increasing total production. Up to this point, we have discussed methods of slowing the rise in total spending. Turning from the demand side to the supply side, what determines the rate of growth of per-capita output? Assuming a constant work-week and a constant ratio of labor force to total population, the answer is productivity, output per manhour. In recent years, productivity has increased at a rate of 2.5 to 3.0 per cent annually, varying substantially from year to year and from industry to industry. Wage increases of an amount proportionately equal to productivity increases would not be inflationary. An increase in wages of a greater amount would either bring about a redistribution of income in favor of wage earners or would tend to be inflationary.

Collective bargaining, as it is presently conducted, is not designed to adjust wage increases in exact proportion to productivity increases.

Nevertheless, collective bargaining is variously affected by such changes, depending on their nature. Improvements in productivity may come about as a result of greater effort on the part of the workers, shifts of labor from less efficient to more efficient lines of trade, better quality in raw materials, and innovations in production technique. Collective bargaining interacts with the first of these methods of improving productivity through its relation to the morale of workers and the controls it exercises over job assignment and rate of work. The second method of improvement is related to the unions' influence over the wage structure and other inducements for changing jobs. The avenue followed to full employment is particularly important here. If the avenue followed places emphasis on those industries exhibiting greatest gains in productivity and thereby allocates a larger part of the labor force to more efficient production, the inflationary pressures on the price level would be reduced. That is, even though wages may be higher in these industries, labor costs per unit of output may be declining because of increases in productivity. The third method is of no consequence here since unions have little influence over the quality of raw materials.

Innovations, the fourth method of raising the level of productivity, provide the most decisive interaction between collective bargaining and productivity changes. Innovations which are labor-saving—substituting capital for labor—tend to reduce the bargaining power of unions unless the demand for the product is very elastic. Efforts of unions to interfere with the adoption of such techniques have been discussed earlier. Innovations which reduce costs and increase profits without replacing labor tend to increase union bargaining power. Innovations leading to new products tend to raise the total demand for labor, unless they replace products having higher per unit labor requirements.

In a dynamically changing economy, new products and new techniques of production are constantly driving out the old and entrenched. Will this happen in a manner which prevents free collective bargaining from pushing wages too high? There are reasons for believing that it might. Many technological changes are of the type which reduce labor requirements per unit of output. The higher the wage, the greater the stimulus to make such changes. As the wage of a given group of workers increases, the pressure to use substitutes for them increases. The substitute may be either in the form of a new production technique (labor-saving innovation) or a new product (interindustrial competition).

What is the effect of continued full employment on the rate of increase in productivity? Although the answer to this is speculative, it appears that the effect should be favorable. Workers and unions may be more willing to give up restrictive practices designed to stretch out the job. Workers may become more willing to give up their seniority and leave low-paying, low-efficiency industries, thus leading to a more productive allocation of the labor force. With the economy operating at a high level, individual firms are more likely to be operating at or near their rated capacity, and hence at lower costs per unit of output, and any increase in sales would require the construction of new (modern and efficient) plant and equipment. Employers, knowing that the bottom will not fall out of their markets, may be more willing to make long-range investments in labor-saving equipment. In fact, being able to count on a long-run rise in demand, with only occasional and brief slack periods, business firms have a potent inducement to make continual improvements in their production facilities. There is, then, reason to be optimistic that the rate of gain in productivity will be sufficient to raise output proportional to the increase in spending.

However, there are also some reasons for pessimism about the effects of full employment on productivity. The employment of inefficient workers, who might otherwise be without jobs, contributes to reductions in output per manhour. Inefficient firms are more likely to find a market for their products, since purchasing power is at a high level. An additional reason for pessimism is that developing and putting into use substitutes for labor is a long-run process. The demand for labor in the short run may be very inelastic, thus giving unions opportunities to make wage gains which become permanently ingrained in the economy. Furthermore, a technological change requiring substantial investment may be hindered by high wages or uncertainty about future wage increases. But with guaranteed full employment, which implies substantial product demand, a labor-saving technique is not likely to be cast aside, particularly under conditions of high wages, even with some degree of uncertainty about future wage levels. In fact, the high wages may have a "shock effect" on otherwise inefficient firms, causing them to adopt labor-saving innovations.

In short, high wages stimulate technological change. At the same time, technological change makes possible high wages and living standards. Whether the rising level of productivity will be sufficient to offset rising wages is not at all certain, particularly if the more rigorous of the two definitions of full employment is adopted. Therefore, it is necessary for the federal government to be prepared to use its fiscal and monetary powers to squeeze profit expectations.

Union Non-Wage Bargaining

Unions are much more than wage bargaining institutions. To the extent that they use up part of their bargaining power to secure such non-wage goals as union security, seniority provisions, and grievance procedures, inflationary pressure is reduced. However, once unions have been recognized and are secure in their position, less of their efforts are needed for some of these non-wage goals. The union may then more vigorously press wage demands, which employers may be inclined to grant rather than give up management prerogatives.

As described earlier, unions have placed a great deal of emphasis on economic security programs since World War II. Although non-wage demands, they are really delayed wage increases. That is, the money that the employer sets aside for the pension plan eventually accrues to the worker. However, it does not represent an increase in the current income of the worker and hence does not lead to an immediate increase in his purchasing power. Nevertheless, it does represent an increase in labor costs and therefore has a limited inflationary impact. When upward pressures on the price level are severe, this use of bargaining power is less destabilizing than a direct wage increase.

As productivity continues to rise, unions and workers may choose to use part of their bargaining power to win reductions in working time. Certainly, this is not an irrational way to attain and enjoy a higher living standard. It may be in the form of shorter work days, three or four-day weekends, more holidays, one or two-month paid vacations to resort areas built and furnished by the employer, or any of a number of other possibilities. Such demands are similar to economic security programs in that they raise the cost of production but do not directly add to the purchasing power of the workers.

The trend toward writing long-term contracts, if it continues, will bring some stability in the rate of wage increase. This does not necessarily mean that the wage increase will be the proper amount from the point of view of combating inflation. Nevertheless, the long-term contracts permit longer-range investment planning and thereby have the effect of increasing productivity. Furthermore, by giving greater predictability to the rate of increase in wages, they aid government policy-makers in developing plans to counteract whatever inflationary tendencies may exist.

Price and Wage Distortions

Since unions dissipate a portion of their bargaining power on non-wage demands, their inflationary potential in a full employment economy is less than it otherwise would be. Whatever inflationary potential they have is at least partially offset by increases in productivity. In spite of these two offsetting factors, the wage concessions they win may contribute to price instability. Employer resistance, of its own accord, cannot be expected to be a sufficiently powerful counteracting force. Therefore, the fiscal and monetary powers of the government must be mobilized for the purpose of withdrawing an appropriate amount of purchasing power from the economy, thus reducing profits and stiffening the resistance of employers.

Whether these conditions will provide price stability at the more ambitious of the two definitions of full employment depends, among other things, on how efficiently resources are allocated. That is, it depends on how quickly resources, particularly labor, shift in response to changes in consumers' demand or changes in the productivity of different industries and occupations. If workers are reluctant to move in response to changing economic opportunity, or if the inducements to mobility are inadequate, then resources will be poorly and inefficiently allocated, leading to distortions in the wage and price structure.

Distortion in the wage structure exists when pay rates (including fringe benefits) do not bring an equilibrium between the number of job openings and the number of workers willing to accept employment in those fields. The persistence of high rates in an industry or occupation that has a relatively large and continuing amount of unemployment in a period of generally full employment would be a clear sign of a distortion in the wage structure. This would tend to foster a distortion of the opposite type: an excess of workers, employed in one or more low-paying industries, who would be capable of filling jobs in the high-paying industry where output is being artificially restricted. Similarly, distortions in the price structure are in evidence when much excess capacity exists in an industry and at the same time the price of the product shows no tendency to decline. Price and wage distortions result from the presence of monopolistic elements in the market and/or inadequate mobility of capital and labor.

What is the relation of collective bargaining to the allocation of resources and price and wage distortions? Of course, distortions may appear for reasons other than collective bargaining, e.g., monopoly practices by business firms or unwise government subsidies to favored industries. Distortions grow out of collective bargaining when there is a high demand for a particular type of labor which is completely unionized. If the union in this case exploits its monopoly power to the fullest extent and at the same time prevents new workers from joining its trade, a wage distortion and a consequent price distortion are likely to appear. For the union to be successful, it would be necessary that no substitutes exist, either for labor or for the final product. That is, the union would have to be able to prevent the work from being done by other groups of workers, either inside or outside of its jurisdictional territory, and prevent it from being done by a different technological process. In an earlier chapter it was argued that a union could practice this type of monopoly restriction over the long run only if it had the cooperation of the employers. In other words, it would be a matter of employers and unions combining to restrict competition, forcing high prices and thus winning high wages and high profits.

Distortions involving restrictions on labor supply occur only where unions have considerable control over entrance into the trade. The construction unions, some of which fall into this category, have frequently been accused of distorting the wage structure. And there is no doubt but that they have actually done so, in at least a few metropolitan areas. However, their restrictive practices tend to be less rigid when nearly all their members are employed. For example, an out-of-town contractor generally has more freedom to bring in his own employees if the level of construction employment is very high in the local area.[7] Hence, a continuing full employment economy might tend to reduce monopoly pressures stemming from construction unions.

Collective bargaining may contribute to another source of wage-price distortion if it prevents resources from shifting as rapidly as changing consumers' tastes would dictate. To the extent that labor is immobile, expanding industries are forced to offer continually rising wages in order to attract additional workers, leading to abnormally high wages and high prices in industries which would otherwise be expanding output at a more rapid pace. Collective bargaining is responsible for immobility if it ties the worker to his job and his union. There may be an increasing degree of immobility if there is a continued expansion in collectively bargained pensions, supplementary unemployment benefits, health and welfare plans, etc. Shifting to new jobs may entail the loss of thousands of dollars' worth of insurance rights.

What is the relation of these price and wage distortions to maintaining stability in a full employment economy? Are they insignificant ripples on the price level, or do they tend to build up to an inflationary fire?

[7] George Strauss, *Unions in the Building Trades* (Buffalo: University of Buffalo Press, 1958).

If some unions, perhaps only a few, are able to win very large wage concessions because of their strong bargaining position, this may be sufficient to upset the entire economy. If these abnormal pay rates are won by unions which set the precedent for the pattern bargaining of that time period, then an inflationary rise in the entire wage level may occur.

One place where a wage distortion may develop with serious inflationary potential is in industries which have made substantial gains in productivity. To illustrate, suppose there are substantial productivity improvements in manufacturing industries and very little in the rest of the economy. Unions in manufacturing now insist on sharing the cost savings proportionately with their employers, i.e., percentage wage increases equal to the percentage increase in output per manhour. Because unionization in manufacturing is relatively high, because many manufacturing industries are oligopolistic, and because full employment causes the demand for the final product to be very high, employers may grant the wage increases and therefore not pass on any of the cost savings through price reductions.

Under these circumstances, wage increases in manufacturing are proportional to increases in output per manhour. At first thought, this may seem to be an appropriate wage-productivity relationship. However, it tends to create a distortion in the wage structure because other workers of equal skill and ability, but in industries where productivity has remained unchanged, are at the moment receiving lower wage rates. With high full employment and strong sympathetic pressures, these workers would be able to win similar wage increases. Therefore, the rise in wages in manufacturing, even though offset by productivity improvements in that industry, would inaugurate a wave of inflationary pressure. Thus, inflationary forces may grow out of a distortion in the wage structure if rates in the most efficient industries are increased more than the *average* increase in productivity for the economy as a whole, and if this in turn causes wages in the remaining industries to increase a like amount.[8]

What public policy actions are available which would ward off these different types of wage-price distortions? If the distortions are the result of collusion between unions and employers, they may be attacked through antitrust prosecution. Sections of the Norris-LaGuardia Act could be

---

[8] James S. Duesenberry, "Underlying Factors in the Postwar Inflation," in Charles A. Myers (editor), *Wages, Prices, Profits and Productivity* (New York: The American Assembly, 1959), pp. 61–89.

modified to increase the possibility of prosecuting a union which has secured a monopoly position, if this is deemed necessary. The Taft-Hartley and Landrum-Griffin restrictions on jurisdictional strikes and secondary boycotts have reduced the opportunity for unions to win and exploit monopoly power. To counteract price and wage distortions growing out of immobility due to private security plans, the government should expand its social security programs.

The government may further counteract price and wage distortions through appropriate changes in fiscal policy. For example, if prices are out of line in the construction industry, spending could be reduced on public construction projects, thus creating unemployed resources. If these unemployed resources are mobile, i.e., if they move into private industrial and residential construction, the distortion would tend to be alleviated. There would then be downward pressures on wages throughout the construction industry, thus causing some workers to look for employment elsewhere. It may be appropriate for the government, in some instances, to use subsidies to encourage mobility out of stagnant or contracting industries and regions. This could include training programs and transportation allotments for workers, and tax concessions to employers to encourage the mobility of capital.

It is not being argued that the government should assume the responsibility for dictating each price in the economy. Nor should it attempt to prohibit everything which threatens to upset the existing wage-price structure; complete rigidity should not be the goal of public policy. In a free market economy, even with a stable price level, individual wages and prices are ceaselessly changing. Distortions constantly develop, and in the process of being integrated into a new wage-price structure, bring about a new allocation of resources. For example, workers employed in an industry which has made a substantially more than average gain in productivity may gain a moderately more than average wage increase and as a consequence additional workers may be attracted to the industry. In other words, shifts in the conditions of supply and demand should be the primary determinant of the allocation of resources, with direct government interference only in extreme cases. Nevertheless, in a full employment economy, waiting for price-wage distortions to take care of themselves may permit irresistible inflationary pressures to develop. If the goal is full employment with price stability, the government must be prepared to counteract serious disequilibriums in the price-wage structure if they tend to persist over long periods of time or if they are not accompanied with an appropriate reallocation of resources.

The Potential Impact on Unions

If serious price-wage distortions are avoided and resources are mobile, does this make the more ambitious of the two full employment goals attainable? An unequivocal answer cannot be given to this question, assuming that price stability is desired. A free economy does not grow at a perfectly even pace, neither in the aggregate nor in its particular parts. Consumption, investment, and government spending change irregularly and unpredictably. Therefore, the pressures on the price level will be different at different times. Perhaps the best that can be hoped for is continual fluctuation between two types of conditions: 1) price stability with the level of employment increasing toward the ambitious full employment goal, and 2) the level of employment decreasing as a consequence of public policy to counteract rising prices. Perhaps there will be plateaus between these periods with high employment and reasonably stable prices.

Fluctuating between these two conditions means inflation, not by smooth progression, but by erratic upward movements in the price level. The choice may be between this and a less ambitious full employment goal, one that would involve making unemployment painful in the sense that new jobs with attractive wage rates are not immediately available. It is quite possible that society will vacillate in its choice of goals, refusing to commit itself permanently to an extreme of absolute price stability or of high full employment.

Assuming this to be the case, what will the impact be on unions and collective bargaining? In those segments of the economy where unions are well organized, their bargaining power will be maintained at a high level because of full employment. However, they will, at various times, run head-on into strong employer resistance, the indirect product of government policy. In these instances unions will need to moderate their demands or face long strikes, perhaps even direct government sanctions. In the segments of the economy where they are weak, unions can expect to grow only at a slow rate, if at all. With full employment, employers will grant concessions to nonunion workers in nearly the same proportion as those won through collective bargaining. Hence, unorganized workers will have little to gain—at least economically—by joining a union.

Direct government sanctions may be necessary if the upward pressure on the price level is too great and employer resistance is unable or unwilling to counteract it. The public may, under these circumstances, give price stability a higher priority than free collective bargaining, still maintaining a full employment economy. If so, the government could directly interfere in collective bargaining with the intention of reducing the money gains that unions would be able to make, by establishing wage controls or requiring all major disputes to be subject to public review.

The argument made in this chapter is not that collective bargaining must, or will, be placed in shackles. Rather, collective bargaining will be affected by the continued pressure of full employment. If productivity increases so fast that inflationary pressures are mild and sporadic, then collective bargaining may continue much as it has been practiced in the past decade, with perhaps less emphasis on work rules designed to make the job last longer. But if inflationary pressures cause considerable price instability, unions and collective bargaining may be forced into a new mold, undoubtedly entailing greater government interference, which in turn would force unions into greater political activity. Some of the possible patterns of government interference will be considered in the latter half of the next chapter.

SUMMARY

One of the most serious maladies which may beset a full employment economy is price instability, and collective bargaining may be one of the important instigators. The pressures on price stability vary with the full employment goal sought through public policy, but even a modest goal places a floor under the demand for labor and enhances the bargaining power of unions. As they push up wages, inflationary pressures are introduced by two different means: rising costs and rising purchasing power. With high full employment, the wages of unorganized workers tend to rise almost proportionately to those of the organized because of sympathetic pressure. It is quite possible, then, that union wage demands will generate overwhelming inflationary pressures.

The primary counteracting pressure is employer resistance to union demands. But employer resistance may be very weak because all employers may be granting approximately the same concessions, therefore no single one of them would fear being at a competitive disadvantage. Even though potential substitutes for labor and interindustrial competition would tend to hold wages in check, in the short run the employer's demand for labor may be too inelastic for these factors to exert any important influence. Consequently, the government may have to use its fiscal and monetary powers to limit total spending, thereby making it more difficult for employers to increase prices and to stiffen their resistance to wage increases. The non-wage demands of unions also serve as a counteracting influence by using up some of their bargaining strength without making immediate additions to purchasing power.

If the average wage increase is offset by a proportionately equal increase in productivity, inflationary pressures would be held in check. Higher wages encourage labor-saving innovations and full employment provides a favorable climate for their adoption. The crucial question is: Will productivity increase rapidly enough to cause output to increase in proportion to rising wages?

The possibility of collective bargaining creating a distortion in the wage structure is one aspect of its influence on prices. If one or two unions are able to win abnormally high wages and at the same time bar entrance to their trade, the consequent price increases in this sector of the economy may act as a leader pulling up the entire price level. Another type of distortion in the wage structure may grow out of those industries which experience the greatest gains in productivity. If they are highly unionized and if the unions are successful in winning wage increases equal to the gains in productivity, then, with other unions, and also nonunion workers, demanding similar wage increases, inflationary pressures are likely to develop.

DISCUSSION QUESTIONS

1. Distinguish between high and low full employment with respect to each of the following: amount of unemployment, total amount of production, mobility of labor, and pressures on the price level.

2. Wage increases have an inflationary impact on both the supply and demand side of prices. Explain.

3. Even if unions secure a 10 per cent wage increase for their members, total consumption spending may rise by only a small fraction of that amount. Explain how this can be true.

4. If unions cannot gain a significant wage advantage for their members, how is it possible that they can generate an inflationary rise in the level of income?

5. Why is it likely that the resistance of many employers to union demands would be weak when inflationary pressures are rampant in the economy?

6. Some employers prefer a strong union and uniform high wage rates for their industry rather than an uneven wage structure determined by the

different bargaining power of each individual employer. Explain why this is so and what its relation is to the development of inflationary pressure.

7. Give two examples of interindustrial competition that restricts the bargaining power of unions even under conditions of high full employment.

8. Each industry should adjust its wage increases in accordance with its own productivity increases. To what extent do you agree with this statement? Explain.

9. If collective bargaining is the cause of price instability under full employment, government policy must be equally restrictive on the two parties: unions and management. Critically appraise this statement.

10. Explain how continued full employment may promote greater output per manhour.

11. What is the impact of non-wage bargaining on the price level?

12. Give an example, real or hypothetical, of collective bargaining upsetting the wage-price structure and thereby creating inflationary pressures.

13. Write an essay expressing your opinion on what the impact of continued full employment will be on the growth of unions.

BIBLIOGRAPHY

Beveridge, William H. *Full Employment in a Free Society.* New York: W. W. Norton & Company, 1945.

Hansen, Alvin H. *Economic Policy and Full Employment.* New York: McGraw-Hill Book Company, 1947.

Lerner, Abba P. *Economics of Employment.* New York: McGraw-Hill Book Company, 1951.

Lindblom, Charles E. "Labor Policy, Full Employment, and Inflation." Millikan, Max F. (editor). *Income Stabilization for a Developing Democracy.* New Haven: Yale University Press, 1953.

———. *Unions and Capitalism.* New Haven: Yale University Press, 1949.

Myers, Charles A. (editor). *Wages, Prices, Profits and Productivity.* New York: The American Assembly, 1959.

Samuelson, Paul A. "Full Employment versus Progress and Other Economic Goals." Millikan, Max F. (editor). *Income Stabilization for a Developing Democracy.* New Haven: Yale University Press, 1953.

U. S. Congress, Joint Economic Committee. *The Effect of Increases in Wages, Salaries, and the Price of Personal Services, Together with Union and Professional Practices upon Prices, Profits, Production and Employment.* Hearings, Part 8, Employment, Growth, and Price Levels. Washington: Government Printing Office, 1959.

Wright, David McCord (editor). *The Impact of the Union.* New York: Harcourt, Brace and Company, 1951.

24

COLLECTIVE BARGAINING IN
A FULL EMPLOYMENT ECONOMY:
THE EVIDENCE

We have examined the question of whether free collective bargaining creates irresistible inflationary pressures in a full employment economy and have found that there is no conclusive answer. In our recent history we have had some experience with the operation of collective bargaining under full employment. Will an analysis of this experience demonstrate the union impact on price stability? Unfortunately, it will not tell us enough even about that time period, much less give us a basis for accurately predicting the impact of the union under full employment conditions in the future.

Nevertheless, a survey of the period since the end of World War II is worthwhile since it illuminates some of the possible relationships between wages and prices. At least a few guides to understanding may be found. And most important, it does demonstrate that it is possible to maintain stable prices with full employment for at least a few years at a time.

RISING WAGES AND INFLATIONARY PRESSURES

The years immediately following World War II were characterized by rapidly rising wages and prices. Although price and wage controls during the war had prevented the rise from being more than 30 per cent, the "return to normalcy" brought such a large increase in demand relative to our productive capacity that prices rose by a larger amount after the war. By the end of 1951 the level of consumers' prices was nearly twice that of 1939; the dollar would buy only as much as fifty cents would buy before the war.

In Table 24-A the statistics for the postwar wage and price increases are presented. Since the statistics are in terms of annual averages, they obscure the sudden bursts by which prices increased. In order to facilitate our analysis, the figures are divided into four time periods. The dates selected for the time periods are designed to emphasize periods of price stability, except for the first one which covers the immediate postwar years. The dates could just as well have been selected to emphasize periods of inflation; however, the purpose here is to indicate the degree of price stability which has been achieved in the American economy. Since the dates have been arbitrarily selected in this manner, special precautions must be taken to avoid concluding that these statistics tell us the complete story about future relationships between collective bargaining and price levels.

1945–1947: Return to Unrestricted Collective Bargaining

The immediate aftermath of World War II was characterized by a large amount of economic confusion. After the cessation of hostilities in Europe, it had been expected that a year would be required to bring Japan to capitulation. When the surrender came in just three months, the government agencies controlling prices and wages were caught completely off-guard. Their time schedules and planning for reconversion to peace-time production and normal economic relationships were sabotaged by international peace. The Office of Price Administration and the National War Labor Board had anticipated continuing inflationary pressures and had hoped to remove controls gradually, recognizing that both prices and wages would probably shift to somewhat higher levels in the postwar era, because of the large increase in the money supply which resulted from financing the war.

After four years of controls over wages and prices—controls which were irritating to everybody concerned—it is not surprising that every economic interest group demanded its freedom. The latent industrial unrest and repressed urges to raise wages and prices exploded in the face of the government's uncertainty and delay. Wage controls were relaxed and government restrictions on strikes and lockouts were ended almost simultaneously. This was most unfortunate timing. The supposedly limited relaxation of controls opened the floodgates, and labor, management, and farmers fought individually and collectively to eliminate the last vestiges of government restrictions.

TABLE 24-A*

	Average Gross Hourly Earnings in Selected Industries					Average Gross Weekly Earnings in Selected Industries				
	Manufacturing			Building construction	Retail trade	Manufacturing			Building construction	Retail trade
	Total	Durable goods	Non-durable goods			Total	Durable goods	Non-durable goods		
1945	1.02	1.11	.90	1.38	.78	44.39	49.05	38.29	53.73	31.55
1946	1.09	1.16	1.02	1.48	.89	43.82	46.49	41.14	56.24	36.35
1947	1.24	1.29	1.17	1.68	1.01	49.97	52.46	46.96	63.30	40.66
Percentage increase 1945 to 1947	21%	16%	30%	22%	30%	13%	7%	23%	18%	29%
1948	1.35	1.41	1.28	1.85 [a]	1.09	54.14	57.11	50.61	68.85 [a]	43.85
1949	1.40	1.47	1.33	1.94	1.14	54.92	58.03	51.41	70.95	45.93
1950	1.47	1.54	1.38	2.03	1.18	59.33	63.32	54.71	73.73	47.63
Percentage increase 1948 to 1950	9%	9%	8%	10%	8%	10%	11%	8%	7%	9%
1951	1.59	1.67	1.48	2.19	1.26	64.71	69.47	58.46	81.47	50.65
1952	1.67	1.77	1.54	2.31	1.32	67.97	73.46	60.98	88.01	52.67
1953	1.77	1.87	1.61	2.48	1.40	71.69	77.23	63.60	91.76	54.88
1954	1.81	1.92	1.66	2.60	1.45	71.86	77.18	64.74	94.12	56.70
1955	1.88	2.01	1.71	2.66	1.50	76.52	83.21	68.06	96.29	58.50
Percentage increase 1952 to 1955	13%	14%	11%	15%	14%	13%	13%	12%	9%	11%
1956	1.98	2.10	1.80	2.80	1.57	79.99	86.31	71.10	101.92	60.60
1957	2.07	2.20	1.88	2.96	1.64	82.39	88.66	73.51	106.86	62.48
1958	2.13	2.28	1.94	3.10	1.70	83.50	90.06	75.27	110.67	64.77
1959	2.22 [b]	2.38 [b]	2.01 [b]	3.21 [b]	1.76 [b]	89.47 [b]	96.87 [b]	79.80 [b]	114.60 [b]	67.06 [b]
Percentage increase 1956 to 1959	12%	13%	12%	15%	12%	12%	12%	12%	12%	11%

TABLE 24-A (continued)

	Wholesale price index all commodities 1947–1949=100	Consumer price index all items 1947–1949=100	Employment (thousands of persons)	Unemployment (thousands of persons)	Unemployment as a percentage of civilian labor force	Gross national product (billions of dollars)	Personal consumption expenditures (billions of dollars)
1945	68.8	76.9	52,820	1,040	1.9	213.6	121.7
1946	78.7	83.4	55,250	2,270	3.9	210.7	147.1
1947	96.4	95.5	57,812 [a]	2,356 [a]	3.9 [a]	234.3	165.4
Percentage increase 1945 to 1947	40%	24%	. . . . .	. . . . .	. . .	10%	36%
1948	104.4	102.8	59,117	2,325	3.8	259.4	178.3
1949	99.2	101.8	58,423	3,682	5.9	258.1	181.2
1950	103.1	102.8	59,748	3,351	5.3	284.6	195.0
Percentage increase 1948 to 1950	–1%	0%	. . . . .	. . . . .	. . .	10%	9%
1951	114.8	111.0	60,784	2,099	3.3	329.0	209.8
1952	111.6	113.5	61,035	1,932	3.1	347.0	219.8
1953	110.1	114.4	61,945	1,870	2.9	365.4	232.6
1954	110.3	114.8	60,890	3,578	5.6	363.1	238.0
1955	110.7	114.5	62,944	2,904	4.4	397.5	256.9
Percentage increase 1952 to 1955	–1%	1%	. . . . .	. . . . .	. . .	15%	17%
1956	114.3	116.2	64,708	2,822	4.2	419.2	269.9
1957	117.6	120.2	65,011 [a]	2,936 [a]	4.3 [a]	442.5	284.8
1958	119.2	123.5	63,966	4,681	6.8	441.7	293.0
1959	119.5 [b]	124.5 [b]	65,581	3,813	5.5	478.8 [b]	311.4 [b]
Percentage increase 1956 to 1959	5%	7%	. . . . .	. . . . .	. . .	14%	15%

* Source: *Economic Report of the President, 1960* (Washington: U. S. Government Printing Office, 1960), Appendix D.
[a] Data not comparable with those for earlier period. [b] Preliminary.

543

A major contributory factor to the government's uncertainty was the generally held belief that there would be much unemployment in the early postwar period and hence the bargaining power of unions and the upward pressure on wages would be reduced. This prediction proved to be incorrect because it was based on an underestimate of the rate at which consumers would spend their accumulated savings—accumulated during the war when their incomes were high and rationing restricted their spending—and an underestimate of the investment spending by business firms in their scramble to convert to peacetime production. The prediction also greatly underestimated the foreign demand for our goods during the period of reconstruction and rehabilitation following the war. The combined increase in consumption, investment, and foreign spending was more than could be matched by the rising output of goods and services. Hence, the ending of controls coincided with tremendous inflationary pressure.

The modified wage controls fell apart under the pressures of a three-way bargaining arrangement—including unions, management, and the government—which developed at the end of 1945. The unions struck to force management to raise wages and at the same time used their political power to secure government approval of their demands. Management, before it would grant concessions to the unions, demanded that the government permit price increases. These pressures precipitated the great strike wave which reached its peak in February, 1946. In that month the government made concessions on both prices and wages in the basic steel industry, with the President personally suggesting 18.5 cents as the appropriate hourly wage increase. A new attempt to hold the line crumbled before an attack by the meat industry, supported by the agricultural interests. All controls, except those over rents, and indirect controls over interest rates were abandoned before the end of 1946.[1]

The period from 1945 to 1947, then, was characterized by high employment and an uncertain government policy. In terms of the annual averages, unemployment was highest in 1946, but even then it was only 2.3 million, less than 4 per cent of the labor force. (Although the

[1] H. M. Douty, "The Development of Wage-Price Policies," in W. Ellison Chalmers, Milton Derber, and William H. McPherson (editors), *Problems and Policies of Dispute Settlement and Wage Stabilization During World War II*, Bureau of Labor Statistics Bulletin No. 1009 (Washington: U. S. Government Printing Office, 1950), pp. 104–54; and John T. Dunlop, "The Decontrol of Wages and Prices," in Colston E. Warne, *Labor in Postwar America* (Brooklyn: Remsen Press, 1949), pp. 3–24.

data in Table 24-A indicate that there was more unemployment in 1947 than in 1946, it was actually greater in the earlier year. The discrepancy results from the application of new definitions of employment and unemployment.) What happened to wages and prices? Hourly wage rates, including overtime, increased approximately 20 per cent in manufacturing, while weekly earnings, as a result of shorter work weeks, increased somewhat less, 13 per cent. In construction and retail trade, the increases in weekly earnings were greater, 18 per cent and 29 per cent respectively. Both the Wholesale Price Index and the Consumers' Price Index rose sharply, 40 per cent and 24 per cent respectively, in this comparatively short period of time, approaching uncontrolled inflation.

There were so many special aspects to this inflation occurring immediately at the end of the war that it tells us little about the problem raised in the previous chapter. Although collective bargaining was certainly not the sole cause of this inflation, wage increases were an important contributing element. We have always had a substantial price rise at the end of a war, regardless of the degree of unionization. Furthermore, the postwar monetary policies added large amounts of fuel to the inflationary flames by making money cheap and abundant.[2] Nevertheless, the period demonstrates the inflationary potential of a full employment economy and indicates the importance of a determined and consistent government policy to counteract it.

1948–1950: Stable Prices with High Employment

Wages and prices continued to rise well into 1948, but toward the end of that year the first postwar recession appeared. Unemployment averaged 3.7 million in 1949 and 3.4 million in 1950, between 5 and 6 per cent of the labor force. This approaches the low full employment goal. Wages continued to rise, but at a much slower rate, increasing slightly less than 10 per cent for the three years. Prices, both wholesale and consumers', averaged the same in 1950 as in 1948. Gross national product rose by 25 billion dollars, about 10 per cent, although the increase in the size of the labor force was even less than 3 per cent, thus indicating a rise in output per worker.

Between the last part of 1948 and the first part of 1950, prices declined while unemployment was approximately 5.5 per cent of the labor force. Does this mean that stable prices can be maintained with 95 or 96

[2] Walter A. Morton, "Trade Unionism, Full Employment and Inflation," *American Economic Review*, Vol. XL (March, 1950), pp. 13–39; and Lester V. Chandler, *Inflation in the United States, 1940–1948* (New York: Harper & Brothers, 1951), especially pp. 325–66.

per cent of the labor force employed? Unfortunately, this proves nothing except that for one time period stability and high employment existed simultaneously. It must be emphasized, however, that high full employment, according to our more ambitious goal, was not attained during this period.

In mid-1950 the United States entered the Korean War and stability in prices came to a sudden halt. Although full employment and collective bargaining were not completely innocent in the price rise that ensued, undoubtedly the primary and initiating cause was scare buying by businessmen and consumers, particularly the latter. Everyone rushed to the market to beat the hoarders. As a consequence, prices rose rapidly, the Consumers' Price Index for 1951 being 8 per cent above that of 1950.

1952–1955: Stable Prices with High Employment

The four years, 1952 through 1955, offer the best illustration that the American economy, under some circumstances, is able to maintain full employment, stable prices, and free collective bargaining, all at the same time. After the initial impact, the economy adjusted rapidly to the Korean War. Wage and price controls, never so restrictive as in World War II, were completely ended in February, 1953, and the economy was able to sustain free collective bargaining thereafter. The gross national product in 1955 was 15 per cent higher than in 1952, almost entirely the result of greater productivity. Almost none of the increase was due to higher prices, and only a small part could be attributed to a larger labor force, since it grew by less than 3 per cent.

During this four-year period there was a modest recession in 1954, when unemployment averaged 3.6 million, 5.6 per cent of the labor force. Otherwise, 96 to 98 per cent of the labor force was employed, with the first two years close to our high full employment goal. Both the Wholesale Price Index and the Consumers' Price Index were remarkably stable over this period with an over-all change of less than 1 per cent in each case, even though consumer spending increased by more than 37 billion dollars, or 17 per cent. This price stability was maintained while hourly wage rates continued their upward march, registering a 13 per cent gain in manufacturing, 15 per cent in construction, and 14 per cent in retail trade. The increases in weekly earnings were not so large proportionately, but were nevertheless quite substantial, being well over 10 per cent, except in construction.

Looking more carefully at the statistics for these four years, it may be noted that hourly wage rates made the greatest gains in construction and durable goods manufacturing, in both instances in comparatively highly unionized industries. Does this represent a distortion in the wage structure? In durable goods manufacturing it perhaps reflected an increase in productivity with the higher wage acting as an inducement to attract more labor. Since the rise in weekly earnings was about proportionate to the rise in hourly rates, employers had made little reduction in overtime, thus indicating a continuation of the same degree of shortage of labor in these industries. That is, large quantities of labor continued to be in demand, relative to the available supply, even at the higher wage rates. On the other hand, weekly earnings in construction rose proportionately much less than hourly rates, perhaps indicating a distortion of the wage structure at this point. That is, at these higher hourly rates, contractors preferred to employ their workers for shorter work weeks, and hence the union policies may have been the cause of some reduction in the amount of construction. However, in 1955 there were other factors which may have been the cause of the decline in the work week of the construction workers. The postwar demand for construction may have been leveling off, after breaking new records for a number of years, regardless of the higher wage rates. Also, the Federal Reserve System was restricting credit and raising interest rates as a part of its anti-inflationary policies at that time. This monetary policy appeared to fall disproportionately hard on mortgage credit for residential construction. Therefore, the decline in the work week of construction workers may have been primarily caused by factors other than union gains through collective bargaining. This example illustrates the difficulty of tracing causation in economic problems. There is a further reason for being uncertain as to whether unions brought about a wage distortion. In the largely unorganized retail trades, hourly rates rose proportionately as much as in the largely organized durable goods manufacturing and construction industries. However, the rise in wage rates in retail trade may have been the result of sympathetic pressure.

1956–1959: Creeping Inflation with Rising Unemployment

During the latter half of the 1950's, price movements followed a different pattern. From 1956 to 1959, consumer prices rose 7 per cent, with some increase occurring each year, and the Wholesale Price Index traced a similar, though slightly more moderate, upward path. Again, these years were marred by a recession, most severe in 1958 when the number of jobless exceeded our proposed standard for low full employment. In fact, unemployment was greater than in any other comparable postwar period. Gross weekly and hourly earnings continued to rise, showing almost no change from their previous trends. The increases in gross national product and personal consumption spending, when deflated for price changes, were considerably less than phenomenal.

As a consequence of the steady upward movement of prices in spite of the relatively loose labor market, new theories of inflation gained popularity. Some economists claimed that prices were being pushed up by rising costs, particularly wages, hence the name "cost-push," or "wage-push," inflation. This was contrasted with the traditional "demand-pull" explanation: total money spending rising faster than output and therefore pulling prices up, as in the immediate postwar years. A theory that would stand somewhere between these two, "structural inflation," pointed to unusually large increases in demand in certain sectors of the economy, e.g., health care, construction, and steel, as initiators of the inflation. Shortages of supply and immobility of resources caused wages and prices in these industries to rise abnormally. Other wages were increased because of sympathetic pressure and the precedent-setting effect of key bargaining agreements, thus pushing up prices even in those sectors where there had been little or no increase in demand.[3]

It may be that the inflation since 1955 is more apparent than real, resulting from the difficulties in measuring price changes over a period of time with an index number. For example, if the cost of a hospital room rises 20 per cent, it is so represented in the index, yet the service rendered may be so greatly improved by advances in medical technology that on a cost-per-cure-of-disease basis, the price has actually declined. Some areas of the economy most plagued by price increases are subject to this difficulty in measurement. Although it is generally agreed that the indexes overstate the amount of inflation, some of the price rise probably represented a genuine decline in the purchasing power of the dollar.

A closer examination of the statistics, beyond those portrayed in Table 24-A, reveals that both wages and prices have risen unevenly,

---

[3] For an extended discussion at both the theoretical and policy levels see the Hearings, Reports, and Study Papers of the Joint Economic Committee on *Employment, Growth, and Price Levels,* especially U. S. Congress, Joint Economic Committee, *Hearings, Part 8: The Effect of Increases in Wages, Salaries, and the Prices of Personal Services, Together with Union and Professional Practices upon Prices, Profits, Production, and Employment* (Washington: Government Printing Office, 1959) and JEC, *Staff Report on Employment, Growth, and Price Levels* (Washington: Government Printing Office, 1959). For a thorough analysis of structural inflation, see Charles L. Schultze, *Recent Inflation in the United States* (Washington: Government Printing Office, 1959), Study Paper No. 1, prepared for the JEC in connection with the study of employment, growth, and price levels.

with steel, machinery, and skilled services making outstanding gains relative to other prices. From 1956 on, wage increases were greater in those manufacturing industries which were more profitable and highly concentrated, having few firms and little danger of new ones entering into competition. In bituminous coal mining and railroads, the wage increases apparently resulted from union bargaining power; the comparatively low levels of profits in these industries would otherwise have restricted gains in pay. The strong position of the construction unions seemed to affect their wage rates favorably, even though they are in a very competitive industry. But in many industries, e.g., lumber, leather, clothing, and textiles, earnings lagged far behind.

Fifteen Years of Erratic Inflation

To sum up, the first decade following World War II was a period alternating between price stability and sudden sharp price increases. The first sharp increase was a postwar readjustment and the second resulted from scare buying at the beginning of the Korean War; together they accounted for 75 per cent of the price increases between 1946 and 1959. Between these inflationary crises, price stability was maintained with a level of employment which averaged well above the low full employment goal. A tentative and preliminary conclusion may be drawn: in a full employment economy, price stability may exist simultaneously with free collective bargaining for three, four, or five years, but during this quiescent period explosive forces are developing. As soon as the trigger mechanism is set off by some chance factor, the price level bursts upward by 5 or 10 per cent to a new temporarily stable equilibrium.

This may be what society is forced to endure if it wants both full employment and free collective bargaining. The burden may be willingly endured if the long-run inflationary tendency is always erratic and unpredictable and therefore never becomes cumulative. That is, if it is never clear how soon or how much prices will rise and if there is always the possibility that prices may decline, consumers and businessmen will not increase their purchases in anticipation of immediate price increases. If the future course of prices follows this description, public policy should perhaps be based on preparedness: always ready to counteract the explosion before it becomes cumulative and so serious that it disrupts production.

The creeping inflation after 1955 may have a different kind of effect, if continued over a long period of time. A slow, steady erosion of the value of the dollar may lead to a decline in the desire to save and to hold cash. If this should occur, the inflation could expand to dangerous proportions. Unions may contribute to a creeping inflation by pushing up earnings in some sectors—where they are strong or demand is rising rapidly—and causing wages to be downwardly rigid in all other sectors. If some pay rates are rising and none can fall, and productivity does not improve fast enough to prevent price increases, unions may be blamed for fostering a wage-push inflation.

If unions regularly act as the trigger mechanism or as the source of cost-push, public policy may be aimed against them. The experience since World War II certainly does not demonstrate to any conclusive extent that unions are the chief culprit in the price rise. With the present degree of unionization, 25 per cent of the labor force, and with the varying degree of strength of sympathetic pressures, unions do not possess sufficient economic power to be the sole cause of a rise in the general price level. At some future date unionization of the labor force may be more complete, or continued full employment—particularly if it is high full employment—may cause sympathetic pressures to become stronger and more consistent. In either case, the union potential for upsetting price stability will be greater, and thus perhaps cause the development of a public policy more restrictive on collective bargaining.

Regardless of whether unions are actually one of the primary causes of inflation, if the general public merely suspects them there will be political pressure on the federal government to interfere with collective bargaining. The interference may take any one of a variety of forms: direct controls of wages and prices, compulsory arbitration, threats of government action if wages rise too rapidly, or pleas to unions, accompanied with much publicity, to hold wage increases to a specified amount. A convenient and useful beginning point for a consideration of this problem is a review of experience in foreign countries.

The British and Swedish economies have maintained full employment since World War II and both have a higher degree of unionization than the United States; hence a brief analysis of collective bargaining in those countries will illustrate possible roles the government may play. Of course, the United States will not—and should not—follow exactly the pattern set by these countries. Although both are democracies with highly developed economies, their customs and traditions differ from ours. The path of development and the present structure of their economies and their collective bargaining institutions also differ from ours in important respects. Nevertheless, a useful insight may be gained even though the analogies are not perfect.

THE BRITISH EXPERIENCE

In the first fifteen years of the postwar period, the level of employment in Great Britain approximated that of Beveridge's definition of full employment.[4] During this time there was a continual upward movement in retail prices and an almost exactly parallel rise in wage rates. By 1955 both were more than 140 per cent above prewar levels. Weekly earnings rose at a more rapid rate because of the greater incidence of overtime payments and an increasing proportion of workers on piece rates. In 1955 weekly earnings, in money terms, were 250 per cent above prewar levels, a far greater increase than occurred in the United States. Between 1949 and 1958 the average annual rates of increase were 4.5 per cent for prices, 6.8 per cent for money wages, and 1.7 per cent for real wages.[5]

The upward pressures on the price level were more potent and more complicated than those in the United States. The fact that the number of job openings exceeded the number of unemployed workers was only one of the reasons for this. Other important causes included the devastation wrought by the war, in terms not only of less housing and consumers' goods, but also of an absolute reduction in the capacity to produce. The existing capital equipment was in great need of modernization. The strategic importance of foreign trade in the British economy complicated the problem. In order to import necessary food and raw materials, Great Britain must sell a large portion of her output to other countries. In 1949 the pound was devalued with the purpose of boosting foreign sales. Since this raised the pound price of imports, and Great Britain imports much of her food and raw materials, further inflationary pressures were generated.

What was the role of unions and collective bargaining in this environ-

[4] For an understanding of conditions in postwar Britain, the following may be consulted: Lloyd G. Reynolds and Cynthia H. Taft, *The Evolution of Wage Structure* (New Haven: Yale University Press, 1956), pp. 251–85; Allan Flanders, "Wage Movements and Wage Policies in Postwar Britain," *The Annals*, Vol. CCCX (March, 1957), pp. 87–98; Barbara Wootton, *The Social Foundations of Wage Policy* (New York: W. W. Norton & Co., 1955), especially pp. 68–160; Paul E. Sultan, "Full Employment on Trial: A Case Study of British Experience," *Canadian Journal of Economics and Political Science*, Vol. XIX (May, 1953), pp. 210–21; Jean T. McKelvey, "Trade Union Wage Policy in Postwar Britain," *Industrial and Labor Relations Review*, Vol. VI (October, 1952), pp. 3–19; Mark W. Leiserson, *A Brief Interpretive Survey of Wage-Price Problems in Europe*, Study Paper No. 11 prepared for the Joint Economic Committee, U. S. Congress (Washington: Government Printing Office, 1959).

[5] Leiserson, *op. cit.*, pp. 36–38.

ment? Before this question can be answered, a brief explanation of the wage setting processes in Great Britain is necessary. At no time during this period of domestic inflation and foreign crises did the government attempt to control wages directly as was done in the United States through the National War Labor Board and the Wage Stabilization Board. Instead, the British reduced the bargaining power of unions by forbidding strikes and increased the resistance of employers by controlling prices.

Within this framework four different techniques were—and still are—used for setting wages. The dominant one is collective bargaining in private industry which covers the majority of workers. The second technique is arbitration, used in the writing of new contracts in Great Britain much more than in the United States. Frequently both parties voluntarily submit their differences to arbitration. Compulsory arbitration can be invoked by either of the parties or by the Minister of Labour. The third technique is used in those industries where unions are weak or nonexistent. Here wages are set by statutory wage councils, the membership of which includes employers, workers, and the public. Finally, the government, as employer of more than 20 per cent of the civilian labor force, including the nationalized industries, directly enters into wage setting. The last three techniques to a large extent follow the lead of collective bargaining; consequently, union policies are of crucial importance in determining the nation's wage level. One major reservation must be made. An employer in need of additional workers may voluntarily offer and pay more than the agreed upon rate, something that is only infrequently done—and almost never openly—in the United States.

Immediately after the war, the Labour Party came into power in Great Britain. Since the Labour Party was—and still is—the political arm of the unions, it was able to win acceptance of its wage policies. However, there was far from full agreement among the political leaders in the Party, the union leaders, and the rank and file. In order to curb inflation and hold down costs, and thereby increase British exports, the Party urged a policy of severe restraint in union wage demands. With much reluctance, this policy was accepted in early 1948 by the Trades Union Congress, the confederation of British unions.

In the three years prior to the TUC acceptance of the policy of wage restraint, retail prices and wage rates had been rising at an annual rate of approximately 7 per cent. For the next two years the rate of annual increase was barely more than one-half of that. During these years labor's political leaders exhorted the General Council of the

TUC to continue the wage restraint, and they in turn continued to sell this policy to the membership. However, in 1950 wage restraint ceased to be a policy of the TUC when the members voted against the leaders. Among the factors motivating this rebellion were the substandard level of real wages received by the lowest-paid workers, the narrowing of traditional differentials between the unskilled, semi-skilled, and skilled workers, the fact that some unions had used their bargaining power to win wage increases leaving other unions behind (some of the unions with the greatest wage increases were the ones whose leaders were members of the TUC General Council), and finally the rising price level and "high" profits. Although the terminology may be different, this is much the same list of reasons for wage increases often cited by unions in the United States.

The two years following the end of wage restraint were marked by rapidly rising prices, at an annual rate of 19 per cent. How much of this may be attributed to the rising wage rates, which increased almost as much as prices, is impossible to say. Certainly, a portion of the inflation was a consequence of the crisis in the balance of payments and the devaluation of the pound. The early stages of the Korean War had their impact as well. The desire of the unions to avoid bearing more than their "fair share" of the austerity program, designed to balance foreign trade, caused them to demand wage increases which were certainly not innocent with respect to the price rise. The Conservative government, which replaced the Labour Party in 1951, had less success than its predecessor in convincing the unions to follow a policy of wage restraint. From 1952 through 1955, wage rates increased at the rate of 6 per cent annually, while the increase in retail prices, though very substantial, was only a little more than half of that. During this time both the British Employers' Confederation and the TUC resisted any suggestions that the government exercise direct wage controls. The British Employers' Confederation urged its members to avoid bidding up wages, the purpose being to cooperate with the Conservative government in achieving a greater degree of stability. But the government itself, bargaining in the nationalized industries, demonstrated a weakness in capitulating to union demands rather than face a strike.

Throughout the postwar years, prices and wages rates rose continually in contrast to the erratic and milder inflation in this country. While we were alternating between periods of upward price spurts and stability, Great Britain had price increases alternating between fast and very fast. From the point of view of the problem with which we are dealing in these two chapters, the significant differences between Great Britain and the United States are: a higher degree of unionization and therefore a higher proportion of wages set through collective bargaining, and secondly, a higher level of full employment. To what extent are these factors responsible for the greater inflation in Great Britain? It is quite possible that wages would have risen at least as much, perhaps more, without the high degree of unionization. The TUC's policy of wage restraint was comparatively successful for at least a few years. In the crises endured by Great Britain in World War II, the Korean War, and its foreign trade balance, it is doubtful if price and wage stability could have been maintained, regardless of union policies; in fact, the importance of collective bargaining in setting wages seemed to have declined during this postwar period. Certainly with the high level of full employment, the upward pressure on wages was irresistible. Is full employment, then, the culprit? If such a high level of full employment is to be maintained without direct wage controls, the risk of a wage-price inflation is bound to be present. To avoid this risk means giving up a certain amount of production and making unemployment more painful. The British chose to run the risk and did suffer a large amount of inflation, though only a part of the price rise can be attributed to the high level of employment.

Lessons from the British Experience

What is to be learned from the British experience that might be relevant to the relation between unions, wages, and prices in the American economy? In order to facilitate answering this question we first make the assumption that although wage increases were not the sole cause of the British price inflation, they were one of the important causative factors. Why did wage rates rise more rapidly than output per manhour? Why was it not possible to hold the average wage to a level which the economy could afford at the existing price level? Although the Labour government and the TUC attempted to hold the line, each constituent union within the TUC believed it had a justification for demanding special concessions. Wage restraint fell to pieces because of the sectional interests of the individual unions.

One lesson, then, is that when wages are one of the primary causes of an upward bias in the price level, and an anti-inflationary wage policy is adopted, it must be binding on all groups of workers.[6] This applies

---

[6] Donald J. Robertson, "Trade Unions and Wage Policy," *The Political Quarterly,* Vol. XXVII (January-March, 1956), pp. 19–30.

to nonunion workers as well as to all segments of the unionized labor force. Although this need not mean an absolute wage freeze, nor even some governmental agency supervising all wage changes, it would require at least enough centralized control over wages to prevent any single group of workers from winning such disproportionate wage gains as to cause other unions to find it necessary to fight for similar gains. Thus, if a few unions secure wage increases far beyond those won by other unions, those left behind would be forced by internal politics to strive for equal wage increases. To avoid this type of situation, central control over wages could be provided by labor itself through a national federation of all unions, requiring more centralized authority than possessed by the TUC. It is not advocated that such policy be adopted in this country. We have not as yet, except during wars, witnessed inflationary pressures which would warrant such a drastic rearrangement of our institutions. But if we ever do, this lesson should not be forgotten.

There was a second factor in the rise of British wage rates from which a lesson may be drawn. The competitive bidding for scarce labor on the part of employers, driving wage rates above agreed upon levels, contributed significantly to the impact of wages on the price level. As long as employers were able to raise prices to compensate for wage increases, they willingly engaged in such competition. The lesson, then, is that if price stability is deemed more necessary than a high level of full employment, the economy's purchasing power must be reduced, thus making it difficult for employers to maintain profit margins after granting wage increases. The British chose the latter goal, maintaining more than our high full employment goal in spite of its inflationary potential.

THE SWEDISH EXPERIENCE

The postwar period in Sweden was one of low unemployment, about matching the high full employment goal, with a little more joblessness than Great Britain but somewhat less than in the United States, and there were considerable upward pressures on prices and wages.[7] The cost of living index rose 40 per cent during World War II, most of this in the first two years. In the following ten years there was an additional 50 per cent increase, approximately two-thirds of this occurring in the early stages of the Korean War. Throughout this period, hourly earnings

[7] For an understanding of conditions in postwar Sweden, the following may be consulted: Reynolds and Taft, *op. cit.,* pp. 228–50; Gosta Rehn, "Swedish Wages and Wage Policies," *The Annals,* Vol. CCCX (March, 1957), pp. 99–108; Walter Galenson, "Scandinavia," in Walter Galenson (editor), *Comparative Labor Movements* (New York: Prentice-Hall, Inc., 1952), pp. 104–72; Leiserson, *op. cit.*

increased each year, but by widely varying amounts, depending to a large extent on government policy. The record of Sweden in the postwar decade has a strong resemblance to that of the United States, alternating between stability and sharp price increases, but the over-all rise in prices was about twice as much as ours.

Some basic characteristics of the collective bargaining mechanism in Sweden differ from those in the United States. The outstanding differences are the greater degree of organization of both workers and employers, and the greater centralization of bargaining. More than 80 per cent of the production workers and about 75 per cent of the white-collar and government workers are organized. The LO (the Swedish federation of trade unions), made up predominantly of industrial unions, represents approximately three-quarters of all organized workers and has the close cooperation of the other important unions. Economic rivalry between the industrial unions is common, but jurisdictional rivalry is almost unknown.

Industry-wide bargaining is well established, and in some years basic agreements—nation-wide agreements for almost all industries, negotiated in one all-inclusive set of bargaining sessions—have been signed by the LO and the SAF (Swedish employers' association). These cover practically all employers. Most contracts are negotiated at about the same time, in the early months of each year, with the first important agreement, usually in the engineering industry, setting a precedent followed by the others.[8] Strikes do not occur until the government mediator feels that no more is to be gained through further negotiation. The LO will not support a strike—and its moral and financial support is extremely valuable—by one of its member unions if it considers that union's demands to be out of line. The SAF also exercises moral and financial pressures over the collective bargaining goals of its members. The great authority of the LO and the SAF, which stems partly from the homogeneity of the Swedish economy, is best demonstrated in the basic agreements which they have signed. The first one came in 1938; there was another during World War II as a technique for stabilizing wages; and there have been several basic agreements between the LO and the SAF in the postwar years as counter-inflationary devices. The centralization of bargaining in Sweden, although much greater than in the United States, is not complete. Individual unions and employers do now and then successfully circumvent the controls of the LO and the SAF.

Not only is Swedish collective bargaining different from that in the

[8] Donald R. Snodgrass, Appendix to Leiserson, *op. cit.*, p. 81.

United States, but it takes place in a different environment. Important from our point of view are the following points. Foreign trade plays a major role in the Swedish economy, and like Great Britain, she devalued her currency in 1949. Through government subsidies and welfare programs, income has been much more equally distributed than in the United States, and because of the broad publicly sponsored social benefits, bargaining concentrates more on wages and less on fringe issues. The LO is closely tied to the Social Democratic Party, which has controlled the Swedish government throughout the postwar decade. Although union members constitute the bulk of the Party membership, the leadership of the unions and the Party are distinctly separate.

A review of the chronology of the wage and price movements in postwar Sweden, and the response of the government to them, reveal that the Swedish government did not hesitate to withdraw purchasing power when the circumstances required this. In 1948, when wage increases were excessive in the opinion of the Minister of Finance, excise taxes were introduced to absorb most of the rise in pay. In each of the next two years, the LO, persuading its member unions to follow, froze wages in a basic agreement with the SAF. After substantial wage increases in 1951, following the opening of the Korean War and the currency devaluation, and more modest wage increases in 1952, the LO successfully promoted a wage restraint program. In 1955 occurred what amounted to a repetition of 1948, first substantial wage increases, then a withdrawal of purchasing power by the government. It was again followed by a single master agreement between the LO and the SAF providing for only modest wage increases, and wage restraint was continued through 1959.

One special aspect of the wage history of Sweden has been the "wage drift," increases in earnings not accounted for by the increased rates negotiated in the collective agreements. This wage drift—or wage glide, as it is sometimes called—was responsible for nearly one-half of the rise in wages after 1945. It was the result of the severe shortage of labor and the consequent bidding for labor by employers. Much of the upward movement in wages was made possible by the large portion —more than 60 per cent—of Swedish labor working on an incentive or piece-rate basis. The effects of the wage drift were particularly noticeable toward the end of each period of wage freeze. While the general level of wages was being held within bounds, specially favored groups of workers made comparatively large gains, thus creating a distortion in the wage structure, with disparities between the wage rates for similar jobs—disparities which could not be maintained for more than a short period of time. Those workers whose wages had remained frozen demanded their share of the full employment pie. Thus, large wage increases were granted all around, putting the wage structure back into a temporary equilibrium.

Lessons from the Swedish Experience

The Swedish were more successful than the British in achieving periods of price stability in the postwar years. Although the different roles played by collective bargaining in the two countries did not entirely account for this difference, some important lessons may be learned from such a comparison. The LO was more effective than the TUC in controlling the wage goals of its member unions, and the SAF was more effective in controlling its constituent employers than was the British Employers' Confederation. As a consequence, wage increases in Sweden did not deviate as far from productivity as in Great Britain. The vigorous action taken by the government was one of the major reasons for the comparative success of the LO. The unions learned by experience that the government could and would use its fiscal power to nullify any money wage increases it believed to be inflationary. Hence, unions, as a total group, had little to lose by moderating their money wage demands. And the LO possessed sufficiently potent weapons to police its members into accepting the basic agreements.

Secondly, both the government and the LO were willing to admit that a wage freeze could not be permanently maintained along with a high level of full employment. An occasional explosion must be permitted to allow repressed bargaining power to express itself and bring about irresistible adjustments in the wage structure. With the large amount of wage drift, this was necessary in 1950 and again in 1955. Recognizing that such adjustments were necessary, the SAF, the LO, and the government cooperated in negotiating them, thus relieving the pressures before they became so strong as to engulf all efforts to maintain stability. These occasional explosions served their purpose, partly because the government was able to prevent the price increases from equaling the wage increases, and workers gained in real income as a result.

One major advantage possessed by the Swedish unions was that of having their Party in power throughout the postwar decade, whereas the Labour Party was in power in Great Britain only for the first half of the decade. Collective bargaining in both countries inevitably involved the government, the unions adjusting their demands with one eye on the government's fiscal and monetary policies. The LO could afford greater confidence in its government, because the Party of its choice was in power. The TUC was better able to hold wages in line while the Labour Party formed the British government. It may be tentatively concluded that unions are more willing to moderate their demands in cooperation with a governmental anti-inflationary policy when the nation's political leaders are more in sympathy with the unions' long-run goals.

A RECAPITULATION

Complete economic stability is both impossible and undesirable. Changes in productivity and in consumers' tastes must and will be reflected in the wage-price structure, and thus bring about a reallocation of resources and a new array of consumers' goods. Within this framework of ceaseless change, is it possible to have stability in the general price level along with full employment and free collective bargaining?

The evidence we have surveyed indicates that there is a strong inflationary bias in a full employment economy. Sudden, and fortunately short, price increases punctuated the price stability in both the United States and Sweden. During the periods of stability, inflationary pressures were generated which were suppressed only for a limited period of time. Only part of the blame for the development of these pressures can be placed on unions and collective bargaining. Leaving out of account war and international tensions, the other two major villains were employers and the government. Unless moderation becomes the policy of each of the three, these repressed pressures will lead to occasional explosions, if not to continual inflation.

Since the government is not a self-interest group in the same sense that unions and employers are, it has the responsibility of initiating the policies of moderation through withdrawing purchasing power when necessary. An economy-wide reduction in purchasing power, perhaps accompanied by an increase in unemployment, affects the profit expectations of all employers, and thus becomes restrictive on all wages, both union and nonunion. Although this will not completely eliminate wage-price distortions, it makes it more difficult for them to develop. The shortage of labor and the high demand for goods under full employment puts the price-wage structure under a severe strain—distortions are likely to appear at many different points—and unless they are relieved by productivity improvements, they develop an explosive potential. Therefore, even with a policy of moderation initiated by the government and forced upon unions and management, occasional explosions in the price-wage structure may occur.

An important qualification must be added to the above paragraphs. We have had comparatively little experience with full employment. Its continuation over several decades will certainly bring about changes in the nature and functioning of unions. Thus the role of collective bargaining in future inflationary periods may be very different from anything we can perceive at this time. Quite possibly the federal government would exercise direct controls over labor-management relations. We turn now to a consideration of some of the possible directions which the government may follow.

DIRECT CONTROLS OVER COLLECTIVE BARGAINING

Perhaps the American economy will enjoy a stable price level and full employment during the next few decades. This pleasant prospect could be the result of rapidly rising output per manhour or of wise and vigorous government policies. In such happy circumstances, direct controls over collective bargaining would receive no political support. Conversely, the American economy could suffer from price inflation. If unions are a major cause of the inflation, or if the public believes they are, direct controls will be considered. What types of direct controls could be imposed by the government?

The most complete control which the government might impose is direct wage regulation, which, for political and economic reasons, would have to include price control. This approach is not likely to be followed during peace-time since it would be a complete rejection of our free price system. The political objections of both labor and management would be unanimous. If such controls were ever adopted, each union and each firm would claim that it was the victim of discrimination by the wage and price setting agency. Even if it could be assumed that the price and wage structure in existence at the time the freeze was initiated was fair and appropriate, this price structure would soon be out of date and require adjustments in the light of changing consumer tastes and changing technology. The criteria for adjusting wages and prices would inevitably become mired in a political crossfire. It is unlikely that a government board—no matter how wise and impartial—could adjust wages and prices so that the output of goods and the allocation of resources would reflect the desires of consumers. Undoubtedly, some industries would enjoy high profit margins and become overexpanded, while others would be severely restricted. There would have to be a considerable change in the attitudes of the American public before direct control over consumption would be permitted to this extent. As consumers, we prefer to make our own decisions on whether to buy more cars, more houses, or more beef. We do not want a government agency making these decisions for us, no matter how democratic it may be.

If blanket controls over wages and prices are rejected, wages may be controlled through government intervention in individual collective bargaining negotiations, which could be accomplished through compulsory arbitration. The advantages and disadvantages of compulsory arbitration were discussed in Chapter 14 and need not be repeated here. It will be recalled that an arbitrator selected by the government makes the final determination on wages and working conditions and that this tends to frustrate normal bargaining procedures. Like wage and price controls, compulsory arbitration probably represents a higher degree of government interference with the free market economy than the American political system would permit.

The government may accomplish a similar result but be somewhat less restrictive on the freedoms of the bargaining parties by appointing investigating boards for major disputes.[9] Such boards would be empowered to investigate the merits of the dispute and to recommend a settlement. Although much publicity would be given to the board's recommendation, the parties would not be compelled to accept it. They would have the freedom to make a somewhat different settlement, or to apply economic sanctions if either one deems it necessary. However, a strike or lockout in opposition to the board's recommendation would mean loss of public sympathy, which might provide sufficient pressure to cause the noncomplying party to modify its position. Furthermore, the government could support the board's recommendation with the threat of a more direct form of interference, e.g., government seizure of the industry. A procedure of this type is beyond the usual practices in the United States, except for the railroad industry, but it does represent less severe restriction than either direct wage and price controls or compulsory arbitration.

There is a fourth technique by which the government could attempt

[9] For a discussion of the problems involved in this method of dealing with wage and price inflation, see Emmette S. Redford, *Potential Public Policies to Deal with Inflation Caused by Market Power*, Study Paper No. 10 prepared for the Joint Economic Committee, U. S. Congress (Washington: Government Printing Office, 1959).

to influence the results of collective bargaining for the purpose of
keeping wage gains within the limits of productivity increases. Following
the Swedish model, the government could announce that it would impose
sales taxes if wage increases exceeded some specified amount. The
amount could perhaps be set by the President's Council of Economic
Advisors, as long as this agency maintains its high level of prestige.
American unions would have difficulty conforming to this procedure,
unless there is a major change in the role performed by the AFL-CIO.
The Federation would need a much greater degree of authority than
it now has in order to police the bargaining goals of its member unions.
It is conceivable, however, that the threat of more direct government
action might cause the international unions to be willing to give up this
much freedom to their Federation. They might prefer to keep the
authority in the family rather than to allow it to be usurped by a
public body.

Under no conditions can collective bargaining be a stagnant institution
in a dynamic economy. And if we maintain full employment, which
turns out to be associated with inflationary pressures, unions may become
the target of restrictive government action, regardless of how guilty they
may be. Management organizations will naturally attempt to have the
blame placed on unions.[10] Although we have discussed only four of the
courses of action open to the government, there are other possibilities:
to declare all union activity to be conspiracy in restraint of trade, make
industry-wide bargaining illegal, or grant all legislative authority over
unions to the state governments. These are probably less attractive
politically than the techniques discussed. In any case, collective bargaining, and particularly the role of the government in collective
bargaining, will change with the coming decades, which in turn will
stimulate changes in the structure of American unions. The possible
directions of change are discussed in the next chapter.

SUMMARY

In a free economy which is dynamic and growing, risks are unavoid-
able. In a full employment economy with free collective bargaining,
one risk is price inflation. The public must decide to what extent it is
willing to bear this risk and its consequences. The risk can be avoided
by accepting less output—a lower standard of living—and by making
unemployment more painful, or the risk may be repressed by direct

---

[10] See, for example, *Inflation, Unions and Wage Policy* (Washington: Chamber of
Commerce of the United States, 1960).

controls over collective bargaining. The nature of this risk is illustrated by the course of events in postwar United States, Great Britain, and Sweden. In the United States and Sweden, full employment was accompanied by alternating periods of stability and sharp price increases and in Britain by alternating periods of price rises and very rapid price rises. It may be that some type of erratic inflation, such as we had in the United States, must be accepted if the economy insists upon a high level of full employment. During the periods of relative stability, pressures are built up which can only be resolved through occasional explosions in the price and wage levels. After each explosion a new temporary equilibrium in the wage-price structure is secured.

The institution of collective bargaining is not the only culprit in creating these inflationary pressures. Even when considering only those inflationary pressures which grow out of wage increases, both business and government have responsibilities as well as the unions. With labor scarce and product demand high, employers are tempted to engage in competitive bidding for workers. To the extent that this upsets the wage structure, explosive forces are created. Likewise, the government must not follow the road of easy money and loose fiscal policy when inflationary pressures are strong. It may have to threaten a withdrawal of purchasing power if either business or unions or both push wages too high, and it must be prepared to carry out that threat when necessary.

The lessons learned from the British and Swedish experiences have important but limited value. The value is limited because collective bargaining is quite different in those countries, because both the workers and the employers are more completely organized, because the federations (TUC and LO) exert more authority over their member unions, and because the government exercises a much greater influence. Both the unions and employers expect to have the government, either formally or informally, participate in their negotiations. Thus, collective bargaining becomes a three-way process. If inflationary pressures in this country become more difficult to control in the future, the government may participate more actively and directly in collective bargaining. Regardless of the direction taken by the increased government participation, it is likely to foster changes in our labor-management institutions. If unions wish to continue to exercise influence over important economic variables, they will have to modify their methods and acquire new characteristics in harmony with changes in the environment. The next chapter will consider some of the prospects for these changes.

DISCUSSION QUESTIONS

1. Using the immediate postwar period, show how inaccurate economic predictions may hamper the development of appropriate policies for dealing with inflationary wage conditions.

2. Write an essay in support of the proposition that price stability, free collective bargaining, and full employment may be maintained simultaneously, making use of the statistics in Table 24–A.

3. Write an essay in opposition to the proposition in the previous question, using the statistics in Table 24–A.

4. Explain why the period 1955 to 1960 presents an unclear picture as to whether unions acted as a powerful inflationary force.

5. Compare the movements in wages and prices during the postwar decade in the United States with those in Great Britain. To what extent to you think collective bargaining was responsible for the difference? Explain.

6. What do you consider to be the major lessons to be learned from the British experience? How do these lessons apply to the United States?

7. Why were the Swedish more successful than the British in holding wages in check during the postwar decade?

8. In a full employment economy, the wage policies of employers may contribute significantly to the growth of inflationary pressures. Drawing on the British and Swedish experience, explain how this is possible.

9. On the basis of the evidence presented in this chapter, explain why it appears necessary to have an occasional wage-price explosion in a full employment economy.

10. If inflationary pressures grow out of collective bargaining, what direct controls may the government employ? How are these direct controls inconsistent with a free market economy?

11. Write an essay on why you do or do not believe that inflationary pressures, assuming that they will be continually strong but not necessarily overwhelming, will drive collective bargaining into a pattern similar to that in Sweden.

BIBLIOGRAPHY

Douty, H. M. "The Development of Wage-Price Policies," in W. Ellison Chalmers, Milton Derber, and William H. McPherson (editors). *Problems and Policies of Dispute Settlement and Wage Stabilization During World War II*, Bureau of Labor Statistics Bulletin No. 1009. Washington: Government Printing Office, 1950.

Dunlop, John T. "The Decontrol of Wages and Prices," in Colston E. Warne, *Labor in Postwar America*. Brooklyn: Remsen Press, 1949.

Flanders, Allan. "Wage Movements and Wage Policies in Postwar Britain." *The Annals,* Vol. CCCX (March, 1957).

Galenson, Walter. *Comparative Labor Movements.* New York: Prentice-Hall, Inc., 1952.

Leiserson, Mark W. *A Brief Interpretive Survey of Wage-Price Problems in Europe.* Study Paper No. 11, Prepared for the Joint Economic Committee, U. S. Congress. Washington: Government Printing Office, 1959.

Meyers, Charles A. (editor). *Wages, Prices, Profits and Productivity.* New York: The American Assembly, 1959.

Rehn, Gosta. "Swedish Wages and Wage Policies," *The Annals,* Vol. CCCX (March, 1957).

Reynolds, Lloyd G., and Taft, Cynthia H. *The Evolution of Wage Structure.* New Haven: Yale University Press, 1956.

Wootton, Barbara. *The Social Foundations of Wage Policy.* New York: W. W. Norton & Co., 1955.

PART

5   THE MAJOR TRENDS

If asked what you mean by labor problems and what were the four or five most important ones of the last fifty years and of the present decade, what would your answer be? Certainly different people would answer these questions differently. A union leader would reply in terms of low wages, unemployment, arbitrary management policies, Taft-Hartley Act restrictions on free collective bargaining, etc. A corporation executive would describe the problems in terms of union restrictions on management prerogatives, union monopolies, high wages, featherbedding, government interference with collective bargaining, etc. The "average citizen" might recall headlines about strikes, corruption, price rises following immediately after wage increases, etc. For the student who has read the first four parts of this book the answer should be in more fundamental and less impassioned terms. Even so, reasonable people will differ on labor questions, since all of us are so personally involved. The following chapter is an effort to review the main theme of the book and to point out the major problem areas. Draw up your own list of four or five major problems of the present time and then predict how they will evolve over the next ten years.

25

WORKERS, UNIONS,

AND THE ECONOMY

Since this is not a mystery novel, most readers will not begin with the final chapter to see "who done it." Yet this chapter has a purpose not dissimilar to the last part of a detective story. The various strands of the book must be pulled together—the important clues must be related to the final solution of the mystery—which in this case is: What is the outlook for workers and unions within the economy? Before proposing an answer to this question, the groundwork must be prepared by considering two preliminary questions: What are the unsolved problems which have continued to plague workers and unions over the past century and a half? What are the areas of continuing conflict between unions and management that inhibit the progressive development of collective bargaining?

There is a major distinction betwen this book and a mystery novel. The fiction writer can manipulate his plot and characters so as to make his conclusions neat, clear, and satisfying. The story we are telling has no conclusion, only different stages of development. And the characters become entangled in a complicated and constantly shifting plot. We shall now attempt to sort out some of the main themes of the plot and project them into the future.

150 YEARS OF DEVELOPMENT

From their beginnings at the start of the nineteenth century, unions in the United States have traveled a long road filled with many detours.

569

They are now sufficiently well established in the United States so that there is no threat to their existence. This was not true a mere thirty years ago. As yet, in terms of the percentage of the labor force unionized, they have not reached the level of development achieved in most European countries, and perhaps they never will. Even though some locals individually are in a precarious position, collectively, "unions are here to stay." Most employers whose employees have been organized for at least a few years accept the fact, and accommodate their management practices to include the union in the decision-making process. The question is not how to get rid of worker organization, but how to deal with it. Unions are now recognized as legitimate institutions by government and the general public, with the expectation that such recognition will last indefinitely into the future. This statement, of course, does not apply equally to all parts of the country. The attitudes toward organized labor expressed by employers, shopkeepers, sheriffs, judges, etc. vary considerably between large cities in the Northeast and small cities in the South.

In the course of its growth, the American labor movement went through long periods of internal struggle, finally arriving at a pragmatic philosophy consistent with the American environment. Along the way, it rejected a number of utopian philosophies which sought to eliminate the private profit system, as well as rejecting the goal of one big union, designed to include all producers. In contrast to some of their European counterparts, American unions adopted bread and butter goals as their objective, seeking these through their own economic power rather than through a political alliance with intellectuals, white-collar workers, small shopkeepers, etc. In short, those union leaders who were successful in guiding permanent organizations concentrated on a job-conscious business unionism, with no direct affiliation with a political party.

One factor which had a decisive influence on unions in their selection of a philosophy was the absence of rigid class lines. In our fluid class system, with its high degree of occupational and father-son mobility, only a fractional part of the members of the labor force feel that their destinies are tied inextricably to a workers' movement. Although millions of workers are employed in factories or mines all of their working lives, many millions more hold white-collar jobs during at least a part of their careers. Most of the first group, particularly if they work in large factories, are comparatively regular union members; however, some of these will long treasure the hope of "rising" to a supervisory position, a white-collar job, or a business of their own. In other words, they hope to improve their economic status independently of union activity. Many of those who have held white-collar jobs for at least a part of their lives—even if for only a year—consider themselves only temporarily attached to the factory; hence, they will resist or be indifferent to unionization.

The lack of a rigid class system has been one reason American unions have been required to spend so much of their energy in organizing reluctant workers. They cannot rely on an automatic affiliation of workers with a strictly workers' group. After once joining, there is no guarantee the worker will remain true-blue. For this reason, as well as employer opposition to the introduction of organization, the union security clause has been a perennial goal of collective bargaining. Since there is no evidence that class lines are becoming more rigid in American society, unions will have to continue to struggle with this problem in the future.

In comparing the balance sheet of today with that of 150 years ago, the improvements in the workers' real standard of living occupy a conspicuous position. The improvements have occurred both in terms of an absolute increase in goods and services enjoyed and in terms of a relative difference between wage earners and higher income groups. The narrowing of the range between the living standards of the industrial workers and of the middle class exerts a profound influence on the outlook for union development. One of the main sources of worker dissatisfaction is largely eliminated. Hence, he has less reason to join a group which is fighting to change the distribution of income.

Of course, if the union movement is responsible for the rise in the workers' standard of living, it has a claim on their allegiance, particularly if it can convince them that it has a continuing effect in this direction. However, there is no clear proof that unions can take much credit for these improvements. The reasoning supporting this belief was developed in Chapter 22.

Associated with the higher real incomes has been an increasing security against complete loss of income, supplied in part through public and private security programs. Unions have been active in developing these programs, using both their political and economic power for this purpose. And they also provide individual workers with greater security against complete loss of income by protecting them against arbitrary discharge. The greater freedom to assert individuality vis-à-vis their employer may be the workers' most valuable gain from membership. Hence, even though it may be true that unions have little independent influence over the economic welfare of workers generally, they contribute significantly to the security and freedom of workers individually.

Despite the fact that organizations of workers first appeared on the American scene more than 150 years ago, their real growth in numbers and influence is hardly a generation old. The leaders in many of the internationals are even today the same persons who fought the picket-line battles to gain initial recognition during the 1930's; but many are reaching their last days and a new generation of leaders is moving up through the echelons. The older leaders conceived of the company as the enemy and looked upon the employer-employee relationship as needing drastic changes. Their waking hours were dedicated to a major overhauling of the status quo, an unremitting pressure on the autocratic controls of employers. The current generation of union officials—and this includes many of the old stalwarts who have adjusted to the modern labor-management conditions—conceive of the firm as an agency requiring their cautious cooperation, their partner in administering the working rules established through collective bargaining.

Expressed somewhat differently, unions are ripening into a mature middle age.[1] The community no longer looks upon them as rabble-rousing organizations dominated by a group of irrational, bomb-throwing communists. The officials spend a smaller fraction of their time winning new members, and, supported by a staff of professionally trained assistants, a larger fraction administering the technical details of contracts and supervising complicated pension and welfare programs. The environment—particularly management—has changed to accommodate worker organization and at the same time unions have settled into a comfortable new status quo.

These observations perhaps underestimate the potential for change within today's labor relations. Collective bargaining continues to act as a mechanism giving direction to shifting currents within our socio-economic system and formalizing the new status positions. Neither unions nor management are satisfied with the present situation, and both have specific proposals for change. Nevertheless, the extent to which their goals and tactics are in fundamental contradiction is not so obvious as it was twenty-five years ago. The American labor movement has ceased to be a movement, in the sense of striving for basic changes in the hierarchy of power groups, and has become an accepted institution within the existing social fabric.

[1] Richard A. Lester, *As Unions Mature* (Princeton: Princeton University Press, 1958).

UNSOLVED PROBLEMS

Although unions have increased their membership many times over and workers enjoy higher incomes with greater security, not all problems have been resolved in the last 150 years. In fact, in many areas where unions and workers have made their greatest progress, the old problems continue to reappear in a somewhat modified form.

Unemployment

The most serious for the individual worker—and for union bargaining strength—is cyclical unemployment. Even though we now know much more about the nature and causes of business cycles than we did three decades ago, we are still a long way from completely eliminating this source of unemployment. Workers, often those with many years of seniority and with families to support, find their incomes drop from $100 or more per week to an unemployment compensation benefit of less than half of that amount, and to zero if their unemployment extends beyond the duration of benefits. Although the unemployed no longer suffer from starvation or the meanest levels of poverty, there is real privation in being without a job.

The best solution to unemployment is to find another job. Since this is not always possible, unions and the government have created what approaches a cradle-to-the-grave system for alleviating the hardships resulting from unemployment, no matter what the cause: old age, physical injury, temporary layoff, etc. However, the American social security system—a crazy-quilt pattern of public and private programs—performs this function in a less than perfect fashion. It leaves much to be desired because of the many gaps in coverage, especially in the unemployment compensation, workmen's compensation, and medical care programs, and because of the inadequate level of benefits.

The shortcomings of the public programs have stimulated a rapid rise in the private programs, many of them through collective bargaining. Private social security, possessing a number of disadvantages as compared with public social security, is threatening to stunt the growth of the latter. Unless the federal and state legislatures show more foresight in expanding our public social security system—and do it very soon—the private programs will dominate the field. Once this happens, it will be exceedingly difficult to replace them with public programs because it will involve undermining the accumulated rights to benefits won by union workers under private economic security plans. Yet, if the government does not expand the public programs, unions have little choice but to provide less satisfactory substitutes through collective bargaining.

Another difficulty created by the continuing threat of unemployment is the possibility of reacting with too much vigor in attempting to prevent its appearance. If policy measures greatly expand the money supply or create conditions which promote wage increases considerably greater than the rise in output per manhour, inflation in the price level will certainly be the consequence. It is quite possible that severe inflation will be a more vexing problem than severe unemployment in the coming decades. If so, unions may become more concerned with adjusting to government regulations of their bargaining power than with devising programs to ameliorate the effects of unemployment.

Discrimination

Some unsolved problems confronting workers and unions are no more than variations of problems facing all of us as citizens. One of these which has special meaning for labor organizations is discrimination against minority groups. In many parts of the country, unions are among the leaders in efforts to bring about treatment of people according to their individual merits rather than on the basis of skin color, religion, or nationality. At the same time, there are some internationals which permit segregated locals or practice other forms of discrimination. In some locals it is almost impossible to become an officer unless you are a member of the accepted religious group or the dominant nationality. Since unions exercise a number of strategic controls over access to the job market, it is most important, from the point of view of civil rights, that they operate on the basis of justice and equality.

Membership Participation

One of the most serious of the unsolved problems which unions face— and one that affects all other problems—is poor membership participation in union affairs, stemming to a large extent from the lack of class consciousness of American workers. And it also stems partly from the penchant of all Americans to join many organizations but be active in few. Why should union members give up their leisure time to work for more effective and more democratic organization? Of course, many do. But for the great majority the union occupies only a peripheral position in their lives. It is easier to take the local and its officials for granted and spend the evening with the family and the television set or at the bowling alleys. If there were a threat to its existence, from the employer or a rival union, the members might be willing to demonstrate the same type of solidarity they show in a strike. Generally, it is only in areas where they are newly organized that the members take a real interest and are willing to sacrifice their time. The political and social power of the labor movement would be substantially enhanced if the members had a higher degree of allegiance.

Largely because of their lack of interest in organizational affairs, the individual members have been "lost in the shuffle" in some unions. Their apathy makes it possible for the leaders to conclude collective bargaining agreements which are not in the best interest of the majority of the workers. And in extreme cases, graft and corruption continue unheeded for years. Unless the members take a more active interest in their locals and internationals, it is unlikely that these sore spots can be effectively eliminated, regardless of any new legislation designed "to clean up the unions." As citizens, all of us have a parallel problem: the lack of interest we show in our city and county governments, despite continuous revelations of graft and corruption.

A tentative solution is interjected at this point: job-conscious business unionism is an inadequate philosophy for the *modern* American labor movement. Would a broader philosophy induce the inactive members to become more personally involved? If political, economic, and social horizons were widened, would workers who now are lukewarm or actively opposed be persuaded to join? If the answers to these questions are yes, then unions would at least know which direction to go in order to cope with some of their thorniest unsolved problems. However, it is possible that they would lose more than they would gain by abandoning their traditional philosophy. It appears that American workers, with their relatively high standard of living, their high degree of occupational mobility, and their unwillingness to consider themselves as a class clearly separated from the rest of society, are not prepared to accept a movement espousing basic changes in our social and political institutions. The rank and file—both union and nonunion—are largely satisfied with the present structure and power balance of our institutions. They do not want to change the good life, they just want more of it. And this trait applies to practically all members of our society.

Corruption in Unions

A further charge against business unionism, particularly when it is combined with autonomy for the individual unions, is that it provides

a safe haven for corruption. The motivating ideology of business unionism is economic improvement for the members, not advancing the social
welfare or developing an enlightened community. And if the organization is a less than perfect democracy and a few of the insiders are
acquiring wealth in an extracurricular fashion, the members are inclined
to look the other way as long as their wages continually rise. Even
though the labor movement as a whole suffers a public "black eye,"
the culprits cannot be disciplined without concentrating much greater
control in the hands of the AFL-CIO.

Would the situation be remedied by adopting some philosophy other
than business unionism? The nature of the American environment makes
it impossible to answer this quesion. A free enterprise economy relies
on economic incentives, with each person striving to win as large a
piece of pie as he can. Success is measured in terms of material wealth
with little concern over how it is earned. Therefore, it is not surprising
if the less scrupulous sell defective goods to unsuspecting consumers, or
charge prices several times the cost of production, or bribe public
officials to gain specially favorable contracts. And it should be no more
surprising if some of the less scrupulous adopt a union as·their vehicle
for ill-gotten gains. Hence, abandoning the business union philosophy
would be feasible only if the total environment changes radically. This
is not to say that business unionism is the same today that it was in
the 1890's, or will be in the 1990's. It is constantly being modified as
unions face new challenges. But the objective is still economic improvement, with major reliance on economic tactics. Of course, corruption is
not a necessary ingredient of business unionism, but the great emphasis
on economic motivation does make it possible for the dishonest to
create almost impregnable strongholds within its materialistic standards.

Jurisdictional Disputes

One outgrowth of job-conscious business unionism is the jealous
guarding of jurisdictional boundaries by each international. As a consequence, unions sometimes fight harder against each other than they
do against employers. The Taft-Hartley Act and the merger of the
AFL and CIO have tended to reduce some of the most overt outbursts
of inter-union rivalry, but events since the merger clearly demonstrate
that jurisdictional disputes have not been eliminated. The manifestations
of the internecine struggles go beyond battling over job territories. They
indicate the lack of cohesion—lack of singleness of purpose—among the

dominant segments of the labor movement. They probably tend to reduce total membership and to blunt the political effectiveness of unions.

AREAS OF CONTINUING CONFLICT

It is only natural that unions have become involved in a number of conflicts which continue decade after decade. After all, unions represent a special interest group in its conflict relationship with an opposing special interest group. Year after year, the unsettled issues are the subject matter of collective bargaining, the technique adopted for making temporary resolutions of the conflicts.

Wage Determination

The most obvious continuing conflict is the determination of wage rates. Regardless of the degree of cooperation between labor and management in promoting efficient production, the two sides have opposite interests when it comes to dividing the total output. This conflict will continue as long as the American economy operates on a free enterprise basis. It is inherent in a system based on private profit and wage employment. Even in a socialistic system, the conflict is not eliminated. It merely takes a different form, with the antagonists being the government, as employer, and the workers, regardless of the nature of their unionization. The conflict then takes place in the political arena as well as on the production line. In other words, no matter how production is organized, there will always be the managers and the managed, and, short of "heaven on earth," they will always have contrary views on what should be done, how it should be done, and who should benefit.

The continuing nature of the conflict may be indicated with the question: How should the increasing output, resulting from advancing productivity, be divided? Perhaps it should be shared proportionately between different producer groups, bringing no change in the relative income shares of labor and capital. Perhaps it should go in larger amounts to capitalists in order to stimulate a greater rate of investment and faster economic growth. Perhaps the distribution should be weighted in favor of labor and thus bring about greater equality in incomes. Or perhaps the increased output should be shared at the consumer level rather than the producer level, with money wages and profits held constant while the price level declines. The discussion of the last few chapters should indicate why this fourth possibility is unlikely.

Whatever share of the increased output goes to labor, there is the continuing question of what form the higher standard of living should take. Should it be in the form of greater material welfare or in the form of greater leisure—shorter work weeks and longer vacations? The answer will undoubtedly be some combination of the two. Shorter work weeks may mean that many workers, placing a low value on leisure, may take a second job. This will lead to divided loyalties, perhaps between two unions or between a union and a nonunion job. Even if the shorter work week does not lead to a second job, it will probably reduce the worker's contacts with his local. It seems unlikely that the typical worker will use additional free time to become more active in union affairs. There will be some exceptions, of course, especially among those who will use the labor movement as a stepping stone to political office or a vehicle for winning greater social prestige.

Management Rights

Management rights are another area of collective bargaining in which there will be unceasing conflict as long as our economy operates on a private enterprise basis. The mere appearance of the union represents a reduction in the authority previously exercised by management. The present unsettled status of management rights is good evidence that this will be a perennial conflict. In some firms, particularly those in smaller cities, management still uses every technique at its disposal to prevent organization of the workers or to eliminate the union if it is already there. At the opposite extreme there are many managers who solicit the full cooperation of the union in almost all aspects of the company's operation, including selection of capital equipment, plant layout, product advertising, incentive payment systems, etc. Between these extremes are the majority of unionized firms, accepting the union, but attempting to restrict its authority to a well-defined area, e.g., economic benefits, seniority, and a grievance procedure with specified limitations.

In a dynamic economy there are continual changes in the roles played by the major institutions. Hence, there will probably never be a clear demarcation of management rights that represents a final solution to the conflict. If the trend turns out to be one of steady expansion of union authority with the end product full partnership in all aspects of management, American business firms will become very different from what they are today. In effect we would have a form of guild socialism— as discussed by Frank Tannenbaum—with the workers holding substantial control over the firms in which they are employed. Even though this is not compatible with our current economic philosophy, the union invasion of management rights does tend in this direction, and it has not reached its culmination yet.

A LOOK INTO THE FUTURE

Given these unsolved problems within the union movement and these continuing conflicts in collective bargaining, what does the future hold for American workers and unions? The answer to this question can at best be only an informed guess, a projection of what one considers to be the most important trends visible at the moment. In our developing society so many things are changing that predictions are of dubious validity. The important trends of today may be insignificant tomorrow.

In order to prepare the groundwork for a look into the future, a number of assumptions need to be made. It is assumed that incomes will continue to rise and that there will be no significant increase in the degree of inequality in income distribution. Consequently, workers will enjoy a steady improvement in their standard of living, although perhaps by varying amounts from year to year. It is also assumed that the most overt forms of employer opposition to unions will continue to be proscribed by law, e.g., the unfair labor practices in the Taft-Hartley Act. And finally, the assumption is made that the economy will not suffer from a severe and prolonged depression; there will be nothing that even approaches the experience of the 1930's. Since the impact of another major world war would be impossible to predict, it is left out of account. Naturally, if any of these assumptions proves to be substantially incorrect, then this look into the future will also be substantially incorrect.

Prospects for Union Growth

There appears to be no good reason for expecting a new burst of union growth in the coming years. At best, membership will be only a slightly rising percentage of the labor force, and more likely will be barely able to maintain a constant percentage: grow at the same rate as the labor force. With the greatest expansion of the labor force occurring in those industries and occupations which have been most resistant to organization, the outlook is not favorable for union growth. There are many students of the labor movement who disagree with this appraisal of the prospects for union growth. They point to opportunities in the retail and service trades and in the professional and technical occupations. The former are ripe for organization, it is argued, because of low wage rates, and the latter because of the declining prestige of their jobs caused by the spread of mass production techniques, particularly among the engineers. Those who claim that unions will grow rapidly in the coming years also expect that further industrialization of the South will eventually enhance union opportunities there. Although these possibilities of union growth cannot be ignored, they should not be overrated. The rising standard of living, with no severe depression—if our assumptions here are correct—will probably encourage a continuing lack of interest in unionization on the part of unorganized workers.

Organization among white-collar workers will be very likely to continue to grow, but probably not to acquire the usual characteristics of unionization nor to affiliate with the AFL-CIO. As professional and technical workers become an increasingly large proportion of the labor force and as they encounter employer-employee problems, their organizations may adopt quasi-bargaining goals. The same may be true of government employees, another group which is becoming larger relative to the labor force. Nurses, engineers, and public schoolteachers have already taken steps in this direction. And even the American Association of University Professors, traditionally concerned with professional ethics and academic freedom, and considering itself above such mundane matters as pay scales, has launched an effective campaign to raise the salaries of college teachers, but only after being shocked by the extent to which educational income has lagged behind other groups. For white-collar groups generally, pressures will develop that will cause them to make concerted efforts to improve their pay and working conditions. However, short of unexpectedly extreme changes, the rising organizations will not amalgamate with the union movement. But a loose informal liaison is conceivable: moral support for the other's bargaining goals and cooperation for certain political objectives. For unions to expect a great deal of material help from these quarters would probably be naïve, but to ignore the possibilities for mutual aid would be foolhardy.

Developments in Collective Bargaining

Regardless of the pace of union growth, collective bargaining will continue to develop and expand into new areas, and its techniques and processes will continue to change. With full employment and the likelihood of intermittent—if not persistent—inflationary pressures, the public may become anxious to take a more active role in influencing the economic consequences of collective bargaining. Even if this interference is something quite short of direct control, unions will have to take cognizance of the government's expanding participation.

Direct control of prices and wages is a possibility at one extreme, but is unlikely for political reasons and the same may be said for compulsory arbitration. The government may simply attempt to influence key bargains, hoping these will set appropriate patterns for other agreements. Or it may announce some permissible upper limit to the percentage increase in wages and threaten to take tax action if this is violated. Even these last two approaches represent a substantial increase in interference in collective bargaining, beyond anything this country has known in peace-time.

What are the possible courses of union reaction? A plausible development would be greater centralization of control over bargaining authority by the AFL-CIO. Assuming inter-union jealousies can be overcome, unions may attempt to manipulate their bargaining timetable to bring their most favorable case to the public's attention at the strategic time; just as the government is about to make its decision on interference, the union with members whose wage rates have lagged behind the economy may be pushed into the limelight. Or something approaching the Swedish system of bargaining may eventually be adopted. Since the Federation has never taken an active role in negotiating new agreements, except to make public pronouncements, even informal regulation of the internationals' bargaining policies and strategy would represent a major departure from the past. The leadership hierarchy in the internationals would not willingly dilute their power, and the membership would probably be reluctant to be one step further removed from control over their working conditions and wage demands. It is hard to imagine that long-standing rivalries among the presidents of competing internationals will be replaced by cooperation to present a common front to both the government and employers. Nevertheless, when the going is toughest, American unions have demonstrated a real capacity to make pragmatic adjustment to their economic and political environment. And even if it is impossible to specify just what organizational changes would occur, greater government interference would encourage more coordination between the internationals in formulating their bargaining strategy.

If greater centralization of control over union collective bargaining policies does occur, what impact will it have on the day-to-day operations of the locals? It is quite possible that there will be no major change on this level. Processing grievances and other aspects of administering the contract in the local plant need not be affected by greater centralization of wage policies. Even where locals have control over negotiating wage rates, e.g., in construction and printing, this power may be retained by the locals, since they have a comparatively small effect on the national wage level. However, if it appears that wage inequities or distortions are developing—a wage drift making it impossible to hold the pattern-setting agreement within noninflationary levels —then even the local wage agreements would have to be controlled. Aside from this, the authority of union locals may be left unmolested. The main changes in union structure would occur in the balance of power between the internationals and the AFL-CIO, with the latter exercising more influence.

There are, however, some developments on the collective bargaining scene which may cause the power of union locals to be reduced, or at least modified. The trend toward industry-wide and pattern bargaining, with three to five-year contracts, is producing changes in the relationship between internationals and locals. When contracts cover long time periods, their administration becomes a matter of vital concern to the international. The settlement of a grievance by one local may act as a precedent which becomes binding on many other locals and cannot be changed until the contract expires. An unsatisfactory settlement may plague the entire union for three or four years. Thus, the locals become more important but at the same time lose some of their independent power. Their importance is increased because of the great weight attached to how they administer contracts at the local level, but their power is reduced as the international exerts more control over the handling of each grievance as it arises, e.g., when the international representative steps into the grievance machinery at an early stage and also decides whether to take a case to arbitration or to wait for a more favorable case to appear later on.

Union Political Activity

One consequence of greater government interference in collective bargaining would probably be an expansion of union political activity. When the government exercises the power of deciding the appropriate amount for wages to increase, unions are compelled to become more active politically. They will want a major voice in determining what is a noninflationary wage increase, and also in the techniques used to secure compliance. In short, the gain or loss to unions from having "friends" or "enemies" in government agencies and in Congress would be much greater than it is today.

From past experience there is not much reason to expect that union political power will be especially effective as long as full employment is maintained. Even if it becomes more urgent for unions to expand their political influence, for reasons related to government anti-inflationary policies, it is quite doubtful whether they will be able to deliver the votes. Union members tend to follow the political advice of their leaders only on matters of extreme and direct urgency. An analogy may be drawn with the union political efforts to eliminate the Taft-Hartley Act. On election day—with the exception of 1948—union members seemed unconcerned about the Act, in spite of the label, "slave labor bill."

Unless the American worker feels that the government is putting its hand directly into his pocketbook, unions will be likely to have great difficulty in winning widespread support for their favorite candidates. However, a wage control decision which is unsatisfactory, particularly if it occurs while profits are rising, would perhaps be sufficient to alter the ballot-box proclivities of blue-collar workers. Certainly, union leaders would "pull out all the stops" in a campaign for solidarity at the next election. In short, repressing inflation through restricting wage increases could very well rearrange the power alignments in the political arena.

SUMMARY

All the previous chapters have been concerned with workers and unions in their *current* problems in the American economy. In this chapter we have consulted our crystal ball in order to forecast the major trends for the coming years. The purpose is not to predict specific future events but rather to focus attention on problem areas in which developments are likely to occur which will have a significant impact on workers and unions. Our approach has been that of the citizen rather than the practitioner. That is, we have discussed the trends from the point of view of their importance to the economy as a whole rather than from the point of view of the partisans: labor leaders and personnel managers.

In our look into the future, we have concluded that there will probably not be any major changes. Union membership will not rise markedly. Many problems of long standing will continue to occupy the attention of the union movement: unemployment, public and private social security programs, integration of minority groups, membership participation in union affairs, corruption, and dealing with jurisdictional disputes and internal rivalries. Areas of continuing conflict in collective bargaining which show no signs of being resolved are wage determination and management rights.

The role played by the government in collective bargaining is one area in which important changes may take place. In order to counteract inflationary pressures in a full employment economy, the government may attempt to restrict the size of wage increases. This may induce a realignment in the union power hierarchy, with more authority placed in the hands of the Federation. Although the greater importance of government in collective bargaining may cause unions to become more active politically, there appears to be little reason to expect their political power to rise substantially.

DISCUSSION QUESTIONS

1. Select what you believe to be one of the chief characteristics of the American labor movement, then sketch the past and portray the future development of this characteristic. Support your look into the future with whatever information and reasoning you consider appropriate.

2. "The American labor movement is well advanced into its 'middle age.'" Explain why you agree or disagree with this statement.

3. "The rising new generation of leaders will guide unions to new frontiers and greater strength." Evaluate this statement, illustrating your answer with references to at least two unions and their leadership.

4. Select some headlines of the past six months and indicate how they relate to the *continuing* problems of labor management relations.

5. How would you expect the structure of the union movement to be changed if price inflation continues for several successive years? Why? What are the primary barriers to the changes you foresee?

BIBLIOGRAPHY

Barbash, Jack. *Unions and Union Leadership*. New York: Harper & Brothers, 1959.

Lester, Richard A. *As Unions Mature*. Princeton: Princeton University Press, 1958.

AUTHOR INDEX

585

SUBJECT INDEX

Additional worker hypothesis, 7-9, *See also* Labor force
Air Line Pilots Association, 191
Allen Bradley case, 259-60, 263, 367
Allied Industrial Workers, 77
Allowances, 442-43
Amalgamated Association of Iron, Steel, and Tin Workers, 56
Amalgamated Clothing Workers of America, 55, 186, 243
Amalgamated Meat Cutters and Butcher Workmen of North America, 70
American Anti-Boycott Association, 252
American Arbitration Association, 231
American Association of University Professors, 580
American Bar Association, 267
American Civil Liberties Union, 127
American Express Company, 472
American Federation of Labor, 39, 46-52, 54-55, 185, 252, 282, *See also* American Federation of Labor-Congress of Industrial Organizations
    Conflict with Congress of Industrial Organizations, 54-55, 62-63
    Conflict with Knights of Labor, 45-46
American Federation of Labor-Congress of Industrial Organizations, 63-78, 105-111, 269, 401, 562, 576, 580-82
    Biennial convention, 110-11
    Executive Committee, 110-11
    Executive Council, 110-11

Functions of the Federation, 107-108
    General Board, 111
    Governing structure, 105-11
    Merger, 63-78
American Federation of State, County and Municipal Employees, 402
American Federation of Teachers, 403
American Medical Association, 445, 464, 481
American Railway Supervisors' Association, 112
American Railway Union, 256, 295
American Train Dispatchers' Association, 112
Anheuser-Busch Company, 258-60
Anti-pirating policy, 333
Antitrust regulation of unions, 246-63
Apex Hosiery case, 258
Apprenticeship, 165-67, 349
Appropriate bargaining unit, 281-82
Arbitration, 229-32, 233-38, 295-98, 301, 552
Atomic Energy Labor-Management Relations Panel, 308-309
Automation, 15, 17, 166-67, 427-29, *See also* Productivity and Technology

Beck, Dave, 73-74, 128, 135
Black International, 44-45
Blacklists, 211
Blough, Roger, 302
Blue Cross, 463-64, 491
Blue Shield, 463-64, 480-81, 491
Brennan, Owen (Bert), 74

589